THE DICTIONARY OF

HERALDRY

THE DICTIONARY OF
HERALDRY

FEUDAL COATS OF ARMS AND PEDIGREES

JOSEPH FOSTER

Introduction by J. P. B. Brooke-Little
Norroy and Ulster King of Arms

STUDIO
EDITIONS

The Dictionary of Heraldry

Previously published in black-and-white as

Some Feudal Coats of Arms

in 1902 by James Parker and Company

This edition published in 1994 by

Studio Editions Ltd, Princess House, 50 Eastcastle Street,

London W1N 7AP,

England

ISBN 1 85170 309 8

Printed in Singapore

CONTENTS

INTRODUCTION

This very handsome volume was first published in 1902 but it lacked that quintessence of the art of heraldry – colour. Now, after nearly eighty years, this omission has been put right in the present edition, in which the old feudal coats, culled from some of the ancient rolls of arms, have been rendered in their true glory. At last the heraldic tyro, unable to interpret the colours of a coat of arms from its blazon (the description given in heraldic terms) will be able to see it as it should be seen. The book has acquired a new, appealing and important dimension.

The alphabetical list of names and blazons of arms from the rolls, many of which are depicted in the margins, has, as the title page indicates, been rather quaintly supplemented by scenes from the Bayeux Tapestry, monumental effigies, arms of living people of ancient lineage, pictures of seals, Greek vases and tiles. There is also a number of chart pedigrees. Much of this is not particularly relevant to the main purpose of the book but it adds to its interest and to the reader's pleasure.

Joseph Foster was born at Sunnyside, Sunderland, on 9 March 1844, being the eldest of the eight children of Joseph Foster, a woollen draper of Bishop Wearmouth by his wife Elizabeth Taylor. Myles Birket Foster, the founder of the London bottling firm of M. B. Foster and Sons, was his grandfather, and an uncle of the same name was the noted illustrator and water-colour painter. Until just before Foster's birth his family had been Quakers for many generations but his father severed the connexion.

After being privately educated Foster became a printer in London but his real hobby and vocation was genealogy and he soon turned to this as a full-time occupation. At first he researched pedigrees, including his own, which were privately printed, but in 1873 he published the first volume of a projected series *Pedigrees of the County Families of England*. This was *Pedigrees of Lancashire Families*, an excellent and well researched collection of a great many extensive chart pedigrees. It was followed in 1874 by *Pedigrees of Yorkshire Families*, an equally valuable work, but there the series ended.

Then, in 1879, he published, in collaboration with Edward Bellasis, Bluemantle Pursuivant and later Lancaster Herald, his *Peerage, Baronetage and Knightage*. This consisted of narrative pedigrees illustrated by original and vigorous drawings of arms. In format it was similar to Sir Bernard Burke's *Peerage Baronetage and Knightage* but the genealogies were more critical and a number of doubtful baronetcies was confined to a section entitled 'Chaos'.

In 1881 Foster produced the first volume of a periodical entitled *Collectanea Genealogica et Heraldica*, which was published from time to time until 1888. It was mainly devoted to genealogical transcripts, notes and comments.

There can be no doubt that Foster was a diligent and critical genealogist, especially when one reflects that he did not have access to much source material and indexed records that are available to genealogists today. For instance the Census Returns, which start in 1841, were not then accessible to the public and County Record Offices, those treasure houses of well-indexed local material, did not exist. It can truthfully be said that Foster was one of the pioneers of modern, critical genealogy and did much to help establish it by publishing valuable, inedited material some of which I detail below; for Foster's other claim to the gratitude and respect of posterity was his love of transcribing, indexing and publishing the results of his prodigious industry.

In 1888 he produced his *Men at the Bar*, having transcribed the admission registers of the Inns of Court. In the next year appeared *Admissions to Gray's Inn and Marriages in Grey's Inn Chapel*. Following this, in 1890, *Index Ecclesiasticus: or Alphabetical Lists of all Ecclesiastical Dignitaries in England and Wales* was published.

One of his most painstaking and useful labours, and one which earned him an honorary Master of Arts degree at Oxford was the publication of *Alumni Oxonienses* in eight volumes, four (1715–1886) appearing in 1886 and the other four (1521–1714) in 1891. These books contain Joseph Lemuel Chester's transcripts of the Oxford Matriculation Registers, much augmented and annotated by Foster. I can testify to this as I have one of the two copies made by Chester and it is jejune in comparison with Foster's published work.

During the last part of his comparatively short life (he died on 29 July 1905) he turned his attention to heraldry. He is known for three handsome volumes published under the auspices of Lord Howard de Walden in what is called the 'De Walden Library', they were: *A Tudor Book of Arms, Some Feudal Lords and their Seals* and *Banners, Standards and Badges*. But just before these were published appeared this present volume, which was reviewed in *The Ancestor* (vol. 1, p. 207) by Mr. Oswald Barron.

Let it be said at once that Barron was an intolerant, pedantic purist in matters heraldic but he had the right to be as he was an undoubted and accepted medieval scholar, as well as being a very able journalist. When these two callings meet in one man, something very explosive is likely to be created. A trenchant example is to be found in his review of Foster's work. After having praised Foster's industry and ability in other fields he continues:

'The making of such a book as *Some Feudal Coats of Arms* demanded a measure of modest scholarship with which Mr. Foster has not equipped himself, a certain patience of research he seems unable to condescend to, and an appreciation of that colour of the middle ages of which Mr. Foster throughout his pages shows himself incapable. In this case the compiler has set himself the work of an antiquary whilst disdaining an antiquary's training. Mr. Foster's preface and introduction show him jubilant, and even though he were in mood to learn, the applause with which this work has been received by a press singularly ill informed in archaeological questions will convince him that there is at least no commercial reason for the antiquarian book compiler to do so. It is this very applause which moves us to review in some detail a book which, otherwise an unimportant one, will by reason of its impressive size and weight inevitably thrust itself amongst English archaeological books of reference'.

Barron continues with an extremely lengthy review tearing to pieces, or rather, expertly butchering, poor Foster's work. His conclusion may be summed up thus: Foster did not know his Norman French sufficiently well and and so was guilty of a number of howlers. He had no skills in palaeography and so, being unable to read many of the original rolls, worked from secondary sources and, not being either an heraldic scholar or a medievalist with a true feeling for or understanding of the Middle Ages, produced a fairly meretricious work.

All this is true, Foster was out of his depth, although he probably did not realize it, but while conceding that Barron's criticisms were well-founded, I feel that it would be unfair not to offer the ghost of Foster some comfort and consolation, even supposing that all may now have been revealed to him or seem to him of little importance in the context of eternal values.

He made a conscious effort to do something which no one before, nor since for that matter, has succeeded in achieving. He extracted arms from all the rolls known to him, put them in order and had them illustrated, admittedly in a way repugnant to Barron, but in my view rather better than adequately. His book therefore serves a purpose for students as a useful reference book to feudal heraldry, the more so as many reliable transcriptions of the rolls have now been published and the student can have recourse to these as well as to recently published scholarly books, in order to check the accuracy of many of Foster's references should he so wish.

Principal among these new works are *A Catalogue of English Mediaeval Rolls of Arms* (Apilogia I) by Anthony (now Sir Anthony) Wagner, (Society of Antiquaries, 1950); *Rolls of Arms of Henry III* (Aspilosia II) edited by T. D. Tremlett and H. S. London and including additions and corrections to Aspilosia I by Sir Anthony Wagner (Society of Antiquaries, 1967); *Anglo-Norman Armory* by Cecil R. Humphery-Smith (Family History, 1973); *Anglo-Norman Armory Two* (same author and publisher, 1984) and *Early Blazon* by Gerard J. Brault (Oxford University Press, 1972).

Perhaps one reason why scholars have been consistently critical of this book is because Foster, instead of stating humbly that it was a first effort to make an alphabet of feudal arms, implied in so many words that he had produced the final and definitive work on the subject. This is a red rag to any informed critic.

I suggest that the reader or viewer of this new and splendid coloured reprint accepts the book at face value, just as if Foster had disclaimed any reference to ultimate scholarship. He will then be rewarded and in no way disappointed.

My own interest in heraldry, which dates from when I was about 12 years old, began with modern heraldry, simply because I was given books which concentrated on the present-day application and conventions of heraldry. Then I received Foster's book and my interest was aroused by early feudal heraldry. In other words because it was pictorially appealing it opened new windows. Now that it is a hundred per cent more visually attractive I hope, indeed I am sure, that it will do the same for others and perhaps eventually lead them to a deeper study of medieval armory in less attractive but intellectually more weighty volumes.

It is important to appreciate that this is a new but not a revised edition of Foster's book. To attempt such an edition would not only be a mammoth task but would also duplicate the work that has been going on for decades compiling a comprehensive Ordinary of medieval and Tudor arms under the aegis of the Society of Antiquaries of London.

My connexion with the production of this book has been simply to advise on the correct colours to be employed. On some occasions either the colours have not been indicated or the written description has not tallied with the tricked shields. I should explain that tricking is a method of indicating colour by using abbreviations of the various tinctures on the actual drawing. Foster employed this system (removed in this edition) and where there is either a lacuna or a discrepancy I have done my best to determine what should properly be done. Beyond this I have in no way edited Foster's work.

John Brooke-Little
Norroy and Ulster King of Arms

March 1989

Here Guy seized Harold. After the Bayeux Tapestry.

HERALDIC INTRODUCTION.

(With Illustrations of the Seals of the Barons, 1300–1.)

CONFUSION of the symbols and devices of the ancients with Heraldry as an exact system has led to much aimless discussion as to its origin and history, and also to much vague theory, as if, forsooth, Heraldry were really an occult science.

Surely in the nature-worshipper we detect the Heraldic protoplasm, the primeval king of arms. He it was who painted the object of his veneration on his skin as a charm against the evil one when at peace, and on his shield in defence of his person when at war; the presence or whereabouts of his chieftain or tribal head he distinguished by a standard, ensign, or banner, as all writers testify, from Moses downwards; in this simple statement may not the Heraldic prototype be surely discerned? Further down the ages it may well have been the bards of every clime who handed down in turn these mystic emblems in their own weird way, inventing as they went the almost forgotten chimera and other monstrosities which were to strike terror into the hearts of the adversary.

Later still, the vases of the Greeks (550, 500 B.C.) are eloquent in examples of the Hellenic equivalent of our Heraldic system. Some of these, by consent of Sir E. Maunde Thompson, Director, I am permitted to reproduce from the Illustrated Catalogue of Greek and Etruscan Vases in the British Museum, edited by H. B. Walters, M.A.; they may be thus described :—

(1) Vase—representation of Heracles and Geryon, who bears on his shield an eagle or other bird displayed—two examples, pp. xiv, xxxvii.

(2) Vase—representation of Achilles lying in wait for Troilos beyond the fountain, on his shield, 2 lyons gardant [the edge of the shield foreshadowing the bordure of later times], p. xxxvii.

(3) Vase—" Caeretan " Hydria, found in a tomb which belongs at the latest to the end of the sixth century B.C. Representation of four warriors in combat. On the shield of one, a demi-boar salient, p. xxiii. See also enlargement, p. xxiii.

(4) Vase—representation of combat of Heracles and Kyknos. On the extreme right is Ares thrusting with a spear, bearded, helmet, visor up, a Bœotian shield black, on a white roundle, a star of twelve points in black and purple, all between two white lyons rampant regardant, p. xxxvi.

ADOMAR DE VALENCE.

ROGER BIGOD.

EDM. DE MORTIMER.

ROB. FITZ WALTER.

JOHN, EARL OF WARREN AND SURREY.

RICHARD, EARL OF ARUNDELL.

xi

d

HENRY DE PERCY.

WILLIAM DE BRAOSE,
LORD OF GOWER.

HUGH DE VERE.

Passing over the *quasi*-Heraldic aspect which some attribute to Totems and other personal distinctions so commonly employed among nations of imperfect civilisation, I may instance the usage of the Celtic tribes of Gaul and Britain who carried symbols or badges on their shields. Their national symbol—the boar—occurs on one such shield, found in the river Witham (see Frontispiece), and dates from the beginning of our era, see "Archæologia," xxiii. 95.

The symbols of the Normans, at the Conquest, represented in the much-debated Bayeux Tapestry next claim our notice. Mr. Fowke, the latest historian of the Tapestry, recites at length the opinions of Bolton Corney, M. Thierry, Dr. Lingard, Mr. Freeman, and many others, with whom he agrees in regarding it as a contemporary work, but in no way associated with Queen Matilda, though probably made under the orders of Bishop Odo by Norman workpeople at Bayeux for their church of Bayeux.*

Of its pre-heraldic devices, represented in the Headpieces of this work, I may, perhaps, be allowed to quote Mr. Fowke's own words :—

HENRY DE GREY.

"As a nearer approach is made to the ages of Chivalry the realistic representations of natural objects give place to those of geometrical figures which were soon systematized as ordinaries, whilst the animals assume the more conventional form in which they were subsequently borne. Thus the place of the wild beasts is taken by crosses, roundles, or besants, interlacing bands, and simple tinctures, and this stage is most clearly shown in the tapestry. We do not here find any particular or distinguished person represented twice as bearing the same device ('Archæologia,' xix. 188), and we must therefore conclude that they are not intended to represent the arms of any individual, or only in some cases and that appropriately, but their representation at all, of course, implies the existence of a system of bearings by which the wearer was known. And this we gather also from Wace, who says—

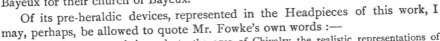

' E tuit ovent fet cognoissances
Ki Norman alter conust
El ke l'autre portuer neuet.'

These were cognizances to distinguish one Norman from another, and no man dared to use another's—showing that the assumption of arms was not the subject of mere caprice.

HUGO BARDOLF.

"The flags which are shown in the tapestry are of two kinds, the Gonfanon and the Pennon, and by them is the rank of the bearer determined. Wace tells us—

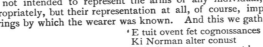

' Li barons ourent gonfanons,
Li chevaliers ourent penons.

The Gonfanon was a peculiar standard, generally borne near the person of the commander-in-chief; such an one occurs thrice in the tapestry, and is invariably Argent, a cross or, in a bordure azure."

Of 39 ensigns

"no less than 30 are triparted, a style of ornament very prevalent with Christian warriors of that period, and considered by Mr. French as emblematic of the Blessed Trinity, and in these points he sees the germ of the pile, a bearing of much disputed origin."

ROBERT DE MONHAUT.

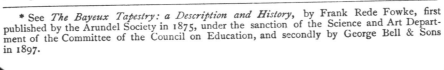

ROBERT DE TATESHAL.

ROBERT DE TONI.

* See *The Bayeux Tapestry: a Description and History*, by Frank Rede Fowke, first published by the Arundel Society in 1875, under the sanction of the Science and Art Department of the Committee of the Council on Education, and secondly by George Bell & Sons in 1897.

PETER DE MAULEY (3).

ROBERT DE CLIFFORD.

WILLIAM DE ROS.

REGINALD DE GREY.

HENRY TEIHEIS.

HENRY DE TREGOZ.

JOHN DE LANCASTER.

WALTER DE FAUCONBERGE.

ROBERT FITZ FAYNE.

WALTER DE HUNTERCOMBE.

ROGER LE STRANGE, OF ELLESMERE.

WILLIAM MARTYN.

RICHARD TALBOT.

JOHN DE BOUTOURT.

THOMAS DE CHAWORTH.

With the spread of Feudalism, then, came the introduction of the linear or geometrical, and from the imaginary per pale, per fess, per chevron, per saltire, &c., would naturally be evolved, the pale, the fess, the chevron, the saltire.* Out of this fortuitous combination of some of the elements of Euclid with the objects of the nature-worshipper, sprang that system we call Heraldry.

Although there is evidence that Heraldic bearings were assuming a definite form in the reign of Stephen (1135-54)† it is not a little remarkable that Richard I. is the first English king who is known to have adopted an heraldic bearing. On his great seal (1189) he bore the two lyons for the Duchies of Normandy and of Poictou or Maine. In his second great seal (1198)‡ he added a third lyon for the Duchy of Aquitaine, or, as some say, for Anjou; this has since been our national arms of dominion; according to Sir Henry Spelman ("Aspilogia," page 67), the earlier kings of England had marks and tokens painted on their shields, which they altered at pleasure. In this connection it would be interesting to know on what authority, if any, Brooke, York Herald, described the Dering Roll as " the names and armes of those Knightes as weare w^t Kinge Richard the firste at the assigge of Acon or Acres," 1191 (Ashmole MS. 1120).

Early instances of these symbols or badges are generally found on standards or banners, and it is worthy of note that in the Crusade of (2 and 3 R. I.) 1191, Richard " had a standard of ye Dragon which he delivered to Peter de Preaus to beare notwithstanding y^t Robert Trusbut chalenged ye carrying thereof as his hereditary right " (Ro. Hoveden, fo. 397, n. 10).

" These symbols or badges were not only borne on shields, but were also paynted on silken surcotes worne over their shirts of mail " (and also upon the caparisons of their horses). See the Arundel or Military Roll and seals. " But these surcotes of silke, being at firste made wide and girt close to them at ye waist, did, by reason of their pleates, oftimes confound the marks so paynted on them, which being discerned they were afterwards made straight and plaine, so that ye same marks which stood eminently to be seen on the shield was also as visible on the surcote both before and behind, and being thus depicted on them gave ye first occasion of calling them cotes of armes " (Stowe MS. 662, fo. 16).

Does not this defect of the early "pleates" supply a cue to the origin of many of the variations in Heraldry? The appearance of a plain fess or a plain bend on a standard would vary, according to the point of view or the strength of the breeze, from different directions; it might suggest, even if it did not appear as, undée, wavy, or dancettée; add to this the proclivities of each arms painter, or the momentary illusion of, say, an engréle for a lozenge, fusil, dancet,

* See also *Antiquities of Heraldry*, by W. Smith Ellis, and " Heraldry, its Laws and its Humours," by Jane MacNeal, *Munsey's Magazine*, September 1901.
† *Geoffrey Mandeville*, by J. H. Round, Appendix A, pp. 388-396.
‡ Richard the First's change of Seal, see *Feudal England*, by J. H. Round, page 545.

JOHN LE STRANGE, OF KNOCKYN.

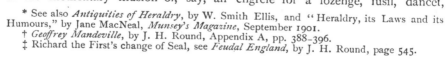

SIMON DE MONTACUTE.

ADAM DE WELLES.

ROB. DE SCALES.

JOHN DE MOLIS.

BOGO DE KNOVILE.

JOHN LOVELL.

RALPH FITZ WILLIAM.

indent, and even a mascle, and their evolution therefrom may be readily accounted for. In Cole's copy of the Parliamentary Roll occurs the ominous note of warning, "Take Hede of his wordes endented and engrayled, and examine such cotes with older Presydents." Nor must we omit to mention the cross moline, patonce, patée and flory, which are often confused, or imperfectly drawn, by the Herald-painter. So with the cross moline, cercellé and recercellé, which are equally confounded in blason and in trick; even crosses crosslet are often drawn as crosses botonnée in early tricks, probably because it was easier so to do. In a less degree the bend, bendlet or baston, the quarter and the canton, fret and fretty, flory and florettée, often represent the caprice or indifference of the Herald or the Herald-painter of each particular roll. So, too, whether a mullet had 5 or 6 points, pierced or not, whether a label had 3 or 5 pendants; and yet the theory has gone forth that the label of three denotes a son, and that a label of five denotes a grandson.

NICHOLAS POYNZ.

WILLIAM PAYNELL.

Perhaps a more interesting feature of these early Rolls is the quaint Norman-French blason; I specially except such illiterate jargon as obtained under the Gartership of the two Dethicks, and of some succeeding kings-of-arms. The rising generation of Heraldic editors, whether of a Family Armorial or of a County History, hardly seem to justify the "out-of-the-mouths-of-babes-and-sucklings" theory by their eagerness to adopt in lieu of universally recognized formula the A-B-C of the "Accedens of Armoury." With equal intelligence might they rehabilitate the author of "Little Jack Horner," and present him to their admirers as the superior of Rudyard Kipling.* But, to be serious, who will solve the blasons of Berkeley and Cromwell in the Boroughbridge Roll (see facsimile and type, pp. xxvi, xxvii), or explain the "wyfers," which occur not only in the arms of Benhale and of Crek, but also in the arms of Sir Edmond de Mauley; for Meyrick, in the "Archæologia," vol. xxxi. page 247, unable to resist a thrust at the expense of the Heralds and their College, supposes them to be vipers' nests? "Tertoleres" in Criel, "voyderis anabeles" in Dolerd, "p'my" in Constable, Dacre and Raynsford, "amptie" in Wellesby, or the "temoyles," "feuilles," "mailles," &c., of Bosville, are also curiosities in their way and worth consideration. The "undée en lung" of the Boroughbridge Roll and "ounde de longe" of Jenyns' Roll seem to have bifurcated and become sometimes palets nebulée, and at others the modern emasculate wavy, in lieu of the bold undulating lines of the old tricks. In this connection the blason of Theobald de Valoines suggests further complications. The "chevron et demi," of Strecche—"une barre et demi" of Twyford, and "une fees et demi" of Pipard, suggest the accommodation of the size of a repetition of charges to artistic effect, 2 chevrons or 2 bars to be equal to 1½.

JOHN DE SULEYE.

ROBERT DE LA WARD.

EUSTACE DE HACCHE.

* See "Archæological Nomenclature," *Literature*, Nos. 194, 5, 6, July 6, 13, 20 (1901).

WALTER DE BEAUCHAMP.

JOHN DE HAVERING.

EDM. STAFFORD.

WALTER DE TEYE.

NICHOLAS DE CAREW.

JOHN LE BRETOUN.

JOHN DE HODLESTON.

ROGER DE HUNTINGFELD.

FULKE LE STRANGE.

HUGH FITZ HENRY.

WALTER DE MOUNCY.

JOHN FITZ MARMADUKE.

MATHEW FITZ JOHN.

EDMUND HASTINGS.

RALPH DE GRENDON.

GILBERT PECCHE.

An early instance of a quarterly coat occurs in the Falkirk Roll, 1298; the coat of Sir Simon de Montagu quartered with Monthermer, which may be considered coeval with the oft-quoted coat of Castile quarterly with Leon, borne by Eleanor, Queen of Edward I., who died in 1296.

The last point to which I will here refer is the ancient practice of adopting the arms, though not the name, of an heiress, and with the further object of drawing attention to this interesting point I append the few instances that occur to me of old families who do not bear the arms of their original paternal family:

Abney assumed Ingwardby; disallowed to Lord Mayor Abney (1701), Harl. MS. 6179, fo. 66.
Congreve assumed Campion.
Coles assumed Knightley.
Croke assumed Blount.
(Croke claims male descent from Blount.)
Fleming assumed Hudleston.

Harpur (Bart.) assumed Rushall.
Hesketh (Bart.) assumed Fytton.
Leigh assumed Lymme.
Lumley (E. Scarborough) assumed Thwenge.
Prideaux assumed Orcharton.
Stanley (E. Derby) assumed Bamville.
Wallop (E. Portsmouth) assumed Barton.
Wrottesley (E.) assumed Basset.

Contemporary with the early Rolls of Arms are the Seals of the Barons who signed and sealed the famous letter to the Pope (12 Feb. 1300-1) on his pretensions to the crown of Scotland. These hundred seals present the earliest and most authentic evidence of the armorials used by the Barons of England in the fourteenth century, or perhaps in the thirteenth century. From the plaster casts in the British Museum it would seem as if many of the seals had been engraved by the same man for the very purpose of this sealing; that used by John de Hastings, lord de Bergavenny, is supposed to be hypothetical, or perhaps a very early example of the fictitious in Heraldry; that of Brian FitzAlan is not heraldic, and that of John de Botetourt is of the nature of a badge or heraldic emblem, while Edmond de Hastings evidently adopted for the occasion the territorial or baronial arms (?) of Drummond, encircling them with a Hastings legend. As will be seen on reference to the engravings the majority of the shields are of the triangular or heater shape. William de Paynell affords the earliest example of arms on a lozenge, and Robert FitzPayne bore his arms on an oval shield. On fourteen seals, those to whom they belonged are represented on horseback in complete armour, but only three of them—namely, Thomas Plantagenet, Earl of Lancaster; Ralph de Monthermer, Earl of Gloucester and Hertford; and John de St. John—are represented as bearing crests on their helmets. The first named was of the blood royal; the second married Joan, the King's daughter, widow of Gilbert de Clare, Earl of Gloucester, &c; the last named, John de St. John, had distinguished himself in the wars of Gascony, France, and Scotland, and was therefore in high military repute. From this fact it is supposed that the bearing of a crest on a helmet was originally limited to those connected with the blood royal, or of the highest military renown, and was in effect the precursor of a much greater honour, eventuating in the Order of the Garter itself. See the "Archæologia."

ROBERT HASSTANG.

HENRY DE PYNKENY.

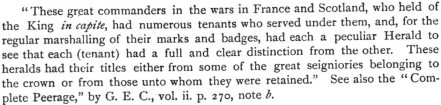

JOHN DE KINGESTON.

WILLIAM DE LEYBURN.

"These great commanders in the wars in France and Scotland, who held of the King *in capite*, had numerous tenants who served under them, and, for the regular marshalling of their marks and badges, had each a peculiar Herald to see that each (tenant) had a full and clear distinction from the other. These heralds had their titles either from some of the great seigniories belonging to the crown or from those unto whom they were retained." See also the "Complete Peerage," by G. E. C., vol. ii. p. 270, note *b*.

Notwithstanding these precautions some heraldic improprieties seem to have occurred subsequent to the battle of Agincourt, for in 5 Hen. v. it was proclaimed that " all such who had taken ye liberty of wearing cotes of armes in any former expedition where neither they nor their ancestors had ever used any were thenceforth prohibited yᵉ farther enjoyment of them unless they could produce a title thereto by Grant from some person who had authority for that purpose, excepting those only who had been with that warlike King in battell of Agincourt (1415), did then bear them in that memorable service." Close Roll 5 H. v. (1417), *in dorso* m. 15.

This brings us within measurable distance of that ill-starred incorporation of the Heralds' College by Richard III., six months after he was crowned. The King gave the Heralds a sometime royal residence, Pulteney Inn or Cold Harbore in Thames Street, built by Lord Mayor Pulteney, temp. E. III. Hardly was the incorporation complete, when Garter Writhe attempted to deprive his brother officers of the advantages of the Royal gift by claiming the house as personal to himself. As a result he resigned his Garter-ship January 4, 1484-5, and the property once more reverted to the Crown. The battle of Bosworth sealed the fate of the Heralds as a Corporation, until the reign of Philip and Mary, when it was re-incorporated, July 18, 1555. But this interregnum failed to allay the spirit of strife inaugurated by Writhe, engendered of personal gain at the expense of his fellows, a spirit which cannot be said to have become extinct.

NICHOLAS DE MEYNIL.

JOHN DE GREYSTOK.

JOHN PAYNELL.

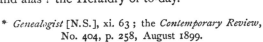

WILL. TOUCHET.

In " Ancestral Families " I shall incidentally show from the more ancient MSS. in the British Museum that the History of official Heraldry is written and embodied in the petty commercial jealousies of the Heralds, in their utter lack of *esprit de corps*, as proved by the sale of their records, and in their unscrupulous Heraldic and genealogical work, which seems to have culminated at that time in the person and name of Lee, Clarenceux King of Arms, to whom, according to Segar, Queen Elizabeth said, that " if he proved no better " than his predecessor Clarenceux Cooke, " yᵗ made no matter yf hee were hanged," such is the Heraldry of history, and alas ! the Heraldry of to-day.*

* *Genealogist* [N.S.], xi. 63 ; the *Contemporary Review*, No. 404, p. 258, August 1899.

TRICK TEMP. H. VI., HARL. MS. 2169, fo. 59*b*.

"William's Messengers." (After the Bayeux Tapestry.) "Here the Messengers came to William."

SOME FEUDAL ARMS

F = Facsimile. † = took up the Cross, i.e., a Crusader 1270.

‡ Dering Roll, see Preface, page vi.

* = probable ancestors of extant Noble and Gentle Families of the name.

John Able

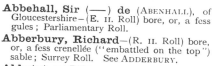

Abbehall, Sir (——) **de** (ABENHALL), of Gloucestershire—(E. II. Roll) bore, or, a fess gules ; Parliamentary Roll.

Abberbury, Richard—(R. II. Roll) bore, or, a fess crenellée ("embattled on the top") sable ; Surrey Roll. See ADDERBURY.

Abbetot, see D'ABBETOT.

Abell, Sir John, of Kent—(E. II. Roll) bore, argent, a saltire engrailed azure ; Parly. Roll.

Abell, John (ABLE)—(E. III. Roll) bore, sable, two bars or, in chief three torteaux (plates, in blason) ; Jenyns' Ordinary. F.

Abelyn, Nicholas (ABLYN)—(E. III. Roll) bore, gules, on a cross patonce argent five escallops azure ; Jenyns' Ordinary. F.

‡**Abelyne, Nicholas**—(H. III. Roll) bore, or, on a cross sable five eaglets argent ; Dering Roll &c. F.

Abernoun v. **Dabernon.**

‡**Abingdon, Philip de**—(H. III. Roll) bore, argent, on a bend gules three eaglets or ; Dering Roll.

Aburgavenny, Le Sr. (BEAUCHAMP)—bore, at the siege of Rouen 1418, gules, crusily and a fess or, a crescent (sable) for difference.

Acclon, Henry—(E. III. Roll) bore, gules, a maunch between six cinquefoyles argent ; (blasoned, gules, a maunch ermine) ; Jenyns' Ordinary. F.

Achard v. **Archard.**

Achard, Piers—(E. III. Roll) bore, undée (barry wavy of ten) argent and gules. Jenyns' Roll : another, undée (6) and a label (3) azure ; Arden Roll, &c. F.

Acherton, William de—(R. II. Roll) bore, argent, two bendlets and a bordure sable ; Surrey Roll. See also ATHERTON.

*****Ackland, John**—(R. II. Roll) bore, checquy argent and sable, a fess gules ; Surrey Roll. F.

Acton (——), an Essex Knight—(H. VI. Roll) bore, gyronny (12) argent and gules, *quarterly with*, gules, on a cross moline argent five escallops of the field ; Arundel Roll.

Acton, Sir John de (AKETON)—bore, at the battle of Boroughbridge 1322, quarterly indented azure and argent ; probably per fess indented is intended, as in the next.

Acton, Sir John de—bore, at the siege of Calais 1345-8, quarterly per fess indented argent and sable (*vel* azure), also ascribed to RICHARD ACTON in Surrey Roll R. II. F.

*[**Acton, Edward de**, of Aldenham, Salop, 1387—bore, gules, crusily or, two lyons passant in pale argent.—Shirley.] F.

[**Acton, Sir Roger,** of Sutton, 1410—bore, gules, a fess ermine within a bordure engrailed of the second.—Shirley.] F.

Acworth (——), a Suffolk Knight—(H. VI. Roll) bore, argent, a gryphon segreant per fess sable and azure ; Arundel Roll.

Adam, Sir John ap, baron 1299—bore, at the battle of Falkirk 1298, argent, on a cross gules five mullets or ; (pierced vert, Jenyns' Ordinary). (F.) The name is often written Badham. He signed, but did not seal, the Barons' letter to the Pope 1301, page xxiv.

Adderbury, Sir John—slain at the siege of Calais 1347, bore, argent, a fess crenellée sable. See also ABBERBURY.

Aglionby, John—(E. II. Roll) bore, argent, two bars and in chief three martlets sable ; Jenyns' Ordinary. F.

‡**Aguillon, Robert** (AGILLUN, AGUILUN or AGULON)—(H. III. Roll) bore, gules, a fleur-de-lys argent. (F.)—WILLIAM (‡) bore it with an azure field ; Dering and Glover Rolls, &c.

de Akeny v. **Dakeny.**

Alanby, Thomas—(E. III. Roll) bore, argent, a chevron within a bordure engrailed azure ; Jenyns' Roll. F., page 5.

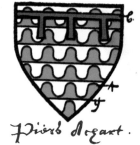

Piers Dogart.

John Acland

Roger Acton

nicholas Abolyn.

Nicol Ablin

Henry Acclon

John de Acton.

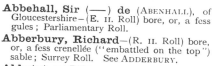

John ap Adam

John Aglomby

Robert Agillun

Edw Acton

B

2

Monto de Albemarle

witt le Alemande

Vasse de Aluogam Rog Anderson

Albemarle, see also AUBEMARLE.

Albemarle, Earl of—(H. III. Roll) bore, gules, a cross patonce vair; Glover Roll, &c. F.

Albini v. Daubeny, and de Albini.

Aldam, Sir Francis, of Kent fil. John—(E. II. Roll) bore, azure, a pile or, Parliamentary Roll; a sun in Harl. 4033; see ALDEHAM.

[Aldeburgh, William de, baron 1371-1386—bore, azure, a fess argent between three crosses crosslet or; Nobility Roll.]

[Aldeburgh, Sir William de, of Aldeburgh, Yorkshire, 1360—bore, a fess dancettée from point to point, between three crosses crosslet (now called botonnée) an annulet for difference. See Monumental Brass.]

Aldefelde, Robert—(E. III. Roll) bore, gules, a lyon rampant argent debruised by a bend sable charged with three crosses crosslet fitchée argent; Jenyns' Roll. F.

‡Aldeham, Thomas de—(H. III. Roll) bore, azure, a sun (16 rays) in his glory or; Dering Roll.

Alderby, Sir Walter—(E. III. Roll) bore, gules, three bulls' heads cabossed argent, horned azure; Ashmole Roll.

*[Aldersey, Hugh de, temp. H. III.—bore, gules, on a bend engrailed argent between two cinquefoyles or three leopards' faces vert—or more anciently, sable, three chargers or dishes argent.—Shirley.]

Alemande, William le—(H. III. Roll) bore vair, on a fess gules three martlets or, Arden Roll; the field, undée argent and azure, in St. George Roll. F.

Alexander (Count Allisander, doubtful if a surname)—(H. III. Roll) bore, barry (6) or and azure, a bordure gules; Arden Roll.

Alneham, Raffe de—(E. III. Roll) bore, azure, five fusils in fess or, a bend gules; Jenyns' Ordinary. F.

Alwent, John—(E. III. Roll) bore, gules, a chevron ermine between three fleurs-de-lys of the last; Jenyns' Ordinary. F.

*Alyngton (——), an Essex Knight—(H. VI. Roll) bore, sable, billettée and a bend engrailed argent; Arundel Roll.

‡Ambras, William (AMBESAS) — (H. III. Roll) bore, or, three dice sable, each charged with an annulet argent, Howard Roll; a plate in Dering Roll.

Amondevill, Robert—(E. III. Roll) bore, vair, three palets gules; Jenyns' Ordinary. F.

Amyas, Drewe de (or AMYAS DE DREWE?)—(H. III. Roll) bore, gules, three palets sable (azure in trick); Howard Roll.

*[Anderson, Roger, of Wrawby, co. Linc. 14th cent.—bore, argent, a chevron between three crosses flory sable.—Shirley.] F.

Andrew, Sir John, of Suffolk—(H. VI. Roll) bore, argent, on a bend engrailed sable three mullets pierced of the field; Arundel Roll.

Angelley, del—(rather DE LANGLEY)·(E. I. Roll) bore, argent, a fess and in chief three escallops sable; Camden Roll.

Anger, Sir Thomas (AWGER), of Kent—(H. VI. Roll) bore, ermine, on a chief azure three lyonceux rampant or; Arundel Roll.

Angervile, Sir John de, of co. Leicr.—(E. II. Roll) bore, gules, a cinquefoyle ermine, within a bordure sable bezantée; Parliamentary Roll. HUGH, took up the cross 1269.

Angevyn, Robert (AUNGEVYN)—(H. III. Roll) bore, gules, un florette (a fleur-de-lys) or; Norfolk Roll.

Angus, Gilbert, Earl of—bore, at the battle of Falkirk 1298, gules, a cinquefoyle pierced or, within an orle of crosses crosslet of the last—more probably, crusily. See also UMFRAVILLE.

Anlaby, Halnath de—(R. II. Roll) bore, argent, a fess between six fleurs-de-lys sable; Surrey Roll.

Ane or Ano, Drew de (ANO DE DREW or DREW DEANE—H. III. Roll) bore, gules, a saltire ermine; Arden Roll.

Anno, Alysaunder de (? DEANE)—(H. III. Roll) bore, gules, frettée argent; Howard Roll.

Anne, Sir William—(E. III. Roll) bore, or, three popinjays between two cotises sable; Ashmole Roll. The arms borne by ANNE (of Burghwallis) were, gules, three bucks' heads cabossed argent.—Yorkshire Visitations, ed. FOSTER.

Anne, William de—(E. III. Roll) bore, gules, on a bend argent cotised or three popinjays vert beaked and legged gules; Jenyns' Ordinary. F.

*Annesley, John de—(R. II. Roll) bore, paly (6) argent and azure a bendlet gules, Jenyns' and Surrey Rolls (F.)—with a bend vaire argent and sable in Cotgrave Roll E. III.—and paly (6) azure and argent a baston gobony or and gules, in Jenyns' Ordinary, E. III. &c. &c. F.

Antingham, —— (E. III. Roll) bore, sable, a bend argent; Ashmole Roll.

Ap Adam v. Adam.

‡Apeldrefeld, Henry de—(H. III. Roll) bore, ermine, a bend gules; HENRY LE FITZ (‡) bore the bend vaire or and gules. WILLIAM (‡) bore, or, a fess lozengy gules and vair; Dering and Howard Rolls.

SIR WILLIAM DE ALDEBURGH.

C. 1360. 33 Ed. III.

Aldborough Church, Yorkshire.

After Stothard.

witt Alington

Robert Amondeville

willm de Anne

John Anneslee

Pedigree of Anne, of Burghwallis.

Arms :—Gu. three bucks' heads caboshed arg. attired or
Crest :—A woman's head, couped at the shoulders ppr.

ROBERT HARRINGWELL, mesne lord of=MARGARET, dau. of
Frickley. (*Arg. on a bend sa. three* | Sir William St.
martlets of the field.) | George, Knt.

Sir William Anne, constable of the=ALICE, dau. | JOAN, dau. and co-heir, | ELIZABETH, dau. and co-heir,
castle of Tickhill, *temp*. Edward II., | and co-heir. | married to Sir Henry | married to John Fitz William,
and 4 Edward III. | | Gramery, Knt. = | of Woodhall. =

2. JOHN ANNE. ALEXANDER ANNE, of Frickley=AGNES.

RALPH ANNE, of Frickley (?) mentioned in the will of Robert=GRACE, sister of Sir Richard Goldsborough, Knt
Wolveden, treasurer of the Church of York, dated 4 Sept., 1432.

THOMAS ANNE, of=ELIZABETH, dau. of John Bosvile, of New Hall, in Darfield, by his | ELIZABETH ANNE.
Frickley. | 2nd wife, Isabel, dau. of Percival Cresacre. (*See* those families.) | ALICE ANNE.

JOHN ANNE, of Frickley, and of Preston and Rowhall, *j. u.*=CATHERINE, dau. and co-heir | MARGERY ANNE.
He is mentioned as John the elder, in will dated 18 March, | of Thomas Preston, of | ELIZABETH ANNE.
1503-4, of Edward Cresacre, sub-dean of York. | Hickleton. | ANNE ANNE.

MARGERY (1st wife),dau.=JOHN ANNE,=CATHERINE (2nd | ANNE. | ALICE. | JOANE, mar. to Sir
of .... Hercy. | of Frickley, | wife),dau. of John | JANE (?) mar. to | ELIZA- | Henry Gramery,
| *Inq. p. m.* 36 | Hotham, of Scor- | John Pecke, | BETH. | and had three
A son, d. y. | H. VIII. | borough, co. Y. | of Wakefield. | | daus. his co-heirs.

CHRISTOPHER | ELIZABETH (1st wife), dau. of Robert=MARTIN | =FRANCES(2nd wife), | GABRIEL ANNE, | =AGNES, dau. | PETER | DOROTHY,mar to
ANNE, son | Nevile, of Ragnall, co. Notts, and | ANNE, of | dau. of Ralph | ofCridlingPark, | of Ralph An- | ANNE. | John Anlaby, of
and heir, died | widow of Thos. Bosvile, of Ardsley | Frickley, | Anger (? Aucher), | co. York, gent., | ger(?Aucher), | WILLIAM | Etton.
without issue. | and Newhall, co. York | brother | of Redness, by his | bd. at Darring- | relict of Wil- | ANNE. | ISABEL, mar. to
| | and heir | wife Alice, dau. of | ton,4 February, | liam Skargill | | Bartholomew
| JOHN, d. y. | (1572). | Wm. Hungate, of | 1588-9. | | | Trigott, of
| | | Saxton (1572). | | | | Kirkby.

GEORGE ANNE,=MARGARET, | GERVAS | ELIZABETH, mar. 1st (as 2nd | DOROTHY, | JANE, mar. 1st to | MARY, m. to | ANNE, mar. | ALICE, mar. to
of Frickley ; | dau. and | ANNE, of | wife) to Francis, brother | mar. to John | Edward Grice, | John Ellis, | to Francis | Richard Dan-
living 1585; | sole heir of | Thorpe, | of the last Sir William | Tindall, of | of Sandal (son | afterwards | Holmes, of | by, of South
died 1620. | Richard | w. p. in | Gascoigne, of Gawthorpe ; | Brotherton, | of ...... Grice, of | Sir Jno. | Hampole, | Cave, co. Yk.
| Fenton, of · | London, | and 2nd to Marmaduke, | co. York, | Wakefield); and | Gascoigne | gent. | FRANCES
Burgh-	20 Sept.,	third son of Sir William	Esq.	2nd to Thomas	Ellis, of	
wallis.	1606.	Tirwhit, of Kettleby, co.		Hopton,of Cold	Kiddal, co.	
		Lincoln.		Hiendley, gent.	York.	

PHILIP ANNE,=ELLEN, dau. and co- | JOHN ANNE, died young. | 1 MARY, mar. to | CATHERINE, | MARTHA, mar. to | ELIZABETH,m. | JANE.
of Frickley, | heir of Hugh Sher- | GEORGE ANNE, d. unmar. | FrancisConyers. | mar. to ... | CharlesForster, | to Thomas | MARGARET.
Esq., eldest | burn, of Esholt, co. | THOMAS ANNE, of Sutton, | 2 BRIDGET and | Bright, of | son and heir of | Lepton, of |
son & heir,æt. | York, Esq., son of | co. Wilts; mar., and had | 3 FRANCES, nuns | Beverley, | Sir Richard | Kebeck, |
22 in 1613, | Sir Richard Sher- | issue. | in Flanders. | M.D. | Forster, of | (?Kepwick) |
died 1647. | burn, of Stonyhurst. | JOHN ANNE, of Ripon. | | | Stokesley, Knt. | co. York. |

JOHN ANNE, | ELEANOR (1st wife), dau. | = MICHAEL ANNE, of Frickley = FRANCES (2nd | PHILIP ANNE, mar. Mar- | JANE.
RICHARD ANNE, and | of Robert Stapleton, of | and Burghwallis, Esq., son | wife), dau. of | garet, dau. of Ambrose | ELIZABETH.
GEORGE ANNE, d. | Temple Hurst, co. | and heir, aged 40, 7 April, | Sir Francis For- | Pudsey,. of Barford, by | ELLEN.
unmarried. | York, Esq. | 1666. | tescue, Bart. | his 2nd wife, Jane Wil- | MARGARET.
| | | | kinson, and d. *s. p.* | All d. unm.

MICHAEL ANNE,=Hon. JANE LANGDALE, dau. of | GEORGE ANNE, of=MARGARET, widow of John, | URSULA, died unmarried
of Frickley, | Marmaduke, the 2nd Lord Lang- | Burghwallis,Esq., | Roundell,ofHuttonWansley, | ELLEN, died unmarried.
Esq., son and | dale, of Holme, living a widow in | 2nd son, aged 10, | and dau. of Thomas Fitzwil- | ELIZABETH, mar. to Anthony Saltmarsh, Esq,
heir, aged 12, 7 | 1728. | 1666. | liam, of Doncaster, gent. | of Strubby, co. Linc. She died 28 Mar., 1672.
April, 1666. · | | | | He died 9 June, 1675, æt. 34.

MICHAEL ANNE, of=ELIZABETH, daughter of | MARMADUKE ANNE,=ELIZABETH, dau. of Robert= | WILLIAM KNIGHT, | ELIZA- | ANNE, wife of
Frickley, Esq.,eldest | Francis Howard, of Corby | of Frickley, Esq., | Plumpton, of Plumpton, | of Frickley, gent. | BETH, | Edward Kil-
son and heir appar- | Castle, Esq., widow of | 2nd son, heir to his | Esq., and co-heir to that | (2nd husband) | died | lingbeck.
ent, died before his | WilliamErrington,of Beau- | father, died at Frick- | ancient family, born 26 | | young. |
father, and without | front, co. Northumber- | ley, 18 Aug. 1722. | May, 1692. | | |
issue. | land, Esq. | | | | |

MICHAEL ANNE, | ELIZABETH (1st wife), dau. of=GEORGE ANNE,= MARY (2nd | PHILIP | ANN, mar. to Arnold | ELIZABETH, | A son and two daugh-
of Frickley and | Thomas Walton, of Winder- | of Burgh- | wife), dau. | and | Knight, of Bus- | a nun, died | ters, one of whom,
Burghwallis, | mere, co. Westmoreland, wi- | wallis, Esq., | of Robert | JANE. | lingthorpe, co. | in a French | FRANCES, married to
Esq, eldest son, | dow of Thomas Cholmley, | died 5 June, | Needham, | Both | Lincoln, and had | prison,1791. | Edward Killingbeck,
sold Frickley, | of Bransby, Esq., marriage | 1785,aged 68; | of Hilston, | died | Alexander, father | | Esq., of Chapel Aller-
and died un- | settlement dated 17 April, | bu. at Burgh- | Monmouth- | young. | of Sir Arnold | | ton. He died 3 Nov.,
married. | 1745, she being then at | wallis. | shire, d. 15 | | Knight, M.D., of | | 1746. She died Sept.
| York | | June, 1816. | | Sheffield. | | 1751, leaving issue.

ELIZABETH, | GEORGE ANNE, of = FRANCES EDI- | MICHAEL ANNE, afterwards TAS- = MARIA AUGUSTA ROSALIA ANNE, dau. and heir
d. aged 16. | Burghwallis,Esq., | THA, dau. | BURGH, of Burghwallis, Esq., | of George Crathorne, Esq., and of Barbara, his
| eldest son, died | and co-heir | brother and heir, born 4 Oct. 1777; | wife, dau. of Thomas FitzHerbert, of Swinnerton,
| without issue, 27 | of William | married 23 April, 1810, when he | Esq., widow of George Tasburgh, Esq., of Bodney,
| July, 1802, aged | Gage, of | assumed, by royal sign manual, | in Norfolk, who left his estates to the said Barbara,
| 27,and was buried | York, Esq., | dated 20 June, 50 George III., the | and her issue· by any future husband, enjoining
| there. | died in 1844. | name and arms of Tasburgh. He | them to take the name and arms of Tasburgh. She
| | | d. at Calais. 10 July,1853, æt. 76. | died May, 1844.

GEORGE ANNE (which patro- | MICHAEL TASBURGH, born | MARY TASBURGH, mar. 28 | FRANCES TASBURGH, mar. 17 Jan., | BARBARA TASBURGH,
nymic he retained), of Burgh- | 20 June, 1818, died 15 | Feb., 1837, to Charles Gre- | 1833, to George Fieschi Heneage, | mar., 20 June, 1839,
wallis Hall, co. York, Esq., J.P. | Jan., 1819. | gory Fairfax, Esq., of Gilling | Esq., of Hainton, D.L., M.P. for | to William Henry
for the West Riding, eldest and | MICHAEL TASBURGH, · born | Castle, co. York, who died | co. Lincoln, and died 13 Nov., | Charlton, Esq., of
only surviving son, born 27 July, | at Versailles, 15 Dec. 1823 ; | 21 April, 1871, æt. 75, *s. p.* | 1842, æt. 31. He d. 11 May, | Hesleyside, co.
1813. | d. in Paris, 4 April, 1827. | | 1864, æt. 64. = | Northumberland =

ERNEST LAMBERT SWINBURNE ANNE,
born 1852, married and has issue.

Jogn Almoont

Robert de Aldefoildo.

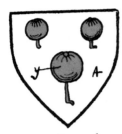

Robert Appolgarte

Jogn Apperley

Sir Walter Arden, 1412,
Aston Church, Warwicks.

Robt. do Appleby

Henry do Apolbi

Apperley, John de—(E. III. Roll) bore, argent a chevron gules between three pine-apples vert, slipped or; Jenyns' Ordinary. F.

Appelby, Sir Henry of Staffordshire—bore, at the first Dunstable tournament 1308, azure, six martlets or; the same are ascribed to Sir WILLIAM (with a label of three), and to EDMUND in other Rolls. (F.)—14 martlets to Sir EDMUND in Ashmole. See also JOHN LE MOINE.

Appleby, Sir Robert—bore, at the battle of Boroughbridge 1322, azure, the bordure of martlets or—tricked as 8 martlets in orle.

Applegarth, Robert—(E. III. Roll) bore, argent, three apples slipped gules; Jenyns' Ordinary. F.

Apr(e)'sby, Christopher de—(R. II. Roll) bore, sable, a cross and in the first quarter a cinquefoyle pierced argent; Surrey Roll.

Arcalowe, Sir William—bore, at the battle of Boroughbridge 1322, argent, three (bars) gemelles sable. F.

Arcas, Sir Alexander, of co. Leicr.—(E. II. Roll) bore, sable, three fleurs-de-lys argent; Parly. Roll. HARCHAS in Harl. Roll.

Archard, Sir Robert of Berkshire—(E. II. Roll) bore, or, a bend engrailed sable; Parliamentary Roll.

Archat, Sir Richard—(E. I. Roll bore, argent, on a bend cotised gules three fleurs-de-lys or, a bordure of the second; Nativity Roll.

Archedeckne, John, baron 1343—bore, at the second Dunstable tournament 1334, argent three chevronels sable; the same is ascribed (1) to ADAM (‡) in the Howard and Dering Rolls, and (2) to Sir THOMAS of Cornwall (in the Parly. Roll) GEFFREY, differenced with a label (5) gules, Arden and St. George Rolls.

Archedekin, Thomas—(H. III. Roll) bore, argent, three chevronels sable bezantée; Glover Roll. F.

Archer, Nicol le—(H. III. Roll) bore, sable, a lyon rampant or; St. George Roll. F.

Arches, Alexander de—slain at the siege of Calais 1347, bore, gules, three arches argent.

Arches, William—bore, at the siege of Rouen 1418, gules, three double arches argent. F.

*Arden, Sir Thomas** and **Sir Robert** (ARDERNE) of Warwickshire—(E. II. Roll) bore, ermine, a fess compony or and azure; Parliamentary and other Rolls. In Jenyns' Ordinary, a fess "Garen" (*i.e.*, Warren) is tricked checquy for John. F.

†**Arderne, Sir John,** of Salop—bore, at the first Dunstable tournament 1308, gules, crusily and a chief or; (F.) Another Sir JOHN—bore, at the siege of Calais 1345-8, gules, crusily fitchée and a chief or (F.), which is also ascribed to HUGH in Jenyns' Ordinary and to WILLIAM with crest in Ballard Roll temp. E. IV.

Arderne, Rauf de—(H. III. Roll) bore, ermine, on a fess gules three lozenges or; Arden Roll. F.

‡**Arderne, Randulph de**—(H. III. Roll) bore, or, crusily a lyon rampant sable; Arden Roll. F.

Arderne, Wakeline de—(E. III. Roll) bore, or, a lyon rampant vert, in Segar Roll, colours reversed, Jenyns' Ordinary (F.) RICHARD, junior, bore, vert, a lyon rampant or debruised by a fess gules.—SIRE DE ARDERNE (‡) bore, argent, a lyon rampant azure, debruised by a bend gules; Dering Roll.

Arderne, William de—(H. III. Roll) bore, sable, three lyons passant or; Arden Roll.

Arfois or **Arforce, ——** (E. III. Roll) bore, argent, three castles triple-turreted gules; Ashmole Roll.

will Arcalon

will Arcgob

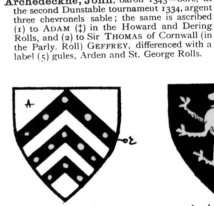

John Ercedeckno

Thomas le Archdekin

Nicol le Archer.

Jogn do Ardorno

Rondulf d'Ardarne.

John Ardorno

Rauf d'Ardarne.

John do Ardorno

wakkin do Ardorno

John Arnsoll

SIR JOHN DE ARGENTINE, 1382.
Horseheath, in Cambs.

Jogn de Argentine

Gilot de Argentine

Giles Argentem

Rauf d. Arras. *Robt de Asseton*

Janico de Artoyes

Le Sire matravers

Barth Asseburnham

Argentine, Sir Giles of Cambridge—bore, at the first Dunstable tournament 1308, gules, crusily and three covered cups argent.

Argentine, Sir John, Knight banneret, 2nd baron—bore, at the first Dunstable tournament 1308, gules, three covered cups argent. (F.) WILLIAM bore the reverse.

Argentine, Reynold de, a baron 1297—bore, gules, crusily fitchée and three covered cups argent, Nobility Roll; father of Sir JOHN, before named, see facsimile GILES.

Armine, *v.* **Ayrmine** and **Ermine.**

Arnes, Robert de—(H. III. Roll) bore, azure, two bends or; Howard Roll.

Arras, Rafe de—(H. III. Roll) bore, argent, on a cross azure five fleurs-de-lys or; Arden Roll. (F.) The Castellan of Arras in Normandy (‡), bore, gules a chief ermine; Dering Roll. See also DARRES.

Arthur, Sir Thomas—bore, at the siege of Rouen 1418, gules, a chevron argent between three clarions or.

Artoys, Janico de—(E. III. Roll) bore, gules, four bars wavy argent; Jenyns' Roll. (F.) See D'ARTOIS.

Arundel, Richard, Earl of, banneret—bore, at the battle of Falkirk, and at the siege of Carlaverock 1300, gules, a lyon rampant or; sealed the Barons' letter to the Pope 1301, pp xv., xxiv. Borne also by Earl EDMUND at the first Dunstable tournament 1308, and by another Earl RICHARD at the siege of Calais 1345-8. MOUNSYER RICHARD DE ARUNDELL and (Earl JOHN) LE SR. MATRAVERS bore, at the siege of Rouen 1418, ARUNDEL, *quarterly with,* MATRAVERS, sable, a fret or. (F.) See also FITZALAN.

*\[**Arundell, Reinfred de,** temp. H. III.—bore, sable, six martlets (*vel* hirondelles) argent.—Shirley.\] F.

Asdale, Thomas—(E. III. Roll) bore, gules, a cygnet passant argent; Jenyns' Roll. F.

****Ashburnham, Sir Bartholomew de**—bore, at the battle of Boroughbridge 1322, gules, a fess (between) six moles (mullets of 6) argent. (F.)—Sir JOHN bore the same with martlets in lieu of mullets, and another SIR JOHN, bore plates instead of mullets; Parliamentary Roll E. II.

‡**Ashburnham, Richard de**—(H. III. Roll) bore, gules, a fess and in chief three spur-rowells argent; Dering Roll.

Ashbye, Sir Robert de—(E. II. Roll) bore, argent, billettée gules and a lyon rampant sable; in another trick the lyon (and not the field) is billettée or; Parliamentary Roll.

Asche, Sire de—(E. I. Roll), bore, argent, a fess azure over all a saltire gules. JOHN DE ASSE, bore, or, a saltire gules over all a fess sable. Camden Roll.

Ashebaston, Sir Richard (ECHEBASTON) of co. Leicester—bore, at the battle of Borough-bridge 1322, argent, a lyon rampant gules, on his shoulder a cinquefoyle of the first, over all a baston azure (in another trick the cinquefoyle is on the baston); Parliamentary Roll. See also EDGBASTON. For same coat without the baston, see Sir ANDREW ASTLEY.

Asherst, Sir Adam—bore, at the siege of Calais 1345-8, gules, a cross engrailed between four fleurs-de-lys argent.

Ashfeld (——), a Suffolk Knight—(H. VI. Roll) bore, sable, a fess engrailed between three fleurs-de-lys argent; Arundel Roll.

As(h)ton, Richard de—(E. IV. Roll) bore, per chevron sable and argent—with crest; Ballard Roll.

Aske, Conan de—(E. III. Roll) bore, or, three bars azure; Grimaldi Roll. F.

Askeby, Sir Robert de—(E. III. Roll), bore, argent, a lyon rampant sable billettée or; Ashmole Roll. F.

Aspall, Sir Robert of Suffolk—(E. III. Roll) bore, azure, three chevronels or; Arundel and Parliamentary Rolls. The field gules in Ashmole Roll.

Asse, John de, *v.* ASCHE.

Asseles, Alan de—(H. III. Roll) bore, gules, a saltire and a chief argent; Arden and St. George Rolls. See LASSELLS.

*\[**Assheton, Sir Robert de,** E. III.—bore, argent, a mullet pierced sable.—Shirley.\] F.

Assi, Sir Robert de—(E. III. Roll) bore, gules, a bend cotised between six martlets or, Ashmole Roll.

Astinn (——? an Essex), Knight—(H. VI. Roll) bore, argent, a chevron between three fleurs-de-lys sable.

Astley, Sir Andrew, a baron 1295—bore, at the battle of Falkirk 1298, argent, a lyon rampant gules, on his shoulder a cinquefoyle of the first; (F.) (Borne with a baston by SIR RICHARD ASHEBASTON.) Borne with a cinquefoyle ermine by THOMAS (F.) in Jenyns' Ordinary, and with a billet ermine in place of the cinquefoyle by Sir NICHOLAS, banneret in Arundel Roll (F.); Sir GILES of co. Leic. *f* Thomas, 3rd lord—bore the cinquefoyle or and a label (3) and azure; Parly. Roll E. II.

Astley, Thomas—bore, in the second Dunstable tournament 1334, azure, a cinquefoyle pierced ermine. (F.) Ascribed also to ANDREW, JOHN, and Sir THOMAS in St. George and Ashmole Rolls and Jenyns' Ordy. **THOMAS, of (Hill) Morton, differenced with a bordure engrailed or; in Surrey Roll R. II. Sir RAUFF—a bordure argent—in Ashmole Roll E. III.; and THOMAS DE—with a label (3) or, on each point two bars gules, in Surrey Roll R. II.

Adam Ashurst

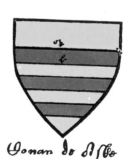

Roger de Askeby

Conan de Asse

Ric̃. de Arundel   *Sr̃ Arthur*   *Thomas Asdale*   *Joĩn de Arundel*   *Thomas Aslanby.*   *Andr. de Estloie*

THE HERALDIC ATCHIEVEMENT

OF

JOHN FRANCIS ARUNDELL, 12TH BARON ARUNDELL
OF WARDOUR.

Jogm Aftlee

Robert Aftoly

Andr. Eftoley

nicg Aftoly

JOHN, LORD AUDLEY.
Shere Church, Surrey, 1491.

Roger de Afton

Lo Conntio
de Afgotil.

Gilbert de Aton

[**Astley, Giles**—bore, gules, a cinquefoyle pierced ermine between three mullets or ; Harl. MS. 1481 fo. 75ᵇ.]

Astley, Robert—(E. III. Roll) bore, azure, crusily or and a lyon passant gardant argent ; Jenyns' Ordinary. F.

Aston, Sir John de, of Northants—(E. II. Roll) bore, sable, a saltire argent ; Parliamentary Roll.

Aston, Sir Richard de, of Gloucestershire —(E. II. Roll) bore, gules, a lyon rampant or, debruised by a bend vair ; Parliamentary Roll.

Aston, Sir Richard of Hants or Wilts.— (E. II. Roll) bore, azure, crusily or, and a bend argent cotised of the second. Parliamentary Roll. One of these names took up the cross 1270.

Aston, Roger de—(E. III. Roll) bore, argent, a dancette (embelif) sable ; Jenyns' Roll. F.

Atherton, —— (E. IV. Roll) bore, gules, three hawks or—with crest ; Ballard Roll.

Atherton, William, see ACHERTON.

✝**Athol, (David) Earl of**—(H. III. Roll) bore, paly or and sable, in Norfolk and Grimaldi Rolls (F.)—paly (6) in Arden Roll—or, 4 palets sable, in Howard Roll and, or three palets azure, in Segar, Camden and St. George Rolls. ADOMAR of Suffolk, younger brother of DAVID DE STRABOLGY, differenced with a bendlet argent. Harl. MS. 1481 fo. 74.

Aton, Sir Gilbert de, a baron 1324— bore, at the battle of Boroughbridge 1322, or, a cross passant argent (by Sir WILLIAM, 2nd baron, in Ashmole) ; and gules, a cross patonce argent (F.), in Parliamentary Roll, &c., another (? platey at the points) in Ashmole.

Atte Hethe *v.* **Hethe.**

Attwater, William, Bishop of Lincoln (6 H. VIII. 1515) bore, undée (barry wavy of six) ermine and gules, on a chevron between three shrimps embowed or, a rose gules seeded argent and leaved vert enclosed by two flowers ; Nobility Roll.

Attewode, John—(R. II. Roll) bore, gules a lyon rampant tail fourchée argent ; Surrey Roll, and as ATWOOD in Ashmole Roll.

Aubemarle, Sir Geffrey of Devon and Hants—(E. II. Roll) bore, gules, crusily or and a bend lozengy ermine ; Parliamentary Roll.

Aucher, Henry—(H. III. Roll) bore, ermine, on a chief azure three lyons rampant or ; Arden Roll.

Audley, Hughe de, Earl of Gloucester, 1337-47—bore, or, three chevronels gules, Nobility Roll H. VI. See also CLARE.

Audley, Sir Nicholas de, of Heligh, baron 1297—bore, at the battle of Falkirk 1298, gules. a fret (*vel* fretty) or ; so borne also by his son JAMES, K.G. (a founder), one of the heroes of Poictiers, and by WILLIAM DE AUDLEY (‡) ; Dering Roll. Sir HUGH of co. Gloucr. differenced with a label (5) azure (F.) ; HUGH and JOHN, a bordure argent (F.), Cotgrave and Jenyns' Ordinary E. III. JAMES, with a label gobony argent and azure, Cotgrave ; and Sir JAMES of co. Gloucr. with a label (3) azure, on each point a lyoncel of the second ; Parliamentary Roll E. II. where Sir NICHOLAS first named, appears among the bannerets. Another JAMES took up the cross 1270.

Auke, Gregory de—(E. III. Roll) bore, gules, two bars and in chief three annulets all argent ; Jenyns' Ordinary. F.

Aunsell, Alexander—(E. III. Roll) bore, ermine, on a fess gules three crosses crosslet or ; Jenyns' Ordinary. F.

Auntesheye, Sir Richard (DAUNTSEY) of Gloucestershire—(E. II. Roll) bore, per fess or and argent, a fess undée gules. (F.) Parliamentary Roll.

Austre(y), William de—(H. III. Roll) bore, gules, a fess argent, a label (5) or ; or AUSTRY *vel* DAUTREY ; Arden Roll.

Autrey, William de (DAUTREY)—(H. III. Roll) bore, azure, a fess dancettée (5) argent, a label (5) gules ; Arden Roll.

Avenbury, Osbern de—(H. III. Roll) bore, gules, three lyons rampant tails fourchée argent ; Arden Roll.

Avene, Sir Leyson de (DAVENEY), of co. Gloucr.—(E. II. Roll) bore, gules, three chevronels argent ; Parly. Roll. See VENE.

Avenel, Sir John de—(E. III. Roll) bore, argent, a fess between six annulets 3 and 3 gules ; Ashmole Roll—the same for Sir WILLIAM of Cambridgeshire in Parliamentary Roll E. II. F.

Awger, Sir Thomas (AUGER) of Kent— (H. VI. Roll) bore, ermine, on a chief azure three lyonceux rampant or ; Arundel Roll.

Awillers *v.* **Davelers.**

Ailesbury, Sir Robert de—bore, at the battle of Boroughbridge 1322, azure, a cross argent and a label (3) gules. JOHN, bore it undifferenced, and another JOHN, with a baston gules, instead of the label ; Jenyns' Ordinary E. III. F.

Ayrmyn, William—(E. III. Roll) bore, argent, a saltire engrailed and a chief gules ; Jenyns' Ordinary. (F.) WM. DE ERMINE, bore, ermine, a saltire engrailed gules, on a chief of the last a lyon passant gardant or. Surrey Roll.

Gregory de Aube.

nicg Auntofhays

Jogn de Aylofbury

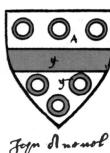
Gilbert de Aton

Huo D Audley

Jogn daudolay

Aloc Aunfoll

Jogn Anonol

miltm Ayrmyn.

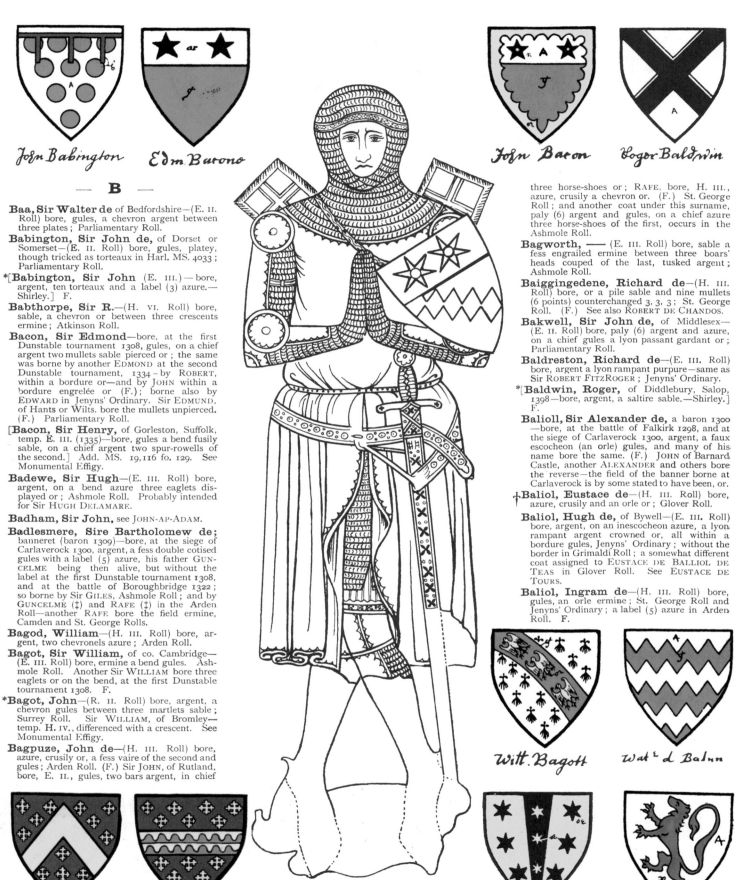

John Babington   Edm Barone   John Bacon   Roger Baldwin

— B —

Baa, Sir Walter de of Bedfordshire—(E. II. Roll) bore, gules, a chevron argent between three plates ; Parliamentary Roll.

Babington, Sir John de, of Dorset or Somerset—(E. II. Roll) bore, gules, platey, though tricked as torteaux in Harl. MS. 4033 ; Parliamentary Roll.

*[**Babington, Sir John** (E. III.)—bore, argent, ten torteaux and a label (3) azure.—Shirley.] F.

Babthorpe, Sir R.—(H. VI. Roll) bore, sable, a chevron or between three crescents ermine ; Atkinson Roll.

Bacon, Sir Edmond—bore, at the first Dunstable tournament 1308, gules, on a chief argent two mullets sable pierced or ; the same was borne by another EDMOND at the second Dunstable tournament, 1334—by ROBERT, within a bordure or—and by JOHN within a bordure engrelée or (F.); borne also by EDWARD in Jenyns' Ordinary. Sir EDMUND, of Hants or Wilts. bore the mullets unpierced. (F.) Parliamentary Roll.

[**Bacon, Sir Henry,** of Gorleston, Suffolk, temp. E. III. (1335)—bore, gules a bend fusily sable, on a chief argent two spur-rowells of the second.] Add. MS. 19,116 fo. 129. See Monumental Effigy.

Badewe, Sir Hugh—(E. III. Roll) bore, argent, on a bend azure three eaglets displayed or ; Ashmole Roll. Probably intended for Sir HUGH DELAMARE.

Badham, Sir John, see JOHN-AP-ADAM.

Badlesmere, Sire Bartholomew de; banneret (baron 1309)—bore, at the siege of Carlaverock 1300, argent, a fess double cotised gules with a label (5) azure, his father GUNCELME being then alive, but without the label at the first Dunstable tournament 1308, and at the battle of Boroughbridge 1322 ; so borne by Sir GILES, Ashmole Roll ; and by GUNCELME (‡) and RAFE (‡) in the Arden Roll—another RAFE bore the field ermine, Camden and St. George Rolls.

Bagod, William—(H. III. Roll) bore, argent, two chevronels azure ; Arden Roll.

Bagot, Sir William, of co. Cambridge—(E. III. Roll) bore, ermine a bend gules. Ashmole Roll. Another Sir WILLIAM bore three eaglets or on the bend, at the first Dunstable tournament 1308. F.

*[**Bagot, John**—(R. II. Roll) bore, argent, a chevron gules between three martlets sable ; Surrey Roll. Sir WILLIAM, of Bromley—temp. H. IV., differenced with a crescent. See Monumental Effigy.

Bagpuze, John de—(H. III. Roll) bore, azure, crusily or, a fess vaire of the second and gules ; Arden Roll. (F.) Sir JOHN, of Rutland, bore, E. II., gules, two bars argent, in chief

three horse-shoes or ; RAFE. bore, H. III., azure, crusily a chevron or. (F.) St. George Roll ; and another coat under this surname, paly (6) argent and gules, on a chief azure three horse-shoes of the first, occurs in the Ashmole Roll.

Bagworth, —— (E. III. Roll) bore, sable a fess engrailed ermine between three boars' heads couped of the last, tusked argent ; Ashmole Roll.

Baiggingedene, Richard de—(H. III. Roll) bore, or a pile sable and nine mullets (6 points) counterchanged 3, 3, 3 ; St. George Roll. (F.) See also ROBERT DE CHANDOS.

Bakwell, Sir John de, of Middlesex—(E. II. Roll) bore, paly (6) argent and azure, on a chief gules a lyon passant gardant or ; Parliamentary Roll.

Baldreston, Richard de—(E. III. Roll) bore, argent a lyon rampant purpure—same as Sir ROBERT FITZROGER ; Jenyns' Ordinary.

*[**Baldwin, Roger,** of Diddlebury, Salop, 1398—bore, argent, a saltire sable.—Shirley.] F.

Balioll, Sir Alexander de, a baron 1300 —bore, at the battle of Falkirk 1298, and at the siege of Carlaverock 1300, argent, a faux escocheon (an orle) gules, and many of his name bore the same. (F.) JOHN of Barnard Castle, another ALEXANDER and others bore the reverse—the field of the banner borne at Carlaverock is by some stated to have been, or.

†**Baliol, Eustace de**—(H. III. Roll) bore, azure, crusily and an orle or ; Glover Roll.

Baliol, Hugh de, of Bywell—(E. III. Roll) bore, argent, on an inescocheon azure, a lyon rampant argent crowned or, all within a bordure gules, Jenyns' Ordinary ; without the border in Grimaldi Roll ; a somewhat different coat assigned to EUSTACE DE BALLIOL DE TEAS in Glover Roll. See EUSTACE DE TOURS.

Baliol, Ingram de—(H. III. Roll) bore, gules, an orle ermine ; St. George Roll and Jenyns' Ordinary ; a label (5) azure in Arden Roll. F.

Witt. Bagott   Watr d Balun

Rauf d bakepus   Joan d' Bakepuz   Ric d' Baigginggedene   Vngard de Baldreston

SIR HENRY BACON.
IN GORLESTON CHURCH, SUFFOLK.
C. 1335. AFTER STOTHARD.

SIR WILLIAM BAGOT,
8 HEN. IV. 1407.
BAGINTON CHURCH, WARWICKSHIRE.
After Boutell.

Baliol, William de—(H. III. Roll) bore, or, an orle vair, a label (5) gules. Another WILLIAM —bore, or, an orle azure, a label (5) gules. Arden and St. George Rolls.

Balnye, William de—(E. III. Roll) bore, argent, an eagle displayed azure, beaked and membered gules. Jenyns' Ordinary. F. See also BILNEY.

‡**Balun, John, and Walter de**—(H. III. Roll) bore, barry dancettée (6 or 8) argent and gules (F.) St. George, Howard and Dering Rolls; THOMAS, gules and or, in Jenyns' Ordinary.

Balun, John—(E. III. Roll) bore, per fess indented argent and gules. Jenyns' Roll. F.

Bam (me), ——, a Kentish Knight—(H. VI. Roll) bore, ermines on a chief pily argent two trefoyles sable; Arundel Roll.

Bamnye *v.* **Bawnd** or **Bownd.**

[**Bampfylde, John** (BAUMFIELD), E. I.— bore, or, on a bend gules, three mullets argent.—Shirley.] F.

Banastre, Sir Adam, of Lancashire—bore, at the first Dunstable tournament 1308, argent, a cross patonce sable, and also by Sir WILLIAM, who was knighted at the capitulation of Calais 1348, and by Sir Thomas K.G. 1376; the cross is variously tricked or blasoned, patée, patonce, and flory, according to the humour of the Herald or his painter, for they were evidently interchangeable, or one and the same. F.

Banastre, Sire William—(E. I. Roll) bore, argent, three chevronels gules, Guillim Roll, and the reverse in the Parliamentary Roll.

Banbury, Gilbert de, and Sir Thomas de, of Oxon—(E. I. Roll) bore, argent a cross patonce (or flory) gules, between four torteaux; Parliamentary Roll.

Banbury, Thomas de—(E. I. Roll) bore, argent, a cross between four mullets (6) pierced gules; Segar Roll. F.

Band, Sir Walter le—(E. II. Roll) bore, gules, three pairs of eagles' wings, or; Parliamentary Roll. See also BAUDE.

Banke, John de—(E. II. Roll) bore, sable a cross between four fleurs-de-lys argent, *quirtering* argent a chevron between three annulets gules, Jenyns' Roll. F.

Bardolf, Sir Hugh, a baron 1299—Sealed the Barons' letter to the Pope 1301, pp. xvii, xxiv; bore, at the battle of Falkirk 1298, and at the siege of Carlaverock 1300, azure, three cinquefoyles or; as also did (1) Sir THOMAS at the first Dunstable tournament 1308, (2) Le Sr. BARDOLPHE at the siege of Rouen 1418, and (3) WILLIAM (‡) in the Dering Roll. A Bardolf coat w thin a bordure engrailed argent in the Ashmole Roll.

Bardolf, John—bore, at the second Dunstable tournament 1334, azure, three cinquefoyles argent (as did Sir WILLIAM, of Norfolk, in Parly. Roll, E. II.), but his cousin JOHN, also of Norfolk, bore a red field.

Bardolfe, Sir Thomas, banneret—(E. II. Roll) bore, or, three cinquefoyles azure. (F.) Parliamentary Roll; the Surrey Roll (R. II.) ascribes argent three cinquefoyles pierced or, to LE SR. DE BARDOLF.

Bardolfe, Thomas—(H. III. Roll) bore, azure, crusily and three cinquefoyles or. Glover and Norfolk Rolls.

Bardwell, William—bore, at the siege of Rouen 1418, gules, a goat saliant, or, *quarterly with,* or, an eagle displayed vert. One Sir WILLIAM bore the goat argent horned or. F. as Bedwell.

Bare, Sir John de—bore, at the battle of Falkirk 1298, and at the siege of Carlaverock 1300, azure, crusily and two barbes or, a bordure indented gules, engrailed in the Carlaverock Roll—the "barbes" blasoned "poissons" in Harl. 6589 fo. 3ᵇ, and "barbeaux" fo. 50; correctly tricked only in Add. 5848 fo. 79, as two barbels addorsed embowed or; in all other MSS. erroneously blasoned or tricked as Heraldic bars. F. RALPH BARRY took up the cross in the last Crusade 1270.

C

Robt. Barboſworz

Tĥ Barnaſtone

Adam de Bartholot

will. Bonnaſ.

Stevene Barret

Bt. Barooſworz

Stevene Barot

will Barantin.

John Barton de ffriton

willm Borome

Roger Bartram Baron de myt forde.

John Barry

Joan d' Baſkervile

Bare, John de—(E. III. Roll) bore, azure two bars or, a bordure engrailed gules ; Jenyns' Ordinary. (F.) See also BARRE.

Barkeworth, Robert (BARCEWORTH) — (E. III. Roll) bore, argent, a saltire sable a label (3) gules ; Jenyns' Ordinary and Roll. (F.) See also BRAKWORTHE.

Barksworth, Sir Robert de, of Suffolk— (E. II. Roll) bore, chequy argent and gules, on a bend azure three lyonceux passant of the first (F.) ; Parliamentary Roll.

Barlow, —— (H. VI. Roll) bore, sable, a double-headed eagle displayed argent ; Arundel Roll.

(Barlye ?), of Essex — (H. VI. Roll) bore, undée (6) sable and ermine (i.e. barry nebulée) ; Arundel Roll.

Barnake, Sir William, of co. Leic.—(E. II. Roll) bore, argent a fess between three barnacles sable ; Parly. Roll ; and in Jenyns' Roll, argent three barnacles sable are ascribed to WILLIAM B., shovellers in lieu of barnacles, are also ascribed to both. F.

Barnam, Henry le—(H. III. Roll) bore, France, and a chief paly argent and gules ; Norfolk Roll.

Barnard, John—(H. VI. Roll) bore, argent, a bear passant sable muzzled, or, quarterly with, gules three lucies naiant (? argent). Arundel Roll, in which two other BARNARD coats appear, (1) gules, three chevronels ermine (2) argent a chevron sable, on a chief gules three mullets or, a crescent for difference.

Barnastone, Thomas—(E. III. Roll) bore, azure, crusily (5, 5) argent and a fesse dancettée ermine ; (F.) Jenyns' Ordinary. This coat seems to have been allowed to, or appropriated by, BARNSTONE of Cheshire and BARNARDISTON of Suffolk.

‡Barnes, Rauf de—(H. III. Roll) bore, quarterly or and azure ; Dering Roll—or, and vert in St. George Roll ; called also BERNERS, see that name.

Barre v. Bare and Barry.

Barre, Robert—(R. II. Roll) bore, gules, three bars crenellée argent ; Surrey Roll.

Barre, Thomas—(R. II. Roll) bore, gules, three bars compony argent and azure, quarterly with, barry (6) or and azure, a bend gules ; Surrey Roll.

Barre, William—(R. II. Roll) bore, azure two lyons passant gardant and a bordure engrailed or ; Surrey Roll.

Barres, (——) de—(H. III. Roll) bore, lozengy or and gules ; Arden Roll.

Barrett, John, of Suffolk—(Hen. VI. Roll) bore, argent, three buckles lozengy gules, tongues to the sinister ; another JOHN bore the same between a bend azure thereon an annulet or ; Arundel Roll.

Barret, Sire Stevene—bore, at the battle of Boroughbridge 1322, argent, crusily and a lyon rampant gules crowned or.

Baret, Sire Stevene—bore, at the battle of Boroughbridge 1322, argent, crusily potent (tricked fitchée in Ashmole) and three fleurs-de-lys sable within a bordure engrailed of the second. F.

Barrentine, Sir Drew de, of Bucks— (E. II. Roll) bore, sable, six eaglets, 3, 2, 1, argent ; Parly. Roll. Three eagles in the Segar Roll ; eaglets or, in the Glover Roll. F. See also Tiles, Neath Abbey, p. ix.

Barrington, Sir Nicholas de, of Essex— (E. II. Roll) bore, argent, three chevronels gules, a label (3) azure ; Parliamentary and Arundel Rolls.

Barington, Sir Philip, of co. Leic.— bore, at the first Dunstable tournament 1308, argent, a lyon rampant sable tail fourchée, on the shoulder a fleur-de-lys or. Parly. Roll.

Barowe, William—(E. III. Roll) bore, argent, on a fess dancette sable three besants ; (F.) Jenyns' Ordinary.

Barry, John—(E. III. Roll) bore, gules two gemelles argent, en manere de barres ; (F.) Jenyns' Ordinary.

Barry, Sir Robert, of Bucks—(E. II. Roll) bore, azure, two lyons passant gardant or ; Arden, St. George, and Parly. Rolls. F.

*[Bartelott, Adam de, 1428—bore, sable, three falconers sinister gloves pendant argent, tasseled or.—Shirley.] F.

Barton, Geoffrey, of Tatton—is heir to the coat of Sir GEOFFRY MASSY of Tatton and also of MASSY—(Ed. IV. Roll) bore, quarterly gules and argent, a label (5) azure. Ballard Roll.

*Barton, John de—(R. II. Roll) bore, argent, a bend wavy sable ; Surrey Roll. See RICHARD DE WALLOP.

Barton, John, of Friton—(E. III. Roll) bore, ermine, on a fess gules three annulets or ; Grimaldi Roll and Jenyns' Ordinary. F.

Bartram, Roger, baron of Mitford—(E. III. Roll) bore, gules, crusily and an orle or ; Jenyns' Ordinary. See also BERTRAM. F.

Barwick, see BERWICK.

Basan, Stephen—(H. III. Roll) bore, undée argent and gules, a quarter sable ; Glover Roll.

‡Basemes, Godfrey de (called also BASEVILE)—(H. III. Roll) bore, gules an inescocheon argent within an orle of cinquefoyles or ; Dering Roll.

Basford, Sir John, knighted at the capitulation of Calais 1348—gules a lyon rampant ermine. F.

Basynges, John—(R. II. Roll) bore, gules, seven barrulets argent ; Surrey Roll.

Robt d' Barri

John de Baſing

will Baſingb

Eno de Baſpeb

walter de Baſkevile

Anfol Baffot

Auncel Baffet

Edmondo de Baffot

Ricg.d Baffot

Rauf Baffot

Rauff Baffott

Sire Rauf Baffot

Gen Baffott

will Baffot

John Baffontt

Roger Bauont

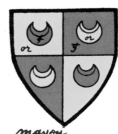

mayou Bafingbourno

warm Baffingborno

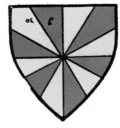

Rog Bamnyo

Baftard

walt. Bonant

Basing, Sir John, of Middlesex — (E. II. Roll) bore, azure, a cross recercelée voided or. (F.) Sir WILLIAM, of Kent, bore the same with a baston gules; Parliamentary Roll. A cross moline in Jenyns' Ordinary. F.

Baskerville, Andrew de—(H. III. Roll) bore, argent, a chevron azure between three torteaux; Arden Roll.

Baskerville, Sir Richard de, banneret— (E. II. Roll) bore, argent, a chevron gules between three hurts; Parliamentary Roll. JOHN and WALTER bore torteaux instead of hurts; Arden and Glover Rolls. F.

*Baskervile, Sir Walter, of co. Glouc.— bore, at the first Dunstable tournament 1308, argent, on a chevron gules between three hurts as many mullets (fleurs-de-lys in Cotgrave Roll) or; in the Parly. Roll, crosses crosslet are substituted for mullets, and in another MS. 5 instead of 3 crosses crosslet are blased crusily. JOHN took up the cross in the last Crusade 1270.

‡Baspes, Sire de—(H. III. Roll) bore, gules, three palets vair, on a chief or a demi fleur-de-lys issuant sable; Dering Roll. F.

Basset, Rauf—(H. III. Roll) bore, or, three piles gules; Arden Roll.

Bassett, Richard, of Weldon, a baron 1299—bore, or, three palets gules, and a bordure azure. RAUFF, also baron, bore the bordure besantée; Surrey Roll.

Basset, Rauff, of Drayton, 1st baron 1264— (E. I. Roll) bore, or, three piles meeting in base gules, a canton ermine. Segar and St. George Rolls (F.)—and so also RALPH 4th Baron K.G. 1369. RALPH 2nd baron bore, at the battle of Falkirk 1298, paly (6) or and gules, a canton ermine. F., probably father of the next named.

Basset, Sir Rauf, banneret—bore, at the first Dunstable tournament 1308, or, three piles meeting in base gules, a canton ermine. Sir SIMON bore them, with a label (3) azure, at the siege of Calais 1345-8, and RAUF LE FITZ also, at the second Dunstable tournament 1334. In tricks for Sir ROBERT or ROGER of Worcestershire the piles are sometimes azure sometimes sable; Parly. Roll. ROGER bore them sable and the canton gules; Segar Roll.

‡Basset, Sir Rauf—(H. III. Roll) bore, or three piles meeting in base gules, a canton vair; Arden and St. George Rolls. JOHN, bore on the canton argent, a gryphon segreant sable armed or; Surrey Roll.

Basset, Lord, slain at the siege of Calais 1347 —bore, gules, three piles meeting in base argent, a canton ermine.

Basset, Rauff—(H. III. Roll) bore, paly (6) or and gules, on a canton argent a cross patée sable; Norfolk Roll.

Basset, Sir Richard—bore, at the first Dunstable tournament 1308, paly (6) or and gules, a bordure sable besantée; (F.) Another Sir RICHARD (E. II.) bore the bordure azure; Parliamentary Roll.

Basset, Sire Rauf—(E. I. Roll) bore, argent, three bars undée gules; Guillim Roll. F.

Basset, Rauf, of Sapcote, a baron 1264, and Simon—(H. III. Roll) bore, undée (6) argent and sable; St. George and Harl. Rolls. Sir JOHN bore the same besantée; Ashmole Roll.

Basset, H.—(H. III. Roll) bore, undée argent and sable a canton gules; St. George Roll.

Basset, Lawrence—(H. III. Roll) bore, undée (6) argent and gules; Arden and St. George Rolls. PHILIP bore, or and gules, St. George Roll; and WILLIAM the reverse in Jenyns' Ordinary. SYMON (‡) bore argent and azure in Howard Roll; and or and azure in Dering Roll.

*[Basset, Sir William, of Tehidy, Cornwall, E. III.—bore, or, three bars undée gules —wavy, in Shirley.] F.

Bassett, Simon—bore, at the second Dunstable tournament 1334, ermine, un partie gules, a mullet or; Collect. and Top., IV. 390.

Bassett, Sir Lawrence and Thomas, of Cornwall—(E. III. Roll) bore, barry dancettée (6) argent and gules; Ashmole Roll, &c.

Bassett, Philip—(H. III. Roll) bore, quarterly or and gules; Glover Roll.

Bassett, Sir Richard, of Rutland, and Sir William—(E. II. Roll) bore, argent, two bars azure, in chief three chaplets gules; Parly. and Ashmole Rolls.

Bassett, Simon—(E. III. Roll) bore, ermine, on a canton gules an orle argent; another a mullet (6) pierced or on the canton; Ashmole and Jenyns' Rolls. F.

‡Bassett, Anscel—(H. III. Roll) bore, ermine, a chief dancettée gules; Dering Roll. F.

Bassett, Sir John—bore, at the siege of Carlaverock 1300, ermine, on a chief dancettée (vel indented), gules, three spur-rowells or. Sir EDMONDE, of co. Glouc., his brother, bore escallops in lieu of the spur-rowells. F.F.

Bassett, Osmond—(E. III. Roll) bore, ermine, on a chief indented gules, two mullets or pierced vert.

Bas(s)ingbourne, Sire Mayeu de— bore, at the battle of Boroughbridge 1322, quarterly or and gules, four crescents counterchanged. F.

‡Bassingbourne, Baldwin, or Jordan— (H. III. Roll) bore, gyrony (12) vair and gules; Arden Roll; for WARREN, in Cotgrave Roll, and for RAFFE in Jenyns' Ordinary.

Bassingbourne, Giles f HUMPHREY— (E. III. Roll) bore, gyrony (6) argent and gules, a baston azure; Cotgrave Roll.

Bassingbourne, Sir Humphrey, of co. Cambridge—(E. II. Roll) bore, gyrony (8) argent and gules, Parliamentary Roll; tricked also 6 and 12 for other Humphreys.

Bassingbourne, Sir John, of Herts— (E. II. Roll) bore, gyrony (8) or and gules; Parliamentary Roll.

Bassingbourne, Sir Warren, of co. Lincs. —(E. II. Roll) bore, gyrony (8, sometimes 12 and 16), or and azure, Parly. Roll and Jenyns' Ordinary. F.

*[Bastard (——), of Kitley, Devon—bore, or, a chevron azure.—Shirley.] F.

Battott, —— (H. VI. Roll) bore, gules, a gryphon segreant or, a bordure engrailed sable; Arundel Roll.

Bause, Sire William, see GAUSE.

Baud, Sir Thomas le—(E. III. Roll) bore, azure, a lyon passant or; Ashmole Roll.

Baud, Sir Walter le, of Essex—(E. II. Roll) bore, gules, three eagles' wings or; Parliamentary Roll.

Bawde, William, of Essex—(E. III. Roll) bore, gules, three chevronels argent; Cotgrave and Surrey Rolls.

Bavent, Sir Roger, a baron 1313—bore, at the first Dunstable tournament 1308, argent, a chief indented sable. (F.) See BAMNYE in margin; bore also by ADAM (‡) in Howard and Dering Rolls. Another ROGER bore it with 3 besants; Jenyns' Ordinary. F.

Bavent, Sire John de—bore, at the battle of Boroughbridge 1322, argent, a chevron gules within a bordure sable besantée; another JOHN bore this coat with the bordure engrailed, at the second Dunstable tournament 1334. F.

Bavant, William—(E. III. Roll) bore, ermine, two bars gules each charged with three spur-rowells or; Jenyns' Ordinary. F.

Jo Baynard | Robt Baynton | Hbt Bayonfo

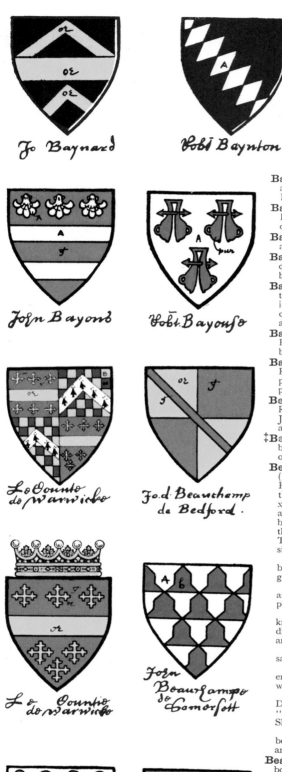

John Bayons | Robt. Bayoufe

Le Counte de Warwicke | Jo.d Beauchamp de Bedford.

Le Countio de Warwick | John Beaurhampe de Somerfott

John Beanchamp. | Jar.d Beauchamp

Bavesar, Walter de—(H. III. Roll) bore, argent, a lyon rampant tail fourchée gules; Dering Roll.

Baynarde, Sir Robert, of Norfolk—(E. I. Roll) bore, sable a fess between two chevronels or; Parly. Roll. For JOHN in Jenyns' Ord. F.

Bayning, William de—(H. III. Roll) bore, argent, three fleurs-de-lys azure; Howard Roll.

Baynton, Sir Robert, knighted at the capitulation of Calais 1348—bore, sable a bend fusily argent. F.

Bayous, Sir John, knighted at the capitulation of Calais 1348—bore, gules, two bars and in chief three escallops argent (F.); the same coat was borne by Sir WILLIAM, of co. Linc., at the first Dunstable tournament 1308.

Bayouse, Herbert, of Merkington—(E. III. Roll) bore, gules, an orle argent over all a bend vair; Jenyns' Ordinary. F.

Bayouse, Sir Robert, of Hunts.—(E. II. Roll) bore, argent three water-bougets purpure; F. Parliamentary Roll; lyonceux rampant in Harl. MS. 6137 f 22.

Beauchamp, William, de Elmeley—(E. I. Roll) bore, gules, a fess or—Grimaldi Roll; JAMES differenced with a label (5) argent (or azure); Arden and St. George Rolls. F.

‡**Beauchamp, Wa(l)ter de**—(H. III. Roll) bore, gules, a fess and in chief three martlets or; Dering and Howard Rolls.

Beauchamp, Sir Walter de, banneret, (3rd son of WILLIAM, 5th Baron of Elmeley)—Sealed, as Dominus de Alcestre, the Barons' letter to the Pope 1301, pp. xx, xxiv, bore, at the battle of Falkirk 1298, and at the siege of Carlaverock 1300, gules, a fess between six martlets or; a Sir WALTER bore the same at the battle of Boroughbridge 1322. They were also borne by Sir GILES, at the siege of Calais 1345-8. (F.)

(1) Another Sir GYLES differenced at the battle of Boroughbridge with a bordure engrelée argent; endentée in Parly. Writs App.

(2) Sir JOHN, son of Sir GILES, differenced at the siege of Calais 1345-8, with a label (3) points argent (or azure).

(3) Sir EDWARD (or Sir GILES) who was knighted at the capitulation of Calais 1348, differenced, with a label (5), pendants gobony argent and azure.

(4) ROGER differenced, with a mullet pierced sable; Surrey Roll.

(5) Sir WILLIAM, of co. Gloucester, differenced at the first Dunstable tournament 1308, with a bordure indented or, Parly. Roll.

(6) Another WILLIAM bore, at the second Dunstable tournament 1334, for difference, " sur le melot devaunt," three chevrons gules; Sloane MS. 1301 fo. 260ᵇ.

(7) Sir WALTER (f 2) JOHN of Powick bore Sir WALTER's coat within a bordure argent; Harl. MS. 1481 fo. 41.

Beauchamp, Guy, 2nd Earl of Warwick—bore, at the battle of Falkirk 1298, at the siege of Carlaverock 1300, and at the first Dunstable tournament 1308, gules crusily (3, 3) and a fess or, as did his son THOMAS, 2nd Earl, at the second Dunstable tournament 1334. (F.) They are ascribed to WILLIAM, banneret, 1st Earl, 24 E. I., 1295-6 in the Parly. Roll. (F.) Earl WILLIAM and Earl GUY also bore it, *quarterly with* ' Le Veyl escu' (de Warwike), checquy or and azure, a chevron ermine—F. —(the latter sealed the Barons' letter to the Pope 1301, pp. xvi, xxiv); Nobility Roll; borne quarterly also by THOMAS, 3rd Earl, at the siege of Calais 1345-8, and RICHARD, 5th Earl, at the siege of Rouen in 1418; tricked crusily (7, 6) in Jenyns' Ordinary. See Monumental Effigies of the 3rd and 4th Earls, and Tiles, Neath Abbey, p. vii.

THOMAS BEAUCHAMP,
4TH EARL OF WARWICK, K.G. 1406.
IN S. MARY CHURCH, WARWICK.
After Waller.

Richard, Erle of Beauchamp, justying at Gynes; he cast to the grounde at his spere poynt behynde the horse tai'e, the Knyght called the Chevaler Ruge c. 1410.
Cotton Ms. Julius E. iv. British Museum.

14

THOMAS BEAUCHAMP,

3RD EARL OF WARWICK, K.G. 1369.

IN ELSING CHURCH, NORFOLK.

From the Hastings Brass.

Beauchamp, Sir John, K.G., brother of Guy, 2nd Earl—bore, at the siege of Calais 1345-8, gules, crusily (3, 3) and a fess or, and for difference, a mullet sable; WILLIAM differenced with a crescent sable, Surrey Roll; as did RICHARD, Lord Abergavenny, at the siege of Rouen 1418; Sir GUY differenced with a label (3) azure; and Sir THOMAS differenced with an annulet azure, both in Ashmole Roll; and another JOHN differenced with a bordure engrelée or.

Beauchamp, Sir John, del County de Warwike—bore, at the first Dunstable tournament 1308, gules billettée and a fess or; 12, 11, 10, 9 and sometimes 6 billets. (F.) Ascribed also to JOHN (‡) in Dering Roll and to Sir JOHN of Essex in Parly. Roll. Another Sir JOHN (6 billets) differenced with a label (3) azure; Harl. Roll.

Beauchamp, Sir John de, of Hache in county Somerset, baron 1299, and banneret—Sealed the Barons' letter to the Pope 1301, pp. xviii, xxiv); and bore, at the battle of Falkirk 1298, and at the siege of Carlaverock 1300, **vair**; borne also by Sir ROGER at the siege of Calais 1345-8, ascribed to ROBERT in Glover Roll (F.), and JOHN (‡) in Dering Roll. Sir MILES, of Bucks, differenced with a label (3) gules, and Sir HUMPHREY with the label or, in Parly. Roll. Sir WILLIAM, "frere" (probably of Sir ROGER), knighted at the capitulation of Calais 1348, bore, vair, on an inescocheon argent, the arms of MORTIMER. (F.) For other differences see Harl. MS. 1481 fo. 89.

Beauchamp, William de, of Eton—(H. III. Roll) bore, gules fretty argent; Glover Roll. RAFE bore, for difference, a label (3) vert; same as THOMAS FLEMING, of Westmorland; Jenyns' Ordinary.

Beauchamp, John, Walter, and **William,** of Bedford—(H. III. Roll) bore, quarterly or and gules a bend of the last; Parliamentary, Norfolk, and St. George Rolls (F.); in other MSS. a bend sable occurs.

Beauchamp, John de—(H. III. Roll) bore, sable, an eagle argent, beaked and legged or; Glover Roll. A second JOHN bore, H. III., undée (6) argent and azure; St. George Roll. F.

Beauchamp, Sir John, of Fyfield in Essex —(E. II. Roll) bore, argent (*vel* or) a lyon rampant sable, crowned gules; Parly. Roll.

Beauchamp, Sir John (BESCHAMP), of Somersetshire—(H. VI. Roll) bore, vert, three besants; Arundel Roll.

Beauchamp, William, of Cumberland—(E. III. Roll) bore, argent on a bend gules three plates; Jenyns' Roll. F.

Beaufitz, Henry—(E. III. Roll) bore, quarterly per fess indented argent and gules; Jenyns' Ordinary. F.

Beaufort, John—(R. II. Roll) bore (before his legitimation), per pale argent and azure on a bend gules, three lyons passant gardant or, a label (3) azure, on each pendant three fleurs-de-lys of the fourth; Surrey Roll.

Beaufoy, John and **William** — (E. III. Roll) bore, argent a chevron between three eaglets gules; Jenyns' Ordinary. F.

Beaulieu, William—(E. III. Roll) bore, same coat as DALSTONE, LASSELLS, of South Cowton, &c., argent a chevron dancettée (i.e. indented) between three daws' heads erased sable; Jenyns' Roll. F.

Beauly, John, of the South—(E. III. Roll) bore, gules and argent embelif battaillée; Jenyns' Roll. See also BEULEE. F.

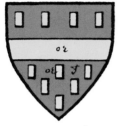

Jo d Beauchamp

Vaffe Beauchamp

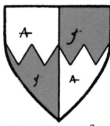

Hy. Beaufitz

want de Bouchamp

John Beaufay.

Will. Beauchampe

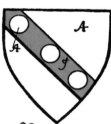

m Beauchamp de Cumberland

Will Beauchamp

m Beaulien

John Beauly

LId Beamond

Godf. d. Beaumond

Tho Boumont

John Beaumond

Lewis Beammond

John Beauple

Robt. Beaupoyl

Michel Booffe

John Booston

Beaumays, Sir (——) de, of Hunts—(E. II. Roll) bore, azure, three garbs banded or; Parliamentary Roll.

*Bea(u)mond, Le Sr.—bore, at the siege of Rouen 1418, azure, florettée and a lyon rampant or, *quarterly with*, azure, three garbs or. (F.) BEAUMONT, of Cole Orton, bears the first quarter as his coat at the present day.

Be(a)umond, Godfrey de—(H. III. Roll) bore, sable, six martlets 3, 2, 1, or, in St. George Roll (F.); sable nine martlets in orle argent in Arden Roll.

Be(a)umond, Sire Henry de, banneret—bore, at the battle of Boroughbridge 1322, azure, florettée and a lyon rampant or, over all a baston gobony argent and gules; this coat is also ascribed to LEWES BEAMMOND in Jenyns' Ordinary. (F.) See BONN.

Beaumond, John, of Devonshire—(E. III. Roll) bore, barry of six ermine and gules in Jenyns' Ordinary (F.); another JOHN, according to Surrey Roll, bore barry (6) vair and gules.

Beaumont, Sir Thomas—bore, at the siege of Calais 1345-8, gules, entoyre of crescents and a lyon rampant argent (F.); his son, Sir THOMAS, junior, bore them at the same time, with a label (3) or.

Be(a)umond, William de—(H. III. Roll) bore, gyrony (12) or and gules; Arden Roll.

Beaupell, John (or BEAUPLE)—(E. III. Roll) bore, gules, a bend cotised argent; Jenyns' Ordinary. F.

Beaupeyl, Sire Robert—bore, at the battle of Boroughbridge 1322, gules, a bend vair (F.); another Sir ROBERT BEAUPLE, of Cornwall (E. II.) bore the same between six escallops argent; Parliamentary Roll.

Beaupré, Ralph de—(E. III. Roll) bore, vert, a lyon rampant or, a baston gules; Jenyns' Ordinary.

Becard (Sir) Piers—(E. II. Roll) bore, or a saltire between four eaglets azure; the saltire is gules in some tricks (F.); Parliamentary Roll.

Beche, Sir John de la, of Berks.—bore, at the first Dunstable tournament 1308, argent, on a bend gules three bucks' heads erased or, in the cantell a martlet sable; Parliamentary Roll.

Beche, John de la, a baron 1342—bore, vaire argent and gules; NICHOL bore the same, and on a canton of the first a martlet sable; Jenyns' Ordinary. F.

Beck, Sire Philip de (Bek)—bore, at the battle of Boroughbridge 1322, argent on a fess gules three bucks' heads cabossed or (F.); his son, Sir JOHAN, bore the same with a martlet sable for difference, but hinds' heads couped, in Ashmole Roll. See also BEK.

Beckebury, Sir William—(E. III. Roll) bore, azure, an eagle or; Ashmole Roll.

Beckham, Roger de, see PECKHAM.

Bedford, John, Duke of, K.G. 1399, bore France and England quarterly, a label (5) per pale ermine and azure, the latter florettée or; K. 400 fo. 6.

*Bedingfeld, Piers de**—(H. III. Roll) bore, gules, an eagle ermine; Howard Roll; the reverse is now borne by the baronet's family.

Beeston, John—(E. III. Roll) bore, vert, a lyon rampant argent crowned gules; Jenyns' Ordinary. F. The same as MENVILE.

Beeston, W.—(E. I. or II. Roll) bore, sable, crusily fitchée and a bend or; Harl. Roll.

‡**Beices, Hameris** (LEICES or LEITES —(H. III. Roll) bore, or a lyon rampant gules crowned azure, a bordure sable besantée, Ashmole Roll; the field argent, and the bordure platey in the Dering Roll.

†**Bek, Antony de,** Bishop of Durham—bore, at the battle of Falkirk 1298, and at the siege of Carlaverock 1300, gules a fer-du-moulin ermine. (F.) The Bishop's name appears among the bannerets in Parliamentary Roll. Brother of the next named.

Bek, John, a baron 1295—(E. III. Roll) bore, gules, a cross moline argent in Jenyns' Ordinary (F.); the cross recercelée in the Arden Roll. Father of the next named.

Bek, Sir Waut de—(E. I. or II. Roll) bore, gules, a cross recercelée argent; Guillim Roll.

Bekeyring, Thomas de—(E. I. Roll) bore, checquy argent and gules; Nativity Roll.

Bekering, Sir Christofer de, knighted at the capitulation of Calais 1348 — bore, checquy argent and gules, a bend sable (F.); THOMAS, bore it with the baston (or bend) azure; Jenyns' Ordinary.

Bekering, Thomas—(R. II. Roll) bore, checquy argent and gules, on a chevron sable three escallops of the first; Surrey Roll. Another THOMAS, bore, E. III., same as a JOHN DE LA RIVER, lozengy or and gules; blasoned "masclée," in Jenyns' Ordinary. F.

Bekuns, Walter—(E. III. Roll) bore, argent, a bend engrailed sable, a label of three gules; Jenyns' Ordinary. F.

Bekynham, Sir (——), a Kentish Knight—(H. VI. Roll) bore, argent, a chevron gules between three bucks' heads cabossed of the last, attires or; Arundel Roll.

Belchamp, Geffry de—(H. III. Roll) bore, quarterly, argent and sable; Glover and Howard Rolls.

Belet, Sir Ingram, of Norfolk—(E. II. Roll) bore, argent, on a chief gules three cinquefoyles argent; Parliamentary Roll. WILLIAM took up the cross in the last Crusade 1270.

Belett, Michael—(E. III. Roll) bore, argent, a fess and in dexter chief point a greyhound courant gules; Jenyns' Ordinary. F.

Pres Bobard.

Ogr Bokorink

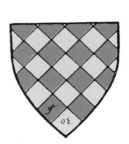

John Bokoringe

Michel Boloff

Antð de Bob
Enesgz. Duram

Joan d. Beck

Peit de Bob

walter Bobnnb

THE HERALDIC ATCHIEVEMENT
(SHIELD III. BROUGHT IN BY BELLASYSE)
OF
HENRY FITZALAN HOWARD, K.G., 15TH DUKE OF NORFOLK.
SEE ALSO PAGES 60 AND 114.

NAMES AND BLAZONS OF THE QUARTERINGS.

It is hoped that the letters in the second column, which indicate the row of quarterings in the shield, will, with the accompanying numerals, facilitate reference to the atchievement on preceding page.

NAMES	SHIELD REFER-BNCES	BLAZONS	REFERENCES TO THE VARIOUS MSS.
			AUGMENTATION
HOWARD	a 1	gules, on a bend between six crosses crosslet fitchée argent, the honorable augmentation for services at the battle of Flodden, 1 Feb., 1513–14	Cott. Jul. C. VII. f. 237 Lansdowne 872, ff. 13, 16 Harl. 1178, f. 45
BELASYSE	a 2	quarterly, 1 and 4 argent, a pale engrailed between two pallets plain sable. 2 and 3, argent, a chevron gules between three fleurs-de-lys azure	
BELLASIS	a 3	or, a fess gules between three torteaux	Visitations of Durham, Ed. FOSTER
SPRING	a 4	{ argent, an inescocheon and an orle of martlets sable . . .	
	a 5	{ argent, three boars' heads within a bordure engrailed sable . .	
BILLINGHAM	a 6	argent, two bars gules on a canton of the second, a lyon passant of the first	
ERRINGTON	a 7	argent, two bars and in chief three escallops azure, a crescent for difference	
BARTON	a 8	azure, a fess between three bucks' heads cabossed or . . .	
RADCLIFFE	a 9	argent, two bends engrailed sable	
NORLEIGH	b 1	gules, a cross engrailed argent	H. 6159, f. 19
RADCLIFFE	b 2	argent, two bends engrailed sable	
NORLEIGH	b 3	gules, a cross engrailed argent	
DAVENPORT (1)	b 4	argent, a chevron between three crosses crosslet fitchée sable, a crescent of the field for difference	
BROMHALL	b 5	sable, a lyon rampant or	
BELLINGHAM	b 6	or, a bugle-horn stringed sable—with ASSHETON on a canton—argent, a mullet sable pierced or	
BURNESHEAD	b 7	argent, three bendlets gules, on a canton of the second a lyon rampant or	H. 1535, ff. 118ᵇ, 249ᵇ, &c.
SUTTON	b 8	or, a lyon rampant queuée forchée vert	
SUTTON—Augmentation . .	b 9	argent, a chevron between three bugle-horns stringed sable .	
CHOLMONDELEY . . .	c 1	gules, in chief two close helmets argent and in base a garb or, a mullet of the second for difference	
WORSLEY	c 2	argent, on a chief gules a mullet or	
HUBBARD	c 3	sable, an estoile or between two flaunches ermine . . .	
GAGE	c 4	per saltire azure and argent a saltire gules	H. 1041, f. 74ᵇ Add. 14, 281, f. 44ᵇ
SUDGROVE	c 5	argent, semée of trefoyles and a double-headed eagle displayed sable	
ST. CLERE	c 6	azure, a sun in splendour or	
LOVAYNE	c 7	azure, on a bend argent cotised or three saltorelles bendways gules	H. 2094, f. 101
DARCY (E. RIVERS). . .	c 8	argent, three cinquefoyles gules	
FITZLANGLEY . . .	c 9	argent, a fess between six (oak ?) leaves slipped gules (H. 807, f. 48ᵇ)	H. 1426, f. 67
HARLESTON	d 1	argent, a fess ermines cotised sable	
LOVELL	d 2	barry of six nebulée or and gules	
WANTON	d 3	argent, a chevron sable, an annulet of the last . (H. 807, f. 59)	
WESTON	d 4	argent, on a chevron sable three leopards' faces or . . .	
BERDWELL	d 5	gules, a goat salient argent horns or	
KITSON	d 6	sable, three fish hauriant argent a chief or	
DONINGTON	d 7	argent, a chevron between three mullets' gules	
BROUGHTON . . .	d 8	paly of six argent and azure, on a chief gules three besants . .	H. 2094, f. 101
DANBY OF YAFFORD . .	d 9	argent, three chevrons interlaced in base, in chief three mullets sable	
BRETVILE	e 1	gules, a fess wavy or.	
CONYERS	e 2	azure, a maunch or in chief a cinquefoyle argent . . .	
PYE	e 3	argent, on a fess azure three escallops of the field . . .	
TANKERVILLE . . .	e 4	gules, an escocheon argent eight martlets in orle or . . .	
CHAMBERLAINE . . .	e 5	gules, a chevron between three escallops or	
GATESDEN	e 6	azure, six lyonceux rampant 3, 2, 1, or	
MORTEYN	e 7	ermine, a chief dancettée gules	H. 1480, f. 23ᵇ
ECKNEY	e 8	azure, two lyons passant guardant or a label of three argent . .	H. 1556, f. 93ᵇ
ST. JOHN OF LAGEHAM . .	e 9	argent on a chief gules two mullets a bordure indented sable .	
LOVAYNE	f 1	azure, on a bend argent cotised or three saltorelles in bend gules	
ABELL v. LOCHER . . .	f 2	argent, a saltire engrailed azure	
BOURCHIER	f 3	(Thomas, of the family of Sir Rafe, H. 1480, f. 23ᵇ and 1557, f. 93ᵇ) argent, a cross engrailed gules between four water-bougets sable, all within a bordure gobony or and gules	H. 1394, f. 341
MIDDLEMORE	f 4	per chevron argent and sable in chief two moor-cocks ppr. . .	H. 1167, f. 125
EDGBASTON	f 5	per pale dancettée argent and azure	
GRESWOLD	f 6	argent, a fess gules between two greyhounds courant sable . .	
GROME	f 7	or, three piles to the base gules, on a chief indented azure two closed helmets in profile of the first	H. 1167, f. 18
GRANGE (2)	f 8	per saltire or and sable four griffins' heads erased counterchanged all within a bordure azure	
STOCKLEY (3)	f 9	argent, a chevron gules between three boars passant sable . .	
BETHAM	g 1	ermine, a chevron between three boars passant sable . . .	H. 1563, f. 92ᵇ
WALLISON	g 2	azure, a stag trippant ermine, attires or, a chief of the last . .	
FOWLER (4)	g 3	azure, on a chevron engrailed argent between three lyons passant guardant or as many crosses moline sable, a canton ermine for Casey	H. 2113, f. 84

Concluded on page 19.

(1) Davenport probably brings in Wettenhall and Alpraham before Bromhall, as in Randal Holme.
(2) Grange brings in Bromley and Hawes } for these no arms have been found.
(3) Stockley brings in Hewett and Sotherne }
(4) Casey should come here, but as no arms are found, *a canton ermine* has been added to Fowler (g 3) for Casey, to indicate the omission of the name or quartering through which the coats from Fowler to Owen ap Edwyn are introduced. The questionable mode of granting a coat to a family long extinct for the mere sake of introducing quarterings should not be upheld.

18

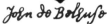

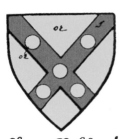
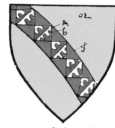

John de Belhuse   Roger Belhouse   Roger Belhous   John de Bellous   Tebaud d' Belhuse

Jo Bolbomore

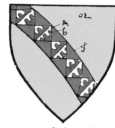

John Bononille

Belhous, Sir John, of Essex—bore, at the first Dunstable tournament 1308, argent, three lyonceux rampant gules (F.); and Sir WILLIAM (E. II.) bore the same, within a bordure indented sable; Parliamentary Roll.

Belhuse, Sir John de; knighted at the capitulation of Calais 1348—bore, or, on a saltire gules another vair. F.

Belhuse, Roger de—(E. III. Roll) bore, or, on a saltire gules five bezants (F.); another bore, sable, a fret enfruct or (F.); Jenyns' Ordinary.

Belhuse, Tebaud de—(H. III. Roll) bore, or, on a bend gules five lozenges vair (F.); St. George Roll.

Belkamore, John de—(E. III. Roll) bore, gules, a bordure engrailed argent, over all a bend of the last (F.); Jenyns' Ordinary. See ROBERT DE BILLEMORE.

Bellasyse, John, of Eltoftes—(E. III. Roll) bore, argent, three chess-rooks sable (F.); Jenyns' Roll.

Bellenden, Sir John de, of co. Glouc.—(E. II. Roll) bore, azure, entoyre of martlets (3, 3, 2, 1) argent; Parliamentary Roll.

Bellers, James—(R. II. Roll) bore, per pale gules and sable, a lyon rampant argent; Surrey Roll.

*Bellewe, John—(E. III. Roll) bore, sable, fretty or; Jenyns' Roll. F.

Belliston, —— (E. III. Roll) bore, or, on a chevron gules, three crosses recercelée argent; Ashmole Roll.

[Bellomont, Robert, Earl of Leicester—"Fitz Pernell" SEAL, a cinquefoyle ermine.]

Belsede, Sir (——), of Norfolk—(E. II. Roll) bore, argent, four bars sable, a canton of the first; Parly. Roll. Harl. MS. 6137.

Beltoft, Les Armes de—(E. III. Roll) bore, or, fretty and a chief azure; Ashmole Roll.

Beltoft, Sir Roger de, of co. Linc.—(E. II. Roll) bore, argent, fretty and a chief azure; Parliamentary Roll. ROBERT bore it, fretty engrailed, in Jenyns' Ordinary. F.

Beltoft, Symon de—(E. III. Roll) bore, argent, three chevronels interlaced azure, a chief of the last; blasoned, argent a frette and a chief azure; Jenyns' Ordinary. F.

*[Bendish, alias Westley, Ralph, of Barrington, co. Cambridge, E. I.—bore, argent, a chevron sable between three rams' heads erased azure.—Shirley.] F.

Beneville, John—(E. III. Roll) bore, or, on a bend sable three mullets pierced argent; Jenyns' Ordinary. See BONEVILE. F.

Bengham, Sire Thomas de—bore, at the battle of Boroughbridge 1322 party, gules and vert, a lyon (rampant) argent. This coat is wrongly ascribed to Sir JOHN DE HOLAND in Bodley's Copy.

Benhale, Robert de—bore, at the second Dunstable tournament 1334, sable, a bend deux wyfres argent—Stowe; six wyfres in Sloane; (cotised wavy) Jenyns' Ordinary (F.) For wyfres = vipers' nests! see "Archæologia," vol. 31, p. 247; see also CREK, post.

Benhale, Sir Robert de, a baron 1360; knighted at the capitulation of Calais 1348—bore, argent, a bend between three fizures (cotises) wavy sable; in another cotises undée.

Benhalle, Robert—(E. III. Roll) bore, gules, a cross recercelée (moline in blason) argent, a baston azure (F.); Ashmole Roll and Jenyns' Ordinary; another with a bordure instead of a baston.

"Bennes DE HAMPTON"—(H. III. Roll) bore, azure, three lyons passant gardant or; Howard Roll.

Bennet, Sir John, of Norfolk—(E. II. Roll) bore, argent, a chevron gules, a bordure sable bezantée; Parl. Roll, Harl. MS. 6137.

Benet, Sir Richard—(E. III. Roll) bore, gules, a lyon rampant ermine, a bordure engrailed of the last; Ashmole Roll.

Benstede, —— (H. VI. Roll) bore, gules, three bars argent; Arundel Roll.

Benstede, Sir John de, a Justice Common Pleas 1309-20—bore, at the battle of Falkirk 1298 [. . . .] a cross pierced and patée and botonné argent.

Benstede, Sir William, of Essex—(E. II. Roll) bore, azure, a fess between two chevronels or; Parliamentary Roll. F.

‡Berbling, Walter or William de—(E. III. Roll) bore, argent, three fleurs-de-lys sable; Dering Roll.

Berbroune, Thomas—(E. III. Roll) bore, or, a cross patée flory gules; Jenyns' Ordinary. F.

Berdone, Walter de—(E. III. Roll) bore, argent, an eagle azure beak and claws gules; Jenyns' Ordinary. F.

Bere, see DE LA BERE.

Bereford, Robert de—bore, at the second Dunstable tournament 1334, sable, a bend engrelée argent. F.

Bereford, Sir Symon, of co. Warwick—(E. II. Roll) bore, argent, three fleurs-de-lys sable; Parliamentary Roll. These arms are ascribed to Sir HENRY DE BERFELD, in the Boroughbridge Roll. See DE BOREFELD.

Bereford, Sir Symon—bore, at the battle of Boroughbridge 1322, argent crusily potent and three fleurs-de-lys sable, a bordure engrailed gules; crusily fitchée in Ashmole Roll.

Bereford, Sir William, of Northants—(E. II. Roll) bore, argent, crusily and three fleurs-de-lys sable; Parly. Roll. BAWDWIN and JOHN—bore crusily fitchée (F.); Surrey Roll and Jenyns' Ordinary.

John Bollasyfe

Tho Bongham

Robert Bongale

Rob: Boltoft   Sym de Boltoft   Ralph Bondyssp   John de Bonestede   Rob. Bonegall   Tho Borbrom

NAMES AND BLAZONS OF BELLASYSE QUARTERINGS—*concluded from p. 17.*

NAMES	SHIELD REFER- ENCES	BLAZONS	REFERENCES TO THE VARIOUS MSS.
LOVEDAY	g 4	per pale argent and sable an eagle displayed counter-changed crowned or	
BARTON	g 5	ermine on a canton gules an owl or	
INGLEFIELD . . .	g 6	argent, three bars gules, on a chief or a lyon passant sable . .	H. 2113, f. 84
CLARKE	g 7	argent, a chevron sable between three Cornish choughs proper .	
FITZLOWE . . .	g 8	argent, three wolves' heads erased gules, a bordure azure billettée or	
GERNON	g 9	vaire argent and gules	
LEE, or LEIGH . . .	h 1	azure, two bars argent a bend counter-compony or and gules .	
GAWSFORD, or TROLLOPE. .	h 2	vert, three stags saliant argent	
HANMER	h 3	argent, two lyons passant guardant azure, a mullet sable .	
RICE AP THEODOR . .	h 4	*gules, a lyon rampant or, a bordure engrailed of the last* .	
OWEN KEVELIOK . .	h 5	*or, a lyon's gamb in bend erased gules*	H. 1241, f. 130
SIR ROGER POWES . .	h 6	*vert, two boars passant or*	H. 1396, f. 159ᵇ
YONAS, or JONAS . .	h 7	*azure, three boars passant in pale argent* . . .	
EDWYN AP JONAS . .	h 8	*argent, a cross engrailed florettée at the points, between four mullets sable*	
OWEN AP EDWYN . .	h 9	*gules, three legs conjoined at the thigh argent* . . .	

(FABULOUS — bracketing h 4 through h 9)

mal. de Bordono

John Boroford

John Boxofford.

Berfield *v.* BORFIELD.

Berhalgh, Richard—(E. III. Roll) bore, argent, three bears passant sable muzzled or (F.); Jenyns' Ordinary.

Beringer, Sir Ingram, of Hants.—(E. II. Roll) bore, or, a cross vert and a bend gules; Parliamentary Roll and Jenyns' Ordinary.

Beringham *v.* Bermingham.

*[Berington, Thomas de—(E. III.) bore, sable, three greyhounds courant in pale argent, collared gules, within a bordure of the last.—Shirley.] F.

‡Berkeley, Morris and Thomas de—(H. III. Roll) bore, gules, a chevron argent; Arden and St. George Rolls.

Berkele, Sir Thomas—bore, at the battle of Boroughbridge 1322, gules "queyntée de la mermounde" for a similar crux, see Sir JOHN DE CROMWELL: Queynty d'argent fretty de ses armes d'ermyne. See facsimile, page xxvi. Parliamentary Writs (Vol. 23), 1830, ii. app. 196. The shields for these coats are left blank in Bodley's Copy of the Roll: their Heraldic interpretation was evidently beyond Brooke, York Herald of that day.

*Berkeley, Sir Thomas, baron 1295—Sealed the Barons' letter to the Pope 1301, pp. xviii, xxiv, and bore, at the battle of Falkirk 1298, gules, crusily patée and a chevron argent, Nobility Rolls; and so borne by Sir MORRIS or THOMAS at the siege of Calais 1345-8, and in Surrey and other Rolls. See Monumental Effigy. Baron THOMAS was father of Sir MAURICE and Sir JOHN, in the next par., and of Sir THOMAS 1308.

Berkeley, Sir Maurice de, banneret, baron 1308—bore, at the battle of Falkirk 1298, and at the siege of Carlaverock 1300, gules, crusily patée and a chevron argent (with a blue label of 3 because his father Thomas was then alive); Parly. Roll. Lord BERKELEY bore it also at the siege of Rouen 1418 (F.). The shield of Sir MORYS, H. VI., has nine crosses patée, in the Arundel Roll; and that of Sir JOHN (brother of Sir MAURICE 1308), of co. Glouc., three (or) in the Parly. Roll; he served also at the battle of Falkirk. JAMES (R. II.) differenced with a crescent azure; Surrey Roll.

Berkeley, Maurice de—bore, in the second Dunstable tournament 1334, gules, crusily argent and a chevron ermine (F.); in Surrey Roll (R. II.), crusily patonce. THOMAS bore the chevron argent in Segar Roll &c. F.

Berkeley, Sir Maurice, of Uley, co. Glouc., a baron 1308—bore, gules, crusily formée argent, a chevron ermine; Atkinson Roll.

Berkeley, Sir Maurice of OM'—(H. VI. Roll) bore, gules, crusily formée and a chevron argent, all within a bordure of the last; Atkinson Roll.

Berkley, Sir John—bore, at the siege of Calais 1345-8, gules, a chevron between ten cinquefoyles argent (F.); ascribed to another JOHN in Surrey Roll, the cinquefoyles pierced.

Berkeley, Sir Thomas—bore, at the first Dunstable tournament 1308, gules, a chevron between ten roses, 6, 4, argent; he served at the battle of Falkirk 1298. In the Parly. Roll as Sir THOMAS, banneret of co. Glouc. (E. II.) he bore, the chevron between 6 roses. Brother of Sir MAURICE 1308 and of Sir JOHN.

Berkeley, Giles de—(H. III. Roll) bore, quarterly or and azure, a bendlet gules in Arden Roll (purpure in St. George); quarterly per fess indented in Harl. MS. 6137 fo. 79. F.

Berkrolls, Sir Roger and Sir William de, of co. Glouc.—(H. III. Roll) bore, azure, a chevron between three crescents or; Ashmole and Parly. Rolls. See also Tiles, Neath Abbey, p. ix.

Berley, John—(E. III. Roll) bore, gules, three mullets pierced or, a quarter ermine; Jenyns' Ordinary. F.

Berlingham, Sir Richard—(E. II. Roll) bore, gules, three bears unmuzzled passant argent; Parliamentary Roll.

Bermingham, Sir Richard de (BERING- HAME)—bore, at the first Dunstable tourna- ment 1308, gules, three owls or. F.

Bermingham, Sir Foulke and John de—(R. II. Roll) bore, per pale dancettée argent and sable; Surrey and Ashmole Rolls. F.

Robt. de Boroford

T... de Borington

John Borley

ffoulke de byrmegh...m

THOMAS DE BERKELEY, 1243.

IN THE WALL OF THE SOUTH AISLE OF THE CHOIR OF BRISTOL CATHEDRAL.

From Gough.

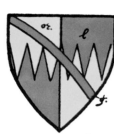

Sir de Barkeloy — Gile d Berkelaie — John Barkeloy — morys Borkoloy — Thomas de Bkoloy — King Borgalge

Rich. de Beringham
Thos de Birmingham
mal. Bornyngham
Walt. de Bermgham

Bermingham, Sir Thomas—bore, at the first Dunstable tournament 1308, azure, a bend engrelée or. (F.) Sir WILLIAM, banneret (a baron 1326) also bore it at the battle of Boroughbridge 1322; the bend tricked as fusily in the Arden, Guillim and St. George Rolls (F.); and, perhaps wrongly, tricked as a bordure in the Arundel Roll, fo. 102b. Sir THOMAS, of co. Worcester, bore it with a label of three gules for difference; Parliamentary Roll.

Bermingham, Sir Walter de (BERYNGHAM)—bore, at the first Dunstable tournament 1308, argent on a bend gules cotised sable, two escallops or (F.). Jenyns' Roll places three escallops on the bend, and the Parliamentary Roll in addition gives or, as the field. F.

*Bernay (——), a Suffolk Kt.—(H. VI. Roll) bore, per pale gules and azure a cross engrailed ermine; Arundel Roll.

Berners, John and Rauf de—(H. III. Roll) bore, quarterly or and vert (F.); Arden, St. George, and Howard Rolls. Another JOHN bore the same with a label gules; Glover and Norfolk Rolls.

Beroun, see also BYRON.

Beroun, Sire John de—bore, at the battle of Boroughbridge 1322, argent, three bendlets gules—and Sir JAMES also, in Parly. Roll.

Beron, Nicholas, of Claiton—(E. IV. Roll) bore, argent, three bendlets enhanced gules and quarterly with, argent on a bend azure three annulets or, a cross crosslet fitchée of the second, with crest; Ballard Roll.

Beronden, Sir Walter de, of Northumberland—(E. II. Roll) bore, argent three roses sable; Parly. Roll.

Beronden, Sir Gilbert de, of Northumberland—(E. II. Roll) bore, gules on a bend argent three roses sable; Parliamentary Roll.

Bertout, —— (H. III. Roll) bore, or, three palets gules, on a canton sable a lyon rampant of the field; Howard Roll. See also BERTRANT.

Bertram, Sir Roger, feudal baron of Bothal—(E. II. Roll) bore, or, "a false escocheon" voided (an orle) azure; Parliamentary Roll (F.). Sir JOHN bore the same, H. VI., quarterly with, argent, a fess between three crescents gules; Atkinson Roll. See also BARTRAM.

Bertram, Roger—(H. III. Roll) bore, gules, crusily and an orle or; Glover Roll. See also BARTRAM.

Bertram, Robert—(H. III. Roll) bore, gules a fess or; Howard Roll.

Bertram, Robert—(H. III. Roll) bore, or, a lyon rampant vert (F.); St. George Roll; crowned azure in Howard Roll.

Bertrant, Walter—(H. III. Roll) bore, per pale or and gules, on a canton azure a rowell argent; Norfolk Roll. See BERTOUT.

Bertto, Hamont de, slain at the siege of Calais 1347—bore, argent, on a chief gules a dexter and sinister hand appaumé pileways of the field. F.

Berwicke, Hugh of—(E. IV. Roll) bore, argent, three bears' heads couped sable muzzled or; with crests; Ballard Roll. One of these names took up the cross in the last Crusade 1270.

Beschamp, Sir John (or BEAUCHAMP), of Somersetshire—(H. VI. Roll) bore, vert three bezants; Arundel Roll.

Besille, John de—(H. III. Roll) bore, argent three torteaux (F.); Arden and St. George Rolls. [JOHN, the nephew, bore the same within a bordure azure (F.); Jenyns' Roll.] Sir THOMAS, E. III., bore a mullet of five or on the first torteaux; Ashmole Roll.

Beslingthorpe, Sir Richard, of co. Linc.—(E. II. Roll) bore, argent, a chevron gules a chief indented sable; Parliamentary Roll.

Besonn, Sir Thomas de, of Cumberland—(E. II. Roll) bore, lozengy argent and sable; Parly. Roll. See BOSON.

*[Betton, Walter de, of Salop—bore, argent, two palets sable, each charged with three crosses crosslet fitchée or.—Shirley.] F.

Betune, Baudewyn de, lord of the manor of Skipton in Craven, brother of the Count of Flanders and Count of Albemarle and Ile; who married Hawisia, Countess D'Albemarle—E. III. Roll, bore, bendy (6) argent and gules (sic) a chief or (F.). Jenyns' Ordinary.

‡Betune, John de—(H. III. Roll) bore, azure, on a chief argent a lyon passant gules; Dering Roll.

Betune, Robert de—(E. I. Roll) bore, or, a lyon rampant sable (F.); Camden Roll.

Betune, William de—(E. I. Roll) bore, argent, a fess gules and in dexter chief point a lyon passant regardant sable (F.); Camden Roll.

Beulee, Richard de—(R. II. Roll) bore, quarterly argent and gules a rose counterchanged seeded or; Surrey Roll. See also BEAULY.

Bevercote, Sir John de—bore, at the battle of Boroughbridge 1322, argent a cross patée (patonce) azure, a label (3) gules. F.

Beynham, Edmund de—(R. II. Roll) bore, sable three mullets, two and one argent; Surrey Roll. See also REYNHAM.

Beyton, Sir William de (BOYTON or BRITTON)—(E. II. Roll) bore, azure, six escallops 3, 2, 1, or; Parliamentary Roll.

Robt. Bertram

Hamont de Bertto

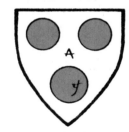

Joan d. Berile

Joan Bofillo lo moyna

Witt d Birmingham — Rauf d. Barnes — Le baron de Botgale — Walt de Botton — Baudewyn de Botune — Volt de Botune

ꝃ꙼ꝛmꝛꝛ] do Betuno

Jo Boꝛoꝛꝛolo

ꝝalꝛoꝛ Biblofꝛoꝛlꝫ

Ꝼꝛꝭ do Biddulpꝫ

Biblesworth, Sir Hugh de, of Herts.—
(E. III. Roll) bore, azure, three eaglets or; (F.)
St. George and Parliamentary Rolls. Sir JOHN
bore six eaglets, 3, 2, 1, or; Ashmole Roll;
both are also ascribed to WALTER. Another
WALTER took up the cross in the last Crusade
1270.

Bicklond, John, see BUCKLAND.

‡Bicknore, John de—(H. III. Roll) bore,
argent a chief azure; Howard Roll.

Bicknore, Sir John de, of Kent—(E. III.
Roll) bore, argent, on a chief azure three
lyonceux rampant of the first (crowned or,
Dering Roll); Parly. Roll. Sir THOMAS bore
the coat with a baston gules; Ashmole and
Parliamentary Rolls.

*[Biddulph (Thomas de), of Staffordshire
(H. III.)—bore, vert, an eagle displayed argent;
another coat—argent, three soldering irons
sable.—Shirley.] F.

Bigod, Roger le, (4th) Earl of Norfolk—
(H. III. Roll) bore, or, a cross gules; Glover
and St. George Rolls.

Bigod, Roger, Earl of Norfolk, Earl Marshal
of England—bore, at the battle of Falkirk
1298, per pale or and vert a lyon rampant
gules, and so sealed the Barons' letter to the
Pope 1301, pp. xv, xxiv. (F.) RAUF bore it
oppressed by a baston argent; Arden Roll.

Bigod, Hugh—(H. III. Roll) bore, gules a lyon
passant or; Norfolk and Glover Rolls.

Bigod, Rauff, of Settrington, Yorks—(H. III.
Roll) bore, or, on a cross gules five escallops
argent. Glover Roll, &c. Ascribed also to
JOHN (F.) in the St. George Roll, and to Sir
RAFFE, of Norfolk, in the Parly. Roll.

Bigod, John (BYGOOD), of Essex, Knight—
(H. VI. Roll) bore, argent, on a chief gules two
crescents of the first (? or); Arundel Roll.

Billemore, Robert de—bore, at the second
Dunstable tournament 1334, argent a bend
gules a bordure engrelé or. (F.) See JOHN
DE BELKAMORE.

Billynge, Nicol—(R. II. Roll) bore, gules,
three fish naiant (in pale) or, a bordure engrailed
argent; Surrey Roll.

Bilney, Sir Roger de, of Norfolk—bore,
at the first Dunstable tournament 1308, argent
an eagle vert, borne also by WILLIAM; (F.)
Jenyns' Ordinary. See also BALNYE.

Binchestre, Robert de—(E. III. Roll) bore,
gules, a chief battaylé argent, tricked, gules a
fess crenellée argent; (F.) Jenyns' Roll.

*[Bingham, Robert de, of Melcombe,
Somerset (H. III.)—bore, azure, a bend cotised
between six crosses patée or.—Shirley.] F.

Bingham, Sire Thos. de, see BENGHAM.

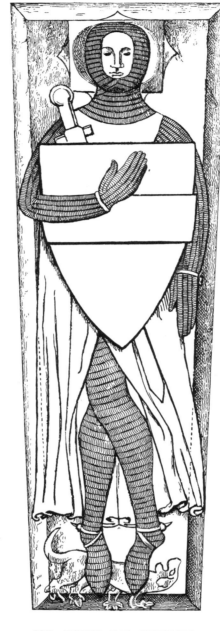

SIR JOHN DE BITTON,

12 HEN. III., 1227.

IN BITTON CHURCH, SOMERSETSHIRE.

After Boutell.

Bingham, John and Richard—(E. III.
Roll) bore, or, on a fess gules, three water-
bougets argent; (F.) Surrey Roll and Jenyns'
Ordinary.

Bingham, Sir Richard—(E. III. Roll) bore,
or two bars gules, charged with three water-
bougets 2 and 1 argent; Ashmole Roll.

Birland, William—(R. II. Roll) bore, gules,
a chevron between three bears' heads couped
argent, muzzled of the field; Surrey Roll.

Bishopbury, Henry—(E. III. Roll) bore,
argent a fess double cotised sable; Jenyns'
Roll. F.

Bishopdonne, John de—(E. III. Roll) bore,
or, four bendlets azure, a quarter ermine;
Jenyns' Ordinary. F.

Bishopsdonne, William—(H. III. Roll)
bore, bendy (10) or and sable; (F.) Arden and
St. George Rolls; and the same with a canton
ermine was borne by Sir JOHN BISHOPSTONE,
of Warwickshire, in Ashmole Roll; bendy of
8 in Parliamentary Roll.

Bissett, Sir John, of co. Worcester—(R. II.
Roll) bore, azure bezanty (3, 3, 2, 1); Parliamentary Roll.

Bittone, Sir John—(R. II. Roll) bore,
ermine a fess gules; Parly. Roll. See Incised
Slab.

Blaen, Sir Raffe (or BLOAN) of Cornwall—
(R. II. Roll) bore, sable, a saltire engrailed
argent; Parliamentary Roll. See BLOYON.

Blakeburne, John de—(H. III. Roll) bore,
paly (6) argent and azure; St. George Roll. F.

Blaked, Sir John, of Bucks—(R. II. Roll)
bore, gules, a chevron vair; Parly. Roll.

Blakenham, Benet de—(H. III. Roll) bore,
barry (6), sable and or, another sable, two
bars or. (F.) St. George Roll; called BEGES
DE BLAKELIG in Arden Roll.

Blakenham, Sir Thomas, of Suffolk—
(R. II. Roll) bore, azure, crusily and two bars
or; Parly. Roll.

Blanchminster, Sir Renaud, Sir
Richard and William—(H. III. Roll)
bore, argent, fretty gules; Glover and Nativity
Rolls. F.

Blande, John—(E. III. Roll) bore, gules, two
bars and 8 martlets in orle or, 3, 2, 2, 1;
Jenyns' Ordinary. F.

Blare, Adam de—(H. III. Roll) bore, sable,
crusily argent and six crescents, 3, 2, 1, or;
Arden and St. George Rolls (which latter gives
another coat, crusily fitchée); (F.) Howard
Roll gives three (not six) crescents.

Otto Mareſcall

Joan Bigod

ꝝoꝛꝛ de Billomore

ꝝoꝛ Builnoyo

ꝝoꝛꝛ de Binggam

Jo. de Byngꝫam

Blenkinsopp of Blenkinsopp Castle.

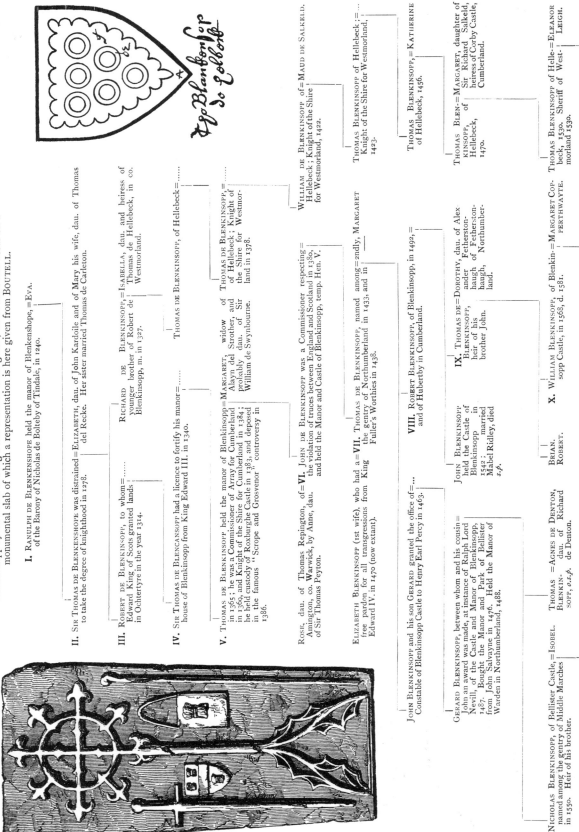

In Haltwhistle Church a mutilated recumbent figure of the 12th or 13th Century is identified as a Blenkinsopp by his shield bearing a fess between three garbs; these arms also occur on a monumental slab of which a representation is here given from BOUTELL.

I. RANULPH DE BLENKENSHOPE held the manor of Blenkenshope, =EVA. of the Barony of Nicholas de Bolteby of Tindale, in 1240.

II. SIR THOMAS DE BLENKENSHOPE was distrained =ELIZABETH, dau. of John Kardoile and of Mary his wife, dau. of Thomas to take the degree of knighthood in 1278. del Recke. Her sister married Thomas de Carleton.

III. ROBERT DE BLENKINSOPP, to whom =...... Edward King of Scots granted lands in Ochtertyre in the year 1314.

RICHARD DE BLENKINSOPP, =ISABELLA, dau. and heiress of younger brother of Robert de Thomas de Hellebeck, in co. Blenkinsopp, m. in 1327. Westmorland.

IV. SIR THOMAS DE BLENCANSOPP had a licence to fortify his manor =...... house of Blenkinsopp from King Edward III. in 1340.

THOMAS DE BLENKINSOPP, of Hellebeck; =......

V. THOMAS DE BLENKINSOPP held the manor of Blenkinsopp =MARGARET, widow of in 1365; he was a Commissioner of Array for Cumberland Alayn del Strother, and in 1360, and Knight of the Shire for Cumberland in 1384; probably dau. of Sir he held custody of Roxburghe Castle in 1383, and deposed William de Swynbourne. in the famous "Scrope and Grosvenor" controversy in 1386.

THOMAS DE BLENKINSOPP, of Hellebeck; Knight of the Shire for Westmor- land in 1378.

ROSE, dau. of Thomas Repington, of =**VI.** JOHN DE BLENKINSOPP was a Commissioner respecting= Amington, co. Warwick, by Anne, dau. the violation of truces between England and Scotland in 1380, of Sir Thomas Peyton. and held the Manor and Castle of Blenkinsopp, temp. Hen. V.

ELIZABETH BLENKINSOPP (1st wife), who had a =**VII.** THOMAS DE BLENKINSOPP, named among the =2ndly, MARGARET free pardon for all transgressions from King gentry of Northumberland in 1433, and in Edward IV. in 1470 (now extant). Fuller's Worthies in 1438.

JOHN BLENKINSOPP and his son GERARD granted the office of =... Constable of Blenkinsopp Castle to Henry Earl Percy in 1465.

VIII. ROBERT BLENKINSOPP, of Blenkinsopp, in 1492, = and of Huberty in Cumberland.

GERARD BLENKINSOPP, between whom and his cousin = John an award was made, at instance of Ralph Lord Nevill, of the Castle and Manor of Blenkinsopp, 1487. Bought the Manor and Park of Bellister from John Salvayne in 1476. Held the Manor of Warden in Northumberland, 1488.

JOHN BLENKINSOPP held the Castle of Blenkinsopp in 1542; married Mabel Ridley, died s.p.

IX. THOMAS DE =DOROTHY, dau. of Alex BLENKINSOPP, ander of Fetherston- heir of his haugh, of Northumber- brother John. land.

NICHOLAS. RICHARD.

BRIAN. ROBERT.

X. WILLIAM BLENKINSOPP, of Blenkin- =MARGARET CO- sopp Castle, in 1568, d. 1581. PERTHWAYTE.

ANNE =CHRISTOPHER RIDLEY of Unthank, North- umberland.

NICHOLAS BLENKINSOPP, of Bellister Castle, =ISOBEL. named among the gentry of Middle Marches in 1550. Heir of his brother.

THOMAS =AGNES DE DENTON, BLENKIN- dau. of Richard SOPP, o.s.p. de Denton.

GEORGE BLENKINSOPP, of Bellis- =JANE, dau. of Albany ter Castle, fought at the Battle Fetherstonhaugh of Pinkie 1547, d. 1580. Fetherstonhaugh.

XI. THOMAS BLENKIN- =JULIAN, dau. of SOPP of Blenkinsopp Leonard Castle, d. 1614. Musgrave

WILLIAM DE BLENKINSOPP of =MAUD DE SALKELD. Hellebeck; Knight of the Shire for Westmorland, 1422.

THOMAS BLENKINSOPP of Hellebeck, = Knight of the Shire for Westmorland, 1423.

THOMAS BLENKINSOPP, =KATHERINE of Hellebeck, 1456.

THOMAS BLEN- =MARGARET, daughter of KINSOPP, of Sir Richard Salkeld, Hellebeck, heiress of Corby Castle, 1470. Cumberland.

THOMAS BLENKINSOPP of Helle- =ELEANOR beck, 1530. Sheriff of West- LEIGH. morland 1530.

THOMAS BLENKINSOPP =MAGDALENE, dau. of Sir H. of Hellebeck. Musgrave of Hartley, in 1553.

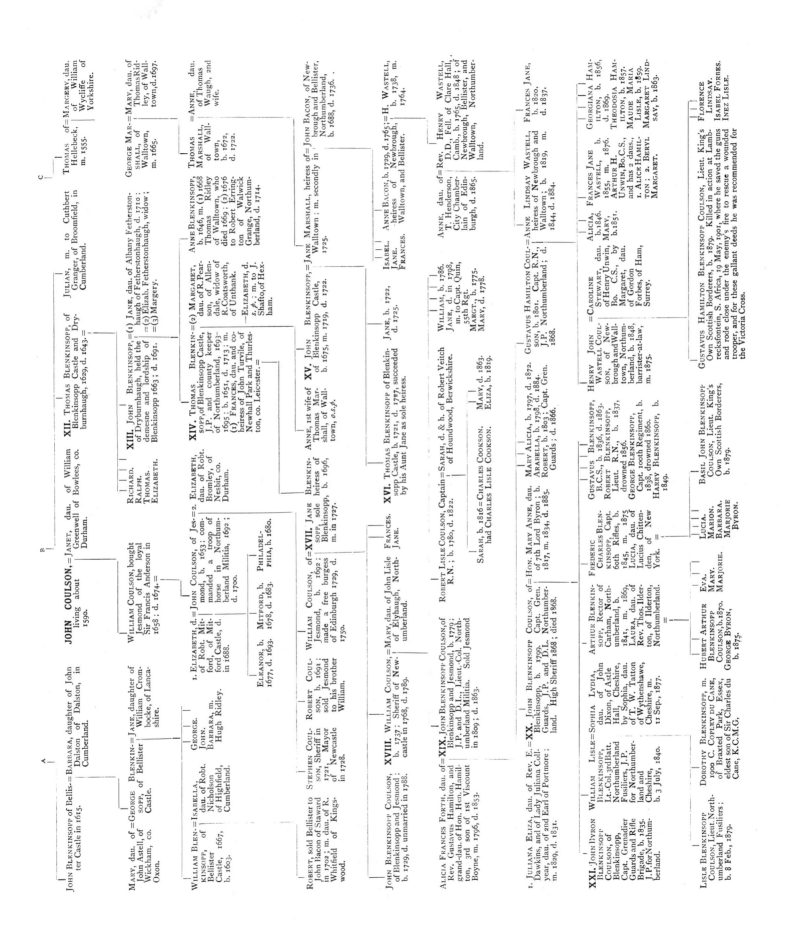

A

JOHN BLENKINSOPP of Bellis- = BARBARA, daughter of John
ter Castle in 1615. | Dalston, of Dalston, in
| Cumberland.

JOHN COULSON, = JANET, dau. of William
living about | Greenwell of Bowlees, co.
1590. | Durham.

B

XII. THOMAS BLENKINSOPP, of
Blenkinsopp Castle and Dry-
burnhaugh, 1629, d. 1643 :—

JULIAN, m. to Cuthbert
Granger, of Broomfield, in
Cumberland.

THOMAS of = MARGERY, dau.
Hellebeck, | of William
m. 1555. | Wycliffe of
| Yorkshire.

C

MARY, dau. of = GEORGE BLENKIN- = JANE, daughter of
John Astell, of | SOPP, of Bellister | William Crom-
Wickham, co. | Castle. | bocke, of Lanca-
Oxon. | | shire.

WILLIAM COULSON, bought
Jesmond of the loyal
Sir Francis Anderson in
1658 ; d. 1674. =

RICHARD.
RALPH.
THOMAS.
ELIZABETH.

XIII. JOHN BLENKINSOPP, = (1) JANE, dau. of Albany Fetherston-
of Dryburnhaugh, held the loyal | haugh of Fetherstonhaugh, d. 1710 :
demesne and lordship of | = (2) Elizab. Fetherstonhaugh, widow ;
Blenkinsopp 1663 ; d. 1691. | = (3) Margery.

GEORGE MAR- = MARY, dau. of
SHALL, of | ThomasRid-
Walltown, | ley, of Wall-
m. 1665. | town,d.1697.

WILLIAM BLEN- = ISABELLA,
KINSOPP, of | dau. of Robt.
Bellister | Nicholson
Castle, 1667, | of Highfield,
b. 1663. | Cumberland.

GEORGE.
JOHN.
BARBARA, m.
Hugh Ridley.

1. ELIZABETH, d. = JOHN COULSON, of = 2. ELIZABETH,
of Robt. Mit- | Jesmond, b. 1653 ; com- | dau. of Robt.
ford, of Mit- | manded a troop of | Bromley, of
ford Castle, d. | horse in Northum- | Nesbit, co.
in 1688. | berland Militia, 1692 ; | Durham.
| d. 1700. |

ELEANOR, b.
1677, d. 1693.

MITFORD, b.
1678, d. 1683.

PHILADEL-
PHIA, b. 1680.

XIV. THOMAS BLENKIN- = (2) MARGARET,
SOPP, of Blenkinsopp Castle, | dau. of R.Pear-
J.P. and county keeper | son, of Allen-
of Northumberland, 1693- | dale, widow of
1695 ; b. 1651, d. 1713 ; m. | R.Coatsworth,
(1) FRANCES, dau. and co- | of Unthank.
heiress of John Turvile, of |
Newhall Park and Thurles- | — ELIZABETH, d.
ton, co. Leicester. = | s.p.; m. to J.
| Shafto,of Hex-
| ham.

ANNE BLENKINSOPP,
b. 1646, m. (1) 1668
Thomas Ridley
of Walltown, who
died 1669 ; (2)1676
ton of Walwick
Grange, Northum-
berland, d. 1714.

ROBERT, sold Bellister to
John Bacon of Staward
in 1702 ; m. dau. of R.
Whitfield of Kings-
wood.

STEPHEN COUL-
SON, Sheriff in
1721, Mayor
of Newcastle
in 1728.

WILLIAM COULSON, of = XVII. JANE, sole
Jesmond, b. 1692 ; | heiress of
made a free burgess | Blenkinsopp,
of Edinburgh 1729, d. | b. 1696,
1750. | m. in 1727.

XV. JOHN BLENKINSOPP, = JANE MARSHALL, heiress of = JOHN BACON, of New-
of Blenkinsopp Castle, | Thomas Mar- | brough and Bellister,
b. 1675, m. 1719, d. 1722. | shall, of Wall- | Northumberland,
| town ; m. secondly in | b. 1688, d. 1736. .
| 1725. |

ANNE, 1st wife of = XVI. THOMAS BLENKINSOPP of Blenkin-
Thomas Mar- | sopp Castle, b. 1721, d. 1787, succeeded
shall, of Wall- | by his Aunt Jane as sole heiress.
town, o.s.p. |

JANE, b. 1722,
d. 1725.

ANNE BACON, b. 1729, d. 1765 ; = H. WASTELL,
heiress of Newbrough, | b. 1738, m.
Walltown, and Bellister. | 1764.

JOHN BLENKINSOPP COULSON, = MARY, dau. of John Lisle
of Blenkinsopp and Jesmond ; | of Elyhaugh, North-
b. 1729, d. unmarried in 1788. | umberland.

FRANCES.
JANE.

ROBERT LISLE COULSON, Captain = SARAH, d. & h. of Robert Veitch
R.N. ; b. 1780, d. 1822. | of Houndwood, Berwickshire.

WILLIAM, b. 1786,
JANE, d. in 1798,
m. to Capt. Quin,
55th Regt.
MARGT., b. 1775.
MARY, d. 1778.

ISABEL.
JANE.
FRANCES.

ANNE, dau. of = Rev. HENRY WASTELL,
T. Henderson, | D.D., Fell. of Clare Hall,
City Chamber- | Camb., b. 1765, d. 1848 ; of
lain of Edin- | Newbrough, Bellister, and
burgh, d. 1865. | Walltown, Northumber-
| land.

FRANCES JANE,
b. 1820,
d. 1837.

ALICIA FRANCES FORTH, dau. of = XIX. JOHN BLENKINSOPP COULSON, of
Rev. Gustavus Hamilton, and | Blenkinsopp and Jesmond, b. 1779;
grand-dau. of Hon. Hen. Hamil- | J.P. and D.L., Lieut.-Col. North-
ton, 3rd son of 1st Viscount | umberland Militia. Sold Jesmond
Boyne, m. 1796, d. 1853. | in 1809 ; d. 1863.

MARY, d. 1863.
ELIZA, b. 1819.

MARY ALICIA, b. 1797, d. 1872.
ARABELLA, b. 1798, d. 1884.
ROBERT, b. 1803 ; Capt. Gren.
Guards ; d. 1866.

GUSTAVUS HAMILTON COUL- = ANNE LINDSAY WASTELL,
SON, b. 1801. Capt. R.N., | heiress of Newbrough and
J.P. Northumberland ; d. | Walltown ; b. 1819, m.
1868. | 1844, d. 1884.

1. JULIANA ELIZA, dau. of Rev. E. = XX. JOHN BLENKINSOPP COULSON, of = HON. MARY ANNE, dau.
Dawkins, and of Lady Juliana Coll- | Blenkinsopp, b. 1799, | of 7th Lord Byron ; b.
year, dau. of 2nd Earl of Portmore ; | Capt. Gren. | 1817, m. 1834, d. 1885.
m. 1829, d. 1831. | Guards, J.P. and D.L. |
| Northumber- |
| land. High Sheriff 1868 ; died 1868. |

SARAH, b. 1816 = CHARLES LISLE COULSON.
had CHARLES LISLE COOKSON.

MARY, d. 1863 = CHARLES COOKSON.
ELIZA, b. 1819.

GUSTAVUS = CAROLINE
BLENKINSOPP, | STEWART, dau.
B.C.S., b. 1836, d. 1863. | of Henry Unwin,
ROBERT BLENKINSOPP, | Bo. C.S., by
Lieut. R.N., b. 1837, | Margaret, dau.
drowned 1856. | of Gordon
GEORGE BLENKINSOPP, | Forbes, of Ham,
Capt. 100th Regiment, b. | Surrey.
1838, drowned 1860. |
HARRY BLENKINSOPP, b. |
1840. |

HENRY JOHN = CAROLINE
WASTELL COUL- | STEWART, dau.
SON, of New- | of Henry Unwin,
brough and Wall- | Bo. C.S., by
town, Northum- | Margaret, dau.
berland, b. 1848, | of Gordon
barrister-at-law, | Forbes, of Ham,
m. 1875. | Surrey.

ALICIA, FRANCES JANE
b.1846. | WASTELL, b.
MARY, | 1855, m. 1876.
b.1851. | ARTHUR H.
| UNWIN,Bo.C.S.,
| and has 2 daus.,
| 1. ALICE HAMIL-
| TON ; 2. BERYL
| MARGARET.

GEORGIANA HAM-
ILTON, b. 1856,
d. 1869.
THEODOSIA HAM-
ILTON, b. 1857.
MAUDE MARIA
LISLE, b. 1859.
MARGARET LIND-
SAY, b. 1863.

WILLIAM LISLE = SOPHIA LYDIA,
BLENKINSOPP, | dau. of John
Lt.-Col.3rdBatt. | Dixon, of Astle
Northumberland | Hall, Cheshire,
Fusiliers, J.P. | by Sophia, dau.
for Northumber- | of T. W. Tatton
land and | of Wythenshawe,
Cheshire, | Cheshire, m.
b. 3 July, 1840. | 11 Sep, 1877.

FREDERIC
CHARLES BLEN-
KINSOPP, Capt.
60th Rifles, b.
1845, m. 1875
LUCIA, dau. of
Lucius Chitten-
den, of New
York. =

ARTHUR BLENKIN-
SOPP, Rector of
Carham, North-
umberland, b.
1841, m., 1869,
LAURA, dau. of
Rev. Thos.Ilder-
ton, of Ilderton,
Northumberland.

LUCIA.
MARION.
BARBARA.
MARJORIE.

EVA.
MARY.
MARJORIE.

BASIL JOHN BLENKINSOPP
COULSON, Lieut. King's
Own Scottish Borderers,
b. 1879.

GUSTAVUS HAMILTON BLENKINSOPP COULSON, Lieut. King's
Own Scottish Borderers, b. 1879. Killed in action at Lamb-
recksfontein, S. Africa, 19 May, 1901, where he saved the guns
and rode close under the enemy's fire to rescue a wounded
trooper, and for these gallant deeds he was recommended for
the Victoria Cross.

FLORENCE
LINDSAY.
ISABEL FORBES.
INEZ LISLE.

LISLE BLENKINSOPP
COULSON, Lieut. North-
umberland Fusiliers ;
b. 8 Feb., 1879.

DOROTHY BLENKINSOPP, m.
1900 C. COPLEY DU CANE,
of Braxted Park, Essex,
eldest son of Sir Charles du
Cane, K.C.M.G.

HUBERT ARTHUR
BLENKINSOPP
COULSON, b.1870.
= GEORGE BYRON,
b. 1875.

XXI. JOHN BYRON
BLENKINSOPP
COULSON, of
Blenkinsopp,
Capt. Grenadier
Guards and Rifle
Brigade, b. 1835.
J.P. for Northum-
berland.

XVIII. WILLIAM COULSON, =
b. 1737 : Sheriff of New-
castle in 1768, d. 1789.

MARY, dau. of New-
umberland.

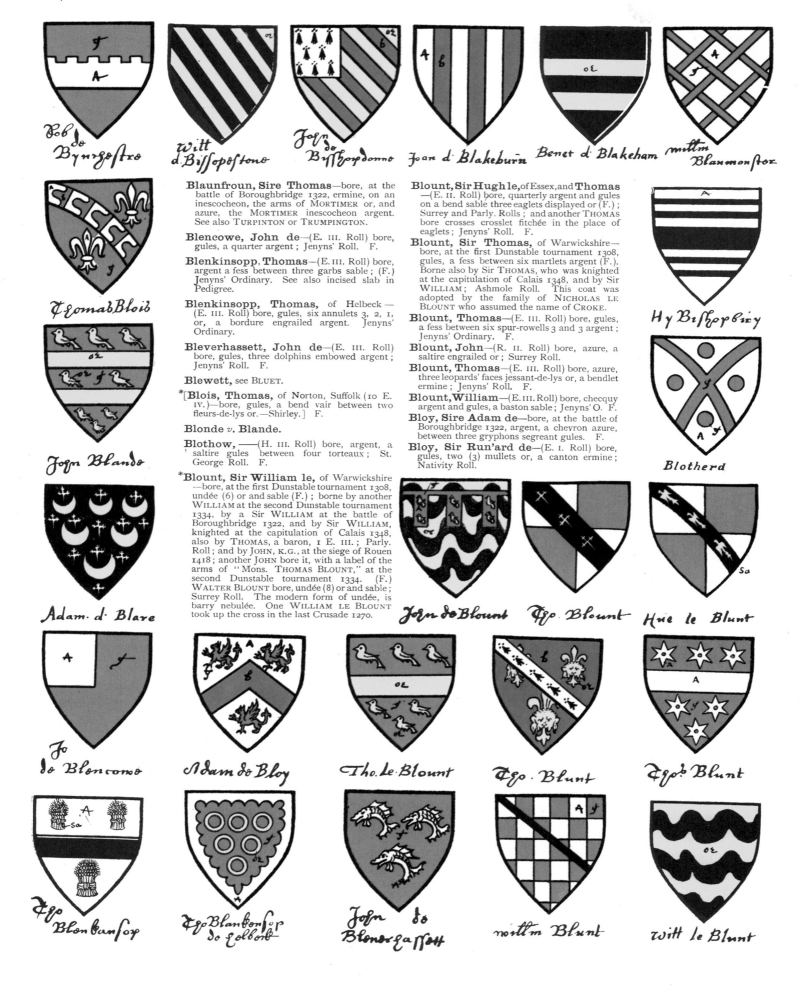

Blaunfroun, Sire Thomas—bore, at the battle of Boroughbridge 1322, ermine, on an inescocheon, the arms of MORTIMER or, and azure, the MORTIMER inescocheon argent. See also TURPINTON or TRUMPINGTON.

Blencowe, John de—(E. III. Roll) bore, gules, a quarter argent; Jenyns' Roll. F.

Blenkinsopp, Thomas—(E. III. Roll) bore, argent a fess between three garbs sable; (F.) Jenyns' Ordinary. See also incised slab in Pedigree.

Blenkinsopp, Thomas, of Helbeck — (E. III. Roll) bore, gules, six annulets 3, 2, 1, or, a bordure engrailed argent. Jenyns' Ordinary.

Bleverhassett, John de—(E. III. Roll) bore, gules, three dolphins embowed argent; Jenyns' Roll. F.

Blewett, see BLUET.

*[**Blois, Thomas**, of Norton, Suffolk (10 E. IV.)—bore, gules, a bend vair between two fleurs-de-lys or.—Shirley.] F.

Blonde v. BLANDE.

Blothow, ——(H. III. Roll) bore, argent, a saltire gules between four torteaux; St. George Roll. F.

***Blount, Sir William le,** of Warwickshire —bore, at the first Dunstable tournament 1308, undée (6) or and sable (F.); borne by another WILLIAM at the second Dunstable tournament 1334, by a Sir WILLIAM at the battle of Boroughbridge 1322, and by Sir WILLIAM, knighted at the capitulation of Calais 1348, also by THOMAS, a baron, 1 E. III.; Parly. Roll; and by JOHN, K.G., at the siege of Rouen 1418; another JOHN bore it, with a label of the arms of "Mons. THOMAS BLOUNT," at the second Dunstable tournament 1334. (F.) WALTER BLOUNT bore, undée (8) or and sable; Surrey Roll. The modern form of undée, is barry nebulée. One WILLIAM LE BLOUNT took up the cross in the last Crusade 1270.

Blount, Sir Hugh le, of Essex, and **Thomas** —(E. II. Roll) bore, quarterly argent and gules on a bend sable three eaglets displayed or (F.); Surrey and Parly. Rolls; and another THOMAS bore crosses crosslet fitchée in the place of eaglets; Jenyns' Roll. F.

Blount, Sir Thomas, of Warwickshire— bore, at the first Dunstable tournament 1308, gules, a fess between six martlets argent (F.). Borne also by Sir THOMAS, who was knighted at the capitulation of Calais 1348, and by Sir WILLIAM; Ashmole Roll. This coat was adopted by the family of NICHOLAS LE BLOUNT who assumed the name of CROKE.

Blount, Thomas—(E. III. Roll) bore, gules, a fess between six spur-rowells 3 and 3 argent; Jenyns' Ordinary. F.

Blount, John—(R. II. Roll) bore, azure, a saltire engrailed or; Surrey Roll.

Blount, Thomas—(E. III. Roll) bore, azure, three leopards' faces jessant-de-lys or, a bendlet ermine; Jenyns' Roll. F.

Blount, William—(E. III. Roll) bore, chequy argent and gules, a baston sable; Jenyns' O. F.

Bloy, Sire Adam de—bore, at the battle of Boroughbridge 1322, argent, a chevron azure, between three gryphons segreant gules. F.

Bloy, Sir Run'ard de—(E. I. Roll) bore, gules, two (3) mullets or, a canton ermine; Nativity Roll.

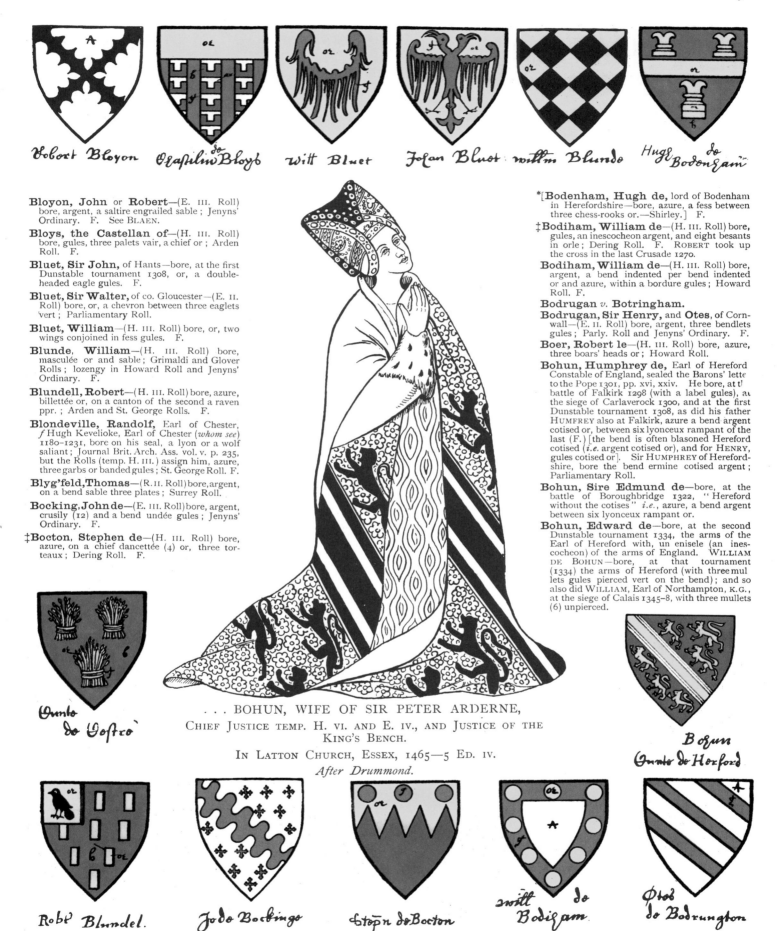

Robert Bloyon   Castilin de Bloys   Will Bluet   Johan Bluet   willm Blunde   Huge de Bodongam

Bloyon, John or **Robert**—(E. III. Roll) bore, argent, a saltire engrailed sable; Jenyns' Ordinary. F. See BLAEN.

Bloys, the Castellan of—(H. III. Roll) bore, gules, three palets vair, a chief or; Arden Roll. F.

Bluet, Sir John, of Hants—bore, at the first Dunstable tournament 1308, or, a double-headed eagle gules. F.

Bluet, Sir Walter, of co. Gloucester—(E. II. Roll) bore, or, a chevron between three eaglets vert.; Parliamentary Roll.

Bluet, William—(H. III. Roll) bore, or, two wings conjoined in fess gules. F.

Blunde, William—(H. III. Roll) bore, masculée or and sable; Grimaldi and Glover Rolls; lozengy in Howard Roll and Jenyns' Ordinary. F.

Blundell, Robert—(H. III. Roll) bore, azure, billettée or, on a canton of the second a raven ppr.; Arden and St. George Rolls. F.

Blondeville, Randolf, Earl of Chester, f Hugh Kevelioke, Earl of Chester (whom see) 1180-1231, bore on his seal, a lyon or a wolf saliant; Journal Brit. Arch. Ass. vol. v. p. 235, but the Rolls (temp. H. III.) assign him, azure, three garbs or banded gules; St. George Roll. F.

Blyg'feld, Thomas—(R. II. Roll) bore, argent, on a bend sable three plates; Surrey Roll.

Bocking, John de—(E. III. Roll) bore, argent, crusily (12) and a bend undée gules; Jenyns' Ordinary.

‡**Bocton, Stephen de**—(H. III. Roll) bore, azure, on a chief dancettée (4) or, three torteaux; Dering Roll. F.

*[**Bodenham, Hugh de,** lord of Bodenham in Herefordshire—bore, azure, a fess between three chess-rooks or.—Shirley.] F.

‡**Bodiham, William de**—(H. III. Roll) bore, gules, an inescocheon argent, and eight besants in orle; Dering Roll. F. ROBERT took up the cross in the last Crusade 1270.

Bodiham, William de—(H. III. Roll) bore, argent, a bend indented per bend indented or and azure, within a bordure gules; Howard Roll. F.

Bodrugan v. **Botringham.**

Bodrugan, Sir Henry, and **Otes,** of Cornwall—(E. II. Roll) bore, argent, three bendlets gules; Parly. Roll and Jenyns' Ordinary. F.

Boer, Robert le—(H. III. Roll) bore, azure, three boars' heads or; Howard Roll.

Bohun, Humphrey de, Earl of Hereford Constable of England, sealed the Barons' letter to the Pope 1301, pp. xvi, xxiv. He bore, at the battle of Falkirk 1298 (with a label gules), at the siege of Carlaverock 1300, and at the first Dunstable tournament 1308, as did his father HUMFREY also at Falkirk, azure a bend argent cotised or, between six lyonceux rampant of the last (F.) [the bend is often blasoned Hereford cotised (i.e. argent cotised or), and for HENRY, gules cotised or]. Sir HUMPHREY of Herefordshire, bore the bend ermine cotised argent; Parliamentary Roll.

Bohun, Sire Edmund de—bore, at the battle of Boroughbridge 1322, "Hereford without the cotises" i.e., azure, a bend argent between six lyonceux rampant or.

Bohun, Edward de—bore, at the second Dunstable tournament 1334, the arms of the Earl of Hereford with, un enisele (an inescocheon) of the arms of England. WILLIAM DE BOHUN—bore, at that tournament (1334) the arms of Hereford (with three mullets gules pierced vert on the bend); and so also did WILLIAM, Earl of Northampton, K.G., at the siege of Calais 1345-8, with three mullets (6) unpierced.

Humfo de Yoftro`

. . . BOHUN, WIFE OF SIR PETER ARDERNE, CHIEF JUSTICE TEMP. H. VI. AND E. IV., AND JUSTICE OF THE KING'S BENCH.

IN LATTON CHURCH, ESSEX, 1465—5 ED. IV.

After Drummond.

Bohun (Erle de Herford)

Robt Blundel.   Johd Bockinge   Stepn de Bocton   willm de Bodigam   Otes de Bodrungton

Johan de Boun

Baron Hugge de Bolbert

Witt de Bolkworthy

Bolron

Tho. Bolron

John Boroforde

Jo de Bolhuno

Robert de Bolton

Robt Bond

Joan d' Bond

Henry Borfield

John Borohont

Robt de Borowde

Bohun, Sir Gilbert de, of co. Hereford-shire—(E. II. Roll) bore, azure on a bend cotised argent between six lyonceux rampant or, three escallops gules ; Parly. and St. George Rolls. JOHN bore the same without the escallops ; St. George Roll.

Bohun, Sir Edmond de, of Herefordshire—(E. II. Roll) bore, azure, a bend per bend indented argent and gules plain cotised of the second, between six lyonceux rampant or ; Parly. Roll.

‡Bohun, John de—(E. I. Roll) bore, or, a cross azure (F.), Dering Roll ; another JOHN, of Midhurst, a baron 1363, bore the same, Segar and Ashmole Rolls ; ascribed also to ROBERT in Surrey Roll.

Bohun, Foulke and Franke, see BOUN.

Bokkesworthe, Sir William de (or BOLKWORTHE)—bore, at the first Dunstable tournament 1308, or, a lyon rampant purpure collared or. F.

Bolde, Sir Henry, of Bold, Lancashire, Kt. —(H. VI. Roll) bore, argent, a gryphon segreant sable beaked and legged gules, quarterly with sable five fusils conjoined in fess argent, a label of three gules ; Arundel and Ballard Rolls.

Bolebec, Hugh—(H. III. Roll) bore, vert, a lyon rampant ermine, Glover Roll ; Sir HUGH, the feudal lord, bore (E. III.), vert, a lyon rampant argent ; Jenyns' Ordinary. F.

Bolesby, William de—(R. II. Roll) bore, sable, a saltire or ; Surrey Roll.

Bolmer, see BULMER.

Bolron,—— (E. IV. Roll) bore, argent, a bend sable between five lozenges in chief and three picks in base sable ; with crest ; Ballard Roll F.

Bolron, Thomas—(E. III. Roll) bore, sable, on a chief argent a fer-de-moulin of the first ; Jenyns' Roll. F.

Boltesham, Sir Thomas, of Rutland—(E. II. Roll) bore, gules, three besons or bird-bolts erect argent ; Parliamentary Roll.

Bolton, John de—(E. I. Roll) bore, argent, on a bend sable three eaglets, or ; Segar Roll. F.

Bolton, Robert de—(E. III. Roll) bore, argent, on a chevron gules three lyons passant gardant or ; Jenyns' Ordinary. Borne also by THOMAS HESLARTON.

Bond, John de—(H. III. Roll) bore, gules, billettée or, and three lyons rampant argent ; St. George Roll. F.

*[Bond, Robert, of Beauchamp Hache, Somerset (9 H. VI.)—bore, sable, a fess or.—Shirley.] F.

Bonetby, Nicol de—(H. III. Roll) bore, azure three estoiles argent ; Glover Roll. F.

‡Bonett, Hamon de—(H. III. Roll) bore, checquy or and gules on a chief azure two spur-rowells argent ; Howard and Dering Rolls. See BOWETT.

Bonevile, Sire Nichol—bore, at the battle of Boroughbridge 1322, or, on a bend sable three mullets (6) argent. F. See BENEVILE.

Bonevile, Sir William, of Sponton, Yorks. —(H. VI. Roll) bore, sable six mullets argent, quarterly with gules, three lyonceux gold ; Atkinson Roll. WILLIAM, Lord BONVILE, K.G., bore the first coat, with the mullets pierced gules ; K. 402 fo. 46.

Bonner, Sir Robert de, of Essex—(E. II. Roll) bore, ermine, a chief indented sable ; Parliamentary Roll.

Booth, Sir John (BOUTHE), of Barton—(E. IV. Roll) bore, argent, three boars' heads erect and erased sable ; with crest ; Ballard Roll.

Booth, Sir William, knighted at the capitulation of Calais 1348—bore, vaire argent and gules, a bendlet sable. F.

Bordeux, Peter de, v. Burdeux.

Bordelys, Sir Geoffrey de, of co. Cambs. —(E. II. Roll) bore, ermine, on a chief gules a lyon passant gardant or ; Parly. Roll.

Bordon, see BURDON.

Bordonn, Sir Walter—(E. III. Roll) bore, argent three cinquefoyles pierced sable ; Ashmole Roll. See also BUROWDON.

Borefield, John—(E. III. Roll) bore, argent, a chevron gules between three pellets 2 and 1 ; Jenyns' Ordinary. F.

Borfeld, Sire Henry de (or BERFIELD)—bore, at the battle of Boroughbridge 1322, or, a chevron sable between three pellets (F.) ; in Ashmole Roll, or, three fleurs-de-lys sable.

Borgate, Sir Peers de, of Suffolk—(E. II. Roll) bore, paly (6) argent and sable ; Parliamentary Roll.

Borges, Sir Thomas, of Kent—(H. VI. Roll) bore, argent, a fess counter-compony or and gules in chief three crosses crosslet of the last ; Arundel Roll.

Borhont, Sir John, of Hants—bore, at the siege of Calais 1345-8, argent a fess between six martlets gules ; (F.). Sir RICHARD, of Wilts., bore the same, E. II. ; Parly. Roll.

[Borowe, Robert de, 1418—bore, gules, a bough erect and eradicated argent. Shirley.] F.

Borowell, (——) Kt.—(H. VI. Roll) bore, paly (6) argent and azure a bend gules ; Arundel Roll. See BROWELL or BURWELL.

Borways v. Burghersh.

*[Boscawen, John de (E. III.) — bore, ermine, a rose gules ; and more anciently, vert, a bull-dog argent !—Shirley.] F.

Bosco, Sir John de (1297)—bore, sable, crusily and three leopards' faces or ; Nobility Roll.

Boson, Sir John and Sir Piers, of Norfolk —(E. III. Roll) bore, argent, three besons (or bird-bolts) erect gules ; Ashmole, Parliamentary, and Surrey Rolls.

Boson, Raf—(H. III. Roll) bore, argent, three bird-bolts, one in pale erect between two pileways gules headed sable ; Arden and St. George Rolls. F.

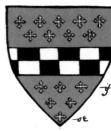

Bork Borways

nicol de Bonotby

nich Bonvillo

witt Booth

John de Boscawon

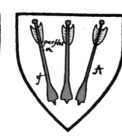

Rauf Bozun

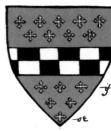

Rauf le Botler

Hugh de Boſſard   Roger Boſopillo

Ego. Boſpillo   Ego. Boſpillo de Dayvillo

Bossard, Sire Hugo—bore, at the battle of Boroughbridge 1322, argent, two bars and in chief three mullets (6) within a bordure, all sable. F.

Bosville, Roger—(E. III. Roll) bore, argent, four fusils in fess gules; Jenyns' Ordinary. F.

Bosvile, Thomas, of Dayvile, in Yorks—(E. III. Roll) bore, argent, five fusils conjoined in fess gules, a crescent sable; Jenyns' Roll. F.

Bosville, Thomas—(E. III. Roll) bore, argent, five fusils in fess gules, in chief three leaves (feuilles in Cotgrave and temoyles in Jenyns' Ordinary) slipped sable (F.); crosslets in Cotton MS. & Harl. 6589; foyles or fermailes in Harl. 1068 and 1577.

Bosvill, John—(R. II. Roll) bore, argent, five fusils in fess gules, in chief three martlets sable; Surrey Roll.

Boteler, Allayne, of Berdon—(E. III. Roll) bore, azure, three covered cups or; Jenyns' Ordinary. F. See also incised slab.

Boteler, Andrew (BUTLER)—bore, at the siege of Rouen 1418, argent six covered cups, 3, 2, 1, sable, *quarterly with*, gules a cross moline argent within a bordure engrailed or; Harl. 6137, reverses the quarterings. F.

Boteler, William de—baron, of Warrington, WILLIAM, of Wem, and Sir THOMAS, of Beausay—(E. II. Roll) bore azure a bend between six covered cups or; Parliamentary, Ballard, and Ashmole Rolls. JOHN, R. II., bore the bend argent in Surrey Roll. This is not the usually accepted coat—see below.

Boteler, James, of Rawcliff, in Lancs., also Sir NICHOLAS, and JOHN—(E. III. Roll) bore, azure, a chevron between three covered cups or; Surrey, Ballard, Ashmole, and Arundel Rolls. WILLIAM, of Kirkland, bore three mullets gules on the chevron; Ballard Roll.

Boteler, Sir William le, of Warrington, a baron, 27 E. I.—bore, gules, crusily or a fess counter-compony (checquy in H. 4033) argent and azure; Parliamentary Roll. RAUF bore this argent and sable, in St. George Roll.

Boteler, William of Wemme, baron 1308, bore, gules, a fess checquy argent and sable, between six crosses patée fitchée at the foot argent; Nobility Roll. Another, gules, a fess checquy (counter-compony in trick), argent and sable between three crosses potent of the second (F.); Jenyns' Ordinary.

Boteler, William — bore, at the second Dunstable tournament 1334, gules, crusily argent, a fess checquy of the last and sable. RAUF bore this crusily or, in Glover Roll. F.

Boteler, Edward and **Sir William**—(E. I. Roll) bore, gules, crusily argent a fess counter-compony or and sable; Arden, Guillim, and Surrey Rolls.

Boteler, Sir Raffe le, of Salop—(E. II. Roll) bore, gules, a fess checquy or and sable (azure, sometimes), in chief two mullets of the second; Parliamentary Roll.

Boteler, Sir William—(E. III. Roll) bore, gules, a chevron counter-compony sable and argent; Ashmole Roll.

Botiler, Theobald, Earl of Ormond—(E. I. Roll) bore, or, a chief dancettée (3) azure; Segar and Ashmole Rolls, &c. (F.) JAMES, 5th Earl, K.G., bore it at the siege of Rouen 1418.

Botiler, Sire Rauf le—bore, at the battle of Boroughbridge 1322, argent, two bendlets gules (F.) RAF bore the bendlets azure (Arden Roll); ermine in Ashmole Roll.

Botiler, Sir Henry le—(E. I. Roll) bore, or, two bends gules a chief sable; Guillim Roll.

Botiler, Sir John (BOALER or BOYLER) knighted at the capitulation of Calais 1348—

SIR JOHN DE BOTILER, 1285.

IN S. BRIDE'S CHURCH,

CO. GLAMORGAN.

After Boutell.

bore, gules, four mascles in fess quarterly argent and sable, between three crosses flory or, H. 6589 (F.); between six crosses crosslet or, in H. 1068.

Botiller DE ST. LYS; le—(E. I. Roll) bore, quarterly argent and gules; Holland Roll.

Botelsham *v.* **Boltesham.**

Boter, Thomas—(E. III. Roll) bore, gyrony (8), ermine and gules; Jenyns' Ordinary. F.

Boterels, Sir William de, banneret—(E. II. Roll) bore, checquy or and gules a chevron azure; Parliamentary Roll. Sir REYNAUD, of Cornwall, bore, three horse-shoes argent on the chevron; Parliamentary Roll.

Boterels, Thomas—(H. III. Roll), bore, gules, bezantée, on a canton argent a cinquefoyle pierced sable; Arden and St. George Rolls. F.

Botetourt, Bartholomew de and **Sir Guy,** of Norfolk—(H. III. Roll) bore, ermine, a saltire engrailed gules; Arden and Parly. Rolls. Sir WILLIAM, of Norfolk, bore a mullet or, for difference at the first Dunstable tournament 1308 (F.); and Sir RALF, also of Norfolk, E. II., bore, a label (3) vert, for difference in Parly. Roll.

Botetourt, Sir John, a baron 1305—bore, at the battle of Falkirk 1298, and at the siege of Carlaverock 1300, or, a saltire engrailed sable; a banneret in the Parliamentary Roll. (F.) Sealed the Barons' letter to the Pope 1301 with a cinquefoyle pierced, on each (foyle) a saltire engrailed, pp. xix, xxiv.

Botetourt, Sir Thomas, of Norfolk—bore, at the first Dunstable tournament 1308, and at the battle of Boroughbridge 1322, or, a saltire engrailed sable, a label (5) gules. Sire JOHAN LE FIZ, bore the same at Boroughbridge, the pendants of the label platey.

Botreaux, Renaud (BOTR'WS)—(H. III. Roll) bore, checquy (also vaire) or and gules, on a chevron azure three horse-shoes argent (F.); Arden and St. George Rolls. Sir WILLIAM reversed the checquy; Harl. Roll.

Botreaux, Le Sire (NICHOLAS) — (E. III. Roll) bore, checquy or and gules, a bend vair. Jenyns' Ordinary. F.

Botreaux, William (BOTREWE)—(R. II. Roll) bore, argent, a gryphon segreant gules armed azure, Surrey Roll; gules and argent in Ashmole Roll.

‡**Botresham, Sire de**—(E. I. Roll) bore, or, three mascles two and one . . . . a chief paly (6) argent and gules; Dering and Camden Rolls. F.

Botringham *v.* **Bodrugan.**

Botringham, Sire Otes de—bore, at the battle of Boroughbridge 1322, argent three bendlets gules (F.). Sir HENRY bore the same; Harl. Roll.

Botringham, William de (BUTTRINGHAM)—bore, at the second Dunstable tournament 1334, argent a bend gules.

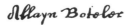
Allayn Botolor   And. Butler   John Botolor
Rauf le Botiller

Rob. le Butilor

William Bottilor

Thom Botor

Thomas Boterel

Johan Botetourte

HENRY BOURCHIER, EARL OF ESSEX, 1483.
IN LITTLE EASTON CHURCH, ESSEX.
After Waller.

Baudwin d. Boulers

Robt. de Boreton

Robert Bousor

Will Bourchor

Off. de Bourne

Botune, Steven de—(H. III. Roll) bore, azure, on a chief indented or three torteaux; Howard Roll.

Boues v. Bucy.

Boughton, Piers de—(R. II. Roll) bore, gules, a goat saliant or; Surrey Roll.

*[**Boughton, Robert de** (BORETON) E. III.— bore, sable, three crescents or.—Shirley.] F.

†**Boulers, Baudwyn de**—(H. III. Roll) bore, sable billettée and a bend argent; Dering and St. George Rolls (F.). See also BULLER.

Boun, see BOHUN.

Boun, Foulke de—(E. III. Roll) bore, sable, three crescents argent; Jenyns' Roll; called JOIR, or JORCE, in the Arden Roll.

Boun, Frank de—(H. III. Roll) bore, gules, a crescent ermine within an orle of martlets ermine; Glover Roll. See BOHUN, of Tressingfield, Suffolk.

†**Bourchalle, Henry de** (BORCHELLE)— (H. III. Roll) bore, paly (6) argent and azure, a fess gules, Dering Roll; tricked also or and azure. See also BURGHILL and BURRELL.

Bourchier, Robert (BURSOUR)—bore, at the second Dunstable tournament 1334, argent, a cross engrelée or. Lord BARNESSE or BERNERS.

‡**Bourchier, Hugh de** (BUCY or BOUES)— (H. III. Roll) bore, or three water-bougets azure; Dering and Howard Rolls. LE SIR BOWCEER, bore, H. VI., azure three water-bougets or; 6th Nobility Roll.

Bourchier, Sir Robert, a baron 1342, knighted at the capitulation of Calais 1348— bore, argent, a cross engrailed gules, between four water-bougets sable (F.), as did Le Sire DE BOUCER, at the siege of Rouen 1418—where WILLIAM B. bore the same (differenced with a martlet or an annulet) *quarterly with* LOVAYNE, gules, billettée or and a fess argent. F.

Bourchier, Bartholomew (BOUSER) — (R. II. Roll) bore, argent, a cross engrailed gules between four water-bougets sable, a label (3) azure; Surrey Roll. WILLIAM, bore, three fleurs-de-lys or on the pendants, and his brother JOHN, 1st Lord Berners, K.G., bore on each pendant a lyon rampant or. Harl. MS. 1418 fo. 52ᵇ.

Bourgyloun, Sir Robert, of Norfolk— (E. II. Roll) bore, quarterly or and gules, in the second and third an annulet argent, over all a bend sable; Parliamentary Roll.

Bourne, Sir Thomas—bore, at the siege of Calais 1345–8, argent, a chevron gules between three lyons rampant sable, ascribed to NICHOLAS (F.) and Richard E. III.; Jenyns' Ordinary.

Bourne, Sir Christopher, knighted at the capitulation of Calais 1348—bore, gules, a lyon rampant argent a bordure engrailed or.

Bourne, Thomas de—bore, at the second Dunstable tournament 1334, gules, a lyon rampant or tail fourchée, a bordure engrelé argent.

‡**Bourne, John de**—(H. III. Roll) bore, ermine on a bend azure three lyons rampant or; Dering Roll; no lyons in Ashmole MS.

Bourneham, Sir Thomas de, of co. Linc. —(E. II. Roll) bore, or a maunch vert; Parliamentary Roll.

Will Botetourt

Otes de Botringham

Le Sire Botrane

Sire de Botresham

Reinaud d' Botrens.

Robt Bouteuillayne

mingʳ Bourde

Witt Bourt

Robt Botenilain

Herebtᵖ d Bonele

Robt de Bonsod

Fgo Bonsott

Henry de Boys del Usburne

John del Boys del Soulfe

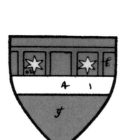

Robt d Brace

Jo. Bracebridge

Jnᵒ d Bracebruge

Bourt, William de—(H. III. Roll) bore, sable a cross patonce argent; Arden and St. George Rolls. F.

Boutevilain, Sir Robert, of Northants——bore, at the first Dunstable tournament 1308, argent three crescents gules, and Sir WILLIAM bore the same; Ashmole Roll and Jenyns' Ordinary.

Boutevilain, John—(R. II. Roll) bore, argent, a chevron between three crescents gules; Surrey Roll. ROBERT, bore, a fess in lieu of the chevron; St. George Roll. F.

Bovile, Herbert, and **Sir William de**—of Suffolk—(H. III. Roll) bore, quarterly or and sable (F.), and Sir JOHN, of Suffolk, a martlet, gules for difference; St. George and Parly. Rolls. WILLIAM bore, a lyon passant gules in the first quarter; Norfolk Roll.

Bovile, Sir John, le fys—(E. III. Roll) bore, gules, four bendlets argent; Ashmole Roll.

Bowes, Robert de, and **William** — (E. III. Roll) bore, ermine, three long bows "tenduz" gules; Jenyns' and Surrey Rolls.

Bowett, Thomas — (E. III. Roll) bore, argent, three reindeers' heads cabossed sable; Jenyns' Roll. F. See BONETT.

Bowles, Sir John—(H. III. Roll) bore, gules, a fess ermine, a bordure engrailed or; Ashmole Roll.

Bownd, Sir Roger — bore, at the first Dunstable tournament 1308, argent, a chief indented sable.

Box, Sir Henry de, of Essex—(E. II. Roll) bore, or, a bendlet between six lyonceux rampant gules; Parliamentary Roll. The lyonceux debruised by the bendlet, H. 6137 fo. 9.

Boxhull, see BUCKESHALL and BUXHULL.

Boxstede, Sir Raffe de, of Essex—(E. II. Roll) bore, quarterly argent and gules, on a bend sable three besants; Parliamentary Roll.

Boxworth, Sir William de, of co. Cambridge—(E. II. Roll) bore, or, a lyon rampant gules, collared argent; Parliamentary Roll.

Boydell, —— (E. IV. Roll) bore, quarterly 1 and 4, vert, a cross patonce or—2, gules, fretty argent a fess or—3, argent, on a fess azure three mullets of the field; and crest; Ballard Roll.

Boyland, —— (E. III. Roll) bore, sable an eagle displayed argent; Ashmole Roll.

Boyland, Sir John, of Norfolk—(E. II. Roll) bore, azure, a saltire engrailed or; Parliamentary Roll.

Boyler, Sir John, see BOTELER.

*__Boynton, Thomas de__—(R. II. Roll) bore, or, a fess between three crescents gules; Surrey Roll. F.

Boys, Sir John, v. BOSCO.

Boys, Sir Robert de, of Suffolk—bore, at the first Dunstable tournament 1308, ermine a cross sable. Another ROBERT bore it at the second Dunstable tournament 1334, as did JOHN, of the South. (F.) Jenyns' Roll.

Boys, Ernald de, Henry, and **James** —(H. III. Roll) bore, argent, two bars and a quarter (or canton) gules; Norfolk Roll, Jenyns' Ordinary, &c. F. Ascribed also to JOHN(‡) in Dering Roll.

Boys, Nicol de—(H. III. Roll) bore, ermine two bars and a quarter gules. Sir JOHN of co. Linc. and ROGER bore, over all, a bendlet sable; Parliamentary and Surrey Rolls.

Boys, Henry de, del Usburne—(E. III. Roll) bore, barry (8) gules and or (or and argent in blason) on a chief indented (3) sable, as many escallops of the second; Jenyns' Roll. F.

Boys, Sir Nichol de, of Bucks, and **John** —(E. III. Roll) bore, argent, a chevron sable bezanty (3 or 5); Parliamentary Roll and Jenyns' Ordinary. F.

Boys, Richard de—(H. III. Roll) bore, MORTIMER'S arms sable and or, the inescocheon argent billettée of the first; Arden, St. George, and Howard Rolls. One of these names took up the cross in the last Crusade 1270.

Boyton, see BEYTON.

‡**Boyville, William de** (E. I. Roll), and SIR WILLIAM, of Northants—(E. II. Roll) bore, gules, three saltorelles argent (F.), Dering and Parliamentary Rolls, &c.; colours reversed in St. George Roll. ROBERT took up the cross in the last Crusade 1269.

Boyvile, John—(R. II. Roll) bore, gules, a fess or between three saltorelles argent; Surrey Roll.

Brabason, Sir Roger, of co. Leic.—(E. II. Roll) bore, gules, on a bend or three martlets sable; Parly. Roll. One of these names with these arms slain at the siege of Calais 1347.

*__Bracebridge, Sir John de,__ of co. Linc.— bore, at the first Dunstable tournament 1308, vaire argent and sable a fess gules (F.); Parly. Roll. Borne also by RAFFE at the siege of Rouen 1418.

Bracebridge, John—(H. III. Roll) bore, or, a cross azure; St. George Roll. F.

Brackonbridge, Sir William, of Arden —(E. III. Roll) bore, argent, a cross pattée voided (i.e. quarter pierced) gules; Ashmole Roll.

Brace, William de—(H. III. Roll) bore, gules, a fess argent two mullets (6) or; Arden Roll [pierced gules St. George]; borne also by ROBERT, with a label (4) azure; St. George Roll. F.

John del Boyd

Fgo de Bointon

John de Boyd

will d Boivile

de Bradburne

THE HERALDIC ATCHIEVEMENT

OF

SIR GRIFFITH HENRY BOYNTON, 12TH BARONET.

wiłł de Braddone   *wiłł Braddone*

Rog d' Bradeleie   *æo Bradscław*

Brace, Sir Robert—(E. III. Roll) bore, gules, a fess or, in chief two mullets argent; Ashmole Roll.

Bradburne, John de—(E. III. Roll) bore, argent, on a bend gules three mullets or voided (*i.e.* quarter pierced) vert; Jenyns' Ordinary. F.

Braddone, Sir Gefferay le, of Northants —(E. II. Roll) bore, sable, a bend engrailed argent (F.); Parliamentary Roll. The bend fusily for WILLIAM, E. I., in Segar Roll. F.

Bradley, John de—(H. III. Roll) bore, argent, a chevron counter-compony or and sable between three ducks "swartish" (black) billed and legged or; Howard Roll.

Bradley, Roger de—(H. III. Roll) bore, or, a fess gules between three buckles azure (F.); St. George Roll and also in Jenyns' Ordinary, where the buckles are blasoned, gules.

Bradshaw, Thomas—(E. III. Roll) bore, argent two bendlets enhanced sable; Jenyns' Roll. F.

Bradshaw, William, of Haw (Haigh)— (E. IV. Roll) bore, argent two bendlets sable; with crest; Ballard Roll.

Bradstone, Roger—(E. III. Roll) bore, argent, an estachés engrailed (5) gules; Jenyns' Roll. F.

Bradeston, Thomas de, baron 1322—bore, at the second Dunstable tournament 1334, argent on a quarter gules a rose or (F.). Sir THOMAS bore this at the siege of Calais 1345–8.

Braibef, John de—(H. III. Roll) bore, gules, a bend fusily or, a label (5) argent; St. George Roll. F.

Brampton, John de—(E. III. Roll) bore, gules, a saltire between four crosses crosslet fitchée argent; Arden Roll. F. BRYAN took up the cross in the last Crusade 1269. See BRUMTONE.

Branche, Piers—(H. III. Roll) bore, ermine, fretty gules; Glover Roll.

Brandon (——), a Suffolk Kt.—(H. VI. Roll) bore, sable, two lyons' gambs per saltire between as many lyons' heads in pale, all erased argent; Arundel Roll.

Branson, Sir John, see BRYANSON.

Braose, see also BREWES and BRUS.

Braose, Sir William de, banneret, baron of Gower 1299, sealed the Barons' letter to the Pope 1301, pp. xvii, xxiv—bore at the battle of Falkirk 1298, azure, crusily and a lyon rampant or tail fourchée; and so for WILLIAM (‡) in Dering Roll; [crusily fitchée and not fourchée in Guillim and Nobility Rolls, &c.] not fourchée in Surrey and Parly. Rolls (F.)—see Monumental Effigy, 1361. So borne by THOMAS, baron 1342; Surrey Roll.

Braose, Sir Giles, of Bucks—(E. II. Roll) bore, azure, crusily and a lyon rampant or, charged on the shoulder with a fleur-de-lys gules; Parly. Roll. Sir JOHN bore the lyons crowned gules, at the siege of Calais 1345–8, and so also PETER, as the last, with a crescent for difference.

Braose, Sir Giles de, banneret—(E. II. Roll) bore, argent, crusily and a lyon rampant gules, tail fourchée renowée; Parly. Roll.

Braose, Sir John, knighted at the capitulation of Calais 1348—bore, gules crusily and a lyon rampant or.

Braose, Sir Peers, of Gloucestershire— (E. II. Roll) bore, or, crusily and a lyon rampant sable, tail fourchée et renowée; Parly. Roll.

Braose, John—(R. II. Roll) bore, argent crusily fitchée and a lyon rampant gules, tail fourchée; Surrey Roll.

Braose, Robert de (BRUIS), of Brecknok, baron 1297—bore, barry (6) vaire (potent counter-potent) ermine and gules, and azure; Nobility Roll. Ascribed also to WM. DE BREWS.

‡Braose, Reynald le (BREWES)—(H. III. Roll) bore, azure, two bars vaire gules and ermine; Howard and Dering Rolls; tricked the reverse (same as JOHN GRESLEY) in Jenyns' Ordinary. F.

Bratworthe, Sire Richard—bore, at the battle of Boroughbridge 1322, argent, a saltire azure, and a label (3) gules; F.; in this roll the arms of Sir JOHN DE BYRON are erroneously applied to him. See also BARKSWORTH.

***[Bray, Thomas** (9 E. III.)—bore, argent, a chevron between three eaglets sable à la cuisse.—Shirley.] F.

Tłō Bradstone   *Rog Bradstone*

Ric Bratworthe   *Thomas Bray*

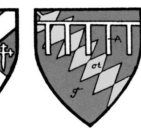
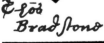

Jhō Brampton   *Joan d Braibef*

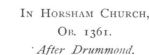

THOMAS LORD BRAOSE.
IN HORSHAM CHURCH,
OB. 1361.
After Drummond.

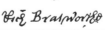

wm de Broose   *Thomas Broose*

SIR REGINALD BRAY, PRIVY COUNCILLOR TO HEN. VII.

IN THE NORTH WINDOW OF

JESUS COLLEGE, PRIORY CHURCH, GREAT MALVERN.

Tho. Braybroke

John Brentisle

Brotologge

Gr. de Brotaigne

Henry de Braylesford

Peirs Breton

Phillip Breton

Rog. Breton

Amyan Brett

John de Brotto

Bray, de —— (Oxon)-(E. III. Roll) bore, quarterly argent and azure, on a bend gules three fleurs-de-lys or ; Cotgrave Roll.

Braye, Sir Robert de, of Northants— (E. II. Roll) bore, vair, three bendlets gules ; Parly. Roll. See Illustration, Sir REGINALD BRAY.

Braybrook, Sir Gerard, of Bucks-(E. II. Roll) bore, argent, seven mascles conjoined 3, 3, 1, gules ; Parliamentary Roll ; another GERARD bore it with a label of three azure ; Surrey Roll ; and another GERARD and a THOMAS–bore, six mascles, 3, 2, 1, gules ; Ashmole Roll and Jenyns' Ordinary. F.

Braylesford, Henry de-(E. III. Roll) bore, or, a cinquefoyle sable ; Jenyns' Ordinary. F.

Bredenhill v. Brudenhill.

Brenley, Sir Lawrence (or BRYNDALE)— (E. III. Roll) bore, gules, a gryphon segreant or ; Ashmole Roll.

Brent, Sir Robert de, of Somerset—(E. II. Roll) bore, gules, a gryphon segreant argent ; Parliamentary Roll.

Brentislee, John de-(E. III. Roll) bore, argent, on a bend engrailed gules three lyonceux passant of the field ; Jenyns' Ordinary. F.

Brereleghe, Thomas-(E. III. Roll) bore, argent, a cross crosslet gules ; Jenyns' Ordinary. F.

Brereley, Sir Thomas-(E. I I. Roll) bore, argent, a cross potent gules ; Ashmole Roll.

Brereton, Andrew of-(E. IV. Roll) bore, argent, two bars sable ; with crest ; Ballard Roll.

Bretagne, John de, nephew of K. Edward (8th Earl of Richmond, ƒ John, Duke of BRITANNY)–bore, at the battle of Falkirk 1298, and at the siege of Carlaverock 1300 ; DREUX, with a quarter of Britanny and a bordure of England, viz., checquy or and azure, a bordure gules poudré with leopards or (i.e., eight lyons of England passant gardant or), over all a canton ermine (F.). Borne also by DE MONTFORT, Earl of Richmond, K.G., 1376.

Breton, Sire Robert—bore, at the battle of Boroughbridge 1322, azure, a bend between six mullets (6) or ; spur-rowells in Jenyns' Ordinary and Surrey Roll ; borne also argent and gules, by PEIRES and Sir WILLIAM, of co. Linc. F.

‡Breton, John—(E. II. Roll) bore, quarterly or and gules, a bordure azure ; Dering Roll ; and for SIR JOHN, of Essex, in Parliamentary Roll. JOHN LE BRETON, D'N'S. DE SPORLE appears to have sealed, with these arms, the Barons' letter to the Pope 1301, pp. xxi, xxiv.

Breton, Sire John, of Essex—(H. VI. Roll) bore, azure, two chevronels or, in chief two mullets pierced argent ; Arundel Roll.

Breton, Philip de Cobburne—(E. III. Roll) bore, sable, fretty argent, a chief or ; Jenyns' Ordinary. F.

Breton, Robert de-(H. III. Roll) bore, per pale gules and azure, a fess between two chevrons argent ; Arden and St. George Rolls.

Breton, Roger—(E. III. Roll) bore, argent, a chevron between three escallops gules ; Jenyns' Ordinary. F.

Brett, Sir Amyan—bore, at the siege of Calais 1345-8, gules, in chief a lyon passant gardant or. F.

Brett, Sir Eumenious (or AMANEU), de la—bore, at the battle of Falkirk 1298, and at the siege of Carlaverock 1300, " gules " ; the arms of the French family of ALBRET, tricked as the next in Harl. MS. 6137 fo. 38ᵇ.

Brett, Sir John and Sir Roger, of Leicestershire—(E. II. Roll) bore, gules billettée and a fess dancettée oʳ. (F.) Ashmole and Parly. Rolls.

Brewes, see also BRAOSE and BRUSE.

Brewes, John de -(E. II. Roll) bore, ermine, a cross lozengy sable ; Jenyns' Roll. F.

Breysy, Sir Piers de—bore, at the first Dunstable tournament 1308, or a lyon rampant azure langued gules. (F.) See BRAOSE.

Bridelshall, Sir Gilbert de, of county Lincoln—(E. II. Roll) bore, argent, two gemelles azure, in chief three mullets gules ; Parliamentary Roll.

Bridmanstone, Sir Stephen de, of Dorset —(E. II. Roll) bore, argent seven mascles conjoined sable ; another trick, six lozenges, 3, 2, 1 ; Parliamentary Roll. See CROUPES.

Brygge (——), an Essex Kt.—(H. VI. Roll) bore, argent, three owls passant sable, beaked and legged or ; Arundel Roll. F.

Brightmere (——), of Essex—(H. VI. Roll) bore, gules, a chevron between three swans' heads and necks erased argent ; Arundel Roll.

Brinton, Adam de-(H. III. Roll) bore, gules, a lyon rampant ermine tail fourchée ; Arden and St. George Rolls. F.

*[Brisco, Isold, of Crofton, Cumberland, 1390—bore, argent, three greyhounds courant sable.—Shirley.] F.

Britby, Robert de -(E. II. Roll) bore, gules, billettée and a fess dancettée argent ; Jenyns' Roll. F.

Britehebury, Avery—(R. II. Roll) bore, argent, two bars azure, on a canton of the last, a martlet or ; Surrey Roll.

Britton, Sir William de (BEYTON or BOYTON), of Suffolk—(E. II. Roll) bore, azure, three escallops or ; Parliamentary Roll.

Brius, or Briwys, see BRAOSE and BRUSE.

Broc, Laurence de—(H. III. Roll) bore, gules, on a chief argent a lyon passant of the field ; St. George Roll.

Brocas, Bernard—(R. II. Roll) bore, sable, a lyon rampant gardant or ; [another BERNARD bore it with a label (3) gules, Surrey Roll] ; and Sir JOHN also bore it at the siege of Calais 1345-8. F.

Am d. Brintone

Rob' de Britby

Isold Brisco

Laurens. d. Broc

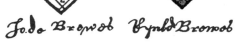

Jo. de Brewos

Reynold Brewos

will. de Breus

will d. Breus.

Brygge

John Brokas

F

34

ThosBrokehole   witt de Bromo   Rog. d. Bromo   W. de Brotherton   John de Broughton   Hue d' Bruges

Adam de la Brooke

Brian d' Bointon

witt de la Brooke

witt Brodonghl

Brockhill, **Sir Thomas** (or BROKETT), of Kent—(H. VI. Roll) bore, gules crusily fitchée or and a cross engrailed argent; Arundel and Ashmole Rolls.

Brockhole, Thomas de—(H. III. Roll) bore, or, crusily and a chevron gules; St. George Roll. (F.) Called also HOLEBROOKE, which see.

Brockholes, Geffrey—(R. II. Roll) bore, argent, a chevron between three brocks' or badgers' heads erased sable; Surrey Roll.

Brocking, Sir Ralffe, of Suffolk—(H. VI. Roll) bore, argent, crusily and a fess undée gules; Arundel Roll.

Broke, Nele de—(H. III. Roll) bore, gules, a chief indented or; Howard Roll.

Broome, Sir Nicholas, of Norfolk—(E. II. Roll) bore ermine, a fess dancettée gules; Parly. Roll.

Brome, Sire William de—bore, at the battle of Boroughbridge 1322, sable a cross passant argent. F.

Brome, Roger de—(H. III. Roll) bore, argent, a chief dancettée gules; St. George Roll. F.

Bromley, Sir John of—(E. IV. Roll) bore, quarterly per fess dancettée gules and or; with two crests; Ballard Roll.

(Bromley?), —— (R. II. Roll) bore, argent, on a chevron gules three besants, a bordure engrailed of the second; Surrey Roll.

Brompton, see BRAMPTON and BRUMTON.

Brontone, Piers de—(H. III. Roll) bore, argent, on a chief gules three escallops or; Arden Roll.

Brony (——), a Suffolk Knight—(H. VI. Roll) bore, argent, a chief indented gules; Arundel Roll.

*[**Brooke, Adam de**, lord of Leighton (H. III.)—bore, or, a cross engrailed per pale gules and sable.—Shirley.] F.

Brooke, Sir Thomas (or BORK)—(E. II. Roll) bore, argent, a fess dancettée (3) sable, bezantée at the points; Parliamentary Roll.

*[**Brooke, William de la**, of Brooke, Somerset, 1231—bore, gules, on a chevron argent, a lyon rampant sable.—Shirley.] F.

Brotherton, Thomas of, Earl Marshal—bore, at the second Dunstable tournament 1334, England and a label (3) argent. F.

*[**Broughton, John de**—(E. II. Roll) bore, argent, two bars gules, on a quarter of the last a cross of the first; Jenyns' Roll. F.

Broughton, Thomas de—(R. II. Roll) bore, azure, a cross engrailed argent; Surrey Roll.

Browe, Hugh de—(R. II. Roll) bore, gules, on a chevron argent, three roses of the field seeded or; Surrey Roll.

Browne, Sir Thomas, of Kent, Kt.—(H. VI. Roll) bore, sable three lyonceux between two bendlets engrailed argent, in the sinister chief point an eagle's head erased or; Arundel Roll.

Bruce, see BRAOSE, BREWES and BRUSE, EARL OF CARRICK.

Bruce, Robert, lord of Annandale, a baron 1295—bore, or, a saltire and chief gules. (F.) See BRUSE.

*[**Brudenell**, *alias* **Bredenhill, William de**, of Dodington, Oxon (E. I.)—bore, argent, a chevron gules between three morions azure.—Shirley.] F.

‡**Bruere, Robert de la**—(H. III. Roll) bore, checquy argent and gules, a chief or and a demi-lyon issuant (sable ?); Dering Roll.

Bruges (——), of Gloucestershire—(E. II. Roll) bore, argent, on a cross sable a leopard's face or, in the first quarter a crescent of the second; Parliamentary Roll.

Bruges, Hue de (or HEGGIOS)—(H. III. Roll) bore, gules, bezantée and a chief ermine; St. George Roll; called KENMAYS, Harl. 246 fo. 33.

Bruili, Roger de—(H. III. Roll) bore, ermine on a bend gules three chevronels or; St. George Roll. F.

Brumtone, Brian de (or BROMPTON)—(E. III. Roll) bore, or, two lyons passant gules (F.); Arden Roll and Jenyns' Ordinary. WALTER bore it with a label (5) sable; Arden and St. George Rolls. F. BRIAN DE BRAMPTON took up the cross in the last Crusade 1270.

Brumton, John de—(H. III. Roll) bore, or, two lyons passant gules, a baston sable (F.), St. George Roll; BAUDWIN bore, three escallops or on a bend; Arden Roll.

Brune, Sir Morys le, a baron 1315—bore, at the first Dunstable tournament 1308, azure, a cross moline or; 8 E. II. (F.). Parly. and Harleian Rolls, and Jenyns' Ordinary; recercelée (in Harl. 337), pearled or, in Ashmole Roll (F.); the cross sarcelée in Jenyns' Ordinary. F. WILLIAM took up the cross in the last Crusade 1270.

Brune, Sir Richard le—(E. III. Roll) bore, azure, a lyon rampant argent guttée de sang; Jenyns' Ordinary. F.

Brune, Thomas—(E. III. Roll) bore, azure, guttée de sang, a lyon rampant argent tail "estans"; Jenyns' Ordinary.

Brune, William—(E. III. Roll) bore, azure, billettée and a lyon rampant or; Jenyns' Ordinary.

Bruse, Sir Barnarde, of Hunts., **Ingram de**(‡), and le frère, **Sir Robert le**—(H. III. Roll) bore, azure, a saltire and a chief or; Howard, Dering, and Holland Rolls.

mario d' Bruno

moro de Bruno

morro le Bruno

Thomas Bruno

willm Bruno

Jo. d. Bromtone

W. d. Brontone.

THE HERALDIC ATCHIEVEMENT

OF

CHARLES GLYNN PRIDEAUX-BRUNE, Esq.,

OF PRIDEAUX PLACE, CORNWALL.

anãderdeel

Robt Brinf.

Cire de Bruffole

Richard le Brut

Robt le Brutun

piorb Bruyb

Le Conte de Carribe

Robord de Brus

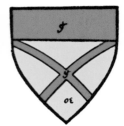

wittm Bruyb

Richard de Brdoufo

Jn. d. Bretafe.

Joan. d. Brutun.

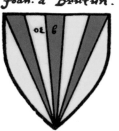

Gwi d. Brian

Otob Brianzon

Jofn Biblonde

‡**Bruse, Richard de**—(H. III. Roll) bore, gules, a saltire and a chief or, Dering Roll; and ROBERT (E. I.) bore the reverse (F.), and another ROBERT (E. I.) bore it with a spur-rowell argent; Camden Roll and Harl. MS. 1481 fo. 43ᵇ.

†**Bruse, Robert de,** Earl of Karric, 1292—bore, or, a saltire gules, on a chief of the second a lyon passant gardant or; Guillim Roll and Jenyns' Ordinary. F. He and his father took up the cross in the last Crusade 1269, 1270.

Brus, Sire William de—bore, at the battle of Boroughbridge 1322, gules, a saltire engrailed and a chief dancettée argent. See Effigy, Sir WILLIAM 1226. In Jenyns' Ordinary the arms are tricked, gules, a saltire engrailed argent, a chief of the second, dancettée throughout gules F.

Brus, Piers, of Skelton, Yorkshire—(E. III. Roll) bore, argent, a lyon rampant azure; Grimaldi and Glover Rolls.

Brus, Richard (BRYS)—bore, at the second Dunstable tournament 1334, argent a lyon rampant gules tail "double tresses et croissele," —fourchée et renowée. Sir RICHARD BREOUSE, of Norfolk (E. II.), bore, the field ermine; Parliamentary and Ashmole Rolls. F.

Brus, John—(H. III. Roll) bore, or, three chevronels gules, a bordure engrailed azure; St. George Roll. F. Indented in Norfolk Roll.

Brus, Robert de (BRUIS or BRIWYS)—(H. III. Roll) bore, gules, a lyon passant gardant ermine; St. George Roll.

Brussele, Sire de—(E. I. Roll) bore, or, a saltire gules; Camden Roll. (F.) See the "Genealogist," XIV. n.s. 10.

Brut, Richard le—(H. III. Roll) bore, checquy argent and sable a bend gules. St. George Roll. F.

Bruton, Robert le, and **Joan le**—(H. III. Roll) bore, quarterly or and gules a bordure engrailed azure; St. George Roll (F.). H. 6137 ff 75, 80, see BRETON.

Bryan, Sir Guy de, K.G., a baron 1350—bore, at the siege of Calais 1345-8, or, three piles meeting in base azure—the colours are often reversed. F. and Effigy.

Bryane, William le—(R. II. Roll) bore, or, three piles meeting in base azure, on a canton paly (4) argent and azure, a bend gules charged with three eagles or; Surrey Roll.

†**Bryanson, Bartholomew**—(H. III. Roll) bore, gyrony (8 or 12) argent and azure; Parly. and Dering Rolls, Jenyns' Ordinary, &c. Ascribed also to SIR JOHN, banneret, and OTES. F.

Bryndale, Sir Lawrence—(E. III. Roll) bore, gules a gryphon segreant or; Ashmole Roll. See BRENLEY.

Bryne (——), of Tervaine—(E. IV. Roll) bore, argent an eagle displayed sable; with crest; Ballard Roll.

Buch, Sr. Captal de—bore, at the battle of Falkirk 1298, paly or and gules, a canton ermine and a bordure sable besantée. Buch or Bucher, the name of a fort near Bordeaux. See BURDEUX, DE FOIX, and GRAILLY. See also pedigree in Anstis' "Order of the Garter," vol. I, Introduction, page 8.

Buchan, the Earl of—(E. III. Roll) bore, azure, three garbs or banded gules; Jenyns' Ordinary. (F. page 39.) See COMYN.

Buchard, Sire Thomas—bore, at the battle of Boroughbridge 1322, gules, and a label (5) sable. See next entry.

SIR WILLIAM DE BRUCE, KT.,
LORD OF UGGLEBARNBY, YORKSHIRE.
IN PICKERING CHURCH, C. 1226.
From Drummond.

Fog de Bokeam

wat. Bukeshull

will Bukemynster

Jo. de Bukton

Alex de Bunbury

Buchard, Sire Will Latymer (BOCHARD) —bore, at the battle of Boroughbridge 1322, gules, a cross (patée or) "Les Armes Latymer"; a label (5) sable charged with a martlet argent (indistinct).

Buckham, Roger de (BOKEHAM) - (E. III. Roll) bore, checquy or and sable, a fess ermine; Jenyns' Ordinary. F.

Buckeshall, Walter (BUKESHALL) — (E. III. Roll) bore, argent, crusily and a lyon rampant gules; Jenyns' Ordinary. F. See also BUXHULL.

Buckland, John, de—(E. III. Roll) bore, gules, two lyonceux rampant argent, a quarter sable fretty or; Jenyns' Ordinary. F.

Buckminster, Sire William—bore, at the battle of Boroughbridge 1322, argent, crusily and a lyon rampant sable (F.); florettée instead of crusily in Ashmole, Cotgrave, and of Lincolnshire in Parliamentary Rolls.

Buckton, John de—(E. II. Roll) bore, argent a goat saliant sable, horned vert; Jenyns' Roll. F.

Buckton, Pyers—bore, at the siege of Rouen 1418, quarterly argent and gules, on the gules quarters three goats passant 2 and 1 of the first horned or. F.

Buckworth *v.* **Bokkesworthe.**

‡**Bucy, Hugh de** (or BOUES)—(H. III. Roll) bore, or, three water-bougets azure; Dering and Howard Rolls. See BOURCHIER.

Bulkley (——), of Aidon—(E. IV. Roll) bore, sable a chevron between three bulls' heads couped argent; with crest; Ballard Roll.

Buller, Baldwyn de—(H. III. Roll) bore, sable, billettée and a bend cotised argent; Howard Roll. See also BOULERS.

*[**Buller, Ralph,** of Woode, in Somerset, 14th cent.—bore, sable, on a plain cross argent quarter pierced, four eaglets of the field.—Shirley.] F.

Bulmer, Ansketell, of Sheriff Hutton, Yorkshire—(E. III. Roll) bore, gules, a lyon rampant or billettée sable; Jenyns' Ordinary.

Bulmer, Sir Raffe, a baron 1342—bore, gules, billettée and a lyon rampant or; Parliamentary, Surrey, Ashmole Rolls, &c.

Bulmer, John de—(E. I. Roll) bore, gules guttée d'or and a lyon rampant of the last (F.); Segar Roll; billettée instead of guttée in Jenyns' Ordinary. F.

*[**Bunbury, Alexander de** (15 H. III.)—bore, argent, on a bend sable three chessrooks of the field.—Shirley.] F.

Bur, William—(R. II. Roll) bore, azure, billettée and a lyon rampant or; Surrey Roll.

Burdeux, Sir Peres, banneret—bore, at the battle of Falkirk 1298, or, a greyhound gules, collared sable, a bordure of the last bezantée. (F.) Sometime Captal de Buch, a fort near Bordeaux. See BUCH and GREILLY.

Burdet, Richard, and **Sir William,** of co. Leic.—(E. III. Roll) bore, azure, two bars or; Jenyns' Ordinary and Parly. Roll.

*[**Burdett, Sir Robert,** of co. Leic.— (E. II.) bore, azure, two bars or, on the sovereign bar three martlets gules; Parliamentary Roll.

Burdet, John, (R. II. Roll) and **Roger**— (E. III. Roll)—bore, azure, two bars or, on each three martlets gules; Surrey and Parliamentary Rolls and Jenyns' Ordinary. F.

Burdon, Sir John, of Notts—(E. II. Roll) bore, gules, three burdons or pilgrims' staves pileways argent (F.), Parliamentary Roll; reversed in Howard and Jenyns' Rolls (F.); borne reversed by WILLIAM, in Arden Roll.

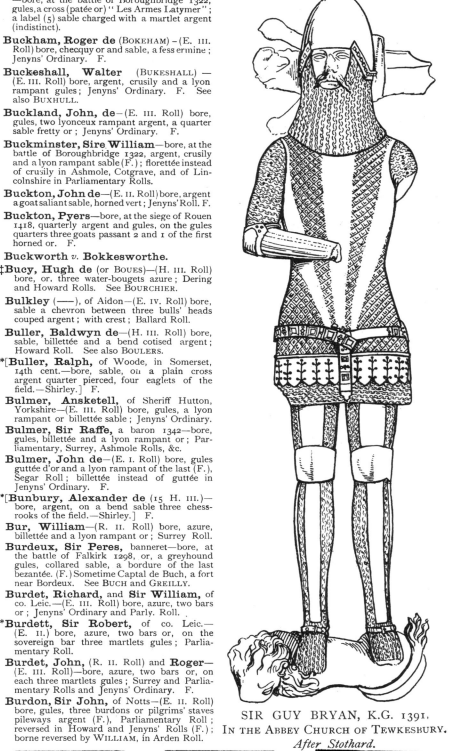

SIR GUY BRYAN, K.G. 1391,
IN THE ABBEY CHURCH OF TEWKESBURY.
After Stothard.

Ansketell Bulmer

Pyers Bukton

Ralfe Buller

Jo de Bolmere

John Bulmer

Peres Burdeux

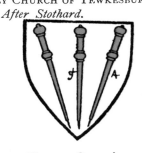

Below, from left to right:

Robt Burdet

Roger Burdoyt

John Burdon

Joan Burdun

SIR ROBERT DE BURES,

C. 1302.

IN ACTON CHURCH, SUFFOLK.

After Waller.

Burdon, William, or **Walter**—(E. II. Roll) bore, azure crusily and three pilgrims' staves or ; Jenyns' and Arundel Rolls.

Bures, Sir Andrew (BOURES)—(E. III. Roll) bore, ermine on a chief dancettée sable two lyonceux rampant or ; Ashmole and Parliamentary Rolls. See Monumental Brass for Sir ROBERT.

Burgh, Walter de, Earl of Ulster—(E. III. Roll) bore, or, a cross gules, the ancient arms of BIGOD, Earl of Norfolk ; Ashmole Roll and Jenyns' Ordinary.

Burgh, Hubert de, Earl of Kent—(E. I. Roll) bore, lozengy vair and gules (F.), Segar Roll ; the same for JOHN (‡), in Camden and Dering Rolls ; and also (1) masculy vair and gules, Norfolk Roll ; and (2) gules, seven mascles, 3, 3, 1, vair ; Howard Roll.

Burgh, Sir John de—(E. III. Roll) bore, argent, on a fess dancettée sable three besants ; Ashmole Roll. F.

Burgh, Thomas de, of Richmondshire—(E. III. Roll) bore, argent, on a fess sable three besants ; Grimaldi Roll. F.

Burgh, Roald de, and **William de**—(E. III. Roll) bore, argent, on a saltire sable five cygnets of the field ; Grimaldi Roll and Jenyns' Ordinary. F.

Burgh, Walter de—(H. III. Roll) bore, quarterly, argent and gules, a cross passant of the second ; Norfolk Roll.

Burgh, William de (BURC)—(H. III. Roll) bore, quarterly, or and azure ; Arden and St. George Rolls. F.

Burghersh, Sir Bartholomew, of Kent, the King's Chamberlain. a baron 1330—bore, at the battle of Boroughbridge 1322, and at the siege of Calais 1345-8, gules, a lyon rampant tail fourchée or (the tinctures reversed in Surrey and other Rolls). Sir STEPHEN bore the same at the first Dunstable tournament 1308 (F.); JOHN bore the same, Jenyns' Ordinary (F.); BARTHOLOMEW or HERBERT (‡) bore it with a label (5) azure, Dering Roll ; and HERBERT bore, gules, a lyon rampant or ; Howard Roll.

✝**Burghill, Henry de**—(H. III. Roll) bore, paly (6) or and azure, over all a fess gules ; Dering and Howard Rolls. See also BURRELL.

Burgoine, Osteleins de—(H. III. Roll) bore, azure, billettée and a lyon rampant or, crowned of the last ; Howard Roll.

Burley (——), a Suffolk Knight—(H. VI. Roll) bore, ermine on a bend or 4 chevronels gules ; Arundel Roll. F.

Burley, Robert, of Wherlsdale — (E. III. Roll) bore, gules, a besant ; Jenyns' Ordinary.

Burley, Simon—(E. II. Roll) bore, barry (6) sable and or, on a chief of the first two palets between as many esquires based of the second, over all an inescocheon gules three bars argent. (F.) Jenyns' Ordinary.

Burley, Sir Simon, K.G., **Sir Richard,** K.G., and **Sir John,** K.G., 1378—bore, or, three bars and in chief two palets sable. on an escocheon of pretence, gules, three bars ermine, a crescent for difference of the second. K. 399 ff. 21, 24, 26.

Burnaby, Sir Nicholas (BRONEBY) — (E. III. Roll) bore, argent, two bars and in chief a lyon passant gules ; Ashmole Roll.

Burne, John de—(H. III. Roll) bore, ermine on a bend azure three lyons rampant argent ; Howard Roll.

Burnell, Sir Edward, banneret, a baron 1311—bore, argent a lyon rampant sable, crowned or, a bordure azure ; Parliamentary and Surrey Rolls. In Jenyns' Ordinary this coat occurs *quarterly with*, or, a saltire sable. F. ; and so borne by HUGH, Lord BURNELL, K.G.,temp. H. IV., the saltire engrailed ; K. 400 fo. 20.

Burnell, Philip—(E. I. Roll) bore, argent, a lyon rampant sable crowned or ; Segar Roll. Sir EDWARD bore this H. VI.—and LE SR. B. also bore (H. VI.) argent, a lyon rampant tail fourchée sable.

Burnell, William—(H. III. Roll) bore, argent, a lyon rampant sable, a label (5) gules ; Howard Roll. ROBERT took up the cross in the last Crusade 1270.

Lo Counte de Bonggan

Tha Burowdon

Burkhulle
Rog d Burkhulle

Tho. Burton

Ralfe Bopgill

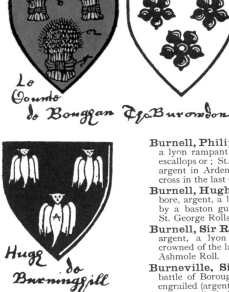
Hugg de Burninghill

Jogn de Birton

Jogn Buffy

Burnell, Philip—(H. III. Roll) bore, argent, a lyon rampant sable, on a bend gules three escallops or ; St. George Roll. Three mullets argent in Arden Roll. ROBERT took up the cross in the last Crusade 1270.

Burnell, Hugh, and **Philip**—(H. III. Roll) bore, argent, a lyon rampant sable, debruised by a baston gules ; Howard, Camden, and St. George Rolls. F.

Burnell, Sir Richard—(E. III. Roll) bore, argent, a lyon rampant azure guttée d'or crowned of the last, langued and armed gules ; Ashmole Roll.

Burneville, Sir John de—bore, at the battle of Boroughbridge 1322, gules, a saltire engrailed (argent) between four cinquefoyles or (F.) ; ascribed also to Sir ROBERT, of Suffolk, in Parliamentary Roll.

Burnham, Sir Thomas, v. **Bourneham.**

Burnham, Sir Walter, of Norfolk—(E. II. Roll) bore, sable, a cross between four crescents argent ; Parliamentary Roll.

Burninghill, Hugh de—(E. II. Roll) bore, sable three bats (or rere-mice) argent ; Jenyns' Roll. F.

Burowdon, Thomas—(E. III. Roll) bore, argent three cinquefoyles sable ; Jenyns' Ordinary. (F.) See also WALTER BORDOWN.

Burrell ——(H. III. Roll) bore, paly (6) or and azure, over all a fess gules ; St. George Roll. See BURGHILL. F.

Burrell, Roger de—(H. III. Roll) bore, paly (10) argent and sable, a bend gules ; St. George Roll. F.

Burton, Sir Rauf de—bore, at the battle of Boroughbridge 1322, paly (6) or and gules on a bend sable three water-bougets argent ; borne also by JOHN ; see Surrey Roll and Jenyns' Ordinary. F.

Burton, Sir John de—(E. III. Roll) bore, gules, three plates on each a chevron sable ; Ashmole Roll.

Burton, Sir Roger de—(E. III. Roll) bore, argent, a fess sable fretty or ; Ashmole Roll.

Burton, Sir William—(E. III. Roll) bore, sable, a chevron between three owls argent (F.); Ashmole Roll. THOMAS, R. II., bore, the owls crowned or ; Surrey Roll.

Buslingthorpe v. **Beslingthorpe.**

Bussy, Sir Hugh, of co. Linc. and **John** —(E. III. Roll) bore, argent three barrulets sable ; Parliamentary and Surrey Rolls and Jenyns' Ordinary. F.

Buterley, Roger or **Stephen**—(H. III. Roll) bore, or, a fess gules in chief three torteaux ; Arden and St. George Rolls. (F.) And another, in Arden Roll, with cinquefoyles pierced gules in lieu of torteaux.

Butler, see BOTELER.

Button, John de—(E. III. Roll) bore, ermine, a fess gules. Jenyns' Roll. F.

Buttringham, William de—bore, at the second Dunstable tournament 1334, argent, a bend gules. See also BODRUGAN and BOTRINGHAM.

Buxhull v. **Buckeshall.**

Buxhull, Sire Alayn de (BOXHULL) of Kent—bore, at the battle of Boroughbridge 1322, or, a lyon rampant azure fretty argent (F.), (or, in H. 6137 ƒ 10ᵇ), Parliamentary Roll ; RAPHE in Jenyns' Ordinary.

Bycovyleyn, William—(R. II. Roll) bore, argent, three crescents 2 and 1 gules ; Surrey Roll.

Byron, Sire John de—bore, at the battle of Boroughbridge 1322, argent, three bendlets gules ; so also Sir JAMES, of co. Linc. R. II., Parliamentary Roll, and Sir RICHARD, E. II., Surrey Roll. In the Boroughbridge Roll, the arms of Sir RICH. BRAKWORTH or BRATWORTH are erroneously assigned to this Sir JOHN.

Byron, Sir John, LE FITZ—knighted at the capitulation of Calais 1348—bore, argent, three bendlets gules and a label (3) azure. So also RICHARD, E. I., Nativity Roll. JAMES (‡), H. III., bore, a label (3) azure (F.), the tinctures reversed in the Dering Roll.

Byron, James de—(H. III. Roll) bore, bendy (10) argent and gules, a label (5) azure ; Howard Roll.

Byron, Nicholas, E. IV. See BERON.

Byye, Sir William—(H. VI. Roll) bore, three azure crescents or ; Arundel Roll.

Rog d Butlere.

Jo. de Button

James d. Biroune.

Guy conducts Harold to William, Duke of the Normans. After the Bayeux Tapestry.

Where a Clerk and Ælfgyva. . . . After the Bayeux Tapestry.

— C —

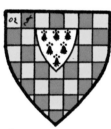

Adam d' Caili

Hugh Valkin

Vicgard Cam

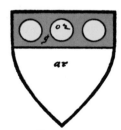

Raffe de Oamoys

Cabery, Alan de, of Hippeswell—(E. III. Roll) bore, gules, a fess vair ; Jenyns' Ordinary.

Caili, Adam de (CAILLY)—(H. III. Roll) bore, checquy or and gules, an inescocheon ermine ; St. George Roll. F.

Caili, Thomas, baron 1309—bore, checquy gules and or, a bend ermine ; Nobility Roll. Ascribed to Sir ADAM DE CAYLE, of Norfolk, in Parliamentary Roll.

Caili, Walter de (CAYLE)—(H. III. Roll) bore, checquy or and azure, on a fess gules three mullets argent ; St. George Roll.

Caili, Sir William (CALY)—(E. III. Roll) bore, quarterly argent and sable, over all on a baston gules three mullets pierced or ; Ashmole Roll.

Caldecott, Richard—(E. III. Roll) bore, per pale argent and azure, a chief gules; Jenyns' Ordinary. SIRE DE CALDECOTT of Norfolk, bore, per pale or and azure, on a chief gules three leopards' faces of the first ; Parliamentary Roll.

Calkin, Sir Hugh, of Flanders—bore, at the siege of Calais 1345-8, argent, a pale between two greyhounds erect sable, (F.) ; respecting each other, in Stowe.

Calthorpe, Sir William, of Norfolk—(E. II. Roll) bore, checquy or and azure a fess ermine, Parliamentary Roll and Jenyns' Ordinary ; also borne, or and sable—another with the fess argent and yet another—checquy or and gules on a fess argent three martlets sable, in the Ashmole Roll.

Calthorpe (——), of Orthenley, Norfolk—(E. III. Roll) bore, ermine, a maunch gules ; Ashmole Roll and Jenyns' Ordinary. See GALTHORP.

Caltofte, Sir John de, of co. Linc.—(E. III. Roll) bore, argent, three roses gules—Parliamentary Roll—this surname occurs also in Cotgrave Roll and for coat " argent, a lyon vaire and a."

Calverley, Sir John—(E. III. Roll) bore, sable, an inescocheon within an orle of owls argent ; Ashmole Roll.

Calverley, Hue, John, and **Walter**—(R. II. Roll) bore, argent, a fess gules between three calves passant sable, see Effigy ; JOHN bore a crescent and HUGH bore a mullet, for difference ; Surrey Roll and Jenyns' Ordinary.

Calvert, Sir Richard (or CULVET)—(E. III. Roll) bore, gules, a bend nebulée argent ; Ashmole Roll.

‡**Cam, Richard**—(H. III. Roll) bore, argent six eaglets 3, 2, 1, displayed sable ; Dering Roll. F.

Camoyes, Le Sr.—bore, at the siege of Rouen 1418, or, on a chief gules three plates—borne also by Sir RAPHE and Sir THOMAS, K.G. In Howard and Dering Rolls, two plates only are ascribed to JOHN (‡)—in the Camden Roll the (3) plates are in fess —in Grimaldi Roll three torteaux are ascribed to RAUF.

Camoyes, Sir Rauf, banneret—bore, at the first Dunstable tournament 1308, argent, on a chief gules three besants. F.

‡**Campaine, Pers de**—(H. III. Roll) bore, argent, a chief gules ; Arden and St. George Rolls. See CHAMPAINE.

Camvile, Sir Geoffrey de, banneret, a baron 1295—bore, azure, three lyons passant in pale argent ; Nobility and Parliamentary Rolls, &c. So ascribed also to HUGH, ROBERT (‡), and WILLIAM. (F.) In the Dering and Howard Rolls the tinctures are reversed for GEOFFREY (‡).

Cantelo, Philip de—(H. III. Roll) bore, argent, a fess gules fretty or ; Howard Roll.

‡**Cantelou, Sire Johan de**—(E. I. Roll) bore, azure, three fleurs-de-lys or ; Dering Roll, &c. —leopards' faces jessant-de-lys in Ashmole MS.

Cantelou, George (E. I. Roll) and **William**—bore, gules, three fleurs-de-lys or (F.) ; Camden Roll, &c. Ascribed also to JORIS *vel* PRES DE, in Howard Roll ; Sir WILLIAM of Salop bore it with a baston argent, in Parliamentary Roll.

Cantelupe, Sir John, banneret—bore, at the battle of Falkirk 1298, azure, three leopards' faces jessant-de-lys or (F.)—perhaps of Snitterfield ; the leopards' faces are often reversed. Sir H. bore a red field in the Atkinson Roll, and so did WILLIAM, with the faces reversed, in the Segar Roll.

Cantelupe, Sir William, of Ravensthorpe, banneret, a baron 1299, bore, at the battle of Falkirk 1298, and at the siege of Carlaverock 1300, gules, a fess vair between three leopards' faces jessant-de-lys or ; F. Parliamentary Roll—faces reversed in Jenyns' Ordinary, &c. Sealed the Barons' letter to the Pope 1301 with (gules) a fess vair between three fleurs-de-lys (or) ; pp. xviii, xxiv.

Capelle, Sir Richard de, of co. Hereford —bore, at the first Dunstable tournament 1308, argent, a chevron gules between three torteaux. F.

roll de Canuuilo

Geo. d' Canetelou

John Dantolu

Vice, d Oapoll

roll de Cantolo

G

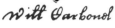

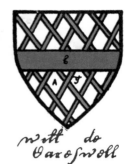

Capon, Sir Robert—(E. III. Roll) bore, gules, three capons and a bordure engrailed argent; Ashmole Roll.

Capps or Cappus (——), a Kentish Knight—(H. VI. Roll) bore, argent, a chevron between three trefoyles sable, an escallop of the first; Arundel Roll.

Caraunt (——), an Essex Knight—(H. VI. Roll) bore, argent, three hurts each charged with as many chevronels gules (sic); Arundel Roll.

Carbonell, John—(E. III. Roll) bore, gules, a cross argent and a bordure or; Jenyns' Ordinary.

Carbonell, William—bore, at the second Dunstable tournament 1334, gules, a cross argent, a bordure engrailed or. (F.) Ascribed also to ROBERT in Surrey Roll, and to Sir JOHN in Ashmole Roll; tricked indented for Sir JOHN, of Suffolk, in Parliamentary Roll.

Carbonell (——), a Suffolk Knight—(H. VI. Roll) bore, gules, a cross argent lozengy sable; Arundel Roll.

Cardelecke, Henry—bore, at the siege of Rouen 1418, azure, a castle triple turreted or. F.

Cardeston, John de—bore, at the second Dunstable tournament 1334, gules, a saltire argent, a label besantée (sic). (F.) See also KERDESTON.

Caresville, Sir William—(E. III. Roll) bore, argent, three gemelles sable; Ashmole Roll, ascribed to JOHN in Jenyns' Roll, with the remark—same as PERS DE CAREW.

Careswelle, William de—bore, at the second Dunstable tournament 1334, argent fretty gules, a fess azure. F.

*Carew, Nicholas de, banneret—bore, at the siege of Carlaverock 1300, or, three lyons passant sable (F.) and as Lord DE MULESFORD sealed the Barons' letter to the Pope 1301, pp. xxi, xxiv. Sir JOHN bore it at the siege of Calais 1345-8, on which occasion Sir JOHN, junior, of co. Glouc., differenced with a label (3) gules. See Baron DE CAREW in Jenyns' Ordinary.

Carew, Pers de—(R. II. Roll) bore, argent, three gemelles sable; Surrey Roll, same as JOHN CARESVILLE.

Carington ——, (E. IV. Roll) bore, sable, on a bend argent three lozenges of the field; with crest; Ballard Roll.

Carlyell, Sir William de, of Cumberland—(E. II. Roll) bore, or, a cross patonce gules; Parliamentary Roll.

Carminow, Thomas—(E. III. Roll) bore, azure, a bend or, and a label (3) gules; Jenyns' Ordinary.

Carnaby, William—(E. III. Roll) bore, argent, two bars azure in chief three hurts; Jenyns' Roll.

Carrick, Earl of—(H. III. Roll) bore, sable, three cinquefoyles 2 and 1, or, Howard Roll; argent in Camden Roll. (F.) This coat probably appertains to the name of Carrick rather than to an Earl of that name.

*[Cary, Sir Robert, of Cary, Devon (H. V.)—bore, argent, on a bend sable three roses of the first.—Shirley.] F.

Casa Nova, Otha de, banneret, v. Sassenau.

Cassynges, Sir William—bore, at the first Dunstable tournament 1308, azure, a cross moline voided or. over all a bendlet gules. F.

Castell, Sir William (or DE CHASTEL), of co. Glouc.—(E. II. Roll) bore, gules, two bars argent on a canton of the last a castle sable; Parly. Roll. ALAN, of the city of London, took up the cross in the last Crusade 1270.

Castelmyne v. Gasceline.

Castilton, Sire de (——), a Knight banneret,—bore, at the battle of Falkirk 1298, gules, a castle or. F.

Castre, Sir John de—bore, at the first Dunstable tournament 1308, azure, an eagle displayed barry (10), argent and gules, (F.); (8) in Ashmole MS.

Castre, Sir John de, of Norfolk—(E. II. Roll) bore, sable, an eagle displayed barry (12) argent and gules; Parly. Roll. THOMAS, bore, the field argent and the eagle barry of 14; Jenyns' Ordinary.

Caterall, Thomas—(E. II. Roll) bore, azure, three mascles or, in trick—blasoned, lozenges pierced; Jenyns' Roll; of Garstang, in Lancs, with crest; Ballard Roll.

Catesbury, Sir Richard de—(E. II. Roll) bore, gules, a fess vair between three goats' heads erased argent; Parliamentary Roll. See GOTESBURY.

SIR HUGH CALVELEY,

OF LEA, IN BUNBURY CHURCH,

CHESHIRE, TEMP. E. III.

After Stothard.

Causton

John Cavondish

John Cayville

mar. de Cayle.

Caundysh, Andrew—(R. II. Roll) bore, sable, three crosses botonnée fitchée 2 and 1 or ; Surrey Roll.

Caunton, Sir John de, of co. Leic.—(E. II. Roll) bore, gules, two bars and in chief as many mullets argent ; Parliamentary Roll.

Causton, Robert de—(E. III. Roll) bore, argent, on a bend sable three crosses crosslet fitchée of the field ; Ashmole Roll and Jenyns' Roll and Ordinary. Another in Ashmole, argent, a bend between six crosses crosslet fitchée 3 and 3 sable.

Caux v. Corbet.

*Cave, William—(E. III. Roll) bore, azure, fretty argent ; Jenyns' Ordinary.

*[Cavendish, Sir John, Chief Justice E. III.—bore, sable, three bucks' heads cabossed argent.—Shirley.] F.

[Cawne, Sir Thomas, of Melcomb, Kent, E. III.—bore, a lyon rampant ermine—see Monumental Effigy.]

Cayville, John—(E. II. Roll) bore, argent, a fess florettée (flory counterflory), gules ; Jenyns' Roll.

Cayle, Walter de—(H. III. Roll) bore, checquy or and azure, on a fess gules three mullets argent. (F.) Arden and St. George Rolls ; sometimes written CAPEL. See also CAILI.

Ceinteyno, John de (or ST. IVE)—(H. III. Roll) bore, or, three lyons passant gules ; Arden Roll.

Cerne, Philip de—(H. III. Roll) bore, per fess argent and gules, a lyon rampant within a bordure all counterchanged. (F.) St. George, Dering and Howard Rolls.

*Chadwick, Sir J., of Chadwick and Healey, co. Lanc.—(H. VI. Roll) bore, gules, an inescocheon within an orle of martlets argent ; Atkinson Roll.

Chalers, Ralph—(E. II. Roll) bore, argent, a fess between two chevronels sable ; Jenyns' Ordinary. An (Essex ?) Knight of the name (H. VI. Roll) bore, argent, a fess between three annulets gules ; Arundel Roll.

†Chaluns, Piers de—(H. III. Roll) bore, gules, five fusils conjoined in fess ermine, a label (3 or 5), azure. (F.) Arden and St. George Rolls, Jenyns' Ordinary.

Chamberlain, Herbert le and Martin (H. III. Roll) bore, gules, three escallops or ; Glover Roll. Sir JOHN bore the same (E. I. or II.) ; Holland Roll.

Chamberlain, Sir Richard, of Lincolnshire—(E. II. Roll) bore, gules, a chevron between three escallops or ; Sir ROBERT bore a fess, Parliamentary and Surrey Rolls ; and for JOHN in Jenyns' Roll.

Chamberlain, Simon—(E. III. Roll) bore, quarterly gules and or, in the first a fer-de-moulin argent ; Jenyns' Ordinary.

‡Chamberlain, Philip—(H. III. Roll) bore; gules, two crossed keys wards to the sinister , Howard Roll. Wards inward in the Dering Roll. F.

‡Chamberlain, William le—(H. III. Roll) bore, azure, three keys erect wards to the dexter 2 and 1 or. (F.) Dering Roll.

Chammon, John (CHANNON or CHAUMOND), of Colthorpe—(E. III. Roll) bore, gules, a lyon rampant argent within a bordure engrailed gobony or and argent (in some azure) ; Jenyns' Ordinary.

†Champaine, Pers de—(H. III. Roll) bore, argent, a chief gules ; Arden and St. George Rolls. See CAMPAINE.

‡Champaine, Robert de—(H. III. Roll) bore, argent, three bars undée gules. (F.) Sometimes blazoned wavy, and in others nebulée ; Howard and Dering Rolls. Sir JOHN of Kent bore the same (E. II.) ; Parliamentary Roll.

Champayne, Sir William—(E. III. Roll) bore, or, fretty sable crusily fitchée at the joints argent ; Ashmole Roll.

‡Champernon, Henry de—(H. III. Roll) bore, gules, a saltire vair ; Howard and Dering Rolls.

Champernoun, Sir Richard—bore, at the battle of Boroughbridge 1322, gules, billettée a saltire vair. (F. p. 45.) JOHN also bore this coat ; Jenyns' Ordinary. HENRY and RICHARD bore the coat crusily (F.) instead of billettée ; St. George Roll and Jenyns' Ordinary.

‡Champernoun, John—(H. III. Roll) bore, gules, a chevron or ; Dering Roll ; the field azure in Ashmole Roll.

Chancellor, Walter—(E. II. Roll) bore, ermine, on a quarter argent a saltire engrailed sable ; Jenyns' Roll.

Chanceux (Hugh) de v. Chauncy.

Perse Chalune

Philip d'Cerne

SIR THOMAS CAWNE,

OF NULCOMB, IN IGHTHAM CHURCH,

KENT, TEMP. E. III.

From Stothard.

Chamberlain

mr) le Chamberlang

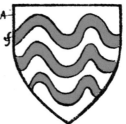

Here d'Chaberun

Robi de Champanis

SERO · SED · SERIO

THE HERALDIC ATCHIEVEMENT

OF

ROBERT, 3rd MARQUIS OF SALISBURY, K.G.

Ricd
de Champernon

Vicz
Chambernoun

Sot de Chanson

Ego de Chausi

Edwd Charlis

Nicolas
d. Charneles.

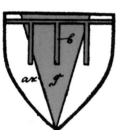
John Chandos

Rob. d. Chandux

Rog. Chandos

Tho. d. Charneles

John
de Charonoll

Pet.
de Chaunry

Chandos, Edward—(E. III. Roll) bore, argent, a pile gules; Jenyns' Ordinary. JOHN bore the reverse; Jenyns' Roll.

Chandos, Sir John, of co. Cambridge—bore, at the first Dunstable tournament 1308, argent, a pile gules, a label (3) azure (F.); Parliamentary Roll. So also did EDWARD at the second Dunstable tournament 1334.

Chandos, Sir John, K.G. (a founder), and **Walter** - (R. II. Roll) bore, or, a pile gules; Surrey Roll.

Chandos, Sir Robert or **Roger** of Cheshire—(E. III. Roll) bore, or, a lyon rampant gules; tail fourchée. (F.) Parliamentary Roll; ascribed also to JOHN, in Jenyns' Ordinary.

Chandos, Robert de—(H. III. Roll) bore or, a pile gules, nine estoiles 3, 3, 3 counterchanged. (F.) St. George Roll. See also BAIGGINGEDENE.

Chanscyre, John (probably a misreading)—(E. III. Roll)—bore, azure, an eagle barry of six argent and gules; Cotgrave Roll.

Chanseus, John de (or **Thomas**)—(H. III. Roll) bore, gules, three eagles displayed 2 and 1 argent. (F.) EMERY DE CHASEUS bore the same sable and or; Arden and St. George Rolls.

Chansi, Thomas de—(E. I. Roll)—bore, burrulée (22) sable and argent, a lyon rampant gules. (F.) Segar Roll. See MONCHENSI.

Charles, Sir Edward, of Norfolk—(E. III. Roll) bore, ermine, on a chief gules three lozenges of the first; Parly. Roll. EDWARD, of Cliffe and Briggenhall, bore this coat with five lozenges conjoined. (F.) Jenyns' Roll and Segar; and as a fess lozengy in Grimaldi Roll.

Charleston, Sir John de, banneret—(E. II. Roll) bore, or, on a chevron vert three eagles displayed of the field; Parliamentary Roll.

Charleton, Le Sr. de (Edward, K.G., a baron 1401-22)—bore, at the siege of Rouen 1418, or, a lyon rampant gules. F.

Charlworth (——), a Suffolk Knight—(H. VI. Roll) bore, ermine on a chief gules five lozenges or; Arundel Roll.

Charnells, Sire Nichol de—bore, at the battle of Boroughbridge 1322, azure, a cross engrailed or. (F.) Sir GEORGE, of Warwickshire, bore the same; Parliamentary Roll. Sir WILLIAM (fys) differenced with a mullet sable; Ashmole Roll.

Charneles, Thomas de—(H. III. Roll) bore, gules, two chevrons and a bordure or. (F.) St. George Roll.

Charnell, Sir John de—bore, at the first Dunstable tournament 1308, or, a fess ermine between two chevronels gules. (F.) Sir JOHN of Warwickshire, bore the reverse—gules and or; Parliamentary Roll and Jenyns' Ordinary.

Charron, Sir Richard de- (E. II. Roll) bore, gules, a chevron between three escallops argent; Parliamentary and Grimaldi Rolls.

Charteray, John—(E. III. Roll) bore, argent, a chevron between three six-foyles gules; Jenyns' Ordinary.

Chaseus, Emery de—(H. III. Roll) bore, sable, three eagles displayed or. (F.) Arden Roll.

Chaston, Thomas—(E. III. Roll) bore, gules, three barrulets vair; Jenyns' Ordinary.

Chaucombe, Sir Thomas de, of Wilts—(E. III. Roll) bore, or, on a cross vert five mullets pierced argent; Ashmole Roll. The mullets or, in Parliamentary Roll.

Chauncy, Thomas, baron of Skirpenbeck in co. Linc.—(E. III. Roll) bore, argent, a chevron gules, a bordure sable besantée (Jenyns' Ordinary); as did Sir PHILIP, also of Lincolnshire; Parliamentary Roll.

Chauncy, Sir Philip de, of Essex—(E. II. Roll) bore, argent, a chevron between three annulets gules; Parliamentary and Cotgrave Rolls. F.

Chavent, Sir Peter, a baron 1299—bore, at the battle of Falkirk 1298, paly (6) argent and azure a fess gules. (F.) Sir JOHN of Somerset bore the same, Parliamentary Roll; azure and argent in Guillim Roll.

Chauvigny, William de—(H. III. Roll) bore, argent, "a fess engrele" (five fusils in fess) gules, a label sable; Norfolk Roll. See next name.

Chaveney, Sr. de—(H. III. Roll) bore. lozenge argent and gules; Arden Roll.

Chaworth, Sir Christopher, knighted at the capitulation of Calais 1348, bore, azure, two chevrons or (F.); borne also by JOHN, THOMAS (‡), Dering Roll, PATRICK and Sir WILLIAM; for Sir THOMAS' quarterly coat see Atkinson Roll, Harl. MS. 1048 fo. 108.

Chaworth, Thomas de, of Norton, baron 1299—sealed the Barons' letter to the Pope 1301, with two chevrons, pp. xix, xxiv.; bore, barry (10), argent and gules, an orle of martlets (10), sable; Nobility Roll.

†**Chaworth, Patrick de** (CHAURCY)—(H. III. Roll) bore, burrulée (14), argent and gules, Glover and Howard Rolls. HENRY bore, (E. III.) burrulée (10, 12), argent and gules, a bend (or baston), sable; Jenyns' Roll.

†**Chaworth, Pain de** (CHAURS)—(H. III. Roll) bore, burrulée (16), argent and gules, an orle of martlets, 4, 2, 2, 1, sable; Arden Roll. Sir PATRICK (14) and 8 martlets; Ashmole Roll; also (14), and 13 martlets (F.), Camden Roll; and another (10 or 12) and 8 martlets, Jenyns' Ordinary. In the Arden, St. George, and Parliamentary Rolls there are coats with four and with six bars, probably tricked in error.

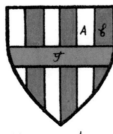
Le Sir
Charleton.

Pores de
Chavent

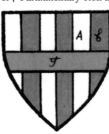
Sr
Chamsorth

Patrich Chamsorth

Emeri d. Chaseul

45

Rauff de Ogolton

Raynold Ogoslunt

John de Ogotwode

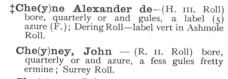

Jo Ogotwyn

Alls'r Ogoworill

†Chaworth, Hervieus de (HEREUI DE CHAURS)–(H. III. Roll) bore, gules, crusily and a bend or; Arden Roll.

Chaworth, William de–bore, burrulée (20) argent and gules three martlets 2 and 1 sable; Harl. MS. 1481 fo. 47.

Checker v. De la Checker.

Chelton, Rauf de–bore, at the second Dunstable tournament 1334, argent on a bend azure three fleurs-de-lys (sic). F.

Cherleton v. Charleton.

Cheshunt, Sir Raynold–bore, at the siege of Calais 1345–8, gules, three bendlets ermine.

Chester, Earl of–bore, azure, three garbs, or, in most of the earliest Rolls. RANDOLPH DE BLONDEVILLE, the last earl, died 26 October 1232, and bore on his seal a lyon or wolf saliant. See BLONDEVILLE and KEVELIOK.

Chester, Earl of–bore, England within a bordure azure; Jenyns' Ordinary. THOMAS HOLLAND, Earl of Kent, bore the bordure argent.

Chester, William–(E. III. Roll) bore, gules, a chevron argent between three arming-buckles tongues to the dexter or; Jenyns' Ordinary.

*[Chetwode, John de (E. III.) — bore, quarterly argent and gules, four crosses patée counterchanged; Shirley.]

*Chetwynd, Sir John–bore, at the battle of Boroughbridge, azure, a chevron between three mullets or. (F.) This coat was also borne by WILLIAM, in the Surrey Roll, the mullets also pierced.

Chetwynd, Sir John de, of Salop–(E. II. Roll) bore, azure, a chevron or between three besants; Parliamentary Roll.

Cheverell, Sir Alexander, of Wilts–bore, at the first Dunstable tournament 1308, argent, three lyonceux rampant sable. F.

Cheveresden, John de–bore, at the second Dunstable tournament 1334, or, on a bend gules three chevrons ermine. F.

Cheveresden, John de–(E. III. Roll) bore, argent, on a bend gules, three "chevres" passant of the field. (F.) Jenyns' Ordinary.

Chevouse, Henry de–(H. III. Roll) bore, argent, a cross gules between four lyons rampant azure; Norfolk Roll.

Cheyndutt, Sir Ralph, of Bucks–(E. II. Roll) bore, azure, a cheyne or, a label of three gules; Parliamentary Roll. F.F.

Che(y)nev (——), de, a Buckinghamshire Knight–(E. II. Roll) bore, argent, a fess and in chief three martlets gules; Parliamentary Roll.

Cheyne (——), an Essex Knight–(H. II. Roll) bore, quarterly sable and argent, six lozenges conjoined in bend sinister (sic); Arundel Roll.

‡Che(y)ne Alexander de–(H. III. Roll) bore, quarterly or and gules, a label (5) azure (F.); Dering Roll–label vert in Ashmole Roll.

Che(y)ney, John — (R. II. Roll) bore, quarterly or and azure, a fess gules fretty ermine; Surrey Roll.

Che(y)ney, John–bore, at the siege of Rouen 1418, checquy or and azure, a fess gules fretty ermine; quarterly with, or, a lyon rampant per fess gules and sable; Ashmole Roll–the quarters sometimes reversed. F.

Che(y)ney, John, Henry and Robert de–(H. III. Roll) bore, checquy or and azure, a fess gules fretty argent. (F.) Arden and St. George Rolls. In Jenyns' Ordinary the tinctures are sometimes reversed.

Cheyne, John–(E. III. Roll) bore, gules, four fusils in fess argent, on each an escallop sable; Jenyns' Ordinary–RAUFF bore this coat within a bordure of the second; Surrey Roll.

Che(y)ney, William–bore, at the siege of Rouen 1418, azure, a cross patonce or, quarterly with, gules five fusils conjoined in fess argent, on each an escallop sable–evidently for CHEYNEY. F.

Cheyny, Robert–(E. III. Roll) bore, azure, semée of estoiles and two lyons passant or; Jenyns' Ordinary.

Cheyne, Thomas–(R. II. Roll) bore, azure on a fess nebulée between three crescents or, a fleur-de-lys gules; Surrey Roll.

Che(yny), Sir William–bore, at the battle of Boroughbridge 1322, gules, frettée or, a label (5) argent. F.

*[Chichester, Richard, of Devon (E. III.)–bore, checquy or and gules, a chief vair; Shirley.] F.

Chicker, see DE LA CHICKER.

Chideoke, Sir John–(E. II. Roll) bore, gules, an inescocheon within a double tressure argent; Parliamentary Roll, as a northern Knight.

Chidiock, John–(E. III. Roll)–bore, gules, a false escocheon within an orle of martlets argent; Jenyns' Ordinary.

Chilton v. Chelton.

Chilton —— (E. III. Roll), bore, argent, a chevron gules; Ashmole Roll.

Chirchingham, Sir Walter de, knighted at Calais 1348–bore, argent, three bars gules in chief as many torteaux, over all a bendlet sable. F.

John de Ogonoroston

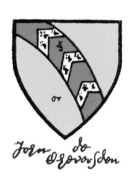

John de Ogoworsdon

Rauff de Ogoyndutt

Allisant de Chene

John Ogpnoy

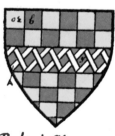

Robt. d. Chennei

Ogoyndutt

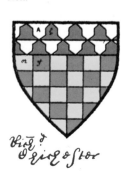

Vic. d. Ogirolostor

walt. de Ogircingyam

witt Ogony

witt Ogpnoy

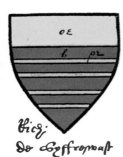

Chiston, Robert de—bore, at the second Dunstable tournament 1334, **argent**, three bends sable crusily fitchée of the field. F.

*[**Cholmondeley, Sir Hugh,** of Cholmondeley in Cheshire (H. III.)—bore, gules, two helmets in chief argent, and in base a garb or ; Shirley.] F.

Chowne, Andrew, slain or drowned at the siege of Calais 1345-8—bore, argent, a fess and in chief three martlets gules.

Chra(c)heth —— (H. III. Roll) bore, gules, five fusils in bend or, a label (5) argent ; Arden Roll. Perhaps CRACHERODE.

Christmas (——), a Kentish Knight—(H. VI. Roll)—bore, gules, on a bend sable three covered cups argent ; Arundel Roll.

Chycheley (——) an Essex (?) Knight — (H. VI. Roll) bore, or, a chevron between three cinquefoyles pierced gules ; Arundel Roll.

Cifrewast, Richard de—(H. III. Roll) bore, azure, two bars gemelles and a chief or. (F.) St. George and Arden Rolls. Three bars gemelles (H. VI. Nobility Roll) and the chief argent in Jenyns' Roll. See SYFFREWAST.

Cir(en)cester, Sir Thomas de, of Glouc.—(E. II. Roll) bore, argent, a chevron azure, a label (3) gules ; Parliamentary Roll.

Clapham, Robert—(E. II. Roll) bore, argent, on a bend sable three covered cups of the first, in chief a quatrefoyle slipped of the second ; Jenyns' Roll.

Clare, Le Seigneur de—(E. II. Roll)—bore, argent a quarter gules ; Jenyns' Roll ; this coat was borne by LYONEL —— at the second Dunstable tournament in 1334.

Clare (——), **de** (E. III. Roll) bore, ermine, three chevronels gules ; Cotgrave Roll : some are of opinion that the original arms of CLARE were the clarions usually ascribed to GRANVILLE, see Tiles, Neath Abbey, p. vii. THOMAS, brother of the Earl of Gloucester, took up the cross in the last Crusade 1270.

Clare, Gilbert de, Earl of Hertford and Gloucester — bore, at the first Dunstable tournament 1308, or, three chevronels gules (see Monumental Effigy). Sire GILBERT and THOMAS differenced with a label (5) azure ; Guillim and Camden Rolls. Sir RICHARD differenced with a label (3) azure at the first Dunstable tournament 1308. (F.) WILLIAM DE CLARE differenced with a label azure ; Glover Roll. See also Audley and Gloucester.

Clare, Robert, 4th brother of Earl Gilbert—bore or, a fess between two chevronels gules—"antecessor" Baron de Fitzwater ; Harl. MS. 1481 ƒƒ 15, 28.

Clare, Sir Nicholas, of co. Glouc.—bore, at the first Dunstable tournament 1308, or, three chevronels gules, a bordure indented sable—engrailed in Harl. 6137 fo. 31b. F.

Clarence, Duke of, LIONEL of Antwerp—bore, France and England quarterly, a label (3) argent on each pendant a canton gules ; Jenyns' Ordinary ; a billet in dexter base of pendant, K. 398 fo. 32 ; 400 fo. 5.

Clarendon, Roger de—(R. II. Roll) bore, gules, a bend or ; Surrey Roll.

Claron, Sir John—(E. I. Roll) bore, gules, a cross recercelée argent, over all a bendlet azure charged with three mullets (6) of the second ; Harleian Roll.

Clavering, Sir John de, 2nd baron, FITZROBERT LE FITZROGER—bore, at the battle of Falkirk 1298, and at the siege of Carlaverock 1300 (when he assumed the name of Clavering by the King's command), quarterly or and gules, a baston sable, a label (3) azure at Falkirk and vert at Carlaverock (F.) wrongly blasoned in Harl. MS. quarterly or and gules fretty argent. See FITZ ROGER. The antient coat, vair, a chief gules ; Nobility Roll 1299.

Clavering, Sir John, banneret—(H. VI. Roll) bore, quarterly or and gules a bend sable, Arundel Roll ; a baston in Ashmole Roll. ROBERT bore a bendlet ; Surrey and Grimaldi Rolls.

Clavering, Sir Allen—bore, at the siege of Calais 1345, quarterly argent and gules, on a bend sable three mullets of the first. The metal is altered to or in the Ashmole MS. (F.) in which the mullets are both argent, and or. Sir ALEXANDER, an Essex Knight, bore this coat (E. II. Roll), with the metal or, in the Parliamentary Roll.

Clederow, Roger, a Kentish Knight—(H. VI. Roll) bore, argent, three covered cups and a bordure engrailed sable ; Arundel Roll.

Clere, John de—(H. III. Roll) bore, argent a fess azure and in chief a lyon passant gules ; Howard Roll.

Clervaux, —— (CLAREVAUX), of Croft—(E. III. Roll) bore, sable, a saltire or, Grimaldi Roll and Jenyns' Ordinary, where the coat is tricked, or, a saltire engrailed gules for JOHN CLAREVAUX. See also JOHN TROMYN.

Cleseby, Asculphus de (HURSQUI)—(E. III. Roll) bore, gules, a fess between three lozenges 2 and 1 argent, Grimaldi Roll (F.) ; JOHN and ROBERT bore the same, Jenyns' Ordinary. F.

Cleseby, John de—(E. II. Roll) bore, gules, "a bend et demi" argent, a quarter ermine, tricked as 2 bends ; Jenyns' Roll.

Cleuisby (or **Clemsby**), **Sir John,** of co. Leic.—(E. II. Roll) bore, argent, a lyon rampant purpure crowned or ; Parliamentary Roll.

Clevedon, see CLIFTON.

Cleville, Sir Thomas (or CHEVILLE)—(E. II. Roll) bore, sable, crusily and a cinquefoyle argent ; Holland Roll.

Cliffe, John OF THE WOLD—(E. II. Roll) bore, argent, three popinjays ppr., Jenyns' Roll ; the Count of Cliffe, de Alemain (H. III. Roll), bore, gules, an orle argent within an escarbuncle or ; Arden Roll.

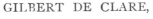

GILBERT DE CLARE,

LORD OF CLARE, EARL OF GLOUCESTER AND HERTFORD, ob. 1230.

After John Carter.

See GLOUCESTER, *post* 95, and FITZ HAMON, 213.

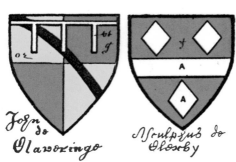

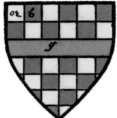

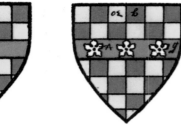

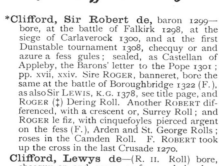

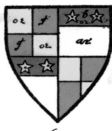

Roj. de Clifford   Rog d' Clifford   Joan d' Clifford   malt. de Clifford   Lo- d E Clinton

Jorn de Olifdone

Jorn de Olovodon

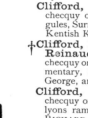

John de Olivodon

Hue d' Clintone

Joan d' Clinton

Joan de Olinton

*Clifford, Sir Robert de, baron 1299— bore, at the battle of Falkirk 1298, at the siege of Carlaverock 1300, and at the first Dunstable tournament 1308, checquy or and azure a fess gules; sealed, as Castellan of Appleby, the Barons' letter to the Pope 1301; pp. xvii, xxiv. Sire ROGER, banneret, bore the same at the battle of Boroughbridge 1322 (F.), as also Sir LEWIS, K.G. 1378, see title page, and ROGER (‡) Dering Roll. Another ROBERT differenced, with a crescent or, Surrey Roll; and ROGER le fiz, with cinquefoyles pierced argent on the fess (F.), Arden and St. George Rolls; roses in the Camden Roll. F. ROBERT took up the cross in the last Crusade 1270.

Clifford, Lewys de—(R. II. Roll) bore, checquy or and azure a fess and bordure gules, Surrey Roll; borne also by CLIFFORD, a Kentish Knight (H. VI.) Arundel Roll.

†Clifford, Roger, Sir John, of Somerset, **Reinaud,** and **Walter**—(H. III. Roll) bore, checquy or and azure, a bend gules (F.), Parliamentary, St. George, Grimaldi, Arden, St. George, and Glover Rolls.

Clifford, John de—(H. III. Roll) bore, checquy or and azure on a bend gules three lyons rampant argent, (F.) St. George Roll. RICHARD of Frampton-upon-Severn, bore the lyons passant or; Harl. MS. 1481 fo. 37.

Clifton, Adam de—(E. III. Roll) bore, checquy or and gules, a bend ermine, Jenyns' Roll; in Jenyns' Ordinary, a mullet azure for difference. In Ashmole Roll (E. III.) occurs, checquy or and gules, a bordure ermine.

Clifton, Sir John de—bore, at the first Dunstable tournament 1308, or, a lyon rampant sable crowned gules (F.); borne also by Sir EDMUND (E. III.) and RENAUD (H. III.), Ashmole and St. George Rolls; Sir JOHN bore the lyon azure, according to the Parliamentary Roll (E. II.).

Clifton, Gervase de—(E. III. Roll) bore, argent, a lyon rampant azure, on its shoulder a fleur-de-lys gules; Jenyns' Ordinary.

Clifton, Sir Gervase—(E. III. Roll) bore, sable, a lyon rampant within an orle of six-foyles pierced argent; Ashmole Roll. Ancestor of the baronets, who bore cinquefoyles.

Clifton, John—(R. II. Roll) bore, argent, a lyon rampant within an orle of cinquefoyles sable; Surrey Roll.

Clifton (——), of Hodsock, Notts.—(E. III. Roll) bore, argent, a lyon rampant sable tail fourchée; Jenyns' Ordinary; same as THOMAS CRECY, v. CRESSY.

Clifton, John de (CLIVEDON)—bore, at the second Dunstable tournament 1334, argent, three escallops gules (F.); Sir JOHN, who was knighted at the capitulation of Calais 1348, bore mascles (F.) alii escallops.

Clifton, Roger de—(H. III. Roll) bore, argent, a chevron sable between three six-foyles pierced gules (F.); Arden and St. George Rolls; roses in Jenyns' Ordinary.

*Clifton, James, of Clifton—(E. IV. Roll), **John** (E. III. Roll), **Robert de** (R. II. and **W.,** E. II. Rolls) bore, sable, on a bend argent three mullets gules; Ballard and Surrey Rolls; mullets pierced in Harl. Roll and Jenyns' Ordinary.

Clifton, Nycol de—(R. II. Roll) bore, sable, on a bend argent three crescents gules, in the cantel a crescent of the second; Surrey Roll.

*Clinton, Sire William de (a baron 1330)—bore, at the battle of Boroughbridge 1322, argent, on a chief azure two mullets (6) or. (F.) JOHN, baron de Clinton 1299, bore the mullets pierced; Nobility and Parliamentary Rolls. THOMAS (R. II.) differenced with a label of three points ermine; Surrey Roll.

Clinton, Le Sr.—bore, at the siege of Rouen 1418, quarterly or and gules, for SAY, quarterly with CLINTON, argent, on a chief azure two mullets pierced or. F.

Clinton, Sir John, of Warwickshire—(E. II. Roll) bore, argent on a chief azure two fleurs-de-lys or; Parliamentary Roll.

Clinton, Sir Thomas de, of Warwickshire—(E. II. Roll) bore, ermine, on a chief azure two mullets or; Parliamentary Roll.

Clinton, Sir John de—bore, at the battle of Boroughbridge 1322, argent, crusily sable, on a chief azure two mullets or; crusily fitchée in Ashmole Roll (F.), and was so borne by WILLIAM at the second Dunstable tournament 1334, and as Earl of Huntingdon at the siege of Calais 1345-8.

Clinton, John de—(E. III. Roll) said to bear the same arms as William de St. Omer—azure a fess between ten crosses crosslet 5 and 5 or; Jenyns' Ordinary.

Clinton, John de—(H. III. Roll) bore, paly (6) or and azure, a canton ermine. (F.) HUGH bore a fess in lieu of the canton. (F.) St. George Roll.

Clinton, Sir John de, of Warwickshire—(E. II. Roll) bore, or, three piles meeting in base azure, a canton ermine; Parly. Roll.

Clitherow v. **Clederow.**

Clivam, William de—(R. II. Roll) bore, argent, a fess gules between three eagles displayed sable armed of the second; Surrey Roll.

*[Clive, Warin de (H. III.)—bore, argent, on a fess sable three mullets or.—Shirley.] F. ROGER ATTE CLIVE took up the cross in the last Crusade 1270.

Clopton (——), a Suffolk Knight—(H. VI Roll) bore, sable on a bend argent between two indents vert, an ermine spot; Surrey Roll.

Clopton, Walter—bore, at the siege of Rouen 1418, sable, a bend argent cotised or. F.

Clovile (——), an Essex Knight—(H. VI. Roll) bore, argent, two chevronels sable each charged with five nails erect or; Surrey Roll.

Roy de Clistone   warm de Olive   wal. Olopton   Lo Cixo de Oobgam   will de Olynton

John Cobham   *Henri d. Cobham*   *Rauf de Cobham*   *Robt de Cobham*

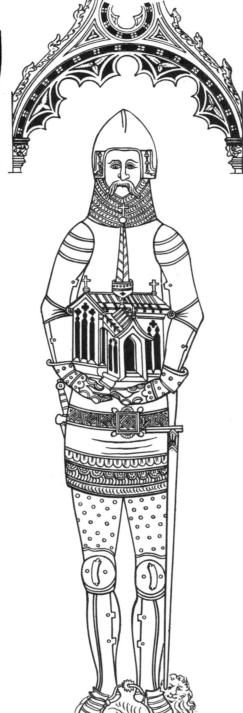

Cobham, Sire Stevene de, a baron 1326—bore, at the battle of Boroughbridge 1322, gules, a cross argent ; so borne also by THOMAS and Sir HENRY, of Kent, uncle of Sir STEPHEN, who differenced with a label (3), azure ; Surrey and Parliamentary Rolls. ROBERT (H. III. Roll) bore, gules, a cross ermine. (F.) Arden and St. George Rolls.

‡**Cobham, Henry de**—(H. III. Roll) bore, gules, florettée or, a cross argent. (F.) Dering and St. George Rolls.

Cobham, Sire Rauf de, a baron 1324—bore, at the battle of Boroughbridge 1322, argent, a lyon (rampant) checquy or and sable. (F.) Sir JOHN *f* RAUF bore it checquy or and azure ; Ashmole Roll.

Cobham, Thomas—(E. II. Roll) bore, ermine, three crescents gules each charged with a besant ; Jenyns' Roll.

Cobham, Le Sr. de (Sir JOHN OLDCASTLE) —bore, at the siege of Rouen 1418, gules, on a chevron or three lyonceux rampant sable, *quarterly with*, argent, a castle sable. F.

Cobham, Sir John, a baron of the Exchequer 1297—bore, gules, on a chevron or three lyonceux rampant sable. Nobility Roll; ascribed to another JOHN (‡) in Dering Roll.

Cobham, Sir Henry de, of Kent—(E. II. Roll) bore, gules, on a chevron or three fleurs-de-lys azure ; Parliamentary Roll. (Ascribed also to JOHN in Howard Roll and Jenyns' Ordinary). Sir RICHARD, of Kent, bore mullets in lieu of fleurs-de-lys.

Cobham, John de—(E. III. Roll) bore, gules, on a chevron or between three fleurs-de-lys azure (*sic*), as many estoiles sable ; Cotgrave Roll.

Cobham, Reginald, a baron 1342, K.G.—bore, at the second Dunstable tournament 1334, gules, on a chevron or three estoiles sable. (F.) Sir JOHN bore the same at the siege of Calais 1345-8, differenced with a label (3) or.

Cobham, Sir Reginald—bore, at the siege of Calais 1345, argent, on a chevron sable three estoiles or ; Cotton MS.

Cobham, Sir John—bore, at the siege of Calais 1345-8 ; gules, on a chevron or three martlets sable ; see Monumental Brass. Borne also by STEPHEN, Bishop of Lincoln, Harl. MS. 1481, fo. 64.

Cobham, John, of Blackburgh in Devon—bore, gules, on a chevron or three eaglets sable ; and THOMAS *fil* Henry of Beluncle in Hoo, Kent, differenced with crescents in lieu of eaglets ; Harl. MS. 1481, fo. 64.

Cobham, Sir Reynold or **Richard de,** of Kent—(E. II. Roll) bore, gules, on a chevron or three mullets azure ; Parly. Roll.

****Codrington, John,** of Codrington, co. Glouc.—arms confirmed 5 July 1441, or 1 July 1442, per R. Leigh clar., altered 23 May 1445, "as worne by him in the service (as standard bearer) of Henry V. in battaile watch and warde," to argent, a fess between three lyonceux passant gules ; and for augmentation 19 Hen. VI. the fess was embattled counter-embattled sable fretted gules (F.) ; in 1473 an additional coat was granted him as a supporter of the House of Lancaster, viz., vert, on a bend argent three roses gules. a dexter hand couped of the second ; Add. MS. 6297 fo. 139, Harl. MS. 1359 Ashmole MS. 857 *ff* 520-1, copy of confirmation in Bodleian Library.

Cokesalton, John de (*v.* KOKESALTON)—(H. III. Roll) bore, argent, fretty gules ; Arden Roll.

Coderinge, Baudewyn de (or CODERUGGE) —(H. III. Roll) bore, gules, three lyonceux rampant or, a label (3 or 5), argent (F.) ; Arden, St. George and Jenyns' Ordinary.

Cogan, John de—(H. III. Roll) bore, lozengy argent and gules ; Howard Roll, same as THOMAS FITZTHOMAS. THOMAS bore gules, three lozenges (2 and 1), argent ; Jenyns' Ordinary.

Cogan, Sir Richard—(E. III. Roll) bore, gules, three leaves vert ; Ashmole Roll.

Cogeshall, William—(R. II. Roll) bore, argent, a cross between four escallops sable ; Surrey and Parly. Rolls for an Essex Knight.

Cokayn, John—(R. II. Roll) bore, argent, three cocks (2 and 1) gules ; Surrey Roll. Argent, three cocks passant sable, in Ashmole Roll. See also THOMAS DE COKEFIELD ; HENRY DE COKINGTON bore the reverse.

[Coke, Hugh,** of Trusley, co. Derby (E. III.)—bore, gules, three crescents and a canton or.—Shirley.] F.

Cokke, Thomas (or COLKE)—(E. III. Roll) bore, sable three bendlets argent ; Jenyns' Ordinary.

†**Cokefeld, Robert** and **Adam**—(H. III. Roll) bore, gules, a fleur-de-lys ermine. (F.) Dering and Howard Rolls.

Cokefeld (? Adam) de—(H. III. Roll) bore, gules, six fleurs-de-lys argent ; St. George Roll. F.

Cokefeld, Thomas de—(E. III. Roll) bore, argent, three cocks (passant) gules ; Jenyns' Ordinary. See COKAYN.

Cokefeld, Sir John de, of Norfolk—E. II. Roll) bore azure, a cross checquy argent and gules ; Parly. Roll and Jenyns' Ordinary.

Cokefield, Sir Richard, of Suffolk—(E. II. Roll) bore, azure, a cross between four cocks passant or ; Parliamentary Roll. See also Tiles in Neath Abbey, p. ix.

Cokefeld, Sire Henry de (COCFELD)—bore, at the battle of Boroughbridge 1322, argent, a saltire engrailed sable, a label (3) gules. Sir SIMON, of Suffolk, bore the same at the first Dunstable tournament 1308 (F.) ; they are ascribed also to ROBERT in Jenyns' Ordinary.

SIR JOHN COBHAM.
IN THE CHANCEL AT COBHAM, 1375-1407.
After Gough.

Badwin d'Coderugge   *John Codrington*   *Sir Cogan*   *Hugh Coke*   *Robt de Cokfeld*   *Ste de Cokefeld*

H

Kokerel

Robt Kokerel

mat: de Cobefor

Henri de Cockington

Roland de Doybond

Simon de Bobofond

mapou de Columbord

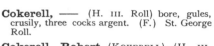

Thomas Colvile de Codwald

witt d. Colevile

Philip d. Colevile

Cokerell, —— (H. III. Roll) bore, gules, crusily, three cocks argent. (F.) St. George Roll.

Cokerell, Robert (KOKERELL)—(H. III. Roll) bore, or, a cross between four cocks gules. (F.) Arden Roll.

Cokerington, Gilbert de—(E. III. Roll) bore, argent, on a cross sable a mullet or; Jenyns' Ordinary.

Cokerington, John de—(E. III. Roll) bore, argent, a chevron between three cocks passant gules; Jenyns' Roll and Ordinary.

Cokesey, Walter de—(H. III. Roll) bore, gules, crusily and a fess argent. (F.) Arden and St. George Rolls.

Cokesey, Walter—(R. II. Roll) bore, argent, on a bend azure three cinquefoyles pierced or; Surrey Roll.

‡Cokington, Henry de—(H. III. Roll) bore, gules, three cocks, 2 and 1, argent; Arden Roll—nine cocks, 3, 3, 2, 1. (F.) in Howard and Dering Rolls.

Cokyn, Sir Renard or Roland de—bore, at the first Dunstable tournament 1308, bendy (6) gules and ermine. (F.) Sir RENARD bore the reverse (E. II.) Parliamentary Roll; and THOMAS bore bendy (6) argent and gules; Jenyns' Roll.

Coldington v. Goldington.

Collay, Sir Robert, of Kent—(H. VI. Roll) bore, sable, three swans' heads and necks erased argent; Arundel Roll.

Collingborne (COLYNGBORN)——an (Essex?) Knight—(H.. VI. Roll) bore, quarterly or and azure, a cross moline counterchanged; Arundel Roll.

Colne, William—(E. III. Roll) bore, sable, a fess between two chevronels argent; Jenyns' Ordinary.

Colpeper, Thomas — (R. II. Roll) bore, argent, a chevron sable between five martlets in chief and two in base gules, *quarterly with*, argent, a bend engrailed gules; Surrey Roll.

Colshill, Thomas—(R. II. Roll) bore, checquy argent and sable (on the second checque), a crescent or, a chief of the last; Surrey Roll. F.

Columbers, Maheu de—(H. III. Roll) bore, (1) argent, a chief gules, Glover Roll; (2) (E. III.) gules a chief argent, a cross-recercelée (moline in trick) counterchanged; Jenyns' Ordinary. In St. George and Arden Rolls the chief becomes per fess argent and gules, and the cross moline counterchanged. F.

*Colvyle, John—(R. II. Roll) bore, azure, a lyon rampant argent; Surrey Roll. (F.) Sir GEOFFREY, of co. Linc. (Parliamentary Roll), bore this coat differenced with a label (3) gules; and JOHN, of Mershland (Jenyns' Ordinary), bore the reverse with the same label.

Colvile, John and Osmond, of Bytham, in Lincolnshire—(E. III. Roll) bore, or, a fess gules; Jenyns' Roll and Ordinary. Sir SYMON or EMOUN, of co. Linc. and WALTER bore the same, and another WALTER differenced his coat with a mullet argent.

Colvile, Sir Thomas—bore, at the siege of Calais 1345-8; or, on a fess gules three lyonceux rampant of the field. (F.) Borne, with the lyonceux argent, by Sir Thomas and Thomas, of Codwald, or Cokewald; Jenyns' Ordinary, Parliamentary Roll.

Colvile, Sir John (and William)—(E. III. Roll) bore, or, on a fess gules three crosses crosslet argent; Ashmole Roll; fitchée in Jenyns' Ordinary. PHILIP took up the cross in the last Crusade 1270.

Colvile, Sir Robert de, of Yorkshire—E. II. Roll) bore, or, a fess gules in chief three torteaux (F.); Parliamentary Roll. Borne also by JOHN in Surrey Roll and ROBERT of Dale in Jenyns' Ordinary.

Colvile, William de—(H. III. Roll) bore, gules, billettée or 4, 5, 4, 3, 2; Arden and St. George Rolls. Six billets and colours reversed in Howard Roll. F.

Colvile, Sir Robert—(E. III. Roll) bore, azure, two bars or, in chief three bezants; (F.) Ashmole Roll.

Colvyle, Sir J.—(H. VI. Roll) bore, or, three chess rooks gules *quarterly with*, azure a lyon rampant argent collared and armed gules; Atkinson Roll.

Colevile, Sir Robert of Blakamor—(E. III. Roll) bore, azure two bars or and in chief three bezants; Ashmole Roll.

Colvile, Henry, of Cambridgeshire—(E. III. Roll) bore, argent a cross patonce gules, borne also by WALTER PERCEHAYE, and are in dispute "et son en debate"; Jenyns' Ordinary. These arms are also ascribed to Sir HENRY (or ROBERT) in Parliamentary Roll, PHILIP (F.) in Arden Roll, and ROBERT and HENRY in Jenyns' Ordinary; in this last BERENGAR LE MOYNE is said to bear the same arms—the cross is variously tricked as moline and flory, patée or patonce and is also blasoned recercelée.

Colwyk (——) a Suffolk Knight—(H. VI. Roll) bore, argent, on a bend azure three besants, in the cantel a cross crosslet fitchée of the second; Arundel Roll.

Colworthe, Richard de—(H. III. Roll) bore, vair argent and gules. (F.) St. George Roll. ROBERT or RICHARD in Jenyns' Ordinary.

Comale, Robert de—(H. III. Roll) bore, azure, a semée of escallops or, a lyon rampant argent; Howard Roll. (F.) See CORMAYLE.

Combe, Sir John (COUMBE)—(E. III. Roll) bore, argent, a chevron engrailed gules between three black birds proper; Ashmole Roll. F.

Combe, Richard de—(E. III. Roll) bore, ermine three ("leopardes lyonceux passant") lyons passant gardant gules; Jenyns' Ordinary. F.

Compton, Sir Robert—bore, sable, three esquires' helmets visors up, or; Cotton MS. Tib. D. 10. F.

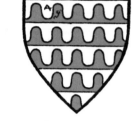

Rich. d' Colewoxpe

Tho Colfhill

John Colvyle

Robt Colonvile

Robt de Comale

John Coumbe

Ric de Combe

§ vo ell ͠g compton

Robt. Compton

Q. Ep. Compton

John Comyn

*[Compton, Thomas de (H. III.)—bore, on a chevron—three fleurs-de-lys—THOMAS, of Fenny Compton, bore, sable three esquires' helmets 2 & 1 argent.—Shirley.] F.

Comyn, John—(E. I. Roll) bore, gules three garbs or. (F.) Ascribed also to Sir JOHN in the Guillim Roll. See BUCHAN.

Comyn, Sir John, of Lincolnshire—(E. II. Roll) bore, argent, crusily and three garbs gules ; Parliamentary Roll.

Comyn, —— (H. III. Roll) bore, azure, semée of estoiles or, and all three garbs argent (sic) (? counterchanged) banded gules. (F.) St. George Roll. Harl. MS. 6137 fo. 78.

*[Congreve, William, E. II.—bore the arms of CAMPION, sable, a chevron between three battle axes argent.—Shirley.] F.

Conquest, Sir John, of Beds.—(E. II. Roll) bore, quarterly argent and sable, a label (3) gules ; Parliamentary Roll.

Constable, Sir William—(E. I. Roll) bore, quarterly vair and gules ; Sir ROBERT bore the same with a bend "engrélé" or ; Nativity Roll, though gules and vair in the Parliamentary Roll. This coat is more often blasoned in the Rolls—quarterly gules and vair a bendlet (vel baston) or, for Sir JOHN, Sir MARMADUKE, RICHARD and ROBERT.

Constable (——), of Flamborough, in Yorks.— (E. III. Roll) bore, quarterly gules and vair a baston argent "parmy" (across) "le gules" ; Cotgrave Roll. For parmy see also DACRE and RAYNSFORD.

Constable, Sir John—Knighted at the capitulation of Calais 1348, bore quarterly vair and gules a border engrailed or. F.

Constable, Roald le, de Richmond— (H. III. Roll), bore, gules, a chief and two gemelles or, Glover Roll : possibly intended to be the same as in the next.

Constable, Robert, of Holderness—(E. III. Roll) bore, barry of six or and azure ; Jenyns' Ordinary.

Constantyn v. Costantyn.

Conway, Henry—(R. II. Roll) bore, sable, on a bend argent cotised ermine a rose gules between two annulets or ; Surrey Roll.

Conyers, Sir John and Robert—(E. II. and E. III. Roll) bore, azure, a maunch or ; Parliamentary Roll and Jenyns' Ordinary (Sir ROBERT bore the reverse—Parliamentary Roll) ; CHRISTOPHER and another, ROBERT, bore the coat differenced with an annulet sable ; Surrey Roll and Jenyns' Ordinary.

Conyers (——), a Yorkshire Knight—(H. VI. Roll) bore, azure, a maunch or charged with a torteaux, quarterly with St. Quintin, or, a chevron gules and a chief vair ; Arundel Roll.

Conyers, Sir Robert—(E. III. Roll) bore, azure, a maunch ermine ; Ashmole and Cotgrave Rolls and Jenyns' Ordinary. Cotgrave also blasons, azure a maunch argent for CONYERS.

Conyers, Robert—(E. II. Roll) bore, or five fusils conjoined in fess sable, quarterly with or, a maunch azure ; Jenyns' Roll.

Coote (——), a Suffolk Knight—(H. VI. Roll) bore, argent, three coots 2 and 1 sable : Arundel Roll.

*Cope, William, of Essex, gentleman—(H. VI. Roll) bore, argent, on a chevron azure between three roses gules slipped and leaved vert as many fleurs-de-lys of the field ; Arundel Roll.

Copuldick, John—(R. II. Roll) bore, argent, a chevron between three crosses crosslet gules ; Surrey Roll. F.

‡Corane, Sire de—(H. III. Roll) bore, argent, an inescocheon sable, a label (5) gules ; Dering Roll. F.

*Corbet, Peter, Baron of Caux 1297—bore, or, a corbyn (or raven) sable ; Nobility, Parliamentary and Ashmole Rolls. This latter gives the same coat also for CORBET within a bordure engrailed gules.

Corbet, Sir Peter—bore, at the battle of Falkirk 1298, or two corbeaux (corbyns) sable (F.), and so sealed the Barons' letter to the Pope 1301, as Lord de Caux, pp. xviii, xxiv. THOMAS DE CAUX, ROBERT (‡) and Sir THOMAS, of Herefordshire, bore the same ; Dering and Parly. Rolls.

Corbet, Sir Roger—(E. III. Roll) bore, two corbyns sable a bordure engrailed gules ; Ashmole Roll.

Corbet, Sir Thomas—bore, at the first Dunstable tournament 1308, or three corbyns 2 and 1 sable. (F.) Borne also by RAFE (E. II.), ROGER (E. I.), and WILLIAM (H. III.) ; Jenyns', Segar and Arden Rolls.

Corbet, Thomas—(H. III. Roll) bore, or, six corbyns 3, 2, 1 sable, on a quarter gules two lyons passant argent ; Arden Roll ; three lyons in St. George Roll. F.

Will Congreve

John Constable

John Coniers

Comyn

John Copaldick

Pers Corbet

Rog. Corbet

Thomas Corbet

Gir. de Gorand

NISI DOMINVS

JE NE CHERCHE QVE VNG

THE HERALDIC ATCHIEVEMENT
OF
WILLIAM, 5th MARQUIS OF NORTHAMPTON.

THE NAMES OF THE QUARTERINGS
WITH REFERENCES TO
THE HERALDIC AUTHORITIES IN THE BRITISH MUSEUM.

It is hoped that the letters in the second column, which indicate the row of quarterings in the shield, will, with the accompanying numerals, facilitate reference to the atchievement opposite.

NAMES	SHIELD REFER-ENCES		BLAZONS	REFERENCES TO THE VARIOUS MSS.
COMPTON (b)	a	1	sable, a lion passant gardant or between three closed helmets argent	
VANNALL (c)	a	2	argent, a chevron vert, a bordure azure bezantée . . .	
AYLWORTH (b). . . .	a	3	argent, a fess engrailed between six billets 3 and 3 or . . .	} H. 1395, f. 44
PAVER (b)	a	4	argent, on a chevron gules three fleurs-de-lys or	Add 14, 305, f. 108
BRERETON (b)	a	5	argent, two bars sable, a mullet for difference gules . . .	
MALPAS, le CLERC . . .	a	6	gules, three pheons 2 and 1 argent	
MALPAS	a	7	argent, a cross flory azure	
EGERTON	a	8	argent, a lyon rampant gules between three pheons sable .	H. 1395, f. 14b
KEVELIOK	a	9	azure, six garbs 3, 2, 1 or	H. 1424, f. 17
BLUNDEVILLE . . .	b	1	azure, three garbs 2, 1 or	H. 1535, f. 67b
LUPUS	b	2	azure, a wolf's head erased argent	H. 2187, f. 97
CORBET	b	3	or, two ravens in pale proper	
SWINNERTON	b	4	argent, a cross patée florettée sable	
BERKELEY (b) . . .	b	5	gules, crusily patée and a chevron argent a bordure of the last .	
HARDINGE	b	6	gules, three Danish axes erect 2 and 1 or	H. 1395, f. 44
ROBERT FITZHARDINGE . .	b	7	gules, a chevron argent, semée of cinquefoyles sable . . .	H. 1073, f. 273
BERKELEY OF DURSLEY . .	b	8	argent, a fess between three martlets 2 and 1 sable . . .	
CREOUN	b	9	azure (? gules), a saltire or (? argent), guttée de sang . . .	H. 1395, f. 62
BETTESHORNE (b) . . .	c	1	argent, on a saltire gules five estoiles or	
WALDEN	c	2	or, on a bend gules cotised azure between six martlets 3 and 3 of the second, three wings argent ; (with TALBOT) on a canton, bendy of ten argent and gules	H. 1395, f. 44 H. 1552, f. 186
OWGAN	c	3	or, on a chief sable, three martlets or, a crescent for difference .	
GREANWIS	c	4	or, a chevron ermine	
STAUNTON	c	5	vair, argent and sable, a canton or	
JOYCE	c	6	argent, a chevron between three leaves vert, slipped gules . .	H. 1552, f. 186
HORFORD	c	7	gules, three eagles displayed argent	
MALYFANT	c	8	argent, on a chief sable, a lyon passant gardant or . . .	} Edmondson's
ROCH	c	9	gules, three roche naiant in pale argent	Baronagium
MILBURNE	d	1	gules, a chevron between three escallops argent . . .	
SPENCER	d	2	argent, two bars gemelles between three eagles displayed sable .	H. 1349, f. 34b
BEAUMONT	d	3	azure, florettée and a lyon rampant or, a crescent sable	
JERUSALEM	d	4	argent, a cross potent between four crosses humettée or . .	
COMYN	d	7	gules, three garbs 2 and 1 or banded gules	
QUINCY	d	8	gules, seven mascles conjoined 3, 3, 1 or	
BLANCHMAINS	d	9	gules, a cinquefoyle ermine	
ROBERT, EARL OF MELLENT .	d	10	lozengy or and azure, a bordure gules platey . . .	H. 1073, f. 22
WAIER	e	1	per pale or and sable, a bend vair	H. 1180, f. 121
BRETVILLE, EARL OF HEREFORD	e	2	gules, a bend argent, over all a fess or	H. 6125, f. 117b
GRENTMESNIL	e	3	gules, a pale or	
ALLEN, LORD GALLOWAY .	e	4	azure, a lyon rampant argent crowned or	
LORD MORVILLE . . .	e	7	azure, florettée and fretty or	
EVERINGHAM	e	8	gules, a lyon rampant vair, crowned or . H. 1487, f. 375b	
BIRKIN	e	9	argent, a fess azure, a label (5) gules	
MAUREWARD	e	10	azure, a fess between three cinquefoyles or	
SHEPEY	f	1	azure, a cross or fretty gules	H. 1180, f. 121
LUCY	f	2	gules, crusily or, three lucies hauriant argent . . .	
FORCHES	f	3	gules, a lyon rampant argent crowned or	
HUGFORD	f	4	or, an eagle displayed sable ducally gorged argent . .	} H. 1563, f. 23b
MIDLETON	f	5	azure, a stag's head cabossed or	
PABENBAM	f	6	barry (6) argent and sable on a bend gules three mullets or .	
DE LA PLANCH . . .	f	7	argent, billettée and a lyon rampant sable, crowned or .	
HAVERSHAM	f	8	azure, a fess between six crosses crosslet argent . . .	} H. 1167, ff. 1, 1b
TRAYLEY	f	9	or, a cross engrailed (? plain) between four mullets gules .	
ACTON	f	10	gules, a fess ermine, within a bordure engrailed argent . .	} H. 1563, f. 23b
KINGSMILL	g	1	argent, crusily fitchée sable, a chevron ermines between three millrinds of the second, a chief of the third	
FAWCONER	g	2	sable, three falcons 2 and 1 argent, beaked and belled . .	
COCK	g	3	quarterly gules and argent	
HAMOND	g	4	or, a chevron engrailed sable between three mullets gules .	} H. 1504, f. 14
ADAMS	g	5	vert, on a cross engrailed or, a mullet gules . . .	
FORSTER	g	6	sable, a chevron ermine between three pheons or . . .	
GOODYER	g	7	gules, a fess between two chevrons vair	
BURY	g	8	vert, a cross crosslet or . . . . . . [sable	
PINCHEPOLE	g	9	argent, an unstringed bugle garnished or between three trefoyles	} H. 1556, f. 102b
WALL	g	10	argent, on a cross sable five lyons rampant or . . .	
SMITH	h	1	1. ermine, on a saltire between three crescents one in chief and two in fess and a dolphin embowed in base azure, an escallop or ; 2. argent, in base on waves of the sea a ship in distress all ppr. ; 3. or, a crescent gules ; 4. azure, a cat, sejant, watching, the dexter paw extended argent	} Douglas Baronage
CLEPHANE			argent, a lyon (of Scotland) rampant gules, a close helmet azure .	
DOUGLAS			1 and 4. argent, a man's heart gules ensigned with an imperial crown ppr. on a chief azure three mullets argent 2 and 3. argent, three piles from the chief gules, in chief two mullets of the first, all within a bordure azure buckled on	} Family Papers
MACLEAN			1. argent, a lyon of Scotland rampant gules ; 2. azure, a castle triple turretted ppr. bannered gules ; 3. or, an armed arm from the sinister ppr. holding a cross crosslet fitchée sable ; 4. per fess or and vert in chief a galley sable, in base a fish naiant argent	
BARING } Escocheon of	d 5 & e 6		1 and 4, azure, on a fess or, in chief a bear's head couped proper muzzled and ringed or	} Modern Grants
HERRING } pretence	d 6 & e 5		2 and 3, gules, crusily or, three lucies haurient 2 and 1 argent, a cross patée fitchée for difference	

(b) Balliol Window.　　(c) In Compton Winyates Church.　　Italic blasons denote the fabulous.

54

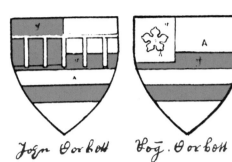

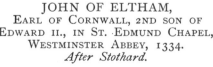

Corbet, Sire Johan—bore, at the battle of Boroughbridge 1322, argent, two bars and a quarter gules, a label argent. F.

Corbet, William—bore, at the second Dunstable tournament 1334, argent two bars gules "un fece d'asure."

Corbet, Sir Roger—Knighted at the capitulation of Calais 1348, bore, argent two bars gules on a canton of the last a cinquefoyle argent. F.

Corbet, Robert—(R. II. Roll) bore, argent, two bars and a canton gules, ROBERT son fitz, differenced with a label (3) argent; Surrey Roll. This coat ascribed to Sir ROBERT (E. III.) in Ashmole Roll.

Corbridge, —— (E. III. Roll) bore, ermine, a fess fusily gules and vair (a better blason may be, ermine on a fess gules five lozenges vair); Ashmole Roll.

Corder, Sir Galyon (altered to Sir WILLIAM in Ashmole Roll)—bore, at the siege of Calais 1345-8, or, on a chief indented (or dancettée) azure, three crosses crosslet of the field. F.

Cormayle, Sir John—(E. III. Roll) bore, argent, three crows proper; Ashmole and Parliamentary Rolls; See also COMALE.

Cormmale, Richard de—(H. III. Roll) bore, argent, on a fess sable three bezants; Howard Roll.

Cornerth, Sir Richard, of Suffolk—Knighted at the capitulation of Calais 1348, when he bore, azure a fess between two chevronels or. (F.) Borne also by THOMAS (R. II.); Surrey Roll; and by Sir THOMAS GRAY in Ashmole Roll.

Cornwall, John of Eltham, EARL OF; f 2 EDWARD II. bore, at the second Dunstable tournament 1334, England within a bordure of France. See Effigy.

Cornwall, Piers Gaveston, Earl of—(E. II. Roll) bore, vert six eagles displayed 3 and 3 or; Arundel Roll (H. VI.).

Cornewall, Sir Edmond de—bore, at the first Dunstable tournament 1308, and at the battle of Boroughbridge 1322, argent, a lyon rampant gules crowned or debruised by a baston sable thereon five bezants. (F.); Add. MS. 5848—(no baston in Harl. MS. 6137 fo. 37). Sir EDMOND, of Oxon. bore, three bezants on the bend; Parly. Roll; as did SYMON in Cotgrave Roll. Sire GEOFFREY bore it at the battle of Boroughbridge 1322, with three mullets (6) or, on the bend. (F.) These two Boroughbridge coats are also ascribed to Sir EDMOND and Sir GEFFREY CURTENEYE in that Roll — an instructive blunder.

Cornwall Richard and Edmund, Earls of—(E. I. Roll) bore, argent, a lyon rampant gules crowned or, within a bordure sable bezantée (F.) in all the Rolls. Sir EDWARD bore the same (E. III.); Ashmole Roll. Sir JOHN, K.G. (H. IV.), bore the bordure engrailed, K. 400 fo. 21.

Cornwall, John, a baron 1433—bore, at the siege of Rouen 1418, ermine, a lyon rampant gules crowned or within a bordure sable bezantée. Borne also by *BRYAN; Surrey Roll.

Cornwall, John de—(R. II. Roll) bore, argent, three fusils in bend between six crosses crosslet fitchée sable; Surrey Roll.

Cornwall, Richard de—(H. III. Roll) bore, argent on a fess sable three besants (plates in the Dering Roll). (F.) Arden and St. George Rolls. ROBERT (‡) bore the same in the Ashmole Copy of the Dering Roll.

Cornwall, Sir Richard—Knighted at the capitulation of Calais 1348, bore argent, on a bend sable three plates; a marginal note adds *puto* or, *i.e.* besants.

Cornwall, Sir Walter de, of the West —(E. II. Roll) bore, argent, a cross sable bezantée (5, 9); Parliamentary Roll. Sir LAURENCE of the North, bore, argent a cross patonce sable bezantée; Parliamentary Roll and Jenyns' Ordinary, in which latter the cross is tricked flory.

Corry, Sir Walter de, of Cumberland— (E. II. Roll) bore, argent, a saltire sable, on a chief azure three cinquefoyles or; Parly. Roll.

Cospatrick, Thomas, of Workington— (E. III. Roll) bore, argent, fretty gules, a chief azure, according to the blason, but tricked, argent, three chevronels interlaced in base gules, a chief azure, same as CHRISTOPHER CURWEN. Jenyns' Ordinary.

Cossington, Stephen—(H. III. Roll) bore, azure three roses or; Howard Roll (a single rose in Jenyns' Ordinary). Ascribed also to Sir WILLIAM of Hants in the Parliamentary and Surrey Rolls.

‡**Cossington, Stephen**—(H. III. Roll) bore, azure, crusily and three cinquefoyles pierced or. (F.) Dering Roll. No crosslets in the Ashmole Copy.

Costantyn, William, of Essex—(H. VI. Roll) bore, argent, a chevron gules between three hurts; Arundel Roll.

Cotel, Sir Ellis, of Somerset—(E. II. Roll) bore, or, a bend gules; Parliamentary Roll. THOMAS also bore it; Jenyns' Ordinary.

Cotenham, John de—(E. II. Roll) bore, barry dancettée (8) argent and gules, tricked as barry dancettée (6) gules and argent; Jenyns' Ordinary.

*[**Cotes (——)** of Cotes, co. Stafford, wrongfully bore the arms of KNIGHTLEY which see,— Erdeswick; Shirley.]

Cotingham, —— (E. IV. Roll) bore, sable, two hinds (perhaps colts) passant counter-passant argent; with crest; Ballard Roll.

Cottingham, John de—(E. III. Roll) bore, sable, a chevron engrailed between three quills (? plumes) argent; Jenyns' Roll.

*[**Cotton, Roger**, of Alkington, Cheshire (R. II.)—bore, azure, a chevron between three hawks' lures (or cotton hanks) argent.—Shirley.] F.

✝**Cotun, Raffe de**—(H. III. Roll) bore, barry (6) argent and azure, in chief three buckles gules tongues to the dexter; Arden and Jenyns' Rolls, where it is also tricked argent two bars azure, &c.

JOHN OF ELTHAM,
EARL OF CORNWALL, 2ND SON OF
EDWARD II., IN ST. EDMUND CHAPEL,
WESTMINSTER ABBEY, 1334.
After Stothard.

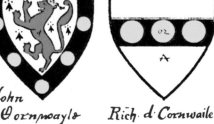

THE HERALDIC ATCHIEVEMENT

OF

AGNES ELIZABETH (*née* Courtenay), VISCOUNTESS HALIFAX.

Robt d· Coury

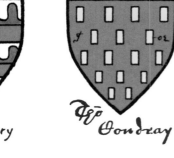

Coudray

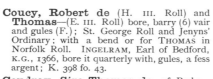

Vaynard de
Coupen

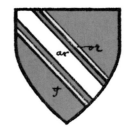

Comte de
Devonshire

Hue
d· Cortenei

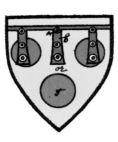

mons· Courtney

John Cove

Coucy, Robert de (H. III. Roll) and **Thomas**—(E. III. Roll) bore, barry (6) vair and gules (F.); St. George Roll and Jenyns' Ordinary; with a bend or for THOMAS in Norfolk Roll. INGELRAM, Earl of Bedford, K.G., 1366, bore it quarterly with, gules, a fess argent; K. 398 fo. 43.

Coudray, Sire Thomas de, of Berks— bore at the first Dunstable tournament 1308, and at the battle of Boroughbridge 1322, gules, billettée or. (F.) Borne also by PIERS and WILLIAM; Arden, St. George, Parly., Cotgrave, and Jenyns' Rolls. Sir THOMAS differenced with a label of three azure; Ashmole Roll.

Coudray or **Caundray,** ——(E. III. Roll) bore, gules, billettée or, and a bend vair; Ashmole Roll.

Coupen, Sir Raymond—(E. II. Roll) bore, gules, six pens erect argent; Parliamentary Roll. F.

Coupland, Sr. de—(E. II. Roll) bore, argent, a chief gules; Jenyns' Roll. Same as WILLIAM FORS, Earl of Albemarle.

Coupland, John de—(R. II. Roll) bore, argent, on a cross sable a mullet of the field; Surrey Roll. The mullet is pierced in Jenyns' Roll.

*****Courtenay, Sir Hugh de,** banneret; a baron 1299, Earl of Devon 1335—bore, at the battle of Falkirk 1298, or, in chief three torteaux, a label azure. The label distinguished the English from the elder branch settled in France.

Courtenay, Hugh de, banneret—bore, at the siege of Carlaverock 1300, or, three torteaux (2 and 1) a label azure (F.) (with a label of five in NICOLAS); as also did Sir PHILIP at the first Dunstable tournament 1308 (F.); borne also by Sir HUGH, K.G., a founder, and Sir PIERS, K.G. Another HUGH bore the same at the second Dunstable tournament 1334, on which occasion THOMAS bore it with a baston azure; Guillim, St. George, and Howard Rolls.

Courtenay, Sir Hugh—bore, at the siege of Calais 1345-8, or, three torteaux, a label (3) azure, each pendant charged with as many crescents of the field—besants, in Cotton MS.— annulets in Harl. MS. (F.) Sir HUGH, who was knighted at the capitulation of Calais 1348, bore, or, three torteaux, a label (5) azure, on each pendant a fleur-de-lys argent (F.); and PHILIP of Powderham differenced with plates in lieu of fleurs-de-lys; Harl. MS. 1481 fo. 55.

Courtenay, (Hugh 4th), Earl of Devon— bore, at the siege of Rouen 1418, or, three torteaux *quarterly with*, or, a lyon rampant azure (for REDVERS). (F.) In the Grimaldi Roll the Earl of Devonshire's coat is blasoned or three gastrels gules (besants) a label azure.

Courtenay, Monsyer—bore, at the siege of Rouen 1418, or, three torteaux, a label (3) azure, on each pendant as many annulets argent (F.); plates in the Ashmole MS., and so borne by Mons. PHILIP (R. II.) Surrey Roll, and Sir PETER, K.G. 1388, K. 399 fo. 25.

Courtenav, Sir Philip, of Somersetshire — (E. II. Roll) bore, or, three torteaux, a bend gobony argent and azure; Parliamentary Roll; Harl. MS. 6137 fo. 7ᵇ; a bend azure in Harl. MS. 4033 fo. 33. See Sir PHILIP, 1308.

Courtenay, Sir Edmond and **Sir Geoffery.** See Sir EDMOND and Sir GEOFFERY CORNEWAYLE.

*[**Courthope** (——), of Goudhurst, Sussex *c.* 1413—bore, argent, a fess azure between three estoiles sable – Shirley.] F.

Cove, Sir John, of Norfolk—bore, at the first Dunstable tournament 1308, gules, a bend argent cotised or; written as COUE, COWE, and TONYE. Parly. Roll, &c.

‡**Covert, Roger le**—(H. III. Roll) bore, gules, a fess ermine, in chief two mullets pierced or, (F.); Dering and Howard Rolls. The fess is between three mullets, or in the Ashmole MS.

Couffolds —— (H. VI. Roll) bore, argent five barrulets and a quarter gules; Arundel Roll.

Cowley, Sir Robert (COVELEY)—(E. III. Roll) bore, argent, on a chevron sable, three leopards' faces or; Ashmole Roll.

Cozans, Sir William — Knighted at the capitulation of Calais 1348, bore, argent, a bend fusily sable, a label (5) gules. F.

Craddok, Richard — (R. II. Roll) bore, argent, on a chevron azure three garbs or; Surrey Roll.

Craili, John—(H. III. Roll) bore, or, a cross between four mullets gules. (F.) St. George Roll. See TRAYLEY.

Crameville, Sire Johan de—bore, at the battle of Boroughbridge 1322, gules, an inescocheon and a bordure mollettée argent—*i.e.* mullets in orle. F.

Crane (——), a Suffolk Knight—(H. VI. Roll) bore, argent, a fess between three crosses crosslet fitchée gules; Arundel Roll.

Crawcestre, John — (E. II. Roll) bore, quarterly or and gules in the first a martlet sable; Jenyns' Roll.

Crek, Walter de — bore, at the second Dunstable tournament 1334, argent a bend azure three "wyfres" *i.e.* cotises wavy. (F.) See also BENHALE *ante* and "Archæologia," Vol. 31, 247, where they are quaintly defined as vipers' nests.

Hog
Le Covert.

Courthorpe

Joan Craili

John
de Cramevilla

walt. de Crek

Will Cozans

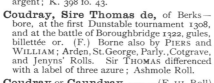

 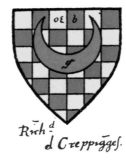  

maurice de Craon   *John de Crepingo*   *Rich.d d Creppigges.*   *Will d Cressi*

John de Cretinge

Simon d. Crey

Will de Crey

[Creke, Sir John de, bore or, on a fess sable three lozenges vair. See Monumental Brass.]

Creon, Maurice de—bore, at the siege of Carlaverock 1300, gules, seven mascles conjoined 3, 3, 1 or. F.

Crepin, William—(H. III. Roll) bore, argent three bars gules "engrélles"; Norfolk Roll. See also CRISPIN.

Creppinge, Sir John de, of Lincolnshire— (E. II. Roll) bore, gules, billettée or, and a lyon rampant argent; Parly. Roll. Guttée d'or in Segar Roll. F.

Creppings, Richard de—(H. III. Roll, bore, checquy or and azure, a crescent gules. (F.) St. George Roll.

Cressner, John—(E. II. Roll) bore, azure on a chief argent three chaplets gules; Jenyns' Roll.

Cressy, William de, banneret, a baron (25 E. I. 1297)—bore, argent, a lyon rampant tail fourchée sable. (F.) Nobility and Arundel Rolls (borne also by CLIFTON, of Hodsall, Notts)—Sir ROGER, of Yorkshire bore it with a label (3) gules; Parliamentary Roll.

Creston, Sir Thomas (or CRISTON)—(H. VI. Roll) bore, gules, a saltire engrailed argent; Atkinson Roll.

Cretinges, John de, a baron 1332—bore, at the siege of Carlaverock 1300, argent, a chevron between three mullets gules. (F.) Borne also by ADAM, JOHN, OSMOND and ROBERT; in some tricks the mullets are pierced, in others they become spur-rowells.

Cretinge, Sir John, of Suffolk—(E. II. Roll) bore, argent, a chevron gules between three torteaux; Parliamentary Roll.

‡Crevequer, Robert and Hamon—(H. III. Roll) bore, or a cross voided gules. (F.) Glover, Dering and Arden Rolls; the cross voided of the field in Camden and Howard.

Creveker, Sir Robert, of Kent—(E. II. Roll), bore, gules, a cross or; Parliamentary Roll.

Crey, Sir Robert de la—bore, at the first Dunstable tournament 1308, argent, an inescocheon gules over all a bendlet sable. F.

Crey, Sir Simon de, of Kent—(E. II. Roll) and John de (E. III. Roll) bore, gules, a cross engrailed or. (F.) Parliamentary Roll and Jenyns' Ordinary—a copy of the Dering Roll adds—for SIMON (‡) "in dexter chief an eagle displayed, Harl. MS. 6137 f 90b."

Crey, Sir William de (KROY), of Kent— bore, at the first Dunstable tournament 1308, gules, a cross engrailed or, over all a baston azure. (F.) See also Parliamentary Roll.

Criketoft, John—(E. III. Roll) bore, lozengy or and sable (F.); Ashmole Roll and Jenyns' Ordinary; blasoned mascles, tricked lozengy— same as WILLIAM BLUNDE.

‡Criell, Nicholas de, baron 1297—bore, gules, a chief or, Nobility Roll—per fess or and gules, in Dering Roll.

Criel, Nychole de (CRYEL)—(H. III. Roll) bore, per fess or and gules, three annulets counterchanged "tertoleres" (F.); Vincent MS. No. 165, 151b and Harl. MS. 1068 fo. 172 (F.). Perhaps ORIEL, which see.

Criol, John (KYRIEL)—bore, at the second Dunstable tournament 1348, or, three chevronels and a canton gules. F.

Criol, Sir Thomas, K.G.—(H. VI. Roll) bore, or two chevronels (a chevron et demye) and a quarter gules; Atkinson Roll. BERTRAM (‡) (F.) or ROBERT, JOHN and Sir NICHOLAS of Kent bore the same; Dering, Parly., Howard, Jenyns' and Surrey Rolls.

‡Crispin, William—(H. III. Roll) bore, lozengy argent and gules (or, in Dering Roll). (F.) JOHN differenced it with a label (5) azure; Howard Roll. See also CREPIN.

Cristemasse. See CHRISTMAS.

Croft, Sir Hugh, of Salop—bore, at the first Dunstable tournament 1308, quarterly per fess indented azure and argent (in the first quarter) a lyon passant gardant or (F.) and Parly. Roll—H. 6137 fo. 27b. In Harl. MS. 4033 the tinctures are reversed, the lyon appearing in the second quarter. In the Ashmole Roll it is erroneously tricked per pale and a chief indented, &c.

Howard Crofts

SIR JOHN DE CREKE.
IN WESTLEY WATERLESS CHURCH,
IN CAMBRIDGESHIRE, 1325.

After Waller.

  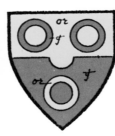  

Robt de la Crey   *Bertram d Criel*   *Criketoft*   *nicholo de Cryol*   *John Kyriol*   *wm Crepin*

I

THE HERALDIC ATCHIEVEMENT

BORNE BY

RALPH CREYKE, .EsQ.,

OF RAWCLIFFE HALL, YORKSHIRE; HIGH SHERIFF, 1894.

Perˀ Crok

Simon d Crombe.

Simon d Cromwell

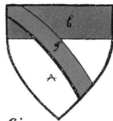

Siꝶ de Crombewell

John de Crumwell

Rich· d Cronpes

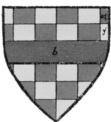

Oliver de Cudgam

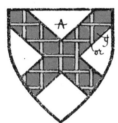

Vaffe Cropshll

nicol de Cuggeho

Croxford

will de Cuggeho

Crofte, Nicholas de—(E. III. Roll) bore, lozengy argent and sable (mascles in blason); Jenyns' Ordinary and Ballard Roll; borne also by Sir PETER LEE of co. Lanc.

Croke v. Sir Thomas Blount.

Croke, Piers—(H. III. Roll) bore, azure three crooks or; St. George Roll. Birds' heads in Harl. MS. 6137, fo. 86ᵇ. F. NICHOLAS and ROBERT took up the cross in the last Crusade 1270.

Crokedayke, Sir Adam de, 1297—bore, ermine three pellets; Nobility Roll.

Crombe, Simon de—(H. III. Roll) bore, argent, a chevron gules on a chief of the last three escallops of the first (F.); St. George Roll. In the Arden Roll, the field ermine and the escallops or, sometimes argent.

Cromwell, John de—bore, at the siege of Carlaverock 1300, azure, a lyon rampant argent tail fourchée, ducally crowned or. F.

Cromwell, Sir John de, banneret—(E. I. Roll) bore, gules, six annulets or; Nativity and Parliamentary Rolls, and Jenyns' Ordinary.

Cromwell, Sire Raufde—(E. I. Roll) bore, argent, a chief azure, surmounted by a bendlet gules, (F.); (SIMON bore the same, E. III. Roll); Guillim and St. George Rolls.

Cromwell, John, of Tatishall, baron 1308—RAUFE (E. I. Roll) and THOMAS of Lamlay (E. III. Roll) bore, argent, a chief gules surmounted by a baston azure; Segar and Arundel Rolls and Jenyns' Ordinary.

Cromwell, Sire Richard de—bore, at the battle of Boroughbridge 1322, argent, a chief gules surmounted by a baston gobony or and azure, (F.) and in Jenyns' Ordinary.

Cromwell, Sir Raulf le (DE TATERSALE) —(R. II. Roll) bore, checquy or and gules, a chief ermine, *quarterly with,* argent a chief gules surmounted by a baston sable; Surrey Roll.

Cromwell, Sire John de—bore, at the battle of Boroughbridge 1322, "Queynty d'argent frettée de ses armes d'Ermyne"; not tricked in the Ashmole Copy, made by BROOKE, York Herald, the blason has yet to be solved, though it rather points to the quarterly coat of RAUF. See also BERKELEY, and facsimile, page xxvi.

Crophill, Raffe—(E. III. Roll) bore, argent, a saltire gules fretty or; Ashmole Roll and Jenyns' Ordinary.

Croupes, Richard de—(H. III. Roll) bore, argent, six lozenges 3, 2, 1 gules; Arden Roll. Sir RICHARD bore mascles (E. II. Roll) with a label (3) azure; Parliamentary Roll; and in the St. George Roll it appears with a label of five also azure. F. See BRIDMANSTONE.

Croxford, —— (E. III. Roll) bore, argent a chevron between three buckles sable garnished with mascles, tongues to the sinister; Ashmole Roll. F.

Crull, ——(E. III. Roll) bore, gules, a chevron between three eagles displayed argent; Ashmole Roll.

Cudemers, John de—(E. I. Roll) bore, gyronny (12) or and sable, (F.), (in the centre what might be mistaken for a pellet); Segar Roll.

‡**Cudham, Oliver and Robert de**—(H. III. Roll) bore, checquy gules and argent a fess azure (F.); Dering Roll; reversed, *i.e.* argent and gules, in the Ashmole MS.

Cuffolds (——), an Essex Knight (? COW-FFOLDS)—(H. VI. Roll) bore, argent, five barrulets and a quarter gules; Arundel Roll.

Cuggeho, Nicol de—(E. I. Roll) bore, gules, a fess between three lozenges argent (F.); Camden Roll.

Cuggeho, William—(H. III. Roll) bore, gules, a fess and in chief three mascles argent (F.); St. George and Parliamentary Rolls; COGGENHO, Northants.

Cuilly, Hugh de—(E. III. Roll) bore, argent a chevron between three mullets sable; Cotgrave Roll. Written TUYLEY in Jenyns' Ordinary. Sir HUGH of Notts bore (E. II. Roll) ogresses in the place of mullets; Parliamentary Roll.

Culcheth, Randolph, alias HINDLEY—(E. IV. Roll) bore, sable, a gryphon segreant argent; with crest; Ballard Roll.

Curson, Sire Roger de—bore at the battle of Boroughbridge 1322, checquy or and sable, a fess argent. (F.) JOHN (E. III. Roll) bore, checquy or and azure, a fess argent, a label (3) gules; Jenyns' Ordinary.

Curson, John—bore, at the siege of Rouen 1418, ermine a bend counter-compony argent and sable (F.) MONSYER CURSON bore on the same occasion this coat differenced with a martlet gules.

Curson, Robert—bore, at the siege of Rouen 1418, gules, on a bend between six billets or, three escallops sable. F.

Curson, Sir John, of Norfolk—(E. II. Roll) bore, or, on a bend gules three besants; Parliamentary Roll.

*****Curson, Roger**—(R. II. Roll) bore, argent, on a bend sable three popinjays or, collared and membered gules—a crescent of the last; Surrey Roll.

Curteis (——), an Essex Knight (CORTEYS)—(H. VI. Roll) bore, ermine on a canton gules an orle argent; Arundel Roll.

Curwen, Thomas de—(H. III. Roll) bore, gules, fretty argent (F.); Arden and St. George Rolls.

Curwen, Christopher—(E. III. Roll) bore, argent, fretty gules, a chief azure; THOMAS bore, argent fretty and a chief gules, Jenyns' Ordinary, but they are tricked, probably in error, argent three chevrons interlaced in base gules, a chief azure for CHRISTOPHER; the chief of the field, for THOMAS; Jenyns' Roll. See COSPATRICK.

Cusance, William—(E. III. Roll) bore, argent, a bend engrailed sable, in chief an escallop of the last; Jenyns' Ordinary.

Johan de Oudomars

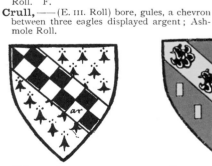

John Curson.

Robert Curson

Roger de Curson

Thõ. d. Corouen

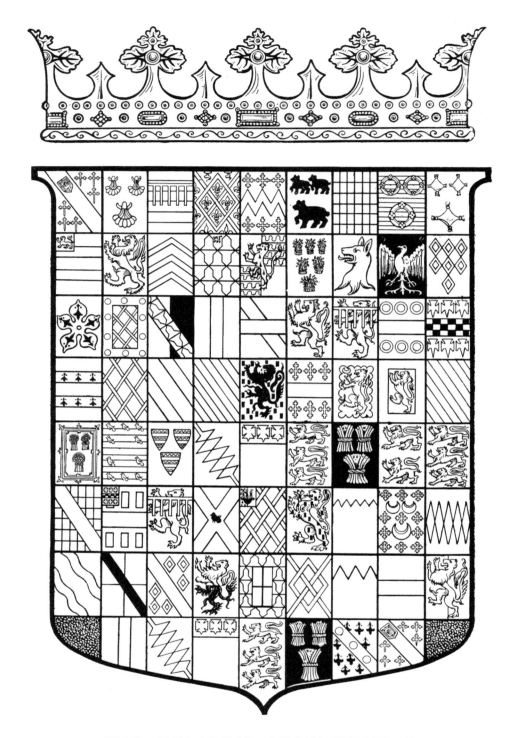

THE HERALDIC ATCHIEVEMENT

(SHIELD II., BROUGHT IN BY DACRE)

OF

HENRY FITZALAN HOWARD, K.G., 15TH DUKE OF NORFOLK.

SEE ALSO PAGES 16 AND 114.

NAMES AND BLAZONS OF THE QUARTERINGS—SHIELD II.

It is hoped that the letters in the second column, which indicate the row of quarterings in the shield, will, with the accompanying numerals, facilitate reference to the atchievement opposite.

NAMES	SHIELD REFER- ENCES	BLAZONS	REFERENCES TO THE VARIOUS MSS.
			AUGMENTATION
HOWARD	a 1	gules, on a bend between six crosses crosslet fitchée argent, the honorable augmentation for services at the battle of Flodden. 1 Feb., 1513–14	Cott. Jul. C. VII. f. 237 Lansdowne 872, ff. 13, 16 Harl. 1178, f. 45
DACRE	a 2	gules, three escallops argent	H. 4259, f. 12ᵇ
MOULTON	a 3	barry of six argent and gules a label (5) azure . . .	H. 1375, f. 49
MORVILLE	a 4	azure, florettée and a fret or	
ENGAYNE	a 5	gules, a fess dancettée between six crosses crosslet or (the field azure in H. 1375)	
TREVES	a 6	argent, three (unmuzzled) bears passant 2 and 1 sable (in pale, in H. 1375)	H. 1425 f. 12ᵇ
VAUX	a 7	checquy or and gules.	
GRYMTHORP . . .	a 8	burulée (14) argent and azure, three chaplets 2 and 1 gules H. 218, f. 39	
GREYSTOKE . . .	a 9	gules, three cushions tasselled or	
LANCASTER . . .	b 1	argent, two bars gules on a canton of the last a lyon passant or .	
BOLEBEC	b 2	vert, a lyon rampant or	H. 1415, f. 119ᵇ
MOUNTFICHET. . . .	b 3	gules, three chevronels or	
FERRERS	b 4	vair or and gules, a lyon in chief or	H. 4259, f. 12ᵇ
PEVERELL	b 5	quarterly gules and vair or and vert, a lyon rampant ermine. .	
KEVELIOK, EARL OF CHESTER .	b 6	gules, six garbs, 3, 2, 1 or	
LUPUS, EARL OF CHESTER .	b 7	*azure, a wolf's head erased sable*	H. 807, ff. 22ᵇ–23
LEOFRIC, EARL OF MERCIA .	b 8	*sable, an eagle displayed or*	
QUINCY	b 9	gules, seven mascles conjoined 3, 3, 1 or	
BELLOMONT . . .	c 1	gules, a cinquefoyle pierced ermine	
MELLENT. . . .	c 2	fretty or and azure a bordure gules platey	Edmondson v. 484
WAIER	c 3	*per pale or and sable a bend vair*	,, v. 483
FITZOSBORNE . . .	c 4	*gules, a bend argent over all a fess or*	
GRENTESMENIL . . .	c 5	gules, a pale or.	H. 807, f. 23
*GALLOWAY . . .	c 6	azure, a lyon rampant argent, crowned or	H. 807, f. 23
MUSCEGROS . . .	c 7	gules, a lyon rampant or a label of five azure	H. 1047, f. 38ᵇ
AVENELL	c 8	gules, a fess between six annulets or	
BOTELER	c 9	gules, a fess checquy argent and sable between six crosses crosslet fitchée of the second	H. 4259, f. 12ᵇ
PANTULF. . . .	d 1	gules, two bars ermine	H. 1047, f. 39
VERDON	d 2	or fretty gules	
SUDLEY	d 3	or two bends gules	
MOUNTFORD . . .	d 4	bendy of ten or and azure	
·DE LA PLANCHE . . .	d 5	argent, billettée and a lyon rampant sable	H. 807, f. 22ᵇ, 70ᵇ
HAVERSHAM . . .	d 6	azure, a fess between six crosses crosslet argent	
RHYS, RICE, or REES, PRINCE OF SOUTH WALES	d 7	*gules, a lyon rampant and a bordure engrailed or a crescent for difference*	
BELISME	d 8	*azure, a lyon rampant and a bordure or*	
TALBOT	d 9	bendy of ten argent and gules	
COMIN	e 1	gules, three garbs 2 and 1, within the Royal tressure of Scotland all or	H. 1396, f. 304
VALENCE. . . .	e 2	barry of ten argent and azure, as many martlets 3, 2, 2, 3 gules .	
MONCHENSI . . .	e 3	or, three escocheons barry of six vair, and gules	
MARSHALL . . .	e 4	gules, four lozenges in bend or	
STRONGBOW . . .	e 5	argent on a chief azure three crosses formée fitchée at the foot of the first	
GIFFARD	e 6	gules, three lyons passant argent	H. 1047, f. 44
MACMORROGH . . .	e 7	*sable, three garbs 2 and 1 argent*	
STRANGE	e 8	argent, two lyons passant gules	H. 1396, f. 304
GIFFARD	e 9	gules, three lyons passant argent	
CLIFFORD . . ·. .	f 1	checquy or and azure a bend gules	
HERDEBURGH . . .	f 2	gules, billettée and a fess argent, with BUTLER of Wem on a canton—gules, a fess counter-compony or and sable six crosses pateé argent	H. 1047, f. 39
COLVILL	f 3	azure, a lyon rampant argent, a label (5) gules	
NEVILL	f 4	gules, on a saltire argent, a martlet sable for difference . .	
UCHTRED, LORD OF RABY .	f 5	or, fretty gules, on a canton per pale ermine and or a galley sable	H. 1396, f. 304
BULMER	f 6	gules, a lyon rampant or, billettée sable	
FITZRANDOLPH, or TALBOYS .	f 7	or, a chief indented azure	
GLANVILE	f 8	azure, crusily and three crescents argent	
PERCY	f 9	azure, five fusils conjoined in fess or	H. 1047, f. 37
BREWER	g 1	gules, two bends wavy or	H. 1411, f. 54
CLAVERING . . .	g 2	quarterly or and gules a bend sable	
FURNIVAL	g 3	argent, a bend between six martlets 3 and 3 gules . . .	
LOVETOT	g 4	argent, a lyon rampant per fess gules and sable . . .	H. 1396, f. 304
FITZJOHN	g 5	quarterly or and gules, a bordure vair	
VERDON	g 6	or, a fret gules (as Earl Marshal only, H. 154, f. 55) . . .	
BOTILER	g 7	or, a chevron dancettée azure	D. ORMONDE
LACY	g 8	or, a fess gules	H. 1395, f. 8
BIGOD	g 9	per pale argent and vert a lyon rampant gules	
GRENTESMENIL . . .	h 1	gules, a pale or	H. 6125, f. 117ᶦ
MARSHALL	h 2	gules, four lozenges in bend or	
STRONGBOW . . .	h 3	argent on a chief azure three crosses formée fitchée at the foot of the first	H. 1396, f. 304 H. 1047, f. 44
GIFFARD	h 4	gules three lyons passant argent.	
MACMORROGH . . .	h 5	*sable, three garbs 2 and 1 argent*	
DAGWORTH . . .	h 6	ermine, on a bend gules, three bezants	Baronage

* Galloway is generally said to bring in Scott and Waltheof but in this connection it is very doubtful ; Alan probably had more than one wife.

Duke William and his army came to Mont Saint-Michel.   After the Bayeux Tapestry.

— D —

D'Abernon, Sir John, of Surrey—(H. III. Roll) bore, azure, a chevron or ; St. George and Howard Rolls ; see Mon. Brass ; his son Sir JOHN differenced with a label (3) argent, at the first Dunstable tournament 1308, and at the battle of Boroughbridge 1322. F.

D'Abitot, Geoffrey, of Hindlip, co. Worc. —(H. III. Roll) bore, per pale gules and vert two lyons passant gardant argent —another, or, two lyons passant gardant that in chief gules, that in base azure. (F.) Arden and St. George Rolls.

D'Abitot, Sir William, of co. Worc. —(E. II. Roll) bore, ermine, a chief bendy (6) or and sable ; Parliamentary Roll.

Dabridgcourt, Sir John (K.G. 1413)—bore, at the siege of Rouen 1418, ermine three bars humettée gules. (F.) Borne also by NICOL and by SANCHET, K.G., a founder ; Surrey Roll (R. II.). This coat by an heraldic illusion may be blasoned the reverse, viz., gules two bars and a bordure ermine.

Dabridgcourt, John de—(R. II. Roll) bore, ermine, three bars humettée gules each charged with as many escallops or ; Parly. Roll.

Dacre, Sir William, of Cumberland—(E. I. Roll) bore, gules, three escallops argent. (F.) Segar, Ashmole and Parliamentary Rolls.

Dacre, Sir Edward, of Cumberland—(E. II. Roll) bore, gules, florettée or, three escallops argent ; Parliamentary Roll.

Dacre, Randolph—(H. III. Roll) bore, azure on a cross or five escallops gules. (F.) Arden and St. George Rolls ; (same as NICHOL VILLERS) ; in Jenyns' Ordinary the cross is described as p'my. See CONSTABLE and RAYNSFORD.

Dagnall, Robert—(H. III. Roll) bore, paly (6) or and azure, a chief gules ; Howard Roll.

Dagworth, Thomas, a baron 1347—bore, ermine on a fess gules three besants. Borne also by Sir JOHN of Suffolk, Parly. Roll—and RALPH, in Ashmole Roll ; torteaux in lieu of besants for NICHOLAS in Surrey Roll (R. II.).

Dagworth, Thomas—(E. III. Roll) bore, ermine on a chevron gules three besants ; Jenyns' Ordinary.

Dakeneye, Sir Baldwin, of Cambridge — (E. II. Roll), **John** and **William** (H. III. Roll) bore, azure, a cross between four lyonceux rampant or. (F.) Parliamentary, St. George and Glover Rolls.

Dakeney, Sir Thomas, of Norfolk—(E. II. Roll) bore, argent, a cross between four lyonceux rampant gules ; Parliamentary Roll.

Dalden, Jordan de—(E. II. Roll) bore, argent, a cross patée (patonce in trick) gules, between four daws proper ; Jenyns' Roll.

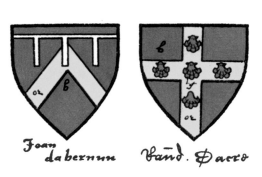

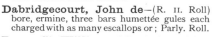

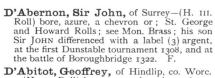

John Darcy   *John Darcyo*   *Nicol d' Arci*   *Norman Darcy*

Dale, Sir Thomas—(E. III. Roll) bore, gules, a swan close argent, membered sable; Ashmole and Surrey Rolls.

Dallingridge, MOUNSYER—bore, at the siege of Rouen 1418, argent, a cross engrailed gules (F.), and in Jenyns' Roll. See Monumental Brass.

D'Alry, Johan (DE ALRE)—(H. III. Roll) bore, argent, three escallops gules; Howard Roll.

Dalston, John de—(E. II. Roll) bore, argent, a chevron engrailed sable between three daws' heads erased of the last; Jenyns' Roll.

Dalton, Sire Robert de—bore at the battle of Boroughbridge 1322 and at the siege of Calais 1345-8, azure, crusily or, a lyon rampant gardant argent.

Dalton, Robert de—(E. III. Roll) bore, azure, a leopard rampant argent—*i.e.* a lyon rampant gardant; Jenyns' Ordinary.

Dalton (——), a Yorkshire Knight—(H. VI. Roll) bore, azure, florettée or, a lyon rampant gardant argent. (F.) Arden Roll.

Dammerell, William—(E. III. Roll) bore, azure, on a chief gules two crescents and another in base argent; Ashmole Roll.

Damory, Sir Richard—bore, at the first Dunstable tournament 1308, undée (6) gules and argent—possibly an error for argent and gules; another Sir RICHARD of Oxon. bore, at the siege of Calais 1345-8, undée (6 or 8) argent and gules—also in Parliamentary Roll. ROBERT bore the same with a label (5) sable; Arden Roll; —In Dering Roll the labels azure, each file being charged with three bezants. (F.) Said to be vairy (modern) argent and gules, &c., in Howard Roll.

Damory, Sir Roger, baron 1317—bore, at the first Dunstable tournament 1308, undée (6) argent and gules a bend azure. (F.) See Tiles, Neath Abbey, page vii.

Dancastre, Robert—(E. III. Roll) bore, or, on a bend azure, three castles triple turreted argent. (F.) Jenyns' Ordinary.

Daneston, John, a Suffolk Knight—(H. VI. Roll) bore, argent three Danish axes gules *quarterly with,* argent, on a chevron sable, a cross patée of the first; Arundel Roll.

Dangervile, Sir John, of co. Leic.—(E. II. Roll) bore, gules, a cinquefoyle ermine, a bordure sable bezantée; Parly. Roll. HUGH took up the cross in the last Crusade 1269.

D'Angle, Sir Guichard, K.G. 1372, Earl of Huntingdon 1377 for life—bore, or, billettée and a lyon rampant azure, K. 398 fo. 44.

Danny, Sir John—(E. III. Roll) bore, argent, on a bend cotised azure three six-foyles pierced or; Ashmole Roll; cinquefoyles argent in Jenyns' Ordinary.

Danny, Nicholas—(E. III. Roll) bore, argent, on a bend vert cotised azure three cinquefoyles or; Jenyns' Ordinary.

Danvers, Sir Thomas (DE ANVERS), of Cheshire, Kt.—(E. II. Roll) bore, gules, a chevron or between three besants; Parliamentary Roll. An Essex (?) Knight bore the same (Hen. VI.); with pierced mullets in lieu of besants; Arundel Roll.

Danyell, (——) of Danby-upon-Yore, in Yorkshire—(E. III. Roll) bore, argent seven mascles 3, 3, 1 gules (blasoned as lozenges pierced); Jenyns' Ordinary.

Danyell, Hugh—(E. III. Roll) bore, azure, two bars argent a chief gules; Jenyns' Ordinary.

Daniell, John—(H. III. Roll) bore, azure, a bend between six escallops or. (F.) St. George Roll.

Danyell, Thomas—(E. III. Roll) bore, argent a pile indented of five points sable. (F.) Jenyns' Ordinary.

Danyell (——), of Cheshire—(E. IV. Roll) bore, argent, a pale lozengy sable, *quarterly with,* argent, a fox regardant sable—with crest; Ballard Roll.

Darcy—The cinquefoyles are often tricked as six-foyles and roses.

Darcye, Sir Adomar (AMOR)—bore, at the siege of Calais 1345-8, argent, an inescocheon within an orle of cinquefoyles gules.

Darcy, Sir John—bore, at the first Dunstable tournament 1308, argent an inescocheon sable between three cinquefoyles gules. F.

Darcy, Sir John—bore, at the battle of Boroughbridge 1322, argent, an inescocheon sable within an orle of six-foyles gules (blasoned in Jenyns' Ordinary for DARCY DE PARKE as sable, a bordure of the arms of DARCY). Sire JOHAN le fiz, bore on the same occasion—argent, on an inescocheon sable an estoile or, all within an orle of cinquefoyles pierced gules.

Darcy, Sir John (of co. Lincoln), knighted at the capitulation of Calais 1348—bore, argent, an inescocheon sable within an orle of cinquefoyles (roses in Parliamentary Roll) gules; also blasoned, as argent, an orle of six-foyles gules and a false escocheon sable. Ascribed to ROBERT in Cotgrave Roll.

Darcy, Sire Norman, le fiz—bore, at the battle of Boroughbridge 1322, argent the bordure of roses (gules) a label (3) azure. F.

Darcy, Sir Rauff—(E. III. Roll) bore, argent, on an inescocheon gules, three crosses crosslet fitchée or, all within an orle of (8) seysfoyles pierced of the second; Ashmole Roll.

Darcy, Sir John, of Knaith, a baron 1332—bore, argent, a cinquefoyle and a bordure indented gules; Nativity Roll.

Darcy, Philip, baron 1299—bore, at the battle of Falkirk 1298, argent, three cinquefoyles gules (incorrectly blasoned as crosses crosslet); Nobility Roll — the cinquefoyles were borne pierced by (1) Sir PHILIP, Knight banneret, (2) NORMAN(‡) (F.), and also (3) by an Essex Knight; Dering and Howard Rolls.

Norman Darcy   *norman Darsy le fiz*

SIR JOHN D'ABERNON.
IN STOKE DABERNON CHURCH,
SURREY, 1277.
After Waller.

Phil Darcy   *Robert Darcy*

THE HERALDIC ATCHIEVEMENT

OF

ROBERT DARCY, 4TH AND LAST EARL OF HOLDERNESSE,

NOW VESTED IN

THE DUKE OF LEEDS, BARONESS CONYERS (CTSS. YARBOROUGH), CTSS. OF POWIS
MRS. C. J. WELD-BLUNDELL, HON. MRS. W. R. FITZWILLIAM, AND OTHERS.

Elyß. d'Aubeni

Philip d'Aubeni   *Rauf d'Aubeni*   *Joßn Danbeney*

Elyß Daubeny

Roßt. Darcy

roill Darcyß

roill de Aubory

Darcy, Sir Norman, knighted at the capitulation of Calais 1348—bore, argent three cinquefoyles gules a label (5) azure. F. Roses for Sir NORMAN, of co. Linc., in Parly. Roll.

Darcy, Sir Robert — bore, at the first Dunstable tournament 1308, argent three cinquefoyles gules a bordure indented sable—engrailed in Harl. MS. 6137 fo. 31ᵇ.

D'Arcy, Sir William—bore, at the siege of Calais 1345-8, azure, crusily and three cinquefoyles argent. (F.) See also Cotgrave. (Sir JOHN, of co. Lincoln, bore roses; in Parliamentary Roll). The same coat was borne at the siege of Rouen 1418 by Le Sr. DE DARCYE—and by DARCY le nepueu; Jenyns' Ordinary (ROGER, 2nd son of JOHN of Knaith, in Yorkshire, bore it within a bordure or, Harl. MS. 1481 fo. 88); and Le Sr. DARCY (R. II. Roll) bore it quarterly with, azure three gemelles and a chief or; Surrey Roll.

Darcy, Norman—bore, at the second Dunstable tournament 1334, argent, three sixfoyles gules; Segar Roll. Borne also by JOHN in Jenyns' Ordinary. Another NORMAN differenced with a label azure; Jenyns' Ordinary. ROBERT bore it (E. I.) within a bordure engrailed sable. (F.) Segar and Harleian Rolls. In Segar tricks roses may be intended.

Darcy, Sire Robert—bore, at the battle of Boroughbridge 1322, argent three six-foyles gules a bordure vair eglettée or. (F.) Tricked in the Ashmole MS. rather like—vert, on an inescocheon gules three six-foyles gules all within an orle of eaglets displayed or.

Darcy, Sir John—bore, at the siege of Calais 1345-8, argent three roses gules. (F.) (See also 6th Nobility Roll, H. vi.) Sir JOHN, the son, bore the same arms at this siege differenced with a label (3) gules. Borne undifferenced by Sir PHILIP, a baron (25 E. I.) and reversed by Sir WILLIAM, of co. Linc., in Parly. Roll.

Darcy, Sir William, of co. Linc.—(E. II. Roll) bore, argent, three roses gules; and Sir ROBERT, also of co. Linc. bore it within a bordure indented sable; Parliamentary Roll.

Darcy, Nicol—(H. III. Roll) bore, sable, a fess or. (F.) St. George Roll.

Darres, Sir Robert—(E. III. Roll)—bore, argent on an orle gules eight escallops or; Ashmole Roll. See Sir JOHN and ROBERT DARCY; see also ARRAS.

D'Artois, Janico (DE ARTOYS)—(E. III. Roll) bore, gules four barrulets wavy argent; Jenyns' Roll. See facsimile, p. 5.

Dassy, Sir Robert (DE ASSI)—(E. III. Roll) bore, gules, a bend cotised or between six martlets of the last; Ashmole Roll.

Daubeney, Le Sr.—(E. II. Roll) bore, gules, three fusils conjoined in fess argent; Jenyns' Roll.

Daubeny, Elias (DE ALBINIACO), baron 1295-1305—bore, gules four lozenges conjoined in fess argent; Nobility Roll. Borne also by Sir GILES, of Devon or Cornwall, Parly. Roll, PHILIP and RAUF, the latter in Segar Roll (E. I.). See also Monumental Slab.

Daubeny, Sir John, of Oxon, 1346—bore, four fusils conjoined, each charged with a mullet (5) pierced; surrounded by three different Daubeny coats here named and a fourth lozenge argent and gules, a bordure of the first. See Monumental Slab.

Daubeny, Elys—(E. I. Roll) bore, gules four fusils conjoined in fess argent, a baston azure. (F.) Segar Roll. WILLIAM bore the same at the second Dunstable tournament 1334, though blasoned as a fess engréle. F.

Daubeny, Felipe—(E. I. Roll) bore, gules four fusils conjoined in fess argent and in chief three martlets or; Segar Roll—five fusils in the St. George Roll, &c. (F.) And so also for RAUFE and WILLIAM (‡) in the Howard and Dering Rolls.

Dawbeney, Sir Ellis, banneret—bore, at the siege of Carlaverock 1300, gules five fusils conjoined in fess argent. (F.) Drawn as a fess engrailed in NICOLAS—Gent's. Mag. xcvi. pt. i, p. 400—an "engréle" is differently interpreted by the earlier arms painters. Sir JOHN, who was knighted at the capitulation of Calais 1348, bore the same coat. So also ELIAS, Baron DAUBENEY, Parly. Roll, and RAUF (‡) Dering Roll, blasoned in the latter as a fess engrailed in Glover Roll.

‡**Dawbeny, Philip**—(E. III. Roll) bore, gules, a fess fusily (vel lozengy vel 5 fusils in fess) argent, and in chief three mullets pierced or; Dering and Howard Rolls.

Dawbneye, Sir John—(E. II. Roll) bore, gules a fess lozengy argent (another ermine, and in a third trick a fess indented ermine) in chief three mullets or. (F.) See also Monumental Slab. Parly. Roll.

Dawbeney, Sir Ralph—(E. III. Roll) bore, gules five fusils conjoined in fess (another a fess engrailed) argent, in chief three escallops or. (F.) Holland and St. George Rolls. WILLIAM bore the same, over all a bend azure; St. George Roll.

Dawbeny, William, de Belvoir—(E. III. Roll) bore, or two chevronels and a bordure gules; Glover and Grimaldi Rolls; the bordure engrailed, on the Monumental Slab.

Daubeny, William (DE AUBENY)—(E. III. Roll) bore, sable, three helmets 2 and 1 argent. (F.) Arden Roll.

Daundelegh, Philip—(E. II. Roll) bore, argent, two bars gules each charged with three crosses crosslet or; Jenyns' Roll and Ordinary.

Daundely, Sir Robert—(E. III. Roll) bore, argent, three bars gules crusily 3, 2, 1 or; Ashmole Roll.

Dauntesey, John (DANDESEYE)—(R. II. Roll)—bore, per pale or and argent three bars undée gules; Surrey Roll.

Dauntesey, Sir Richard (AUNTESHEYE), of co. Glouc.—(E. II. Roll) bore, per fess or and argent a fess undée gules; Parly. Roll. F.

Dautrey, Geffrey (DE ALTA RIPA)—(E. III. Roll) bore, azure five fusils conjoined in fess argent, a baston gules; Jenyns' Ordinary.

Dautrey, Lyon—(E. III. Roll) bore, gules, a bend argent between two cotises engrailed or; Jenyns' Ordinary.

Dautrey, John—(R. II. Roll) bore, sable, five fusils conjoined in fess argent; Surrey Roll. WILLIAM (‡) differenced it with a label (5) gules. (F.) Arden, Dering and Howard Rolls—blasoned also as a fess dancettée of five. In Cotgrave Roll, fusils gules, for DAWTRYNE.

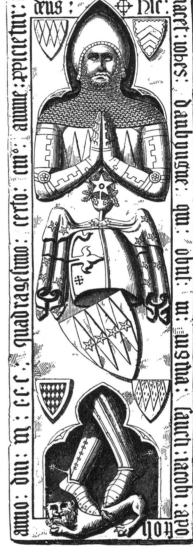

SIR JOHN DAUBENY.
IN NORTON BRIZE CHURCH,
OXON., 1346.
After Boutell.

Joan d'Aubeni

Joan Dabeni

roill d'Aubeni

roill d'Antrene

Þobt Daventry

Boðk Dauðoeð

John Dawnay

Hið Dayroll

Dautrey, Richard—(E. III. Roll) bore, or five fusils conjoined in fess sable; ARNOLD PERCY, bore the same; Jenyns' Ordinary.

Daveney v. **Avene** and **Vene.**

*****Davenport, William**—(E. IV. Roll) bore, argent, a chevron between three crosses crosslet fitchée sable—with crest; Ballard and Arundel Rolls.

Daventree, John — (E. III. Roll) bore, ermine, a fess checquy (counter compony in trick) or and azure; Jenyns' Ordinary.

Daventry, Robert—bore, at the second Dunstable tournament 1334, ermine, a fess gules. (F.) A cross in Jenyns' Ordinary.

Daveye, Philip—(R. II. Roll) bore, argent, on a chevron sable between three mullets pierced gules, a crescent of the field; Surrey Roll.

Davelers, Sire Bartholomew, of Suffolk —bore, at the battle of Boroughbridge 1322, argent, three inescocheons gules. (F.) DE AWILLERS in Parliamentary Roll.

Davereignes. See DE VALOIGNES.

*****[Dawnay, John**, 17 E. II.—bore, argent, on a bend cotised sable three annulets of the field. —Shirley.] F.

Dawney, John — (E. III. Roll) bore, per decision of Earl Percy, or five fusils conjoined in fess azure, a bordure azure besantée " per Darell (sic) Earl Percy"; Jenyns' Ordinary.

Dawtrey v. **Dautrey.**

*****[Dayrell, Richard**, of Lillingston, Bucks, c. 1200 — bore, azure, a lyon rampant or crowned argent.--Shirley.] F.

de Albini, Nigel (of whom the MOWBRAYS) —(H. I. Roll) bore, gules, a lyon rampant argent; his brother WILLIAM, chief butler of England (father of WILLIAM, Earl of ARUNDEL), bore, gules, a lyon rampant or— Harl. MS. 1481 fo. 34ᵇ.

De Alta Ripa, Geoffray—(E. III. Roll) bore, azure, five fusils conjoined in fess argent, a baston gules; Jenyns' Ordinary. See also DAUTREY.

Deane, Sir William (DE DEN), of Essex— (E. II. Roll) bore, argent, a fess dancettée gules; Parliamentary Roll.

Deane, Sir Henry (DE DEN) of Northants —bore, at the first Dunstable tournament 1308, argent, a fess dancettée between three crescents gules. (F.) See also Parly. Roll.

Deen, Sire Johan de—bore, at the battle of Boroughbridge 1322, argent, two bars sable crusily patée or. (F.); three on each bar in Ashmole MS.—in Parliamentary Roll for DEN, of Hunts, Knight (E. II.), the bars gules, and the crosses patonce.

Deane (ALYSAUNDER DE ANNO)—(E. III. Roll) bore, gules, fretty argent; Howard Roll.

Deane, Drew (DE ANE)—(E. III. Roll) bore, gules a saltire ermine; another coat—argent guttée de poix. (F.) Arden and St. George Rolls.

Dene, Sir John de, of co. Leic.—(E II. Roll —bore, argent, a lyon rampant purpure; Parliamentary Roll.

Dene, John—(E. III. Roll) bore, gules, three bars a quarter argent and a torell de sable; tricked as, barry (6) gules and argent, on a quarter of the last a bull passant gardant sable; Jenyns' Ordinary.

Deane, Robert (DENE) of Sussex—(E. II. Roll) bore, per bend sinister enhanced azure and gules, a maunch argent (also tricked with the maunch over all); Jenyns' Roll.

Deincourt v. **Deyncourt.**

De Insula, Sir John, 1297—bore, or, a fess between two chevrons sable; Nobility Roll. He signed, but did not seal, the Barons' letter to the Pope 1301, p. xxiv. See also DE LISLE and LISLE.

Deiville v. **Deyville.**

De la Beche, John, a baron 1342—bore, vaire, argent and gules. NICHOL, added, on a canton of the first, a martlet sable; Jenyns' Ordinary. F., vide BECHE.

De la Beche, Sir John, of Berks.—(E. II. Roll) bore, argent, on a bend gules three bucks' heads erased or (cabossed in Harl. 4033); in the cantell a martlet sable; Parliamentary Roll. See DE LA VACHE.

De la Bere, John—(E. II. Roll) bore, azure, crusily fitchée and three boars' heads couped or. (F.) Jenyns' Roll. One of these names took up the cross in the last Crusade 1270.

De la Bere, Simon—(E. III. Roll) bore, azure, a bend cotised argent between six martlets or. (F.) Surrey Roll. Cotised or, in St. George Roll.

De la Checker, Sir Laurence—(E. II. Roll) bore, checquy argent and azure; Holland Roll.

De la Ferret, Sir John—(E. I. Roll) bore, gules, a double-headed eagle displayed or; Holland Roll.

De la fforde, Sir Adam, of Wilts.—bore, at the siege of Carlaverock 1300, azure, three lyonceux rampant 2 and 1 crowned or. (F.) Parliamentary Roll. Sir RICHARD bore the same; Holland Roll.

De la Freign, Sir Foulk, of Ireland —bore, at the siege of Calais 1345-8, azure on a saltire or, a saltorelle gules. F.

De là Hacche, Sir Eustace, banneret, a baron 1299—bore, at the battle of Falkirk 1298 and at the siege of Carlaverock 1300, or a cross engrailed gules; Guillim and Parly. Rolls.

SIR — DALYNGRUGGE.
IN FLETCHING CHURCH, SUSSEX,
1395; 8 RIC. II.
After Boutell.

Dren deane

Henry de Don

John de Doon

Þobort Dono

Simon d' la bere

Jogn la Bore

Adam de la fforde

ffulko de la ffroyno of Jreland

mir de la Hosse

Jogn de la Hay

Henri de la Launde

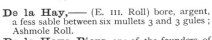

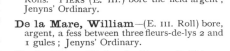

De la Hay,—— (E. III. Roll) bore, argent, a fess sable between six mullets 3 and 3 gules ; Ashmole Roll.

De la Haye, Piers, one of the founders of Swine Abbey, postea Melton modo Darcij— bore, argent three escallops in bend gules between two cotises sable ; Jenyns' Roll.

‡**De la Haye, John**—(E. I. Roll) argent, a sun in his splendour gules. (F.) 12, 13, 16, and 24 rays ; Dering and St. George Rolls.

De la Hay, Rauf—(H. III. Roll) bore, argent a ray (of the sun) gules ; Glover Roll. Called a ruell in Norfolk Roll.

De la Hoese, Sir John (or HESE), a Berkshire Knight—(E. II. Roll) bore, argent, a fess sable between three lyonceux rampant gules ; Parliamentary Roll and Jenyns' Ordinary.

‡**De la Hose, Nicholas** (HESE or HEUSE)— (E. I. Roll) bore, argent three hose (men's) 2 and 1 gules ; Camden, Dering, and other Rolls (F.) ; or and sable, in the illustration.

De la Launde, Henry—(E. I. Roll) bore, per pale gules and azure three lyons passant gardant in pale or. (F.) Segar Roll.

De la Lee, Sir John, of Herts—(E. II. Roll) bore, argent, a cross checquy or and azure ; Parliamentary Roll.

De la Lee, John, of Herts—(E. III. Roll) bore, gules, billettée argent a fess counter compony or and azure. (F.) St. George Roll.

De la Leye, Gilbert of Kilvington—(E. III. Roll) bore, or, a fess crenellée between six mullets 3 and 3 gules ; Jenyns' Ordinary.

De la Leye, Thomas—(E. III. Roll) bore, azure, three chevronels argent (F.) ; St. George Roll.

De la Ley, Wauter (LEEY)—(R. II. Roll) bore, argent, a fess between three crescents sable ; Surrey Roll.

De la Lynde, John (E. III. Roll) and **Sir Walter,** of Sussex—(E. II. Roll) bore, argent, a cross engrailed gules (F.) ; St. George and Parliamentary Rolls. Borne also by JOHN LE FITZ HENRY, ANDREW LEVAAT, and PAINE TIBTOT.

De la March —— (H. III. Roll) bore, "burulée de argent et d'azure de un menue burules ; " Norfolk Roll.

De la Mare, Sir John, banneret, baron 1299—bore, at the battle of Falkirk 1298, and at the siege of Carlaverock 1300, gules, a maunch argent (F.) ; Dering and Arundel Rolls. Sir JOHN of Oxon. (E. II.) bore the maunch ermine ; Parly. Roll. JOHN and ROBERT (E. I.) bore it issuing from the sinister chief (F.) ; Segar Roll.

De la Mare, John—(E. III. Roll) bore, gules, a leon leopard rampant argent, i.e. a lyon rampant gardant ; Jenyns' Ordinary.

De la Mare, Sir Piers, knighted at the capitulation of Calais 1348—bore, gules, two lyons passant gardant argent (F.), as also did JOHN and Sir ROBERT of Hants ; Surrey and Parliamentary Rolls.

De la Mare, Sir Geoffrey, of Surrey or Sussex—(E. II. Roll) bore, or a fess double cotised azure ; Parliamentary and Ashmole Rolls. PIERS (E. III.) bore the field argent ; Jenyns' Ordinary.

De la Mare, William—(E. III. Roll) bore, argent, a fess between three fleurs-de-lys 2 and 1 gules ; Jenyns' Ordinary.

De la Mare, Daland—(E. III. Roll) bore, azure, a bend between six crosses crosslet fitchée 3 and 3 or ; Jenyns' Roll.

De la Mare, Sir John, of Essex—(E. II. Roll) bore, argent on a bend azure three eaglets displayed or ; Parliamentary Roll.

De la Mare, Piers (c. R. II. Roll) and **Sir Reginald** (E. III. Roll)—bore, barry dancettée (6) or and gules ; Surrey and Ashmole Rolls.

De la More, Bartholomew—(E. III. Roll) bore, argent seven barrulets azure, a chevron gules ; Arden and St. George Rolls.

De la More, John—(E. II. Roll) bore, gules a cross patée (patonce in trick) and an escallop argent ; Jenyns' Roll.

De la More, Richard—(E. III. Roll) bore, quarterly indented argent and azure ; Norfolk Roll. One of these names took up the cross in the last Crusade 1270. See also ACTON, page 1.

De la More, William—(E. III. Roll) bore, sable a cross argent ; Jenyns' Ordinary.

De la Mote, William—(E. III. Roll) bore, vair, a bend engrailed gules ; another, vair, a bend gules and a label (3) argent ; Jenyns' Ordinary.

De la Penne, Sir John of Bucks—(E. II. Roll) bore, argent, on a fess sable three plates ; Parliamentary Roll. F.

De la Penre, Sir Guy (surname illegible)— (E. III. Roll) bore, or three bendlets gules a label (3) azure ; Ashmole Roll.

De la Planche, Sir James of Bucks, Kt.— (E. II. Roll) bore, argent, billettée and a lyon rampant sable crowned or (F.) ; Parliamentary Roll. In Segar the billets resemble guttée de poix, and they suggest ermine.

De la Pole, John—(R. II. Roll) bore, or, a stag's head cabossed gules, between the antlers a fleur-de-lys of the last ; Surrey Roll.

De la Pole, Michel and **Simon**—(R. II. Roll) bore, azure, a fess between three leopards faces or ; Surrey Roll. (F.) Borne also by WILLIAM, K.G., Earl of Suffolk, at the siege of Rouen 1418 ; quarterly with, WINGFIELD, K. 401 fo. 22.

De la Pole, Sir Walter—bore, at the siege of Calais 1345-8, azure two bars wavy or (F.) Not wavy in Cotton MS. ; argent two bars, nebulée azure, in Parliamentary Roll, for POOLE, a Norfolk Knight.

Jogn de la Lindo

Richard de la maro

Joan de la Lee

Thos d la Leie

Pers d la Mare

Gilbert de la Leye

Barthot de la mor

de la Planto

Jogn de la Honno

Jogn de la maro

68

Le Counts de Suffolke

Walt. Polapole

Guy de la Roce

Roger de la Warre

Vicô de la Warre

John d'la river

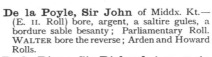

Vicô de la Vypox

Robt de la warde

Roger d. la Ware

De la Poyle, Sir John of Middx. Kt.—(E. II. Roll) bore, argent, a saltire gules, a bordure sable besanty ; Parliamentary Roll. WALTER bore the reverse ; Arden and Howard Rolls.

De la River, Sir Richard—bore, at the battle of Boroughbridge 1322, argent, fretty sable and an inescocheon gules (F.) ; Jenyns', Ashmole, and Arundel Rolls.

De la Ryver, Sir Nicholas—(E. II. Roll) bore, vaire argent and gules, a bordure azure besantée ; Parliamentary Roll.

De la River, Sir John (of Berks)—bore, at the first Dunstable tournament 1308, azure two dancets or (F.) (two bars dancettée in Parly. Roll.) He signed but did not seal the Barons' letter to the Pope 1301, p. xxiv. Another JOHN bore this coat at the second Dunstable tournament 1334 ; RICHARD bore it also ; St. George and Arden Rolls. Sir R. bore three dancets ; Atkinson Roll. H. VI.

‡**De la Roce, Guy**—(E. III. Roll) bore, or, three bends azure, within a bordure gules entoyre of fleurs-de-lys argent. (F.) Dering Roll.

De la Roch, Thomas, a baron 1300—bore, sable, two lyons passant gardant argent ; Nobility Roll ; (ascribed to JOHN in Jenyns' Ordinary). Sealed the Barons' letter to the Pope 1301, pp. xxi, xxiv.

De la Roche, William—(H. III. Roll) bore, gules, two bends argent, each charged with as many lozenges bendways azure ; Howard Roll.

De la Vache, Hugh v. **Vache.**

De la Vache, Sir John (of Berks)—bore, at the first Dunstable tournament 1308, argent on a bend gules three (" deym ") deer heads erased or, in the cantell a martlet sable. Called DE LA BECHE in the Parly. Roll, where the heads are cabossed.

De la Vach, Sir Richard, of Bucks, K.G. 1356—bore, at the siege of Calais 1345-8, gules, three lyonceux rampant argent crowned or. (F.) Ashmole Roll ; as did Sir PHILIP, K.G. 1399 ; K. 399 fo. 19. Sir RICHARD bore it (E. II.) differenced with a label (3) gobony or and argent ; Parly. Roll. See also DELAFFORDE.

De la Vale, Gilbert, de la Marche—(H. III. Roll) bore, argent a cross fourchée gules ; Glover Roll.

De la Val, Guy—(H. III. Roll) bore, or, eglettée 4, 4, 3, 3, azure on a cross gules five escallops argent ; Howard Roll.

De la Val, John—(E. II. Roll) bore, ermine two bars vert ; Jenyns' Roll. Another, ermine two gemelles and a chief or ; Jenyns' Ordinary.

De la Ward, Sir Robert, baron 1299—bore, at the battle of Falkirk 1298, and at the siege of Carlaverock 1300, vaire argent and sable. (F.) Dering and Camden Rolls. Sealed the Barons' letter to the Pope 1301, pp. xx, xxiv. Ascribed also to JOHN in Jenyns' Ordinary.

De la Warde, Robert—(E. III. Roll) bore, undée (6) argent and sable ; Jenyns' Ordinary.

De la Warr, Roger—bore, at the siege of Carlaverock 1300, gules, crusily (fitchée in NICOLAS, but wrongly) and a lyon rampant argent ; Dering and Howard Rolls. Ascribed also to JOHN (E. III.), Sir JOHN, a baron (27 E. I.), and Sir JOHN, Kt. banneret. For JOHN, second baron, see next entry also.

(De) La Warr, Roger, baron, of Isfield, signed, but did not seal, the Barons' letter to the Pope 1301, p. xxiv. He bore (E. I. Roll) gules, crusily fitchée and a lyon rampant argent. (F.) (See preceding entry.) Ascribed also to a JOHN and a ROBERT ; the latter perhaps took up the cross in the last Crusade 1270. JOHN, son of ROGER, differenced with a label (3) azure, at the first Dunstable tournament 1308 ; Nobility Rolls.

De la Warre, Sir William, knighted at the capitulation of Calais 1348—bore, gules crusily fitchée argent a lyon rampant or.

Delefend, Sir Gilbert—bore, at the first Dunstable tournament 1308, undée (6) sable and argent a label (3) gules. JOHN bore or two bars undée sable. F.

De Le Fend, Sir John—bore, at the first Dunstable tournament 1308, " argent two barres unde de sa."

De L'Isle, Gerard—(E. III. Roll) bore, gules, a lyon passant argent crowned or ; Jenyns' Ordinary. Same as WARIN DEL IDLE, whom see.

De Lisle, Sir John, banneret—(E. II. Roll) —bore, or, on a chief azure three lyons rampant of the first ; Parliamentary Roll.

De Lisle, Sire John—bore, at the battle of Boroughbridge 1322, ermine two chevrons sable. F.

De Lisle, Sir John, K.G., a founder, and **Robert**—(E. III. Roll) bore, or a fess between two chevronels sable. (F.) St. George Roll and Jenyns' Ordinary. See also (1) Sir ROBERT DEL IDLE, who bore the same at the battle of Boroughbridge, 1322, and (2) JOHN, Baron Lisle.

De Lisle, John, of Hants—(E. III. Roll)—bore, gules, a chevron between three " foyles de gletvers " gules ; Parly. Roll (leaves slipped), or, in Jenyns' Ordinary.

Delves, —— (E. IV. Roll) bore, argent, a chevron gules between three billets (delves) sable ; with crest ; Ballard Roll.

Dengayne v. **Engayne.**

Denham, Sir John (DENOM)—(E. III. Roll) bore, argent, a bend sable lozengy or cotised gules ; Ashmole Roll.

Dennardeston, Sir Peers de, of Suffolk—(E. II. Roll) bore, azure, two bars argent, on a chief gules a lyon passant (gardant in H. 4033 fo. 15) or ; Parly. Roll.

John de lo ffend

John del Jsle

Johan de Lisle

Robt d. Lile

INCISED SLAB.
JOHANNES DE DENTON,
DOMINUS DE AINSTAPLI.

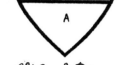

nicole de Ore   Richard de Ore   Richard Doring   Nich ffitz Doring

Dennis (——), a Kentish Knight—(H. VI. Roll) bore, argent, a fess undée gules between six fleurs-de-lys 3 and 3 azure ; Arundel Roll.

Dennis —— (R. II. Roll) bore, sable three hatchets erect 2 and 1 argent ; Surrey Roll.

Dent, William de—(E. II. Roll) bore, vert, a buck's head cabossed or, a bordure engrailed of the last ; Jenyns' Roll.

Denton, John de, of Ainstable—bore, two bars in chief three martlets. See Incised Slab, from Boutell.

Denton, Richard—(E. III. Roll) bore, gules, a chevron between three crescents argent.

Denton, Sir Richard—(E. III. Roll) bore, argent, two bars gules in chief three cinquefoyles pierced sable ; Ashmole Roll.

De Ore, Nicole—(H. III. Roll) bore, a cross gules frettée or between four jackdaws proper. (F.) Dering Roll.

De Ore, Richard—(H. III. Roll) bore, barry (6) argent and azure on a bend gules five bezants. (F.) Dering Roll.

Depden, John—(R. II. Roll) bore, argent, on a chief azure three lyons rampant or ; Surrey Roll.

Depham, Sir Stephen of Norfolk, Kt.—(E. II. Roll) bore, argent on a fess gules three lyonceux passant gardant or ; Parliamentary Roll.

Derby (Henry), Earl of (E. II.)—bore, England and a baston azure ; Cotgrave Roll. According to the 6th Nobility Roll, temp. H. VI., bore England undifferenced.

Derby, Henry "of Bolingbroke," **Earl of**—(R. II. Roll) bore, France and England quarterly, differenced with a label (5) per pale (2) ermine and (3) azure florettée or ; Surrey Roll.

[**Dering, Richard**, fil. ; de Haute, bore, SEAL, 19 Hen. IV.—argent, a fess azure in chief three torteaux :—Shirley.] F. Said to be father of the next-named.

‡**Dering, Ric.** le fiz—(H. III. Roll) bore, or, a saltire sable (F.) ; Dering Roll. The arms of DE MORINIS.

De River. See RIVER.

Dernford, William—(H. III. Roll) bore, sable, an eagle displayed argent (F.) ; Arden and Howard Rolls. Another WILLIAM bore argent two wings conjoined sable (F.), and a third WILLIAM bore three fish hauriant conjoined in triangle (Y)—(F.) ; Arden and St. George Rolls.

Derward (——), an Essex Knight—(H. VI. Roll) bore, ermine on a chevron sable three crescents or ; Arundel Roll.

Derwentwater, John—(E. III. Roll) bore, argent ("a fez et demy") two bars gules on a quarter of the last a cinquefoyle pierced of the first ; Jenyns' Roll and Ordinary ; pierced or, in Surrey Roll.

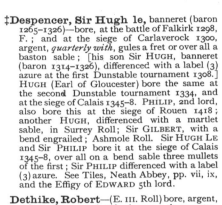

EDWARD, LORD DESPENCER.

IN THE

ABBEY CHURCH AT TEWKESBURY,

1375.

After Carter.

‡**Despencer, Sir Hugh le**, banneret (baron 1265–1326)—bore, at the battle of Falkirk 1298, F. ; and at the siege of Carlaverock 1300, argent, *quarterly with*, gules a fret or over all a baston sable ; [his son Sir HUGH, banneret (baron 1314–1326), differenced with a label (3) azure at the first Dunstable tournament 1308.] HUGH (Earl of Gloucester) bore the same at the second Dunstable tournament 1334, and at the siege of Calais 1345–8. PHILIP, 2nd lord, also bore this at the siege of Rouen 1418 ; another HUGH, differenced with a martlet sable, in Surrey Roll ; Sir GILBERT, with a bend engrailed ; Ashmole Roll. Sir HUGH LE and Sir PHILIP bore it at the siege of Calais 1345–8, over all on a bend sable three mullets of the first ; Sir PHILIP differenced with a label (3) azure. See Tiles, Neath Abbey, pp. vii, ix, and the Effigy of EDWARD 5th lord.

Dethike, Robert—(E. III. Roll) bore, argent, a fess vaire or and gules between three waterbougets azure (sable in trick) ; Jenyns' Ordy.

‡**Detling, William de**—(E. I. Roll) bore, sable, six lyonceux rampant 3, 2, 1 argent (F.) ; Dering and Camden Rolls. Called ECLYNGE or OCLYNE in Jenyns' Ordinary.

Devereux (——) bore, at the siege of Rouen 1418, argent, a fess gules and in chief three torteaux (F.) ; borne also by WALTER, 6th LORD FERRERS, K.G. 1472, see title page ; attributed to WALTER in Arden and St. George Rolls, and to Sir JOHN, K.G., baron 1384–94, differenced with a mullet pierced or ; K. 399 fo. 22. JOHN differenced it with a mullet or (R. II.) ; Surrey Roll.

Devereux, John (E. III. Roll), and **Sir William**, of Cheshire—bore, the reverse *i.e.* gules, a fess argent, in chief three plates ; Ashmole, Glover and Parliamentary Rolls ; besants in Harl. MS. 4033 fo. 49b, probably an error for the first coat.

Hue le de Espenser   Hue le Despenser

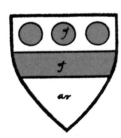

witt de Dornsford   witt d Derneford   witt d Doenford   Witt de Detling   mon Devereux

Le Sire de Deyncourt

Edmond Deyncourte

Hue denacurt

Ansel de wile

Jorn de De Euyle

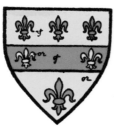

Johan de Ejuile

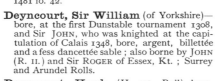

Robert Dinant

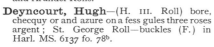

Geoff de Dinaunt

Devonshire, Earl of. See COURTENAY and REDVERS.

Deyncourt, Sir Edmund, baron, 1299—bore, at the battle of Falkirk 1298, azure, billettée and a fess dancettée or (F.)—sealed the Barons' letter to the Pope 1301, pp. xviii, xxiv—his sons EDMUND and JOHN bore the same at the siege of Carlaverock 1300, and also WILLIAM, baron, (1310) in Nobility Roll, and Sir HENRY, baron, at the siege of Calais 1348. Le Sr DAYNCOURTE bore them at the siege of Rouen 1418; Sir JOHN, baron (1 E. II. 1308), and Sir JOHN, banneret, bore the same; Parliamentary and Arundel Rolls. WILLIAM, brother of EDMUND of Granaby, differenced with a baston gobony argent and gules; Harl. MS. 1481 fo. 42.

Deyncourt, Sir William (of Yorkshire)—bore, at the first Dunstable tournament 1308, and Sir JOHN, who was knighted at the capitulation of Calais 1348, bore, argent, billettée and a fess dancettée sable; also borne by JOHN (R. II.) and Sir ROGER of Essex, Kt.; Surrey and Arundel Rolls.

Deyncourt, Hugh—(H. III. Roll) bore, chequy or and azure on a fess gules three roses argent; St. George Roll—buckles (F.) in Harl. MS. 6137 fo. 78ᵇ.

Deyncourt, Raf—(H. III. Roll) bore, gules, billettée and a fess dancettée or; Arden and St. George Rolls.

Deyncourt, Sir William—(E. I. Roll) bore, ermine a fess dancettée sable; a note in Jenyns' Ordinary, an earlier coat than that of, argent billettée dansey sable. See Sir WILLIAM above.

Deyvill, Sir John—bore, at the battle of Falkirk 1298, or, a fess gules, florettée counterchanged—3, 3, 2, 1—3, 2, 1 (F.) 2, 2, 2. Borne also by ROBERT; Jenyns' Ordinary.

Deyvill, Roger—(E. III. Roll) bore, or, a fess sable, florettée counterchanged; Jenyns' Ordinary.

Deyvile, Sir John, banneret—bore, at the battle of Boroughbridge 1322, gules, florettée and a lyon rampant argent. (F.) Parliamentary Roll.

‡**Deyvile, Ansele** (DE VILE)—(H. III. Roll) bore, argent a fess between six mullets (6) pierced gules; (F.) Dering Roll; three pierced mullets (5) in chief only, in Ashmole MS.

Dichant, John and **Robert**—(E. III. Roll) bore, ermine two gemelles and a chief gules—tricked as two bars cotised; Jenyns' Roll and Ordinary.

*Digby, Sir John de,** of co. Leicester—(E. II. Roll) bore, azure, a fleur-de-lys argent; Parliamentary Roll.

Digges (——), a Kentish Knight—(H. VI. Roll) bore, gules, on a cross argent five eaglets displayed sable; Arundel Roll.

Dinant, Sire Oliver, banneret, a baron 1295—bore, gules, five fusils conjoined in fess ermine; Nobility Roll; ascribed to another OLIVER (‡) in Dering Roll; blazoned also as a fess dancettée, a fess of fusils and a fess fusily—four lozenges conjoined in Parliamentary Roll. ROBERT bore 3 escallops in chief ermine; Howard Roll. Another ROBERT (‡) bore the fess between four escallops 3 and 1 ermine. (F.) Dering Roll.

Dinant, Roillans de—(H. III. Roll) bore, gules five fusils conjoined in fess between six roundles ermine; Howard Roll.

Dinant, Geoffrey de—(H. III. Roll) bore, gules, crusily or five fusils conjoined ermine. (F.) St. George Roll.

Dinawesbran, Sr. (——) **de**—(H. III. Roll) bore, azure, crusily an orle or; Arden Roll.

Dinham v. **Dynham.**

Disney, William—(R. II. Roll) bore, argent, three lyons passant in pale gules; Surrey and Cotgrave Rolls.

*[**Disney, Sir William** (H. III.)—bore, argent, on a fess gules three fleurs-de-lys or. Shirley.] F. See Monumental Slab.

D'Obehale v. **Obehale.**

Dockseye, Sir Richard de, of Salop—(E. II. Roll) bore, a lyon rampant azure, a baston gobony or and gules; Parliamentary Roll.

*[**Dod, Hugo,** of Cloverly, Salop (H. IV.)—bore, argent a fess gules between two cotises wavy sable. DOD of Edge bore, three crescents or, on the fess.—Shirley.] F.

Doddingsells, John (v. ODINGSELLS)—(R. II. Roll) bore, argent, a fess gules; Surrey Roll.

Dodingsells, Sir John (v. ODINGSELLS), banneret—bore, at the first Dunstable tournament 1308, argent, a fess and in the dexter chief point a mullet (6) gules; Parliamentary Roll. (—— ODINGSELLS, le filz, differenced with a label azure, at the second Dunstable tournament 1334); borne also (F.) by HUGH (E. I.) and RALF (E. III.) in Jenyns' Ordinary. Another HUGH and WILLIAM of Long Ichendon, bore two mullets (6) in chief (F.) Jenyns' Ordinary and Segar Roll; spur-rowells in Dering Roll, but in the Ashmole Copy the fess is between three spur-rowells.

Dodingsells, Nicolas (v. ODINGSELLS) (f WILLIAM)—(H. III. Roll) bore, argent on a fess gules three escallops or in chief two spur-rowells of the second. (F.) St. George Roll; the fess between three spur-rowells, in Harl. MS. 1481 fo. 87ᵇ.

MONUMENTAL SLAB.
—— DISNEY,
IN KINGERBY CHURCH,
LINCOLNSHIRE, C. 1350.
After Boutell.

will Disney

Hugo Dod

Hue do Oddingcol

will do Oddingcolod

Nicol d. Oddiggeseles

jon de dointon

H Dolerd

Joan. d. Domare

william Drope

Or Dronsfield

Jo Drokesford

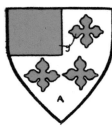

will Dryby

Dointon, John de—(H. III. Roll) bore, azure two trumpets (*vel* hautboys) pileways or. (F.) Arden and St. George Rolls.

Dokesworth, Sir John, of co. Cambridge —(E. II. Roll) bore, azure, a cross between four lyonceux rampant argent ; Parl. Roll.

Dolerd, Sir H.—(H. VI. Roll) bore, gules, two flaunches (voyderis anabelees) argent, a bordure sable ; Atkinson Roll. F.

Domare, John de (?DONMARE)—(H. II. Roll) bore, azure, billettée and a crescent or. (F.) St. George Roll.

Donneworthe, Robert de—(E. I. Roll) bore, gules a cross argent between four besants. (F.) Segar Roll.

Dordant, Sir John, fell at the siege of Calais 1348—bore, per fess indented azure and argent a pipe gules.

Dovedale, Sir John (or DE UVEDALE), of Surrey or Sussex—(E. II. Roll) bore, argent a cross moline gules in trick, blasoned, recercelée ; Parliamentary and Jenyns' Rolls. THOMAS bore it (E. III. Roll) *quarterly with,* azure fretty or ; Jenyns' Roll.

Dovre, Richard de—(H. III. Roll) bore, gules, two leopards (*i.e.* lyons) passant or ; Glover Roll.

Doyley, John—(E. III. Roll) bore, or, two bends gules ; Jenyns' Ordinary.

Draicott, Richard de, baron—bore, 1297, paly (6) argent and gules a bend ermine ; 1st Nobility Roll. BERTRAM took up the cross in the last Crusade 1270.

Drayton, Sire Symon de—bore, at the battle of Boroughbridge 1322, argent a cross engrélé gules. F.

[**Drewe, William,** of Orcheston, Devon, *c.* 1300—bore, ermine a lyon passant gules— Shirley.] F.

Drewell, Sir John (or DURWEL), of Bucks —(E. II. Roll) bore, quarterly argent and sable, in the first a crescent gules ; Parl. Roll.

Driffield, William, of the Wold—(E. III. Roll) bore, argent, a chevron between three lyons' heads erased sable ; Jenyns' Roll.

Drokenesford, John de (DROCHFORD)— bore, at the battle of Falkirk 1298, quarterly or and azure (4) roses counterchanged (F.) ; Keeper of the Wardrobe, Bishop of Bath and Wells 1309-29.

Dronsfield, Christopher—(E. II. Roll) bore, gules, two bastons couped in " guise du chevron " or, tricked, gules a chevron raguly fracted in the centre argent (F.) ; Jenyns' Roll.

Drummond, Sir John, of Inchmahome, 1301—bore, three bars wavy. See Monumental Slab. He was taken prisoner in the Scottish wars, his lands were conferred on Sir Edmund Hastings, who signed the Barons' letter to the Pope 1301, and sealed it with this Sir John's seal, p. xxii. See *post* 107.

Drury (——) a Knight—(H. VI. Roll) bore, argent on a chief vert two mullets or ; Arundel Roll. Mullets pierced in Ashmole Roll ; NICHOLAS of Saxham. Suff. bore a cross Tau between the mullets ; Harl. MS. 1481 fo. 84.

Dryby, William—(E. II. Roll) bore, argent, three quartrefoyles and a quarter gules—tricked argent three cinquefoyles pierced and a quarter gules ; Jenyns' Roll.

Dryland (——) a Kentish Knight—(H. VI. Roll) bore, gules guttée d'eau, on a fess undée (nebulée) argent an ermine spot ; Arundel Roll.

SIR JOHN DRUMMOND.
IN THE CHOIR OF INCHMAHOME.
OB. 1301.
After Drummond.

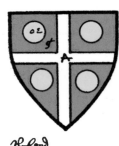

Robert de Donewort

Symon Drayton

Patrie de Dunbar ff itz le Conte

malte de Donstanville

Jon Durenasval

Emon Durosmo

piers of Dutton

Du Bois, James. See BOYS.

Duckinfield —— (R. II. Roll) bore, argent, a cross voided sable, *quarterly with*, argent six annulets 3 and 3 gules, for PLECY; Surrey Roll.

Dunbar, Patrick, Earl of—bore, at the battle of Falkirk 1298, gules, a lyon rampant argent, a bordure of the second charged with roses of the first; he bore this also at the siege of Carlaverock 1300, when he was styled "Conte de Laonis" (Lothian); at the same siege his son PATRICK differenced the arms with a label (3) gules (F.); though according to NICOLAS a blue label of 5 points; most of the Rolls blazon the roses (fraises) as cinquefoyles. The bordure is omitted from the Norfolk Roll.

‡**Dunstanville, Walter de**—(H. III. Roll) bore, argent, fretty (6) gules, on a quarter of the second a lyon passant gardant or (F.); Dering, Glover, and Howard Rolls.

Dunsta(n)ville, Sir Robert, K.G.—(R. II.) bore, argent a fret gules within a bordure engrailed sable, over all on a canton of the second a lyon passant or; K. 399 fo. 30. This K.G. is doubtful.

Dunyton, Reynald de—(E. III. Roll) bore, argent three crosses moline gules—fer-de-moline in trick; Jenyns' Ordinary.

Durace v. **Derace, le Conte**—(E. III. Roll) bore, gules, three palets vair, on a chief or a demi fleur-de-lys issuant sable; Jenyns' Ordinary.

Duresme, Sir Emon (or GELEM) of Essex—(E. III. Roll) bore, argent on a cross of St. George (gules) five fleurs-de-lys or; Parliamentary Roll and Jenyns' Ordinary; six fleurs-de-lys in Ashmole Roll. F.

A TOURNAMENT, CIRCA 1500; BRITISH MUSEUM, ADD. MS. 24,098.

Durevassal, John (DURON-ASPAL)—(H. III. Roll) bore, vert, three fleurs-de-lys or (F.); Arden and St. George Rolls. The field also azure in the latter roll.

Durwell v. **Drewell.**

Dutton, Laurence de—(R. II. Roll) bore, argent *quarterly with*, gules a fret or; Surrey Roll (F.); ascribed to Sir PIERS in the Atkinson Roll. See also ALAYN DE ELLESFELD.

*[**Dykes, William de,** of Dovenby in Cumberland (E. III.)—bore, or, three cinquefoyles sable; Shirley.] F.

Dyk(e)s, William de—(R. II. Roll) bore, argent, a fess vaire or and gules between three water-bougets sable; Surrey Roll. F.

*[**Dymoke, John**—(R. II. Roll) bore, sable, two lyonceux passant in pale argent crowned or; Surrey Roll and Jenyns' Ordinary. F.

Dymot, Sir David, of co. Lanc.—(E. II. Roll) bore, gules, on a chief or a lyon passant sable (another of the field); Parliamentary Roll.

Dyne, Sir John of Oxon—(E. II. Roll) bore, or a fess sable; Parliamentary Roll.

Dynham, Sir Oliver, knighted at the capitulation of Calais 1348—bore, gules, four fusils conjoined in fess ermine, a bordure engrailed argent (F.) JOHN bore the arms without the bordure; Surrey Roll and Jenyns' Ordinary. Sometimes five fusils and sometimes ermines.

Dynham, Oliver de—(E. III. Roll) bore, gules, three bezants; Jenyns' Ordinary.

Dyve (——) a Suffolk Knight—(H. VI. Roll) bore, gules, a chevron between three dyvers sable, the breasts argent; Arundel Roll. F.

will de Dykes

will. de Dykes

John Dymoke

Oliver Dingam

Dyve

FROM THE HASTINGS BRASS IN ELSING CHURCH.

"Here they gave the King's Crown to Harold." His Coronation. After the Bayeux Tapestry.

— E —

Henry Eam

Wm de Echingham

Ric Edgcumbe

Rob Edenham

Ric de Egebaston

Edwardes of Kilhendro

John Dongayno

will Elmodon

[Eam, Sir Henry, K.G., a founder—bore, or, a fess sable, issuant therefrom a demi-lyon rampant gules; K. 398 fo. 28. F.]

Eccleshall, Sir Robert de—(E. II. Roll) bore, gules, a bend between six martlets 3 and 3 argent; another sable and or; Parliamentary Roll.

Echebaston, Sir Richard (or ASHEBASTON). See EDGEBASTON.

Echingham, William de, a baron, 8 E. II. —(E. I. Roll) bore, azure fretty argent. (F.) Camden Roll. Borne also at the siege of Rouen 1418. Ascribed also to another WILLIAM(‡) in the Dering Roll.

Echingham, Sir Robert de, of Kent— (E. II. Roll) bore, azure, fretty argent, a bordure indented or; Parliamentary and Ashmole Rolls. Le Sir DE E. bore the bordure engrailed in Jenyns' Ordinary.

Eclynge, William de (or OCLYNE)—(E. III. Roll) bore, sable, six lyonceux rampant argent; Jenyns' Ordinary. Called DETLING in the Camden Roll.

Eden (——), a Suffolk Knight – (H. VI. Roll) bore, azure, a chevron between three close helmets or; Arundel Roll.

Edenham, Robert, of Swaledale—(E. II. Roll) bore, azure, on a bend gules three dolphins embowed argent. (F.) Jenyns' Roll.

*[Edgcumbe, Richard, 1292 –bore, gules, on a bend ermine cotised or, three boars' heads couped argent.—Shirley.] F.

Edgebaston, Sir Richard de, of co. Linc. —bore, at the battle of Boroughbridge 1322, argent, a lyon (rampant) sable, a baston azure a cinquefoyle ermine. (F.) The lyon gules and the cinquefoyle argent in the Parliamentary Roll—the cinquefoyle sometimes on the lyon's shoulder and at other times on the baston.

Edlington v. Erdington.

[Edwardes (——) of Kilhendre, Salop—bore, gules, a chevron engrailed between three tygers' heads erased argent.—Shirley.] F.

*[Egerton, Uryan, of Egerton, in Cheshire, 14th cent.—bore, MALPAS, argent (a lyon rampant gules between) three pheons sable.— Shirley.] F.

Eglescliff, Walter de—(E. III. Roll) bore, or, on a saltire azure five plates; Jenyns' Ordinary.

Eglesfield, John de—(E. I. Roll) bore, argent, three eaglets displayed gules; Jenyns' Roll.

Eglestone, Adam de, of Wilberfosse— (E. I. Roll) bore, argent an eagle displayed sable, membered purpure; Jenyns' Roll.

Ekont v. Glanvile.

Elande, Sir Hugh—(E. II. Roll) bore, argent, on a bend gules three escallops or; Parliamentary Roll.

Elande, Thomas de—(R. II. Roll) bore, gules two bars argent between eight martlets 3, 2, 3 of the last; Surrey Roll.

Ellerton, Roger de, of Swaledale—(E. III. Roll) bore, argent, a chevron between three bucks' heads cabossed sable; Jenyns' Roll.

Ellesfield, Sire Gilbert de (or ELMESFIELD), of Oxon—bore, at the battle of Boroughbridge 1322, undée (6) argent and sable (F.). (Three bars in Ashmole Roll.) Sir JOHN of Oxon bore the same; another Sir GILBERT differenced it with a label (3) gules; Parliamentary Roll.

Ellesfeld, Sir John (ELCHESFIELD) of Oxon—(E. II. Roll) bore, argent two bars undée sable; Parliamentary Roll.

Ellesfeld, Alayn de—(E. I. Roll) bore, DUTTON, over all on a bendlet sable three mullets (6) of the third (or). (F.) Segar Roll.

Ellis (——), of Thornton Rust, Yorks.—(E. III. Roll) bore, sable, three (" haches batantz ") battle axes argent; Grimaldi Roll.

Ellis, Sir Henry, of Yorkshire—(E. II. Roll) bore, or, on a cross sable five crescents argent; Parliamentary Roll. JOHN bore escallops; Surrey Roll.

Uryan Egerton

Alayn de Ellesfeld

Sir John Dollesfeld

Adam delmerugge

KING EDWARD VII.

The Dynasty of Saxe-Coburg and Gotha

AS TRACED FROM

Hengist, King of the Saxons. 434,

BY JEROME HENNINGES, 1583.

Revised with the Genealogies of the Margraves of Meissen by Dr. Gosse.

This pedigree rather suggests that one may contemplate the Accession of King Edward VII., 23 January, 1901, as a regaining of Britain by the Saxon.

HENGST or HENGIST, King of the Saxons on the death of his father, Witigislaus (4th from Woden) in 434. Upon the invitation of Vortiger, King of the Britons, to assist him against his Northern enemies, the Scots and Picts, he set sail for Britain in 447 with his Angles or first Englishmen, and landed in Thanet. It is said that he became King of Kent, and that he received the whole country of Kent on giving his daughter Rowena in marriage with King Vortiger. Hengist is said to have died in 474 or 488, father of Hadwaker (or Audoacre), father of Hattwigate, father of Hulderic, father of Bodicus, father of Berthold, father of Sighard, father of Dietrich, father of Wernekind, who was father of Wittekind, next named =

HORSA or HORSTUS sailed with his brother into Britain, and was slain at the Battle of Ailsford, in Kent.

WITTEKIND THE GREAT, last King and first Duke of = SVATANA, Duchess of Saxony, A.D. 789, warred with Charlemagne, by whom he was conquered; d. 807. | Saxony (2nd wife).

CHARLEMAGNE, or CHARLES THE GREAT, = HILDEGARDE, dau. of King of France, Italy, and Germany; d. 1, bd. 24 Jan., 814. | Hildebrand, Duke of Swabia (1st wife).

WITTEKIND II., Count of Wettin, near Halla, = JULIANA or YOLANTHA, dau. of d. 825. | Theodoric, Count of Rochiltz.

LEWIS, PIUS, d. 840. = JUDITH, dau. of Guelph, Count of Altorf, d. 843 (2nd wife).

DITGREM, Count of Wettin and Burgrave = BOSSENA, Countess of of Zörbig, d. about 850. | Pleissen.

CHARLES II., Calvus or the = HERMENTRUDE, dau. of Odo, Count Bald, d. 6 Oct., 878. | of Orleans (1st wife).

DITMAR, Count of Wettin and Burgrave of Zorbig, = WILLA, dau. of Otto, Count d. 933 (83 years after his father!) | of Raveningen.

LEWIS III., Balbus, d. 10 April, 879. = ADELAIDE (2nd wife).

DIETRICH or THEODORE, = JUDITH, dau. of Bion, Count of Wettin, d. | Count of Merseburg. about 970.

DEDO I. Von Wettin, = 953-7. Hopf, p. 150.

EDGINA, dau. of Edward, = CHARLES III., the Simple, = FREDERUNE (1st King of England (2nd d. 7 Oct. 929. | wife). wife).

DEDO II., Count of = TITBURGA, dau. of Wettin, d. 1009. | Theodoric, Margrave of Brandenburg.

DIETRICH I. Von Wettin, = 982-1009.

LEWIS IV., of = GERBEGA, dau. = GISILBERT, GISELA [An- = ROLLO, France, d, | of Henry, Duke of derson makes Duke of 15 Oct. 954. | Auceps, the Lorrain. her sister, not Nor- Emperor. daughter, of mandy. CHARLES III.]

MARGRAVES OF MEISSEN.

LANDGRAVES OF THURINGIA.

DIETRIC or THEODORE II., Count of Wettin = MATILDA, dau. of Echard, Mar- and Landsberg, d. 1034. | grave of Misnia or Meissen.

CHARLES, made Duke of Lorrain in = AGNES, Countess of Vermandois 987, d. 992. | (2nd wife).

THIMO, Margrave of Meissen, d. 1091 = ITHA, dau. of Otto, Duke of (57 years after his father!) | Saxony, on the Weser.

LEWIS I., surnamed the Bearded, made Landgrave = CECILIA, Countess of Thuringia by Emperor Conrad II., 1039, d. 1055. | of Sangerhausen.

A

B

CONTINUED ON NEXT PAGE.

CONTINUED FROM PRECEDING PAGE :—

A

MARGRAVES OF MEISSEN.

B

LANDGRAVES OF THURINGIA.

CONRAD, surnamed the Great, succ. = LUITGARDIS, sister of Emperor his cousin Henry, Count of Eulenburg (nephew to Dietrich, Count of Wettin and Margrave of Meissen), in 1127; he was invested with the dignity of Margrave of Meissen by the Emperor Lothair, who also conferred on him the Margravate of Lower Lusatia in 1136. He d. 1157 (66 years after his father!) Conrad III.

LEWIS II., surnamed the Leaper, Landgrave of = ADELHEID (2nd wife), dau. of Udo, Thuringia, d. 1123. Margrave of Stade.

LEWIS III., made Landgrave of Thuringia, with = HEDWIG, dau. of the Saxon special privileges, 1130, d. 1149. Emperor Lothair.

LEWIS IV., surnamed the Iron, Landgrave of = JUDITH, dau. of Emperor Conrad Thuringia, d. 14 Oct. 1172. III.

OTTO, Margrave of Meissen, surnamed = HEDWIG, dau. of Albert the Rich, d. 1189–90. (Ursus), the first elector of Brandenburg.

HERMAN I., Landgrave of Thuringia, = SOPHIA, dau. of Frederick V. of Saxony (1st wife). d. 1215.

ALBERT, Margrave of Meissen, surnamed = SOPHIA, dau. of Frederick, the Proud, was poisoned by one of his Duke of Bohemia. servants, 1195.

DIETRICH or THEODORE, Margrave of = JUDITH, heiress of Thuringia after her Meissen, Count of Weissenfels, only brother brother Henry; she re-m. to Poppo XIII., of Albert; poisoned by his physician, 1222 Count of Henneburg. (1st husband).

MEISSEN AND THURINGIA UNITED.

CONSTANTIA (1st wife) dau. of = HENRY, surnamed the Illustrious, youngest son, = AGNES (2nd wife), sister of = ELIZABETH, of Maltitz DIETRICH, Bishop of Leopold, Duke of Austria, d. b. 1218; Margrave of Meissen through his Wenceslaus IV., King (3rd wife). Naumberg, 1245–72. before 1262. father, and Landgrave of Thuringia through of Bohemia. his mother; d. 1287–8, aged 70.

ALBERT, surnamed the Froward, obtained the = MARGARET, dau. of Emperor Frederick II., DIETRICH or HENRY. HERMAN the long. FREDERIC, province of Thuringia for his portion; dis- 1256; to avoid assassination she fled from THEODORE. = FREDERIC the little. junior. = tinguished himself in wars in Prussia, 1265; her husband, who m. Cunigunda von Eisen- ⼂ ⼂ d. at Erfurt, 1314, aged 74. berg, one of her ladies.

HENRY, a lord without AGNES (1st wife), dau. = FREDERICK I., Mar- = ELIZABETH, Countess of DIETRICH, dwelt at AGNES. = HENRY, Duke of Bruns- land, d. at Altenberg, of Mainhard, Duke of grave of Meissen and Arnshaugh (2nd wife), Leipzic, murdered in wick in Grubenhagen. 1299. Corinthia, m. 1286. Landgrave of Thu- the Church 24 Dec. ringia, b. 1257, d. 1307, aged 37. 1323.

FREDERICK II., Margrave of Meissen and Landgrave = MATILDA, dau. of Emperor FREDERICK, the Crooked, ELIZABETH, = HENRY, Ironside, Land- of Thuringia, surnamed the Grave, d. 2 Feb. Lewis VI., of Bavaria. slain 1315. d. 1368. grave of Hesse. 1349, aged 40.

FREDERICK III., – CATHERINE, dau. SIGISMUND, Bishop WILLIAM, got Up- BALTHASAR, got ELIZABETH, m. BEATRICE, m. ANN and Margrave of Meis- of Count Henry, of Mersburg. per Meissen 1376. Thuringia, 1376; to Frederick V., to Bernard IV., CLARA sen and Land- of Henneberg; LEWIS, Archbp. of d. 10 Feb. 1407. m. Margaret, dau. Burgrave of of Anhalt. (twins). grave of Thu- she had Coburg Magdeburg. of Albert, Bur- Nurnberg. ringia, surnamed which was thus grave of Nurn- the Valiant; b. added to Saxony; berg. = 14 Oct. 1332; d. m. 1346. ⼂ 25 May, 1381.

ELECTORS OF SAXONY.

FREDERICK I. and IV., surnamed the Warlike, reigned jointly with his brothers as = CATHERINE, dau. of WILLIAM, the Rich, pur- GEORGE, dwelt at Coburg, Margrave, and with them purchased Saalfeld of the Counts of Schwartzburg. On Henry, Duke of Bruns- chased the Margravate d. unm. 9 Dec. 1401. the extinction of the Ascanian line of the electors of Saxony in 1422, the Duchy of wick, d. 28 Dec. 1422. of Brandenburg, d. 30 FREDERICK and KATHE- Upper Saxony and the dignity of Elector and Arch-marshal of the Roman Empire March, 1425. RINE died young. attached to it, devolved on Frederick IV.; d. 4 Jan. 1428, aged 61.

FREDERICK II., Elector of = MARGARET, dau. of SIGISMUND, Bishop of WILLIAM, got Thuringia, ANN, wife to Lewis II., KATHARINE, m. 11 June, Saxony, surnamed the Ernest I. Ironside, Arch- Wurtzburg, 1440–3; refused the Crown of Landgrave of Hesse, 1441, to Frederick II., Gentle; b. 22 Aug. duke of Austria; m. d. 24 Dec. 1471. Bohemia, m. twice; 1436. Elector of Brandenburg. 1412; d. 7 Sept. 1464. 1431; d. 12 Feb. 1486. d. 17 Sept. 1482 = ⼂

A

CONTINUED ON NEXT PAGE.

CONTINUED FROM PRECEDING PAGE :—
A

THE ERNESTINE LINE.

ERNEST, Elector of Saxony, governed jointly = ELIZABETH, dau. with his brother Albert for 20 years, and of Albert III., then divided their territories. Ernest got Duke of Bavaria; Thuringia, with the Electoral dignity, and m. 1460, d. 1484. Albert became owner of Meissen. This partition originated the distinction of the Ernestine and Albertine lines, still observed in the House of Saxony; b. 24 Mar. 1441; d. 26 Aug. 1486.

THE ALBERTINE LINE.

ALBERT, Margrave of Meissen, surnamed the Courageous, founder of the Albertine line; b. 31 July, 1443; d. at the siege of Groeningen 12 Sept. 1500, leaving two sons, George and Henry, ancestor of the Kings of Saxony; this line received the Electorate in 1547 on the deprivation of John Frederick I.

AMALIA, wife of Lewis, Duke of Landshut, in Bavaria, and d. 18 Nov. 1502.

ANN, wife of Albert, Elector of Brandenburg; d. Oct. 1512.

HEDWIG, Abbess of Quedlingburg.
MARGARET, Abbess of Seuselitz.

FREDERICK, Elector of Saxony, surnamed the Wise, founded the University of Wittenberg 1502, 'the protector of Martin Luther'; b. 17 Jan. 1463; d. unm. 5 May, 1525, just upon the rising of the Boors in rebellion.

SOPHIA (1st wife), dau. of = JOHN, Elector of Saxony = MARGARET (2nd wife), Magnus, Duke of Mecklenberg, betrothed 23 Oct. 1499; d. 12 July, 1503.

JOHN, Elector of Saxony on the death of his brother, 1525, surnamed the Constant, gave a total defeat to the rebellious Boors, taking Thomas Mantzer, their leader, prisoner; b. 30 June, 1468; d. 16 Aug. 1532.

MARGARET (2nd wife), dau. of Waldemar, Prince of Anhalt; m. 13 Nov. 1513; d. 7 Oct. 1521.

ALBERT, administrator of Mentz, 1480; d. 1 May, 1484.
ERNEST, Archbishop of Magdeburg, 1476; d. 3 Aug. 1513.

CHRISTIAN, m. 1478, to John, King of Denmark.
MARGARET, m. 27 Feb. 1487, to Henry, Duke of Brunswick.

JOHN FREDERICK I., Elector of Saxony, surnamed the Magnanimous, taken prisoner at the battle near Mulberg, 24 April, 1547, and deprived of the Electorate; b. 30 June, 1503; d. 3 Mar. 1554.

SYBILLA, dau. of John, Duke of Cleve, and sister of Anne of Cleve, Queen of Henry VIII. of England; m. 2 June, 1527; d. 21 Feb. 1554.

MARY, m. 27 Feb., 1536, to Philip, Duke of Pomerania, and d. 7 Jan. 1583.

JOHN ERNEST, dwelt = CATHERINE, dau. of at Coburg, d. 8 Feb. 1553.

CATHERINE, dau. of Philip, Duke of Brunswick. She remarried to PHILIP, of Schwartzburg.

---

(1) JOHN FREDERICK II., Duke and founder of the temporary division of Saxe-Gotha, deposed 1567, founded the University of Jena, 1548; d. 9 May, 1595; line extinct on the death of his son, John Ernest, of Eisenach, 23 Oct. 1638, s.p.

(2) JOHN WILLIAM, founder of the House of Saxe-Weimar, = DOROTHY SUSANNA, dau. of Frederick III. and succ. his brother in Gotha. He solicited the hand of Queen Elizabeth on her accession to the English throne, and was refused; b. 11 Mar. 1530; d. 2 Mar. 1573.

DOROTHY SUSANNA, dau. of Frederick III. Elector Palatine of Simmern; m. 15 June, 1560; d. 29 Mar. 1592.

FREDERICK WILLIAM, founder of the Altenburg line, which became extinct on the death of his grandson, 14 April, 1672.

DOROTHEA MARIA (1st wife), dau. of = JOHN, Duke of Weimar, b. 22 May, = CATHARINE (2nd wife), dau. of Wm., Joachin Ernest, Prince of Anhalt; m. 7 Jan. 1593; d. 18 July, 1617.

JOHN, Duke of Weimar, b. 22 May, 1570; d. 31 Oct. 1605.

CATHARINE (2nd wife), dau. of Wm., Landgrave of Hesse; m. 14 May, 1598; d. 19 Aug. 1658.

WILLIAM, Duke of Weimar, b. 11 April, 1598; d. 17 May, 1662; his son, John Ernest, was founder of the line of Saxe-Weimar.

JOHN ERNEST, b. 1594; d. in Hungary, 6 Dec. 1626.
FREDERICK, slain in battle in Brabant, 19 Aug. 1622.

ALBERT, Duke of Saxe-Eisenach, m. 1633, Dorothy, dau. of Frederick Wm., Duke of Saxe-Altenburg.
JOHN, b. 19 Sept. 1600; died a prisoner 17 Oct. 1628.

BERNARD, the Brave, Duke of Weimar, 'an incomparable Hero,' distinguished at Lutzen, one of the heroes of the Thirty Years' War; d. at Newburg on the Rhine, 8 July, 1639.

ERNEST, Duke of Saxe-Gotha, surnamed the = DUCHESS ELIZA-Pious (9th son) founder of the Modern House of Saxe-Gotha, and of the Houses of Saxe-Coburg-Gotha, Saxe-Meiningen, and Saxe-Altenberg (Hildburghausen), having, according to the custom of the House, divided his dominions among his seven sons; b. 25 Dec. 1601; d. 26 Mar. 1675.

DUCHESS ELIZABETH SOPHIA, only dau. of John Philip, Duke of Altenburg; m. 24 Oct. 1636; d. 20 Dec. 1680.

FREDERICK I., Duke of Saxe-Gotha, b. 15 July, 1646; d. 2 Aug. 1691, having m. 14 Nov. 1669, Magdalene Sibylla, Duke of Sar-Halle or Weisenfels. She d. 7 Jan. 1681. On the death s.p. of his descendant, Frederick IV., 11 Feb. 1825, the House of Saxe-Coburg inherited Gotha, when Saalfeld passed to Saxe-Meiningen.

ALBERT, of Saxe-Coburg, b. 24 May, 1648; d. s.p.s. 6 Aug. 1699, having married twice.

BERNARD, of Saxe-Meiningen, b. 10 Sept. 1649; d. 27 April, 1706, leaving issue by both his wives.
⊥
SAXE-MEININGEN.

HENRY, of Saxe-Romhild, b. 19 Nov. 1650; d. s.p., 13 May, 1710, having m. 1 Mar. 1676, Elizabeth, dau. of Lewis VI., Landgrave of Hesse Darmstadt; she d. 16 Aug. 1715.

CHRISTIAN, of Saxe-Eisenberg, b. 6 Jan. 1653; d. 28 April,1707, having married twice—left an only dau.

ERNEST, of Saxe-Hildburghausen, b. 12 July, 1655; d. 17 Oct., 1715, having m. 30 Nov. 1680, Sophia Henrietta, dau. of George Frederic, Prince of Waldeck; she d. 15 Oct. 1702.
=
⊥
SAXE-ALTENBURG.

SOPHIA HEDWIG, = JOHN ERNEST, = CHARLOTTE (1st wife), dau. of Christian, Duke of Saxe-Merseburg, m. 18 Feb. 1680; d. 2 Aug. 1686.

JOHN ERNEST, Duke of Saxe-Saalfeld (7th son), b. 22 Aug. 1658; d. 17 Dec. 1729.

CHARLOTTE JOANNA (2nd wife), dau. of Josias, Prince of Waldeck, m. 2 Dec. 1690; d. 1 Feb. 1699.

CHRISTIAN ERNEST, Duke = CHRISTIAN FREDE-of Saxe-Saalfeld, reigned jointly with his brother after his father's death; b. 18 Aug. 1683; d. 1745.

CHRISTIAN FREDERICA, of Coss, m. 18 Aug. 1724.

CHARLOTTE WILHELMINA, m. 26 Dec. 1705, to Philip Reinard, Count of Hanau.

FRANCIS JOSIAS, Duke of Saxe-Saalfeld = ANNE SOPHIA, dau. of and Coburg (which was received from Saxe-Meiningen), jointly until 1745. He introduced the law of primogeniture into his family 1746; b. 25 Sept. 1697; d. 16 Sept. 1764.

ANNE SOPHIA, dau. of Lewis Frederick I., Prince of Schwartzburg Rudelstadt, m. 2 Jan. 1723; d. 11 Dec. 1780.

SOPHIA WILHELMINA, m. 8 Feb. 1720, to Frederic Anthony of Schwartzburg Rudelstadt.
HENRIETTA ALBERTINE, b. 20 Nov. 1698.

ERNEST FREDE-RICK II., Duke of Saxe-Saalfeld-Coburg, b. 8 Mar. 1724; d. 8 Sept. 1800.

= SOPHIA ANTOINETTE, dau. of Ferdinand Albert II., Duke of Brunswick Wolfenbüttell, m. 23 April, 1749; d. 17 May, 1802.

JOHN WILLIAM, b. 11 May, 1726; d. 4 June, 1745.

CHRISTIAN FRANCIS, an Austrian general, b. 25 Jan. 1730; d. 18 Sept. 1797.

FREDERICK JOSIAS, an Austrian general, b. 26 Dec. 1737; d. 26 Feb. 1815.

ANN SOPHIA, b. 3 Sept. 1727.
CHARLOTTE SOPHIA, b. 24 Sept. 1731; d. 2 Aug. 1810; m. 13 May, 1755, to Ludovick, Prince von Mecklenburg Schwerin, who d. 12 Sept. 1778. =
⊥

FREDERICA CAROLINE, b. 24 June, 1735; d. 18 Feb. 1791, having m. 22 Nov. 1754, to Christian, Margrave von Brandenburg Anspach, who d. 1806.

⊥
CONTINUED ON NEXT PAGE.

CONCLUDED FROM PRECEDING PAGE :—   A

ERNESTINE FREDERICA SOPHIA (1st wife), dau. of = FRANCIS FREDERICK ANTHONY, Duke of Saxe-Saalfeld- = AUGUSTA CAROLINA SOPHIA (2nd wife), dau. of
Ernest Frederick Charles, of Saxe-Hildburghausen,   Coburg, b. 15 July, 1750; d. 9 Dec. 1806.   Henry XXIV., Count of Reuss Ebersdorff, m. 13
m. 6 Mar. 1776; d. 28 Oct. following.   June, 1777; d. 16 Nov. 1831.

ERNEST FREDERICK = LOUISA DOROTHEA   MARY LOUISA   = EDWARD, Duke   FERDINAND   = MARIA   LEOPOLD GEORGE = CHARLOTTE
ANTHONY   (1st wife), only   VICTORIA, b.   of Kent and   GEORGE   ANTOINETTE,   FREDERICK   AUGUSTA,
CHARLES LEWIS I.   child of Augustus,   17 Aug. 1786;   Strathearn,   AUGUSTUS,   only child and   CHRISTIAN, King   Princess of Wales
Duke of Saxe-   Duke of Saxe-   d. 16 Mar.   (2nd husband)   Duke of Saxe-   heir of Francis   of the Belgians   (1st wife), only
Coburg and Gotha   Gotha Altenbur;   1861; m. first   K.G., G.C.B.,   Coburg; b.   Joseph, Prince   (elected) 21 July,   child of Geo. IV.;
(K.G.), to which   m. 31 July 1817;   21 Dec. 1803,   Field-Marshal,   28 Mar. 1785;   of Kohary, in   1831, K.G.;   m. 2 May, 1816;
latter he succeeded   d. 30 Aug. 1831.   as 2nd wife to   4th son of   d. 27 Aug.   Hungary;   b. 16 Dec. 1790;   d. s.p. 6 Nov.
12 Nov. 1826,   = ANTOINETTA   Emich Charles,   George III.,   1851.   m. 30 Nov. 1815;   d. 10 Dec. 1865.   1817.
when Saalfeld   FREDERICA (2nd   Prince of Lein-   King of Eng-   d. 25 Sept. 1862.   = LOUISE MARIE
passed to Saxe-   wife), dau. of   ingen, who   land; b. 2   THERESE (2nd
Meiningen;   Alexander, Duke   died 4 July,   Nov. 1767;   wife), eldest dau.
b. 2 Jan. 1784;   of Wurtemburg;   1814. =   d. 23 Jan.   of Louis Philippe,
d. 29 Jan. 1844.   m. 23 Dec. 1832;   ⋏   1820.   King of France;
    d. 24 Sept. 1860.   m. 9 Aug. 1832;
    d. 11 Oct. 1850.

FERDINAND, Regent of = MARIA DA GLORIA
Portugal, b. 29 Oct.   Queen of Portu-
1816; d. 17 Dec. 1885   gal, 1836; d. 15
(2nd husband).   Nov. 1853.

ERNEST AUGUSTUS,   ALBERT FRANCIS   = VICTORIA, Queen of   PEDRO V., King of   LOUIS I., King of = MARIA, dau.   LEOPOLD II., King   PHILIP EUGENE,
Duke of Saxe-Co-   AUGUSTUS CHARLES   Great Britain and   Portugal, d. s.p.   Portugal, 1861,   of Victor   of the Belgians,   Count of Flan-
burg-Gotha, K.G.,   EMANUEL,   Ireland, Empress of   11 Nov. 1861.   K.G., b. 31   Emanuel II.,   1865, K.G., b. 9   ders, Duke of
b. 21 June, 1818;   Duke of Saxony,   India, crowned   Oct. 1838; m. 6   King of   April, 1835; m. 22   Saxe-Coburg,
died s.p. 22 Aug.   Prince of Saxe-   in Westminster   Oct. 1862; d. 19   Italy, m. 6   Aug. 1853, Maria,   m. 1867, Princess
1893; m. 3 May,   Coburg and Gotha,   Abbey, 28 June,   Oct. 1889.   Oct. 1862.   Archduchess of   Mary Louisa,
1842, Alexandrine,   PRINCE CONSORT,   1838, and pro-   Austria, 2nd dau.   dau. of Charles,
dau. of Leopold,   K.G., K.T., K.P.,   claimed Empress of   of Archduke   Prince of
Grand Duke of   G.C.M.G., Field-   India at Delhi,   Joseph. =   Hohenzollern-
Baden.   Marshal in the   1 Jan. 1877;   Sigmaringen.
    English Army;   b. 24 May, 1819;   4 daughters   =
    b. 26 Aug. 1819;   m. 10 Feb. 1840;   ⋏
    m. 10 Feb. 1840;   d. at Osborne,
    d. 14 Dec. 1861.   23 Jan. 1901.

CARLOS, King of Portugal, 1885, = MARIE   AMELIE,   ALPHONSO, Duke   PRINCE ALBERT
K.G., b. 28 Sept. 1863, ENTITLED   Princess of   of Oporto,   LEOPOLD,
TO QUARTER THE ANCIENT   France, m. 22   b. 31 July, 1865.   b. 8 April, 1875.
ROYAL ARMS OF ENGLAND.   May, 1886.

LOUIS PHILIPPE, Duke de Braganza,   MANUEL, Duke de Béja,
b. 21 March, 1887.   b. 15 Nov. 1889.

EDWARD VII., of the = ALEXANDRA   ALFRED   = MARIE   ARTHUR   = LOUISE,   LEOPOLD,   VICTORIA,   = FREDERICK   PRINCESS ALICE,
United Kingdom of   CAROLINE,   ERNEST   ALEXAN-   WILLIAM,   Princess of   DUKE OF   Princess   III., GER-   Grand Duchess
Great Britain and Ire-   eldest dau.   ALBERT,   DROVNA   DUKE OF   Prussia   ALBANY,   Royal of   MAN   of Hesse.
land, and of all the   of Christian   Duke of   (V.A.,C.I.),   CON-   (V.A., C.I.,   1881, K.G.,   the United   EMPEROR   PRINCESS
British Dominions be-   IX., King of   Saxe-Co-   only dau. of   NAUGHT   R.C.), 3rd   K.T., &c.,   Kingdom   AND KING   (HELENA) CHRIS-
yond the Seas, King,   Denmark,   burg-Gotha,   Alexis   AND STRAT-   dau. of   b. 7 April,   (V.A.,C.I.),   OF PRUSSIA,   TIAN of Schleswig
Defender of the Faith,   Lady of the   1893, DUKE   Emperor of   HEARN,   Prince   1853; d. 28   GERMAN   1887, K.G.,   Holstein.
Emperor of India,   Order of the   OF EDIN-   all the   1874, K.G.,   Frederick   Mar. 1884;   EMPRESS   d. 15 June,   PRINCESS LOUISE,
ascended the Throne   Garter;   BURGH,   Russias;   K.T., K.P.,   Charles of   m. 27 April,   AND QUEEN   1888.   Duchess of Argyll.
23 Jan. 1901; pro-   m. 10 Mar.   1866, K.G.,   m. 23 Jan.   &c., Grand-   Prussia,   1882,   FREDERICK   PRINCESS
claimed King next   1863.   K.T.,K.P.,   1874.   master of   G.C.B., m.   Princess   OF PRUSSIA,   (BEATRICE)
day; born at Bucking-   P.C.,G.C.B.   the United   13 Mar.   Hélène   b. 21 Nov.   HENRY OF
ham Palace, 9 Nov.   &c., &c.; b.   Grand   1879.   (V.A.,   1840; m. 25   BATTENBURG.
1841; created Prince of   6 Aug. 1844;   Lodge of   C.I.,   Jan. 1858;
Wales and Earl of   d. 30 July,   Freemasons   R.C.), dau.   d. 5 Aug.
Chester, 4 Dec. 1841;   1900.   of England,   of late   1901.
Earl of Dublin (attached   1901, a   George
to the Crown), 17 Jan.   General in   Victor,
1850; bapt.   3 daughters.   the Army;   Prince of
at St.   born 1 May,   Waldeck
George's   1850.   and Pyr-
Chapel,   mont. =
Windsor,
25 Jan. 1842.

PRINCE ARTHUR,   PRINCESS MARGARET.
b. 13 Jan. 1883.   PRINCESS VICTORIA.

PRINCE ALBERT   PRINCE GEORGE   = PRINCESS   PRINCE ALEX.   PRINCESS VICTORIA   PRINCE LEOPOLD   PRINCESS   WILLIAM II. = AUGUSTA
VICTOR   FREDERICK ERNEST   VICTORIA   JOHN CHARLES   (V.A., C.I.), b.   CHARLES EDWARD,   ALICE   GERMAN   VICTORIA,
CHRISTIAN   ALBERT, K.G., K.T.,   MARY   ALBERT, b. 6,   1868.   Duke of Saxe-   MARY   EMPEROR   eldest dau.
EDWARD, DUKE   K.P., G.C.V.O.,   (MAY),   d. 7 April, 1871.   PRINCESS MAUD, m.   Coburg and Gotha,   VICTORIA.   AND KING   of Frederick
OF CLARENCE   DUKE OF CORNWALL,   V.A., C.I.,   PRINCESS   22 July, 1896, to   1900, Duke of   OF PRUSSIA,   Christian,
AND AVONDALE,   1901, created BARON   only dau.   LOUISE (V.A.,   PRINCE CHRISTIAN   Albany, Earl of   K.G., Hon.   Grand Duke
AND EARL OF   KILLARNEY, EARL   of H.R.H.   C.I.), m. 27 July,   FREDERIC OF   Clarence, and   Admiral of   of Schleswig
ATHLONE, K.G.,   OF INVERNESS AND   the   1889, to Alex.,   DENMARK.   Baron Arklow from   the Fleet, Field-Mar-   Holstein
K.P., d. unm. 14   DUKE OF YORK,   Duchess   1st Duke of Fife,   his birth (posthu-   shal in the Army, Col.-   Sonderburg
Jan. 1892.   24 May, 1892, Admiral   and H.H.   K.T., P.C. =   mous), 19 July,   in-Chief 1st Dragoons,   Augusten-
R.N., &c., b. 3 June,   the Duke   1884.   b. 27 Jan. 1859.   burg, m. 27
1865, m. 6 July, 1893.   of Teck.   Feb. 1881.

PRINCE EDWARD ALBERT   PRINCE HENRY WILLIAM,   LADY ALEXANDRA VICTORIA, b.   PRINCE FREDERICK WILLIAM,   PRINCE AUGUST, b. 29 Jany.
CHRISTIAN, b. 23 June,   b. 31 March, 1900.   17 May, 1891.   K.G., CROWN PRINCE OF   1887.
1894.   PRINCESS VICTORIA ALEX-   LADY MAUD ALEXANDRA, b.   GERMANY AND OF PRUSSIA,   PRINCE OSCAR, b. 27 July,
PRINCE ALBERT FREDERICK   ANDRA, b. 25 April, 1897.   3 April, 1893.   b. 6 May, 1882.   1888.
ARTHUR GEORGE, b. 24   PRINCE WILLIAM EITEL,   PRINCE JOACHIM, b. 17 Dec.
Dec. 1895.   b. 7 July, 1883.   1890.
PRINCE ADALBERT, b. 14   PRINCESS VICTORIA LOUISE,
July, 1884.   b. 13 Sept. 1892.

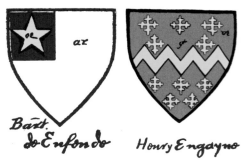

Bart. de Enfonde — *Henry Engayne*

Elmbride (ELMINDBRIGHT) ——, (E. III. Roll) bore, gules, on a chief or three tremoyles vert; Cotgrave Roll. See next blazon.

Elmeden, William—(E. II. Roll) bore, argent, on a bend sable three crescents of the first. (F.) Jenyns' Roll.

Elmerugge, Adam de—(H. III. Roll) bore, chequy argent and sable on a chief or three elm leaves slipped vert. (F.) Arden and St. George Rolls.

Elmham, Sir W., of Elingham or Elmham, in Norfolk, Knight — (H. VI. Roll) bore, argent a fess gules between three eagles displayed sable; Atkinson and Arundel Rolls. THOMAS bore it also; Jenyns' Ordinary.

Eltham, Thomas de—(H. III. Roll) bore, azure, an estoile of 15 points or; Howard Roll.

Emerike, John—(E. III. Roll) bore, barry (6) or and sable, a baston ermine; Cotgrave Roll.

Empryngham, Sir Johan de—bore, at the battle of Boroughbridge 1322, vert, an inescocheon within an orle of (am'oles) martlets argent; the field sable in the Cotgrave Roll. See also ERPINGHAM.

Eneby, Robert—(H. III. Roll) bore, paly (6) argent and gules, a bend sable. (F.) Dering and Howard Rolls.

Enfende, Sir Bartholomew de, of Middlesex—bore, at the first Dunstable tournament 1308, argent, on a canton sable a mullet or—the canton gules (F.) in the Parliamentary Roll; the mullet pierced in the Cotgrave Roll.

Enfield, Sir Henry de, 1297—bore, gules, an inescocheon within an orle of martlets or; 1st Nobility Roll; also borne by HUGH in Jenyns' Roll, and thus blazoned —gules, an orle of martlets or, a false escocheon of the same.

Engayne, Sir John de and **Sir Thomas de**—both knighted at the capitulation of Calais 1348, the latter bore, or a fess dancey sable; the former bore, gules, a fess dancey or (F.), which is also ascribed to RAFE in Jenyns' Ordinary, in which MS. azure, a fess dancettée argent, occurs for WILLIAM.

Engayne, John de, banneret, a baron 1299—bore, at the battle of Falkirk 1298 and at the siege of Carlaverock 1300, gules, crusily and a fess dancettée or; he signed, but did not seal, the Barons' letter to the Pope 1301, p. xxiv. Sir HENRY bore this also at the siege of Calais 1345-8 (F.), and they are ascribed to WILLIAM in Howard Roll and Jenyns' Ordinary.

Engayne, Eustace (DENGAYNE)—(E. III. Roll) bore, azure, billettée and a fess dancettée or, a label (3) gules; Jenyns' Ordinary.

Engayne, John—(R. II. Roll) bore, azure, on a fess dancettée between six escallops argent, a mullet pierced gules; Surrey Roll.

Engaine, Sir Nicholas de, of Essex—(E. II. Roll) bore, azure, crusily and a fess dancettée or, over all a bend gules; Parliamentary Roll.

Engham, Oliver de (see INGHAM)—(E. III. Roll) bore, per pale or and vert, a cross moline gules; Jenyns' Ordinary.

England, Kings of—See SEALS.

England, Edward I. King of—bore, at the battle of Falkirk 1298, and at the siege of Carlaverock 1300, gules, three leopards passant or—i.e. lyons passant gardant. See Tiles, Neath Abbey, p. vii.

England, Edward II. King of—bore, as Edward le Fitzroy, at the siege of Carlaverock 1300; England with a label (3, sometimes 5) azure

KING EDWARD III.

From a rubbing of the Hastings Brass, in Elsing Church, Norfolk.

Bartholmu d Ertingdone — *Rauf de Eslingo*

Robert Eueby — *T Erpinggam*

England, Edward III. King of—bore the arms of France and England quarterly—Monumental Brass in Elsing Church, Norfolk. EDWARD THE BLACK PRINCE differenced with a label (3) at the siege of Calais 1345-8; see Monumental Effigy next page.

England, Henry V. King of—bore, at the siege of Rouen 1418, France and England quarterly.

England's Royal Princes—See Bedford, Chester, Clarence, Cornwall, Derby, Exeter, Gloucester, Huntingdon, Kent, Lancaster, Richmond, Rutland, Wales, York, &c. &c.

Englefield, Sir Roger de, of Berks.—(E. II. Roll) bore, barry (6) argent and gules, on a chief or a lyon passant azure; Parliamentary Roll; argent, three bars gules, &c., in Arundel Roll.

Englethorpe (——), an Essex Knight—(H. VI. Roll) bore, gules, a cross engrailed ermine, an annulet argent; Arundel Roll. See INGLETHORPE.

Englishe, Sir John le (ENGLEYS), of Cumberland—(E. II. Roll) bore, sable, three lyonceux rampant 2 and 1 argent; Parliamentary Roll. Sir ROBERT and WILLIAM bore the same; a second trick in Ashmole Roll makes the lyons ermine. See also INGLOWE.

Englosse, Sr. (——) bore, at the siege of Rouen 1418, gules, three gemelles or, and a canton argent billety sable; Ashmole Roll.

Enneyse, Sr. (——) de, of Bucks—(E. II. Roll) bore, gules, a fess dancettée ermine; Parl. Roll.

Erde (——), a Kentish Knight—(H. VI. Roll) bore, ermine three saltorelles gules; Arundel Roll.

Erdern, (——) de—(H. III. Roll) bore, checquy azure and or, a chevron gules; Arden Roll. See also MAURUS, *post.*

Erdington, Thomas de—(R. II. Roll) bore, azure, two lyons passant in pale or; Surrey Roll.

Erdington, Sir Henry (EDRINGTON), of Warwickshire, a baron 1336—bore, azure, two lyons passant or a bordure gules; Parliamentary and Arden Rolls. ? Same as PERCEVALL DE SOMERI, in St. George Roll.

Ere, Nichole de—(H III. Roll) bore, ermine, a cross gules fretty or; Howard Roll. See ORE.

Erington, John de—(E. III. Roll) bore, argent, two bars and in chief three escallops azure; Jenyns' Roll.

Ermine, William de—(R. II. Roll) bore, ermine, a saltire engrailed gules, on a chief of the last a lyon passant gardant or; Surrey Roll. See also AYRMYN.

Erpingham *v.* **Empringham.**

Erpingham, Sir Thomas, K.G. 1401—bore, at the siege of Rouen 1418, vert, an inescocheon within an orle of martlets argent (F.), and so ascribed to Sir THOMAS of Norfolk, in Parliamentary Roll.

Erpingham, Thomas de—(R. II. Roll) bore, azure an inescocheon within an orle of (8) martlets argent, another or; Surrey Roll.

Ertingdene, Bartholomew de—(H. III. Roll) bore, gyronny (12) or and sable (F.); St. George Roll.

Eryholme, William—(E. III. Roll) bore, argent, a chevron between three martlets sable; Jenyns' Ordinary.

Eschallers, John—(E. III. Roll) bore, argent, a fess between two chevronels sable; Jenyns' Ordinary.

Hue de Eſteote   Walt. de la Eſtcourt

Johan de Eſtorling   Robt. le ſtottot

Eschallers, Sir Thomas of Cambridgeshire—(E. II. Roll) bore, argent a fess between three annulets gules; Parliamentary Roll. ESCALES, Harl. MS. 6137 fo. 18b.

Escote v. **Estcote.**

‡**Eslynge, Raufe de**—(H. III. Roll) bore, azure, a bend gules cotised or between six boars' heads 3 and 3 couped of the last (F.); Dering and Howard Rolls.

Eslynton, John de—(E. III. Roll) bore, argent, two bars and in chief three mullets azure; Jenyns' Ordinary.

Essex and Gloucester, Earl of. See GEOFFREY DE MANDEVILLE.

Estave, Sir Bawdewyn de (or ESTONWE), of co. Cambridge—(E. II. Roll) bore, sable, a cross patonce argent; Parliamentary Roll.

Estcote, Hugh de—(E. II. Roll) bore, sable six escallops 3, 2, 1 or; Jenyns' Roll. 4, 3, 2, 1 (F.) in Arden and St. George Rolls.

[**Estcourt, Walter de la**, c. 1326—bore, ermine, on a chief indented gules, three estoiles or; Shirley.] F.

Esterling, John de—(E. I. Roll) bore, paly (6) argent and azure on a bend gules three fleurs-de-lys or (F.); Segar Roll.

Estonwe v. **Estave.**

Estoteville, Sir Nicholas de, of Norfolk (E. II. Roll), and **Walter** (H. III, Roll)—bore, burulée argent and gules over all three lyonceux rampant sable; Parliamentary and Norfolk Rolls. Sir ROBERT, banneret (E. II. Roll), and ROBERT LE NORMAND (H. III. Roll) bore one lyon only; Parliamentary and Glover Rolls.

Estoteville, William, de la March—(H. III. Roll) bore, burulée, argent and gules, over all three cocks sable; Glover Roll.

‡**Estotot, Robert l'**—(H. III. Roll) bore, ermine on a cross gules five martlets or (F.); Arden and St. George Rolls. Written also SCOTHE, SCOTTO and STOTOT.

Estrateshull, Sir Nicholas de (EST'USHULLE), of Norfolk—(E. II. Roll) bore, argent, three cinquefoyles gules; Parly. Roll.

Estun (——), an Essex (?) Knight—(H. VI. Roll) bore, or, three covered cups gules, a label (3) azure; Arundel Roll.

Etone v. **Stone.**

Etton, Sir J.—(H. VI. Roll) bore, burulée gules and argent on a quarter sable a cross patée or; Atkinson Roll and Jenyns' Ordinary, differenced by a label (3) azure in Surrey Roll for — DE ETTON.

Eure, Henry de, Sir John de, and Raufe de—(H. III. Roll) bore, quarterly or and gules, on a bend sable three escallops argent (F.); St. George and Parliamentary Rolls, &c. See FITZ-JOHN.

Everard, Osmond—(E. II. Roll) bore, argent, on a chief gules three mullets pierced of the field; Jenyns' Roll.

Everingham, Adam, baron 1310—bore, gules a lyon rampant vair; Nobility Roll. Borne also by Sir ADAM, knight banneret; Arundel, Nativity, and Parliamentary Rolls, and by JOHN, in Jenyns' Ordinary; an ADAM bore the lyon crowned or in St. George Roll; EDMUND bore it charged with an annulet gules, Ashmole Roll; and THOMAS bore the original coat with a baston or; Cotgrave Roll.

Everingham, Reynold de—(R. II. Roll) bore, gules, a lyon rampant vair *quarterly with*, sable, a bend between six crosses crosslet argent; Surrey Roll.

Everingham, Adam de, of Birkin, Yorkshire, and **John**—(E. III. Roll) bore, argent, a fess azure, a label (3) gules (azure, in Nativity Roll); Jenyns' Ordinary and Ashmole Roll.

Everingham, Sir Adam, and **John** of Rockley—(E. III. Roll) bore, quarterly argent and sable a baston gules. LAURANCE bore the baston sable; Surrey Roll.

Everley, Walter de—(H. III. Roll) bore, or on a bend azure three escallops of the first; Arden and St. George Rolls. WILLIAM took up the cross in the last Crusade 1270.

Evington, Sir John de—bore, at the first Dunstable tournament 1308, argent, on a chief azure two fleurs-de-lys or. See also OVINGTON.

Ewen, John, an Essex Knight—(H. VI. Roll) bore, sable a chevron between three fleurs-de-lys or; Arundel Roll.

Exeter, Duke of, THOMAS BEAUFORT, K.G. 1400—bore, France and England quarterly, within a bordure gobony ermine and azure. K. 400 fo. 8.

Eynes, Sir (——) of Salop—(E. II. Roll) bore, argent, on a fess gules between three hounds (talbots) courant azure, as many besants; Parliamentary Roll.

Eynesford, John and **William**—(E. III. Roll) bore, gules, a fret ermine at each joint; Arden, Ashmole, and Surrey Rolls.

Eynesford, William—bore, at the second Dunstable tournament 1334, gules, a fret engrailed ermine at each joint (F.), ascribed also to JOHN in the Surrey Roll, and to Sir JOHN in the Ashmole Roll, where the trick as an illusion appears as ermine, semée of quatrefoyles gules. THOMAS bore the same differenced with a bordure azure in Jenyns' Ordinary.

Eynegrove, Walter de—(H. III. Roll) bore, ermine, a chief dancettée gules (F.); St. George Roll.

*[**Eyre, William le**, of Hope (H. III.)—bore, argent on a chevron sable three quatrefoyles or.—Shirley.] F. RICHARD LE EYR took up the cross in the last Crusade 1270.

*[**Eyston, John** (H. VI.)—bore, sable, three lyons rampant or.—Shirley.] F.

*[**Eyton, John de,** 1394—bore, or, a fret azure *quarterly with*, gules, two bars ermine.— Shirley.] F.

EDWARD, THE BLACK PRINCE.
OB. 1376.
IN THE CHAPEL OF S. THOMAS BECKETT,
CANTERBURY CATHEDRAL. *After Stothard.*

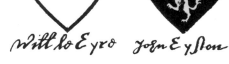

Henri D enere   wal d' Einegroue   jno. Eynoffordo   Willʒ le Eyro   John Eyſton   John Eyton

Eyre of Lindley Hall, co. Leicester, and Eyre of Upper Court, co. Kilkenny.

One of the most intelligible and best proofs of the ancient consequence of this family is that STEPHEN LE EYRE was commissioned with another person in 11 Ed. III. to take into the King's hands the Alien Houses (Priories), in the county of Nottingham.—JOSEPH HUNTER.

RICHARD LE EYRE, held the fourth part of a knight's fee at Barton, in Warwickshire, with his brother-in-law, Robert Marshall, of Brough, near Hope, 36 Hen. III. 1251-2, TESTA DE NEVILL. A namesake Richard, the crusader, having taken up the cross, was named with others in letter of protection dated at Westminster, 26 June, 1270, 54 H. III.

RICHARD, WILLIAM and JOHN EYRE—also RICHARD and EDWARD HEYRE, occur in the Agincourt Roll, 1415.—Public Record Office.

RICHARD and HUGH EYRE, gen.—with 4 archers—were summoned to serve the King in Normandy for one whole year. 21 Nov. 14 E. IV. 1474.

ARTHUR EYR (possibly Sir ARTHUR), and THOMAS EYR his brodyr, his Pety Captayn, were with the army in France. 5 Hen. VIII. 1513.

WILLIAM LE EYRE, of Hope, in Derbyshire, temp. Hen. III., held one bovate of land there, = of the King *in capite* by service of the custody (or forestership) of the Forest of High Peak, in Hopedale, died seised thereof before 4 Dec., 28 Ed. I., 1291. Inq. p.m. 3 Feb. 28 Ed. I. 1299-1300.

ROBERT LE EYR, of Hope, aged 30 in 1291, when he did homage for his lands, = had summons to perform military service in person against the Scots, 29 Ed. I. | PETER HEYR, 1319.

ROBERT LE EYRE, = of Hope. | STEPHEN, 1362. | JOHN, of Chesterfield, co. = JOAN, dau. and co-heir of Walter = HUGH TOTHILL, Derby, E. II. | Tinslow, of Tinslow, in Yorkshire. 1336.

WILLIAM LE EYR, of Hope, forester of the Forest of High Peak, 19 Ed. III. Patent Roll, died *s.p.*, 4 Nov. 1362, Inq. p.m. 30 Nov., 36 Edw. III. ; Nicholas, his brother and heir. | NICHOLAS LE EYRE, of Hope, heir of his brother, = confirmed in his lands together with the custody of the Forest of High Peak, 23 Jany. 1362-3.

NICHOLAS LE EYRE, of Hope, temp. H. 4. = JOANNA, dau. and heir of Edward Barlow, of Barlow, in Lancashire.

| NICHOLAS EYRE, of Hope, 12 H. VI.; ancestor of Nicholas, of London, 1670. | ROBERT EYRE, of Padley, in Derbyshire, in right of = his wife; Feet of Fines, 1432, 1442, 1448; d. 21 March, 1459, buried in the church of Hathersage, to which he was a great benefactor; brass in the chancel. | JOANNA, dau. and sole heir of Robert Padley, lord of Hathersage and of Padley, d. 9 March, 1463, buried with her husband; brass in the chancel. | WILLIAM, of North Lees, in Hathersage. THOMAS, and six daughters, who married. |

| ROBERT EYRE, of Padley, High Sheriff Derbyshire 1482, ancestor of Will Archer (formerly Eyre), M.P. Berks, 1734. | NICHOLAS EYRE, of Normanton-upon-Soar, Notts, where his descendants continued for five generations. | ROGER EYRE, of Holme = Hall, nr. Chesterfield, in Derbyshire, in right of his wife, buried at Whittington, painted in glass in the window behind the altar. | ELIZABETH, dau. and sole heir of Robert Whittington, of Holme Hall, cousin and heir of Henry Bakewell. | RALPH, of Offerton-in-the-Peak, m. MARGARET, dau. & co-heir of George Oxspringe, of Oxspringe Hall, in Yorks. = | PHILIP, parson, of Ashover. EDMUND, ancestor of Robert of Rayton, Notts, 1614. STEPHEN, of Hassop, ancestor of Thomas, who died 1792. |

| ROBERT, *o.s.p.* ROGER, *o.s.p.* | THOMAS EYRE, of Dunston = Hall and of Holme Hall, benefactor to the Church of Chesterfield. | MARGARET, daughter of Alured or Alfred Barwick, of Bulcotes, Notts. | GRACE, wife of Robert Fitzherbert, of Tissington. AGNES, wife of Nicholas Stafford, of Eyam. | ANNE, wife of Adam Beresford, of Bentley. ELIZABETH, wife of —— Allestree of Allestree. |

PHILIP, 1503. | ROGER EYRE, of Holme Hall, lord of the manors of Whittington, Newbold, Dunston, Rampton, = ELIZABETH, dau. of Robert Barley, of Barley, in &c., 1501-2, d. 22 Aug., 1516; will dated 7 Aug. 7 H. 8, to be buried at Chesterfield, but if he died | Derbyshire. at Lenton to be buried in the Abbey. Feet of Fines, 1503.

| ELIZABETH (1st wife), = widow of John Bosvile, of Newhall, dau. of Ralph Reresby, of Thriberg, both in Yorks. | EDWARD EYRE, of Holme = Hall and of Newbold, aged 30 at his father's death, d. 5 July, 1557. | ALICE, dau. of Robert Pursglove, and sister of Robert, Suffragan Bishop of Hull and York, Prior of Gisbourne, and Provost of Rotheram, &c. &c. &c | CHRISTOPHER, of Weston-upon-Trent. = | ROWLAND. | MICHAEL, a priest. | ANNE, wife of Randle Rye, of Whitwell, in Derbyshire. ELIZABETH, wife of —— Denman of Retford, Notts. JOAN, wife of John Bullock, of Winston, in Derbyshire. |

A   B

CONTINUED ON NEXT PAGE.

CONTINUED FROM PRECEDING PAGE.

A   B

ANTHONY EYRE, of Newbold and of Keeton, or Keveton, Yorks, ancestor of Colonel Henry Eyre, C.B., of Rampton, Notts, and of the late Vice-Admiral Sir George Eyre, K.C.B., K.C.M.G., father of the late Lieut.-Genl. Sir William Eyre, K.C.B.

ELIZABETH, wife of John Rollesley, of Rollesley.
ANNE, wife of Thomas Revell, of Carnthwaite, Carnfield.
LUCY, wife of Humphrey Stafford, of Eyam.

FAITH (1st wife), dau. of Sir John Chaworth, of Wyverton, Notts. = THOMAS EYRE, of Dunston and Holme, sometime of Amerton, all in Derbyshire, a zealous Catholic and great sufferer, temp. 6 Eliz.; sold Whittington to procure the pardon of his father-in-law, Fitzherbert; buried at Dunston, 1 May, 1593; m., 3rdly, MARY YORK. = JANE (2nd wife), dau. of John Fitzherbert, of Padley aforesaid.

MARY.   JANE = Sir JOHN ROUTH.

BARBARA (1st wife), dau. and heir of Sir Philip Draycott, of Paynsley, Staff., Kt. = EDWARD EYRE, of Newbold and of Dunston Hall, a great sufferer by the penal laws in 1648. = ELLEN (2nd wife), dau. of Thomas Lowicke, of Osmotherley, in York, md. 1610.

VINCENT, of Rossington, married Mary, dau. of Robert Fitzherbert, of Somersall.

JANE, wife of William Plumpton.

ELIZABETH, wife of John Horn.

ROGER, 'Religious,' baptized at Chesterfield-in-the-Peak, 26 July, 1612.

THOMAS EYRE, of Woodhouse in Dronfield and of Newbold, a zealous loyalist, captain in Sir John Fitzherbert's regiment of horse, raised a troop at his own expense, the first raised in Derbyshire; was in nine battles, ex parte regis; is said to have fought hand-to-hand at Edge Hill with Oliver Cromwell, then a colonel, thrice in one battle; Governor of Welbeck under the Earl of Newcastle; fought at Newark, taken prisoner near Derby in the retreat from Naseby, died in Derby Gaol 1645, from a fever, the result of neglect of his wounds. Buried at West Hallam; admon. 23 June, 1647, and again 19 May, 1648. = ELIZABETH, dau. of Robert Outram, of Woodhouse, and niece and next heir to Michal and Thomas Burton, of Holmesfield, co. Derby. A runaway match, she not quite twelve years old; 'twas said that when three sons were born, the total ages of mother and sons were under twenty-one years. Baptized at Dronfield, 13 May, 1624; m. at Barton Blount, 19 May, 1636; she died 29 Nov., 1688, the widow of Francis Lowe, of Youlgrave.

STEPHEN EYRE, a volunteer in his brother's troop: married twice.

THOMAS EYRE, of Newbold, b. 22 Aug., 1641, d. 29 June, 1682, buried at Newbold. = ISABELLA, eldest dau. and co-heir of John Catterick, of Stanwick, in Yorkshire.

MICHAEL, o.s.p.

ROBERT, of Holmesfield, parish of Dronfield, w.d. 9 April, 1680, proved 22 Jan., 1681. = MARY, dau. of Richard Washington, of Adwick-le-Street, Yorks.

EDWARD, d. 28 Nov., 1700, buried in Newbold Chapel.

VINCENT EYRE, of Woodhouse in Dronfield, a good herald and genealogist, and great friend of Thomas and Edward, 8th and 9th Dukes of Norfolk, b. 1 Nov., 1673, d. at Glossop 20 Jan., 1759. = ANN, dau. of Nathaniel Bostock, M.D., of Whixall, Salop, by Anne, eldest dau. and co-heir of John Stafford, of Bury St. Edmunds, b. 18 Sept., 1684, m. 1 Nov., 1703, d. 10 Dec., 1746.

ELIZABETH, wife of Henry Balguy, of Derwent; he buried at Hope 27 Nov., 1737.

MARY, wife of Nich. Bagnel, of Hodsock, Notts.

VINCENT EYRE, of Highfield, in Chesterfield, a solicitor in Gray's Inn, unable to practise as he refused to take the oath. Secretary to Thomas, 8th Duke of Norfolk, and Secretary and Gentleman of the Horse to Edward, 9th Duke of Norfolk; born at Whixall 23 Jan., 1703-4, married, and died, s.p., 23 Oct., 1761.

EDWARD EYRE, of London, Silkmercer, ancestor of Lieut.-Col. Eyre, of Middleton Tyas, of the late Major-Gen. Sir Vincent Eyre, C.B., K.C.S.I., and others.

NATHANIEL EYRE, of Glossop, in Derbyshire, steward to Edward, Duke of Norfolk, at Worksop, b. 25 Jan., 1713, d. 20 Aug., 1781. = JANE, dau. of John Bromhead, of Lidgate, near Sheffield, m. 1742, d. May, 1807.

TERESA.
MARY.
ANN.
MARGARET.
CATHERINE.
URSULA.
All died unmarried.

VINCENT EYRE, of Highfield, and Newbold, in Derbyshire, b. Oct., 1744, d. 7 April, 1801. = CATHERINE, only child of William Parker, of Rainhill, co. Lancs., m. 3 April, 1774, d. 2 Nov., 1840.

EDWARD, a priest, d. 10 Dec., 1777.
JOHN, a priest, d. 19 Feb., 1786, and other children died in infancy.

THOMAS, first President of Crook Hall and Ushaw College, Durham, d. 7 May, 1810, buried in the Ushaw Cemetery.

JANE, b. 5 Sep., 1839, m. 30 June, 1779, to John Wheble, of St. Mary Abbot, Kensington, merchant, of the Bulmershe family; d. 9 June, 1801.

VINCENT HENRY EYRE, of Highfield and Newbold, High Sheriff Derbyshire, b. 20 Jan., 1775, d. 5 June, 1851. = MARY, dau. of Anthony Wright, of FitzWaters, Essex, m. 1808, d. 19 Dec., 1854.

CHARLES NATHANIEL EYRE, died at St. Croix lez Bruges, 28 Jan., 1859, leaving THOS. JOSEPH, who died unmarried 17 Sep., 1866.

SARAH (1st wife), dau. of William Parker, of Kingston-upon-Hull, Yorks, m. Aug. 1811, d. 3 May, 1825. = JOHN LEWIS EYRE, Count Eyre of the Lateran Hall and Apostolic Palace in the Papal Dominions, b. 3 Jan., 1789, d. 11 Nov., 1880. = AUGUSTINE CECILE PULCHERIE (2nd wife), dau. of Armand Dumesnill, Marquis de Sommery, m. 13 May, 1828, d. 20 Feb., 1876.

WILLIAM FRANCIS EYRE, b. 14 July, 1793, married twice and had three sons.

VINCENT ANTHONY EYRE, of Lindley Hall, co. Leic., b. 8 August, 1809, d. 22 March, 1887. = JANE (1st wife), dau. of Edward Huddleston, of Sawston Hall, co. Camb., m. 5 April, 1842, d. 19 April, 1881. = HON. MARGARET PRESTON (2nd wife), dau. of Edward, 13th Vis. Gormanstown, m. 1882, d. 1887.

ANNE MARY, wife of John Errington, of High Warden, Northumberland, High Sheriff, 1865.

VINCENT WILLIAM, a priest, Hon. Chamberlain to the Sovereign Pontiff, d. 22 Jan., 1871.
JOHN LEWIS EYRE, a priest, d. 14 Oct., 1842.
WILLIAM HENRY EYRE, a priest S.J., d. 6 Mar. 1898.

Most Rev. CHARLES PETER EYRE, Roman Catholic Archbishop of Glasgow, 1878, &c.
ANNE MARIA, d. 7 Aug., 1897, m. 4 April, 1842, to WILLIAM HENRY GRAINGER, of Causestown, co. Meath, who died July 1872.

THOMAS JOSEPH EYRE, of Upper Court, co. Kilkenny, High Sheriff 1868, and of Thorpe Lee, Egham, Surrey, b. 11 June, 1821, m. 4 June, 1861, Anne Jane, 4th dau. of William Forward Howard, Earl of Wicklow, K.P., and widow of Richard, Baron Milford.

PULCHERIE, died in infancy.

VINCENT THOMAS EYRE, of Lindley Hall, Capt. 6th Inniskiling Dragoons, b. 29 Jan., 1843, d. 26 Sep., 1893. = BARBARA, 3rd dau. of Thomas Gifford, of Chillington, co. Stafford, m. 8 Sep., 1873.

ARTHUR HENRY EYRE, b. 13 Sep., 1851. = JULIA O'CONNOR, m. 6 June, 1874.

ARTHUR NEVILL.

FERDINAND JOHN EYRE, of Moreton Hall, Suffolk, High Sheriff 1893, b. 1854. = MARY, dau. of Sir H. R. Paston-Bedingfeld, 6th Bart., m. 1880.

VINCENT THOMAS JOSEPH EYRE, of Lindley Hall, co. Leic., b. 17 Nov., 1880.

REGINALD THOMAS, b. 5 June, 1882.
VALENTINE WILLIAM, b. 16 Sep., 1888.

BARBARA GERTRUDE MAY.
MURIEL FRANCES.

M

THE HERALDIC ATCHIEVEMENT

OF

THOMAS JOHN EYRE, Esq.,

OF UPPER COURT, CO. KILKENNY.

"*Here Duke William's soldiers fight against the men of Dinan, and Conan reached out the keys.*"
After the Bayeux Tapestry.

— F —

wlt ffairfax

*Bārt
de ffanecourt*

*Ġerard
d ffanecour*

*[Fairfax, William (H. III.)—bore, argent, three bars gemelles gules, surmounted by a lyon rampant sable crowned or.—Shirley.] F.

*[Fane, John (VANE), of Hilden, Kent (H. VI.)—bore, azure, three dexter gauntlets or.—Shirley.] F.

Falvesley, John de (FAWSLEY), a baron 1383—bore, or, two chevron gules; Surrey Roll.

Fanecourt, Sire Bartholomew de—bore, at the battle of Boroughbridge 1322, sable a cross patonce (flory) argent a bordure indented or—engrailed in Ashmole MS. (F.); and Jenyns' Ordinary.

†Fanecourt, Gerard de—(H. III. Roll) bore azure, billetée or, a quarter ermine (F.); Arden Roll and Jenyns' Ordinary. The field gules in St. George Roll; another argent, billetée sable, Harl. MS. 6137 fo. 56.

Fannell, John—(E. III. Roll) bore, sable a cross or; Jenyns' Ordinary.

Fannell, Sir William, of Rutland (E. II. Roll) and Roger (E. III. Roll) bore, argent, a bend gules, a bordure sable bezantée; Parliamentary Roll and Jenyns' Ordinary. Allowed to FAVELL, of Northants.

‡Farynges, Richard de (FERINGES) — (H. III. Roll) bore two (bars) gemelles and in chief a lyon passant gules. (F.) Dering and Howard Rolls.

Farington, William—(R. II. Roll)—bore, gules, three cinquefoyles 2 and 1 or; Surrey Roll. FFARINGTON of ffarington, Kt., bore the same (E. IV.) *quarterly with*, argent, a chevron gules between three leopards' faces sable; Ballard Roll.

Farmingham v. Framlingham.

Farnham, Sir Robert de, of co. Staff.—(E. II. Roll) bore, quarterly argent and azure four crescents counterchanged; Parly. Roll.

*[Farnham, John, 1393—bore, quarterly or and azure, in the first and second quarters a crescent counterchanged.—Shirley.] F.

Farnhill, John—(E. II. Roll) bore, bendy (6) ermine and azure; Jenyns' Roll.

Fastolf, John—(R. II. Roll) bore, quarterly or and azure on a bend gules three escallops argent; Surrey Roll. Ascribed to Sir JOHN, K.G. temp. H. VI.; K. 402 fo. 6.

Faucombe, Walter de—(H. III. Roll) bore, sable, a cinquefoyle within an orle of martlets argent; Glover Roll. See also FAUKEHAM.

Fauconberg, Sir Walter, banneret, a baron (27 E. I. Roll)—bore, argent, a lyon rampant azure; Parly., Arundel, Surrey, and Ashmole Rolls (same as PIERS BRUS, of Skelton). ROGER bore the lyon differenced on the shoulder with a fleur-de-lys; Surrey Roll.

Fauconberg, John—bore, at the second Dunstable tournament 1334, argent, a lyon rampant azure, a baston gobony or and gules. (F.) The same coat is ascribed to Sir WALTER, the baron, in the Nobility, Parliamentary and Nativity Rolls. JOHN bore the field ermine; Harl. MS. 1481 fo. 44.

Fauconberg (——) of the South—(E. III. Roll) bore, argent three leopards passant gules, *i.e.* three lyons passant gardant gules; Jenyns' Ordinary.

Fauconberge, Peres, of Ketelwell—(E. III. Roll) bore, azure, a cinquefoyle between five martlets 3 and 2 or; Jenyns' Ordinary.

Fauconberge, Walter de—(H. III. Roll) bore, sable, a cinquefoyle within an orle of martlets argent; Norfolk Roll.

Fauconberge, Walter, of Ryse—(E. III. Roll) bore, or, a fess azure, in chief three palets gules—St. George Roll, and so sealed the Barons' letter to the Pope 1301, pp. xix, xxiv; in Jenyns' Ordinary, the trick and blazon is three "peus recoupée" (piles couped). F.

Fauconbridge, Sir Henry—(E. II. Roll) bore, argent, ten lozenges (or fusils) conjoined 5, 5 barways sable (azure for WILLIAM). (F.) Parliamentary Roll and Jenyns' Ordinary ff. 21, 32ᵇ—but in folio 18ᵇ tricked as argent, two bars engrailed sable.

Fauconer, Sir John le, of Notts—(E. II. Roll) bore, argent, three falcons close, belled gules; Parliamentary Roll.

‡Faukeham, William de—(H. III. Roll) bore, argent, a fess between three annulets gules. (F.) Dering and Howard Rolls. See also FAUCOMBE.

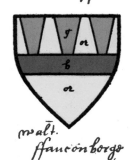

*John
ffauconberg*

*walt
ffauconborgo
de Ryso*

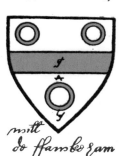

*walt.
ffauconborgo*

John ffano

*Ricd
de fforingos*

John ffarnham

*wllt
de ffauenborgo*

*wllt
de ffaukegam*

 John ffildyng

Rog ffolbridge

willt ffolton

John ffolton

SIR GEORGE FELBRIGGE.
IN PLAYFORD CHURCH,
SUFFOLK, 1400.
After Boutell.

*[**Feilding, John** (FILDYNG), of Newnham (12 H. VI.)—bore, argent, on a fess azure three fusils or. Seals E. III., R. II.—Shirley.] F.

Felbridge, Sir Roger, of Norfolk, knighted at the capitulation of Calais 1348—bore, or, a lyon rampant gules (F.), and so also did a knight and an esquire of the family at the siege of Rouen 1418. Borne also by Sir ROBERT and Sir SIMON, K.G., the Standard bearer, see Monumental Brass; Parliamentary, Guillim and Ashmole Rolls. GEORGE bore the lyon differenced with a mullet pierced argent on his shoulder. See Monumental Brass, Sir GEORGE.

Felbrigge, John—(E. III. Roll) bore, or a lyon "embelife" rampant gules—*i.e.* saliant. (Jenyns' Ordinary), and so blasoned for Sir ROGER, of Norfolk, in the Parliamentary Roll.

Feltgrave, John—(E. II. Roll) bore, or, three chevronels gules each charged with as many fleurs-de-lys argent; Jenyns' Roll. Same as Sir WM. FITZRAFFE.

Felton, John de—(E. III. Roll) bore, gules, a buck's head cabossed or; Jenyns' Roll.

Felton, Sir Amand and **William**—(E. III. Roll) bore, gules two lyons passant ermine; Ashmole Roll and Jenyns' Ordinary. Sir ROBERT and Sir THOMAS, K.G., bore the lyons crowned or—as in the next; Gloucester and Ashmole Rolls.

Felton, Sir John de, le filz—bore, at the first Dunstable tournament 1308, gules, two lyons passant ermine crowned or. Sir WILLIAM bore it also at the siege of Calais 1345-8, and Le Sr. DE FELTON bore it at the siege of Rouen 1418 [one MS. gives two lyons argent (F.) another three uncrowned lyons argent]. Sire ROGER bore it also differenced with a mullet (6) or on the cantel, at the battle of Boroughbridge 1322. F.

Felton, Sir Robert de, of co. Glouc.—(E. II. Roll) bore, gules two lyons passant ermine, a baston gobony or and azure. Sir WILLIAM bore the lyons argent; Parliamentary Roll. Sir JOHN, also of Gloucester, bore the lyons crowned or.

Felton, John and **Will de**—(E. III. Roll) bore, gules, two lyons passant argent within a double tressure flory counterflory of the second; Jenyns' Roll and Crdinary. In Surrey Roll the tressure is *or*, for JOHN.

Fenes, Sir John de—(E. II. Roll) bore, or, a lyon rampant sable; Parliamentary Roll; the field argent for the Sire (‡) DE FENES in the Dering and Camden Rolls, and the lyon rampant regardant in the latter. F.

Fenes, Sir R. and **Sir J.** (with difference)—(H. VI. Roll) bore, argent two lyons passant azure; Atkinson Roll.

Fenes, Sir Gyles de, of Sussex—(E. II. Roll) bore, azure, three lyonceux 2 and 1 rampant or, a label (3, 5) gules; Parliamentary and Howard Rolls. ROGER bore the coat undifferenced in Jenyns' Ordinary. GILES, WILLIAM, and INGRAM took up the cross in the last Crusade 1270.

Fenton, Thomas de—(E. III. Roll) bore, argent, a cross between four fleurs-de-lys sable; Jenyns' Ordinary.

Fenwick, Sir John—(E. III. Roll) bore, argent a chief gules, six martlets 3, 2, 1 counterchanged (F.); Ashmole Roll and Jenyns' Ordinary; blasoned as, per fess gules and argent, six martlets 3, 2, 1 counterchanged, in Surrey Roll.

Feringes v. **Faringes.**

Ferlington, Henry—(E. III. Roll) bore, sable, five fusils in fess or; Jenyns' Ordinary.

Ferlington, Henry—(E. III. Roll) bore, gules, three palets vair and a chief or; Jenyns' Ordinary and Grimaldi Roll.

SIR SIMON DE FELBRIGGE, K.G.,
STANDARD BEARER TO RICHARD II.,
IN FELBRIGG CHURCH, NORFOLK,
1416, 4 H. V.
After Boutell.

Roger ffolton

Sire de fenes

JE RESPONDERAY

THE HERALDIC ATCHIEVEMENT

OF

HENRY STORMOUNT FINCH-HATTON, 13TH EARL OF WINCHILSEA
AND 8TH EARL OF NOTTINGHAM.

Jogn do Ffonmick

ffolipo do ffono

Guy forro

Dounto do foxob

will fforrob

Edw. fforrob

Ffp do fforrorob

Richard Filol

will do fforrob

Jogan ffilol

Ferne v. **Cerne** and **Frene.**

‡**Ferne, Philip de**—(H. III. Roll) bore, per fess argent and gules a lyon rampant within a bordure all counterchanged (F.); Ashmole copy of Dering Roll. Called also CERNE.

Ferre, Sir Guy (FERE) of Suffolk—(E. II. Roll) bore, gules, a fer-de-moulin argent, a baston azure; Parliamentary Roll; a cross recercelée in Segar and Harleian Rolls. F. JOHN took up the cross in the last Crusade 1270.

Ferrers, (William 7th) Earl of Derby—(H. III. Roll) bore, vaire or and gules (F.); Glover, Arden, and Howard Rolls; argent and gules in St. George Roll. ROBERT (called RALF) baron of Chartley, bore the same arms at the siege of Calais 1345-8, also as Sir ROBERT when knighted at the capitulation of Calais 1348, by Sir JOHN, banneret, 1st baron of Chartley (1299), and WILLIAM (E. II.); Nobility and Parliamentary Rolls.

Ferrers, Sir Thomas de, of Herefordshire—(E. II. Roll) bore, vaire or and gules, a baston azure: Parliamentary Roll.

Ferrers, Hugh de—(H. III. Roll) bore, vair; Glover Roll.

Ferrers, Sir William of Groby, banneret, a baron 1297—bore, the DE QUINCI coat, viz.: gules, seven mascles conjoined 3, 3, 1 or (F.), at the battle of Falkirk 1298, and at the siege of Carlaverock 1300, Nobility and Parliamentary Rolls; he sealed the Barons' letter to the Pope 1301, pp. xviii, xxiv. Perhaps grandfather of Sir RALPH who differenced with a label (3) argent at the siege of Calais 1345 8. Another Sir WILLIAM, knighted at the capitulation of Calais 1348, differenced with a baston azure. WILLIAM, 5th Lord FERRERS of Groby, bore the coat undifferenced at the siege of Rouen 1418, ascribed also to HENRY in Jenyns' Ordinary; another Sir RAUFF bore them (E. III.) within a bordure engrailed argent; Ashmole Roll. The BADDESLEY-CLINTON line added a canton ermine to the DE QUINCI coat.

Ferrers, Sir John de—bore, at the first Dunstable tournament 1308, vaire or and gules, (Add. MS. 5848) a lyon passant of the first, Harl. MS. 6137 fo. 32; ROBERT of Wem, baron 1375, bore the coat with a lyon passant gardant or, in the sautreme point; Jenyns' Ordinary.

Ferrers, Sir Thomas de—bore, at the first Dunstable tournament 1308, vaire or and gules, on a quarter the arms of BOHUN, azure, a bend argent cotised or between six lyonceux rampant of the last. F.

Ferrers, William—(H. III. Roll) bore, vaire (old form) or and gules a bordure azure; Arden Roll. F.

Ferrers, William—(E. III. Roll) bore, vaire or and gules, a bordure azure, entoyre of de-crescents or; Jenyns' Ordinary.

Ferrers, Richard (E. III. Roll), **William** (H. III. Roll) bore, vaire, or and gules, a bordure· azure, entoyre of horse-shoes argent; Jenyns' Ordinary, St. George Roll, and Harl. MS. 1481 fo. 46; in the Howard and Camden Rolls the bordure is sable for WILLIAM. F.

Ferrers, Sir John and **William** of Cornwall—(E. III. Roll) bore, or, on a bend sable three horse-shoes argent; Ashmole Roll and Jenyns' Ordinary. F.

Ferret, Sir John de la—(E. I. Roll) bore, gules, a double headed eagle displayed or; Holland Roll.

Fetheir, William—(E. II. Roll) bore, gules, a chevron ermine between three plumes (feathers in trick) argent; Jenyns' Roll. Harl. MS. 6589 gives a single ermine spot on the chevron.

Fifehead v. **Fishead.**

Fyffe, Earl of—(E. III. Roll) bore, paly gules and or; Grimaldi Roll.

*[**Filmer (Robert)**, of Herst, in Otterden (E. II.)—bore, sable, three bars and in chief as many cinquefoyles or.—Shirley.] F.

*[**Finch**, alias **Herbert, Vincent** (E. II.)—bore, argent, a chevron between three gryphons sable.—Shirley.] F.

Fineux, Sir John, of Kent, Kt.—(H. VI. Roll) bore, vert, a chevron between three eagles displayed or, *quarterly with*, gules, a lyon rampant argent; Arundel Roll.

Fishacre —— (E. III. Roll) bore, azure six lucies or; Cotgrave Roll.

Fishacre, William—(E. II. Roll) bore, gules, a dolphin hauriant embowed argent; Jenyns' Roll.

Fisheade, William—(E. III. Roll) bore, or, three water-bougets azure; Jenyns' Ordinary. F.

Fisseburn, Giles de—(H. III. Roll) bore, gules, a dolphin naiant embowed argent; St. George Roll. F. Called FISSHMAN in Arden Roll.

Fytton, Richard — (R. II. Roll) bore, argent on a bend azure three garbs or, a crescent of the second; Surrey Roll. See HESKETH.

Fitton, Sir Thomas, of Gawsworth—(E. IV. Roll) bore, argent, two chevronels and a quarter gules; with crest; Ballard Roll.

Richard Filol

Gile d. Fisseburne

Jon fforoob

Robert ffismor

Vincent ffinch

will ffissoado

will ffilol

Brian
ffitz Allen

John
le ffitz Alain

will
fitz aloyne

Wa
ffitz Barnard

Fitz Alan, Sir Bryan le, banneret, baron of Bedale 1295, sealed the Barons' letter to the Pope 1301, with a strange device, pp. xviii, xxiv. He bore, at the battle of Falkirk 1298, and at the siege of Carlaverock 1300, barry or and gules (F.) blasoned (1) as barry (10) in the Nobility Rolls 1297, 1299, 1300; (2) as barry (8) at Carlaverock; these arms are said to be the same as HUGH POINTZ and to be disputed, see also Glover, Grimaldi, Howard and St. George Rolls and Jenyns' Ordinary; (3) attributed to BRYAN (‡) as barry (6) in Dering and Guillim Rolls, and (4) as, or three bars gules in the Arundel and Parly. Rolls.

Fitz Alan, Sir Richard, Earl of ARUNDEL, banneret—sealed the Barons' letter to the Pope 1301 (pp. xv, xxiv), at the battle of Falkirk 1298, and at the siege of Carlaverock 1300, gules, a lyon rampant or; ascribed to JOHN (‡) in the Dering Roll (F.); another Earl JOHN bore it at the siege of Rouen 1418 *quarterly with* MALTRAVERS, sable a fret or; fretty in Monumental Effigy. See also ARUNDEL.

Fitz Aleyne William—(E. III. Roll) bore, azure, three boars' heads erect couped paly (8) azure and or; F. Ashmole Roll.

Fitz Aucher, Henry—(E. III. Roll) bore, ermine, on a chief azure three lyons rampant or; Jenyns' Ordinary. See FITZ HENRY.

Fitz Barnard, John—(E. II. Roll) bore, vair a fess gules in chief two mullets pierced or; Jenyns' Ordinary.

Fitz Barnard, Ralf le—(H. III. Roll) bore, vair, on a chief gules a cross patonce argent. (F.) St. George Roll. See FITZ ROGER.

Fitz Bernard, Sir Thomas le, of Kent, baron (8 E. II.)—bore, vair, on a chief gules two mullets or; Parly. Roll. RAFE also bore this coat; Arden Roll. JOHN and RAFE bore the mullets pierced in Jenyns' Ordinary and Roll.

Fitz Ellis, Robert, of Newton—(E. III. Roll) bore, argent, a dancettée in chief azure. (F.) Grimaldi Roll and Jenyns' Roll.

Fitz Edmund, Athelward—(H. III. Roll) bore, argent, an eagle displayed azure on a chief of the second a lyon of the first. REYNAUD bore it or and azure. WYCHARD bore the reverse, and RICHARD bore it sable and or. Howard Roll.

Fitz Ernys (or FITZ ERMYS), **Sir Philip,** of Hunts—(E. II. Roll) bore, argent, three torteaux; Parliamentary Roll.

Fitz Eustace, Sir Thomas, of Lincolnshire—(E. II. Roll) bore, azure, crusily or, a bend argent; Parliamentary Roll.

Fitz Geoffrey, John le—(H. III. Roll) bore, quarterly or and gules a bordure vair; Glover and Grimaldi Rolls, Jenyns' Ordinary. Same as RICHARD LE FITZ JOHN. HENRY, of Horsede, took up the cross in the last Crusade 1270.

Fitz Gerald, Maurice, 4th Earl of Kildare—bore, at the siege of Calais 1345-8, argent, a saltire gules. (F.) Howard, Camden and other Rolls. Ascribed to another MAURICE (‡) in Dering Roll.

Fitzgerald, Sire Thomas, Earl of Desmond—(E. I. Roll) bore, ermine a saltire gules; Guillim Roll and Jenyns' Ordinary.

Fitz Gerald, Warine le—(H. III. Roll) bore, gules a leopard (a lyon rampant) argent, crowned or; Glover Roll.

Fitz Henry, Sir Aucher le, of Essex, baron 1310—bore, ermine on a chief azure three lyonceux rampant or; Nobility and Parliamentary Rolls; borne also by ROBERT, son of HENRY, in Parly. Roll. See FITZ AUCHER.

Fitz Henry, Conan, of Kelfield, in Yorkshire—(E. III. Roll) and THOMAS (R. II. Roll) bore, argent a cross engrailed sable; Jenyns' Ordinary and Surrey Roll. JOHN LE FITZ HENRY bore the cross gules (St. George Roll), where it is said that the same arms were borne also by ANDR. LEVAAT and JOHN DE LA LINDE. HENRY, of Sconebrok, took up the cross in the last Crusade 1270.

Fitz Henry, Hugh, lord of Ravenswath 1294, sealed the Barons' letter to the Pope 1301, pp. xxi, xxiv; SIR HENRY, knighted at the capitulation of Calais 1348; and RANDOLPH (E. III.) all bore azure fretty and a chief or. (F.) St. George and Grimaldi Rolls. See FITZ HUGH.

Fitz Henry, Adam, of Ellerton, Yorkshire—(E. III. Roll) bore, argent seven mascles conjoined 3, 3, 1 gules, on a quarter ermine a covered cup or; Jenyns' Ordinary.

Fitz Herbert, —— (E. III. Roll) bore, gules, three lyonceux rampant or; Ashmole Roll. See FITZ PIERS and FITZ REGINALD.

Fitz Herbert, Thomas—(E. II. Roll) bore, argent, six martlets and two cotises engrailed sable—tricked as argent a plain bend between two cotises engrailed sable; Jenyns' Roll.

*[**Fitz Herbert, Sir Henry** (E. I.)—bore, argent, a chief vaire or and gules, over all a bend sable.—Shirley.] F.

Fitz Hugh, Sir Henry le, banneret—bore, at the battle of Falkirk 1298, azure fretty and a chief or. His son Sir HENRY differenced with a label (3) gules at the first Dunstable tournament 1308; Ashmole Roll and Jenyns' Ordinary; azure, a fret or, in Cotgrave Roll. See FITZ HENRY.

Fitz Hugh, Sir Henry le, banneret and a baron 1321—bore, azure, three chevronels interlaced in base and a chief or; Arundel, Parliamentary and Surrey Rolls. F.

Fitz Hugh, Edmond—(R. II. Roll) bore, gules, three lyons rampant 2 and 1 or, a bordure engrailed argent; Surrey Roll. See Sir REYNOLD FITZ REGINALD.

Fitz Hugh, Jernegan, of Tanfelde—(E. III. Roll) bore, or three bars azure, over all an eagle displayed gules; Grimaldi Roll—barry (6) in Howard Roll, and (14) azure and or in Jenyns' Ordinary.

JOHN FITZ ALAN, EARL OF ARUNDEL.

IN THE FITZALAN CHAPEL, ARUNDEL, 1434. *After Stothard.*

Robert ffitz Ellys
do newton

morris le
fitz Gerard

Hugh d' filHary

willm
fitz Garide

Henry
ffitz gorbert

Hy
ffitz Horogh

‡**Fitz Humfrey, Walter**—(E. II. Roll) bore, quarterly argent and sable. (F.) Parly., Dering and Howard Rolls. Ascribed also to Sir WALTER, of Essex, in Parly. Roll. Same as HANITUNE.

Fitz John, Richard le, a baron 1295 (ƒ JOHN, baron 1264)—bore, quarterly or and gules, a bordure vair. (F.F.) Borne also by MATTHEW fil, JOHN, Parliamentary Roll, and by JOHN (‡) in Dering, Howard and Norfolk Rolls. Same as JOHN LE FITZ GEFFREY.

Fitz John, Roger le, de Evre—(H. III. Roll) bore quarterly or and gules, a bend sable ; Glover Roll. (THOMAS FITZ NICOL bore the bendlet argent in Surrey Roll.) Same as Sir ROBERT LE FITZ ROGER.

Fitz John, Mathew, D'n's de Stokeham 1297, sealed the Barons' letter to the Pope 1301, pp. xxi, xxiv, and bore, per pale (azure and gules) three lyonceux rampant (or) ; ascribed to HERBERT and JOHN LE FITZ MAHEU (see) in Glover and Segar Rolls. (F.)

Fitz John, Sir Robert le—(E. I. Roll) bore, checquy or and gules ; Holland Roll. RICHARD bore it with a chief ermine in Jenyns' Ordinary.

Fitz John, Randolf, of Woodhall—(E. III. Roll) bore, azure a chief indented (or) ; Grimaldi Roll ; dancettée in Surrey Roll. See FJTZ RANDOLPH.

Fitz John, Sir Adam de, of Lincolnshire—(E. II. Roll) bore, sable, two bars argent, in chief three plates ; Parliamentary Roll.

‡**Fitz Lee** or **Fitz Lel, William**—(E. III. Roll) bore, sable, crusily and three crescents 2 and 1 argent. (F.) Dering Roll.

Fitz Maheu, Philip le—(H. III. Roll)—bore, per pale gules and azure three lyonceux rampant ermine. (F.) Arden and St. George Rolls. See FITZ JOHN.

Fitz Marmaduke, John le, banneret (eldest son of Marm. Fitz Geoffry, lord of Hordern *vel* Hawthorne, co. Durham)—bore, at the siege of Carlaverock 1300, gules a fess between three popinjays argent (F.) ; sealed the Barons' letter to the Pope 1301, pp. xxi, xxiv ; ascribed also to THWENG of Lumley in Jenyns' Roll and Ordinary. (F.) Sir RICHARD bore it (E. II.) with a baston, over all, azure ; Parly., Jenyns' and Glover Rolls. See also THWENGE.

Fitz Martin, Nicol le—(H. III. Roll) bore, argent, two bars gules, a label (3) azure ; Glover and Jenyns' Rolls.

Fitz Michaell, Michael, of Siggeston—(E. III. Roll) bore, barry (8) or and gules, a quarter ermine ; Jenyns' Ordinary.

Fitz Nele, Sir Robert—bore, at the first Dunstable tournament 1308, paly (6) argent and gules ; borne also (E. II.) by Sir RAUF of Bucks, Parliamentary Roll ; and THOMAS (E. III.) Jenyns' Ordinary.

(SIR WILLIAM) FITZ RALPH.
IN PEBMARSH CHURCH IN ESSEX, 1323.
After Waller.

‡**Fitz Nel, Robert**—(H. III. Roll) bore, paly (6) argent and gules a fess azure ; Dering Roll three bezants on the fess in the Ashmole Copy ; three spur-rowells or (F.) in the Howard and Segar Rolls.

Fitzneel, Thomas—(E. II. Roll) — bore, argent, three palets gules, on a fess azure as many martlets or ; Jenyns' Roll. JOHN in Cotgrave, the martlets argent.

Fitz Nicol, Rauf le—(H. III. Roll) bore, gules, semée of escallops argent, a cinquefoyle or ; Glover Roll. Ascribed also to RICHARD in the Norfolk Roll.

Fitz Nicol, Thomas—(R. II. Roll) bore, quarterly or and gules, a bendlet argent ; Surrey Roll. See also ROGER LE FITZ JOHN.

Fitz Oberne, Sir Roger—(E. II. Roll) bore, three gemelles and a canton argent ; Parliamentary Roll.

†**Fitz Otes, Hugh le**—(H. III. Roll) bore, bendy (6) or and azure a quarter ermine. (F.) St. George and Camden Rolls—three bends in the Howard Roll—bendy (8) argent and azure a quarter ermine, in Jenyns' Ordinary.

Fitz Payne, Robert le, a baron 1299, sealed the Barons' letter to the Pope 1301, pp. xix, xxiv. He bore, at the battle of Falkirk 1298, and at the siege of Carlaverock 1300, gules, three lyons passant in pale argent, a baston azure. (F.) Parliamentary, Segar and other Rolls (save the Nobility Rolls, in which, as Baron of Lammer 1297-1308, he has only two lyons). Sir ROBERT, Kt. banneret, bore the same without a baston ; Arundel Roll (H. VI.) and SIR JOHN or ROBERT of Gloucestershire bore, the baston gobony or and azure ; Parliamentary Roll and Jenyns' Ordinary.

Fitz Payne, John le—(E. II. Roll) bore argent, a hawk's lure gules ; Jenyns' Roll.

Fitzpiers, Reginald (REYNALD, REYNARD or RENAUD le—(H. III. Roll) bore, gules, three lyonceux rampant or. (F.) Howard, Glover, St. George and Camden Rolls. See FITZ HERBERT and FITZ REGINALD.

Fitz Rauff, Sir Robert le—bore, at the first Dunstable tournament 1308, burulée (10) argent and azure three buckles 2 and 1 gules tongues to the sinister.

Fitz Raffe, Sir Robert, of Yorkshire—(E. II. Roll) bore, barry (8) argent and azure three chaplets gules, a label (3) or ; Parly. and Nativity Rolls ; WILLIAM bore, burulée (14) in Arden Roll. Some MSS. assign him buckles, in lieu of chaplets gules, tongues to the dexter. F. See FITZ WILLIAM.

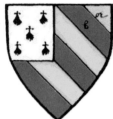

Rainand le fil' ff

Robt le ffitzrauf

Randolfo fitz Bapo do midolgam

Reynald le ffiz Reynald

Hamond le ffitz Richard

Joan le fil' Simon

Rauf le ffitz Richard

Robt le fil' roger

Robt le ffitz roger

Fitz Rauffe, Raffe, of Multon in Richmondshire, founder of the Abbey of Egglestone—(E. III. Roll) bore, barry (6) or and azure, tricked as or two bars azure, in Jenyns' Ord.

Fitz Rauff, Hugh le—(H. III. Roll) bore, gules, a fess vair; Glover Roll. WILLIAM took up the cross in the last Crusade 1269.

Fitz Raffe, Sir William of Essex—(E. II. Roll) bore, or, three chevrons gules on each as many fleurs-de-lys argent; Parliamentary Roll. See Monumental Brass. Same as JOHN FELTGRAVE, in Jenyns' Roll.

Fitz Rauf, Sire Randolf—bore, at the battle of Boroughbridge 1322, purpure a chief indented or (F.); Ashmole Roll.

Fitz Randolph, John, of Spenythorne, and **Randolph Fitz John,** of Woodall—(E. III. Roll) bore azure a chief indented or, and **Rauf** of Midleham bore the reverse; Jenyns' Ordinary. HENRY bore azure a chief fretty or; Glover Roll. See also FITZ ROBERT.

Fitz Reginald, John, baron of Blenleveny in Wales (25 E. I.), sealed the Barons' letter to the Pope 1301, pp. xviii, xxiv—bore, gules, three lyonceux rampant or; Nobility and Parly. Rolls; called FITZ RAYMOND in Arundel Roll. See FITZ HERBERT and FITZ PIERS.

Fitz Reginald, Sire Reynald le—bore, at the battle of Boroughbridge 1322, gules, three lyonceux (rampant) or within a bordure indented argent (F.); tricked engrailed in Ashmole Roll; and so ascribed to EDMOND FITZ HUGH in Surrey Roll.

Fitz Reynarde, Sir John, of Bucks—(E. II. Roll) bore, or, two chevrons gules, on a canton of the last a lyon passant argent; Parliamentary Roll. Called JACOB in Harl. MS. 4033 fo. 36b.

Fitz Richard, Sire Hamond le—bore, at the battle of Boroughbridge 1322, gules, a chevron (between) three unicorns argent. F.

Fitz Richard, Sire Rauf—bore, at the battle of Boroughbridge 1322, ermine, a chief bendy (10) or and azure. F.

Fitz Robert, Randolph (of Midleham) or RANDOLPH DE MIDLEHAM—(E. III. Roll) bore, or, a chief azure; Grimaldi Roll. See FITZ JOHN and FITZ RANDOLPH.

Fitz Robert, Sir Walter le, of Rutland—(E. II. Roll) bore, or two chevrons gules; Parly. Roll. Another WALTER bore it with a fess gules; Grimaldi Roll. See FITZWALTER.

Fitz Roger, Sire Robert le—(E. I. Roll) bore, argent a lyon rampant purpure (sable in Dering and Howard Rolls) (F.); Guillim Roll and Jenyns' Ordinary. RICHARD BALDERSTON bears the same.

Fitz Roger, Sir Robert le, banneret, lord of Clavering—bore, at the battle of Falkirk 1298, and at the siege of Carlaverock 1300, quarterly or and gules a baston sable (F.); signed, but did not seal, the letter to the Pope 1301, p. xxiv; Nobility, Parly. and other Rolls. Ascribed also to JOHN(‡), in the Ashmole Copy of the Dering Roll; same as Sir ROGER LE FITZ JOHN. See also Sir JOHN DE CLAVERING.

Fitz Roger, Rauf le—(H. III. Roll) bore vair, a chief gules, (F.); St. George Roll; ascribed also to JOHN, Baron FITZ ROGER, in the 2nd Nobility Roll 1299. See also CLAVERING and FITZ BARNARD.

Fitz Simon, Sir Hugh and John—(E. III. Roll) bore, gules, three false escocheons argent (F.); Ashmole and St. George Rolls. RICHARD, K.G., a founder, bore the reverse in Arundel and Surrey Rolls.

Fitz Simon, Sir John, of Norfolk—bore, at the battle of Boroughbridge 1322, sable, a fess (between) three crescents argent (F.); Parliamentary Roll; another Sir JOHN bore the same, knighted at the capitulation of Calais 1348.

Fitz Simon, Sir John, of Herts—(E. II. Roll) bore, azure three eaglets displayed or a canton ermine; Parliamentary Roll; four eaglets 2 and 2 in Harl. MS. 6137 fo. 13.

Fitz Symond, Richard le—bore, at the second Dunstable tournament 1334, gules, a chief or (F.); THOMAS bore the reverse in Surrey Roll.

Fitz Simon, Sir Raffe, of Lincolnshire—(E. II. Roll) bore, azure, a lyon rampant ermine; Parly. Roll. ROBERT DE WY' took up the cross in the last Crusade 1270.

Fitz Simon, Simon le—(E. III. Roll) bore, gules, three roses ermine; Jenyns' Ordinary. Another SIMON (H. III.) bore gules, three chess-rooks ermine (F.); St. George Roll.

Fitz Stevens, Raffe of Thornton Rust, Yorks—(E. III. Roll) bore, azure, three martlets or, tricked as martels (hammers with claws); Jenyns' Roll. See MATHEW of Thornton Steward.

Fitz Thomas, Thomas le—(H. III. Roll) bore, lozengy argent and gules (F.); St. George Roll, called FITZ COLOM, in Arden Roll; same arms as JOHN COGAN. See also FITZ WILLIAM. JOHN, of Wrastulingwrth, took up the cross in the last Crusade 1270.

Fitz Urse, Reginald—(H. III. Roll) bore, or, a bear passant sable, muzzled argent; Howard Roll. F.

John ffitzsimond

Rich de ffitzsimon

Rauf le ffitz roger

Simon le fil Simon

Tho le ffitz Thomas

Rog ffitz-urse

Robert le ffitz walter

fuke le fz marin

will fitzmaryn

Alayn ffitz warin

Rauf fitzwilliam

will fflemingo

John ffloyer

ar
fg
will fitzwillia

ar

Fre ffogge

gu
a
Jon ffitzwilliam

gu

Tho Folegambe

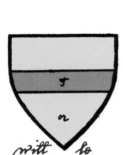

g
or
will le ffitzwilliam

Gaston de ffoix

Baldwin de ffflandord

or
g

Ric ffukeram

Fitz Walter, Sir Robert le, banneret, a baron 1295, sealed the Barons' letter to the Pope 1301, pp. xv, xxiv. He bore, at the battle of Falkirk 1298 and at the siege of Carlaverock 1300, or a fess between two chevronels gules. (F.) Nobility and Parly. Rolls. See also Tiles, Neath Abbey, p. ix. Borne also by ——, knighted at the capitulation of Calais 1348, and by Sir RICHARD, Kt. banneret in the Arundel Roll (H. VI.) also by Le Sr. —— at the siege of Rouen 1418, he probably WALTER 7th Lord. Ascribed also to ROBERT(‡) in the Dering Roll. See FITZ ROBERT.

Fitwaryn, Sir Fouke, of Whittington, banneret and baron 1295—bore, quarterly per fess indented (tricked, dancettée) argent and gules, Nobility Roll, (quarterly indented in the Parly. Roll) ; ascribed also to FOUK (‡) in Dering Roll ; sealed the Barons' letter to the Pope 1301, pp. xviii, xxiv. See also Tiles, Neath Abbey, p. ix. Another Sir FOUKE bore it at the first Dunstable tournament 1308 differenced with a mullet sable. (F.) See also WM. FITZ WILLIAM, in Cotgrave. Sir WILLIAM, baron, bore it (undifferenced) at the siege of Calais 1345-8, on which occasion Sir JOHN differenced with a label (3) azure, and so ascribed to PHILIP in the Norfolk Roll (H. III.) —reversed for Sir FOUKE in Ashmole Roll, where tricked per pale with a chief indented counterchanged—probably in error.

Fitzwarren, Sire William—bore, at the battle of Boroughbridge 1322, quarterly per fess indented (tricked, dancettée) argent and sable. (F.) Parly., Arden, St. George and Segar Rolls ; reversed in Guillim Roll. This Sir WILLIAM may be identical with the preceding Sir WILLIAM of Calais. Another WILLIAM and EUDO took up the cross in the last Crusade 1270.

Fitz Waren, Alayn—bore, at the second Dunstable tournament 1334, quarterly argent and gules, on a canton of the first a martlet sable. F.

Fitz Warren, Sir Foulke, K.G.—(E. III. Roll) and **Sir William**, a baron 1342—bore, quarterly per fess indented (tricked, dancettée) ermine and gules ; Cotgrave, Surrey and Arundel Rolls ; reversed in Jenyns' Ordinary, and in the Ashmole Roll ; where tricked per pale with a chief indented counterchanged —probably in error.

Fitz William, Sir Rauffe le, banneret, baron 1295, sealed the Barons' letter to the Pope 1301, pp. xx, xxiv. He bore, at the battle of Falkirk 1298 and at the siege of Carlaverock 1300, burulée (12) argent and azure, three chaplets gules (F.)—barry (6) &c., in the Nobility Rolls 1297-1310, and Segar Roll ; argent four bars azure, &c., Parly. Roll ; barry (10) Arundel and Jenyns' Roll ; burulée (18) in Guillim Roll. WILLIAM, of Coleston, took up the cross in the last Crusade 1270. See FITZ RAFFE and GREYSTOCK.

*****Fitz William, Sir William**, a baron 1327—bore, at the first Dunstable tournament 1308, lozengy argent and gules. (F.) Parliamentary, Ashmole and Surrey Rolls—masculée in Nativity and Parliamentary Rolls and Jenyns' Ordinary. See also FITZ THOMAS.

Fitzwilliam, Sir John—(E. III. Roll) bore, lozengy gules and argent ; Ashmole Roll.

Fitz William, Thomas le—(H. III. Roll) bore, masculée ermine and gules ; Glover Roll.

Fitzwilliam, Sir William—bore, at the battle of Falkirk 1298, or, a fess gules. F. Called FLUMAN in the Wrest Park copy of the Roll.

Fitz Wyth, Sir Geoffrey, of Norfolk— (E. II. Roll) bore, azure, three gryphons passant or ; Parliamentary Roll. See WYTHE.

Fitz W(——), John le—(H. III. Roll) bore, ermine, two bars gules ; Arden Roll.

Flamville, Sir William—(E. III. Roll) bore, argent, a maunche azure ; Ashmole and Surrey Rolls.

Flamville, Sir Roger, of co. Leicr.—(E. II. Roll) bore, argent, a maunche gules, besantée ; Parliamentary Roll.

‡**Flandres, Baudwin de**—(H. III. Roll) bore, or, a lyon rampant sable within a bordure gules. (F.) Dering Roll—bordure engrailed in Ashmole MS. The Constable of Flanders bore, argent, an inescocheon gules, in Dering Roll.

Flaunder, Sir Henry, of Flanders—bore, at the siege of Calais 1345-8, sable, fretty or.

Fleming, Sir Baldwin and **Robert**— (E. III. Roll) bore, vair, a chief checquy or and gules ; Ashmole Roll and Jenyns' Ordinary ; in the latter tricked per fess, &c.

Fleming, John, of Layland—(E. III. Roll)— bore, the arms of RICHARD GRAY (azure, two bars argent on a chief of the last) with three cushions erect gules ; Jenyns' Ordinary.

*****Fleming, John**, and **Thomas**, of Westmorland—(E. III. Roll) bore gules, fretty argent, a label (3) vert ; Jenyns' Ordinary. Same arms as RAUFE BEAUCHAMP.

Flemyng, Sir William, of Gloucestershire —bore, at the first Dunstable tournament 1308, and at the battle of Boroughbridge 1322, gules, fretty argent and a fess azure. (F.) Parliamentary Roll.

Fleming, Thomas—(R. II. Roll) bore, barry (6) argent and azure in chief three lozenges gules ; Surrey Roll. Compare this JOHN F. of Layland.

Fletham, John de—(E. II. Roll) bore, sable, three unicorns' heads couped argent ; Jenyns' Roll.

Flitwick, Sir David, of Beds.—(E. II. Roll) bore, argent, two lyons passant gardant sable ; Parliamentary Roll and Jenyns' Ordinary.

*****[Floyer, John**, of Floyer Hayes, E. I.—bore, sable, a chevron between three arrows argent. —Shirley.] F.

Fluman, Sir William—bore at the battle of Falkirk 1298, or, a fess gules. See FITZ WILLIAM.

Fogge (——), a Kentish Knight—(H. VI. Roll) bore, argent, a fess between three annulets sable ; Arundel Roll.

Fogge, Thomas—bore, at the siege of Rouen 1418, argent on a fess between three annulets sable as many spur-rowells of the field. (F.) Surrey Roll.

Foix, Gaston de, K.G. 1438-9, Earl of Longueville, and his son, JOHN, K.G. 1445, Earl of Kendal, Captal de Buch—bore, or, three palets gules, *quarterly with*, or, two bulls passant gules, a riband round the neck vert, over all a label (3) the pendants cruceiform sable, each charged (for JOHN) with 5 escallops in cross argent ; K. 402 fo. 22. See also BUCH, BURDEUX, and GRAILLY. Pedigree in Anstis' "Order of the Garter," vol. I. Introduction, page 8. F.

Foljambe, Godfrey—(R. II. Roll) bore, sable a bend or between six escallops argent ; Surrey Roll. THOMAS bore the bend or (F.) ; St. George Roll.

Folkeram, Sir Richard, of Berks—(R. II. Roll) bore, or, a bend engrailed azure ; Parliamentary Roll—a bend of fusils (F.), in St. George Roll—a bend endentée *vel* lozengy in Jenyns' Ordinary.

Folliot, Jordan, a baron 1295—bore, gules, a bend argent (F.) as did Sir Richard (of Norfolk) at the first Dunstable tournament 1308.

Foliott, Sr. Edmond or Osmond, of Lincolnshire—(E. ii. Roll) bore, gules, a bend argent, a label (3) or; Parliamentary Roll (called Simon in Harl. MS. 4033 fo. 43); another Osmond bore it, with the bend between six crescents argent; Jenyns' Ordinary.

Folliott, Osmonde—(E. iii. Roll) bore, gules, a bend argent between six increscents 3 and 3 or; Jenyns' Ordinary.

[Folliott, Richard, Ed. iii., bore, undée. See Monumental Brass of his widow, who became the second wife of Sir Roger Northwoode.]

Folliott, Samson (or Saunsuin)—(E. iii. Roll) bore, argent, two lyons passant gardant gules (F.); St. George Roll.

Folvile, Sir Christopher—(E. iii. Roll) bore, per fess ermine and or a cross moline (recercelée) gules; Sir John bore it per fess argent and or; Ashmole Roll.

Folvile, John—(E. iii. Roll) bore, or, a chief argent, over all a cross recercelée (tricked moline) gules; Jenyns' Ordinary.

Folvile, Sir Matthew—(E. iii. Roll) bore, argent, two bars undée sable a canton gules; Ashmole Roll.

Folvile, Philip—(E. iii. Roll) bore, undée (6) argent and sable, a quarter gules.

*[Forester (Richard), of Willey (c. 1325)—bore, quarterly per fess dancettée argent and sable, in the first and fourth quarters a bugle horn of the last.—Shirley.] F.

Forde v. de la Forde.

Forneus, Sir Robert, of Norfolk—(E. ii. Roll) bore, argent, a pile engrailed sable; Parliamentary Roll.

Forneus, Sire John de—bore, at the battle of Boroughbridge 1322, sable a pile engrelée argent (F.); as also did another Sir John who was knighted at the capitulation of Calais 1348, then blasoned as a pale fusily; as a pile indented of five, in Jenyns' Ordinary; and as a pale lozengy of three pieces, in Ashmole Roll.

Forneus, St. Maheu—(E. i. Roll) bore, gules, crusily and bend or; Harleian Roll.

Forneus, Maheu de—(E. i. Roll) bore, gules, a bend between six martlets or (F.); Segar Roll.

Forneus, Sir Simond—(E. iii. Roll) bore, or, a bordure indented gules and a label of three azure; Ashmole Roll.

Fors, William de, Earl of Albemarle, and Sr. de Coupland—(E. iii. Roll) bore, argent, a chief gules; Glover, Grimaldi, and Jenyns' Rolls.

*[Fortescue, (Adam) (31 E. i.)—bore, azure, a bend engrailed argent plain cotised or.—Shirley.] F.

Fossard, Amaund—bore, at the second Dunstable tournament, gules six bendlets or. F.

Fossard, Robert—(E. ii. Roll) bore, or, a bend sable; Grimaldi and Jenyns' Rolls, borne also by Bigod and Le Sire Mauley.

Fotheringay, John—(E. iii. Roll) bore, argent, two lyons passant rere-regardant sable, reversed in the trick; Jenyns' Ordinary.

‡Fouche, Roger la—(H. iii. Roll) bore, ermine, on a fess gules three bezants; Dering Roll.

Fouleshurst, Robert—(R. ii. Roll) bore, gules, fretty or, on a chief argent two spur-rowells sable; Surrey Roll.

Fox ——, an (?) Essex Knight—(H. vi. Roll) bore, per pale vert and sable a cross potent argent; Arundel Roll.

Foxley, Sir John de, of Bucks—(E. ii. Roll) bore, gules two bars argent; Parliamentary and Surrey Rolls. See Monumental Brass.

Framlingham (——), a Suffolk Kt.—(H. vi. Roll) bore, argent, a fess gules between three ravens proper quarterly with, argent, a chevron between three crescents sable; Arundel Roll.

*[Frampton, John de, (E. iii.)—bore, argent, a bend gules cotised sable.—Shirley.] F.

Franceis, Adam — (R. ii. Roll) bore, per bend sinister sable and or a lyon rampant counterchanged, Surrey Roll; per bend or and sable &c., in Jenyns' Ordinary.

Frances, Sr. (——), of Norfolk—(E. ii. Roll) bore [. . . .] a saltire between four crosses crosslet fitchée all argent; Parliamentary Roll.

Frauneys, Robert — (R. ii. Roll) bore, argent, a chevron between three eagles displayed gules; Surrey Roll.

ELIZABETH
2ND WIFE OF SIR ROGER NORTHWOODE,
WIDOW OF RICHARD FOLLIOTT
AND
DAUGHTER OF SIR JOHN DE SEGRAVE.
MONUMENTAL BRASS
IN MINSTER CHURCH, ISLE OF
SHEPPEY, 1361.
After Stothard.

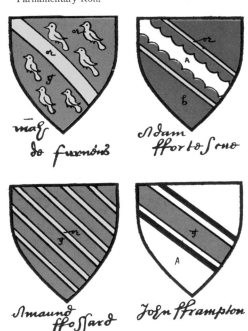

Nicȝ ffrowll

Alex. Frivile

Frivile

Baudwin ffrowill

Franks, Sir William—bore, at the siege of Calais 1345-8 (knighted at the capitulation 1348) vert, a saltire engrailed or (F.) ; Ashmole Roll and Jenyns' Ordinary.

Fraser, Sir Symond—summoned to Scotland among the barons 1298, served at Falkirk and Carlaverock. See FRYSELL.

Freford, John de—(E. III. Roll) bore, gules, a bend between six mascles argent ; Jenyns' Ordinary.

Frembaude, Sir Nicholas, of Bucks—(E. II. Roll) bore, gules, crusily and a cross or ; Parliamentary Roll.

Frene, Sir Gerard (FRENYE) (E. II. Roll) bore, or, a fleur-de-lys sable and a bordure gules ; Parliamentary and Harleian Rolls. See also DE LA FREIGN.

Frene, Hugh de (a baron 1336)—bore, at the second Dunstable tournament 1334, gules two bars "endente" argent and azure—indented from point to point (F.) ; Ashmole Roll and Jenyns' Ordinary ; the bars, per fess indented in St. George Roll ; bends, per bend indented, in Parliamentary Roll, and for Sir WALTER, of Herefordshire, also, one bend only ; H. 6137 fo. 27.

Freschville, Raff de, Baron of Stavely 1297 —bore, azure, a bend between six escallops argent ; Nobility Roll ; ascribed also to AUKER and JOHN in Howard Roll and Jenyns' Ordinary ; RAUFF differenced with a mullet gules ; Surrey Roll.

Frevile, Alexander—(H. III. Roll) bore, or, a saltire lozengy vair and gules. (F.) ; Arden and St. George Rolls.

Frevile, Sir Alexander de, of co. Worc.— (E. II. Roll) bore, or, a cross lozengy gules and vair. (F.) Sir BALDWIN bore or, on a cross gules five lozenges vair ; Parliamentary Roll ; (cross flory in Jenyns' Ordinary) ; 12 lozenges (F.) in St. George Roll.

Frevile, John—(E. III. Roll) bore, or, on a cross vair 9 lozenges in cross gules ; Jenyns' Ordinary. Although the blason of these crosses differ, it should probably be the same in all.

Frevile, Sir Baldwin—(E. II. Roll) bore, or, a cross patonce gules ; Ashmole and Surrey Rolls. Sir PIERS differenced with an annulet azure ; Ashmole Roll.

Frevile, Baudwin de—(H. III. Roll) bore, vair, a cross "passant" gules ; Norfolk Roll.

Frevile, Sir John de, of Cambridgeshire, and RICHARD and ROBERT—(E. II. Roll) bore, gules, three crescents ermine. (F.) Parliamentary, Arden, St. George, and Jenyns' Rolls. Another RICHARD (E. I.) bore, or three crescents gules. (F.) Segar Roll. See FREISLE and FRIVILE.

Fritherby, Edmond de—(R. II. Roll) bore, argent, three fleurs-de-lys 2 and 1 gules ; Surrey Roll.

Frodsam (——), an Essex Kt.—(H. VI. Roll) bore, argent, on a cross engrailed sable five mullets (8) gules ; Arundel Roll.

Frognal (——), a Kentish Kt.—(H. VI. Roll) bore, sable, two bars or, a chief argent ; Arundel Roll.

Frowick (——), a Suffolk Kt.—(H. VI. Roll) bore, azure, a chevron between three leopards' faces or ; Arundel Roll.

Frysell, Sir Symond (FRESELL or FRASER) —bore, at the battle of Falkirk 1298, sable, six roses (fraises) argent (F.) ; and nine roses (fraises) 3, 3, 2, 1 at the siege of Carlaverock 1300.

Fulborne, Sir John de, of Cambridgeshire —(E. II. Roll) bore, argent, a chevron between two wyverns (tails nowed) sable ; Parliamentary Roll—tricked in Harl. MS. 6137 fo. 18, or a chevron and in chief two wyverns sable.

*[**Fulford, Sir Henry,** (E. III.)—bore, gules, a chevron argent.—Shirley.] F.

Fulthorp, Alan—(E. III. Roll) bore, argent, a cross moline sable. WILLIAM differenced with a crescent argent ; Surrey Roll and Jenyns' Ordinary.

Furneus v. **Forneus.**

Furnivall, Thomas, D'nus de Sheffield, a baron 1295 and a banneret, sealed the Barons' letter to the Pope 1301, pp. xviii, xxiv ; bore, at the battle of Falkirk 1298 and at the siege of Carlaverock 1300, argent, a bend between six martlets gules. (F.) Nobility, Parly. and Arundel Rolls ; borne also by GERARD (of Munden), Sir THOMAS and WALTER ; Glover, Guillim and Norfolk Rolls. WILLIAM differenced with a label azure ; Glover Roll. In the Glover Roll the field is tricked or for GERARD (Harl. MS. 1481 fo. 38) and also for THOMAS in the St. George Roll.

Furnivall, Le Sr.—(E. III. Roll) bore, gules, on a cross patonce or five mullets of the field ; Ashmole Roll and Jenyns' Ordinary. Same as Sir THOMAS UGHTRED.

*[**Fursdon, Walter,** (E. I.)—bore, argent, a chevron azure between three fire-balls proper. —Shirley.] F.

†**Fyliol, Richard**—(H. III. Roll) bore, sable three covered cups or. (F.) St. George Roll.

Fyliol, Sir Thomas, of Essex—(E. II. Roll) bore, or, on a fess between two chevronels gules, three trefoyles argent ; Parliamentary Roll.

Fyliol, Sir John, of Essex—(E. II. Roll) bore, vair, a canton gules (F.) ; Parliamentary and Arden Rolls. His son Sir JOHN differenced with a mullet (on the canton) or, at the first Dunstable tournament 1308.

SIR JOHN DE FOXLEY.
IN BRAY CHURCH, IN BERKSHIRE,
1378.
After Boutell.

Richard Frivile

Richard de Froile

Simon de ffrisollos

Henry ffulford

Thọ̃ d'Furnival

Walt. ffursdon

"Here Duke William crossed over the sea in a great ship." *After the Bayeux Tapestry.*

— G —

Gabriell, Bartholomew—(E. III. Roll) bore, or billety (6) sable ; Cotgrave Roll. See GASELYN.

*[**Gage, John** (9 H. IV.)—bore, per saltire argent and azure a saltire gules.—Shirley.] F.

Gainsforde (——) an Essex ? Knight—(H. VI. Roll) bore, argent, a chevron gules between three greyhounds courant sable ; Arundel Roll.

Galeys, William de—(E. I. Roll) bore, gules, a fess between two chevronels or ; Segar Roll. (F.) See also WALEIS.

Galloway, Alan, lord of—(E. III. Roll) bore, azure, a lyon rampant argent, crowned or ; Jenyns' Ordinary. F.

Galthorp, Bartholomew, of Orthenley, Norfolk—(E. III. Roll) bore, ermine, a maunch gules ; Ashmole Roll and Jenyns' Ordinary.

Gammage, Payne de—(H. III. Roll) bore, argent, a chief azure, over all five fusils in bend gules (F.) ; ADAM, differenced with a label (5) of the first ; a label or, for NICHOL ; Arden and St. George Rolls. In Jenyns' Ordinary the bend is engrailed.

Gant, Gilbert de, baron (of Lindsey) 1295— bore, barry (6) or and azure a bend gules ; Nobility and Parliamentary Rolls. Ascribed also to GEOFFREY (H. III.), Norfolk Roll ; WILLIAM (H. III.), Glover Roll ; and to GILBERT of Swaledale (E. II.) in Jenyns' Ordinary.

Gard, Hugh, of Denmark—(E. III. Roll) bore, azure, a sun or ; H. 6589 fo. 37. See ANDREW HUGARDE.

Gardyn, Sir Thomas de, of Cambridge-shire—(E. II. Roll) bore, argent, two bars sable, a label (3) gules ; Parly. Roll.

Gargrave (——) of Suffolk, Kt. (Sir JOHN, Master of the Ordnance to King Henry in France)—(H. VI. Roll) bore, lozengy argent and sable on a bend of the last three crescents of the first ; Arundel Roll.

Garshall, Sir Thomas, of Warwickshire—(E. II. Roll) bore, quarterly argent and sable on a bend gules three fleurs-de-lys of the first ; Parliamentary Roll.

Gascoigne, William—(E. III. Roll) bore, argent, on a pale sable a lucie's head couped hauriant of the first ; Jenyns' Ordinary.

Gaselyn, Sire Edmond, of Hants—bore, at the battle of Boroughbridge 1322, or, billettée sable (F.) (azure, in Parliamentary Roll.) An-other EDMOND bore it with a label (5) gules fretty of the second ; Arden and St. George Rolls, and GEOFFREY bore it with a label gules. Another GEFFREY took up the cross in the last Crusade 1270.

Gaselyn, Sir Walter, of Hants—bore, at the first Dunstable tournament 1308, or billettée azure with a label (3) gules ; no label in Parliamentary Roll. Sir JOHN of Hants bore it with a bend gules (F.), Parliamentary Roll ; and Sir SIMOND bore the first coat with a label (5) gules ; Guillim Roll.

*[**Gatacre, Humphrey,** esquire of the body to Hen. VI.—bore, quarterly gules and ermine a fess azure bezantée between in the second and third quarters three piles meeting in base of the first.—Shirley.] F.

‡**Gatton, Hamon de**—(H. III. Roll) bore, checquy argent and azure (F.) ; Dering and Camden Rolls. GARTUNE in the Howard Roll.

Gaunte, Le Chastelyn de—(E. III. Roll) bore, azure, a false escocheon argent (an inescocheon) ; Jenyns' Ordinary.

Gaunt, Simon de—(E. II. Roll) bore. gules, three dexter gauntlets apaumée argent (F.) ; Jenyns' Roll.

Gause, Sire William—bore, at the battle of Boroughbridge 1322, gules, two bars and (in chief) three escallops argent. (F.)

Gaveston, Piers, Earl of Cornwall 1308, banneret—bore, vert, three eaglets displayed or ; Nobility Roll ; six eaglets, 3, 2, 1, in Parly. Roll ; 3 and 3 in Arundel Roll ; the field azure, both in Jenyns' Roll and Ordinary.

Gayton, Sir John de, of Rutland, Kt.—(E. II. Roll) bore, argent a fess between six fleurs-de-lys 3 and 3 gules ; Parliamentary Roll (F.) ; the fess between three in Arden Roll.

John Gago

will de Galeys

Alan of Galloway

pain d. Gamage

Hamun de Gatton

Sim de Gaunt

will Gause

John de Gayton

Edmond Gaselyn

John Gaselyne

Hump. Gatacre

Goff Genyville   *will le Conne*   *John Gont*   *nicz Gontill*   *will Gerard*   *will Germyn*

Gayton, Sir Philip de, of Rutland—(E. II. Roll) bore, argent, crusily and three fleurs-de-lys azure; Parly. Roll. HAMOND, JOHN, WILLIAM and WALTER took up the cross in the last Crusade 1270.

Geddinge, Sir John de, of Suffolk—(E. II. Roll, bore, checquy argent and gules on a fess azure three round buckles or, tongues to the dexter; Parliamentary Roll.

Geddinge (——) a Kentish Knight—(H. VI. Roll) bore, gules, a chevron argent between three gryphons' heads erased or; Arundel Roll.

Gelres, The Count de (or GUELDRES in Flanders)—(E. III. Roll) bore, azure, billettée and a lyon rampant or; Jenyns' Ordinary. Possibly of the family of the author of the famous " Armorial de Gelres." See page xxxvi.

Genevill, Geffray de, a baron 1299—bore, azure, three pairs of barnacles expanded in pale or, on a chief ermine a demi lyon rampant issuant gules (F.); Nobility Roll, &c. (the barnacles argent in the Harl. Roll). Attributed to another GEFFREY (‡) in Dering Roll. A GEFFREY and WILLIAM took up the cross in the last Crusade 1270.

Genevile, Simon de (or JOINVILLE)—(H. III. Roll) bore, sable three pairs of barnacles expanded or, on a chief argent a demi lyon rampant issuant gules; Glover Roll.

‡Genne, William le—(H. III. Roll) bore, argent, three lyons rampant 2 and 1 sable (F.); Dering Roll.

Genney, Sir Roger, of Norfolk—(E. II. Roll) bore, paly (4) or and gules a chief ermine; Parly. Roll. See also GENY.

*[Gent (John), of Wymbish, in Essex, 1328—bore, ermine, a chief indented sable (F.), and, adds Shirley, a chevron sable is sometimes borne on the shield.]

Gentill, Sir Nicholas—(E. II. Roll) bore, argent, two bars sable on a chief of the last two mullets pierced of the first; Parliamentary Roll.

Gentill, Sir Nicholl, of Sussex or Surrey—bore, at the first Dunstable tournament 1308, or, on a chief sable two mullets argent pierced gules (F.); pierced argent, in Parliamentary Roll, and gules in Jenyns' Ordinary.

Geny, Sir Thomas—(E. III. Roll) bore, azure, a false escocheon within an orle of martlets or; Ashmole Roll, an orle *vel* in-escocheon voided.

Gerard, Sir Thomas of the Bryne—(E. IV. Roll) bore, azure, a lyon rampant ermine, ducally crowned or; with crest. Ballard Roll—see Monumental Brass for PETER, 1492.

Gerard, Thomas — (E. III. Roll) bore, gules, three inescocheons ermine; Jenyns' Ordinary. See WILLIAM GERMINE.

*[Gerard, William (16 E. I.)—bore, argent, a saltire gules, in Shirley.] F.

Gerberge, John and **Raffe**—(E. III. Roll) bore, ermine, on a chief gules, three lozenges or; Jenyns' Roll and Ordinary—the lozenges vair, in Ashmole Roll.

Gerberge, Thomas — (R. II. Roll) bore, sable, a fess between two chevrons or; Surrey Roll.

Gercomvile v. **Jerkavile** and **Marconvile.**

Germyn v. **Jermyn.**

Germine, William—(E. III. Roll) bore, gules three false escocheons ermine a mullet (6) argent. (F.) Jenyns' Ordinary. See THOMAS GERARD.

Gernons, see BLUNDEVILE, Earl of CHESTER.

Gernoun, Sir William de, of Essex—(E. II. Roll) bore, argent, three piles undée meeting in base gules; Parliamentary Roll. Wavy in Harl. 6137 fo. 14ᵇ—paly wavy argent and gules in Glover Roll.

Gerthestone, Robert de—(E. III. Roll) bore, argent, on a fess sable three crosses patonce or; Jenyns' Ordinary.

Gerveys, Robert—(E. II. Roll) bore, argent, a chevron azure between three escallops sable; Jenyns' Roll.

Gery, Sir John—(E. III. Roll) bore, paly (6) or and gules, a chief ermine; Ashmole and Surrey Rolls.

Getingdon, Nicholas—(E. III. Roll) bore, gyronny (8) or and sable; Jenyns' Ordinary.

Gey, Walter de—(H. III. Roll) bore, argent a lyon rampant sable debruised of a bend gules (Arden Roll); charged with three buckles or. (F.); in St. George Roll.

Ghisnes, Ingelram de, a baron 1295—bore, gules, a chief vair (potent counter potent); Nobility Roll.

Giffarde, Sir John, of co. Worc.—(E. II. Roll) bore, argent, nine torteaux 3, 3, 2, 1; Parliamentary Roll. ALEXANDER, JOHN and RAFFE bore ten torteaux. (F.) St. George and Surrey Rolls and Jenyns' Ordinary.

Giffard, William—(E. III. Roll) bore, argent, three stirrups and straps gules; Jenyns' Roll—the reverse in Howard Roll (H. III.). Sir PEIRS bore, at the battle of Boroughbridge 1322, azure, three stirrups with a bordure indented all or. (F.) Tricked engrailed in Ashmole MS. *PETER GIFFORD (H. III.) bore the last coat without the bordure.—Shirley.

Giffard, John de, banneret, a baron 1295—bore, gules, three lyons passant in pale argent. (F.) Nobility, Parliamentary and Arundel Rolls—ascribed also to WILLIAM in Jenyns' Ordinary. Sir JOHN LE BOEF, of Oxon, bore it (E. II.) differenced with a label (3, 5) azure; Parliamentary Roll. Ascribed to another JOHN (‡) in Dering Roll. Ascribed to another JOHN of co. Glouc. (E. II.) bore the same difference—but sable in Harl. MS. 4033 fo. 48, and so also one OSBERT, baron 1297; Nobility Roll.

walter de G'oi   *Alos Giffard*

PETER GERARD, ESQ.
IN WINWICK CHURCH, LANCASHIRE
1492. *After Waller.*

John Giffard   *Piers Giffard*

Osborn Giffard   *Will Giffard*   *Robt de Giffard*   *Robt de Gifford*   *E. Ekont Glanvill*

‡**Giffard, Ellis**—(H. III. Roll) bore, gules, three lyons passant in pale argent within a bordure or ; Dering Roll—the bordure engrailed in Howard Roll.

†**Giffard, Walter**—(H. III. Roll) bore, azure, three lyons passant in pale argent crowned or ; Dering and Howard Rolls.

Giffard, William—(H. III. Roll), bore, argent, crusily and a lyon rampant gules. (F.) Jenyns' Ordinary ; (WALTER BUKESHALL bears 'the same)—crusily sable in Arden and St. George Rolls. A WILLIAM took up the cross in the last Crusade 1270.

Giffard, Osberne—(H. III. Roll) bore, ermine, two bars gules on a chief of the last a lyon (of England) passant gardant or ; St. George Roll and Jenyns' Roll—(a fess in lieu of the bars (F.) Segar Roll) ; attributed to another OSBERNE (‡), the field and lyon or, in the Dering Roll ; the field argent in the Ashmole MS.

Giffard, Osburne—(H. III. Roll) bore, argent, two bars gemelles and a chief gules ; Howard Roll.

Giffard, Robert de—(H. III. Roll) bore, or a cross engrailed sable. (F.) St. George Roll ; blasoned fusily and tricked dancettée in Arden Roll.

†**Gifford, Robert**—(H. III. Roll) bore, argent, a cross engrailed sable, over all a gorge azure. (F.) Dering Roll.

Gifford, Hugh—(E. III. Roll) bore, gules, fretty engrailed ermine ; Jenyns' Ordinary. WAREYN DE VALOYNES bears the same.

Gilder, Sir Gawayne—(E. III. Roll) bore, gules, three estoiles or, a bordure engrailed argent. Ashmole Roll.

Gillott, Nicholas DE MERKINGTON—(E. II. Roll) bore, per bend indented sable and argent ; Jenyns' Roll.

Gise *v.* **Guise.**

Gisell or **Oysell, Roger**—(E. III. Roll) bore, argent, a saltire engrailed between four birds (oiseau) sable ; Jenyns' Ordinary.

Gissing, Sir Thomas—(E. III. Roll) bore, argent on a fess (between two crosses crosslet fitchée) azure three eagles displayed or ; Ashmole Roll—a bend in lieu of a fess and without crosslets in Surrey Roll.

Gistell, Walter de—(H. III. Roll) bore, gules, a chevron ermine ; Norfolk Roll.

Glamvile, Randolf de (or GLANVILE)—(E. III. Roll) bore, or, a chief indented (4) azure ; Jenyns' Ordinary.

[**Glanvile** (——), of Catchfrench (*c.* 1400), bore azure, three saltorelles or.—Shirley.]

Glanville, *sive* **Ekont** ——— (H. III. Roll), bore, azure, crusily three crescents argent. (F.) St. George Roll.

Glastonbury, Sir Henry de, of Somerset —bore, at the first Dunstable tournament 1308, argent a bend engrailed sable (F.) ; blasoned as fusily for the Sir HENRY who was knighted at the capitulation of Calais 1348 ; ascribed as lozeny to JOHN (E. III.) in Jenyns' Ordinary—probably engrailed ; fusily and lozengy are synonymous.

Gloucester, Earl of, GILBERT DE CLARE— bore, at the first Dunstable tournament 1308, or three chevronels gules (F.) ; Nobility and Arundel Rolls, &c. See AUDLEY and CLARE.

Gloucester, Duke of, THOMAS of Woodstock K.G.—(R. II. Roll) bore, quarterly 1, England, 2 and 3, France, all within a bordure argent, 4, azure, a bend argent between two cotises and six lyons rampant or ; Surrey Roll ; K. 399 fo. 4.

[**Gloucester, Robert** (of Caen), Earl of ; surnamed CONSUL, fil. nat. Hen. I.—to him is improperly ascribed gules three clarions or. See Monumental Effigy.]

Gloucester, Sire Walter de (of co. Glouc.) —bore, at the battle of Boroughbridge 1322, argent three lyonceux (rampant) gules, within a bordure indented azure (F.) ; Parliamentary Roll ; tricked engrailed in Ashmole MS. ; blasoned " cersele " in Cotgrave Roll.

Gobaud, Sire Johan, of co. Linc.—bore, at the battle of Boroughbridge 1322, gules, a fess and in chief three besants (F.) ; Holland Roll ; two bars or, &c., in Jenyns' Ordinary and Parliamentary Roll.

Gobion, Sir Hugh, of Yorkshire—(H. III. Roll) bore, barry (8) argent and gules a label (3, 5) azure ; St. George (F.) and Parliamentary Rolls ; burulée (18) in Arden Roll.

Godard, Sir Hugh, of Cheshire—(E. II. Roll) bore, ermine, a cross patonce sable ; Parliamentary Roll.

Godard, John—(E. III. Roll) bore, quarterly gules and argent, in the second and third quarters an eagle displayed sable ; Jenyns' Ordinary.

Goddyston, Sir John, of Essex—(H. VI. Roll) bore, ermine, a saltire engrailed gules ; Arundel Roll.

Godemontone, John de—(H. III. Roll) bore, argent, an eagle displayed gules (F.) ; Arden and St. George Rolls.

Goderiche, William—(R. II. Roll) bore, argent, two lyons passant gardant in pale sable ; Surrey Roll.

Goldesborow, Richard de—(R. II. Roll) bore, azure, a cross patonce argent ; Surrey Roll ; cross, tricked flory in Jenyns' Ordinary.

In Memoriam.

———

ROBERT THE CONSUL,
EARL OF GLOUCESTER, 1119, II. F.NAT. II. I.
IN THE CHOIR OF TEWKESBURY ABBEY,
OB. 1147.
See also CLARE 47, and FITZ HAMON 213.

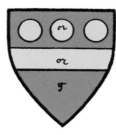

Le County de Gloucestre   *Walt de Gloucestre*   *Hy. de Glastonbury*   *John Gobaude*   *Hue Gobiun*   *John de Godemontone*

John de Goldinton

Brian de Gonua

Rauf de Gorges

John de Gorge

Raffe de Gorges

Ada de Gurdun

Mal de Gogala

Nich de Gower

Hy. de Graham

Wat d. Graunture

John de Goring

Wat. d. Graunture

Otes Grandison

Will Grandison

Goldingham, Sir Allen de, of Suffolk—(E. II. Roll) bore, undée (6) argent and gules, a label (3) azure; Parliamentary Roll. Argent a bend nebulée gules is ascribed to another Suffolk Knight; Arundel Roll.

Goldingham, Alexander—(R. II. Roll) bore, barry nebulée (6) ermine and gules; Surrey Roll.

Goldingham, William de—(H. III. Roll) bore, ermine, three bars wavy gules; Howard Roll.

Goldington, Sire John de—bore, at the battle of Boroughbridge 1322, or, two lyons passant sable, a label (3) gules; borne without the label but with the lyons gardant by Sir JOHN, who was knighted at the capitulation of Calais 1348. F.

Goldington, Sir Raffe de, of Beds—(E. II. Roll) bore, argent two lyons passant in pale azure; Parliamentary Roll.

Golofree, Sir John—(E. III. Roll) bore, undée (6) argent and gules on a baston sable four besants, Ashmole Roll; three besants for JOHN and THOMAS, in Surrey Roll and Jenyns' Ordinary.

Gondronville, Gerard de, of Loreyne—bore, at the siege of Carlaverock 1300, vair; sometimes called HUNTERCOMBE. See NICOLAS edn.

Gonnis, Bryan de (E. III. Roll) bore, vair, a bend lozengy (vel engrailed) gules (F.); St. George Roll and Jenyns' Ordinary, where it is blasoned vaire or and azure a bend gules.

Gonnis, Walter de—(E. III. Roll) bore, quarterly vair and gules; Jenyns' Ordinary.

Gonnyes, de —— (E. III. Roll) bore, gules, a chevron ermine; Jenyns' Roll and Ordinary; borne also by LODBROOKE.

Gonvile, Sir Richard—(E. III. Roll) bore, or, on a bend sable three mullets argent pierced gules; Ashmole Roll.

Gordon, Sir Adam, of Hants or Wilts—(E. II. Roll) bore, gules, three leopards' faces jessant-de-lys argent; Parliamentary Roll.

‡**Gordon, Adam**—(H. III. Roll) bore, or, a fleur-de-lys gules; Dering and Howard Rolls.

Gordon, Adam de—(H. III. Roll) bore, gules, three fleurs-de-lys argent (F.); Arden and St. George Rolls. See also Sir ADAM GORDON.

Gordon, Sir Thomas, or GARDYN, of co. Cambridge—(E. II. Roll) bore, argent, two bars sable, a label (3) gules; Parliamentary Roll.

Gorges, Raffe de—bore, at the siege of Carlaverock 1300, and at the first Dunstable tournament 1308, lozengy or and azure (F.); this coat appears in many rolls, sometimes the tinctures are reversed, at others six lozenges 3, 2, 1 are tricked for lozengy; the mascles are tricked five lozenges for Sir RAFFE, banneret, in Parliamentary and Arundel Rolls; masculée argent and azure is ascribed to JOHN, in Jenyns' Roll.

Gorges (——), a Suffolk Knight—(H. VI. Roll) bore, lozengy or and azure a chevron gules (F.), quarterly with, argent, on a chief gules three bezants; Arundel Roll.

Gorges, Rafe de—(H. III. Roll) bore, argent, a gorge azure (F.); Arden, Jenyns', Howard and Glover Rolls; (successfully claimed by WARBURTON of Cheshire); a RAFE took up the cross in the last Crusade 1270.

*[**Goring, John de** (E. II.)—bore, argent, a chevron between three annulets gules.—Shirley.] F.

Gornay v. **Gurnay.**

Goschalle, Walter de—(E. III. Roll) bore, or, a hurt charged with a cinquefoyle of the first, on a chief dancettée (4 indents) azure, two besants (F.); Ashmole Roll. In the Dering Roll the coat is tricked per fess dancettée, &c., for RAFFE or WALTER (‡).

Gotesbury, Sir Richard de, of Herts—(E. II. Roll) bore, gules, a fess vair between three goats' heads erased argent: Parliamentary Roll.

Gounis v. **Gonnis.**

Gousell, John—(E. III. Roll) bore, argent, a fess between six martlets 3 and 3 sable; Jenyns' Ordinary.

Gousell, John—(E. III. Roll) bore, paly (6) argent and gules on a chief azure a fess dancettée or, RAFE bore it with the colours of the chief and fess reversed; Jenyns' Ordinary.

Gousell, Thomas (GAUSIL)—(E. III. Roll) bore, argent, on a bend sable three trefoils or; Jenyns' Roll.

Goushull, Nicoll—(R. II.) bore, barry (6) or and gules, a canton ermine, his son NICHOLL differenced with a label (3) azure; Surrey Roll.

Gower, Sir Robert—(E. III. Roll) bore, argent, on a chevron sable three leopards' faces or; Ashmole Roll. JOHN DE GUER took up the cross in the last Crusade 1270.

Gower, Thomas, of Stittenham (? Stainsby) (E. III. Roll) bore, ermine, a cross flory gules, blasoned as patée; Jenyns' Ordinary.

*[**Gower, Sir Nicholas,** of Stittenham (12 E. III.)—bore, barry (8), argent and gules, a cross flory gules—blasoned patonce by Shirley.] F.

Grabom, William (or GABOM)—(H. III. Roll) bore, argent, on a bend gules three eagles displayed or; Arden Roll.

Graham, Henry de, banneret—bore, at the siege of Carlaverock 1300, gules, a saltire argent on a chief of the last three escallops gules. F.

Grailly v. **Buch, Greilly.**

Gramary, Henry—(E. III. Roll) bore, gules, crusily botonnée and a lyon rampant argent; Jenyns' Ordinary.

Gramary, Sir William—(E. III. Roll) bore, gules, billettée or, and a lyon rampant argent, Ashmole Roll; billettée argent in the coat ascribed to WILLIAM; Jenyns' Ordinary.

Grancourt, Walter de (GRAUNCURT)—(H. III. Roll) bore, sable, florettée or, (F.); St. George Roll and Arden Roll sable, six fleurs-de-lys 3, 2, 1, or.

Grandall v. **Grendole.**

✝**Grandin, William**—(E. I. Roll) bore, azure, three mullets 2 and 1 or, (F.); Dering and Camden Rolls.

Grandison, de —— (E. III. Roll) bore, paly (6) argent and azure on a bend gules a castle or. Another (see OTHO)—azure, on a bend argent three escallops gules; Cotgrave Roll.

Grandison, Oto de, a baron 1299—bore, paly (6) argent and azure on a bend gules three escallops or, (F.); Nobility Roll, &c. (ascribed to another OTES (‡) in Dering Roll); paly (4) Harl. Roll; paly (8) in Jenyns' Ordinary; azure, three palets argent, &c.; Guillim Roll.

Grandison, Sir Otho de, knighted at the capitulation of Calais 1348—bore, paly (6) argent and azure, on a bend gules three buckles, tongues erect bendwise or (F.); Ashmole Roll.

THE HERALDIC ATCHIEVEMENT

OF

SIR ROBERT GRESLEY, 11TH BARONET,

OF DRAKELOW, DERBYSHIRE; HELD OF THE CONQUEROR IN 1086.

FACSIMILE OF AN OLD TRICK SHOWING CORRECTLY THE RED HAND OF ULSTER.

Guillm de Graundsonn

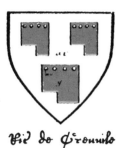

Wil de Greuule

nicole de Gras

Roy de Paliologro

John Gregory

Johan de Grelli

Gauff de Grondont

Joan de Graundone

Euſt. Gronville

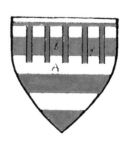

Gefrai d. Greſelere

Pers d' Grete

Will Grevol

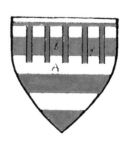

Henry de Grey

Henri de Grey

Grandison, Sir William de, banneret, a baron 1299—bore, at the battle of Falkirk 1298, and at the siege of Carlaverock 1300, paly (6) argent and azure, on a bend gules three eaglets displayed or (F.) ; Nobility, Parliamentary, and Arundel Rolls. Borne also by Sir PIERS at the battle of Boroughbridge 1322, by Sir WILLIAM at the siege of Calais 1345-8, by another WILLIAM at the siege of Rouen 1418, and by Sir THOMAS, K.G., 1370.

Granem, William (or GRAVEM)—(H. III. Roll) bore, azure, six spur-rowells or, a label (5) gules ; Howard Roll. See GRANDIN.

Granville, Richard de—(H. III. Roll) bore, argent three clarions gules garnished argent (F.) ; Arden Roll. It is surmised that the clarions were originally the canting coat of CLARE, and that their arms were erroneously ascribed at an early period to GRANVILLE. See Tiles, Neath Abbey, p. v.

‡**Gras, Nicole le**—(H. III. Roll) bore, azure, three lyonceux rampant 2 and 1 or, a chief argent (F.) ; Dering and Howard Rolls.

Grauncurt v. **Grancourt.**

Gravesend, Sir Stephen, of Kent—(E. II. Roll) bore, or, four eagles displayed sable, a canton ermine ; Parliamentary Roll.

Greece; The Palialologi; Emperors of —(H. III. Roll) bore, or a sea lyon sable. Segar Roll. F.

Greenacre, Richard—(R. II. Roll) bore, sable, three covered cups 2 and 1 argent (ROBERT bore it with an annulet argent), Surrey Roll ; ascribed, colours reversed and a torteux for difference, to another RICHARD in Jenyns' Ordinary.

Greene (——), a Knight—(H. VI. Roll) bore, argent, a bugle horn between three gryphons' heads erased sable ; Arundel Roll.

Greene, Henry—(R. II. Roll) bore, argent, a cross engrailed gules ; Surrey Roll.

Greene, John—(E. II. Roll) bore, checquy or and azure, a bordure gules ; Jenyns' Roll. THOMAS MAUDUIT bore these arms.

Greene, Richard — (E III. Roll) bore, argent, a fess dancettée sable, in chief three leopards' faces of the last ; Jenyns' Ordinary.

Greene, Thomas—(R. II. Roll) bore, azure three bucks passant (perhaps statant) 2 and 1 or ; Surrey Roll.

Greenford, John—(E. III. Roll) bore, verta lyon rampant tail estant or ; Jenyns' Ordinary.

Greet v. **Grete.**

Gregory, Sir Henry, Knight banneret— (H. VI. Roll) bore, azure two bars double cotised or, in chief a lyon passant of the last ; Arundel Roll.

*[**Gregory, John** (E. I.)—bore, or, two bars and in chief a lyon passant azure.—Shirley.] F.

Greilly, Piers de (GRELY)—(H. III. Roll) bore, or, on a cross sable five escallops argent ; Howard Roll ; and so in Surrey Roll for MONS. PIERS LE CAPITOU DE BOUCH, K.G. and a founder. See pedigree Anstis' "Order of the Garter," vol. I. Introduction, page 8. See also BUCH ante.

Grelle, Thomas de, banneret, and a baron 1308—bore, gules, three bendlets enhanced or (F.), a bend and two bendlets above ; Nobility Roll 1308, Gresley 131c, borne also by JOHN, ROBERT, and Sir THOMAS. (Another JOHN bore the field argent, JOHN MAUVEISIN carried the same). Another ROBERT bore four bendlets. The coat for Sir THOMAS is tricked in Harl. 6137, fo. 40b, probably erroneously, as bendy (8) or and gules.

Greley, Sir William, Knight banneret— (H. VI. Roll) bore, gules three bars or ; Arundel Roll.

Grendale, Sir Walter de, of Yorkshire— (E. II. Roll) bore, ermine, a cross patonce gules ; Parliamentary Roll.

Grendon, Raffe de, banneret, a baron 1299, sealed the Barons' letter to the Pope 1301, pp. xxi, xxiv. He bore, at the battle of Falkirk 1298, argent, two chevrons (a chevron et demy) gules (F.) ; Nobility, Parliamentary, and Arundel Rolls. Ascribed also to a ROBERT in Arden and St. George Rolls.

Grendon, Sir Robert de, of co. Leic.— (E. II. Roll) bore, argent, two chevronels gules, a label (3) vert, Parliamentary Roll—(ascribed also to a JOHN, in Jenyns' Ordinary)—a label (3) argent, each point vaire of the last and sable ; Ashmole Roll.

Grendon, Sir John, of Warwicks.—bore, at the first Dunstable tournament 1308, vaire argent and sable a baston or (F.) ; Ashmole and Parliamentary Rolls.

Grensted v. **Grimsted.**

[**Grenville, Sir Eustace,** of Wootton (E. I.)—bore, vert, on a cross argent five torteaux.—Shirley.] F.

[Gresley, Sir Piers** and **Geffray**—(E. II. Roll) bore, vaire, ermine and gules ; Parly., Arden and St. George Rolls. Sir PIERS DE GREYLLIE, Knight banneret (H. VI. Roll), and JOHN (E. II. Roll) bore the reverse ; another JOHN bore, vaire argent and gules ; Surrey Roll.

Gresley, John—(E. III. Roll) bore, barry (6) azure and ermine, tricked, vaire ermine and gules, two bars azure ; Jenyns' Ordinary. RAYNELL DE BREWES bears the same arms.

Grete, Pers de—(H. III. Roll) bore, argent, a saltire engrailed azure (F.) ; Arden and St. George Rolls.

*[**Grevel, William,** of Milcote 1401—bore, sable, on a cross engrailed or five pellets, a bordure engrailed argent ; borne by WILLIAM of Campden, with the addition of a mullet in the first quarter, and his son JOHN bore 10 annulets in lieu of the pellets.—Shirley.] F.

Grey—For differences see Harleian MS. 1481 folios 17, 19, 20, 21, 23, 25, 26, 27.

Grey, Henry le, of Codnor, banneret, a baron 1299, sealed the Barons' letter to the Pope 1301, pp. xvii, xxiv. He bore, at the battle of Falkirk 1298, and at the siege of Carlaverock 1300, barry (6) argent and azure (F.) ; Nobility and Parly. Rolls ; borne also by JOHN, K.G. (? of Rotherfield, a founder, see), in Surrey, Arden and St. George Rolls ; by REGINALD or REYNAUD in the Segar Roll ; by Sir RICHARD, Kt. banneret in Arundel, Parliamentary, Dering, Glover and Howard Rolls. Le Sr de GRAYE also bore these arms at the siege of Rouen in 1418 (? Baron DE WILTON). The Camden Roll affords the solitary example of the colours reversed, Harl. MS. 6137 fo. 70.

Grey, Sir Reginald de, of Wilton, banneret, a baron 1297, sealed the Barons' letter to the Pope 1301, pp. xvii, xxiv. He bore, at the battle of Falkirk 1298, barry (6) argent and azure a label (3, 5) gules ; Nobility and Dering Rolls, &c. Sir HENRY bore the same at the battle of Boroughbridge 1322 (F.) ; Segar Roll, also ascribed to Sir JOHN, Knight banneret ; Parly Roll.

Grey, John DE SANDIACRE — bore, at the second Dunstable tournament 1334, barry (6) argent and azure a label gules besantée, borne also by RICHARD of Sandiacre, in Ashmole Roll and Jenyns' Ordinary.

VIX EA NOSTRA VOCO

THE HERALDIC ATCHIEVEMENT

OF

FRANCIS RICHARD GREVILLE, 5TH EARL OF WARWICK AND BROOKE.

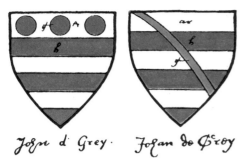

Jopu d' Grey. *Jofan do Grcoy*

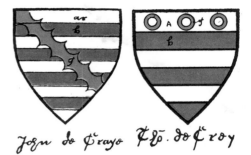

Jofn do Grayo *Ꝉꝺ. do Grcoy*

Grey, Sir John de—bore, at the first Dunstable tournament 1308, barry (6) or and azure in chief three torteaux (F.), borne also by ADAM (H. III.); St. George Roll, and Le Sr DE RYTHYNE (temp. H. VI.); Nobility and Surrey Rolls (R. II.). See Monumental Brass for ROGER, 1st Lord Grey de Ruthyn; and title page for THOMAS, Marquis of Dorset, K.G. 1476. See Sir THOMAS.

Grey, Sir John de, banneret, of Rotherfield, Oxon—bore, at the battle of Falkill 1298, and at the siege of Carlaverock 1300, barry (6) argent and azure a baston gules (F.); as did his son JOHN, of Rotherfield. K.G. and a founder (a baron in 1338), at the second Dunstable tournament 1334; the same arms are ascribed with a baston, bendlet or bend to Sir JOHN of Essex, RICHARD, and ROBERT in the Parliamentary, Surrey, and Arden Rolls. In the Carlaverock Roll the arms for Sir JOHN are argent four bars azure a bend engrailed gules. F.

Grey, Sire Nichol de—bore, at the battle of Boroughbridge 1322, barry (6) azure and argent, a baston gobony of the second and gules (F.) (gobony or and gules in Nativity Roll); tricked, barry argent and azure in the Ashmole MS.

Grey, Sir Nichol, of Essex—(E. III. Roll) bore, barry (6) argent and azure a baston gobony or and gules; gules and or for ROBERT of Barton in Rydal; Parliamentary Roll and Jenyns' Ordinary.

Grey ——, (E. III. Roll) bore, barry (6) argent and azure on a bend gules three fleurs-de-lys or; Ashmole Roll.

Grey, John de—(H. III. Roll) bore, barry (6) argent and azure, a bend of lozenges gules (F.) Howard Roll;—argent, a bend fusily gules, St. George Roll.

Grey, Sir Richard—(E. I. Roll) bore, barry azure and argent florettée or; Nativity Roll.

Grey, Reginald de—(H. III. Roll) bore, argent, three bars azure, a label (5) gules, probably a mistake for barry, as before; Howard Roll.

Grey, Richard de—(H. III. Roll) bore, argent, three bars azure over all a bend gules bezantée, probably a mistake for barry, as before; Howard Roll.

Gray, Sir R.—(H. VI. Roll), and **Sir Thomas**—(E. III. Roll) bore, gules, a lyon rampant and a bordure engrailed argent; Atkinson and Ashmole Rolls. Borne also by Sir JOHN, K.G., temp. H. V.

*****Gray, Thomas**, of Heton—(E. III. Roll) bore, gules, a lyon rampant argent and a bordure engrailed or; Jenyns' Ordinary. See HETON.

Grey, Sr (——) LE BASTARD—Knighted at the capitulation of Calais 1348, bore, gules, a lyon rampant and a border engrailed argent, a baston sable. F.

ROGER, LORD GREY DE RUTHYN,
1352–3.
*From a Rubbing of the Hastings Brass in
Elsing Church, Norfolk.*

Grey, Sir Thomas—(E. I. Roll) bore, gules, a lyon rampant and a bordure indented argent, a baston azure; Nativity Roll.

Gray (——), a Knight—(H. VI. Roll) bore, gules, a lyon rampant argent a bordure engrailed gobony of the second and or; Arundel Roll.

Grey, Sir Thomas, of co. Lancs.—(E. II. Roll) bore, gules, seven mascles 3, 3, 1 conjoined or, a baston gobony argent and azure; Parliamentary Roll.

*****[Grey, Sir Thomas de**, of Suffolk, E. I.— bore, barry (6) argent and azure, in chief three annulets gules.—Shirley.] F. Ancestor of the Earls of Stamford, who discarded the annulets; this family also bore the coat of CORNERTHE, as in the next entry.

Gray, Sir Thomas, of Cambridgeshire— (E. III. Roll) bore, azure, a fess between two chevronels gules; Ashmole Roll. The coat of CORNERTHE.

Grey, Sir Thomas, of Suffolk—(E. II. Roll) bore, azure, a fess between two chevronels or a label (3) gules; Parliamentary Roll.

Greystoke, Sire Rauf de (formerly FITZ WILLIAM)—bore, at the battle of Boroughbridge 1322, burulée (12) azure and argent, three chaplets gules (F.), also burulée (14, 16) argent and azure, &c.; Ashmole and Surrey Rolls and Jenyns' Ordinary; grandson of RALPH FITZ WILLIAM. See that name.

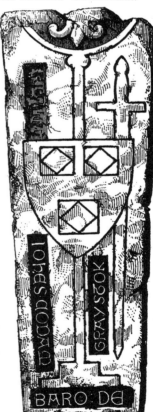

JOHN,
BARON OF GREYSTOKE, 1305.
MON. SLAB AT GREYSTOKE.

nuꝛol do Grey *Joan d' Grey* *Lo Baſtarꝺ do Grey* *Le Baron d' Creſtoc* *Ꝑauf do Grꝛoſtoꝛo*

Jrvan ap Griffid

Dauid ap Griffid

Roes ap Griffith

Roes ap Griffith

Roger Grimstone

Robt. le Grosvenor

will Gronou

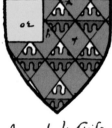

Auncel d' Gise

Thomas de Gorney

Jmbord de Gu

Greystoke, John de, a baron 1295, sealed the Barons' letter to the Pope 1301, with 3 lozenges; see pp. xxiii, xxiv, and also Monumental Slab—according to the Rolls he bore, gules, three cushions or (F.) Nobility Roll; (? argent), in St. George Roll; or and gules in Jenyns' Roll, and apparently in the Holland Roll.

Greyton, Sir John v. **Gayton.**

Griffith, Evan ap, of Wenunwyn—(H. III. Roll) bore, or, a lyon rampant gules (F.); Arden and St. George Rolls. See also Tiles, Neath Abbey, p. ix.

Griffith, David ap—(H. III. Roll) bore, quarterly or and azure four lyonceux passant gardant counterchanged (F.); St. George Roll.

Griffith, Llewellin ap—(H. III. Roll) bore, quarterly or and gules four lyons passant counterchanged; St. George and Norfolk Rolls. See also Tiles, Neath Abbey, p. vii.

Griffin, John (E. III. Roll) and **Thomas** (R. II. Roll)—bore, sable, a gryphon segreant argent, armed or; Cotgrave and Surrey Rolls.

Griffith, Ydon, lord of—(H. VI. Roll) bore, azure, a gryphon segreant armed and membered gules; "his daughter married to Lord Hoo"; Atkinson Roll.

Griffith, Owen ap—(H. III. Roll) bore, gules, a cross or between four eagles displayed argent; Arden Roll.

Griffith, Rees, ap—bore, at the second Dunstable tournament 1334, gules on a fess dancettée argent between three lyonceux passant or as many martlets sable (F.); six lyonceux passant in the Surrey Roll. F.

Grimeles, Robert de—(H. III. Roll) bore, argent, on a cross gules five spur-rowells or; Howard Roll.

Grimsby, John de—(R. II. Roll) bore, per chevron sable and argent in chief two cinquefoyles pierced of the field; Surrey Roll.

Grimsted, Sir Andrew (or GRENSTED), of Somerset—(E. II. Roll) bore, gules three barrulets vair; Parliamentary Roll.

*****Grimston, Gerrard de** and **Roger de**—(E. III. Roll) bore, argent on a fess sable, three mullets (6) or pierced gules (F.); Surrey Roll and Jenyns' Ordinary.

Grimston, Roger—(E. III. Roll) bore, argent, on a fess vert three mullets pierced or; Jenyns' Ordinary.

Grindale, John—(E. III. Roll) bore, burulée (12) argent and gules a cross patonce (flory in trick) sable; Jenyns' Ordinary.

Groney, Sir William, of Normandy—bore, at the siege of Calais 1345-8, argent, a bend engrailed azure (F.); surname uncertain, perhaps BORNEY or GORNEY.

*****[Grosvenor, Sir Robert le,** 1389—bore, azure, a garb or, on the determination of the Scrope and Grosvenor controversy.—Shirley.] F.

Grose v. **le Grose.**

Guise, Auncell de (GYSE)—(H. III. Roll) bore, lozengy gules and vair a canton (sometimes a quarter) or (F.); St. George and Howard Rolls—tricked vair and gules in the Dering Roll (perhaps erroneously tricked paly for lozengy as in facsimile from Camden Roll)—masculée in Jenyns' Ordinary, &c., blasoned by Jenyns as the arms of the Earl of Kent reversed and a canton or. In Arden Roll another AUNCEL bears a spur-rowell sable, on the quarter, see Sir JOHN.

Guyse, Walter de—(E. II. Roll) bore, masculée vair and gules, on a quarter or a fleur-de-lys azure; tricked, lozengy gules and vert, &c.; Jenyns' Roll.

Guise, Sir John (GYSE), of Bucks—(E. II. Roll) bore, gules, six lozenges 3, 2, 1, vair, on a canton or a spur-rowell sable.

Gu(y), Imberd—(H. III. Roll) bore, azure, three pheons 2 and 1 argent; St. George Roll. Names doubtful. See also GEY.

Guldeford, Sir John de, of the North—(E. II. Roll) bore, argent, two bars gemelles sable; Parliamentary Roll; three bars H. 6137 fo. 28ᵇ.

Gurney, Sir Thomas de, of Somerset—bore, at the first Dunstable tournament 1308, paly (6) or and gules; paly (8) or and azure in Parliamentary Roll. F.; and so ascribed to AUNCELL and MAHEU, in St. George and Surrey Rolls.

Gurnay, Sir John, of Essex, Knight—(H. VI. Roll) bore, azure, on a bend cotised argent, three leopards' faces gules jessant-de-lys or; Arundel Roll.

†**Gurney, Johan de**—(H. III. Roll) bore, argent, a cross engrélée gules; Norfolk Roll.

Gurnay, Maheu—(E. II. Roll) bore, or, three piles meeting "in poynt" gules; Jenyns' Roll. Sir MATHEW said by some to have been a Companion of the Garter 1386.

Gurney, Robert de—(H. III. Roll) bore, or, a lyon rampant sable a border gules; Glover Roll.

Gurney, Sir William (BORNEY or GORNEY), of Normandy—bore, at the siege of Calais 1345-8, argent, a bend engrailed azure; name doubtful.

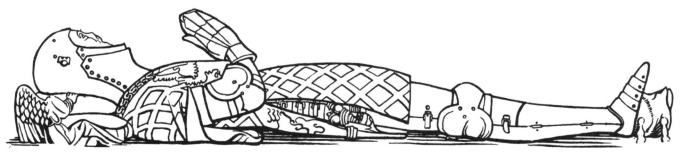

JOHN FITZALAN, EARL OF ARUNDEL, DIED 1434. IN THE FITZALAN CHAPEL, ARUNDEL.
After Stothard.

Ibaig of Bemersyde, co. Berwick.

I. PETER DE HAGA, c. 1150–1200. Witness, as 'Petrus del Hage' to a Charter of Richard de Moreville, Con-=GODA.
stable of Scotland, c. 1162–6 (Dip. Scot. No. 75), and to a number of Charters of the period.

II. PETER DE HAGA, c. 1200–28. Granted a Charter of part of his forest of Threepwood with two oxgates of land=ADA, dau. of Sir Henry Sinclair, of Carfrae (Mylne MS.).
and a house and garden in Bemersyde—'that of my mother Goda of good memory'—to the Abbey of
Dryburgh 'for the soul of Ada, my late wife,' &c. (Liber de Dryburgh, pp. 269–71). Douglas states that their
burying-place in Dryburgh Abbey was given to the Haigs in the time of this Petrus.

III. HENRY DE HAGA, c. 1228–40. Witness, as 'Henricus de la Hage' to a Charter circa 1230 of Alan=ADELIZA, dau. of Sir Anchitell de Riddel (Mylne MS.).
FitzRoland, Constable of Scotland (Liber de Melros, i. 202, 203).

PETER DE HAGA (IV.).

IV. PETER DE HAGA, c. 1240–80. Granted half a stone of wax to the Abbey=KATHARINE, dau. of Sir
of Old Melrose by a Charter to which the name of 'Thomas Rymor de William Bellocampo or
Ercildune' is appended as a witness. The Seal of Petrus de Haga Beauchamp (Mylne MS.).
attached to this Charter bears as cognisance three barulets. The Saltire,
or St. Andrew's Cross, may have been assumed by the Haigs for service in
the Holy Land. Patrick, Earl of Dunbar, who had lands at Ercildoune,
near Bemersyde, sold his brood-mares in 1247 to the Monks of Melrose on
his departure for the Holy Land (Liber de Melros, i. 204).

V. JOHN DE HAGA, c. 1280–1326. Confirmed to the Monks of Dryburgh his=ERMEGARDE, dau. of Sir
father's gift of the forest of Flatwood (Liber de Dryburgh, p. 96). Adam de Gordon in the
His name appears on the list of those who swore fealty to Edward I. in Merse (Mylne MS.).
1296, but he subsequently joined Sir William Wallace. 'When Wallace
came to Gladswood Cross, Haig of Bemersyde met him with many good
horse' (Old Monkish couplet). To his time is ascribed the prophecy of
Thomas the Rhymer—'Tyde What May Betyde, Haig shall be Haig of
Bemersyde.'

Azure, a saltire between a mull[...] chief and base, and a decresc[...] and increscent in fess, argent[...]

VI. PETER DE HAGA, c. 1326–33. Was at battle of Bannockburn, 1314; at that of Duplin, 1332; and=MARGARET, dau. of Alan Purves,
was killed at battle of Halidon Hill, 1333 (Douglas's Baronage, p. 134). of Ercildoune (Mylne MS.).

VII. HENRY DE HAGA, 1333–68, d. unmd. Witness to a   **VIII.** JOHN DE HAGA, 1368–88. Witness to a Charter=MARY, daughter of John Mautland, Lord of
Charter of Sir William de Abernethy, Knight (Liber of John Mautland, Lord of Thirlestane (Liber de Thirlestane (Mylne MS.).
de Dryburgh, pp. 259, 260, 274). Dryburgh, p. 230), and is said to have fallen at
Otterburn, 1388.

IX. SIR ANDREW HAIG, 1388–1414. Witness as 'Dominus Andreas=BLANCHE, widow of Sir Edmund de Bradeston, Kt. Grant from Ric. II. 13 May, 1395, to Sir   WILL[...]
Haig' to a Charter of David Menyheis de Weme, dated 1412 Andrew Hage, Kt., and Blanche his wife, formerly widow of Sir Edmund de Bradeston,
(Registrum de Dunfermelyn, p. 279). Kt., of two annuities of 40 marks and £40. ''Calendar of Documents relating to
Scotland,'' ed. J. Bain, p. 99.

X. JOHN HAIG, 1414–36. Maintained a long feud with the Abbot of Melrose, for which he was excommunicated in 1422=ELIZABETH, dau. of Archibald Mure of Rowallan.
(Liber de Melros, ii. 542–44). Killed at Piperdean, 1436.

XI. GILBERT HAIG, 1436–58. Excommunicated with his father in 1422; at=BARBARA (his cousin),   DAVID (mentioned in deed of ex-
battle of Sark, 1450; and joined the E. of Angus against the E. of Douglas, dau. of McDougal of communication).
1455. Makerstoun.

XII. JAMES HAIG, 1458–90. Fought for King James III. at Sauchieburn, 1488; his son taking up arms for the=MARGARET, dau. of Sir David
Prince. Obliged by James IV. to resign Bemersyde to his son, 12th Feb., 1490. His seal, 'S. Jacobi Haig,' Scott, of Branxholm (The Scotts
shows the saltire on the shield, but is much worn. of Buccleuch, i. 56).

XIII. WILLIAM HAIG, 1490–1513. Invested with Bemersyde, at hands of=ISOBELL, dau. of Mungo Home, of Cowdenknowes, and Elizabeth, dau. of   ELIZABETH.
King James IV., 'by staff and baton,' Feb. 13, 1490. Fell at Flodden, James Stuart, Earl of Buchan, son of Sir James Stuart (Black Knight
Sept. 20, 1513. of Lorn) and Joan Beaufort, widow of James I. of Scotland.

XIV. ROBERT HAIG, 1513–54. A notorious freebooter (Acta Dom. Concil. et Sessionis, vol. iv. o. 89, 90). Dis-=BARBARA, dau. of William Spottiswood, of that Ilk.
tinguished himself at Ancrum Moor, 1544, and for his bravery received a 'discharge of many bygone debts
owing to the King.' Took 'assurance' of Somerset, 1547. Resigned Bemersyde to his son, 1554.

XV. ANDREW HAIG, 1554–83. Received Charter of=ELIZABETH, dau. of   JAMES.   GEORGE, farmer in=ISABEL, dau. of
Bemersyde from Mary, Queen of Scots, dated William McDougal   Bemersyde. Robson, of
June 3, 1554. Restored Bemersyde Tower, of Makerstoun diswood.
where a stone bears the arms of Haig and Mar. Contract dated Sept. 16, 1540
McDougal, with 'A.H.E.M. 1581.' (Prot. Bk. of W. Corbet, No. 7, fo. [...]

XVI. ROBERT HAIG, 1583–1602. 'Robert Hege, of=MARGARET, dau. of George Kerr, of Faldonside. Her   ANDREW.
Bemersyde,' on Feb. 11, 1585, is surety for peace- brother, Andrew, was one of Rizzio's murderers;
able behaviour of the Kerrs of Faldonside, towards and implicated in Raid of Ruthven, 1582.
James Sinclair (Reg. Priv. Council, iii. 721).

XVII. JAMES HAIG, =ELIZABETH, dau.   **XIX.** WILLIAM, 1627–36. King's Solicitor for Scotland, d. unm. in   GEORGE, d. un[...]
1602–1619. Dis- of Thomas Holland 1639. Received Charter of Bemersyde Jan. 29, 1611, and MARGARET, m[...]
poned Bemersyde McDougal, of resigned it to his nephew, Andrew, Dec. 14, 1619, at whose death James Halit[...]
July 9, 1610, to his brother William, and d. on Continent Stodrig. in 1627 he resumed possession. Identified in 1634 as author of of Dryburg[...]
before Nov. 1623, when he is referred to as 'umquhil' James 'The Supplication,' he fled to Holland. In April 1635, as security was ancestr[...]
Haig, of Bemersyde. for a loan of 5,300 marks he assigned to Wm. McDougal in Sir Walter S[...]
Groningen his equity of redemption of Lord Hay's mortgage over
Bemersyde.

A
CONTINUED ON NEXT PAGE.

CONTINUED FROM PRECEDING PAGE.

A

ANDREW, 1620 – 27. ...ceived Bemersyde from uncle, William Haig. ...arter under Great Seal, ...ed Jan. 13, 1620. Seisin Feb. 5, 1620 ; died at ...nersyde, unm. 1627.

2. ROBERT. Consents as 'brother and heir of umquhil Andrew Haig' to transfer of Bemersyde mortgage to Lord Hay, of Yester, the right of redemption being expressly reserved to William Haig and his heirs or assignees. Dated May 15, 1627. = ELSPETH, dau. of John Abercromby, of Abbots Throsk, and Agnes, sister of Sir Alex. Drummond, of Carnock, co. Stirling. Proved her husband's will, Oct., 1664. Reg. Test. Stirling.

3. GEORGE.
4. JAMES, an officer in Dutch Service.
5. ALEXANDER.
6. WILLIAM.
8 & 9 sons.
10. FREDERICK.

XX. DAVID, 1636–54 (7th son), living in 1635 with his uncle, Wm. McDougal, in Groningen. On his marriage in 1636, received from William Haig a disposition of Bemersyde, and from William McDougal the right of redemption of Lord Hay's mortgage. = HIBERNIA SCHOLES (m. 27 Oct. 1636), widow of Anthony Gunter Prott, and descended from the Hohenzollen family,

... HAIG, Orchard Farm, ...r Alloa. = ISOBEL, dau. of Alexander Ramsay, of Alloa ; m. Mar. 1, 1660.

Other issue.

XXI. ANTHONY HAIG, 1654–1712. His title having been impugned by a decision of the Court of Session in 1671, he resigned Bemersyde to the Crown, and received a new Charter dated Feb. 16, 1672. = JEAN, dau. and heir of James Home, of Harieheugh.

...RGE HAIG, b. Aug. 27, ...2, of Newbigging, near ...oa. = JANET ANDERSON ; m. Mar. 22, 1684.

Other issue.

XXII. ZERUBABEL HAIG, 1712–32, of Bemersyde. Connected with the Jacobite party in 1715, d. 1732. = ELIZABETH, dau. of Thomas Gordon, of the Strathearn family, Clerk of the Justiciary, Edinburgh ; m. April 13, 1698.

... HAIG, b. 1688, ...Alloa ; m. Dec. 31, ...1. = ELSPETH NICOL, of a well-known family in Alloa, who matriculated their arms in 1733.

5. JAMES HAIG, of Alloa ; m. Aug. 7, 1718. = MARY, dau. of John Mackenzie, of Alloa.

Other issue.

XXIII. JAMES ANTHONY HAIG, 1732–90, of Bemersyde, b. 1718, d. 1790. A Jacobite. = BARBARA, dau. of William Robertson, of Ladykirk ; m. Sep. 25, 1757.

...RGE HAIG, b. Settled in S. ...lina ; m. 1742. ...d by Indians 1749. = ELIZABETH WATSON, m. 2, Lieut. Mercier ; 3, William Webb.

Other issue.

2. JOHN HAIG, b. Sept. 9, 1720, of the Gartlands, near Alloa ; m. Feb. 11, 1751. = MARGARET, dau. of John Stein, of Kennetpans, Clackmannanshire.

Other issue.

XXIV. JAMES ZERUBABEL HAIG, 1790–1840, of Bemersyde. Capt. 93rd Regt. ; m. Dec. 9, 1794. = ISABELLA, dau. of Samuel Watson, Solicitor, Edinburgh.

...RGE = MARY, dau. ...s, b. of Colonel ...d. 1790, Hezekiah ...arleston, Maham. Will ...ed Sep. ...90, exe...s, John ...s Haig, Blake, ...les, and ...ashing-

1. JAMES, b. 1755, d. 1833, of Blairhill, co. Perth. = HELEN, dau. of John Higgins, of Neuk ; m. May 6, 1784.

2. JOHN, b. 1758, d. 1819, of Bonnington, nr. Edinburgh. = CHRISTINA, dau. of John Jameson, of Leith ; m. 1787.

4. ROBERT, b. 1764, d. 1845, of Roebuck, co. Dublin ; m. Aug. 7, 1798. = CAROLINE MARY, dau. of Sir William Wolseley, of Wolseley, co. Staff.

6. WILLIAM, b. 1771, d. 1847, of Seggie, co. Fife ; m. Oct. 13, 1794. = JANET, dau. of John Stein, of Kennetpans.

XXV. JAMES HAIG, 1840–54, of Bemersyde, Writer to the Signet, b. 1795, d. unmarried Jan. 14, 1854. In 1866, Barbara, Sophia, and Mary Haig executed a deed conveying Bemersyde, at death of last survivor of them, to their 'cousin Arthur Balfour Haig.'

BARBARA, d. unm. 1873.
SOPHIA, d. unm. 1878.
MARY, d. unm. 1871.

HEZEKIAH-...AM HAIG, ...harleston, b. ...d. 1836. = AGNES RITCHIE ; m. 1808.

6. DAVID, b. 1796, d. 1848, of Glenogil, co. Forfar ; m. Mar. 17, 1828. = ELIZABETH, dau. and heir of Richard Price, of Highfields Park, Sussex.

3. ROBERT, b. 1796, d. 1878, of Fane Valley, Dundalk ; m. Nov. 1, 1823. = MAGDALENE, dau. of David Murray, of Whitehouse, Musselburgh.

8. GEORGE-AUGUSTUS, of Pen-Ithon, co. Radnor ; b. 1820. = ANNE ELIZA, dau. of Capt. M. E. Fell ; m. July 28, 1848.

3. JOHN, b. 1802, d. 1878, of Cameron House, Fife. = RACHEL - MACKERRAS, dau. and co-heir of Hugh Veitch, of Stewartfield, nr. Edinburgh ; m. Aug. 20, 1839. Of the family of Veitch of Eliock.

...DER - RITCHIE ...2, d. 1855, m. ANN MARR, ...of Dr. Robert ...own Haig. =

JAMES-RICHARD, b. 1831, d. 1896, of Blairhill, co. Perth, and Highfields Park, Sussex. = JANE, dau. of James Thompson ; m. May 8, 1857.

XXVI. ARTHUR BALFOUR, Lieut.-Col. R.E., C.M.G., succeeded to Bemersyde at death of Sophia Haig, of Bemersyde, 6th and youngest son, born 1840. = FRANCES-CHARLOTTE, only dau. of George Francis, 3rd Lord Harris, m. Apl. 9, 1874.

1. JOHN ADAIR.
2. MURRAY, Capt. H.E.I.C.S.
3. FELIX, M.-Gen. R.E.
4. MALCOLM, M.-Gen. I.S.C.
5. EDWIN, Lieut. 5th Fusiliers, fell at Lucknow 1857.
1. ISABELLA.
2. EMILY.
3. CATHARINE.

1. CHARLES-EDWIN, b. 1849, Barrister, Inner Temple, m. Orchardwood, Ascot. = JANET-STEIN, dau. of John Haig, of Cameron House, Fife ; m. Apl. 18, 1871

2. ALEXANDER.
4. CECIL.
5. EDRIC.
1. JANET, m. G. F. Boyd.
2. EDITH, m. J. A. H. Jameson.
3. ROSE, m. J. H. Thomas.
4. SYBIL, m. D. A. Thomas, M.P.
5. CHARLOTTE.

2. HUGH-VEITCH, of Ramornie, Fifeshire, b. 1845, m. June 3, 1872. = ARCHIE ANN LINDSAY, dau. of W. N. Fraser, of Findrack, Aberdeenshire.

1. WILLIAM, m. 1871, left issue.
3. JOHN.
4. GEORGE.
5. DOUGLAS, Lt.-Col. 7th Hussars.
1. MARY, m. (1) Lt.-Col. De Prée, R.A., and (2) John Jameson.
2. JANET.
3. HENRIETTA, m. W. G. Jameson.

...DER - RITCHIE ...b. 1844, of ...of Charleston, ...eston, S.C. ; ...LIZABETH ...ELL. =

1. ALEXANDER-PRICE, of Blairhill, b. 1863, Lieut. 5th Dragoon Guards ; m. Aug. 1, 1885. = JESSIE-LOUISA, dau. of George Armstrong, of the Elms, Gosforth.

2. DAVID PRICE, of Highfields Park, Sussex, b. 1868. = EDITH-MARY, dau. of C. Wacher ; m. 25 March, 1896.

3. J. RICHARD P.
4. WILLIAM P.
1. MARGARET, m. Alex. Stuart.
2. JESSIE, m. A.C. Anderson.
3. ELIZABETH.
4. MARY-ANNE.
5. KATHERINE.

1. GUY-ARTHUR-GEORGE, b. 1876.
2. NIGEL ESME, b. 1887.
1. DOROTHY-BARBARA.
2. CICELY-PHOEBE.

ROLAND-CHARLES, Capt. 7th Dragoon Guards, b. 1873 ; m. 20 Apl., 1899, Geraldine-Dorothy, dau. of Rev. Beauchamp K. W. Kerr-Pearse, of Batts Park, Somerset, Rector of Ascot.

RACHEL DOROTHY WOLSELEY.

1. OLIVER, b. 1876, Lieut. 7th Hussars.
1. RUTH, m. Cecil G. De Prée, 15th Hussars.
2. ALTHEA-VIRGINIA JOSEPHINE.

...XANDER-RITCHIE, b. 1878.
...RENCE-WITSELL, b. 1880.
...ERT-McKEOWN, b. 1882.
...HARD-LINING, b. 1886.
...-ELIZABETH.

1. JAMES-LESLIE, b. 1886.
2. ALASTAIR-NIGEL, b. 1900.
EILEEN-ALEXANDRA.

RONALD-PRICE, b. 10 Jan., 1899.

FESTINA· VERV NT: ḣESTINGA: VT CIBVM· RAPERENTVR:

" Here the Knights pushed on to Hastings to find food." *After the Bayeux Tapestry.*

— **H** —

Henri Habervile

Euſtace de Hacqe

Rauf Haket

Habervile, Henry—(H. III. Roll) bore, azure, in dexter chief point a lyon passant gardant or, in sinister chief point and in base a cinquefoyle pierced of the last ; Arden and St. George Rolls. (F.) See TUBERVILLE.

Hacche, Sir Eustace de, banneret, baron 1299, sealed the Barons' letter to the Pope, 1301, pp. xx, xxiv. He bore, at the battle of Falkirk 1298, and at the siege of Carlaverock 1300 or, a cross engrailed gules (F.) ; ascribed also to JOHN in Jenyns' Ordinary.

Haccombe, Sir Stephen, of Devon— (E. II. Roll), and JOHN (E. III. Roll)—bore, argent, three bendlets sable ; Parliamentary Roll and Jenyns' Ordinary.

Ha(c)ket, Henry—(H. III. Roll) bore, or, three bendlets gules, a label (5) azure ; Arden Roll.

‡**Hacket, Rauf de**—(H. III. Roll) bore, sable, crusily and three hake-fish hauriant 2 and 1 (F.), Dering Roll ; hauriant in pale in Ashmole MS. ; ascribed to WILLIAM in Howard Roll.

Ha(c)ket, Sir Walter, of Derbyshire—bore at the first Dunstable tournament 1308, argent, two bends gules (F.), Parliamentary and Ashmole Rolls ; ascribed also to JOHN in Jenyns' Ordinary.

Ha(c)kley (——), armiger ; slain at the siege of Calais 1347—bore, azure, a chevron between three bugles argent, a crescent for difference.

Ha(c)klute, Sir Edmond, of Salop— (E. II. Roll) bore, argent, on a (plain) bend between two cotises dancettée gules three mullets or. Sir RICHARD bore it with trefoyles in place of mullets on the bend ; Parliamentary and Ashmole Rolls.

Hacklute, Sir Richard—bore, at the first Dunstable tournament 1308, argent, on a bend gules cotised sable three fleurs-de-lys or (F.) LEONARD (R. II. Roll) bore, mullets or pierced azure, instead of fleurs-de-lys, on the bend— another trick makes the bend and cotises sable, both in Surrey Roll.

Hacklute, John de—(E. III. Roll) bore, argent, a fess gules and another in chief dancettée of the last ; Jenyns' Ordinary.

Ha(c)kelute, Sir Walter, of Salop—(E. II. Roll) bore, gules, a fess dancettée between three Danish hatchets erect or, Parly. Roll ; fess indented argent, Harl. 6137, fo. 27ᵇ.

Hacon, Sir Hubert (HAKON), of Norfolk —(E. II. Roll) bore, sable, two bars vaire argent and vert ; Parliamentary Roll.

Hadham, Thomas—(E. III. Roll) bore, argent a bend between six round buckles 3 and 3 azure, tongues to the base ; Jenyns' Ordinary.

*****Haggerston, Robert**—(E. III. Roll) bore, azure, on a bend cotised argent three chess-rooks (? rightly billets) in bend of the field (F.) ; Jenyns' Ordinary. Originally, a scaling ladder between two leaves in allusion to a Hazlerigg heiress ; Shirley.

Hake, Andrew—(E. III. Roll) bore, azure, three bars or, a bordure engrailed argent ; Jenyns' Roll.

Hakenbeche, Reginald—(R. II.) bore, or two bars azure ; Surrey Roll.

Hales, Sir Stephen de—(E. III. Roll) bore, sable, a chevron between three lyonceaux rampant argent ; Ashmole and Surrey Rolls.

Hallys ——, (E. III. Roll) bore, burulée (12) argent and azure, on a canton gules a lyon passant or ; Ashmole Roll.

Halnsby (——), a Knight—(H. VI. Roll) bore, or, a saltire sable ; Arundel Roll.

Halouton, Sir Robert de, of co. Cambridge—(E. II. Roll) bore, argent on a bend gules three eaglets displayed or (F.) ; Parliamentary Roll and Harl. MS. 6137, fo. 63. ROBERT DE HAULTON took up the cross in the last Crusade 1270.

Hal(o)uton, Sir Thomas de, neyr.—bore, at the battle of Boroughbridge 1322, and another THOMAS bore at the second Dunstable tournament 1334, gules a lyon rampant argent crowned or, and so also did Sir THOMAS, knighted at the capitulation of Calais 1348 ; (F.) Ashmole Roll.

Hal(o)ughton, Thomas de—(H. III. Roll) bore, gules, three bucks' heads cabossed or (F.), St. George Roll ; one buck's head in Arden Roll.

Robert de Halroot un

Rȝo de Halnoton

Robert Hagorſton

Walter Habott

Richard Hackluto

Henry Halȝgum

ffranc Halȝgum

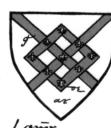

Lamr de Hamoldono

Rȝob de Halnȝono

Lawr de Hamerton

John Hamlyns

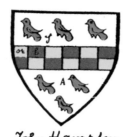

John Hampton

Andrew de Harterley

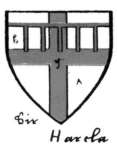

Sir Harcla

Le Sire Harrington

Joh de Hambune

Vic. de Harloo

Halowton, Thomas de—(E. II. Roll) bore, gules "a palme" argent—a sinister hand apaumée couped in trick; Jenyns' Roll.

Halsham, Sir Henry—bore, at the siege of Rouen 1418, or, a chevron engrailed between three lyons' heads erased gules (F.)—the field argent and leopards' faces for a Suffolk Knight; Arundel Roll.

Haltham, Sire Francis de—bore, at the battle of Boroughbridge 1322, azure an escarbuncle or. F.

Halton, John de—(E. III. Roll) bore, argent, two bars azure in chief two escallops gules—ROBERT bore three hurts in chief; Jenyns' Ordinary. See HALOUTON.

Hameldene, Sir Laurence de, of Suffolk, Knight—bore at the first Dunstable tournament 1308, argent, fretty gules, florettée at the points or—a fret in Parliamentary Roll. F.

Hamerton, John — (E. III. Roll) bore, argent, a fess between three lyonceux rampant, tails fourchée, sable; Jenyns' Ordinary.

*Hamerton, Lawrence—(E. II. Roll) bore, argent, three martels (vel hammers) sable (F.); Jenyns' Roll.

Hamlowe v. Hanlowe.

Hamlyn, Sir John, of Leicestershire, Knight—bore, at the first Dunstable tournament 1308, and at the battle of Boroughbridge 1322, gules, a lyon rampant ermine crowned or (F.); Parliamentary and Ashmole Rolls. Cotgrave gives—gules, a lyon or guttée de poix, for HAMLYN. F.

Hamme v. Hawnes.

Hamme, Sir John de, of Surrey—(E. II. Roll) bore, azure, a chevron between three demi lyons rampant or; Parliamentary Roll.

Hammon, Sir John (or HANLOWE), of Oxon. —(E. II. Roll) bore, argent, a lyon rampant azure guttée d'or; Parliamentary Roll.

Hampton, Sir John (HOPTON)—bore, at the siege of Calais 1345-8, argent, a fess counter compony or and azure, between six martlets gules. F.

Hancett, Hamond (or HAMO HAUTEYN)— (H. III. Roll) bore, gules, three bends or; Arden Roll; a label (5, 6) argent; St. George Roll. Compare with tricks in copies of the Arden Roll. F.

Haningfylde, Sir William, of Essex— (E. II. Roll) bore, or, a chevron sable; Parliamentary Roll.

Haninvile, Henry de—(H. III. Roll) bore, sable, crusily fitchée and a bend or (F.); St. George Roll. Surname doubtful. See also HANVILE.

Hanitune, John de—(E. I. Roll) bore, quarterly argent and sable (F.), same as FITZ UMFREY; Guillim and Segar Rolls.

Hankeford —— (E. III. Roll) bore, argent, two cotises dancettée sable; Ashmole Roll.

Hanley (——) a Kentish Knight—(H. VI. Roll) bore, vert, a saltire engrailed argent; Arundel Roll.

Hanle(y), Sir John (of Kent)—bore, at the first Dunstable tournament 1308, gules, three crescents or; argent in Parliamentary Roll. F.

‡Hanlo, Nichole de—(H. III. Roll) bore, or, two chevronels gules on a quarter of the second a crescent argent (F.); Dering, Howard and Camden Rolls.

Hanlowe, Sir John de (of Oxon.)—bore, at the first Dunstable tournament 1308, argent, a lyon rampant azure guttée d'or (F.); Parliamentary Roll (as of Kent) and Jenyns' Ordinary. See also HAMLYN and HAMMON.

Hansarde, Robert de—bore, at the siege of Carlaverock 1300, gules, three mullets argent (F.); ascribed also to GILBERT, JOHN, Sir JOHN, and to Sir ROBERT of co. Lincs., Parliamentary, Nativity, and Ashmole Rolls; in some the mullets are pierced, in others mullets of six pierced occur, i.e. spur-rowells; estoiles, not mullets for GILBERT are tricked in Glover Roll; and azure, not gules, for the field is ascribed to WILLIAM in Norfolk Roll.

Hansard, Sir John, of Lincolnshire — (E. II. Roll) bore, gules, a bend between six mullets 3 and 3 argent; Parliamentary Roll.

Hansted v. Hausted—Hawsted.

Hanvile, Sir Thomas de, of Bucks—(E. II. Roll) bore, azure, a fess dancettée between three "girfauks" (falcons) or, tricked as martlets; Parliamentary Roll—a plain fess gules in Ashmole Roll. See HANINVILE.

Harcla, Sir Andrew, of Cumberland baron 1321, Earl of Carlisle 1322—bore, at the first Dunstable tournament 1308, argent, a cross gules, in the cantel a martlet sable (F.) (as HARTECLEY); Parliamentary and Nativity Rolls.

Harcla, Sir Nicholas (or MICHEL HERTE-CLAWE) of Cumberland—(E. II. Roll) bore, argent, a cross gules; Parliamentary Roll; borne also by one of this name with a label (5) azure (F.) knighted at the capitulation of Calais 1348.

*Harcourt, Sir John de, of co. Leic., banneret—bore, at the first Dunstable tournament 1308, gules two bars or, as also did ROGER, K.G., slain at the siege of Calais 1347. (F.) Parliamentary Roll [borne by JOHN f Sir JOHN, with a label (3, 5) azure] the reverse ascribed to another JOHN, RICHARD, THOMAS, and WILLIAM; Parliamentary, Segar, Glover, and St. George Rolls.

Harecourte, Robert de—(H. III. Roll) bore, gules, two bars ermine; Howard Roll.

Harlyns

Hartwell

Hamo Hanteyn

nicholab Hanlo

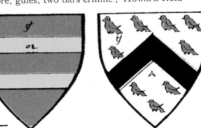

John de Hamlono

John Hardeshull

Roba de Hardres

de Harecourt

P

Hardeshull, Sire Johan de—bore, at the battle of Boroughbridge 1322, and at the second Dunstable tournament 1334, argent, semée of martlets gules, a chevron sable (F.), in Ashmole MS. ; 3 and 3 martlets at Dunstable, 7 and 4 in Ashmole Roll, and in Jenyns' Ordinary for THOMAS.

Hardeshull, Sir William, of co. Leic.—(E. II. Roll) bore, or a cross engrailed gules in the first quarter a martlet vert ; Parliamentary Roll. See HARCLA.

Harding, Sir Edmond, of Kent, Kt.—(H. VI. Roll) bore, gules, a lyon rampant ermine over all a chevron or ; Arundel Roll.

†**Hardres, Robert de**—(H. III. Roll) bore, ermine, a lyon rampant gules debruised by a chevron or ; Dering Roll ; the field argent in Howard Roll. F.

Harlaston (——) a Suffolk Knight—(H. VI. Roll) bore, argent, a chevron sable, *quarterly with,* argent a fess ermine cotised sable ; Arundel Roll.

Harleston, Thomas—(E. III. Roll) bore, argent, a saltire gules between four fleurs-de-lys azure ; Jenyns' Ordinary ; JOHN NEVILL, of Lincolnshire, bears these arms.

Harley, Sir Richard (HARLEE) of Salop—(E. II. Roll) bore, or, a bend cotised sable ; Parliamentary Roll. F.

Harling, ——, (E. III. Roll) bore, azure, florettée argent ; Ashmole Roll.

Harlyns (——), a Suffolk Kt.—(H. VI. Roll) bore, argent, a unicorn rampant sable horned and unguled or ; Arundel Roll. F.

Harington *v.* **Haverington.**

***Harington, Sir John de** (HAVERINGTON) a baron 1324—bore, at the first Dunstable tournament 1308, sable fretty argent (F.) ; Parliamentary Roll, &c. ; this coat was also carried at the siege of Rouen 1418. Sir JOHN, Sir MICHAEL and Sir JOHN appear to have differenced with a label (3) gules ; Ashmole, Nativity, and Surrey Rolls.

Harington (——), a Knight—(H. VI. Roll) bore, quarterly (1) sable fretty argent, a label (3) gules ; (2) argent, a saltire gules ; (3) gules, three escallops argent ; (4) argent, a cross patonce sable ; Arundel Roll.

Harington, Sir T.—(H. VI. Roll) bore, sable, a fret argent, a label (5) gules, *quarterly with,* argent a cross patée sable ; Atkinson Roll.

Harington, Sir James, of Hornby—(E. IV. Roll) bore, argent, fretty sable ; with crest ; Ballard Roll.

Harington, Sir John de—(E. II. Roll) bore, or, a chief gules, over all a bend azure ; Parliamentary Roll ; the field argent, Harl. MS. 6137 fo. 19.

Harington, John de—(E. III. Roll) bore, or, a chief gules over all a bend sable ; Jenyns' Ordinary.

SIR JOHN HARSYCK.
IN SOUTHACRE CHURCH, NORFOLK, 1384, 8 R. II.
From Boutell.

Harpden, Sir William de, of Oxon.—(E. II. Roll) bore, argent a mullet pierced gules, Parliamentary Roll ; a Suffolk Knight of this surname, bore (H. VI.) argent on a mullet gules, a besant charged with a martlet sable ; Arundel Roll.

[**Harpur** (——) of Rushall—a plain cross—but bore the arms of Rushall, argent, a lyon rampant within a bordure engrailed sable.—Shirley.]

Harsick, John de—(E. III. Roll) bore, or, a chief indented (4) sable ; Jenyns' Ordinary, a fess in Ashmole Roll. See Monumental Brass.

Hartford *v.* **Hertford.**

Hartford, Robert—(E. III. Roll) bore, argent, on a fess sable three harts' heads cabossed or ; Jenyns' Ordinary.

Hartford, Thomas, of Badsworth—(E. III. Roll) bore, argent, a lyon purpure masculy or ; Jenyns' Ordinary.

Harthull, Sir Richard de, of co. Derby—(E. II. Roll) bore, argent two bars vert ; Parliamentary Roll — also ascribed to JOHN HERTHILL, though tricked vair, in Jenyns' Ordinary.

Hartwell, —— (HAREWELL), an Essex ? Knight—(H. VI. Roll) bore, sable, a buck's head cabossed argent between the attires a cross patée of the last ; Arundel Roll. F.

Haseley (——) a Suffolk Knight—(H. VI. Roll) bore, argent, a fess gules between three hazle nuts or, husks and stalks vert ; Arundel Roll. F.

*[**Hasilrig, Thomas,** of Fawdon — bore, argent, a chevron between three hazel leaves slipped vert.—Shirley.] F.

Haslarton *v.* **Heslarton.**

Hassell *v.* **Hansard.**

Hastang, Sir Robert de, of co. Staff., a baron 1311—bore, at the first Dunstable tournament 1308, azure, a chief gules, over all a lyon rampant or—Guillim, Segar and Parliamentary Rolls. Sir ROBERT signed the Barons' letter to the Pope 1301 and sealed with a lyon fourchée over all a barrulet in chief, pp. xxii, xxiv ; see also Jenyns' Ordinary and Parliamentary Roll.

Fre Ho Hasilrig   Fre do Hasting

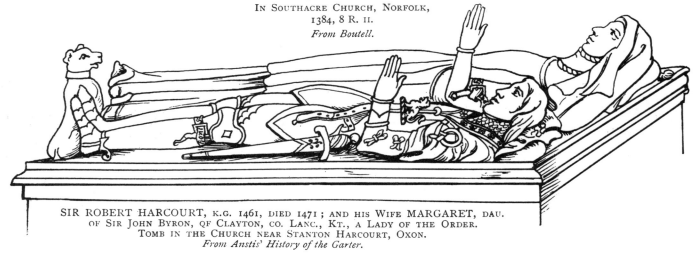

SIR ROBERT HARCOURT, K.G. 1461, DIED 1471 ; AND HIS WIFE MARGARET, DAU. OF SIR JOHN BYRON, QF CLAYTON, CO. LANC., KT., A LADY OF THE ORDER. TOMB IN THE CHURCH NEAR STANTON HARCOURT, OXON.
From Anstis' History of the Garter.

Haſoloy

nuɔ̃ do Haſtango

John do Haſtorp

John do Haſtings

Hastang, Sir John de (HASTINGES)—bore at the first Dunstable tournament 1308, azure, a chief gules over all a lyon rampant argent; ascribed also to HUMFRY in Arden and St. George Rolls, and to Sir PHILIP, of Staff., in Parliamentary Roll.

Hastang, Sire Thomas de—bore, at the battle of Boroughbridge 1322, azure, a chief gules over all a lyon rampant or, and a label argent; ascribed also to Sir JOHN, ƒ Sir ROBERT, of co. Staff., in Parliamentary Roll.

Hastang, Sir Nichol de (of co. Staff.)—bore, at the first Dunstable tournament 1308, azure, a chief gules, a lyon rampant or debruised by a baston argent (F.); Parly. Roll.

Hastang, Rafe de—(H. III. Roll) bore, azure, a chief or and over all a lyon rampant gules; Howard Roll.

Hasthorp, Sire Johan de—bore, at the battle of Boroughbridge 1322, argent on a bend sable three martlets or. F.

Hasting [Drew de—bore, before the Conquest per fess or and vert, a bull rampant counterchanged!! Jenyns' Roll, Add. MS. 12,224 fo. 48b.]

Hastings, John de, Baron of Bergeueny 1299, signed the Barons' letter to the Pope 1301 and sealed with a cross which with the field is charged with fleurs-de-lys, pp. xvi, xxiv. He bore, at the siege of Carlaverock 1300, or, a maunch gules (F.); Nobility, Parliamentary and Arundel Rolls; borne also by HENRY, Sir HENRY, and by JOHN (‡) in Dering Roll; also by Le Seigneur DE HASTINGES at the battle of Boroughbridge 1322—and by LAURENCE, Earl of PEMBROKE, at the siege of Calais 1345-8; HASTINGS is borne quarterly with VALENCE on the Monumental Brass.

Hastings, Sir Edmund de, banneret, a baron 1299 (brother of JOHN, Baron of Bergavenny)—bore, at the battle of Falkirk 1298, and also at the siege of Carlaverock 1300, or, a maunch gules a label (5) sable (argent, in Nobility Roll; vert in Parly. Roll.) Sir EDMUND had from Edward I. the Scottish Earldom of Menteith on the deprivation of Earl ALAN. On becoming surety for Sir JOHN DRUMMOND, a prisoner in England, and having succeeded to his lands and apparently his arms, barry wavy of six, he so sealed the Barons' letter to the Pope 1301, pp. xxi, xxiv, describing himself as "D'n's de Enchimcholmok" = Inchmahome; see Sir JOHN'S effigy, p. 71.

Hastings, Sir Hugh, of Gressing, Norfolk, summoned to a council in 1342—bore, at the siege of Calais 1345, or a maunch gules a label (3) azure (F.) see Monumental Brass; borne also by Sir NICHOLAS at the first Dunstable

LAURENCE HASTINGS, EARL OF PEMBROKE.
IN ELSING CHURCH, NORFOLK. OB. 1348.
From a rubbing of the Hastings Brass.

tournament 1308; Cotgrave and Parliamentary Rolls, and by Sir WILLIAM (E. I.) Harl. Roll. Another Sir WILLIAM, banneret (E. II. Roll), bore, a label (3) charged with the arms of Pembroke, checquy argent and azure three martlets gules; Parliamentary Roll.

Hastings, Sir William de—bore, at the first Dunstable tournament 1308, or, a maunch within an orle of martlets gules, a label (3) argent, each pendant charged with four barrulets azure, for Valence.

Hastings, Le Sr. de (——) bore at the siege of Rouen 1418, or, a maunch gules, *quarterly with*, gules, a bend argent.

Hastings, Sir John, of co. Glouc. (brother of Sir WILLIAM)—bore, at the first Dunstable tournament 1308, HASTINGS within a bordure of Valence, also blasoned burulée argent and azure, eight martlets in orle gules, over all on an escocheon (of HASTINGS), or a maunch gules. (F.) Sir WILLIAM, banneret, bore it also (E. II.); Parliamentary Roll. See another Sir WILLIAM, who bore HASTINGS, with a label of PEMBROKE.

Hastings, Sir Edmund, bore (erroneously it is said) at the battle of Falkirk 1298, or, three maunches gules a label azure (F.) (see Sir EDMUND above); tricked without the label in Jenyns' Ordinary for OSMOND and EDMOND—the field argent for another EDMUND in Jenyns' and Arundel Rolls.

Hastyng (——) Knight (H. VI. Roll)—bore, argent a fess gules between three maunches sable; Arundel Roll.

Hastings, Sir Rafe—Knighted at the capitulation of Calais 1348, argent, a maunch sable. (F.) Ashmole and Cotgrave Rolls, &c.; borne also by William, Lord Hastings, K.G. 1462; see title-page.

Hastings, Sir Miles de, of Oxon.—(E. II. Roll) bore, or, a fess in chief two mullets gules; Parliamentary Roll. Sir PHILIP bore it differenced with a label (3) azure at the first Dunstable tournament 1308.

Hastings, Sir Robert de, of Cambridgeshire—(E. II. Roll) bore, ermine, on a chief azure two mullets or; Parliamentary Roll.

‡**Hastings, William de**—(H. III. Roll) bore, argent, a fess between three lozenges azure. (F.) Dering, Howard and Camden Rolls.

Hatfeld, Thomas, Bishop of Durham—bore, at the siege of Calais 1345-8, ermine a chevron sable (sometimes gules) impaled on the dexter with the arms of the See of Durham. F.

Hugo Haſtings

John de Haſtings

Edm. Haſtings

Rafe de Haſtings

n̄ do Haſtings

Ꞇ Ꞑ Hatfiold
Biſhop of Durham

THE HERALDIC ATCHIEVEMENT

OF

SIR CHRISTOPHER HATTON, K.G., OF HOLDENBY HALL, NORTHANTS,

LORD CHANCELLOR OF ENGLAND.

Robt. Haunfard

Robt Hanftodo

Jorn de Hauftodo

Gooff de Hautovillo

L. do Hantot

Joan d. Hauerigges

Hatfeild, Thomas—(E. II. Roll) bore, sable, a chevron between three lyonceux rampant argent, Jenyns' Roll; the chevron or and a mullet sable in Jenyns' Ordinary.

Hatthorpe, Robert—(E. III. Roll) bore, sable, a chevron engrailed or; Jenyns' Ordinary.

Hauberk, John—(R. II. Roll) bore, argent on a bend sable three cinquefoyles pierced or. Surrey Roll.

Hausted, Sire John de, of Rutland, a baron 1322—bore, at the battle of Boroughbridge 1322, and at the second Dunstable tournament 1334, gules a chief checquy (counter-compony in trick) or and azure, a baston ermine; Jenyns' Ordinary, Parliamentary Roll and Ashmole MS. Sir ROBERT bore it at the first Dunstable tournament 1308 with a bend argent (F.); Parliamentary and Harl. Rolls—ascribed with a bend sable to another JOHN in Jenyns' Ordinary.

Hausted, Sir John de—bore, at the first Dunstable tournament 1308, argent on a bend vert three eaglets displayed or. F.

Haute, Sir William, of Kent, Kt.—(H. VI. Roll) bore, per pale azure and gules, a lyon rampant argent, *quarterly with,* or, a cross engrailed gules; Arundel Roll. See HAWTE.

Hauteville, Sir Geffrey (of Devon or Cornwall)—bore, at the battle of Boroughbridge 1322, sable crusily and a lyon rampant argent. (F.) Parliamentary Roll—ascribed crusily fitchée to THOMAS in Jenyns' Ordinary.

Hauteyn, Hamo, v. Hancett.

Hautot, Richard de—(H. III. Roll) bore, ermine, on a chief gules three mullets (6) or. (F.) Arden and St. George Rolls. See HOTTOT.

Havering, Sir John de, banneret, baron of Grafton 1299—bore, at the battle of Falkirk 1298 (argent) a lyon rampant, gules collared or; tail fourchée and collared azure in Nobility and Parly. Rolls; on his seal affixed to the Barons' letter to the Pope, the lyon is fourchée but not collared, pp. xx, xxiv.

Havering, Richard and **William de**—(H. II. Roll) bore, argent, a lyon rampant tail fourchée gules; St. George Roll and Jenyns' Ordinary.

Havering, Sir John—(E. III. Roll)—bore, argent, crusily fitchée and a lyon rampant tail fourchée and renowée all gules (F.); Ashmole Roll; ascribed in the same Roll with a label (3) azure to—HAVERINGHAM.

Havering, John ap, of Essex—(H. II. Roll) bore, argent, three lyons' heads erased sable. Arundel Roll. F.

Havering, John de—(H. III. Roll) bore, azure, on a fess argent, three escallops gules. (F.) St. George Roll.

Haveringham, v. Sir John Havering.

Haverington, Sir John de—(E. II. Roll) bore, argent, three hinds' heads couped gules, a label (3) or; Parliamentary Roll.

Haverington, Sir John de (v. HARINGTON)—bore, at the first Dunstable tournament 1308, sable fretty argent; St. George and Nativity Rolls. Sir MICHAEL differenced with a label (3) or, at the first Dunstable tournament 1308—but with a label gules (F.) in Nativity Roll.

Haversage, Matthew de (HAYERSEGGE) (H. III. Roll) bore, paly argent and gules, a chief of the first; Glover Roll.

Haversham, Nicol de—(H. III. Roll) bore, azure, crusily and a fess argent; St. George Roll.

Haward v. Howard.

Hawarde, Sire William, of Norfolk, baron 1296 – bore, gules crusily and a bend argent; Nobility and Parliamentary Rolls.—Sire WILLIAM HAUWARDE v. HAYWARDE, bore the same at the battle of Boroughbridge 1322. See also HOWARD.

Hawkewoode, John—(R. II. Roll) bore, argent, on a chevron sable three escallops of the field; Surrey Roll.

Hawkston, Sir Thomas — bore, at the siege of Calais 1345-8 argent, on a fess gules three hawks or. F.

Hawley, Thomas — (R. II. Roll) bore, azure, a saltire engrailed argent; Surrey Roll.

Hawnes —— (HAMME), of Suffolk, Kt.—(H. VI. Roll) bore, vert, two fish (lucies) hauriant addorsed and embowed argent; Arundel Roll. F.

Hawte, Nicholas — bore, at the siege of Rouen 1418 argent, on a bend azure three lyons passant or. (F.) Called HAWE in Ashmole MS. See HAUTE.

Haye, see De la Haye.

SIR HUGH HASTINGS.
FROM THE HASTINGS BRASS IN
ELSING CHURCH, NORFOLK, 1347.

John Havoring

Richard d. Haveringef

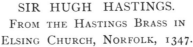

michaol de Haverington

nicol de Havorffam

Hawkfton

Hanmo

nich Hawto

Hugh Horcy

Henne del Horcie

Herei d. Hereford

Robt d. Hereford

Roger Horgam

Rich Heigham

Rob. Horswarde

Richard Hekin

Henri de Heriet

malt de Helinn

wm Horingand

malt de Holion

witt Herun

John Honoago

Joan Herun

Heath v. Hethe.

Heaton v. Heton.

Heaton, William—(E. IV. Roll) bore, argent, on a bend engrailed sable three bulls' heads erased of the field, *quarterly with*, argent, a Moor's head wreathed ppr. between three fleurs-de-lys sable ; with crest ; Ballard Roll.

Hebden, William—(E. III. Roll) bore, ermine, five fusils conjoined in fess gules ; Surrey Roll and Jenyns' Roll and Ordinary.

Hedingham, Richard de—(E. III. Roll) bore, argent a chevron between three fleurs-de-lys sable, ermine in blason ; Jenyns' Ordinary.

Heggios, Huge (*sive* BRUGES)—(H. III. Roll) bore, gules, bezantée and a chief ermine ; St. George Roll.

*[**Heigham, Richard**, *c.* 1340—bore, sable, a fess checquy or and azure, between three horses' heads erased argent.—Shirley.] F.

Hekin, Sir Richard, knighted at the siege of Calais 1348—bore, sable, a gryphon segreant argent. F.

Hellifield, William de—(E. III. Roll) bore, argent, two bends undée sable—same as RIC. DE STAPLETON ; Jenyns' Ordinary.

Hellis, Raufe de—(H. III. Roll) bore, sable, a bend argent ; Howard Roll.

Helyon, Richard and **Walter**—(H. III. Roll) bore, or, a buck's head cabossed sable ; Arden Roll and Jenyns' Ordinary. F.

‡**Helyon, Walter**—(H. III. Roll) bore, or three bucks' heads couped sable (F.) (azure in Ashmole MS.) ; Dering and Howard Rolls.

Heminghall, Sir Raffe de, of Norfolk—(E. II. Roll) bore, or, on a fess between two chevronels gules three escallops argent ; Parliamentary and Ashmole Rolls. THOMAS bore the escallops or ; Surrey Roll.

*[**Heneage, John**, 10 E. III.—bore, or, a greyhound courant sable between three leopards' faces azure, a border engrailed or.—Shirley.] F.

Hengrave, Sir Edward, of Suffolk—(E. II. Roll) bore argent, a chief dancettée (4) gules ; Parliamentary, Ashmole and Surrey Rolls, dancettée of 3 points in Jenyns' trick.

‡**Henre, William de**—(H. III. Roll) bore, gules, a cross argent, a label (5) azure ; Dering and Howard Rolls.

Henyngham (——), of Suffolk, Kt.—(H. VI. Roll) bore, quarterly or and gules a bordure sable poudré of escallops argent ; Arundel Roll.

Herbert, H—— (E. I. Roll) bore, ermine, a chief vaire or and gules over all a baston sable ; Harl. Roll.

Herbert, ——, (E. III. Roll) bore, per pale azure and gules three lyonceux rampant or ; Ashmole Roll. See FITZHERBERT.

Hercy, Sir Hugh, of Langford, co. Derby —(E. III. Roll) bore, gules, a chief argent ; Ashmole Roll. Sir HUGH, of co. Leic. (E. II.) differenced with a label (3) azure ; Parliamentary Roll—reversed in Jenyns' Roll. F.

Hercy, Henry del—(H. III. Roll) bore, azure, a cross or. (F.) St. George Roll.

Herdebye, John de—(E. III. Roll) bore, gules, billettée (5, 5) and a fess dancettée argent ; Jenyns' Ordinary.

Hereford, Earl of, v. Bohun.

Her(e)ford, Sir Henry de—(E. III. Roll) bore, gules, three eaglets displayed argent ; Ashmole Roll. HENRY, differenced with a label (5) azure ; St. George Roll. F.

Hereford, Robert de—(H. III. Roll) bore, or on a chief dancettée azure three annulets argent. (F.) Arden Roll.

Hereford (——) de—(H. III. Roll) bore, or, a pair of wings conjoined gules ; Arden Roll.

Hereward, Sir Robert, of Norfolk—(E. II. Roll) bore, azure, a fess gobony gules and vert between three owls argent ; Parly. Roll. F.

Hereward, Sir Robert, of Cambridgeshire — (E. II. Roll) bore, checquy or and azure on a bend gules three eagles displayed argent ; Parly. Roll—in some checquy azure and or, &c.

Herham, Sir Roger, Knighted at the capitulation of Calais 1348—bore, undée en lung argent and gules. F.

‡**Herice, Henry de**—(H. III. Roll) bore, or three hedgehogs passant in pale sable (F.) ; Howard Roll—2 and 1 passant sable in Dering Roll. Boars in Ashmole MS.

‡**Heringod, William**, and **Sir John**, of Sussex—(E. II. Roll) bore, azure, crusily and six herrings hauriant 3, 2, 1, or (F.) ; Dering, Camden, Parly., and Howard Rolls.

Herle, Sir Robert—(E. III. Roll) bore, gules, a chevron between three drakes (shovellers) argent ; Ashmole and Surrey Rolls.

Heron, Sir Godard, Sir Roger, John, (F.), **Sir John**, of Essex, **Sir Odinel**, of Northumberland—(E. II. and E. III. Rolls) bore, azure three herons passant argent ; Nativity, Glover, Parly., and St. George Rolls—tinctures reversed in Parly. Roll for Sir ODINELL. See HERONVILE, THOS.

Heron, Sir Roger and **Sir William**—(E. II. Roll) bore, gules, three herons passant argent ; Parly. and Ashmole Rolls—GERARD differenced with an annulet, and WALTER with a cross crosslet, both in chief, or ; Surrey Roll.

Heron, John—(R. II. Roll) bore, gules, a chevron between three herons argent—WILLIAM bore the chevron engrailed ; Surrey Roll and Jenyns' Ordinary.

Heron, William—(H. III. Roll) bore, gules, crusily or, a heron argent ; Arden and St. George Rolls.

Herondel, John de—(H. III. Roll) bore, gules, billettée and three lyons rampant or ; Arden Roll.

Heronvile, John de—(H. III. Roll) bore, sable, two lyons passant argent crowned or ; Arden Roll.

Heronvile, Thomas—(E. II. Roll) bore, azure, three herons passant argent, same as HERON ; Jenyns' Roll.

Hersham, Simon de (or HERSTUN)—(H. III. Roll) bore, sable three spur-rowells gules ; Arden Roll. Written HERSHEW in Harl. MS. 4965 fo. 10.

Herswell, Simon de—(H. III. Roll) bore, sable, three mullets (6) or (F.) ; St. George Roll.

ΠΛΕΟΝ ΗΜΙΣΥ ΠΑΝΤΟΣ.

THE HERALDIC ATCHIEVEMENT

OF

JOHN   ARUNDELL   HILDYARD, J.P., D.L.

OF HUTTON BONVILLE, YORKSHIRE.

112

Simon d. Herswell

Horpy

Henr' Hose

de Hotgoman

william Hill

Roger Hillary

will Hoskote

John Atte Hethe

Gilbert de Hirton

Robt d Hilton

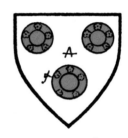

Robert Hilton

Hodey

Hertford, Earl of, v. Clare.

Hertford, ——, (E. III. Roll) bore, sable, five lozenges in bend or ; Ashmole Roll.

Herthill, John—(E. III. Roll) bore, argent two bars vert ; tricked vair ; Jenyns' Ordinary. See HARTHILL.

Hertlington, Henry—(E. III. Roll) bore, argent, a lyon rampant crowned gules ; Jenyns' Ordinary.

Hertlow, Sir William—(E. III. Roll) bore, argent, three gemelles gules ; Ashmole Roll.

*Hervy (——), an Essex Knight—(H. VI. Roll) bore, gules, on a bend argent three trefoyles vert ; Arundel Roll, F. See HOUN.

Hese v. DE LA HESE, HOSE, and HUSSEY.

Hese, Henry—(H. III. Roll) bore, or, three eagles displayed 2 and 1 sable (F.) ; Arden and St. George Rolls.

Hesy, Hugh le—(R. II. Roll) bore, or, on a fess sable a lyon passant gardant argent ; Surrey Roll.

Hese, John de la—(E. III. Roll) bore, argent, a fess sable between three lyonceux rampant 2 and 1 gules ; Jenyns' Ordinary, and in Roll as HESSEE, and as Sir JOHN DE LA HOESE, a Berkshire Knight, in Parly. Roll.

Hesilton, Elynaud de—(E. III. Roll) bore, argent, a saltire gules between four torteaux ; Jenyns' Ordinary.

*[Heskayte, Sir William, 1275—bore the arms of FYTTON—argent, on a bend sable three garbs or ; Shirley.] F.

Heslarton, Sir Thomas de, of Yorkshire —(E. II. Roll) bore, gules, six lyonceux rampant 3, 2, 1, argent crowned or ; Parly. Roll—borne also by WALTER in Jenyns' Ordinary and by Sir RAFFE in Ashmole Roll—in which is the same coat, within a bordure engrailed argent – but without Christian name.

Heslarton, Thomas—(E. II. Roll) bore, argent, on a chevron gules three lyonceux passant gardant or ; Jenyns' Roll and Ordinary, borne also by ROBERT DE BOLTON.

Heslington, Richard de—(H. III. Roll) bore, argent, three crescents sable ; Norfolk Roll.

Hethe, John Atte—(E. III. Roll) bore, gules, on a bend cotised argent three heathcocks sable ; Ashmole Roll. F.

Hethersett, ——, (E. III. Roll) bore, azure, a lyon rampant gardant or—another with a mullet sable on the lyon's shoulder ; Ashmole Roll.

Hethman, Sir Raol (or ROOS) de—bore, at the first Dunstable tournament 1308, azure, fretty argent, a bordure indented or. F.

Heton, Sir Gilbert de—bore, at the first Dunstable tournament 1308, gules, a cross flory or (F.) same arms as Sir WILLIAM LATYMER.

Heton, Henry de — (R. II. Roll) bore, azure, a lyon rampant argent ; Surrey Roll.

Heton, Sir John — (E. III. Roll) bore, argent, on a chief indented sable two fleurs-de-lys or ; Ashmole Roll.

Heton, Thomas de—(E. III. Roll) bore, gules, a lyon passant argent ; Jenyns' Ordinary.

Heton, Thomas de—(E. II. Roll) bore, vert, a lyon rampant and a bordure engrailed argent ; Jenyns' Roll. See GREY of Heton.

Hevere, William de—(E. I. Roll) bore, gules, a cross argent and a label (5) azure. (F.) Camden Roll.

Heverley, Walter—(E. III. Roll) bore, or, on a bend azure three escallops of the first. Jenyns' Ordinary.

Hewes, Sir Richard, of Cornwall or Devon —(E. II. Roll) bore, gules, fretty and a quarter argent ; Parliamentary Roll.

Hewys, Thomas—(E. IV. Roll) bore, argent, fretty gules, and a quarter ermine ; Jenyns' Ordinary.

Hewick, Sir Nicholas – (E. III. Roll) bore, gules, bezantée and a lyon rampant argent ; Ashmole Roll. MALTHAM RATCLIFFE carryes the same ; Jenyns' Ordinary. NICHOLAS bore, vair (tricked vert), six besants 3, 2, 1 ; Jenyns' Ordinary.

Heworth, Thomas—(E. III. Roll) bore, argent, a saltire between four mullets pierced gules ; Jenyns' Ordinary.

Heyham, Sir Roger de, of Beds.—(E. II. Roll) bore, paly (6) argent and azure on a chief gules three escallops or ; Parliamentary Roll.

Heyham, Sir William—(E. I. Roll) bore, bendy (6) argent and gules a label (3) azure ; Holland Roll—gules three bends argent and a label azure in Harl. MS. 6137 fo. 40.

Hildyard, Sir Robert—(E. I. Roll) bore, azure, three mullets or ; Nativity Roll.

*[Hill, William, R. II.—bore, ermine, on a fess sable a castle argent.—Shirley.] F.

Hillarye, Sir Walter, of Norfolk—(E. II. Roll) bore, argent, a fess checquy or and sable, a mullet of the last ; Parliamentary Roll. F.

Hillary, Roger—(E. III. Roll) bore, sable, crusily fitchée and three fleurs-de-lys argent ; Ashmole and Surrey Rolls. F.

Hilton, Sir Robert de, banneret, a baron 1297—bore, at the battle of Falkirk 1298, argent, two bars azure. (F.) Nobility, Parliamentary and St. George Rolls.

Hilton, Sir Robert de—bore, at the battle of Boroughbridge 1322, argent, three chaplets gules. (F.) Borne also by ROBERT, of Swyne, in Holderness, one of the founders of the Abbey there ; Jenyns' Roll and Ordinary.

Hilton, John, of Westmorland — (E. III. Roll) bore, sable, three annulets or, in chief two saltorelles argent ; Jenyns' Roll.

Hincle(y), Sir John de—(E. III. Roll) bore, gules, a chevron engrailed argent ; Ashmole Roll.

Hindley, Randolph (alias CULCHETH)—(E. IV. Roll) bore, sable a gryphon segreant argent ; with crest ; Ballard Roll.

Hingham, Sir John, of Norfolk—(E. II. Roll) bore, per pale or and vert a fer de moulin gules ; Parliamentary Roll.

Hinlington, William de (HINELYNTON) —(H. III. Roll) bore, argent, a label (5) gules ; Howard Roll—probably a foreigner.

Hinton, John de—(E. III. Roll) bore, gules, on a bend argent cotised or three martlets sable ; Jenyns' Ordinary.

Hippeswell, Alan de—(E. III. Roll) bore, argent, a fer de moulin sable ; Grimaldi Roll.

Hodey (——), a Suffolk Kt.—(H. VI. Roll) bore, argent, a fess indented point in point, vert and sable, plain cotised counterchanged, a bordure engrailed of the second ; Arundel Roll. F.

Hodnet, Ede de — (H. III. Roll) bore, quarterly per fess indented argent and gules, a label (5) azure. (F.) Arden and St. George Rolls—as EDGAR.

Ede de Hodenet

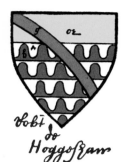

Hoese, Sir John de la, v. Hese.

Hoggesharde, Sir Thomas—bore, at the siege of Calais 1345–8, vaire argent and gules, a bordure sable bezantée. (F.) ? HOGHSHEAD.

Hoggeshawe, Robert de (or SHIREBROK) (H. III. Roll) bore, vair, a chief or, over all a bend gules. (F.) St. George Roll—on the bend three mullets of six points; Harl. MS. 6589.

Hoghton, Sir Alexander, of Hoghton, in Lancs.—(E. IV. Roll) bore, argent, three bars sable; Ballard and Ashmole Rolls.

*__Hoghton, Richard de__—(E. I. Roll) bore, sable, three bars argent; Arundel, Surrey and Jenyns' Rolls. JOHN (E. I.) differenced with a mullet sable; Jenyns' Roll. Another RICHARD differenced with a label (3) gules; Surrey Roll.

Hoghton, Sir Robert (or HOUGHTON), of Notts—(E. III. Roll) bore, azure, three bars humettée argent; Ashmole Roll.

Holand v. Holland.

Holbech (——), an Essex? Kt.—(H. VI. Roll) bore, argent, a chevron engrailed sable Arundel Roll.

Holebrooke, Sr. (——) **de,** a Suffolk Kt.— (E. II. Roll) bore, or crusily and a chevron gules; Parliamentary and Ashmole Rolls; ascribed also to RICHARD in Arden and St. George Rolls—same as THOMAS DE BROKEHOLE in Glover Roll.

Holewell, Sire Walter—bore, at the battle of Boroughbridge 1322, ermine, on a bend gules three crescents or.

(Holester) —— (E. I.); bore, or, a cross gules; Harleian Roll; OLWESTER or OLUNSTER.

Holford, Sir George—(E. IV. Roll) bore, argent, a greyhound passant sable; with crest; Ballard Roll.

Holgomb, John de (? HOLCOMBE)—(R. II. Roll) bore, or, on a bend sable three mullets argent; Surrey Roll.

Holland v. Hoyland.

Holland, Sire Richard de—bore, at the battle of Boroughbridge 1322, azure, semée of escallops and a lyon rampant gardant, argent. F.

Holland, Richard—(E. III. Roll) bore, sable, semée of escallops and a lyon rampant argent; Jenyns' Roll.

Holland, Thomas, K.G. 1376, a founder, Earl of Kent (1381) bore, England within a bordure argent. Seal 1371—represented without the bordure in the Monumental Brass to JOICE, Lady TIPTOFT.

Holland, John, K.G. 1381, Earl of Holland, Duke of Exeter 1443–7—bore, England within a bordure azure florettée or; Surrey Roll.

JOICE,
Widow of Sir JOHN TIPTOFT, daughter of EDWARD CHARLETON, LORD POWIS.

MON. BRASS IN ENFIELD CHURCH, MIDDLESEX, OB. 1446.

After Boutell.

Arms of Holland and Charleton.

Holand, Sir Robert de, banneret, a baron 1314—bore, at the first Dunstable tournament 1308, azure, florettée and a lyon rampant gardant argent (F.); Parly. and Arundel Rolls; borne also by HENRY and JOHN, Surrey Roll and Jenyns' Ordinary, and by Sir OTES, K.G. (a founder), and Sir THOMAS, K.G., at the siege of Calais 1345–8, the former then differenced with a cross patée gules on the lyon; ALAN (ancestor of HOLLAND of Denton) differenced with a bendlet gules; Harl. MS. 1481 fo. 58ᵇ.

Holand, Sir John—bore, at the battle of Boroughbridge 1322, gules, two bars, the martlets in bordure argent (F.); generally blasoned and tricked six martlets 3, 2, 1 argent, see next blason. This coat is wrongly ascribed to Sir THOMAS BENGHAM in the Ashmole MS.

Holande, Sir Hugh—(E. III. Roll) bore, argent, two bars and nine martlets in orle, 4, 2, 3 gules; Ashmole Roll.

Hollingshed, Sir Hugh de—(E. II. Roll) bore, argent on a cross sable a mullet or; Parliamentary Roll.

Holme, John, of North Holme—(E. II. Roll) bore, or, three fleurs-de-lys azure; Jenyns' Roll.

Holteby, Sir Henry de, of Lincolnshire— (E. II. Roll) bore, azure, fretty argent, a chief of the last; Parliamentary Roll.

Hondesacre, Rafe (E. III.) and **William** (H. III. Roll) bore, ermine, three chess-rooks 2 and 1 gules (F.); Jenyns', Arden, and St. George Rolls.

Honford, ——, (E. IV. Roll) bore, sable, an estoile argent; with crest; Ballard Roll.

*__[Honywood, Edmund de,__ of Postling, Hen. III.—bore, argent, a chevron between three hawks' heads erased azure.—Shirley.] F.

Hoo, St. John (E. III. Roll) bore, gules, on a fess indented argent two mullets pierced sable; Ashmole Roll.

Hoo, Sir Robert de, of Beds—(E. II. Roll) bore, quarterly argent and sable a bend gules; Parliamentary Roll.

Hoo, Robert de — (H. III. Roll) bore, quarterly sable and argent, a bendlet or; Arden and St. George Rolls.

Hoo, Thomas and **William de**—(E. II. Roll) bore, quarterly argent and sable (F.); Jenyns' and Surrey Rolls. To MOUNSYER HOO (Sir THOMAS) the reverse are ascribed at the siege of Rouen 1418; borne also by THOMAS, Lord HOO and HASTINGS, K.G. 1445; K. 402 fo. 27.

Hookes, Sir William, of Yorkshire—(E. II. Roll) bore, azure, a fess between three fleurs-de-lys or; Parliamentary Roll.

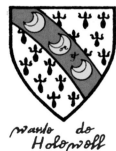

THE HERALDIC ATCHIEVEMENT (Shield I.)

of

HENRY FITZALAN HOWARD, K.G., 15TH DUKE OF NORFOLK.

Shield II., see p. 60.   Shield III., see p. 16.

THE NAMES OF THE QUARTERINGS

WITH REFERENCES TO

THE HERALDIC AUTHORITIES IN THE BRITISH MUSEUM.

It is hoped that the letters in the second column, which indicate the row of quarterings in the shield, will, with the accompanying numerals, facilitate reference to the atchievement opposite.

NAMES	SHIELD REFER-ENCES	BLAZONS	REFERENCES TO THE VARIOUS MSS.
			AUGMENTATION
HOWARD	a 1	gules, on a bend between six crosses crosslet fitchée argent, and—as an honorable augmentation—an escocheon or, charged with a demi lyon rampant pierced through the mouth with an arrow, within the Royal tressure of Scotland; granted to Thomas, 1st Duke of Norfolk, K.G., "et heredibus suis"; for services at the battle of Flodden, 1 Feb., 1513-14	Cotton, Julius C. VII. f. 237 Lansdowne 872, ff. 13, 16 Harl. 1178, f. 45
FITTON	a 2	azure, three cinquefoyles argent . . . . . Blomefield's	Norfolk, IX. 157
BOIS	a 3	ermine, a cross sable	} H. 1411, f. 1ᵇ
SCALES	a 4	gules, six escallops, 3, 2, 1, argent	} H. 1411, f. 1ᵇ
UFFORD¹	a 5	sable, a cross engrailed or	H. 1411, ff. 50, 54
DE VALOINES² . . .	a 6	argent, three palets wavy gules	} H. 1484, f. 50
BLOND	a 7	lozengy or and sable	} H. 1484, f. 50
TENDRING . . .	a 8	azure, a fess between two chevronels argent . H. 1047, f. 20ᵇ	Add 19, 151, f. 143
KERDESTON . . .	a 9	gules, a saltire engrailed argent between four crosses crosslet fitchée of the last	Add 19, 138, f. 146
GANT	b 1	barry of six or and azure, a bend gules	Add 19, 138, f. 154ᵇ
BACON	b 2	gules, three boars passant or . . . Add 19, 116, ff. 33-65 and 118	
MYLDE	b 3	argent, a lyon rampant sable depressed by a fess counter-compony of the first and or	H. 1047, f. 26ᵇ
MOWBRAY . . .	b 4	gules, a lyon rampant argent	H. 1411, f. 1ᵇ
DE ALBINI . . .	b 5	bendy of eight argent and gules	)
BEAUCHAMP . .	b 6	quarterly or and gules a bend sable	
BRAOSE	b 7	azure, crusily and a lyon rampant or	} H. 1411, f. 4
MILES, EARL OF HEREFORD .	b 8	gules, two bends the uppermost or the other argent . .	
BALUN, OF ABERGAVENNY .	b 9	argent, three bars dancettée gules	)
NEWMARCH . . .	c 1	gules, five fusils conjoined in fess or	
SEGRAVE	c 2	sable, three garbs or	} H. 1411, f. 53
SEGRAVE	c 3	sable, a lyon rampant argent crowned or	} H. 1411, f. 53
CHAUCOMBE . . .	c 4	or, a chief azure, over all a bend gules	H. 2188, f. 43
BROTHERTON . . .	c 5	England, and a label of three argent	H. 1411, f. 53
FITZALAN	c 6	gules, a lyon rampant or	)
FITZFLAEL . . .	c 7	barry of eight or and gules³	
CLUN	c 8	argent, a chief azure	} H. 807, f. 73ᵇ
PEVERELL . . .	c 9	or, a cross engrailed azure	H. 1411, ff. 23ᵇ, 43*
DE ALBINI . . .	d 1	gules, a lyon rampant or	)
ST. HILLARY	d 2	argent, on a chief azure, two saltorelles or . . Edmondson's	Baronagium, 361
BLUNDEVILLE, EARL OF CHESTER	d 3	azure, three garbs or	
KEVELIOK, EARL OF CHESTER .	d 4	azure, six garbs, 3, 2, 1, or	)
LUPUS, EARL OF CHESTER .	d 5	azure, a wolf's head erased argent	
HAMLIN PLANTAGENET . .	d 6	azure, florettée or, on a bordure gules eight lyons of England .	} H. 1411, ff. 40, 43*
WARREN	d 7	checquy or and azure	
MARSHALL . . .	d 8	gules, five fusils in bend or	
STRONGBOW⁴ . . .	d 9	argent on a chief azure three crosses patée fitchée at the foot or .	)
MACMORROGH . . .	e 1	sable, three garbs or .	
TILNEY	e 2	argent, a chevron between three griffins' heads erased gules .	
ROCHFORD . . .	e 3	quarterly or and gules, a bordure sable bezantée, in the second quarter an annulet for difference	H. 1411, f. 68 H. 4031, f. 238
ROOS	e 4	gules, three water-bougets argent	H. 1552, f. 189ᵇ
THORPE	e 5	gules, three crescents argent	H. 1560, f. 139
ASPALL	e 6	azure, three chevronels or	)
NORWOOD . . .	e 7	ermine, a cross engrailed gules	
FITZALAN . . .	e 8	gules, a lyon rampant or	)
FITZFLAEL . . .	e 9	barry of eight or and gules³	
CLUN	f 1	argent, a chief azure	} H. 1411, f. 43ᵇ
PEVERELL . . .	f 2	or, a cross engrailed azure	
DE ALBINI . . .	f 3	gules, a lyon rampant or	)
ST. HILLARY . . .	f 4	argent, on a chief azure, two saltorelles or . . Edmondson's	Baronagium, 361
BLUNDEVILLE, EARL OF CHESTER	f 5	azure, three garbs or	
KEVELIOK, EARL OF CHESTER .	f 6	azure, six garbs, 3, 2, 1, or	)
LUPUS, EARL OF CHESTER .	f 7	azure, a wolf's head erased argent	
HAMLIN PLANTAGENET . .	f 8	azure, florettée or, on a bordure gules eight lyons of England .	} H. 1411, ff. 40, 43*
WARREN	f 9	checquy or and azure	
MARSHALL . . .	g 1	gules, five fusils in bend or	
STRONGBOW⁴ . . .	g 2	argent on a chief azure three crosses patée fitchée at the foot or .	)
MACMORROGH . . .	g 3	sable, three garbs or	
MATRAVERS . . .	g 4	sable, a fret or	} H. 890, f. 1
WYDVILLE . . .	g 5	argent, a fess and canton gules	} H. 890, f. 1
LYONS OF WARKWORTH .	g 6	argent, a lyon rampant gules	
S. LIS	g 7	argent, two bars and in chief three fleurs-de-lys gules . .	} H. 2156, f. 115ᵇ

¹ Ufford is usually made to bring in Vesey and Glanville. They are, however, omitted from this atchievement, as the late Chester Waters rejects the early pedigree of Ufford in his History of the Chesters of Chichele, vol. 1. 244, 253.
² Valoines, John de, married Isabel, apparently heir in her issue of John de Creke, Harl. 1393, f. 104, but doubt is rather thrown on this in Add. MS. 19, 125, ff. 165 and 169; the usual quarterings of Creke and Glanville are therefore omitted, see also Valoines in Add. MS. 19, 153, f. 80.
³ This the Coat borne by FitzAlan of Bedale is included on the authority of Glover, Somerset Herald, and others.
⁴ Strongbow brings in Giffard, Harl. MS. 1047, f. 44, see Shield II.

116

Robt Hopton   Walt d Hopetone   John de Horbyre   John Hore   Will de Hornes   John de Hotrum

Will deHotot

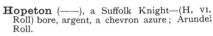

John de la Huse

Hue d· Houile

John Hovile

Will Haward

Hopeton (——), a Suffolk Knight—(H. VI. Roll) bore, argent, a chevron azure; Arundel Roll.

Hopton, Sir John (or HAMPTON)—bore, at the siege of Calais 1345–8, argent, a fess counter-compony or and azure between six martlets gules—blasoned checquy.

Hopton, Robert—(E. II. Roll) bore, argent, two bars sable each charged with three mullets pierced or; Jenyns' Roll. F.

Hopton, Walter de, of co. Glouc.—(H. III. Roll) bore, gules crusily and a lyon rampant or (F.); Arden, St. George, and Parliamentary Rolls. Sir WALTER bore it crusily fitchée (E. III.), Ashmole Roll.

Horbourne, Sir John (or HORBURY), of Yorkshire—(E. II. Roll) bore, barry (8) argent and azure, a bend gules (F.); Parliamentary Roll; barry of six and a bendlet; Guillim and Camden Rolls.

Hore, John—bore, at the siege of Rouen 1418, sable, three cinquefoyles argent pierced gules. F.

Horkesley, Sir William, of Essex, Kt.—(E. II. Roll) bore, ermine, on a chief indented azure three lyonceux rampant or; Parliamentary Roll.

Horne, Gerard, v. Hournis.

Horne, Sir John de, of Sussex—(E. II. Roll) bore, gules, a fret vair; Parliamentary Roll.

Horne (——), an Essex? Knight—(H. VI. Roll) bore, gules, three bugle horns sable, another impaling, gules, crusily fitchée and three crescents argent; Arundel Roll.

‡Hornes, William de—(H. III. Roll) bore, argent, three hunting horns in pale gules garnished sable. (F.) Dering Roll.

Horsley, Robert—(E. II.) bore, gules, three horses' heads erased argent bridled sable; Jenyns' Roll.

Horsele, Robert de—(R. II. Roll) bore, sable, three cinquefoyles 2 and 1 pierced argent —Surrey Roll and Jenyns' Ordinary.

Hoscarle, Sir Thomas—(E. III. Roll) bore, azure, three battle axes erect argent; Ashmole Roll—see HURSTAL; surname doubtful.

Hoscott, Sir Robert de, of Bedfordshire—(E. II. Roll) bore, azure, a cross patée ermine between four roses gules; (tricked patonce); Parliamentary Roll; a cross patée argent, Guillim Roll; and a cross formée argent; Surrey Roll.

Hose, Nichole de la (HESE or HEUSE)—(H. III. Roll)—bore, argent, three (men's) hose 2 and 1 gules; Arden and Howard Rolls. F.

Hoter, Thomas—(H. III. Roll) bore, gyronny (12) ermine and gules; Arden Roll.

Hotham, John de—(E. III. Roll) bore, or, on a bend sable three mullets argent pierced gules (F.), being the arms of DE MAULEY with three mullets on the bend; Jenyns' Ordy. Sir JOHN differenced it with a martlet gules, at the battle of Boroughbridge 1322.

*Hotham, John, of Boudlay—(E. III. Roll) bore, burulée (12) argent and azure, on a canton or a martlet sable; Jenyns' Ordinary.

Hotote (——), a Suffolk Kt.—(H. VI. Roll) bore, azure, a cross moline argent; Arundel Roll.

Hotot, Sir John, of co. Glouc.—(E. II. Roll) bore, azure, on a chevron cotised or between three crescents argent, two bars gemelles of the first; Parly. Roll—chevron plain in Harl. 6137 fo. 26.

Hotot, Richard v. Hautot and Hoscott.

Hotot, Sir William de, of co. Glouc.—(E. II. Roll) bore, azure, a chevron or, between three crescents argent; Parliamentary Roll. F.

Houghton, Sir Robert, of Notts—(E. III. Roll) bore, azure, three bars humettée argent; Ashmole Roll. STEPHEN DE HOUTON took up the cross in the last Crusade 1270. See also HOGHTON.

Houn, Hervey de—(H. III. Roll) bore, vert, on a bend argent three escallops gules; Arden Roll.

Hournis, Gerard — (E. III. Roll) bore, argent, a lyon rampant gardant gules—another with a label (3) azure; Ashmole Roll—surname almost illegible.

Hovell, Sir Hugh, of Suffolk, Richard, Robert and Sir Robert—(H. III. Roll) bore, sable, a cross or; Arden, Parly. and St. George Rolls. Sir STEVEN, also of Suffolk, bore it at the first Dunstable tournament 1308, differenced with a label (3) argent (F.) in Parly. Roll.

Hovile, Hugh—(H. III. Roll) bore, argent, a bend azure, a label (5) gules. (F.) Arden and St. George Rolls.

Hovile, Sir John—bore, at the first Dunstable tournament 1308, quarterly or and gules, a martlet of the second. F.

*Howard, Sir John, of Norfolk—(E. II. Roll) bore, gules, crusily and a bend argent; Parliamentary Roll. Sir WILLIAM bore it at the battle of Boroughbridge 1322 (F.), tricked crusily fitchée in the Ashmolean MS.; Arden and St. George Rolls (F.) in Arundel Roll; WILLIAM in Jenyns' Ordinary.

*Howard, Sir William—bore (1297) gules, crusily fitchée and a bend argent; Nobility Roll; his son, Sir WILLIAM, bore it also at the battle of Boroughbridge 1322; Ashmole MS., as before mentioned. Sir JOHN, Admiral of the North fleete, bore it at the siege of Calais 1345–8 (F.); Surrey Roll, Jenyns' Roll and Ordinary (borne also by HUNTINGFIELD). See JOHN, Lord Howard, K.G. 1472, after Duke of Norfolk, on title page. This coat appears in the Ashmole Roll differenced with a fleur-de-lys azure, and apparently with an ermine spot on the bend in Harl. MS. 1481 fo. 83.

Hoyland, Sir William de, of Lancashire—(E. II. Roll) bore, sable, a cross patonce or; Parliamentary Roll.

Huband, Henry—(H. III. Roll) bore, sable three fleurs-de-lys argent. (F.) St. George Roll.

Esteven Hoscott   John de Howard   Henry. Huband.

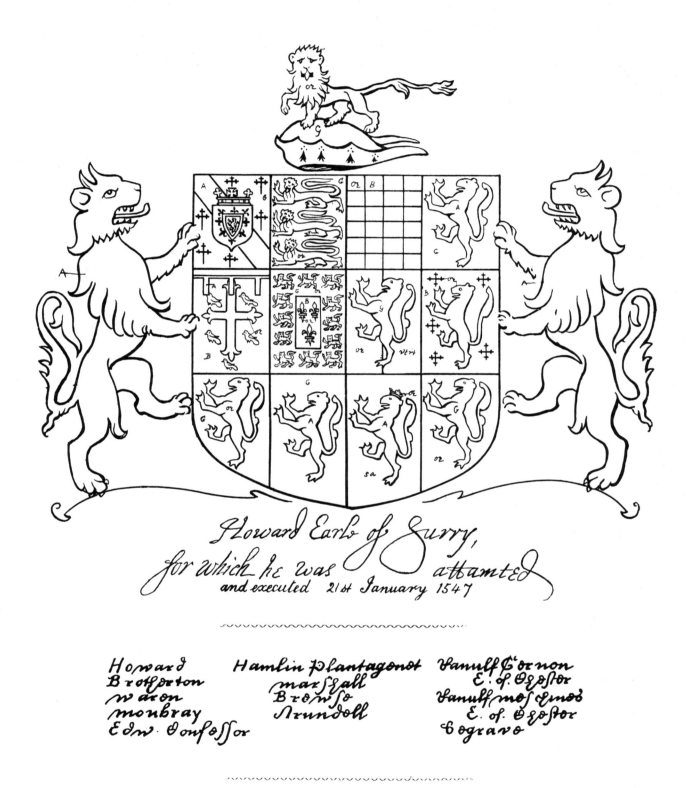

Howard Earl of Surry,
for which he was attainted
and executed 21st January 1547

Howard	Hamlin Plantagenet	Vanulf Gernon
Brotherton	marshall	E. of Oxestor
waron	Brewse	Vanulf mes Emes
monbray	Arundell	E. of Oxestor
Edw. Confessor		Bograve

It does seem rather hard that a man should lose his head for using arms fabulously ascribed to a person who never bore arms—those of Edward the Confessor.

Josan de Hovilo

Johan de Hodolistuno

Witt d Hugeford

Robt. de Hugham

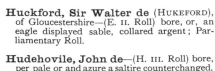

Joan d. Hulle

Seer d. Huntingfeld

Vis̄ de Hulton

Gmo de Hundiscote

malk. de Hungerford

mittm de Hungerford

mat de Honterbubo

Perob de Huntingfoild

Witt d. Hursthalo

Witt Hurleton

Henri Houso

Josn de Huysso

Huckford, Sir Walter de (HUKEFORD), of Gloucestershire—(E. II. Roll) bore, or, an eagle displayed sable, collared argent ; Parliamentary Roll.

Hudehovile, John de—(H. III. Roll) bore, per pale or and azure a saltire counterchanged. St. George Roll. See HUNTE.

*****Hudleston, Sir John de,** banneret, sealed the Barons' letter to the Pope 1301, pp. xxi, xxiv. He bore, at the battle of Falkirk 1298, and at the siege of Carlaverock 1300, gules, fretty (6) argent. (F.) Arundel, Parliamentary and Guillim Rolls—a fret for JOHN, in Surrey Roll. JOHN DE KOKESALTON bore the reverse ; Arden Roll.

Hudleston, Sir Adam—bore, at the first Dunstable tournament 1308, and at the battle of Boroughbridge 1322, gules, fretty argent, a label (3) azure ; Nativity Roll (in which RICHARD occurs without the label). Also ascribed to Sir RICHARD in the Parliamentary and Ashmole Rolls, and to Sir RICHARD, THE NEPHEW, also in Parliamentary Roll—the label is sometimes tricked.

Hudleston, Sir Adam de—(E. II. Roll) bore, gules, fretty argent, a bordure indented or , Parliamentary Roll.

Hugarde, Andrew, of Danemarke—(E. III. Roll) bore, azure, a sun argent ; Jenyns' Roll. HUGH GARD bore, azure a sun or ; Harl. MS. 6589 fo. 37. See OGARD.

Hugford, William de—(H. III. Roll) bore, azure, three bucks' heads cabossed or. (F.) Arden and St. George Rolls.

Hugford, William de (or HUNGERFORD) —(E. II. Roll) bore, azure, three palmes (? quills in trick) 2 and 1 or. (F.) Jenyns' Roll.

‡Hugham, Robert de—(H. III. Roll) bore, argent, five chevronels sable. (F.) Dering Roll ; six in Ashmole MS., four in Howard Roll, are ascribed to ROBERT DE HUHAM.

Hull, Sir Edward, K.G. (H. VI.)—bore, argent three crosses crosslet fitchée in bend azure between two bendlets gules ; K. 402, fo. 35.

Hulle, John de—(H. III. Roll) bore, azure, an eagle displayed argent. (F.) Arden and St. George Rolls.

Hulls, Sir Richard de, of Cambridgeshire —(E. II. Roll) bore, azure an eagle displayed argent, a baston gules ; Parliamentary Roll.

*****[Hulton, Richard de** (32 E. I.) — bore, argent, a lyon rampant gules.—Shirley.] F.

Hundescote, Sire de —— (E. I. Roll) bore, ermine, a bordure gules. (F.) Camden Roll.

Hungerford, Walter, K.G., a baron 1426— bore, at the siege of Rouen 1418, sable, two bars argent, in chief three plates, *quarterly with,* per pale dancettée gules and vert a chevron or (F.) tricked in the Ashmole MS., gules, a chevron and in chief a dancettée (3) argent— the paternal coat in Jenyns' Ordinary. Sir E. with his proper difference (unnamed) and Sir R. with a label (5)—in Atkinson Roll. HUNGERFORD, THE BASTARD, slain at the siege of Calais 1345-8, bore, barry (6) sable and argent, in chief three plates.

Hunte, Sir Oswald, Kt. banneret—(H. VI. Roll) bore, per pale argent and sable a saltire counterchanged ; Arundel Roll.

Huntercombe, Sir Walter, banneret, a baron 1295, sealed the Barons' letter to the Pope 1301, pp. xix, xxiv. He bore, at the battle of Falkirk 1298, and at the siege of Carlaverock 1300, ermine two gemelles gules. (F.) Nobility, Arundel and Parliamentary Rolls— ascribed to RAUF in St. George Roll. WILLIAM took up the cross in the last Crusade 1270.

Huntercombe, Gerard de, of Loreyne— HONDERCOMBE, rightly GONDRONVILLE.

Huntingdon, Earl of. See SCOTT.

Huntingfield, Roger de, of Bradenham, a baron 1297, sealed the Barons' letter to the Pope 1301, pp. xxi, xxiv. He bore, or, on a fess gules three plates ; Nobility Roll. Sir WILLIAM, banneret, (F.) bore the same ; Parliamentary, Arundel and other Rolls.

Huntingfield, Sir Piers de, of Kent— (E. II. Roll) bore, quarterly or and gules a bordure sable ; Parliamentary Roll.

‡Huntingfield, Peres de—(H. III. Roll) bore, quarterly or and gules, a label (5) sable ; Howard Roll—on each pendant three plates (F.) Dering Roll ; besants in Ashmole Roll.

Huntingfield, Sir Walter, of Herts— (E. II. Roll) bore, gules, on a bend three lyonceux passant sable. (F.) Parliamentary Roll. Ascribed also to JOHN in Jenyns' Roll and Ordinary. WILLIAM took up the cross 1270.

‡Huntingfield, Cael, Sael, or **Saer de**— (H. III. Roll) bore, gules, crusily fitchée and a bend argent. (F.) Dering, Howard, and St. George Rolls. Same arms as HOWARD.

Huntingfield, Sir William de—(E. I.) bore, argent, crusily (8, 13) and a bend gules ; Holland Roll.

Hurleton, William—(E. IV. Roll) bore, four ermine spots in cross (F.) with crest ; Ballard Roll.

Hurstal, William—(H. III. Roll) bore, azure, three axes argent. (F.) St. George and Arden Rolls—ascribed to Sir THOMAS HOSCARLE in Ashmole Roll.

Hussey, Henry de, of Sussex, baron 1295 —bore, ermine three bars gules ; Nobility, Parliamentary and Ashmole Rolls ; ascribed to another HENRY (‡) in the Dering Roll ; tricked, barry (6) in Arden and Norfolk Rolls.

Hussey, Sir John (of Hants or Wilts.), knighted at the capitulation of Calais 1348 – bore, or, a cross vert. (F.) Ascribed also to Sir ROGER in Ashmole Roll — another Sir JOHN (E. II.) differenced with a label (3) gules ; Parliamentary Roll and Jenyns' Ordinary.

Hussee, John de la—(E. III. Roll) – bore, gules, a fess between two chevronels ermine ; Jenyns' Ordinary.

Hutton, William, of the Forest—(E. II. Roll)—bore, gules, a fess sable between three cushions tasselled argent ; Jenyns' Roll.

*****[Huyshe, John de** (13th cent.), bore, argent, on a bend sable three lucies naiant of the first. —Shirley.] F.

Hyde ——, a Knight — (H. VI. Roll) bore, gules, a saltire engrailed or, a chief ermine ; Arundel Roll.

Hyde ——, (E. IV. Roll) bore, azure, a chevron between three lozenges or ; with crest ; Ballard Roll.

Pedigree of Hunter=Weston of Hunterston, Ayrshire.

NORMAN THE HUNTER, circa 1080–1165.

AYLMER DE LA HUNTAR, of the County of Ayr, one of the "Magnates Scotiæ" who signed the submission to Edward I. of England, 1296, when the Scottish succession was in dispute between Bruce and Baliol.

WILLIAM HUNTER, of Arneil, or Ardneil, obtained a Crown charter from K. Robert II. 2 May, 1374, " of all that land of Arnele which had been held by ' Andre Cambell militis' "; died about 1436.

WILLIAM HUNTER, laird of Arnele-Huntar, paid on his entry to the estate 1447, eleven years' arrears of blench duty, in addition to double entry money—infeft in his estate 1447, and in Hielies in the Barony of Dalry 1452. Custos or hereditary Keeper of the Forest of the Little Cumray (1453), an island, then a royal forest; died about 1454. =

JOHN, Hereditary forester on the death of his brother, had son ARCHIBALD, 1465.

The Arms of ABBOT ANDREW HUNTER, Lord High Treasurer of Scotland, 1449–53, found in Melrose Abbey, carved at the base of a niche on the fifth buttress from the south transept of Melrose Abbey.

Two abbots croziers in saltire between a rose in chief and three bugle horns 2 in fess, that in base resting on a mell—a device for Melrose. Two remaining characters on the shield have been identified as A. H.

ARCHIBALD HUNTAR, of Arnele-Huntar, infeft in his estate on coming of age, 1456; ob. 1487. = MARGARET, dau. of William Ker, laird of Kersland; mar. before 1462.

JOHN HUNTAR, of Huntarstone (so styled in sasine 9 Apl. 1511), or of that ilk, Hereditary forester of Little Cumray, his fee twenty shillings, 1461; fell at Flodden 9 Sept. 1513. = MARGARET, dau. of John, 2nd Lord Cathcart, by Margaret, dau. of Sir William Douglas, of Drumlanrig.

ROBERT HUNTAR, of Huntarston, or of that ilk, under age at the death of his father. The King granted him the ile of Cumray by charter, 31 May, 1527, and which was confirmed 12 Nov. 1534—he however sold it shortly after to the Earl of Eglintoun; obtained a charter 25 Feb. 1535, of the lands of Annanhill, within the lordship of Roberton and bailliary of Cuninghame, confirmed by Royal charters 16 March following and 1 Jany. 1541—acquired the lands of Campbeltown; died 1546. = JONET, dau. of John Montgomerie, of Giffen, and widow of John Craufurd, of Craufurdland; died 1547.

KENTIGERN, or MUNGO HUNTAR, of Easter Arneil, infeft 1537, and of Huntarstone 8 May, 1546; at Dumbarton with the Army of the King, 1546; died "at the faith and peace of Queen Mary, under her standard at the battle of Pinkiescleuth," 10 Sept. 1547. = MARION, dau. of James Hamilton, of Torrance, co. Lanark, and she in possession of the tower, fortalice and manor place of Hunterston for upwards of 48 years; living 1594.

ISOBEL, mar. to John Crauford, of Giffordland, who fell at the battle of Pinkie, 1547.

ROBERT HUNTAR, of Huntarstoune, or of that ilk, an infant at the death of his father, one of those Ayrshire gentlemen who subscribed the Principal Band in defence of the reformed religion, 4 Sept. 1562. Obtained a Crown charter, of South Cames, now the town of Milport, in the island of Gt. Cumbrae, 29 Nov. 1578; died 1580. = MARGARET, dau. of Thomas Craufurd, of Auchinames. She re-mar. to John Stewart, burgess, of Glasgow.

JOHN HUNTAR, tutor, of Huntarstoun, m. Janet Lindsay.

ROBERT HUNTER, of Huntarstown, under age at his father's death, had a Royal charter of South Cames, in Bute, 1580, and in 1609 a Royal charter of Arneil-Huntar, with "tower fortalice," &c.; died s.p. May 1616. = MARGARET, dau. of Patrick Peibles, of Broomlands.

JEAN, m. (2nd) 1608, to Rev. Alex. Scrymgeour, minister at Irvine. = 1. REV. ROBERT CUNNINGHAME, minister of Barnwell, 1st husband.

MARION, m. to Robert Peibles, a baillie of Irvine, who died 16 Sept. 1605.
KATHERINE, m. (1st) to Hugh Garven, of Irvine, who died 29 June, 1607, and (2nd?) 4 May, 1616, to Robert Cunninghame, of Auchinharvie.

JEAN CUNINGHAME, elder dau. and co-heir. = PATRICK HUNTER, laird of Hunterstone, by devise of Robert 27 Sept. 1611, son of William, of Beneberrie Yairds, co. Ayr, by his wife Marion Hamilton—died 1665, aged 74—epitaphs in Latin and English.

CATHERINE, died before 1613. = ROBERT CUNINGHAME, of Auchinharvie—husband also of Catherine's aunt.

KATHERINE.
MARION.

ROBERT HUNTER, laird of Hunterstone, entered Glasgow College 27 July, 1627; died Dec. 1679. = 1. ELIZABETH, dau. of Patrick Craufurd, of Auchinames. = 2. MARION, eldest dau. of James Cuninghame, of Aiket.

HENRY, a minister of the Church of Scotland, laureated in Glasgow University 1650, settled at Dromore in Ireland, ejected 1661; died unmar. 1673.

FRANCIS, said to be ancestor of Hunter of Long Calderwood.

1. ———, m. to Alex. Cuninghame, of Carlung.
2. JEAN, m., about 1653, to David Kennedy, of Balmaclanachan and Craig.

PATRICK HUNTER, laird of Hunterston, and of Langmuir, j.u.; died in 1699. = MARION, dau. of John Cuninghame, of Langmuir; mar. 15 Aug. 1662.

ROBERT, M.A. Glasgow Uny. 1643, minister of Kilbride, ancestor of Hunter, of Kirkland.

JAMES, bred to the bar; m. Margt., sister of Rev. John Spalding, minister at Dreghorn, ancestor of Orby Hunter, of Croyland Abbey.

HUGH, a physician in Kilmarnock.

JEAN, m. (contract 3 Nov. 1658) to Rev. John Spalding, minister of Dreghorn.

PATRICK HUNTER, laird of Hunterston; m. 5 May, 1704; d. 9 Nov. 1738. = MARION, eldest dau. of Thomas Craufurd, of Crawfurdsburn, or Cartsburn, co. Renfrew.

HENRY, minister of Mearns in 1713; d. 1733.
JOHN.

DOROTHEA, m. to Hy. Cuninghame, of Carlung.
=
⊥

MARIAN, m. 1694 to John Peebles, of Crawfield.

ANNE, m. 1702 to Alexander Cuninghame, of Clogher, co. Tyrone.
MARGARET.

ROBERT HUNTER, laird of Hunterston; m. 1762; d. 1796, aged 86. = JANE, dau. of Matthew Aitcheson, by Eleanora, dau. of John McGilchrist, of Easter Porsill; died in 1787.

DAVID.
=
⊥

ELIZABETH, m. to John Hyndman, of Lunderston.
MARION, m. to Hugh Muir.

DOROTHEA, m. (1st) to William Kelso, of Hullerhirst, and (2nd) to Hugh Weir, of Kirkhall.

MARGARET, m. to Robert Caldwell. =

2 sons and 3 daus. died young or unmar.

ELEANORA, only surviving child and heiress of Hunterston; b. 22 Oct. 1764; d. 24 Dec. 1851. = ROBERT CALDWELL, assumed the additional name and arms of Hunter, of Hunterston; died 22 Aug. 1826. Built Hunterston.

ROBERT HUNTER, of Hunterston House and Castle, J.P., D.L., of Ayrshire; b. 1 Oct. 1799; d. 14 March, 1880. = CHRISTIAN MACKNIGHT, eldest dau. of William M. Crawford, of Cartsburn, co. Renfrew; m. 23 Nov. 1836.

3 sons and 4 daus. died young or unmar.

JANE, elder dau. and co-heir of Hunterston, Lady of Justice of the Order of St. John of Jerusalem; mar. (as 2nd wife) 8 July, 1863. = GOULD READ HUNTER-WESTON, of Hunterston, j.u., J.P., D.L., Ayrshire, F.S.A., Lt.-Col. (retd.) H.M. Indian Army, served at Oudh and Lucknow, 1857, medal and clasps, assumed addl. surname and arms of Hunter, of Hunterston, by Royal licence 8 May, 1880; b. 16 Apl. 1823.

ELEANORA, 2nd dau. and co-heir; m. 31 Oct. 1866; d. 29 March, 1884. = ROBERT WILLIAM COCHRAN PATRICK, of Ladyland and Woodside, Ayrshire.
⊥

AYLMER GOULD HUNTER-WESTON, brevet Lt.-Col. Royal Engineers, D.S.O. for services in South Africa. See Official Quarterly Army List; born 23 Sept. 1864.

REGINALD HUGH HUNTER-WESTON, late Lieut. Seaforth Highlanders; born 11 Apl. 1869. = AGNES, dau. of John Roberts, C.M.G., of Littlebourne. Dunedin, N.Z.; m. 9 Aug. 1899.

The Camp at Hastings. Tidings of Harold brought to William. A house is burnt. After the Bayeux Tapestry.

— I—J—K —

Lo Siro
Jecinggam

Robert del Hdlo

Nicol d Jnēule

Counte
vernondel Hdlo

Ichingham, le Sire—bore, at the siege of Rouen 1418, azure, fretty argent. (F.) See ECHINGHAM.

Idle, Sire John del—bore, at the battle of Boroughbridge 1322, gules crusily and a lyon passant argent ; not gardant in Ashmole MS.

Idle, Sire Robert del, banneret—bore, at the battle of Boroughbridge 1322, or, a fess between two chevrons sable ; and with the chevrons gules, ascribed to ROBERT in Camden Roll. Same as JOHN and ROBERT DE LISLE.

Idle, Count Vernon del—(E. I. Roll) bore, or, a lyon rampant azure. (F.) Camden Roll. See ISLE.

Idle, Sire Warin del, banneret—bore, at the battle of Boroughbridge 1322, gules, a lyon passant (gardant) argent, crowned or (F.) ; not gardant in the Ashmole copy. Same as GERARD DE L'ISLE.

Ilderton, John—(E. III. Roll) bore, argent, three water-bougets sable ; Jenyns' Ordinary. F.

Illey, Sir Philip de, of Lincolnshire—(E. II. Roll) bore, gules, an eagle displayed or, a baston azure ; Parliamentary Roll. WILLIAM took up the cross in the last Crusade 1270.

Illey, John de—(E. III. Roll) bore, ermine, two chevrons sable. (F.) Ashmole Roll. Same as Sir JOHN DE LISLE.

Ilsley, Sir Robert de—(E. III. Roll) bore, or, two gemelles sable and in chief three ogresses ; Ashmole Roll.

Imberd, William or **Guy**—(H. III. Roll) bore, azure, three fleurs-de-lys 2 and 1 argent. Arden and St. George Rolls—these names are usually reversed, and the surname written GU. F.

Incule, Nichol de—(H. III. Roll) bore, or, on a chief azure three lyonceux rampant argent. (F.) Arden and St. George Rolls ; same as DE MENNE. See also LISLEY.

Inge, Sir William, of Beds.—(E. II. Roll) bore, or, a chevron vert ; Ashmole, Parliamentary and Nobility Rolls.

Inglefield v. **Englefield**.

Inglethorpe, John, of Norfolk—(E. II. Roll) bore, gules a cross engrailed argent ; Parliamentary, Ashmole and Surrey Rolls. Sir JOHN, differenced it with a label (3) or, at the battle of Boroughbridge 1322. (F.) An Essex Knight (H. VI. Roll) bore, gules, a cross engrailed ermine, an annulet argent Arundel Roll.

†**Inglethorpe, John**—(H. III. Roll) bore, gules a saltire engrailed or. (F.) Arden Roll.

Ingham, Robert—(E. III. Roll) bore, ermine, on a fess gules three escallops or ; Jenyns' Ordinary. Perhaps INGRAM.

Ingham, Oliver de, a baron 1328—bore, per pale or and vert, a cross moline gules ; Jenyns' Ordinary.

Ingleby, John de—(E. II. Roll) bore, sable an estoile argent ; Jenyns' Roll.

Inglish and **Inglosse** v. **English** and **Englosse**.

Inglows, Henry — (R. II. Roll) — bore, quarterly or and azure in the first quarter a lyon rampant sable. Surrey Roll.

Ingram, John—(E. II. Roll) bore, ermine on a fess gules three escallops argent ; Jenyns' Roll. ROBERT bore the escallops or ; Grimaldi Roll and Jenyns' Ordinary.

Insula v. **de Insula**.

Ipre v. **Ypre**.

Irby, John de—(R. II. Roll) bore, argent, fretty sable, a quarter of the last ; Surrey Roll.

Irby, Sir Thomas, of Cumberland—(E. II. Roll) bore, argent, fretty sable, on a canton gules a cinquefoyle or ; Parliamentary Roll.

Ireland, John, of Hutt—(E. IV. Roll) bore, gules, six fleurs-de-lys 3, 2, 1, argent—with crest ; Ballard Roll.

‡**Irie, Maheu de**—(H. III. Roll) bore, argent a bend azure ; Dering Roll.

[**Irton, Roger de**, 1292—bore, argent, a fess sable in chief three mullet gules.—Shirley.] F.

*[**Isham, Robert de**, 2 R. II.—bore, gules, a fess and in chief three piles wavy meeting in the centre argent.—Shirley.] F.

Warin del Jdle

Jogn do yloo

Roger do Jrlon

Jogn do Jggulucstrop   malt. d. Jgguluostrop   Robt. do JSsam

John Ylderton

Will Islip

Edm Jonnoy

Dany Jorbauilo

Watt. Jorningham

Jho Jorolyn

John Jos

Robert Jorce

John Jolly

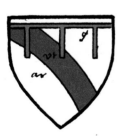

Edw. de Kendale

Iskynsall, —— (E. III. Roll) bore, or, a fess between two chevronels gules, a canton ermine; Ashmole Roll.

Isle, Earl of the, Baldwin; EARL OF DEVON or EXETER and LORD OF THE ISLE OF WIGHT—(E. I. Roll) bore, or a lyon rampant azure; Segar and St. George Rolls. See also VERNON and WARREN DEL IDLE.

Islip, William, Keeper of the Privy Seal—bore, at the siege of Calais 1345-8 ermine, a fess engrailed between three weasels passant gules. F.

*[Jenney, Edmund, c. 1400 – bore, ermine, a bend gules cotised or.—Shirley.] F.

Jerkavile, Davy de—(E. I. Roll) bore, quarterly or and azure in the first quarter a lyon rampant gules. (F.) Camden Roll - called GERCOMVILE in Howard Roll. See also MARCONVILE in Dering Roll.

Jermyn, Sir John, of Suffolk, Kt. – (H. VI. Roll) bore, argent, a lyon rampant gardant gules; Arundel Roll.

*[Jerningham Sir Walter, (22 E. I.) bore, argent, three buckles, tongues to the dexter gules.—Shirley.] F.

Joce, Sir John (or JOS)—bore, at the first Dunstable tournament 1308 argent, an eagle displayed sable a bendlet gobony or and gules. (F.) Sir JOHN, of Middlesex (E. II.) bore the baston gules; Parliamentary Roll.

* Jocelyn, Thomas, (13 E. I.) bore, azure, a circular wreath argent and sable with four hawks' bells affixed in quadrature or. - Shirley.] F.

John, Lewis (or JONES), an Essex Knight - (H. VI. Roll) bore, sable, a chevron between three trefoyles argent; Arundel Roll.

Jorce, John—(E. III. Roll) bore, per pale azure and gules, an eagle displayed argent membered of the second; Jenyns' Ordinary.

Jorcee, Robert—(E. III. Roll) bore, argent, on a bend or. three water-bougets azure. (F.) Jenyns' Ordinary.

Jove, William le — (H. III. Roll) bore, argent, three lyons rampant sable; Howard Roll.

Jumper, William (? INNPERE)—(H. III. Roll) bore, argent, a fess between three crescents argent; Arden Roll.

Justine, Adam de—(H. III. Roll) bore, barry (6) argent and azure, in chief three torteaux; Arden Roll.

Kekitmore, Piers de—(E. III. Roll) bore, gules, three text S's 2 and 1 or; Arden Roll.

°[Kelly, Sir John, (44 E. III.)—bore, argent, a chevron between three billets gules; Shirley.] F.

Kendale, Sir Edmonde de, of the North —(E. II. Roll) bore, argent, a bend vert cotised gules. all dancettée; Parly. Roll—cotises vert, in Glover Roll.

Kendale, Sir Robert de, of Herts.—bore, at the first Dunstable tournament 1308, argent, a bend vert, a label (3), Parly. Roll; EDWARD, bore it at the second Dunstable tournament 1334. (F.) Ascribed also to RICHARD in Jenyns' Ordinary.

Kendale, Robert—(R. II. Roll) argent, on a bend azure three mullets pierced or; Surrey Roll.

°[Kendall, Richard, 43 E. III. — bore, argent, a chevron between three dolphins naiant embowed sable.—Shirley.] F.

Kene (——) of Essex? Knight—(H. VI. Roll) bore, ermine a cross florettée sable, quarterly with, azure, on a fess between two chevronels or three eaglets displayed gules; Arundel Roll. ROBERT LE KEN, took up the cross in the last Crusade 1270.

Kenney, Alexander de—(H. III. Roll) bore, quarterly or and gules a label (5) sable bezanty (F.); St. George Roll.

Kennings, Sir John, of Norfolk—(E. II. Roll) bore, azure, a fess engrailed between three escallops argent; Parly. Roll.

Kenette, Pers de—(H. III. Roll) bore, gules, three talbots-on-the-scent argent; Arden Roll.

Kent, Earl of—HUBERT DE BURGH 1227-43 —bore, lozengy vel mascuily vair and gules; Grimaldi and Parly. Rolls; reversed in Arden and Nobility Rolls.

Kent, Earl of, EDMUND of Woodstock—bore, 1321, England within a bordure argent; Parly. Roll and Jenyns' Ordinary; borne also by HOLLAND, Earl of Kent; Surrey Roll.

‡Kent, Thomas de—(H. III. Roll) bore, argent, a fess gules (F.); Dering and Howard Rolls.

Kentwode, John—(R. II. Roll) bore, gules, three roses ermine; Surrey Roll.

Kerdeston, Sir William de, of Norfolk, knighted at the capitulation of Calais 1348 — bore, gules, a saltire engrailed argent (F.); Parlv. Roll—ascribed also to JOHN, FOUKE, and WILLIAM in Arden and Norfolk Rolls and Jenyns' Ordinary Sir ROGER differenced with a label (3) or; Parly. and Ashmole Rolls.

Kerdeston, John—bore, at the second Dunstable tournament 1334, gules a saltire argent a label besantée (sic).

Kerdiff, Paul de—(H. III. Roll) bore, azure, a fess or (F.) (St. George Roll); between six martlets (3. 3) or, in Arden Roll.

Kevelioke, Hugh, EARL OF CHESTER—(E. III. Roll) bore, azure, six garbs 3, 2, 1, or; Jenyns' Ordinary, but see BLONDEVILLE.

Kidesby, Sir William—bore, at the siege of Calais 1345-8, sable, a fess or, between two chevrons argent. F.

Kidley, Thomas (KYDELEY)—(R. II. Roll) bore, sable, a saltire embattled argent; Surrey Roll.

Kighley, Sir Henry (KEIGHLEY)—(E. IV. Roll) bore, argent, a fess sable—with crest—Ballard Roll; ascribed to WILLIAM in Jenyns' Ordinary.

Alixand d. Kenei

Tomas de Kent

Paul d'Kerdif

Will Kerdoftone

Sir R. Kendall

Will Kidofby

R

Kildare, Earl of—bore, argent, a saltire gules ; Jenyns' Ordinary. See FitzGerald.

Kilkelely v. Milkeley.

Killom, Aleyn de—(E. III. Roll) bore, azure, three covered cups or—same as Allayn Boteler ; Grimaldi Roll and Jenyns' Ordinary.

Kimbe, William de (Kymball)—(H. III. Roll) bore, or, a chevron gules, a bordure sable ; Glover Roll.

Kinardsley, Sir Hugh de, of Salop—(E. II. Roll) and Richard (H. III. Roll) bore, azure, crusily and a lyon rampant argent (F.) ; Parly. and St. George Rolls.

Kingesmede, Sir Walter de, of Salop—(E. II. Roll) bore, barry (8) or and azure, on a bend argent three escallops gules ; Parly. Roll.

***[Kingscote, Nigell de**, E. I.—bore, argent, nine (perhaps 10) escallops shells sable, on a canton gules a mullet pierced or ; Shirley.] F.

Kingston, John, D'n's de Kingeston, sealed the Barons' letter to the Pope 1301 with a lyon rampant tail fourchée, pp. xxii, xxiv. Another John bore, at the second Dunstable tournament 1334, sable a lyon rampant tail fourchée or—ascribed also to Sir John, banneret, and to Thomas, in Arundel and Parly. Rolls. Sir Nicholas, of Yorkshire, differenced with a label (3) gules, and Sir John with a label (3) argent, Sir Walter, also of Yorkshire, differenced with a baston sable ; Parly. Roll. See Kynaston.

Kirham, Nichol (or Will) **de**—(H. III. Roll) bore, argent three lyonceux rampant gules, a bordure sable (F.) ; Arden and St. George Rolls.

Kiriell v. Criol.

Kirkan, Piers (Kerkan)—(E. II. Roll) bore, argent, three "clete" leaves vert (F.) ; Jenyns' Ordinary.

Kirkbride, Thomas—(E. III. Roll) bore, vert, a cross engrailed argent, tricked the reverse ; Jenyns' Ordinary.

Kirkbride, Sir Richard, of Cumberland—bore, at the siege of Carlaverock 1300, argent, a saltire engrailed vert ; Parly. Roll—a cross in Nicolas.

Kirkby, Sir John and **Richard de**—(E. III. Roll) bore, argent 2 bars gules on a canton of the last a cross moline (recercelée) or ; Ashmole and Surrey Rolls.

Kirkby, Richard de—(E. II. Roll) bore, argent a fess et demy (2 bars) sable, on a quarter of the last a fer-de-moulin of the second ; Jenyns' Roll.

Kirkland, William (or Richard)—(E. III. Roll) bore, argent, three gemelles sable ; Jenyns' Ordinary.

Kirkton, John de, a baron 1362—bore, at the second Dunstable tournament 1334, barry ermine and gules (F.) ; gules, three bars ermine in Ashmole Roll and Jenyns' Ordinary.

Kirkton, Rauf de — (E. III. Roll) bore, azure, three water-bougets 2 and 1 argent ; Jenyns' Ordinary.

‡**Kirkton, Raufe de**—(H. III. Roll) bore, argent, six eaglets displayed 3, 2, 1 sable ; Dering and Howard Rolls - three eaglets (F.) in St. George Roll, and so ascribed to Thomas in Jenyns' Ordinary.

Kirktott, William de (Kirktoft)—bore, at the second Dunstable tournament 1334, masculy or and sable (F.)—ascribed also to Sir —— Kirketott, knighted at the capitulation of Calais 1348.

Kirktot, Sir William, of Suffolk, Kt.—(E. II. Roll) bore, azure, on a cross argent five escallops gules ; Parliamentary Roll.

•[**Knatchbull, John** (E. III.)—bore, azure, three crosses crosslet fitchée in bend between two cotises or.—Shirley.] F.

Knevet (——), an Essex Knight—(H. VI. Roll) bore, argent, a bend engrailed gules, *quarterly with*, argent three inescocheons each charged with a lyon rampant gules ; Arundel Roll.

***[Knightley, Sir Robert de** (Knyteley), 30 E. I.—bore, ermine, *quarterly with*, paly (6) or and gules.—Shirley.] F.

Knolle, Ellis de—(E. III. Roll) bore, argent, a bend cotised sable ; Jenyns' Ordinary.

Knolles, Robert, K.G.—(E. II. Roll) bore, gules, on a chevron argent three roses of the field ; Surrey and Jenyns' Rolls. K. 399, fo. 20.

Knovill, Sir Bogo, a baron 1295—bore, argent, three spur-rowells gules ; Nobility Roll. Sealed the Barons' letter to the Pope 1301, differenced with a label of three, pp. xx, xxiv (reversed—no label—in Dering and Ashmole Rolls - gules, three mullets or pierced vert in Cotgrave Roll).

Sir Gilbert, of co. Glouc., also bore argent, three spur-rowells gules ; Arden, Dering and Howard Rolls. Another Bogo, Boges, or Bevis differenced with a label (5) azure (F.) ; Howard and Camden Rolls, and Sir John, of co. Glouc. (f Sir Gilbert aforesaid) differenced with a label (3) azure at the first Dunstable tournament 1308 ; Parly. Roll.

Knovill, Bogo, or **Boege**, or **Beges**—(H. III. Roll) bore, gules, six spur-rowells or, a label (3, 5) azure ; Arden, St. George and Jenyns' Rolls.

Knoville, Thomas—(E. III. Roll) bore, gules, three water-bougets ermine ; Jenyns' Ordinary—borne also by James Roos.

Kokesalton, John de—(H. III. Roll) bore, argent fretty gules ; Arden Roll. See Hudleston.

Kymball v. Kimbe.

Kyme, Philip de, banneret, a baron 1295—sealed the Barons' letter to the Pope 1301, pp. xviii, xxiv, and bore, at the siege of Carlaverock 1300, gules crusily and a chevron or ; Ashmole and Dering Rolls—ascribed also to Sir Simon, of Lincolnshire (E. II.) Parly. and Segar Rolls, and to Sir William (E. II.) Parly. and Arundel Rolls - the crosses crosslet are omitted from the blason of the Howard Roll.

Kyme, Sir William de—bore, at the first Dunstable tournament 1308 and at the battle of Boroughbridge 1322, gules, crusily and a chevron or, a label (3) argent. (F.) ; azure in Nativity Roll.

[**Kynaston, Sir John de**, (E. II.)—bore, sable, a lyon rampant tail fourchée or.—Shirley.] (F.) See also Kingston.

Kynes, Sir John—(E. III. Roll) bore, barry (6) vair and gules ; Ashmole Roll.

Kyriel, Sir Thomas, K.G. 1460—bore, or, two chevrons and a quarter gules. K. 402, fo. 48. See Criol.

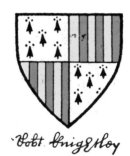

The Battle of Hastings—the Norman horsemen (unsuccessfully) attack. After the Bayeux Tapestry.

— L —

Honri do Laci

Adam d' Laci

witt d' Lāburne

John Lambton

Lacy, Henry de, banneret, Earl of Lincoln 1257—bore, at the battle of Falkirk 1298 and at the siege of Carlaverock 1300, or, a lyon rampant purpure (F.) ; Nobility and Parliamentary Rolls. JOHN, his grandfather, bore, quarterly or and gules, a baston sable, a label (5) argent " Le veyl escu de Nicol." See Earls of LINCOLN.

Lacy, Adam de—(H. III. Roll) and **Sir John,** of Herefordshire –(E. II. Roll) bore, or, a fess in chief three martlets gules. (F.) Parliamentary and St. George Rolls.

Lacy, Sir John de, of Rutland—(E. II. Roll) bore, undée (6) gules and ermine ; Parliamentary Roll.

Lacy, Sir Robert de, of Cambridgeshire— (E. II. Roll) bore, argent an orle gules, over all a bendlet sable ; Parliamentary Roll.

Lacy (——), a Cornish Knight –(H. VI. Roll) bore, azure, three shovellers' heads and necks erased argent ; Arundel Roll.

Lakenham, William—(E. III. Roll)) bore, argent, a cross between four lyonceux rampant gules ; Jenyns' Ordinary.

Lakenheath, John (LAKYNGHYTHE) — (R. II. Roll) bore, argent, a chevron sable between three caps of the last, turned up gules ; Surrey Roll.

‡**Lambourne, Sir William de,** of Essex— (E. II. Roll) bore, argent, two chevrons sable (F.) ; Parly., Dering and Howard Rolls. Ascribed to MILES in Arden Roll—a trick with label (3) gules in Ashmole Roll.

Lambourne, William—(R. II. Roll) bore, argent, on a bend sable cotised gules three lyons' heads erased of the field (another or) ; Surrey Roll.

Lambton (——), a Kentish Knight—(H. VI. Roll) bore, gules, a chevron between three lambs' heads couped argent, *quarterly with,* argent, a chevron sable between three ravens (? Cornish choughs) ppr. beaked and legged gules ; Arundel Roll.

*[**Lambton, Robert de,** 1314—bore, sable, a fess between three lambs passant argent.—Shirley.] F.

Lampet, Sir John, of Bardwell, Suffolk, Kt.—(H. VI. Roll) bore, argent a bend engrailed azure three rams' heads couped of the first horned or ; Arundel Roll.

Lampette, Sir John, of Suffolk, Kt.— (H. VI. Roll) bore, argent, on a cross engrailed gules between four escallops sable five besants ; Arundel Roll.

Lamplewe, Sir John de, of Cumberland —(E. II. Roll) bore, or (argent in Glover Roll) a cross florettée at the points sable ; Parliamentary Roll (peculiarly tricked in Harl. MS. 4033 fo. 50) – ascribed also to ROBERT (F.) and THOMAS in Segar and Surrey Rolls.

Lamplogh, Thomas—(E. II. Roll) bore, argent, a chevron between three lyons' heads erased sable ; Jenyns' Roll.

Lancaster, Edmund, Earl of (1267-76)— (*fil* H. III.) bore, England, with a label (3) France, a label (4) on his tomb ; Grimaldi Roll and Jenyns' Ordinary. Father of the next named. See illustration, page 125.

Lancaster, Thomas, banneret, **Earl of** (1296-1322)—sealed the Barons' letter to the Pope 1301, pp. xvi, xxiv, bore at the battle of Falkirk 1298, at the siege of Carlaverock 1300, and at the first Dunstable tournament 1308, England, and a label (3) of France ; Arundel and Parliamentary Rolls—a label (5) in Guillim and-St. George Rolls.

Lancaster, Sir Henry de, banneret (brother of THOMAS, last-named) bore, at the battle of Falkirk 1298 and at the siege of Carlaverock 1300 (Earl of LANCASTER, restored 1327)—England and a baston azure (F.) ; Parliamentary and Arundel Rolls ; sealed the Barons' letter to the Pope 1301, as lord of MONMOUTH, pp. xvi, xxiv ; styled Baron in the Nobility Roll – his son HENRY bore the same at the second Dunstable tournament 1334.

Lancaster, Henry, K.G., **Duke of** (1345-62) —bore, at the siege of Calais 1345-8, England with a label of France. (F.) See Monumental Brass.

Lancaster, John, OF GAUNT, **Duke of** (1362-99) bore, France and England quarterly ; over all a label (3) ermine on each pendant three ermine spots ; Surrey Roll and Jenyns' Ordinary.

Lancaster, John de, banneret, baron 1299 —bore at the siege of Carlaverock 1300, argent two bars gules, on a canton of the second a lyon passant gardant or, (sealed the Barons' letter to the Pope 1301, pp. xix, xxiv) ; barry (6) in lieu of 2 bars, &c., ascribed to JOHN of Holgill in Jenyns' Ordinary and to ROGER and WILLIAM in St. George Roll. In the Nobility Roll the canton is charged with a cinquefoyle or.

Lancaster, Sir Thomas—bore at the siege of Calais 1345-8, argent, two bars gules, on a canton of the second a rose or – in the margin also—gules, a lyon rampant gardant or, collared azure ; Ashmole Roll.

Robord do Laġîlowo

Hy do Lancaftro

Ț ęoō Lancaftor

Joõn d· Lancaſt'

Richard Lane   John Langford

Lancastre, John de—(R. II. Roll) bore, argent, a chevron between three eagles legs à la cuisse gules, a bordure engrailed sable; Surrey Roll.

Landles, John de—(E. III. Roll) bore, gules, an orle or; Nativity Roll and Jenyns' Ordinary. See also LAUNDELES.

Lane *v.* **Lone.**

Langford, Sir John de—bore, at the battle of Boroughbridge 1322, paly (6) argent and gules, on a chief azure a lyon passant or (F.); gardant in Ashmole and so borne by Sir CHRISTOPHER, knighted at the capitulation of Calais 1348. Ascribed also to THOMAS in Jenyns' Ordinary.

Langford, Sir Nichol de—bore, at the battle of Boroughbridge 1322, vert, six lyonceux rampant 3, 2, 1 or. (F.) See next entry for another.

Langford, Sir Nichol de—bore, at the battle of Boroughbridge 1322 and at the siege of Calais 1345–8. paly (6) or and gules, a bend, bendlet or baston argent (F.); Ashmole Roll and for Sir JOHN, of Derby or Notts, in Parliamentary Roll. Another NICHOL bore it at the second Dunstable tournament 1334 and he was probably knighted at the capitulation of Calais 1348.

Langford, Sir Rauff, see Longford.

Langley, Sir Edmonde de, of Warwickshire—(E. II. Roll) bore, argent, a fess and in chief three escallops sable (F.); Parly., Camden, and Harl. Rolls. (WALTER bore ogresses in place of escallops (F.); St. George Roll.) Ascribed to GEOFFREY (‡) in Howard Roll, and with the escallops 2 and 1 between the fess in Camden and Dering Rolls.

Langley, Sir Thomas—(E. III. Roll) bore, gules, two bars and in chief as many bucks' heads cabossed or; Ashmole Roll.

Langton (——), baron of Walton in Lanc., knighted at the capitulation of Calais 1348—bore. argent, three chevronels gules (F.); ascribed (with crest) also to Sir JOHN, of Walton, E. IV., Ballard Roll, and also to THOMAS, baron of Newton, in Jenyns' Ordinary; CHRISTOPHER, differenced with a label (3) azure; Surrey Roll.

War.
d. Langelleg

HENRY, DUKE OF LANCASTER, K.G.,
GRANDSON OF H. III.
IN ELSING CHURCH, NORFOLK,
1347, 21 E. III.
From a rubbing of the Hastings Brass.

nichol de Langford   Richard de Langford

Langton (——) a Knight—(H. VI. Roll) bore, gules, a chevron argent between three lyonceux rampant or; Arundel Roll.

Langton, John de—(E. III. Roll) bore, per pale or and vert, a cross recercelée (moline, in trick) gules, over all a baston sable; Jenyns' Ordinary.

Langton, Raffe—(E. III. Roll) bore, gules, an orle argent, a bend sable; Jenyns' Ordinary.

Langton, Thomas, of Wingarde—(E. II. Roll) bore, or, a lyon rampant sable vulned on the shoulder proper; Jenyns' Roll.

*[**Langton** —— of Langton, co. Linc.—(temp. H. II.) bore, paly (6) argent and sable, a bend or.—Shirley.] F.

Langtree, Gilbert—(E. IV. Roll) bore, three ermine spots 2 and 1—with crest; Ballard Roll.

Lansladron, Serlo de, of Cornwall, baron 1299 - bore, sable, three chevronels argent; Nobility and Parly. Rolls.

Lanthony, —— (E. I. Roll) bore, or, on a chief indented azure, three plates; Harl. Roll.

Lapare *v.* **Larpare,** —— (E. III. Roll) bore, gules crusily and a lyon rampant argent; Ashmole Roll. Name and blason doubtful.

Lapun, Robert de—(H. III. Roll) bore, gules, fretty vair (F.); St. George Roll. See LATHUN.

Lascelles, Allen—(E. III. Roll) bore, gules, a saltire and a chief argent (F.); Jenyns' Ordinary, where it is blasoned, probably in confusion with EGLESCLIFFE, gules on a saltire five besants argent. See also ASSELES.

Lascelles, John de, of Allerthorpe—(E. III. Roll) bore, sable, a cross patée (flory in trick) or; Jenyns' Ordinary.

*[**Lascelles, John de,** of Hinderskelfe (9 E. II.) 1315–16—bore, sable, a cross patonce and a bordure or.—Shirley.] F.

Lassels, John, of Langthorn—(E. III. Roll) bore, argent, six roses 3, 2, 1 gules; Jenyns' Ordinary.

Lascelles, Pigot—(E. II. Roll) bore, argent, three chaplets gules; Jenyns' Roll. ROGER, differenced with a bordure engrailed of the last; Jenyns' Ordinary.

Lascelles, Thomas, of South Cowton—(E. III. Roll) bore, gules, on a chevron sable between three eagles' heads erased as many mullets (6) all argent; Jenyns' Ordinary.

dol Angolley   Langton Baron de Walton   Langton   Robt d. lapun   Alain de Lassols   John de Lascelles

Lathom, Sir Thomas—bore, at the siege of Calais 1345–8, argent (? or) on a chief dancettée azure three plates (F.), besants in Ashmole MS.—the field or with besants in Ashmole Roll and Jenyns' Ordinary.

Lathom, Philip, of Knowesley—(E. iv. Roll) bore, or on a chief dancettée azure three plates, over all a bendlet gules ; with crest ; Ballard Roll and Harl. MS. 1481 fo. 82.

Lathun, Robert de—(H. iii. Roll) bore, gules, fretty vair; St. George Roll. See LAPUN.

✝**Latimer, William le,** of Corby, banneret, a baron 1299—bore, at the battle of Falkirk 1298 and at the siege of Carlaverock 1300, gules, a cross patonce or (F.) ; sealed the Barons' letter to the Pope 1301, pp. xviii, xxiv. His son WILLIAM, also a baron, having precedency over his father, bore the same at Falkirk 1298 with a label argent, but without at the first Dunstable tournament 1308, and probably at the battle of Boroughbridge 1322, then styled banneret, his son may, however, be intended, who certainly bore the same at the second Dunstable tournament 1334. JOHN and THOMAS differenced with a label (3, 5) azure ; St. George and Surrey Rolls.

Latimer, John de—bore, at the battle of Boroughbridge 1322, and Sir THOMAS bore, at the first Dunstable tournament 1308, gules, a cross patonce or, a label (3) of France ; Parly. Roll. Another THOMAS bore it also at the second Dunstable tournament 1334, and it is also ascribed in Jenyns' Ordinary to THOMAS, of Norfolk ; it was also carried at the siege of Rouen 1418 ; and with a bordure argent at the second Dunstable tournament 1334.

Latimer, Thomas de, of Braybrooke, a baron 1299—bore, gules, a cross patonce or, a label (sable) ; Nobility and Parly. Rolls. Sir THOMAS, LE BOURSARY, or BOUCHARI, differenced with a label (3) sable, on each pendant a plate (F.), at the first Dunstable tournament 1308. Ascribed also to Sir WILLIAM in the Parly. Roll. Sire WILLIAM LE BOCHARDE further differenced, at the battle of Boroughbridge 1322, with a martlet argent on the label. In the Nobility Roll the label is differenced bezantée for (1) Sir WILLIAM ; and for (2) Sir JOHN sable florettée or (F. as THO.), and for (3) Sir THOMAS the label is azure.

Latimer, Sire John le—(E. I. Roll) bore, gules, on a cross patonce or five covered cups sable ; Guillim Roll.

Latimer, Sir John le, of Yorkshire—(E. II. Roll) bore, gules, on a cross patonce or, four escallops sable ; Parly. Roll (the father of Sir WARYN). Sir THOMAS bore five escallops ; Harl. Roll and Harl. MS. 1481 fo. 86.

EDMUND CROUCHBACK,
EARL OF LANCASTER 1295
(BROTHER OF EDWARD I.),
AND PROBABLY HIS PATRON SAINT ST. GEORGE.
From an Illumination prefixed to a Missal,
"*Archæologia,*" xii. 200.

Latimer, Sir Waryn—bore, at the battle of Boroughbridge 1322, and another Sir WARYN, knighted at the capitulation of Calais 1348, bore, gules, on a cross patonce or five maunches of the field (F.) ; Jenyns' Ordinary and Harl. MS. 1481 fo. 86.

Latymer, Sire Nicholas—bore, at the battle of Boroughbridge 1322, LATYMER, and bend of France, *i.e.* on a bend azure three fleurs-de-lys or (F.) To Sir NICHOLAS, of Yorkshire, a later hand in Parly. Roll (E. II.) adds " Noe bende nor fleur-de-luces," Harl. MS. 6137 fo. 22 ; for differences see Harl. 1481 fo. 86.

Laton, Sir Christopher de (LAYTON)--Knighted at the capitulation of Calais 1348, argent, crusily fitchée (3, 3) a cross sable (F.) ; ascribed also to THOMAS in Grimaldi Roll and Jenyns' Ordinary. ROBERT differenced with a cinquefoyle pierced of the field ; Surrey Roll.

Laton, William de—(E. II. Roll) bore, argent, on a bend gules three escallops of the field ; Jenyns' Roll. F.

Laton, William de—(R. II. Roll) bore, or, a cross moline gules ; Surrey Roll.

Launde *v.* De la Launde.

Laundeles, Sir John de—(E. III. Roll) bore, azure an orle or ; the field gules for LANDLES ; Nativity Roll and Jenyns' Ordinary.

Laurence, Sir James, of Asheton—(E. IV. Roll) bore, argent, a cross ragulée gules— with crest ; Ballard Roll. F.

La Ware *v.* De la Ware.

*✱[**Lawley, Thomas,** 1471—bore, argent, a cross formée checquy or and sable.—Shirley.] F.

*✱[**Lawton, Hugh,** Hen. VI.—bore, argent, on a fess between three crosses crosslet fitchée sable, a cinquefoyle of the first.—Shirley.] F.

Lebaud, Sir Thomas—(E. III. Roll) bore, azure, a lyon passant or ; Ashmole Roll.

John Leche

Adam Lechmore

Piers Leighton

Henri Lekebourne

John Leycester

Beronge le moye

Hughe le Spencer

Piers de Legh

John Leigh

Simon de Leycester

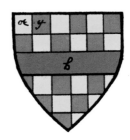

Joan le Sor

Roger le Straunge

Fouke Le Estrange

John Le Estraunge

*[Leche, John, 1475—bore, ermine, on a chief indented gules, three crowns or.—Shirley.] F.

*[Lechmere, Adam de—bore, gules a fess, and in chief two pelicans or, vulning themselves ppr.—Shirley.] F.

Le Despencer, Hugh—bore, at the second Dunstable tournament 1334, quarterly argent and gules (sic) a baston sable; the fret or in the 2nd and 3rd quarters is probably omitted. See DESPENCER and SPENCER. F.

Ledye, Roger—(R. II. Roll) bore, argent, a fess gules between three eaglets displayed sable; Surrey Roll.

Lee, Ley, v. De la Lee and De la Ley.

Leeham v. Leigham.

Leeke, Andrew de (LEYKE)—(R. II. Roll) bore, argent, a chief gules surmounted by a bend engrailed azure. ROBERT differenced it with a mullet pierced or; Surrey Roll.

Leeke, John de (LEYKE) — (R. II. Roll) bore, argent, on a saltire engrailed sable nine annulets or; Surrey Roll.

Leeke, John de (LEKE)—(E. III. Roll) bore, sable, six annulets 3, 2, 1, or; Jenyns' Ordinary.

Leem (——) a Norfolk Knight—(E. II. Roll) bore, or, a saltire engrailed vert; Parliamentary Roll, an addition. See LE MOYNE.

Legh, Sir Peter (LEE), of co. Lanc.—(E. III. Roll) bore, masculy argent and sable, tricked lozengy; Jenyns' Ordinary—modo NICHOLAS DE CROFTE.

Legh (William) of the Boothes—(E. IV. Roll) bore, azure, two bars argent, over all a bendlet counter compony or and gules—with crest; Ballard Roll; blasoned checquy but tricked counter-compony in Jenyns' Roll. Harl. MS. 1481 fo. 80.

Legh, Sir Piers á, of Bradley—(E. IV. Roll) bore, quarterly (1), argent, a cross sable a fleur-de-lys of the last, (2), gules, a cross engrailed argent (3), argent, a mullet sable (4), vert, a chevron between three crosses patonce or—with crest; Ballard Roll.

Legh, Thomas, of Adlington—(E. IV. Roll) bore, azure, a plate between three crowns or, a bordure argent; quarterly with, argent, a cross patonce sable, with crest; Ballard Roll.

*[Legh, John, 12 Hen. VI.—bore, gules, a cross engrailed and a fusil argent.—Shirley.] ' F.

*[Legh, Thomas de, H. III.—bore the arms of Lymme, gules, a pale fusily argent.—Shirley.] (F.) Or, a lyon rampant gules, was subsequently allowed to LEIGH of West Hall and a silver lyon to LEGH of East Hall.

Le Grose, Sir Renaud, of Norfolk—(E. II. Roll) bore, quarterly, argent and azure, on a bendlet sable three martlets or; Parliamentary Roll—ascribed to Sir JOHN in the Ashmole Roll.

Leices or Leites v. Beices.

Leicester, Earl of, SIMON DE MONTFORT, 1230-65—bore, gules, a lyon rampant, tail fourchée argent. (F.) Arden, Glover, St. George and other Rolls; bore on his banner—per pale dancettée argent and gules; Glover, Grimaldi and other Rolls.

Leicester, John, of Cheshire—(E. IV. Roll) bore, azure, a fess or fretty gules between three fleurs-de-lys 2 and 1 of the 2nd—with crest; Ballard Roll. (F.) See also LEYCESTER.

Leigham, Sir John de (LEEHAM), of Berks—(E. II. Roll) bore, sable, florettée (3, 2, 1) or; Parliamentary Roll; in another MS. 2, 2, 1.

*[Leighton, Sir Richard, 1313 bore (Seal) quarterly per fess indented or and gules, over all a bendlet.—Shirley.] F.

Lekebourne, Sir Henry de—bore, at the first Dunstable tournament 1308, argent crusily and a fess dancettée sable. F.

Lekebourne, Sir Henry de, of co. Lincs.—(E. II. Roll), and Hugh (E. III. Roll) bore, argent, crusily (6, 4) and a chevron sable; Nativity and Parliamentary Rolls and Jenyns' Ordinary.

‡Le Leu, Nicole—(H. III. Roll) bore, gules two heraldic wolves passant argent; Dering Roll—greyhounds in Ashmole MS. See LOW.

Le Mare v. De la Mare.

Le Moy(n)e, Berenger—(E. I. Roll) bore, gules, crusily and a cross patée argent. (F.) Segar Roll. See MOYNE.

Le Moyne, Sir John, of Suffolk—(E. II. Roll) bore, or a saltire engrailed gules; Parliamentary Roll. See LEEM.

‡Le Poer, Robert—(H. III. Roll) bore, quarterly ermine and azure two leopards' faces or; Dering Roll.

Le Sor, John—(H. III. Roll) bore, checquy or and gules a fess azure. (F.) St. George Roll.

Le Strange, Sir John, of co. Glouc.—(E. II. Roll) bore, gules, two lyons passant argent, a bordure indented or, over all a baston azure; Parliamentary Roll.

Le Strange, Roger, of Ellesmere, baron 1295—bore, gules, two lyons passant argent and a bordure engrailed or; sealed the Barons' letter to the Pope 1301, pp. xix, xxiv; Nobility, Howard and Arundel Rolls, &c. (F.) Ascribed also to Sir JOHN in Harleian Roll.

Le Strange, Sir Fouke, banneret, baron 1309—bore, at the first Dunstable tournament 1308, argent two lyons passant gules (F.); sealed the Barons' letter to the Pope 1301, pp. xxi, xxiv; borne also by (‡) JOHN, in Dering, Camden and St. George Rolls; his son JOHN differenced with a label azure in Glover Roll.

L'Estrange, Sir John, of Knockyn, banneret, baron 1299—bore, at the siege of Carlaverock 1300, gules two lyons passant argent, sealed the Barons' letter to the Pope 1301, pp. xix, xxiv. (His son JOHN, of Corsham and of Blanchminster, bore the reverse; Harl. MS. 1481 ff. 16, 18); and by Sir ROGER at the siege of Calais 1345-8. Borne also by EUBULUS, Baron Strange 1325, and JOHN and HAMON, in Segar, Surrey and St. George Rolls, and by LE SR.—at the siege of Rouen 1418. Another JOHN (brother of EUBULUS) differenced with a bendlet or; Surrey Roll—as did his son HAMON, of Hunston, Norfolk. EUBULUS, younger brother of JOHN (the father of HAMON) differenced with a label (3) or, on each pendant a lyon rampant gules; Harl. MS. 1481 fo. 19b.

L'Estrange, Sir John—bore, at the first Dunstable tournament 1308, gules, two lyons passant argent within an orle (8) martlets or. (F.) Of co. Gloucester in Parliamentary Roll.

L'Estrange, Fowke—bore, at the second Dunstable tournament 1334, gules, two lyons passant argent crowned or.

John Strange

Hamūd d'Estrange

Robt̃ de Le Strang

Joan le struim

Rauf de Louoland

John Leycostor

Eric Lomyne

Roger de Lowknor

John Lobonour

will de Loyburne

Symon de Loybourne

de Lillebon

piers de Limesey

Rauf de Limesey

Rauf de Limesey

folipe de Lindesore

Le Strange, John—bore, at the siege of Rouen 1418, gules, two lyons passant on the shoulder of each a fleur-de-lys sable. F.

Le Strange, Sir Hamon—bore, at the first Dunstable tournament 1308, gules, two lyons passant argent oppressed by a baston or (F.); of co. Glouc. in Parliamentary Roll.

Le Strange, Robert—(H. III. Roll) bore, gules crusily and two lyons passant argent; St. George Roll—crusily fitchée in Harl. MS. 6137 fo. 77ᵇ. F.

Le Strunn John (or LE STURMY?)—(H. III. Roll) bore, gules, a chevron between three mullets (6) argent. (F.) Arden and St. George Rolls.

Lesume, Adam—(E. II. Roll) bore, barry (10) argent and azure in chief three torteaux; Jenyns' Ordinary.

Leu v. **Le Leu** and **Low**.

Levaat, Andrew—(H. III. Roll) bore, argent, a cross engrailed gules; St. George Roll. Borne also by JOHN LE FITZ HENRY and JOHN DE LA LINDE.

‡**Leveland, Raufe de**—(H. III. Roll) bore, sable, three bears' heads bendways couped 2 and 1 argent. (F.) Dering Roll; boars' heads in Howard Roll.

Leventhorpe (——), Knight—(H. VI. Roll) bore, argent, a bend gobony gules and sable cotised sable; Arundel Roll.

Leversage, ——, (E. IV. Roll) bore, argent, a chevron between three levers erect 2 and 1 sable—with crest; Ballard Roll. F.

Levett v. **Livett**.

Levinton, John de—(E. II. Roll) bore, gules, on a chevron argent three cinquefoyles sable; Jenyns' Roll.

Leving, Richard (LEWYNE)—(E. II. Roll) bore, ermine, on a bend gules three escallops or. (F.) Jenyns' Roll. WILLIAM DE LEOYN, of Brampton, took up the cross in the last Crusade 1270.

Lewknor, Sir John—bore, at the siege of Calais 1345-8 azure, three chevronels argent; ascribed also to ROGER (‡) and Sir THOMAS, of Sussex; Dering and Parliamentary Rolls. Another ROGER differenced with a label (5) or (F.); Camden Roll.

Lewknor, John—bore, at the second Dunstable tournament 1334, gules, two bends depressed by a chevron argent. F.

Lewknor, Sir John—(E. III. Roll) bore, gules, a chevron between three talbots passant argent; Ashmole Roll.

Lexington, John de—(H. III. Roll) bore, argent, a cross fourchée azure—"au kanee"—Glover Roll.

Leyburn, Sir William, banneret, a baron 1299—bore, at the siege of Cariaverock 1300, azure, six lyonceux rampant 3, 2, 1, argent. (F.); Nobility, Parliamentary and Arundel Rolls; sealed the Barons' letter to the Pope 1301, pp. xxii, xxiv—ascribed also to JOHN of Kent,

ROGER (‡) and another WILLIAM (‡); Jenyns' Ordinary, Dering and Norfolk Rolls. ROGER took up the cross in the last Crusade 1270.

Leyburn, Sir Henry de—bore, at the first Dunstable tournament 1308, azure, six lyonceux rampant, 3, 2, 1, argent, a label (3) gules. Sir JOHN, knighted at the capitulation of Calais 1348, differenced with a bordure engrailed or; ascribed also to SIMON in Segar Roll (F.)—and in the Parliamentary Roll to Sir SIMON, of Kent, with a bordure indented or; ROGER and THOMAS a label (4) gules; Segar Roll. Sir HENRY of Kent, with a label gobony or and gules; Parly. Roll

Leyborne (——), of the household of the Earl of Salisbury—(E. III. Roll) bore, azure, five lyons rampant 2, 2, 1 argent, a bordure engrailed or, over all a quarter ermine; Jenyns' Ordinary—ascribed to THOMAS, without the bordure; Jenyns' Ordinary.

Leyburn, Sir William, banneret—(H. VI. Roll) bore, argent, six lyonceux rampant 3, 2, 1 sable; Arundel Roll.

Leyburn, Sir de (?JOHN), knighted at the capitulation of Calais 1348—bore, gules, six lyons rampant 3, 2, 1 argent—ascribed also to Sir RICHARD of Yorks, and THOMAS; Parliamentary and Surrey Rolls. Sir NICHOLAS of Yorks differenced with a label (3) azure.

Leyborne, John, of the North, banneret—(E. III. Roll) bore, or six lyonceux rampant 3, 2, 1 sable; Jenyns' Ordinary. Ascribed also to ROGER and Sir WILLIAM, of the North; Howard and Parly. Rolls (see WILLIAM above—the field argent)—THOMAS MALLORY bore the same; JOHN DE ST. MARTIN bore the reverse.

Leycester v. **Leicester**.

*[**Leycester, John,** c. 1390—bore, azure, a fess of fretty gules, between two fleurs-de-lys of the second; Shirley.] F.

Leye v. **de la Leye**.

Leyland, Sir Thomas—(E. III. Roll) bore, argent a bend gules cotised sable; Ashmole Roll, surname doubtful.

Lille, Ancels de (LYLLE)—(H. III. Roll) bore, argent, a fess between six mullets (6) gules; Howard Roll—in other Rolls a label (5) azure.

Lillebon, Walter de—(H. III. Roll) bore, per pale argent and sable a chevron counterchanged. (F.) Arden Roll.

Lilleburne, John de—(E. III. Roll) bore, sable, three dossers (or water-bougets) argent; Ashmole and Surrey Rolls.

Limbury v. **Lymbury**.

Limesy, Sir Piers de (of Warwickshire)—bore, at the battle of Boroughbridge 1322, gules, an eagle displayed or. (F.) Ascribed to RICHARD in Segar Roll and to Sir RICHARD of Warwickshire, with a baston of MONTFORD, or four bendlets azure, in Parliamentary Roll—and in Jenyns' Ordinary to JOHN, with and without a bend azure, and another JOHN or an eagle purpure membered gules.

Limesy, Raf de—(H. III. Roll) bore, gules, three eagles displayed or. (F.) Arden and St. George Rolls—another RAUF (‡) bore, six eagles 3, 2, 1 (F.) Dering and Holland Rolls (Sir RAFE)—and in a note, a label (5) azure for Sir RICHARD; Holland and Howard Rolls. See Harl. MS. 1481 fo. 67ᵇ.

Limsoy, Sir Philip (LINDESEY) of the North—(E. II. Roll) bore, or, an eagle displayed purpure; Parliamentary Roll; ?azure and oppressed by a baston argent; Harl. Roll—(the eagle sable) oppressed by a baston gobony azure and gules (F.) (perhaps the baston of MONTFORT is intended); Segar Roll.

Lowor Soggo

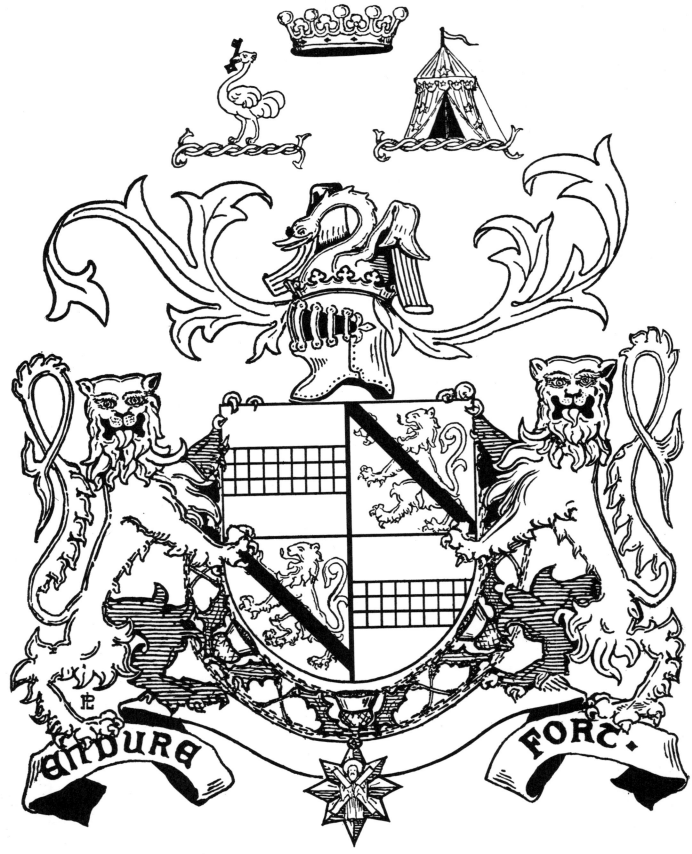

THE HERALDIC ATCHIEVEMENT

OF

JAMES, 26TH EARL OF CRAWFORD, AND 8TH EARL OF BALCARRES, K.T.

Cûle de Nicol

Ûûte de Nitolo

Alex Lyndſey

wilt de Lindoſtas

Limsey, Sir Simon de, of the North—(E. I. Roll) bore, or an eagle displayed purpure; Ashmole Roll; sable in Segar Roll and differenced with the baston (? MONTFORT) gobony argent and azure; Parliamentary Roll.

Lincoln, Earl of (JOHN DE LACY), 1232 – (E. I. Roll) bore, quarterly or and gules a baston sable, a label (5) argent. (F.) "Le veyl escu de Nicol." Segar, Camden, Nobility and other Rolls; no label in Nobility Roll H. VI.

Lincoln, Earl of (HENRY DE LACY), 1257– 1311—bore, at the battle of Falkirk 1298, and at the siege of Carlaverock 1300, or a lyon rampant purpure (F.); lyon sable in Howard Roll.

Lindsay, Sir Alexander—bore, at the battle of Falkirk 1298; gules, a fess chequy or (in error for argent) and azure. (F.) Jenyns' Ordinary.

Lindsay, Sir Gilbert de, of Hunts—(E. II. Roll) bore, gules, crusily or an orle vair; Parliamentary Roll; ascribed also to WILLIAM (F.) in St. George Roll.

Lindsay, Walter de—(H. III. Roll) bore, gules, an orle vair; Arden and Glover Rolls. WALTER le fitz, differenced with a label (3) azure; Jenyns' Ordinary.

*****Lingayn, Sir Rauff**—(E. III. Roll) bore, barry (6) or and azure, on a bend gules three cinquefoyles pierced argent; Ashmole Roll – escallops on the bend (F.) in Arden and St. George Rolls.

Lisle, v. **De Insula** and **De Lisle.**

Lisle, John de, of Wotton, baron 1299, signed but did not seal the Barons' letter to the Pope 1301, page xxiv. He bore, or, a fess between two chevronels sable; ascribed also to his son JOHN, 2nd baron, K.G. (a founder), who served at the siege of Calais 1345–8; Nobility and Surrey Rolls—ascribed also to Sir ROBERT, Banneret, in Guillim, Parliamentary and Arundel Rolls; to another ROBERT (‡) in Dering Roll; to WARREN in Segar Roll, and to WILLIAM (F.) at the siege of Rouen 1418; another WILLIAM differenced with a martlet or.

Lisle, Sir Baldwin de, of Rutland—(E. II. Roll) bore, or, on a fess between two chevronels sable three roses argent; Parly. Roll.

Lisle, Robert de, of Rougemont, baron 1311, appears to be referred to in the first entry. Sir JOHN, his son or grandson, knighted at the capitulation of Calais 1348—bore, gules, a lyon passant gardant argent crowned or (F.), one of the founders of the Order of the Garter, Sir GERARD and Sir WARIN, of Rutland, both bore the arms at the first Dunstable tournament 1308; Parly. Roll; ascribed to another GERARD in Dering Roll. They are also ascribed to Sir FOULK in Harleian Roll.

SIR HUMPHREY LITTELBURY.
IN HOLBEACH CHURCH IN LINCOLNSHIRE.
After Stothard.

Lisle, Gerard de—(E. III. Roll) bore, gules, crusily fitchée or, a lyon passant gardant, argent; Parliamentary Roll and Jenyns' Ordinary. Sir ROBERT, of Rutland, bore it crusily in Parliamentary Roll.

Lisle, Sir Warren de, knighted at the capitulation of Calais 1348—bore, argent, a lyon passant gardant gules crowned or.

Lisle—Le Count de le Ille—(H. III. Roll) bore, gules, three bars or "diaspres" (? diapered). Norfolk Roll.

Lisley, Sir John de, banneret—(H. VI. Roll) bore, or, on a chief azure three lyonceux rampant of the first. (F.) Arundel and St. George Rolls. See also INCULE.

Lisley, Sir John de, of Hants – (E II. Roll) bore, or, a chevron between three leaves ("foyles of gletuers") gules; Parliamentary Roll. See also DE LISLE. F.

Lisley, John de, Seigneur of Laybourne— (E. III. Roll) bore, gules, a chevron between three "foyles" or; Grimaldi Roll. (F.) Sir WALTER bore the reverse and a label azure; Nativity Roll.

Lisoures, John—(E. III. Roll) bore, azure, two chevronels and a mullet or – tricked as a martlet; Jenyns' Ordinary and Roll.

Lisours, John—bore, at the second Dunstable tournament 1334, azure, a chief or. (F.) Ashmole Roll and Jenyns' Ordinary.

*****[Lister, John,** 6 E. II.—bore, ermine, on a fess sable, three mullets or.—Shirley.] F.

Littlebury, John de—(R. II. Roll) bore, argent, two lyons passant gardant gules; Surrey Roll. Sir ROBERT differenced, with a label (3) azure; Ashmole Roll. See Monumental Effigy of Sir HUMPHREY.

Littlebury, Humphrey and **William**— (E. III. Roll) bore, argent, two lyons passant gardant gules on a bend vert three eaglets displayed or; Jenyns' Ordinary.

Littlebury, Robert—bore, at the second Dunstable tournament 1334, argent two lyons passant gules, a label azure (F.)—apparently not gardant

John Liſurs

John Liſter

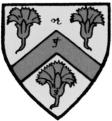

Raf de Lingoynt

witt de Lyſlo

John de Liſlo

Liſley

John de Lyſley

Robt. Luttelbury

S

THE HERALDIC ATCHIEVEMENT

OF

REAR-ADMIRAL SIR LAMBTON LORAINE, 11TH BARONET.

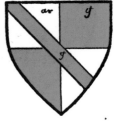

‡**Livett, Robert**—(H. III. Roll) bore, argent, crusily gules a lyon rampant sable. (F.) Dering and Howard Rolls.

Lockton, Roger de (LOKINTONE)—(H. III. Roll) bore, argent, a chief azure, a label (5) gules. (F.) St. George Roll.

Lodbrooke, Sir John, of Warwickshire—(E. II. Roll) bore, azure, a chevron ermine. (F.) Harleian, Parliamentary, and St. George Rolls. See also GONNYES.

Lodiham *v.* **Bodiham**.

Londe, William de—(E. III. Roll) bore, argent, two bars sable, a bordure engrailed gules; Jenyns' Ordinary.

*[**Lone, Richard de le**, DE HAMPTON—1315 bore, per fess or and azure, a chevron gules between three mullets counterchanged.—Shirley.] F.

Longchamp, Henry—(E. III. Roll) bore, or, three crescents gules on each a mullet argent. See HENRY DE THANI; Jenyns' Ordinary.

Longe, Sir William—(E. I. Roll) bore, or, a saltire gules; Harl. Roll, Jenyns' Ordinary.

[**Longespée, Mauld**, dau. of WILLIAM, Duke of Normandy, and wife to HUGH MORTIMER, who came with the Conqueror—(Roll E. I.) bore, gules, three espées (swords erect), argent, Jenyns' Roll—a fable.]

Longespée, William, Earl of Salisbury—(H. III. Roll) bore, azure, six lyonceux rampant (3, 2, 1) or; Howard, Glover and Grimaldi Rolls; see Monumental Effigy. ESTIENN differenced with a label gules, Glover Roll—and another with a "cantell" ermine, Norfolk Roll.

Langford *v.* **Langford**.

Longford, Sir Rauff—(E. IV. Roll)—bore, paly (6) or and gules a bendlet argent, *quarterly with*, quarterly gules and argent—and crest; Ballard Roll.

Longueville, Sir Gerard—(E. III. Roll) bore, gules, crusily argent 4, 3, 2, 1, a fess dancettée ermine; Ashmole Roll. HENRY and Sir JOHN, of Hunts., bore the fess argent (F.); Segar, Parly., and Jenyns' Rolls.

Longvale, John—(E. I. Roll) bore, gules, three bends vair; Jenyns' Ordinary.

Longvilliers, Sir John, of Whatton—(E. III. Roll) and Sire THOMAS, who fought at the battle of Boroughbridge 1322, bore, sable, crusily and a bend argent (F.); Ashmole Roll and Jenyns' Ordinary.

Lonye, Sir John de, of co. Linc.—(E. I. Roll) bore, checquy argent and azure, on a chief gules three mullets or; Parly. Roll. F.

*[**Loraine, William**, H. IV.—bore, quarterly sable and argent, a plain cross counterchanged.—Shirley.] F.

Loring, Nele, K.G. (a founder) 1344—bore, quarterly argent and gules, a bend sable; K. 398 fo. 24; at the siege of Calais 1345-8 the coat is blasoned, quarterly or and gules a bend of the last; and in the Surrey Roll (R. II.) quarterly argent and gules a bend engrailed of the last; Sir PIERS, of Beds, bore the bend plain; Parly. Roll; as did Sir WILLIAM at the siege of Rouen 1418.

L'Orti vel de **Urtiaco, Henry de**, baron 1299—bore, vert a pale or; Nobility Roll.

Lorty, Sir Henry de, of Somerset—(E. II. Roll) and JOHN (E. III. Roll) bore, azure a cross or; Parly. Roll and Jenyns' Ordinary.

Loudham, Sir John de, of Suffolk—(E. II. Roll) bore, argent, three inescocheons sable; Parly. and Ashmole Rolls. Ascribed to RAFFE in Jenyns' Ordinary.

Loudham, Sir John, of Derby—(E. II. Roll) bore, argent, on a bend azure, three crosses crosslet or; Parly. Roll. Crusily on the bend in Ashmole Roll and Harl. MS. 6137 fo. 19.

Lounde, Henry—(E. I. Roll) bore, argent, fretty azure; Jenyns' Roll.

Loundres, Robert de—(H. III. Roll) bore, per pale argent and sable, a chevron gules; Howard Roll. Sir ROBERT bore the chevron per pale gules and or; Ashmole Roll.

Louthe, Richard—(E. I. Roll) bore, "partie endentée" or and gules—tricked per pale dancettée or and gules; Jenyns' Roll.

Lovayne, the Chastelain de—(E. I. Roll) bore, bendy (6) gules and or; Camden Roll. F.

Lovayne, Sire de—(E. I. Roll) bore, sable, a lyon rampant argent, crowned or (F.), Camden Roll; uncrowned in Howard Roll; his brother EDMUND differenced with a label (5) gules.

WILLIAM LONGESPÉE, EARL OF SALISBURY, SON OF HEN. II. BY FAIR ROSAMOND. IN SALISBURY CATHEDRAL, 1226-7. *After Stothard.*

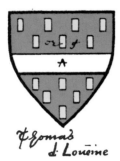

Thomas d. Louëine

John do Lovedale

Rog . Lovedai

Richard Lovell

Robert Lovell

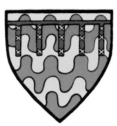

Johan Lovel

Henry Lowther

with Lovell.

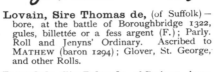

Thomas Lovell

Lovain, Sire Thomas de, (of Suffolk)—bore, at the battle of Boroughbridge 1322, gules, billettée or a fess argent (F.) ; Parly. Roll and Jenyns' Ordinary. Ascribed to MATHEW (baron 1294) ; Glover, St. George, and other Rolls.

Lovedale, Sir John de, of Brabant—bore, at the siege of Calais 1345-8, sable, a bugle horn argent, on a chief of the second a lyon passant gardant or. F.

Lovedaye, Sir Richard, of Essex—(E. II. Roll) bore, azure, three bars dancettée or ; Parly. Roll ; colours reversed in Harl. MS. 6137 fo. 14. ROGER, bore dancée (6) or and sable (F.) ; St. George Roll.

Lovell, John, of Tichmarsh, banneret, baron, 1299—bore, at the battle of Falkirk 1298, undée (6) or and gules ; Nobility, Parly., and Arundel Rolls. JOHN, Lord de Dackingg, sealed the Barons' letter to the Pope 1301, with these arms differenced with a label (3) on each pendant 3 mullets, pp. xx, xxiv ; see JOHN (2) below. Another JOHN bore them (undifferenced) at the second Dunstable tournament 1334 ; ascribed also to THOMAS, of Tichmarsh, in Jenyns' Ordinary, tricked or and azure in Ashmole Roll ; and as, or three bars nebulée gules for Sir JOHN in Harleian and Guillim Rolls.

(1) JAMES, brother of JOHN, first-named, differenced with a quarter ermine, Harl. MS. 1481 fo. 43.

(2) JOHN, differenced with a label (5) azure, Camden and St. George Rolls ; each charged with three mullets (6) or ; Segar Roll. F.

(3) Sir WILLIAM, knighted at the capitulation of Calais 1348, differenced with a label (3) gobony argent and azure (F.) ; the label tricked in Ashmole MS. as barry (8) argent and azure, perhaps identical with trick of Sir WILLIAM, of Oxford, in Parly. Roll, who bore a label of VALENCE, viz., barry, argent and azure, on each pendant, a martlet gules.

(4) WILLIAM, differenced with a label of France at the second Dunstable tournament 1334.

(5) Sir JOHN, the bastard (of Oxford), differenced with a label (3) azure, each charged with a mullet argent ; Parly. Roll.

Lovell, Sir Thomas (of Oxon.), who tilted at the first Dunstable tournament 1308—bore undée (6) or and gules, a baston or azure (F.) in Parly. and Ashmole Rolls. JOHN LE FITZ bore the baston argent in Camden Roll, and another JOHN differenced with a baston sable in Arden Roll.

Lovell, Le Sr. (William) de—bore, at the siege of Rouen 1418, undée (6) or and gules *quarterly with*, azure, florettée and a lyon rampant gardant argent (F. ; Surrey Roll, as LE SR. DE LOVEL and HOLLAND. Borne also by his grandfather, JOHN, K.G. 1405 ; K. 400 fo. 19.

Lovell, Sir Richard, banneret—bore, at the first Dunstable tournament 1308, or, crusily and a lyon rampant azure (F.) ; Parly. and Arundel Rolls. Not crusily in Glover Roll. JOHN took up the cross in the last Crusade 1270.

Lovetot, John de—(H. III. Roll) bore, argent, a lyon rampant per fess gules and sable, Arden and St. George Rolls ; (sable and gules, Jenyns' Ordinary) ; NIGEL, of Hunts, bore the field or ; Harl. MS. 1481 fo. 39.

*[**Lovett, Robert** (33 E. I.)—bore, argent, three wolves passant in pale sable.—Shirley.] F.

Low, Sir John le, of Bucks—(E. II. Roll) bore, argent, two bars and in chief three wolves' heads erased gules ; Parly. Roll.

Low, Nichole le—(H. III. Roll) bore, gules, two wolves passant argent. (F.) Dering and Howard Rolls.

***Lowther, Henry**—(E. III. Roll) bore, argent, six annulets 3, 2, 1 sable ; Jenyns' Ordinary—HUGH bore the field or ; Jenyns' Ordinary and Ashmole Roll. Borne also by Sir JEFFRY, a Kentish Knight. See Incised Slab.

Lucien, Piers—(E. III. Roll) bore, argent, a lyon rampant gules, over all a baston gobony or and azure ; Jenyns' Ordinary.

Luckyn, Sir Roland de (LOKYN)—bore, at the first Dunstable tournament 1308, bendy (6) gules and ermine. Surname doubtful ; rather COKYN or QUKIN.

Lucre, William—(E. III. Roll) bore, argent, an orle sable ; Jenyns' Ordinary.

Lucy, Sir Geffrey—(E. II. Roll) bore, gules, two lucies pileways argent ; Holland Roll.

Lucy, Geffrey de, of Cockermouth, baron 1297—bore, gules, three lucies hauriant 2 and 1 argent (F.) Ashmole Roll ; or, in Arden and Glover Rolls—ascribed to RICHARD in the Grimaldi Roll, and so carried at the siege of Rouen 1418. THOMAS, differenced at the second Dunstable tournament 1334 with a label azure and a bordure engrailed argent (F.) ; also by ANTHONY or AMERY in Jenyns' Ordinary—4 lucies in blason. Sir WILLIAM bore the paternal coat crusily argent ; Harl. 1481, ff. 59-65.

Lucy, Sir Amery (AYMER or EMERY), or Kent—(H. III. Roll) bore, azure crusily and three lucies 2 and 1 hauriant or ; Parliamentary, Howard, St. George and Dering Rolls. Sir THOMAS, of Kent. bore the lucies argent ; Parliamentary Roll¶

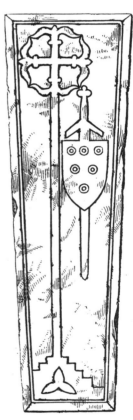

Incised Slab, Kirkby Stephen.

LOWTHER.
From Boutell.

Le Sire Lovell

nicolo do Lou

Le Sire de Lucye

Tho . de Lucye

Geoffrey de Luci

RETINENS VESTIGIA FAMÆ

EX LIBRIS

CHARLES BYBIE LYSTER:

Christopher Ludlowe   Tho Lodilowe   Rauf Lumley   Tho Loterel   Henry Lutterell

Lucy, Geoffrey, of Kent—(H. III. Roll) bore, gules, crusily three lucies hauriant 2 and 1 or (F.); Parliamentary Roll, &c. REYNOLD differenced with a label (3) azure; Surrey Roll. See Harl. 1481 ff. 59, 65.

Ludburgh, John de—(E. III. Roll) bore, gules, a chevron argent between three leopards' faces or; Jenyns' Ordinary. F.

Ludlowe, Sir Christopher de, knighted at the capitulation of Calais 1348—bore, or, a lyon rampant sable. (F.) So also JOHN, in Surrey Roll and Jenyns' Ordinary.

Ludlow, Sir Thomas, of Salop (E. II. Roll) and **John** (E. III.)—bore, azure, three lyons passant gardant argent; Parliamentary Roll and Jenyns' Ordinary. F.

Ludlow, Thomas—bore, at the second Dunstable tournament 1334, gules, crusily a lyon rampant and a border engrailed all argent (F.) (gardant in Parliamentary Roll); crusily or in Ashmole Roll.

Lukard ——, (E. III. Roll) bore, argent three (? wolves) heads couped gules; Ashmole Roll.

*__Lumley, Rauf__ and **Sir T.**—(R. II. Roll) bore, argent, a fess gules between three popinjays ppr. (F.); Surrey and Atkinson Rolls.

Lumley, Marmaduke (R. II. Roll) bore, gules, on a fess between three popinjays argent as many mullets pierced of the last. Sir ROBERT DE, of co. Durham (E. III), bore the mullets sable. (F.) Surrey and Parliamentary Rolls.

Lusignan, Sir Geoffrey—(H. III. Roll) bore, burulée (12) or and azure, a lyon rampant gules; Arden Roll. See also VALENCE and Harl. MS. 1418 fo. 29.

*[**Luttley, Philip de,** 20 E. I.—bore, quarterly, or and azure four lyons rampant counterchanged.—Shirley.] F.

Luttrell, Andrew, and **Sir Geoffrey,** of co. Linc., **Robert** and **Thomas** (F.)—(H. III. Roll) bore azure, a bend between six martlets argent; St. George and Guillim Rolls. ALEXANDER took up the cross in the last Crusade 1270.

Luttrell, Sir Andrew, of co. Linc. (E. II. Roll), and **Sir Hugh** (H. VI. Roll) bore, or, a bend between six martlets sable; Parliamentary and Atkinson Rolls.

Luttrell, Hugh—bore, at the siege of Rouen 1418, or, a bend between six martlets sable a bordure engrailed of the second. (F.) Surrey Roll.

Lydevusers, Sir John, of France—bore, at the battle of Boroughbridge 1322, azure on a bend argent, an inescocheon or charged with a bend dancettée sable. F.

Lye (——), a Knight—(H. VI. Roll) bore, argent, a bend fusily sable, a crescent of the second; Arundel Roll.

Lymbury, Sir John, knighted at the capitulation of Calais 1348—bore, argent an escocheon sable within an orle of cinquefoyles gules. F.

Lymbury, Sire William de—bore, at the battle of Boroughbridge 1322, argent five cinquefoyles 2, 2, 1 sable. (F.) Six-foyles ascribed to JOHN in Jenyns' Ordinary.

Lynde v. de la Lynde.

Lyons, Sir John—bore, at the second Dunstable tournament 1334, argent, a lyon rampant gules. (F.) Ashmole Roll.

[**Lyster, John,** 6 E. II.—bore, ermine, on a fess sable three mullets or; Shirley.] See Bookplate, preceding page.

Lythegranes, John—(E. III. Roll) bore, gules, an orle argent, over all a bend or; Jenyns' Ordinary.

*[**Lyttelton, Thomas**—bore (H. IV. Seal) argent, a chevron between three escallops sable.—Shirley.] F.

John Ludburgh   Tho Ludlow

John de Lydevuford   Wm de Lymbury

AN UNIDENTIFIED EFFIGY IN THE TEMPLE CHURCH.

From the "Herald and Genealogist."

Sir Laurence and Thomas Bassett of Cornwall bore similar Arms, as did Sir Richard Lovedaye of Essex.

Phil. de Luttley   John de Lyouns

John Lynbury   Tho Lyttelton

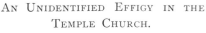

The Norman horsemen (unsuccessfully) attack the English. After the Bayeux Tapestry.

— M —

Ozarlos vongo do la mayno

John machell

Giles de maili

witt Mailot

M . . . seles, Edmond de—(H. III. Roll) bore, per pale argent and sable a fess counterchanged; St. George Roll—borne also by CUSACKE and FITZ PAINE. See WINCELES.

Mac Culloch, Patrick (MAKCOLAGH), of Scotland—(E. III. Roll)—bore, ermine, fretty gules; Jenyns' Ordinary.

Mac Donnell, Sir Duncan, of Scotland—(E. I. Roll) bore, or, three lyonceux sable; Nativity Roll.

Machell, John—(E. I. Roll) bore, argent, three greyhounds courant in pale sable collared (? gemelles) or. (F.) Jenyns' Ordinary.

Mac Moylin, Clarus (O'MOILLCHONRYE), Archdeacon of Elphin, founded the Abbey of Loughkee 1215 and also the Church of Deryndoyne, co. Roscommon, (ARCHDALE)—bore, argent, a dexter arm issuant from the sinister gules. (F.) Jenyns' Ordinary as CHARLES DE LA ROUGE MAYNE.

Madrestone, Philip de—(H. III. Roll) bore, gules, a double headed eagle displayed . . . . membered or; Howard Roll.

Magnaby, Hugh de—(E. III. Roll) bore, argent, three bars sable, a maunch gules; Grimaldi Roll. See MANBY.

‡**Maili, Giles de**—(H. III. Roll) bore, or, three mallets (or martels) gules. (F.) Dering Roll.

Mailott, William—(H. III. Roll) bore, gules, fretty or, a chief ermine. (F.) St. George Roll.

Mainwaring, John, of Pever—(E. IV. Roll) bore, gules, two bars argent, a crescent azure——M. of Ightfield bore the same, *quarterly with,* checquy argent and sable; Ballard Roll.

***Man(waring), William**—(E. III. Roll) bore, argent, two bars gules; Grimaldi Roll.

Malebys, Sir John—(E. II. Roll) bore, argent, three (heads " de bis ") hinds' heads couped gules; Parliamentary Roll.

Malbys, Sir William—(E. III. Roll) bore, argent, a chevron between three hinds' heads erased gules; Ashmole Roll—byses in Jenyns' Ordinary.

‡**Males, John**—(H. III. Roll) bore, gules, three Catherine wheels (F.) altered to round buckles, tongues to the dexter or; Dering and Howard Rolls.

Malessour, Sir Thomas—(E. III. Roll) bore, per pale azure and gules, three crescents argent; Ashmole Roll. ROBERT fil. HENRY took up the cross in the last Crusade 1270.

ˣ[**Malet, Baldwin,** E. I.—bore, azure, three escallops or.—Shirley.] F.

‡**Malett, Robert**—(H. III. Roll) bore, sable, three round buckles, tongues to the dexter, 2 and 1, argent. (F.) Dering, Howard and St. George Rolls.

Mallet, Sir Thomas, of Notts—(E. II. Roll) bore, gules, a fess ermine between six buckles tongues to the dexter, or; Parliamentary Roll—the fess or, in Harl. MS. 6137 fo. 19ᵇ.

Malett, Richard and **Sir Robert,** of Bucks—(E. II. Roll) bore, sable, a chevron between three buckles tongues to the dexter argent; Jenyns' and Parliamentary Roll.

Maleverer, John, Oliver, Robert — (E. III. Roll) bore, gules, three greyhounds courant in pale argent collared gemelles or; Surrey Roll and Jenyns' Ordinary. (ROBERT bore the field sable—and the collar blasoned gobonée or and sable.) Sir THOMAS and Sir WILLIAM seem to have borne the greyhounds uncollared; Arden, Parliamentary, Ballard and Arundel Rolls.

Maleverer, Sir John, Knight banneret—(H. VI. Roll) bore, sable, fretty or. Arundel Roll.

Maleverer, Sir Michael—bore, at the first Dunstable tournament 1308, argent, a bend engrailed gules—purpure in Harl. MS. 6137. (F.) But see MALMAINS.

Maleverer, Sir John—(E. I. Roll) bore, gules, a chief or, over all a baston gobony (6) argent and azure; Nativity and Parliamentary Rolls and Jenyns' Ordinary.

Malignee, Reynold — (R. II. Roll) bore, ermine, on a fess gules, three palets or; Surrey Roll.

Malise, Roger de (MELESE)—(H. III. Roll) bore, argent, two bars and in chief three escallops gules; Arden Roll. See also STRATHERNE.

Mallory, Antony and **Sir Peter** (1227)—bore, or, a lyon rampant tail fourchée gules; Ashmole, Nobility and Surrey Rolls.

Mallory, Sir Piers, of co. Leicester—(E. II. Roll) bore, or, three lyonceux passant gardant sable; Parliamentary Roll.

Mallory, Thomas—(E. III. Roll) bore, or, six lyonceux rampant, 3, 2, 1, sable; Jenyns' Ordinary. JOHN DE LAYBOURNE bore the same, and JOHN DE ST. MARTIN bore the reverse.

John malos

Robt Malet

Baldwin malot

michaell malovororo

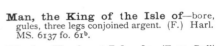

Mallory, William (MAULARE)—(H. III. Roll) bore, or a demi-lyon tail fourchée in chief gules. (F.) St. George Roll.

Malmains, (Sir) Thomas—bore, at the second Dunstable tournament 1334, gules (three dexter hands apaumée an), ermine (spot in each palm); Ashmole Roll.

*Malmains, Henry — (H. III. Roll) bore, gules, three dexter hands apaumée 2 and 1 argent, Dering Roll; hands, or (F.) in Howard Roll; gules in Ashmole Roll; NICOLE bore them argent in Dering and Howard Rolls. F.

Malmains, Sir Nicole, of Kent—(H. III. Roll) bore, gules, three sinister hands 2 and 1 couped ermine. (F.) Arden and St. George Rolls—argent in Camden Roll.

Malmains, Sir Nicholas—bore, at the first Dunstable tournament 1308, argent, a bend engrailed purpure (F.) (azure in Harl. MS. 6137 fo. 10); Parliamentary Roll and Jenyns' Ordinary—bend, plain in Nativity Roll.

Malmains, Thomas—(E. I. Roll) bore, sable, a bend lozengy argent. (F.) Jenyns' Ordinary.

Malolacu, Peter de, v. Mauley.

Maltham, Ratcliffe—(E. III. Roll) bore, gules, bezantée and a lyon rampant argent; Jenyns' Ordinary.

Malton, Henry de—(E. I. Roll) bore, sable, a lyon rampant or, within an orle of annulets argent; Jenyns' Ordinary.

Malton, Sir Henry de—(E. III. Roll) bore, sable, a lyon rampant argent crowned or, a bordure of the second charged with annulets (13) of the first; Ashmole Roll.

Malton v. Multon.

Maltravers, Sir John, banneret, a baron 1330—bore, at the first Dunstable tournament 1308 (as le fitz) and at the battle of Boroughbridge 1322, sable, fretty or, a label (3) argent; another Sir John bore it without the label (F.) at the siege of Calais 1345-8. Sire GAWYN bore the same, Howard Roll (H. III.) as often tricked and blasoned, a fret. See also ARUNDEL and FITZALAN. Ascribed to another JOHN (‡) in the Dering Roll.

*Maltravers, William—(H. III. Roll) bore, sable, fretty or, on a quarter argent, three lyons passant in pale gules (F.); Dering Roll.

Malvesyn v. Mavesyn.

Man, the King of the Isle of—bore, gules, three legs conjoined argent. (F.) Harl. MS. 6137 fo. 61ᵇ.

Manby, Hugh and John de—(E. III. Roll) bore, argent, three barrulets sable, over all a maunch gules; Jenyns' Ordinary. MAGNABY in Grimaldi Roll.

Manby, Sir Walter de, banneret—(E. II. Roll) bore, azure, a cross or; Parliamentary Roll.

Mancestre, Sir Grey de—bore, at the battle of Boroughbridge 1322, vair, a baston gules—vaire, argent and sable (F.); in the Ashmole MS., Harl. and Ashmole Rolls, and so also for JOHN in the St. George Roll.

Mancestre, Sir Simon de, of Warwick-shire, bore, at the first Dunstable tournament 1308, vaire, or and sable on a bend gules three eaglets displayed or; Parliamentary Roll.

Manclerk v. Menclerk.

Mandevile (Geffrey de) Earl of (Essex and Gloucester 1213-16)—bore, quarterly or and gules; Glover and Grimaldi Rolls. See Mr. Round's GEOFFREY DE MANDEVILLE 392-6. Borne also by the family of DE SAY.

Mandevile, Sir John de, of Hants. or Wilts.—(E. II. Roll) bore, quarterly vair and gules; Parliamentary Roll.

Mandevile, John de—(H. III. Roll) bore, quarterly argent and azure within a bordure vaire or and gules; Howard Roll.

Mandevile, Sir John or Richard de, of Warwickshire (E. II. Roll) bore, azure, fretty or; Parliamentary &c. (argent in Ashmole Roll). Sire RICHARD differenced it at the battle of Boroughbridge 1322 with a label (3) gules. F. Ascribed to another RICHARD in Dering Roll.

Mandevile, Richard de—(H. III. Roll) bore, azure, fretty argent a fess gules; Glover and Grimaldi Rolls. RICHARD and THOMAS—the fretty or in Jenyns' Ordinary.

Mandeville, Sir Thomas de, of Essex—(E. II. Roll) bore, argent, on a chief indented gules, three martlets or; Parliamentary Roll. JOHN in Harl. MS. 6137.

Mandeville, Thomas—(E. III. Roll) bore, or three barrulets azure; Jenyns' Ordinary.

Manfee, Sir William, of Sussex—(H. III. Roll) bore, argent, a lyon rampant sable between nine escallops in orle gules. (F.) Dering (as MANBY), Camden and Parliamentary Rolls. Borne also by MANBY, of Elsham, in co. Linc.

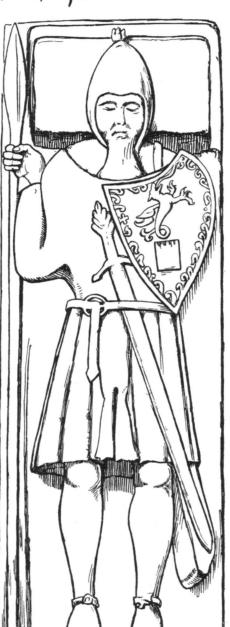

MACLEAN OF DUART.

From Drummond's "Sculptured Monuments in Iona."

Bawodynn de mant   *Watt mannby*   *Raulf do Marconvile*   *Tobaud do maroli*   *Thomas de Marines.*   *John markham*

Manners, Sir Bawdwyn de, of co. Cambridge—bore, at the first Dunstable tournament 1308. argent, a saltire engrailed sable. (F.) Ascribed also to HENRY, in Arden Roll (H. III.)—JOHN BLOYON bears the same; Jenyns' Ordinary.

*****Manners, John** and **Sir Robert**—(E. III. Roll)—bore, or, two bars azure and a chief gules (azure, in Nativity Roll); Ashmole Roll and Jenyns' Ordinary.

Manningham (——), Knight (H. VI. Roll) —bore, argent a chevron between three moorcocks sable; Arundel Roll.

Manny, Terry de—(E. III. Roll)—bore, or, three chevronels sable; Ashmole Roll and Jenyns' Ordinary. RICHARD SUTTON, of Norfolk, bore the same.

Manny, Sir Walter de, K.B. 1331, K.G. 1359, a baron 1347—bore, at the second Dunstable tournament 1334, and at the siege of Calais 1345-8, or three chevronels sable, on the second a lyon passant of the first (F.); a lyon passant guardant on the premier chevronel, in K. 398 fo. 50—two chevronels only in Jenyns' Ordinary.

Mansell *v.* **Maunsell.**

Manston (——), a Kentish Knight—(H. VI. Roll) bore, gules, a fess ermine between three mullets pierced argent; Arundel Roll.

Maneston, Richard de — (H. III. Roll) bore, argent, a fess gules between three eagles displayed sable; Howard Roll.

Mantell (——), an Essex Knight—(H. VI. Roll) bore, argent, a cross engrailed between four martlets sable; Arundel Roll.

Mapertishall, Sir John—(E. III. Roll) bore, argent, fretty sable, on a chief gules a lyon passant gardant or; Ashmole Roll.

March and Ulster, Earl of, *v.* **Edmund Mortimer.**

March *v.* **de la March.**

Marchington, Thomas—(R. II. Roll) bore, or, a fret sable, and a canton gules; Surrey Roll. See also MARKINGTON.

‡**Marconville, Raulf de**—(H. III. Roll) bore, quarterly argent (or, in Ashmole MS.) and azure, in the first quarter a lyon rampant gules. (F.) Dering Roll—same arms as DAVY GERCOMVILE alias JERKAVILE.

Mardestone, Sir Peers de, of Suffolk— (E. II. Roll) bore, azure, two bars argent, on a chief gules a lyon passant (gardant—H. 4033 *f* 15ᵇ) or; Parly. Roll. See DENNARDESTON.

Mare, Mareli, Mareys, Mardac, *v.* **de la Mare, Marley, Smareys, Murdac.**

‡**Marines, Thomas de**—(H. III. Roll) bore, or, a cross engrailed gules. (F.) Dering and St. George Rolls.

Marke, Ingram, Robert and **William** (MERC or MERKE)—(H. III. Roll) bore, gules, a lyon rampant argent; Arden and Norfolk Rolls — "sautant embelif" (F.) in Jenyns' Ordinary. Sir JOHN of Essex bore it within a bordure indented or; Parly. Roll—engrailed (F.) in St. George Roll.

Markham, Sir Robert (*f* Sir JOHN, King's Sergeant E. II.)—bore, azure, on a chief or a demi lyon rampant issuant gules. (F.) Sir JOHN of Sedbrooke bore it within a bordure (? argent). Harl. MS. 1481 fo. 84.

Markinfield, Andrew—(H. III. Roll) bore, argent, on a bend sable three besants; Jenyns' Ordy. (—) a Yorkshire Knight bore it—H. VI. Roll,—*quarterly with*, gules, three closed helmets argent, garnished sable—Arundel Roll.

Markington, Henry de—(E. III. Roll) bore, gules, an orle argent, over all a bend ermines; Jenyns' Ordinary.

Marley, Roger de (MERLEY)—(H. III. Roll) bore, barry, argent and gules, a bordure azure charged with martlets or; Glover Roll.

‡**Marley, Tebaud de** (MARELI)—(H. III. Roll) bore, or, a cross gules fretty argent, between four eaglets displayed azure. (F.) Dering Roll.

Marmaduke *v.* **Fitz Marmaduke.**

Marmion, John, banneret, baron 1297— bore, vair, a fess gules; Nobility Roll—as also did PHILIP (F.), Sir ROBERT in Norfolk, Ashmole and Arden Rolls; and WILLIAM (‡) in Dering Roll. F.

Marmion, Philip—(H. III. Roll) bore, vair, a fess gules fretty or. (F.) St. George and Glover Rolls.

Marmion, Sir John, Knight banneret— (H. VI. Roll)—bore, vert, a fess gules—and, added—between six lyons rampant 3 and 3 argent; Arundel Roll.

Marmion, Sir William—bore, at the siege of Calais 1345-8, vair, a fess gules, a label (3) or. F.

Marmion, Geoffrey, of Checkendon, Bucks, bore, vair, three mascles 2 and 1 gules—Harl. MS. 1481 fo. 71.

Marmion, Sir William—bore, at the first Dunstable tournament 1308, gules, a lyon rampant vair crowned or (F.); (uncrowned in Jenyns' Ordinary)—ascribed to a Suffolk Knight in Arundel Roll, and to Sir WILLIAM, of co. Leic. in Parly. Roll, though in Harl. MS. 6137 fo. 24, the field is argent and the lyon vert.

‡**Marmion, Philip** — (H. III. Roll) bore, sable, a sword erect in pale, point in chief argent; Dering and Howard Rolls—point in base (F.) Camden Roll.

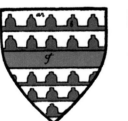

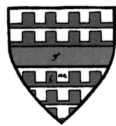

MACLEAN OF ROSS.
From Drummond's " Sculptured Monuments in Iona."

Pphilip marmiun   *will marmiun*   *Phelip Marmion*   *Pfillip marmyon*

T

W^m de marmion — *will marmion* — *will to Mareschale* — *Ric̃ martel* — *will martin* — *Lamb massingbord*

John martell

Joan de Merc

Rob̃ de morc

Hugh massio

Marnell, Stephen de—(H. III. Roll) bore, azure, on a chief or, a lyon passant gules; Howard Roll.

Marney, Robert—(R. II. Roll) bore, gules, a lyon rampant gardant argent; WILLIAM differenced with a label (3) or; Surrey Roll.

Marr, Earl of—(H. III. Roll) bore, azure, crusily fitchée and a bend or; Vincent 162 fo. 133ᵇ. In Norfolk Roll—azure, billettée and a bend or.

Marshall, The (Earl of Pembroke)—(H. III. Roll) bore, per pale or and vert a lyon rampant gules; Glover, Howard and Norfolk Rolls. See Monumental Effigy.

Marshall, William, banneret, baron 1309—bore, at the siege of Carlaverock 1300 (sealed the Barons' letter to the Pope 1301, pp. xviii, xxiv), and at the first Dunstable tournament 1308, gules a bend lozengy or (F.) (blasoned, engrailed); Parly. Roll. Sire ANCEL, of Norfolk, then differenced it with a label (3) argent. Another Sire ANCEL bore it undifferenced at the battle of Boroughbridge 1322 (Parly. Roll). Ascribed also to ‡JOHN in Dering and Harl. Rolls—variously blasoned and tricked as, a bend fusily or lozengy, or a bend of fusils or lozenges conjoined—which last appears to be the recognised form. The Marshal of Ireland bore the bend argent; Jenyns' Ordinary.

Marshall, Sir Raffe le, of Hants—(E. II. Roll) bore, or, a cross moline gules, sometimes blasoned récercelée; Parliamentary Roll.

Martell, Sir John, of Essex, Kt.—(H. VI. Roll) bore, gules three martels or, handles argent (F.); Arundel Roll; martels argent for WALTER, H. III.; Norfolk Roll; RICHARD bore it or and gules; Dering Roll. Sir ADAM, of Berks, and RICHARD bore it sable and argent. (F.) Parly. and St. George Rolls.

‡**Martel, Richard**—(E. I. Roll) bore, or, three martels gules; Dering Roll.

Martel, Sir John—(E. I. Roll) bore, gules, a bend fusily or; Harleian Roll—same arms as MARSHALL.

Martell, Sir William—(E. I. Roll) bore, argent, two bars gules and in chief three torteaux.—Harleian Roll. See MOELS.

Martin, Sir William, of Kemeys, banneret, baron 1295—bore, at the battle of Falkirk 1298, argent, two bars gules — (same as WILLIAM MAUDUYT) sealed the Barons' letter to the Pope 1301, pp. xix, xxiv. Another Sir WILLIAM, differenced with a label (5) azure, bezanty. (F.) Guillim and Segar Rolls. See also St. MARTIN and WINTERSHULLE.

Martyne, Sir Waryne, of co. Glouc.—(E. II. Roll) bore, argent, two bars gules each charged with three bezants; Parly. Roll.

Martyn, Warryn—(H. III. Roll) bore, ermine three bars gules. WILLIAM differenced with a label (5) azure; Howard Roll. NICHOLAS and ROBERT took up the cross in the last Crusade 1270.

Martinaux, Anketyn—(E. III. Roll) bore, argent, a cinquefoyle gules; Jenyns' Ordinary.

Martindale, William de—(E. I. Roll) bore, barry (6) argent and gules, a baston sable; Jenyns' Roll.

*[**Massie, Hugh**, of Coddington, R. II.—bore, quarterly gules and or, in the first and fourth three fleurs-de-lys argent, a canton of the third.—Shirley.] F.

*[**Massingberd, Lambert**, (E. I.)—bore, azure, three quatrefoyles (two and one) in chief a boar passant or, charged on the shoulder with a cross patée gules.—Shirley.] F.

Massy, Sir Geoffrey, of Tatton—(E. IV. Roll) bore, quarterly gules and argent, a label (5) azure—with crest. GEOFFREY BARTON, of Tatton, is heir to this cote of MASSEY and also of MASSY; Ballard Roll.

Massy, Hamond — (E. III. Roll) bore, quarterly gules and or in the first a lyon rampant argent; Jenyns' Ordinary. Another cote is thus obscurely blasoned from the Howard Roll, bendy of lozenges conjoined or and gules a lyon rampant sable.

Massy, John—(R. II. Roll) bore, sable, a cross patonce or; Surrey Roll.

Mateflon, Guy de—(H. III. Roll) bore, chevronny (8) gules and or; Howard Roll.

Mathew (——), of Thornton Steward, Yorks. (E. I. Roll) bore, gules, three martlets argent, tricked as martels; Jenyns' Roll. See FITZ STEVEN, of Thornton Rust.

Mauduit, Sir John—bore, at the first Dunstable tournament 1308, gules, three piles wavy meeting in base or. Undée or and gules "en lung" (F.) was carried by Le Sire . . . MAUDUYT at the battle of Boroughbridge 1322, i.e., paly wavy (6) or and gules; tricked as three palets nebulée in Ashmole Roll for Sir JOHN of Swinford, and as three piles dancettée meeting in base for Sir JOHN of Hants or Wilts. in Parly. Roll. JOHN, carried "gules" (sic)—at the second Dunstable tournament 1334—and in Jenyns' Roll (E. I.) paly undée (6) or and sable is ascribed to another JOHN.

Mauduit, Sir Roger, of Northumberland—bore, at the battle of Boroughbridge 1322, ermine, two bars gules (F.); Parly. and Nativity Rolls. WALTER and WILLIAM bore the field argent; Sir WILLIAM MARTYN bears the same; Glover and Jenyns' Rolls.

Mauduit, Sir John, of Warminster, and **Thomas**—(E. III. Rolls) bore, checquy or and azure, a bordure gules (F.) (tricked bezanty in Jenyns' Ordinary), Ashmole and St. George Rolls. THOMAS took up the cross in the last Crusade 1270.

Bogot manduit

Thõ. Mandut

Siro Manduyt

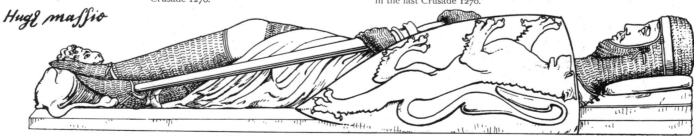

EFFIGY OF WILLIAM MARSHALL, EARL OF PEMBROKE 1219. IN THE TEMPLE CHURCH. *From Richardson.*

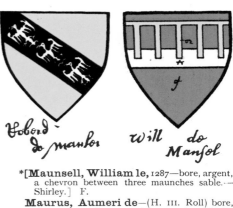

Maulare, William v. **Mallory**.

Mauley, Piers de—(H. III. Roll) bore, vair, a maunch gules (F.); Glover and St. George Rolls.

Mauley, Sir Piers de, banneret, baron 1295—bore, at the battle of Falkirk 1298, or, a bend sable (F.) and sealed the Barons' letter to the Pope 1301, pp. xviii, xxiv. Sir ROBERT, or rather, perhaps, Sir PIERS (3rd baron), bore it at the siege of Calais 1345–8, and Sir PIERS, banneret (4th baron), bore it at the siege of Rouen 1418; Arundel Roll. In Jenyns' Roll Le Sire MAULEY bore or, a bend sable *quarterly with* BIGOD, same as ROBERT FOSSARD. His brothers (1) ROBERT, bore, on the bend, three eaglets displayed argent and (2) JOHN, bore on the bend, as many dolphins embowed argent; Harl. MS. 1481 fo. 87. See following entries.

Mauley, Sir Robert de, of Yorkshire—(E. I. Roll) bore, or, on a bend sable three eaglets displayed argent (F.); Segar and Harleian Rolls; see Monumental Effigy, and "Archæologia," vol. 31, p. 47—the bend azure in Ashmole Roll.

Mauley, Sir John de, of Yorkshire—(E. II. Roll) bore, or, on a bend sable three dolphins embowed argent; Parly. Roll.

Mauley, Sir Ed. de, of Yorkshire—(E. I. Roll) bore, or, on a bend sable between two lyons rampant of the second, three dolphins embowed argent, Harleian Roll; another coat—or, on a bend sable, three eight foyles (imperfectly drawn) argent; Harleian Roll.

Mauley, Sir Edmond de, of Yorkshire—(E. II. Roll) bore, or, on a bend sable, three wyverns, tails nowed, argent—F. (Harl. MS. 4033 fo. 43b); three bunches of grapes argent; Harl. MS. 6137, Parliamentary Roll. F.

Maunsell, John—(E. I. Roll) bore, sable, a chevron between three mullets pierced or; Jenyns' Roll.

Maunsell, Thomas and **Sir William**, of co. Glouc.—(E. II. Roll) bore, gules, a fess argent, a label (3, 5) argent—sometimes or (F.); St. George and Parly. Rolls, Jenyns' Ordinary; ascribed to another WILLIAM in Dering Roll

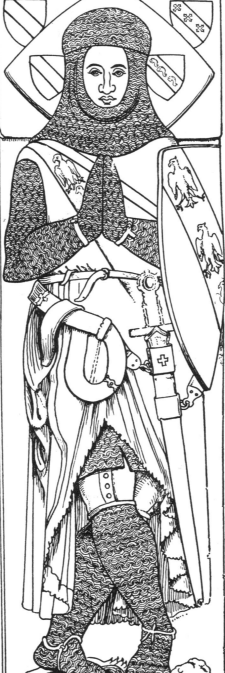

SIR ROBERT DE MAULEY.
(FORMERLY) IN YORK MINSTER, TEMP. E. II.
From the "Archæologia."

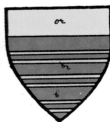

*[**Maunsell, William le**, 1287—bore, argent, a chevron between three maunches sable.—Shirley.] F.

Maurus, Aumeri de—(H. III. Roll) bore, checquy or and azure, a chevron gules. (F.) St. George Roll. Variously called DE ERDERNE and DE MANES.

Maurewarde, Thomas—(R. II. Roll) bore, azure, a fess argent between three cinquefoyles pierced or; Surrey Roll.

Mause, William—(R. II. Roll) bore, argent, semée of escallops gules and a lyon rampant sable; Howard Roll.

Mautas, William—(H. III. Roll) bore, azure, seven mascles conjoined 3, 3, 1 or; Howard Roll.

Maveysyn, Guy—(H. III. Roll) bore, or two bars gules; Howard Roll.

‡**Maveysyn, Henry, John** and **Robert**—(H. III. Roll) bore, gules, three bendlets argent; Dering, Howard and Surrey Rolls. JOHN GRELEY, carries the same.

Mawburney ——, (E. I. Roll) bore, masculy gules and ermine, on a quarter azure a cross recercelée or — tricked masculy and a cross moline; Jenyns' Roll.

Medhope ——, (E. III. Roll) bore, ermine, a lyon rampant azure; Jenyns' Ordinary.

Meldone, Sir William—(E. III. Roll) bore, argent, a saltire sable; Ashmole Roll.

Melise, Roger de—(H. III. Roll) bore, argent two bars and in chief three escallops gules; Arden Roll. See MALISE.

Melsanby, Walter de—(E. I. Roll) bore, sable, two gemelles and a chief argent; Jenyns' Roll.

Melton, John and **William de**—(E. III. Roll) bore, azure, a cross patonce voided argent; Jenyns', Surrey, and Cotgrave Rolls, in which last it is not voided.

Melton, John de—(E. III. Roll) bore, azure, a cross patonce voided gules—pecé botonée. (F.) Jenyns' Ordinary.

Menclerk, Peres de—(H. III. Roll) bore, azure, three cinquefoyles argent; Norfolk Roll.

***Menell, Sir Hugh** (MENYLE, MENYLL, MEYNELL), of co. Cambridge—bore, at the first Dunstable tournament 1308, vaire argent and sable, a label (3) gules. (F.) Sir GYLES, bore it undifferenced, and RICHARD bore the label gobony or and gules. (F.) Jenyns' Ordinary.

***Menill, Sir Nichol de**, of Whorlton, banneret, Baron Meinell, 1295—bore, at the battle of Falkirk 1298, azure, three gemelles and a chief or. (F.) St. George Roll and Jenyns' Ordinary; sealed the Barons' letter to the Pope 1301, pp. xxii, xxiv; borne also (H. III. Roll) by TREMON (or TREVOR) DE MENYLL in Glover Roll; two gemelles in Nobility, Guillim and Parly. Rolls.

Henry menylo

night de monno

Howel ap Meurit

Geoffrey de Moromond

John de Morowortz

Robt de moofi

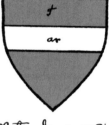

Geo de motolam

Godfrey de Mons

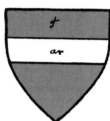

Andr motstodo

Menell, Gilbert de—(E. III. Roll) bore, paly (6) argent and gules, on a bend sable three horse-shoes or ; Cotgrave Roll.

Menyle, Henry (E. III. Roll) bore, paly (12) and **William,** paly (8) argent and gules, on a bend azure three horse-shoes or. (F.) Jenyns' Ordinary.

Menell, Ralph (MENVILE)—(E. III. Roll) bore, vert, a lyon rampant argent crowned gules ; Jenyns' Ordinary. Same as JOHN BEESTON.

Menne, Nichol de—(H. III. Roll) bore, or, on a chief azure three lyonceux rampant argent. (F.) Arden and St. George Rolls ; same as D'INCULE.

Merc v. **Marke.**

Menteth, the Earl of—(E. III. Roll) bore, gules, a fess checquy or and azure—tricked compony ; Jenyns' Ordinary.

Meredith, Howell ap—(H. III. Roll) bore, paly (6) or and azure on a fess gules three mullets argent. (F.) St. George Roll.

‡**Meremond, Geffrey de** - (H. III. Roll) bore, argent two bars sable (F.) Dering Roll ; and in chief a mullet pierced gules, in the Ashmole copy.

‡**Mereworth, William** and **John**—(H. III. Roll) bore, argent, crusily sable and a chevron gules. (F.) Dering and Howard Rolls and Jenyns' Ordinary.

Meriett, Sir John de (MERYETT or MERIEL) of Hants or Wilts.—(E. II. Roll) bore, barry (6) or and sable (barry 8 in Ashmole). Sir JOHN, the nephew, differenced with a bend ermine ; Parliamentary Roll.

Merton, Sir Richard—(E. III. Roll) bore, vert, three bendlets argent ; Ashmole Roll ; argent and azure in Jenyns' Ordinary.

Merville v. **Henry le Sturmin.**

Meschines v. **Randolf Blondeville.** Page 25.

Mesi, Robert de—(H. III. Roll) bore, gules, a fess argent. (F.) Arden and St. George Rolls ; reversed in Harl. MS. 6137 fo. 55, " Mezi " fo. 82.

Metford (——), an Essex Knight—(H. VI. Roll) bore, or, a fess gules, between three martlets sable, *quarterly with,* sable, a lyon rampant tail fourchée and renowée argent ; Arundel Roll.

Metham, Thomas — bore, at the second Dunstable tournament 1334, quarterly azure and argent a fleur-de-lys or. (F.) Surrey Roll and Jenyns' Ordinary. Sir THOMAS in Ashmole Roll, reversed in Howard Roll.

Metstede, Andrew—(E. III. Roll) bore, quarterly or and gules four escallops counter-changed ; Jenyns' Ordinary.

Mette, Semkyn, of Kent, Kt.—(H. VI. Roll) bore, azure, on a bend or three mascles gules ; a fleur-de-lys argent ; Arundel Roll.

Meus, Sir Godfrey de (MEUX)—bore, at the first Dunstable tournament 1308, azure, six gryphons segreant 3, 2, 1 or. (F.) Ascribed also to Sir GEFFREY and Sir JOHN ; Ashmole and Nativity Rolls.

Middleton (——) a Yorkshire Knight—(H. VI. Roll) bore, gules, a lyon rampant argent, on a bend azure three escallops or ; Arundel Roll.

***Midelton, John** of Northumberland, and **William de**—(H. III. Roll) bore, quarterly gules and or, in the first quarter a cross patonce (patée in blason) argent ; St. George Roll and Jenyns' Ordinary. (F.) GILBERT took up the cross in the last Crusade 1270.

Midelton, Pieres de—(E. III. Roll) bore, argent, fretty and a quarter sable ; Jenyns' Ordinary.

Milkeley, Sir Robert de, of Herts, Kt.— (E. II. Roll) bore, gules, three chevronels argent ; Parliamentary Roll.

‡**Mingee, Adam de**—(H. III. Roll) bore, or, on a quarter azure, a cat-a-mountain's head erased argent ; Dering Roll.

Mynyot, John—(E. I. Roll) bore, gules, three helmets argent, crested or—ROGER of Calton differenced with a label (3) azure ; Jenyns' Roll.

Missenden, Edmond de—(R. II. Roll) bore, or, a cross engrailed gules, in the dexter canton a raven proper ; Surrey Roll. See MUSSENDEN.

*[**Mitford, John de,** R. II.—bore, argent, a fess between three moles sable.—Shirley.] F. ROBERT took up the cross in the last Crusade 1270.

Moels, Sir John, of Cadbury, banneret, baron 1299—bore, at the battle of Falkirk 1298 argent, two bars gules, in chief three torteaux (F.) sealed the Barons' letter to the Pope 1301, pp. xx, xxiv ; borne also by JOHN MULES at the second Dunstable tournament 1334 ; Arundel, Nobility, and Parly. Rolls, by ROGER in St. George Roll ; mullets ascribed to NICHOLAS in Glover Roll.

Mohaut v. **Monhaute** and **Monthalt.**

Mohun, Sire John de, of Dunster, banneret, baron 1299—sealed the Barons' letter to the Pope 1301, pp. xviii, xxiv. He bore at the battle of Falkirk 1298, and at the siege of Carlaverock 1300, or, a cross engrailed sable (F.) ; when his son Sir JOHN (father of Sir JOHN, 2nd baron, K.G., and a founder) also bore it, with a label (3) gules ; Nobility, Arundel, and Ashmole Rolls. Sir REIGNOLD, knighted at the capitulation of Calais 1348—differenced it with a label (5) gobony argent and gules. See also Tiles, Neath Abbey, p. ix.

Mohun, Reginald de—(E. III. Roll) bore, gules, a maunch ermine ; Grimaldi Roll— the maunch argent, in Glover Roll—and so ascribed to WILLIAM differenced by a label (5) azure (F.) in St. George Roll.

Mohun, John de—(H. III. Roll) bore, gules, a maunch ermine, a fleur-de-lys issuant or. (F.) Howard Roll and Jenyns' Ordinary.

Moigne v. **Moyne** and **Le Moigne.**

witt d. Midleton

John de mitford

John d Moles

Jo. de moun   John mohun   witt d Moun

Wal' d'Molecaſtre

watt moloſworþ

Symon de moloun

will mollynorþ

Giloo de monpoſin

Bertram do mountbocgor

Bertram do mountbocgor

A da do montgaut

Molcaster, Sir Robert—(E. III. Roll) bore, barry (6) argent and gules, a baston azure; Ashmole Roll. Burulée (12); as MONCASTRE in Surrey Roll.

Molcastre, Walter de—(H. III. Roll) bore, burulée (12) argent and azure on a bend azure three escallops or. (F.) St. George and Parliamentary Rolls tricked in the latter, barry 8 and 10—the bend sable.

*****Molesworth, Sir Walter de**, of Hunts—(E. II. Roll) bore, vair, a bordure gules crusily or; Parliamentary Roll. F.

Moleyns, Sir John and **Richard**—(E. III. Roll) bore, sable, on a chief azure three lozenges conjoined gules; Ashmole Roll and Jenyns' Ordinary—the field azure, in the coat carried by Lord MOLEYNS, who was slain at the capitulation of Calais 1348.

Moleyns, John—(R. II. Roll) bore, or, three palets wavy gules; Surrey Roll.

Molington, Sir John de, of Suffolk—(E. II. Roll) bore, argent, a fess between two chevronels azure; Parliamentary Roll.

‡**Moloun, Symon de**—(H. III. Roll) bore, azure, bezanty 3, 2, 1 (sometimes platey) on a chief argent (sometimes or) a demi-lyon rampant issuant sable. (F.) Dering Roll, gules in Ashmole MS.

Molton v. **Moton.**

*****Molyneux, William**—(E. III. Roll) bore, azure, a fer-de-moulin pierced or; Jenyns' Ordinary and Ballard Roll; on an escutcheon of pretence, the atchievement of Sir THOMAS of Sefton, in Ballard Roll; unpierced in Jenyns' Roll. F.

Mompesson, Sir Giles, of Norfolk—(E. II. Roll) bore, argent, a lyon sable, on his shoulder a "pynzon" or; Parliamentary Roll.

Mompesson, Giles de—(E. I. Roll) bore, argent twelve birds (?"pynzon") 3, 3, 3, 2, 1 azure, beaked vert and membered gules. (F.) Segar Roll.

Monbocher, Bertram de—bore, at the siege of Carlaverock 1300, argent, three pitchers sable, a bordure of the second bezanty (F.) (piles meeting in base gules (F.) in Harl. MS. 6137 fo. 39ᵇ); Sire BERTRAM bore the pitchers gules at the battle of Boroughbridge 1322; Surrey and Harleian Rolls; piles as before in Parliamentary Roll.

Monbocher, Raffe—(E. I. Roll) bore, argent, three "possenetts" gules; Jenyns' Roll.

Monchensi v. **Munchensi.**

Monceaux, Hamond—(E. I. Roll) bore, gules, a cross recercelée (tricked moline) and an escallop or; Jenyns' Roll.

Moncell, William de—(H. III. Roll) bore, gules, a fess argent, a label (5) or; Howard Roll

Monhaute v. **Monthalt.**

†**Monhaute, Adam de**—(H. III. Roll) bore, argent, three gemelles over all a lyon rampant gules (F.); Howard Roll and Jenyns' Ordinary; borne also by Sir JAMES, of Lincolnshire, in Parliamentary Roll. JOHN and SIMON also took up the cross in the last Crusade 1270.

Monmouth, Guy and **John de**—(H. III. Roll)—bore, or, three chevronels gules, over all a fess azure (F.) (argent in Norfolk Roll and Jenyns' Ordy.); Arden and Glover Rolls.

*****[Monson, John**, 1378—bore, or, two chevronels gules.—Shirley.] F.

Montagu, Sir Simon de, baron 1300, bore, at the battle of Falkirk 1298, quarterly 1 and 4, argent, three lozenges conjoined in fess gules; 2 and 3, azure, a gryphon segreant or; one of the earliest examples of a quarterly coat. With the first he sealed the Barons' letter to the Pope 1301, pp. xix, xxiv; but at the siege of Carlaverock 1300 he carried the gryphon only, which is supposed to be the original arms of the family; a male gryphon is ascribed to OSMOND in Jenyns' Roll.

Montagu, Sir William, baron 1317-18—bore, at the first Dunstable tournament 1308, argent, three lozenges conjoined in fess gules (see Tiles, Neath Abbey, pp. vii and ix), as did WILLIAM (Earl of Salisbury 1337-44) at the second Dunstable tournament 1334; when Lyonel differenced with, a quarter gules. (F.) At the siege of Calais 1345-8, Sir EDMUND differenced with a label or on each pendant an eagle displayed vert; JOHN bore it within a bordure sable in lieu of the label, Surrey Roll, and his son RICHARD of Stowe in Somerset differenced with three pellets 2 and 1 in lieu of the bordure, Harl. MS. 1481 fo. 45.

Montagu, William, 2nd Earl of Salisbury 1344, K.G., a founder—bore, argent three lozenges conjoined in fess gules, *quarterly with*, gules, three armed legs flexed and conjoined argent garnished or, for the lordship of Man, in Surrey Roll; in the same Roll the quarters are also given in the reverse order. THOMAS, 4th Earl of Salisbury, 1409, K.G.—bore, at the siege of Rouen 1418, argent three lozenges conjoined in fess gules *quarterly with*, MONTHERMER, or an eagle displayed vert.

Montagu, Edward—(E. II. Roll) bore, ermine, three lozenges conjoined in fess gules; Jenyns' Ordinary.

Montfichet, Richard de—(H. III. Roll) bore, gules, three chevronels or, a label azure; Glover Roll.

Montfort, Simon de, Earl of Leicester 1230-65—bore, gules, a lyon rampant tail fourchée argent (F.); Arden and Camden Rolls. PHILIP differenced with a label azure; Norfolk Roll—a coat with the tinctures reversed in Ashmole Roll.

Simon de montagu

Simon de mountagu

Le Counte do Saliſburþ

Jon do monoun

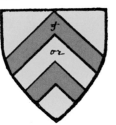

John monſon

Simo de mountford

Lyono montagu

will montaguo

Dorb de mountfort

Adam d Mungomen

will de Montgomory

John montgomory

Rob de mungaut

Saffo de Mountgormor

John montfort

Edward mountgormor

Andrew mongault

Edw. mountgormor

will mordaunt

will morolo

Robt Morley

will d Moreres

Montfort, Sir Alexander, Sir John, of Dorset, **Sir Lawrence** and **Thomas**—(E. III. Roll) bore, argent, crusily gules and a lyon rampant azure ; Ashmole, Parliamentary, Grimaldi and Jenyns' Ordinary.

Montfort, Sir John de, banneret—bore, bendy (10) or and azure ; Parliamentary and Jenyns' Rolls. (‡) PIERS (F.) has (1) bendy of 12 in Camden Roll, (2) or, four bendlets sinister azure in Dering and Arden Rolls, and (3) azure six bendlets or, in Segar Roll.

Montfort, Robert and **Sir William**—(E. III. Roll) bore, bendy (10) or and azure a label (5) gules (azure in St. George) ; Dering and Howard Rolls ; a label (3) gules for Sir WILLIAM, of Surrey or Sussex ; Parliamentary Roll.

Montfort, Sir John—(E. III. Roll) bore, azure, three bendlets or ; Guillim Roll ; another four bendlets or, a label (3) gules ; Ashmole Roll ; or, four bendlets azure ; Nobility Roll. H. 6.

Montfort, Sir John, banneret—(H. III. Roll) bore, barry undée (10) argent and azure ; Arundel Roll. F.

Montfort, Sir W.—(H. VI. Roll) bore, argent, on a chief azure two fleurs-de-lys or ; Atkinson Roll.

Montford, John de (otherwise DE BRETAGNE), Duke of Britanny, Earl of Richmond 1372, K.G. 1376—bore, chequy or and azure a bordure of England, over all a canton ermine ; K. 398 fo. 35. See BRETAGNE.

Mon(tford), le Count de—bore, or four bendlets azure ; Nobility Roll, temp. H. VI. 1422-60 ; more like MONTHERMER in Roll.

Montgomery, Adam de—(H. III. Roll) bore, or, three lyons passant in pale sable (F.) ; Arden and St. George Rolls.

Montgomery, John—(E. III. Roll) bore, argent, a cross engrailed between four mullets gules ; Jenyns' Ordinary. F.

Montgomery, John—(E. III. Roll) bore, gules, a false escocheon ermine, within an orle of horse-shoes argent, nailed sable ; Jenyns' Ordinary ; the same is ascribed to WILLIAM in the Glover Roll, and is blasoned ermine, a bordure gules, entoyre of horse-shoes argent nailed sable ; in Arden Roll the tinctures are argent gules or and sable.

Montgomery, Sir William de (of Derby or Notts)—bore, at the battle of Boroughbridge 1322, or, an eagle displayed azure (F.) ; borne also by Sir JOHN at the siege of Calais 1345-8, and also by NICOL and Sir WALTER.

Monthalt, Sir Roger (MOHAUT, MUHATT, MUNHAUT) baron 1295 (H. III. Roll)—bore, azure, a lyon rampant argent ; Glover and Howard Rolls ; his brother Sir ROBERT, banneret, baron 1299, bore the same at the battle of Falkirk 1298, and at the siege of Carlaverock 1300 (sealed the Barons' letter to the Pope 1301, pp. xvii, xxiv) ; Nobility, Parly. and Arundel Rolls. (JOHN ORTON bore the same.) JOHN differenced it with a label (3) or, Jenyns' Ordinary ; a label (5) gules, Arden and St. George Rolls, and so also with the field or, also in Arden Roll.

Monthalt, Sir Andrew (MONHAULT), of Masenden—bore, at the siege of Calais 1345-8, azure, a lyon rampant argent, a bordure or. F.

Monthaute v. Monhaute.

Monthermer, Sir Edward, knighted at the capitulation of Calais 1348—bore, or, an eagle displayed vert, on a bordure gules 8 or 10 lyons of England (F.) ; Ashmole Roll. Ascribed also to another EDWARD (F.) without the bordure in Jenyns' Ordinary.

Monthermer, Sir Raffe, banneret, Earl of Gloucester and Hertford 1209—bore, at the battle of Falkirk 1298, or, an eagle displayed vert, and at the siege of Carlaverock 1300, or, three chevronels gules for CLARE, Earl of Gloucester, though he was then vested in his own arms as borne at Falkirk. Sealed, with an eagle, the Barons' letter to the Pope 1301, pp. xvi, xxiv. See Tiles, Neath Abbey, p. vii.

Montjoy v. Mountjoy.

Montmorency, John de—(H. III. Roll) bore, or, poudrée of eagles azure, a cross gules ; Norfolk Roll.

Montryvell —— (E. III. Roll)—bore, azure, a lyon tail fourchée or, armed and crowned argent ; Cotgrave Roll.

Moran, Sir Thomas—(E. III. Roll) bore, argent, on a fess sable three six-foyles pierced or, in chief a lyon passant gules ; Ashmole Roll.

Mordac v. Murdac.

*[**Mordaunt, William** (25 E. I.)—bore, argent, a chevron between three estoiles sable. —Shirley.] F.

More v. de la More.

More —— (E. III. Roll) bore, argent, a fess dancettée (3) paly (6) or and gules, between three spur-rowells sable ; Ashmole Roll.

More, Sir Thomas—(E. III. Roll) bore, gules, a bend argent billettée sable ; Ashmole Roll. Same as MORREWES.

Morell, Sir William—bore, at the battle of Boroughbridge 1322, azure, florettée or, a demi-lyon (rampant) couped argent, over all a bend gules. F.

Moresby, Sir Hugh—(E. III. Roll) bore, sable a cross or, a cinquefoyle pierced argent ; Ashmole Roll. A six-foyle tricked in Jenyns' Ordinary.

Morgan (——), a Kentish Knight—(H. VI. Roll) bore, sable, a chevron between three spear-heads erect argent ; Arundel Roll.

Morley, Sir William, of Norfolk, baron 1299—bore, at the battle of Falkirk 1298, argent, a lyon rampant tail fourchée sable— crowned or, in Parly. and Segar Rolls.

Morley, Sir Robert de—bore, at the battle of Boroughbridge 1322, argent, a lyon rampant sable crowned or (F.) Another Sir ROBERT bore the same at the siege of Calais 1345-8 ; borne also by THOMAS, 4th Lord, K.G., father of THOMAS (5th Lord) who bore it at the siege of Rouen 1418 ; Surrey Roll and Jenyns' Ordinary.

Morley, Robert de — (R. II. Rol bore, argent, a lyon rampant sable, a label (3) gules ; Surrey Roll. Another ROBERT bore, sable, a lyon rampant argent, a baston gules ; Cotgrave Roll.

Morley, John de, of Craven—(E. III. Roll) bore, sable, a leopard's face or jessant-de-lys argent ; Jenyns' Ordinary.

Mor(r)ice, John—(E. III. Roll) bore, sable, a saltire engrailed argent —on an E. P. the arms of the Earl of Ulster ; viz., or, a cross gules ; Jenyns' Ordinary.

Morice, John (MORYS or NORYS)—(E. III. Roll) bore, azure, billettée and a cross recercelée argent—moline in trick ; Jenyns' Ordinary.

Morieus, Sir Hugh de, of Suffolk, Kt.—(E. II. Roll) bore, azure three meures (mulberry) leaves or ; Parly. Roll. See MURIELL.

Mor(r)eres, William de—(H. III. Roll) bore, ermine, on a fess or four bendlets azure (F.) ; Arden and St. George Rolls.

Barth de morston

Witt d' Morriton

Robt de mortoygne

Oouft de mortimor

Henj de morton

Howgf de mortimor

Robt de Mortimor

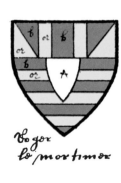

Roger le mortimor

Gefray d'Mortimer

Roger de mortou

Roger de mortimor le fitz

Witt molton

Watt de mouncey

Morrewes, Thomas—(R. ii. Roll) bore, gules, a bend argent billettée sable; Surrey Roll. Same as Sir THOMAS MORE.

‡**Moristone, Bartholomew de**—(H. iii. Roll), bore, argent, on a chief gules three birds or (F.); Dering and Howard Rolls.

Morritone, William de, v. **Morteyn.**

Morteyn v. **Norteyn,** or **Norton.**

Morteyn, Robert de, and **William de**—(H. iii. Roll) bore, ermine a chief gules; Glover and Jenyns' Rolls; called MORRITONE (F.) in St. George Roll. Sir JOHN, of Beds (E. ii. Roll), bore the chief indented; Parly. Roll.

Morteyne, Sir Roger, banneret—bore, at the siege of Carlaverock 1300, or, six lyonceux rampant 3, 2, 1 azure—sable (F.) in Harl. MS. 6137 fo. 39, and in Arundel and Parly. Rolls, where the tails are fourchée.

Morteyn, Sir Roger—(E. i. Roll) bore, azure, three lyons rampant argent (sometimes, or); Guillim Roll.

Moton, Sir William—(E. iii. Roll) bore, argent, a cinquefoyle pierced azure; Ashmole and Surrey Rolls.

Mortimer, William, of Attleborough, baron 1294—bore, or, florettée sable, Nobility Roll; his son, Sir CONSTANTINE, bore the same 3, 2, 1 at the first Dunstable tournament 1308, and as florettée (F.) at the battle of Boroughbridge 1322. Ascribed also to WILLIAM in Arden and St. George Rolls. In the Ashmole Roll, the coat also occurs differenced with a label (3) gules; another, with a bordure engrailed argent.

Mortimer, John—bore, at the second Dunstable tournament 1334, as also, Sir WILLIAM, knighted at the capitulation of Calais 1348, azure, florettée argent.

Mortimer, Henry de, of Foxcote—(H. iii. Roll) bore, argent on a cross azure five escallops of the field; Arden Roll. WILLIAM, bore the escallops or (F.), in St. George Roll.

Mortimer, Sir Hugh de, of Richard's Castle, baron 1299—bore, at the (F.) battle of Falkirk 1298, and at the siege of Carlaverock 1300, gules, two bars vair. (F.) Ascribed also to JOHN in Jenyns' Ordinary and to ROBERT (‡) in Dering Roll. F.

Mortimer, Robert de—(H. iii. Roll) bore, barry or and vert florettée; Norfolk Roll.

Mortimer, Walron—(E. iii. Roll) bore, argent, two bars gules, on a chief of the last three six-foyles of the first—cinquefoyles in the trick; Jenyns' Ordinary.

Mortimer, William de—(E. iii. Roll) bore, gules, crusily or, two bars vair; Arden Roll.

Mortimer, Sir William, banneret—(H. vi. Roll) bore, gules, a cross flory or, Arundel Roll; in which the name is doubtful, perhaps LATYMER is intended.

Mortimer, Edmund, of Wigmore, baron 1295—bore, as did ROGER his father, barry (6) or and azure, on a chief of the first three palets between two esquires based of the second, over all an inescocheon argent (sealed the Barons' letter to the Pope 1301, pp. xv, xxiv); Camden and Guillim Rolls. [EDMUND, last Earl of March and Ulster, K.B.; quartered DE BURGH or, a cross gules; Surrey Roll.] His brethren differenced

   (1) Sir WILLIAM with a baston, and
   (2) Sir GEOFFREY, with a saltire over all gules (F.); ascribed also to Sir JOHN of Herefordshire in Parly. Roll.

Mortimer, Sir Roger, of Chirke, a baron 1307, bore, MORTIMER'S arms with the inescocheon ermine (F.) (wrongly argent in the Nobility Roll) at the battle of Falkirk 1298 and at the siege of Carlaverock 1300; sealed the Barons' letter to the Pope 1301, pp. xviii, xxiv; see also Harl. MS. 1481 ff 33, 66.

   The field is as often as not tricked the reverse and bars (3) rather than barry. The seals of EDMUND and ROGER show one palet only on the chief.

Mortimer, Hugh, lord of Chilmarsh, uncle to EDMUND above-named, bore, at the battle of Boroughbridge 1322, MORTIMER'S arms or and gules—the inescocheon argent—Harl. MS. 1481 ff 33, 66; ascribed also to Sir HENRY of Herefordshire in the Parly. Roll; the reverse, gules and or, ascribed to JOHN, in Norfolk and St. George Rolls.

Mortimer, Sir Roger de, le fiz (f ROGER, 2nd baron) of Herefordshire, bore, at the first Dunstable tournament 1308, MORTIMER'S arms or and azure, the inescocheon (argent) charged with a lyon rampant purpure (F.); Parly. Roll. HENRY bore the reverse azure and or, the inescocheon (argent) billettée sable; Arden Roll.

Mortimer, Raf de—(H. iii. Roll) bore, MORTIMER'S arms sable and or—the inescocheon argent; Arden Roll.

Mote v. **De la Mote.**

Moton, Sir William—(E. iii. Roll) bore, argent, a cinquefoyle pierced azure; Ashmole and Surrey Rolls.

Moton, Sir William (or MOLTON), knighted at the capitulation of Calais 1348—bore, argent, crusily and three fleurs-de-lys within a bordure engrailed all sable. F.

Moulton v. **Multon.**

Moulton, Sir Edmond—(E. iii. Roll) bore, azure a cross patonce voided argent; Ashmole Roll. See MULTON.

Moulton, Thomas de—bore, at the second Dunstable tournament 1334, gules, a baston azure. See MULTON.

Mounce, Sir Eble or **Ellis de**—(E. ii. Roll) bore, or, a bend cotised gules, a label (3) azure; Parliamentary Roll.

Mounceaux, Hamond—(E. i. Roll) bore, gules a cross recercelée (moline, in trick) and an escallop or; Jenyns' Roll.

Mounchensi v. **Munchensi.**

Mouncy, Sir Walter de, baron 1299—bore, at the battle of Falkirk 1298 and at the siege of Carlaverock 1300, chequy argent and gules. (F.) Nobility and Guillim Rolls; sealed the Barons' letter to the Pope, 1301, pp. xxii, xxiv.

Mounferant, Hubert—(E. iii. Roll) bore, paly (6) argent and sable, on a chief gules three six-foyles or, cinquefoyles in trick; Jenyns' Ordinary.

✝**Mounteney, Sir Ernaud** (MUNCENI), of Essex, and ✝**Robert**—(H. iii. Roll) bore, azure, a bend between six martlets or; Glover and Howard Rolls. Sir JOHN, differenced with a mullet gules at the first Dunstable tournament 1308; St. George Roll, attributes a label (5) gules to ERNAUD.

HERALDIC ATCHIEVEMENT, ORIGINALLY OUTSIDE THE DOGE'S PALACE, VENICE,

ATTRIBUTED IN THE "ARCHÆOLOGIA," 1842, VOL. XXIX., App. 387, TO

THOMAS MOWBRAY, DUKE OF NORFOLK, WHO DIED 1400.

Mr. Courthope, Somerset Herald, regarded this rather as a memorial of a visit of Henry IV. as Earl of Derby.

Thos̄ de Mounteney   *John de mounteny*   *Robt. de muntein*   *John de mūbay*   *will moigne*

John mountney

mulso

Mounteney, Sir Thomas de—bore, at the battle of Boroughbridge 1322, gules, a bend between six martlets or. (F.) Parly. Roll; ascribed to JOHN also in Surrey Roll.

Mounteney, Sir John de—bore, at the battle of Boroughbridge 1322, gules, a bend cotised or between six martlets of the last. (F.) Ashmole MS. and Parliamentary Roll. Ascribed to THOMAS in Jenyns' Ordinary.

‡**Mounteney, Robert de**—(H. III. Roll) bore, azure, a bend or. (F.) Dering Roll.

Mounteney, John and Rauffe—(E. III. Roll) bore, vaire argent and sable, a chief or over all a baston gules; Jenyns' Ordinary. F.

Mountfort v. **Montford.**

‡**Mountjoy, Stephen de**—(H. III. Roll) bore, gules, three inescocheons or. (F.) Dering and Howard Rolls.

Mowbray, Sir John, banneret—bore, at the first Dunstable tournament 1308, gules, a lyon rampant argent (F.); borne also by his father, ROGER, of Axholme, baron 1295; Nobility and Parly. Rolls. See also Tiles, Neath Abbey, p. ix. Ascribed to ROGER (‡) in Dering Roll, in Arden Roll to ROBERT (possibly in error for ROGER), and in the Arundel Roll to Sir THOMAS, banneret. Sir PHILIP, of Scotland, differenced with a bend "engréle" sable; Nativity Roll.

Mowbray, Sr. de, the Earl Marshal (THOMAS, K.G., Duke of Norfolk 1397-8)—bore, England, differenced with a label (5) argent *quarterly with,* gules a lyon rampant argent; Surrey Roll. Another coat in the same Roll attributed to THOMAS MOWBRAY, is England differenced with a label (3) argent charged with three eagles displayed of the first *quarterly with,* gules, a lyon rampant argent, a label (3) azure.

‡**Mowin, John**—(H. III. Roll) bore, argent, three cinquefoyles pierced and a quarter gules. (F.) Dering Roll.

†**Moyne, Berenger le**—(E. III. Roll) bore, argent, a cross patonce (*vel* patée) gules, flory in trick—same as HENRY COLVILE; Jenyns' Ordinary; colours reversed in Segar Roll, there called "LE MOYE." F.

Moyne, Jacques le and Sir John, of Suffolk—(E. II. Roll) bore, or a saltire engrailed gules; Jenyns' Ordinary and Parliamentary Roll. F.

Moyne, Sir John—(E. III. Roll) bore, or, three bars vert; Ashmole Roll. F.

Moyne, John le (MOINS)—(H. III. Roll) bore, azure, six martlets 3, 2, 1 or; Arden Roll. (F.) Ascribed to HENRY DE APPLEBY in St. George Roll.

Moyne, John—(E. I. Roll) bore, argent, a bend between six mullets gules; Jenyns' Roll. F.

Moyn, John, VEL MOYZ—(H. III. Roll) bore, argent a canton gules—the field diapered masculy; Howard Roll.

Moyle, Sir Thomas le—(E. III. Roll) bore, argent, on a canton gules a lyon passant gardant or; Ashmole Roll.

Moyle, Sir William le, of Hunts.—(E. II. Roll) bore, azure, crusily and a fess dancettée argent; Parliamentary Roll.

Moyne, William (MOIGNE)—(E. III. Roll) bore, argent, two bars and in chief three mullets (6) sable; Surrey Roll and Jenyns' Ordinary. F.

Mules, John—bore, at the second Dunstable tournament 1334, argent, two bars gules, on a chief of the last three torteaux. See MOELS.

Mulso (——), a Suffolk Kt.—(H. VI. Roll) bore, ermine on a bend sable three goats' heads erased argent, horned or; Arundel Roll. F.

Multon, Sir Thomas de, of Egremont, banneret, baron 1299—bore, at the battle of Falkirk 1298, barry argent and gules (F.); sealed the Barons' letter to the Pope 1301, pp. xviii, xxiv; and bore, at the siege of Carlaverock 1300, argent, three bars gules (F.); (no doubt his banner was the same on both occasions, though Falkirk seems in error); Arundel, Glover and Nobility Rolls (reversed in Arden, Guillim and St. George Rolls). The latter coat borne also by RAFFE, of Egremont and Tebauld; Howard Roll and Jenyns' Ordinary, and at the second Dunstable tournament 1334, by JOHN.

Multon, Thomas de, of Frankton, bore, at the second Dunstable tournament 1334 (argent three bars) gules, a baston azure (gules, three bars argent in Cotgrave Roll, and so in Ashmole, with the baston azure); THOMAS of Gillesland differenced with a label (3) vert (n) baston), Jenyns' Ordinary (no label in Cotgrave Roll), and THOMAS LE FORRESTIER with a label sable; Glover Roll.

Multon, John, of Frankton—(E. III. Roll) bore, gules, three bars argent, in chief as many crescents or; Jenyns' Ordinary. F.

Multon, John de—(E. III. Roll) bore, sable three bars, in chief as many annulets all argent; Jenyns' Ordinary. F.

Multon, Thomas—(E. III. Roll) bore, argent, two bars gules, a label (3) vert; Jenyns' Ordinary.

John Mowin

Thō d Moletene

Thō de moltoun

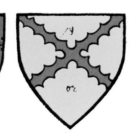

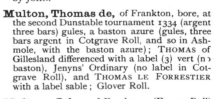

Berong le moys   *John le moyno*   *Jon de moines*   *John moyno*   *John multon*   *John de multon*

Hubord de molotono

James de mltuno

witt de mouncols

vice de monteansi

Rauf d' Muchasi

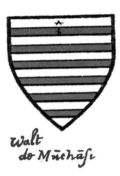

Walt de Muchasi

witt de monteansi

maryn de monteansi

Multon, Thomas de, of Gillesland, baron 1307 – bore (Vaux, *i.e.*), checquy or and gules; Nobility Roll 1310 and Parliamentary Roll; according to Cotgrave Roll he subsequently bore argent three bars gules; a label (3) vert is added in Jenyns' Ordinary, see above; Arden and St. George Rolls ascribe the Vaux coat to HUBERT DE MOLETONE. F.

Multon, Sir James and **Sir Thomas,** both of Lincolnshire – (E. II. Roll) bore, checquy, or and sable (F.); Harleian, Parly. and Segar Rolls.

Multon, Sir Edmond – (E. III. Roll) bore, azure a cross patonce voided argent; Ashmole Roll.

‡**Muncells, William,** or **Walran** (MUN- CEUS, MUNCELTH) – (H. III. Roll) bore, argent, a bend sable (F.); Dering, Howard, and Camden Rolls. See MUNCY.

†**Munceny, Ernulphus** and **Robert** *v.* **Mounteney.**

Munchensi, Sir Richard de – bore, at the battle of Boroughbridge 1322, argent, a chevron between three billets azure (F.); ascribed to RAFFE, the billets sable in Jenyns' Ordinary.

Munchensi, Rauf de – (H. III. Roll) bore, quarterly sable and or (F.); St. George Roll; differenced with a mullet (6) argent; Arden Roll.

Munchensi, Randolph – (E. III. Roll) bore gyronny (8) sable and or, an inescocheon ermine, a mullet (6) gules, tricked sable; Jenyns' Ordinary. F.

Munchensi, Sir William, of Herts – (E. II. Roll) bore, burulée (14) argent and azure. Sir RANDOLPH differenced with a label (3) gules, Parly. Roll; barry of 8 Harl. MS. 6137 fo. 13; barry of 10 in Jenyns' Ordinary.

Munchensi, Walter – (H. III. Roll) bore, argent, seven barrulets azure (F.); Arden Roll, six in St. George Roll.

‡**Munchensi, William de** – (E. I. Roll) bore, or, three inescocheons vair (F.); Camden Roll. In Dering Roll the inescocheons are [barry (6)] vair and gules, and are so ascribed to WARREN in Glover and Howard Rolls.

Munchensi, Sir Warren de – (E. I. Roll) bore, or, three inescocheons bendy (6) vair and gules; Grimaldi Roll and Jenyns' Ordinary.

Munchensi, Sir William de – (E. II. Roll) bore, lozengy vair and gules (F.) Parly. Roll. Harl. MS. 4033 fo. 51.

‡**Muncy, John de** – (H. III. Roll) bore, gules, a maunch or (F.); Dering and Howard Rolls.

Murdac, Sir Thomas, of Northants – bore, at the first Dunstable tournament 1308, or, fretty sable (F.); Parly. Roll. Borne also by Sir JOHN at the battle of Boroughbridge 1322, and by another Sir JOHN who was knighted at the capitulation of Calais 1348; Ashmole and Surrey and H. VI. Nobility Rolls; ascribed to WILLIAM in St. George Roll.

Muriell, Thomas, of Scremby – (E. III. Roll) bore, argent a chevron between three "roses crochees" sable, Catherine wheels in trick; Jenyns' Ordinary. F.

‡**Musard, Raufde** – (H. III. Roll) bore, gules three plates (F.); Dering, Howard and St. George Rolls.

Muscegros, John and **Robert** – (E. I. Roll) bore, or, a lyon rampant gules; Camden Roll and Jenyns' Ordinary; apparently borne also by GRIFFITH LE FITZ OWEN and by WILLIAM POLE.

Muscegros, John de – (E. I. Roll) bore, gules, a lyon rampant or, a label (6) azure (F.); Segar Roll.

***Musgrave, Sir Thomas** – (E. III. Roll) bore, azure, six annulets 3, 2, 1 or; Ashmole Roll and Jenyns' Ordinary. F.

Mussenden, Edmond de – (R. II. Roll) bore, or, a cross engrailed gules, a Cornish chough proper; Surrey Roll. Sir THOMAS, slain at the siege of Calais 1347, bore the field argent and a martlet sable. F.

Mustell, Henry – (H. III. Roll) bore, sable, platey and a quarter ermine (F.); Arden and St. George Rolls.

Mustone, William de – (E. I. Roll) bore, argent, a chevron between three crosses patée sable – patonce in trick; Jenyns' Roll.

Myland, Amary de – (H. III. Roll) bore, sable, billettée and a lyon rampant tail fourchée argent; Norfolk Roll. See NEIRNWYST.

Jofn de muncout

Jeo de mortegot

Jol. de muscegros

Vand mounteonsio

Jeo muriell

Rauf Musart

Jeo musgrave

Jeo de Mussondon

Henri Mustel

" Here fell Leofwine and Gyrth, the brothers of King Harold."   After the Bayeux Tapestry.

— N—O —

narburgh.

Rauf de molo

Henri le nolfun

Jofin de noreford

Nalinghurst *v.* **Naylyngest.**

Namar, Sir Robert, K.G. 1370—bore, or, a lyon rampant sable, oppressed by a baston gules ; K. 398 fo. 57.

Nancovenant, Sir Geoffrey, of Lincolnshire—(E. II. Roll) bore, argent, a bend sable, cotised gules ; Parliamentary Roll and Jenyns' Ordinary.

Napton, John de—(E. III. Roll) bore, or, on a fess azure three escallops argent ; Harleian Roll and Jenyns' Ordinary.

[**Narburgh** (——) bore, ermine a chief gules. (F.) Arden Roll—added in "a newe hand."]

Naunton, Bartholomew de—(E. I. Roll) bore, sable, three martlets argent ; Ashmole and Jenyns' Rolls.

Nautur *v.* **Vautur.**

Naylyngest, Sir Hew, of Essex, Kt.— (H. VI. Roll) bore, gules, a cross engrailed or —*quarterly with*—argent, a bend sable cotised or ; Arundel Roll.

Neirnwyst, Sir John (or NEYRMIST), of Bucks—(E. II. Roll) bore, sable, billettée and a lyon rampant argent ; Parliamentary Roll.

Nele, John de—(H. III. Roll) bore, burulée (12) argent and azure, a bend gules ; Howard Roll.

‡**Nele, Rauf de**—(H. III. Roll) bore, gules, two fish (? eel) hauriant addorsed argent. (F.) Dering Roll ; or, in Ashmole MS.

Nelson, Henry le—(H. III. Roll) bore, paly (6) argent and purpure a bend (new put in with colours) vaire or and sable. (F.) Arden Roll—paly argent and sable in Add. MS. 4965.

Nerford, John de (or NEIRFORD)—bore, at the second Dunstable tournament 1334, gules, a lyon rampant ermine. (F.) Borne also by Sir WILLIAM of Norfolk (probably father of JOHN), summoned to advise on the affairs of the realm 1294, 1297. See also WILLIAM in Dering Roll.

Nertoft, Sir Adam de, of Essex—(E. II. Roll) bore, sable, a lyon rampant or ; Parliamentary Roll.

‡**Nervile, Laurence,** and **Sir Jarvis** (or JAMES NEVILE), of Sussex — (H. III. Roll) bore, gules crusily two hunting-horns addorsed or ; (F.F.)—trumpets or hautboys ; Dering, Arden and Howard Rolls.

Nevesfeld, Sir Guy de, of Essex—(E. II. Roll) bore, vert, an eagle displayed or ; Parliamentary Roll. See STEINEFELD.

Neville, Geffray de—(E. I. Roll) bore, or, une nief, maste, cables and phane sable. (F.) Grimaldi Roll.

Nevill, John de, of Hornby, Yorks.—bore, at the second Dunstable tournament 1334, argent, a saltire gules. (F.) Ascribed also to GEFFREY in St. George Roll, to ROBERT of Hornby, in Jenyns' Ordinary, and to Sir JOHN Guillim and Parly. Rolls. JOHN of Lincolnshire bore the same between four fleurs-delys azure ; Jenyns' Ordinary—same as THOMAS HARLESTONE.

Nevill, Raff, of Raby, baron 1295—bore, gules, a saltire argent ; Nobility Roll—sealed the Barons' letter to the Pope 1301, pp. xviii, xxiv. Borne by JOHN, 3rd Lord Nevill of Raby, K.G. 1369, see title page, and at the siege of Rouen 1418 by RALPH, Earl of Westmoreland, K.G., see Monumental Effigy ; ascribed also to Sir RANDOLPH, banneret, in Arundel Roll, and to ROBERT of Raby, in Grimaldi Roll ; and to another ROBERT‡ in Dering Roll.   RICHARD, K.G. 1436, Earl of Salisbury (and his son RICHARD, K.G., Earl of Warwick), differenced, with a label (3) gobony argent and azure, his brother (*a*) WILLIAM, lord FAUCONBERG, with a mullet sable, (*b*) his brother GEORGE, lord LATIMER, with a pellet, and (*c*) his brother *EDWARD, lord of Abergavenny, with a rose gules. (F.) Harl. MS. 1418 fo. 49ᵇ.

(1) ALEXANDER of Condal differenced with a mullet pierced sable ; Surrey Roll and Jenyns' Ordinary.

(2) ALEXANDER of Raskelfe differenced with a martlet gules ; Jenyns' Ordinary.

(3) Sir JOHN differenced with a label (3) azure ; Ashmole Roll.

(4) Sir RALPH differenced with an annulet sable ; Ashmole Roll

(5) Sir ROBERT differenced with a mullet sable ; Ashmole Roll.

(6) THOMAS, differenced as ALEXANDER of Raskelf ; Surrey Roll.

(7) WILLIAM, differenced with a saltire azure ; Surrey Roll.

Nevile, Rauf de—bore, at the second Dunstable tournament 1334, gules, a saltire "engréle" argent. F.

Jarvis d' Nervik

Lorom do noville

Johan do novile

Goffry nopill   *Edm. noville*   *Rauf de novile*

Joan d' Neiule

Phillip de nouilo

Phillip de nouilo

Tebaud d' Neiule

Nevil, Robert, DE PYKALE—(E. III. Roll)
bore, gules, a saltire ermine ; Jenyns' Ordinary.

Nevil, John de—(E. I. Roll) bore, gules, a
saltire or ; Segar Roll—the reverse borne by
JOHN DE VAUTUR.

Nevile, Sir Hugh, banneret, and **John,** of
Essex—(H. III. Roll) bore, azure, a lyon
rampant or. (F.) Arundel and Norfolk Rolls
and Jenyns' Ordinary.

Nevill, John, "the forester"—(E. III. Roll)
bore, gules, a lyon rampant argent guttée de
poix ; Jenyns' Ordinary. See below.

Neville, Sir Philip, of Lincolnshire—(E. II.
Roll) bore, argent, a fess dancettée gules, a
bend sable. (F.) Parly. Roll—a bordure
sable bezantée (no bend), Jenyns' Ordinary.

Neville, Sir Philip, of co. Leic.—(E. II.
Roll) bore, gules, five fusils conjoined in fess
argent, in chief three mullets or. (F.) Sir
RICHARD, differenced with a label (3) azure
instead of the mullets ; Parliamentary Roll.

Nevile, Sir Roger (or ROBERT)—bore, at
the siege of Calais 1345-8, gules, a fess dancettée argent, a bordure indented or. (F.)
Ascribed to Sir ROBERT, of co. Leic., in
Parly. Roll.

Neville, Sir Philip—bore, at the battle of
Boroughbridge 1322, gules, a chief engrailed
(dancettée in trick) argent, within a bordure
indented (engrailed in trick) or—a label (3)
azure each file charged with 2 bars of the
second, blasoned, barruly of the second and
azure. F.

Nevill, Sir Thomas, of Lincolnshire—
(E. II. Roll)—bore, argent, a chief indented
vert, a bend gules ; Parliamentary Roll.

Nevylle, Raffe, of Cotham or Cletham—
(E. III. Roll) bore, ermine, a chief indented
azure ; Jenyns' Ordinary.

Nevile, Walter de (NEIUILE)—(H. III. Roll)
bore, azure, two gemelles in chief a lyon
passant gardant argent. (F.) St. George Roll.

Nevile, John de—(H. III. Roll) bore, paly
(6) azure and or, on a chief gules three escallops argent ; Howard Roll.

Neville, Geoffrey, of Sheriff Hutton—
(E. III. Roll) bore, masculy (tricked lozengy)
or and gules, a quarter ermine ; Jenyns' Ordinary—ascribed in the Glover Roll to JOHN
DE NEVILL, cowerde.

Nevill, John le, LE FORRESTIER—(H. III.
Roll) bore, or, crusily sable, a bend gules ;
Glover Roll. See above.

Nevile, Tebaud de (NEIUILE)—(H. III.
Roll) bore, azure, crusily three garbs argent
banded gules (F.) ; St. George Roll—another
crusily or, and a chief argent, added.

Nevile, Sir Theobald de, of Northants or
Rutland—(E. II. Roll) bore, azure, crusily
three fleurs-de-lys argent ; Parly. Roll—
leopards' faces jessant-de-lys ; Harl. MS. 6137
fo. 23.

Nevile, Sir John de, of Northants or Rutland—(E. II. Roll) bore, gules, crusily and
three fleurs-de-lys argent ; Parly. Roll.

Nevill, Henry—(H. III. Roll) bore, gules,
crusily fitchée and three leopards' faces jessant-
de-lys or, on the first, a crescent azure ; Surrey
Roll.

Nevyll, John—(H. III. Roll) bore, gules,
crusily fitchée or three leopards' faces of the
last jessant-de-lys argent ; Surrey Roll.

Newborough, Robert de—bore, at the
second Dunstable tournament 1334, bendy (6)
or and azure, a bordure engrelée gules (F.)
Borne also by Sir ROBERT, knighted at the
capitulation of Calais 1348.

Newby, John de—(E. I. Roll) bore, sable
on a fess argent three roses gules ; Jenyns'
Roll.

Newenham, Sir John de, of Surrey—
(E. II. Roll) bore, argent a cross gules over
all a bendlet azure ; Parly. Roll.

Newenton, Sir Adam de, of Essex—
(E. II. Roll) bore, azure, six eaglets displayed
3, 2, 1 or ; Parly. Roll—three eaglets (F.) in
Arden Roll and Jenyns' Ordinary.

Newen *v.* **Nowers.**

Newmarch, Adam and **Sir Thomas**—
(E. III. Roll) bore, argent five fusils conjoined
in fess gules ; Jenyns' Ordinary, Ashmole and
Parly. Rolls ; (4 fusils in H. 6137 fo. 19) a fess
engrelée in Nativity Roll.

Newmarch, Sir Adam, Sir John, and
Roger—(E. II. Roll) bore, gules, five fusils
conjoined in fess or (F.) ; Jenyns' Ordinary,
Holland, Parly. and St. George Rolls—(a fess
engrailed in Glover Roll)—the reverse ascribed
to Sir ROBERT in Guillim Roll.

Newson, John de—(E. I. Roll) bore, azure,
on a fess argent three crosses gules ; patée in
trick ; Jenyns' Roll.

**RALPH NEVILL,
EARL OF WESTMORLAND.**
IN STAINDROP CHURCH, CO. DURHAM, 1425.
After Stothard.

Roger de nouilo

Phillip de nouilo

Wat. d' neiuilo

Robt. de now burgg

Adam d' Newenton

Adam d' Neumart

Robert noel

Johnn norbury

Virard do norfolk

John de norays

*[**Noel, Robert** (*c.* H. III.)—bore, or, fretty gules, a canton ermine.—Shirley.] F.

Noon, Edmond—(H. III. Roll) bore, or, a cross engrailed vert; Surrey Roll.

Norbury, Hugh de (NORTHBURGH)—(H. III. Roll) bore, gules, crusily fitchée and three roses argent; Surrey Roll.

Norbury, Sir John—bore, at the siege of Rouen 1418, sable, on a chevron between three bulls' heads cabossed argent, a fleur-de-lys of the field (F.); Arundel Roll.

Norfolk, Earl of, *v.* BIGOD.

Norfolk, Richard—(E. I. Roll) bore, gules, a fess between two chevronels argent (F.); Segar Roll.

Norland, Richard—(H. III. Roll) bore sable, a chevron argent between three wolves' heads of the second couped gules; Surrey Roll.

‡**Normanvile, Rafe de**—(H. III. Roll) bore, gules, a fess double cotised argent; Dering, Surrey, and Camden Rolls. F.

Normanvile, Rafe—(E. I. Roll) bore, argent, on a fess double cotised gules three fleurs-de-lys of the first; Jenyns' Roll and Ordinary—being the arms of BADLESMERE with the fleurs-de-lys added.

Norris, Sir John de (NORAIS)—bore, at the first Dunstable tournament 1308, sable, billettée and a cross florettée argent. (F.) See also Tiles, Neath Abbey, p. vii. In the Parly. Roll the cross ascribed to Sir JOHN, of co. Glouc., seems to be patée florettée fitchée at the foot in Harl. MS. 6137—differently tricked in Harl. MS. 4033, fo. 48. F.

Norrys, Sir John—(E. III. Roll) bore, azure, billettée and a cross recercelée argent—moline in trick; Jenyns' Ordinary.

Northam, Thomas de—(E. III. Roll) bore, per pale gules and sable, a lyon rampant argent crowned or; Jenyns' Ordinary.

*[**Northcote, Andrew** (17 E. I.)—bore, or, a chief gules fretty of the first.—Shirley.] F.

‡**Northey, William de**—(H. III. Roll) bore, quarterly argent and azure (F.); Dering and Howard Rolls.

Northwich, Northwood *v.* NORWICH, NORWOOD.

Norton, Sir — (NORTEYN)—bore, at the siege of Rouen 1418, per pale gules and azure a lyon rampant ermine. (F.) same as NORWICH.

Norton, Sir James de, of Hants.—(E. II. Roll) bore, vert, a lyon rampant or; Parly. Roll. WILLIAM took up the cross in the last Crusade 1270.

Norton, Sir John, of Kent—(H. VI. Roll) bore, gules, a cross potent ermine; Arundel Roll.

Norton, Richard—(E. I. Roll) bore, argent, three cushions sable; Jenyns' Roll.

Norton, Robert de—(E. I. Roll) bore, sable, three piles florettée at the points, issuant from the sinister argent (F.); Jenyns' Roll.

Norton, Sir Robert de—bore, at the battle of Boroughbridge 1322, argent, a chevron between three buckles sable; tongues to the base in the Ashmole MS. F.

Norton, Roger—(E. III. Roll) bore, argent, a chevron between three cushions sable; Jenyns' Ordinary. RICHARD bore this without the chevron, as above.

[**Norton, Roger,** formerly CONYERS, E. III.—bore, azure, a maunch ermine, over all a bend gules.—Shirley.] F.

Norwich, Sir John de (NORTHWICH)—bore, at the battle of Boroughbridge 1322, per pale gules and azure a lyon rampant ermine, a label (3) or. Ascribed to . . . NORTEYN, undifferenced at the siege of Rouen 1418.

Norwich, John de (NORTHWYCHE)—bore, at the second Dunstable tournament 1334, per pale azure and gules, a lyon rampant ermine (F.), as did Sir JOHN, knighted at the capitulation of Calais 1348; Jenyns' Roll and Ordinary.

Norwoode, Sir John de—bore, at the first Dunstable tournament 1308, argent, a cross engrailed gules, a label (3) azure.

Norwoode, Sir John de, baron 1313—bore, ermine a cross engrailed gules (a saltire in Jenyns' Ordinary); Arundel and Howard Roll; ascribed to ROGER‡ in Dering Roll; see Monumental Brass for Sir ROGER 1361. Sir JOHN, of Kent, differenced with a label of three azure (F.); and another, ermine a cross patonce gules, Harleian Roll.

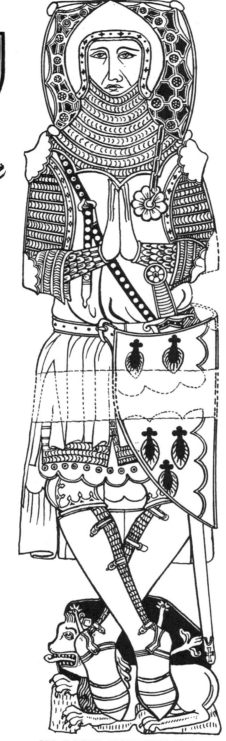

SIR ROGER NORTHWOODE.
IN MINSTER CHURCH, ISLE OF SHEPPEY,
1361.
After Stothard. For his wife see Foliot.

Roger norton

do norton

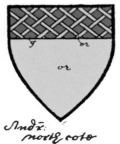

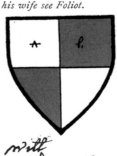

Raufe de normanvile

John le norrys

Andr. northcote

will de northy

Robt. do norton

John do northwick

Roger norwort

Joan de norwode

David de Offringtone

Roland de Okestod

Joan d. Okinton

Rog nun wike

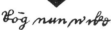

Rauf d. obehale

Michel d. Oppeshale

Jon de Orbebi

Nowell, John—(E. III. Roll) bore, argent, three covered cups sable ; Jenyns' Ordinary.

Nowers, John and **Sir Simon**, of Norfolk —(E. II. Roll) bore, vaire argent and gules ; Parly. Roll and Jenyns' Ordinary. RICHARD COLEWORTH bears the same. F.

Nowers, Sir John and **Roger**—(E. III. Roll) bore, azure, a fess argent between three garbs or ; Ashmole and Jenyns' Rolls. F.

Nowers, Sir (——), a Bucks Knight—(E. II. Roll) bore, argent, two bars and in chief three crescents gules ; Parliamentary Roll.

Nunwike, Roger de—(E. III. Roll) bore, sable, an eagle displayed or ; Jenyns' Ordinary. F.

Nutbeme, Thomas—(H. III. Roll) bore, gules, a fess undée ermine ; Surrey Roll.

*[**Oakeley, Philip**, H. III.—bore, argent, on a fess between three crescents gules as many fleurs-de-lys or ; Shirley.] F.

Obehale, Raufe d'—(H. III. Roll) bore, or, a fess gules. (F.) St. George Roll.

Oc —— v. Ok ——.

O'Clare'ce, Sir B.—(H. VI. Roll) bore, azure, a fleur-de-lys or, on a chief (? of the last) gussett gules, two lyons combatant or ; another blason, per chevron gules and azure in the chief or two lyons rampant combatant or ; and for the Honour of CLARE or CLARENCE, a fleur-de-lys of the third in base ; Atkinson Roll.

Odingsells v. Doddingsells.

Offingtone, David de—(H. III. Roll) bore, azure, a saltire engrailed or. (F.) Arden and St. George Rolls.

Ogard (——), a Yorkshire (?) Knight—(H. VI. Roll) bore, azure, a mullet of seven points argent ; Arundel Roll. See HUGARD.

[**Oglander, Roger**, H. III.—bore, azure, a stork between three crosses crosslet fitchée or. —Shirley.] F.

*[**Ogle, Robert** (or RICHARD) **de**—(E. I. Roll) bore, argent, a fess between three crescents gules (Jenyns' Roll) F. ; *quarterly with*, or an orle azure ; Surrey Roll.

*[**Oker, Philip de** (OKEOVER)—(H. III. Roll) bore, ermine, on a chief gules three besants. (F.) Surrey Roll.

Okham, Nicholas de—(E. III. Roll) bore, gules, a fess between three crescents, 2 and 1 argent ; Jenyns' Ordinary.

Okindon v. Wokindon.

Okinton, John d'—(H. III. Roll) bore, or, three cinquefoyles pierced gules ; St. George Roll ; roses (F.) in Harl. MS. 6137 fo. 88.

Okinton (OLZETON) **John de**—(H. III. Roll) bore, or a fess vert between three cinquefoyles pierced gules. (F.) Arden Roll.

Okstede, Roland de—(H. III. Roll) bore, or, a " kene " gules ; Glover Roll.

‡**Okstede, Roland**—(H. III. Roll) bore, argent, an oak eradicated proper acorned or. (F.) Dering and Howard Rolls.

Oldcastle, Sir John, baron Cobham 1409— bore, at the siege of Rouen 1418, gules, on a chevron or three lyonceux rampant sable *quarterly with*, argent a castle sable.

Oldhall, —— (E. III. Roll) bore, per pale azure and gules, a lyon rampant ermine, a label (3) or ; another with lyon ducally crowned or, but no label ; Ashmole Roll. Sir WILLIAM in Atkinson Roll, without arms ; Harl. MS. 1408 fo. 108[b].

Olney, Sir John de, of Bucks.—(E. II. Roll) bore, azure, crusily and a fess argent ; Parly. Roll ; ?[another barry (6) argent and azure, a bordure indented gules ; "Genealogist," XI. 181.]

*[**Ondeslow, Roger de,** E. I.—bore, argent, a fess gules between six Cornish choughs proper.—Shirley.] F.

Opshale, Michel de—(H. III. Roll) bore, argent, a cross sable fretty or. (F.) Arden and St. George Rolls. See UPSALE.

Orbebe, John de—(H. III. Roll) bore, argent, two chevrons gules, on a quarter of the second as many lyons passant of the first (F.) ; Arden Roll.

Ore, Nichol de (ERE)—(H. III. Roll) bore, ermine, a cross gules fretty or ; Howard Roll.

‡**Ore, Nicole de**—(H. III. Roll) bore, argent, a cross gules fretty or, between four daws ppr. ; Dering Roll.

‡**Ore, Richarde de**—(H. III. Roll) bore, barry (6) argent and azure, on a bend gules five besants ; Dering Roll. F.

Oreyle, John—(E. III. Roll) bore, argent, a cross between four martlets gules ; Jenyns' Ordinary. F.

Oriel, Nichole de (CRYEL)—(H. III. Roll) bore, " or and gules partie per fess three annulets counterchanged tertoleres " ; Howard Roll. See (F.) CRIOL.

Orkablin —— (H. III. Roll) bore, or, on a cross vert five escallops argent (F.) ; Arden Roll. See WALTAUBIN ; same arms as THORLEY.

Roger Oglander

Richard de Oglo

Philip Okeover

Jon de olzeton

Richard de Ore

DRAWN BY JOHN HENRY METCALFE FOR
"ALUMNI OXONIENSES."

John Oroylo

Orbablm

Rafe de Ottingdon

Sire de Oudenarde

John de Quington

Le Counte de Ormaund

John Orby

Rand de Otteby

John de Ousthorpe

willm Onyngton

Solomon Oxondon

E' de Oxford

‡**Orlaston, William de**—(H. III. Roll) bore, or, two chevrons gules, on a quarter of the second a lyon rampant or; Dering Roll; argent (F.) in Howard and Camden Rolls.

Ormonde, James Butler, Earl of—bore, at the siege of Rouen 1418, or, a chief dancettée (3) azure. F. See also BOTELER.

Ornesby, John—(E. III. Roll) bore, gules, crusily botonnée and a bend argent; tricked, gules, a bend argent; Jenyns' Ordinary.

Ornesby, Sir William de, of Norfolk—(E. II. Roll) bore, gules, crusily argent, a bend checquy or and azure (argent and azure Harl. 6137 fo. 17); Sir JOHN differenced with a mullet; Parliamentary Roll.

Orphill v. **Crophill.**

Orreby, Sir John, of Dalby in Cheshire, baron 1309—bore, gules, two lyons passant argent, a label (3) or; Parliamentary, Nobility and Ashmole Rolls (F.); undifferenced in Jenyns' Ordinary.

Orton, John de—(E. III. Roll) bore, azure, a lyon rampant argent; Jenyns' Ordinary; same as ROBERT DE MONHAUT.

Otteby, Sir Randolph de, of Lincs.—(E. II. Roll) bore, gules, two bars argent, in chief three plates; Parliamentary Roll. F.

Otterburne, John—(E. III. Roll) bore, argent, on a chief dancettée (3) gules three crosses crosslet fitchée of the first; Jenyns' Ordinary.

‡**Otringden, Rafe de**—(H. III. Roll) bore, ermine, a cross voided gules; Dering and Howard Rolls; a cross gules voided argent in Arden Roll, voided or (F.) in Camden Roll; sometimes blasoned, a cross surmounted of another.

‡**Oudenarde, Sire de**—(H. III. Roll) bore, barry (6, 12) or and gules, a bend · azure; Dering and Camden Rolls.

Oughtred, Sir Thomas, K.G. 1356—bore, at the siege of Calais 1345–8, gules, on a cross flory (patonce) or five mullets pierced of the field; K. 398 fo. 58. See UGHTRED.

Oulwenne, Gilbert—(H. III. Roll) bore argent, fretty gules, a chief azure; Surrey Roll.

Ousthorpe, John de—(E. I. Roll) bore, gules, three "dewe" leaves argent; Jenyns' Roll. F.

Ovington, Sir John de (QUINGTON)—bore, at the first Dunstable tournament 1308, argent on a chief azure two fleurs-de-lys or. See also EVINGTON.

Ovington, William—(E. III. Roll) bore, gules, on a bend argent three martlets sable (F.); Jenyns' Ordinary.

Owen, Griffith, LE FITZ WEN-UN-WEN (? FITZ OWEN-OWEN)—(E. III. Roll) bore, or, a lyon rampant gules; Jenyns' Ordinary. Same as JOHN MUSCEGROS and WILLIAM POLE.

Oxcliff, William—(E. I. Roll) bore, argent, three bulls' heads cabossed sable; Jenyns' Roll.

*[**Oxenden, Solomon** (E. III.)—bore, argent, a chevron gules between three oxen passant sable.—Shirley.] F., confirmed 24 H. VI. 1445–6.

Oxford, Earl of—(H. III. Roll) bore, quarterly, gules and or, a mullet argent (F.); Arden, Glover and Surrey Rolls; carried also at the siege of Rouen 1418.

[**Oxford, Earl of,** ROBERT DE VERE, 9th, bore, azure, three crowns or, a bordure argent *quarterly with*, VERE; grant 3 Jan. 1386, pat. I. m. 1; Cotton MS. Julius C. VII. fo. 237.]

Oysell, Richard and **Roger**—(E. III. Roll) bore, argent, a saltire engrailed between four "Choughes de Cornwaille" sable; Grimaldi Roll and Jenyns' Ordinary.

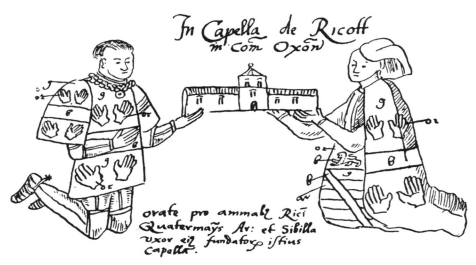

In Capella de Ricott m̃ Com̃ Oxon̄

orate pro amma Rici Quatermay̅s Ar: et Sibilla vxor ei̅ fundator̅ istius Capellæ.

Here English and French fell in battle. After the Bayeux Tapestry.

— P—Q —

Edmͨ Pagenham

Jorn Palis

Pallat

Pagenham, Sir Edward or **Sir Edmund**, of Suffolk, and **John**—(E. II. Roll) bore, quarterly or and gules, an eagle displayed vert; Ashmole and Parliamentary Rolls and Jenyns' Ordinary. F.

Pagham (——), an Essex ? Knight—(H. VI. Roll) bore, argent, three chevronels gules; Arundel Roll.

Pakenham, Sir John, of Beds.—(E. II. Roll) bore, barry (6) argent and azure, on a bend gules three mullets or. Sir JOHN LE FITZ, bore pierced mullets for difference; Parliamentary Roll; and so borne by LAWRENCE in Surrey Roll.

Pakenham, Myles—(E. I. Roll) bore, gules, a chevron between three crosses crosslet fitchée argent; Jenyns' Roll.

Palie, Sir John de, knighted at the capitulation of Calais 1348—bore, gules, a bend vair between six crosses potent or. F.

Palialogi, the; Emperors of Greece—bore, or, a sea lyon sable. Segar Roll. See Greece.

Pallat, ——, Kt., slain at the siege of Calais 1348—bore, gules, three swords, points to the centre argent. F. See PAULET.

*[**Palmer, William** (9 H. IV.)—bore, sable, a chevron or between three crescents argent.—Shirley.] F.

*[**Palmes, William,** 1300—bore, gules, three fleurs-de-lys argent, a chief vair.—Shirley.] F.

Paltoun, Sir F., of Suffolk, Kt.—(H. VI. Roll) bore, argent, six roses 3, 2, 1 gules; Arundel Roll. Sir JOHN bore six-foyles; Ashmole Roll. F.

Pantu'e, James de—(H. III. Roll) bore, argent, six barrulets and a canton gules; Arden Roll. See PAUNTON.

Pappeworth, William de—(H. III. Roll) bore, gules, a fess dancettée argent; Surrey Roll.

Parys, Sir William de—bore, at the battle of Boroughbridge 1322, sable, crusily and a chevron argent. (F.) Arundel Roll and Jenyns' Ordinary.

‡**Parke, Henry de** (PERKE)—(H. III. Roll) bore, argent, a stag's head cabossed gules. (F.) Dering and Howard Rolls.

Parke, Richard del—(E. III. Roll)—bore, sable, an eagle displayed argent, a bordure azure—argent in trick; Jenyns' Ordinary.

*[**Parker, Thomas,** R. II.—bore, gules, a chevron between three leopards' faces or.—Shirley.] F.

Paslew, Sir John, of Essex, Kt.—(H. VI. Roll) bore, azure, a fess argent between three cups or; Arundel Roll. See WAKYRLEY.

Paslew, John—(E. I. Roll) bore, argent, a fess between three mullets pierced azure; Jenyns' Roll.

Paslew, Sir John (PASSELEWE), of Essex—(E. II. Roll) bore, bendy (10) or and azure, on a canton argent a lyon passant gardant gules; Parliamentary Roll—or, four bends azure, &c. in Harl. MS. 6137 fo. 14.

Passele, Robert de—(H. III. Roll) bore, gules, a lyon rampant or; Surrey Roll.

Patishulle, Sir John (of Rutland)—bore, at the battle of Boroughbridge 1322, argent, a fess sable, between three crescents gules. Ascribed to Sir WALTER in the Ashmole Roll, and with the fess undée, to Sir WALTER, of Essex, in the Parliamentary Roll.

Pateshull, Sir Walter de—bore, at the battle of Boroughbridge 1322, argent, a fess engrélée between three crescents sable. (F.) Ascribed to SIMON, but with a plain fess in Jenyns' Ordinary.

wittm Paris

Henry do parke

Ftͦ Parker

witt Palmer

wilham Palmes

F. Paltoun

Robt de Passele

Joan d. Pateshulle

walter Pateshulle

witt Patric

John Patton

John Paulett

Grimbald Pauncefott

Thomas Paynoll

watt d' Paueli

Watt Pavoley

willia painoll

Gilbort porge

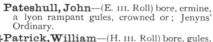

Pateshull, John—(E. III. Roll) bore, ermine, a lyon rampant gules, crowned or; Jenyns' Ordinary.

†**Patrick, William**—(H. III. Roll) bore, gules, three mullets (6) or. (F.) Arden and St. George Rolls—spur-rowells in Jenyns' Ordinary.

[**Patten, John**, 1376—bore, lozengy ermine and sable, a canton gules.—Shirley.] F.

Paule, John—(E. I. Roll) bore, ermine, on a fess azure three crosses crosslet or; Jenyns' Roll.

*[**Paulet, Sir John**, ob. 1356—bore, sable, three swords in pile points to the base proper—his son Sir JOHN bore (15 R. II.) gules, a pair of wings conjoined in lure argent—being the coat of his mother, the heiress of Reyney.—Shirley.] F.

Paulys, Sir Walter, of Stratton—(E. III. Roll) bore, gules, three lyons passant argent on a baston azure three mullets or; Ashmole Roll.

‡**Pauncefot, Sir Grimbald**—(H. III. Roll) bore, gules, three lyonceux rampant argent. (F.) Deringland Howard Rolls. Sir GILBERT, of Gloucestershire, bore the same; Parliamentary Roll E. II.

Pauncefot, William—(H. III. Roll) bore, azure, two bars or; Arden Roll.

Paunton, (——), an Essex? Knight—(H. VI. Roll) bore, barry (10) argent and gules, a quarter of the last; Arundel Roll. JAMES DE PANTU'E (H. III. Roll) bore, argent, six barrulets and a canton gules; Arden Roll.

Paunton, Sir Hugh, of the North—(E. II. Roll) bore, gules two bars and, in the cantel a fer-de-moulin ermine; Parliamentary Roll.

Paveley, Sire Walter de—bore, at the battle of Boroughbridge 1322, azure, a cross florettée and a martlet or "in the quarter." (F.) JOHN, RENAUD and Sir WALTER bore it without the martlet; Jenyns' Ordinary, St. George and Harl. Rolls. Sir JOHN bore the martlet argent; knighted at the capitulation of Calais 1348. REGINALD and WILLIAM took up the cross in the last Crusade 1270.

Paveley, Sir Walter, K.G., a founder—(H. III. Roll) bore, azure, a cross patonce or; Surrey Roll and K. 398 fo. 30.

Paveley, Edward — (H. III. Roll) bore, azure, a cross recercelée or; Norfolk Roll.

Paveley, Sir Walter (of Oxon.), knighted at the capitulation of Calais 1348—bore, gules, three lyons passant argent, on a bend azure three mullets or (F.); a baston in Cotgrave Roll.

Pavent, John—(E. I. Roll) bore, argent, on a bend gules three eaglets or; Jenyns' Roll and Arundel.

Payfote, Sir Fouke—bore, at the first Dunstable tournament 1308, argent, five fleurs-de-lys 3, 1, 1, sable, a label (3) gules: another florettée. (F.)

Payn, Sir Geoffrey and **Sir John**, both slain at the siege of Calais 1347—bore, two bars and in chief three escallops, azure—sable for Sir JOHN. GEOFFREY took up the cross in the last Crusade 1270.

Payne, Walter—(E. I. Roll) bore, gules, a lyon rampant tail fourchée argent *quarterly with* PAVELEY, azure a cross florettée or; Jenyns' Roll—called WALTER PAYUELI in Jenyns' Ordinary.

Paynell, Sir Raffe, of Caythorpe, co. Linc.—(E. II. Roll) bore, argent, a bend sable; Parly. Roll. Ascribed to RALPH PAYNE in Jenyns' Ordinary—STOPHAM bears the same.

Paynell, Sir John, of co. Linc.—(E. II. Roll) bore, gules, a cinquefoyle argent; Parly. Roll.

Paynell, John—(E. III. Roll) bore, gules a cross argent; STEPHEN PENCESTER bears the same arms; Jenyns' Ordinary.

Paynell (Sir) John, DE KNAPTOFT—(E. III. Roll) bore, gules, a cross patonce argent; Ashmole and Surrey Rolls.

Paynell, Sir William—bore, at the first Dunstable tournament 1308, argent, five bars sable, eight martlets in orle gules; tricked also with 4 bars. F.

Paynell, Sir John, banneret—bore, at the battle of Falkirk 1298 and at the siege of Carlaverock 1300, vert, a maunch or (F.); but the reverse appears for JOHN, Baron of Otteley, in Nobility Roll 1300; and for WILLIAM in Nobility Roll 1310; and for JOHN in Harl. and Parly. Rolls. See next.

Paynell, William, lord of Fracynton, baron 1303-17, and his brother **John**, lord of Otteley, baron 1317-18, sealed the Barons' letter to the Pope 1301 (*the former on a lozenge*), with two bars and an orle of eight martlets, pp. xx, xxii, xxiv. See next.

Paynell, Hugh, Sir Thomas, of Wilts, and **Sir William**—(H. III. Roll) bore, or, two bars azure, nine (8 or 6) martlets in orle gules. (F.) Arden, Howard, Parly., Harleian and other Rolls—(the field argent ascribed to WILLIAM in Jenyns' Ordinary); another Sir WILLIAM, of Wilts, bore the bars sable and the martlets " in manner of bordure assis"; Parly. and Howard Rolls; THOMAS‡ and WILLIAM (‡) in Dering Roll.

Paynell, Sir William—(E. I. Roll) bore, argent, three bars azure in chief three martlets gules; Holland Roll.

Paynell, ffouke de—(H. III. Roll) bore, or, two lyons passant gules, crowned azure; Howard Roll.

Paynell, John—(R. II. Roll) bore, gules, two chevronels and a bordure argent; Surrey Roll.

Payver (PAYCUR) —— (H. III. Roll) bore, argent three martlets gules; Arden Roll—surname uncertain. See PEYVERE.

Pecham v. Peckam, and Petham.

Peche, Sir Gilbert, of Corby, banneret, baron 1299, sealed the Barons' letter to the Pope 1301, pp. xxi, xxiv. He bore, at the battle of Falkirk 1298, and at the first Dunstable tournament 1308, argent a fess between two chevronels gules. (F.) Nobility and Howard Rolls; another GILBERT (‡) in Dering Roll; ascribed also to HAMOND in the St. George Roll, to JOHN in Jenyns' Ordinary, and to Sir ROBERT, of Kent, banneret, in Arundel Roll. (Sir WILLIAM, of Suffolk, bore the chevronels sable.) Sir HUGH, of Suffolk, differenced with a label (3) azure—to this, Sir ROBERT, also of Kent, perhaps a baron 1321, added a besant on each point of the label; Parly. Roll. SIMON and WILLIAM took up the cross 1270.

Peche, Sir Edmund, of Suffolk—(E. II. Roll) bore, argent a fess between two chevronels gules, as many martlets in chief and one in base sable (F.); Parly. Roll. In Harl. MS. 6137, a semée of martlets sable is added.

Pecche, Sir John, of Warwickshire—bore, at the first Dunstable tournament 1308 and as a banneret at the battle of Boroughbridge 1322, gules, crusily and a fess argent (F.); at the latter Sir JOHN *soun fiz*, differenced with a label (3) azure; ascribed also to THOMAS, but with six crosses crosslet (2 and 3) in Jenyns' Roll.

Edmond porge

John Pesore

John Paynoll

Paulett Marchio Wintoniæ

AIMES : LOYAVLTE :

FACSIMILE
FROM
COOKE'S BARONAGE,
CIRCA 1580.
ADD. MS. 5504.

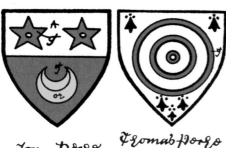

Jon perge   Tromab porge

Peche, Sir (——), of Suffolk—(E. II. Roll) bore, argent, a chevron gules a bordure sable besantée ; Parliamentary Roll.

Peche, Sir Robert, an error for Sir GILBERT —bore, at the battle of Falkirk 1298, argent (a fess between two chevronels gules. (F.) Jenyns' Ordinary.

Peche, John—(R. II. Roll) bore, azure, a lyon rampant tail fourchée ermine, crowned or ; Surrey Roll.

‡**Peche, John**—(H. III. Roll) bore, gules, a crescent or and on a chief argent two mullets (5) pierced of the field. (F.) Dering Roll ; spur-rowels in Howard Roll.

Peche, Baldwin—(H. III. Roll) bore, vaire or and gules ; Norfolk Roll.

Peche, Sir Thomas, of co. Cambridge— (E. II. Roll) bore, azure an eagle displayed argent, on the dexter wing a maunch gules. Parliamentary Roll.

Peche, Sir Thomas—(E. III. Roll) bore, ermine, a gorge gules ; Ashmole Roll. F.

‡**Peckham, John de** (PECHAM)—(H. III. Roll) bore, azure, six annulets 3, 2, 1 or. (F.) Dering and Howard Rolls. See PETHAM.

Peckham (——) a Kentish Knight—(H. VI. Roll) bore, ermine a chief quarterly gules and or ; Arundel Roll. St. NICOLAS bears the same, with the chief reversed (?)

Peckham, Roger, de (BECKHAM)—(R. II. Roll) bore, checquy or and sable, a fess ermine ; Surrey Roll.

Pedwardyne, Sir Roger—bore, at the battle of Boroughbridge 1322, or, crusily and three crescents gules, each charged with a plate. F.

Pedwardwyn, Thomas, Walter and **William**—(E. III. Roll) bore, gules, two lyons passant in pale or. (F.) Arden and Surrey Rolls, Jenyns' Ordinary. ROBERT differenced with a label (3) argent ; Surrey Roll.

Pedwardyne, Walter de—(H. III. Roll) bore, or, three lyons passant in pale gules ; Howard Roll.

*****Pelham, (Sir John)**—bore, at the siege of Rouen 1418, azure, three pelicans argent 2 and 1 vulning themselves proper. F.

Pembroke v. Marshall and **Valence.**

Pembroke, Earl of—bore, at the siege of Rouen 1418, barry (10) argent and azure an orle of martlets gules, *quarterly with,* or a maunch gules. (F.) JOHN (HASTINGS) last Earl of Pembroke of that line was accidentally killed in a tournament at Woodstock 1389, aged about 17.

A KNIGHT OF THE PEMBRIDGE FAMILY.
IN CLEHONGER CHURCH, HEREFORDSHIRE.
After Hollis.

Ingor de Pedwardin   Walter d' Pedwerdin

Penbrige, Sir John de (PENBRUGGE)— bore, at the first Dunstable tournament 1308, azure, a chief gules and a bend engrailed argent. F.

Pembrugge, (Sir John, of Cheshire)—bore, at the second Dunstable tournament 1334, argent, a chief azure, a bordure engrailed gules ; Parliamentary Roll.

Pembrugge, Fouk de—(E. I. Roll) bore, barry (6) or and azure ; Harleian Roll ; for HENRY, barry 6, 8 and 14 (F.) are tricked in Dering, Howard, St. George, and Camden Rolls (and differenced with a label (5) 'gules in Arden Roll). Sir RICHARD, K.G. 1369, barry of eight.

Penbryg, Sir Henry de—bore, at the first Dunstable tournament 1308, barry (6) or and azure, a bend gules (F.) ; Arden Roll ; barry (8) for Sir HENRY of Herefordshire in Parly. Roll.

Penbruge, Sir John, of Herefordshire— (E. II. Roll) bore, barry (8) or and azure, on a bend gules three mullets argent ; Parly. Roll. See Monumental Effigy of a member of this family—leopards' faces on the bend.

Penbrugge, John—(R. II. Roll) bore, or, a fess double cotised azure, a bendlet gules ; Surrey Roll.

‡**Pencestre, Stephen**—(H. III. Roll) bore, gules, a cross argent (F.) ; Dering Roll ; borne also by JOHN PAYNELL ; the cross or, for JOHN in Jenyns' Ordinary.

Penedoke, Henry de—(H. III. Roll) bore, sable, a lyon rampant argent (F.) ; St. George Roll.

Penley, Sir Richard—(E. III. Roll) bore, or, a lyon rampant purpure ; Ashmole Roll.

Penne. See DE LA PENNE.

Stevene de Poncestre   Henry de Pendoke

Jon de Porgam

monñ. Polgam

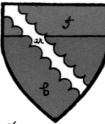

Oounto de Ponbrook

Jorn de Penbridge

Henry de Penbrugge   Henry de Pembridge

Pennington, Baron Muncaster, of Muncaster

AND

Legh, of Norbury Booths Hall in Cheshire.

Condensed from "Penningtoniana," by J. Foster, Hon. M.A., Oxon.

GAMEL DE PENINGTON, temp. Hen. II. ; a great benefactor to Conishead Priory, to = which he gave the churches (with all their appurtenances) of Penington, Molcastre, with chapels [of Aldeburg], Wytebec and Skeroverton, cos. Lanc. and Cumb.

BENEDICT DE PENINGTON. He, jointly with his brother Meldred gave = Agnes. Skeldon Moor to the Abbey of Russyn, in the Isle of Man.

MELDRED DE PENINGTON. He gave to Conishead Priory two bovates of land in Burgh, and three acres of land, with a messuage, in "Langliferga."

ALAN DE PENINGTON, son and heir. Richard de Lucy, by fine at Carlisle, 1 Dec., 1208, 1 John, *granted to Alan* = *all his tenement of Mulecastre, to hold by the service of one-twelfth part of one knight's fee and foreign service, belonging to the king. In 1363 Sir Wm. de Penitone* was found to hold by the same service, see below.

ALEXANDER.

THOMAS DE PENINGTON, son and = AGNES, dau. of Sir John de Longvillers, knt. = Thomas de Greistock 1254 (39 Hen. III.) heir, dead in 1240.

ALAN, living July, 1242.

Sir ALAN DE PENINGTON, a knight in 1276, 4 Edw. I. By fine at Westm. 54 Hen. III. (1270) for fifty marks of silver he parted with the advowsons of Mulecastre (Cumb.) and Overton (Westm.) to the Prior of Conishead, living 1292, and supposed to be identical with Sir Alan de Penington, "who coming from the wars beyond seas, died at Canterbury, and was buried in the church of the White Fryars " (*Weever's Funeral Monuments*).

Sir WILLIAM DE PENITONE, dispute with the Abbot of Furness in 1318, as to the services by which he held the manor of = Penington (Peniton), co. Lanc. ; dead before 1323.

Sir JOHN DE PENITONE, son and heir, a minor in 1323, = JOAN, widow of Sir John, had dower from the Abbot of of age by 1326 ; held the manor of Penington by service Furness, 7 Jany., 1332/3. May be identical with Joan of a tenth part of a knight's fee ; dispute with the Abbot (d. 16 or 17 June, 1363) eldest sister and co-heir of John of Furness, who had taken John's cattle, 1328/9 ; died de Multon, of Egremont, & wife of Robert Fitz-Walter. about 1332.

MAUDE, mar. to John, son and heir of Sir Richard de Hodleston, and Alice his wife, 1317/18. 11 Edw. II.

JOAN, living 7 Jany., 1351/2.

Sir WILLIAM DE PENITONE, son and heir, abbot's ward for nineteen years ; of age before 26 Edward III. = ELIZABETH, dau. and co-heir of Thomas de Malton, of East (1352 3), at which date he was already married to the dau. of Sir W. de Leghe, but without the licence of the Gevedale, or Givendale, co. York. She was æt. 60 in 1404, abbot, by whom his marriage had been previously sold to Sir William de Threlkeld, while under age. (By 5 H. IV. Re-mar. to Hugh Standysshe, and living, 1411/12, an inquisition taken at Egremont, 8 September, 1363, after the death of Joan, wife of Robert FitzWalter, who 13 H. IV., but pre-deceased him, who died 30 April, 1421, died 16 or 17 June, 37 Edward III., 1363, *it was found that William de Penitone held of the said Joan the manor* 9 Hen. V. *of Mulcaster by homage, fealty and service of one-twelfth part of a knight's fee, etc.*, as granted to Alan de Penington first mentioned. Living 29 Sept., 1368.

Sir ALAN DE PENINGTON, "chivaler," under age at his father's death. Died 27 Sept., 1415. Inq. taken at Lancaster = KATHERINE, daughter and co-heir of Sir Richard 13 April, 1416. de Preston, 1390, M. 1.

Sir JOHN DE PENINGTON, son and heir, æt. 22 years at his father's death. Appointed Commissioner in = KATHERINE, daughter of Sir Thomas de Tunstall, knight, by Cumberland to raise archers, by Act of Parliament, 1457/8, 36 H. VI. Henry VI. took refuge at Muncaster Isabel, daughter to Sir Nicholas Harrington, knight ; dispen- in 1461, after the battle of Towton Field (29 March), and gave Sir John the "luck of Muncaster." He sation for marriage to Sir John, son of Sir Alan de Penington, died 6 July, 1470 ; inq. p.m., 20 Feb., 1503/4. granted 28 April, 1412, related in the third degree.

A

CONTINUED ON NEXT PAGE.

158

CONTINUED FROM PRECEDING PAGE :—
A

JOHN PENNINGTON, Knight of the Shire for Cumberland 1446-7, died = ELIZABETH, living 1482, daughter of Sir   ANNE, mar.   CATHERINE, mar. to Jno. Rigmayden, of
in the lifetime of his father. John, Earl of Shrewsbury, appointed   Nicolas Radcliffe, of Derwentwater,   to Sir   Wedacre, in Lanc., Vis. Lanc. 1567.
one John Pennington steward of Weysford by patent dated at Weys-   M.I.   Christopher
ford, 27 Aug., 1450.   Curwen.

ISABEL, dau. = Sir JOHN PENNINGTON, heir to his grandfather, Inq., = JOANE, dau. of Sir William Eure, of = Sir ROBERT   WILLIAM PENNINGTON, of Hundisdon
of John   20 February, 1503/4. Was in the vanguard of the   Witton Castle, by Maud, dau. of   OGLE, knt.   (? Hunsdon, Herts), of the King's
Broughton,   English army at the invasion of Scotland in 1482,   Lord FitzHugh, of Ravenswath   1st husband.   Household, 1495/6, styled " William
M.I., and   and was made a knight banneret 24 July of that   Castle. On 13 Aug., 1467, an ora-   [53.]   Penyngton senior." The king granted
sister to Sir   year by the Earl of Northumberland. Sheriff of   tory was granted to Dame Jane Ogle   him the reversion of the office of
Thos.   Cumb., 9 Nov., 1510. He married Joane Ogle at   and Henry Eure, Esq., within the   bailiff of the lordship of Cheshunt,
Broughton.   Beverley, 15 Oct., 1472. He died 3 May, 1512, inq.   diocese of York. She died at Mun-   Herts, 2 Jan., 1513/4. He was dead
   at Penrith, 26 Aug. 1518. His will, dated at Mul-   caster, 13 Oct., 23 Hen. VII., 1507.   in 1522.   =
   caster, 4 May, 1505, which he acknowledged 1 June,
   2 Hen. VIII., 1510.

JOHN PEN- = MARY, da.   ALAN   WILLIAM PEN- = ANNE, dau. and   ELIZABETH PENNING-   MARGARET,   Sir WILLIAM PENNINGTON, = FRANCES, dau.   Sir RICHD.
NINGTON,   of Sir Jno.   PEN-   NINGTON, of   heir of Geo.   TON, mar. (? 1st to   mar. 1st. to J.   cousin and heir male to   of Henry   PENNING-
of Mun-   Hudleston.   NING-   Newton,   Martindale, of   —— Salkeld, and,   Lamplew, of   John, son of Wm. Penning-   Pagrave, of   TON.
caster, ad-   She died   TON,   Cumb., j.u.   the diocese of   2ndly, by dispensa-   Lamplew,   ton, of Newton aforesaid,   Pagrave, Nor-
mitted to   20 May,   living,   1495, " Ju-   Carlisle ; on 10   tion, dated 14 July,   and, 2ndly, to   æt. 40 years, 28 Oct., 19   folk, by Anne,
Lincoln's   1525, 17   1505,   nior," eschea-   Aug., 1488, she   1491) to Sir Walter   Thos. Ley-   H. VIII., 1527. Knighted   dau. of Jno.
Inn 1   Hen. VIII.   o.v.p.   tor for Cumb.,   had licence to   Strickland. He died   borne, of   at Valenciennes (in the   Glemham, of
Dec., 20   Inq. p.m.   s. p.   26 Nov., 1512,   mar. W. Pen   26 Sept., 1506. She   Cunswick.   wars in France), 3 Dec.,   Glemham,
E. IV.,   at Carlisle,   until his death,   nington, of the   mar., after 9 Aug.,   15 H. VIII., 1523, by the   Suffolk, by his
1480, of   17 Jan.,   on Friday, 9   diocese of York;   1508, and " before   ELLEN, mar. to   Earl of Suffolk. Sheriff of   wife Alianore,
the King's   1525/6.   Sept., 1513, 5   related in the   the fest. of Seynt   —— Kighley.   Cumb., 20 H. VIII. He   who was aunt
Household   Hen. VIII.   3rd and 4th de-   Michell tharchangell   died 20 April, 1532, Inq.   to Charles
1495/6.   Inq. 26 Aug.,   grees. She   next comyng," to Sir   ANN, mar. to   p.m., at Penrith, 20 Sept.,   Brandon,
Inqs.   1519, and at   died before her   Richd. Cholmeley.*   Richd. Bar-   1532, and at Appleby, 23   Duke of Suf-
p.m. 1518   Penrith, 25   husband. Inq.   He died 27, 28, or   wis.   Oct. following. Inventory   folk. She was
and 1525.   Sept., 1520.   p.m.   29 Dec., 1521. Wife   dated 4 Dec., 1533.   mar. before 3
He died   of Sir Wm. Gas-   Feb., 17 H.
28 June,   coigne, of Carding-   VIII., 1525/6.
1516, 8 H.   ton, Beds., in 1527.
VIII.

ISABEL, = THOMAS   JOHN PENNINGTON, heir male to his   JOAN (1st wife, = WILLIAM PENNINGTON, jun., son and heir (aged = BRIDGET (2nd wife, = SIR HUGH
dau. and   DYKES,   uncle, John Pennington, under the   M.I.), dau. of   14 years and 9 months at his father's death, 20   M.I.), 2nd dau. of   ASKEW,
heir, æt.   of War-   will of his grandfather, æt. 19   Thomas, Lord   April, 1532). He and all his tried horsemen   John Hudleston,   of Seaton,
40 years   thall.   years, 28 June, 1516. Had livery   Wharton, by   were called out upon service of the borders,   by his 3rd wife,   Cumb., and
at her   of his lands, 12 Feb., 1521. Died   Eleanor, dau.   1543, M.I. Sheriff of Cumb., 6 Ed. VI., and 1   Joyce, dau. and   Blyborough,
mother's   14 June, 14 Henry VIII., 1522.   of Sir Bryan   & 8 Eliz. Died 14 Mar., 15 Eliz., 1573. Inq.   heir of John Prick-   Linc. (1st
death.   Inq. p.m., at Penrith, 28 Oct., 19   Stapleton, knt.   p.m., at Cockermouth, 12 Mar., 1573/4.   ley, of Prickley, co.   husband).
   Henry VIII. (1527).   of Wighill,   Worcester.   His will dated
    Yorks.   1 Sept., 1561.

A quibus Dykes, of
Dovenby, Cumb.

JOSEPH PENNINGTON, son and heir, aged 8 years, 9 = ISABEL, dau. of = Sir ROBERT   JOHN,   M.I. = ANN, dau. of Christopher Cracken-   WILLIAM, M.I.   JOYCE, mar.
months, and 27 days at his father's death in 1573, in   Alvary Copley,   SAVILE, of   (—— Pening-   thorpe of Newbiggin, md. be-   to Anthony
ward of Anthony Huddleston and Ralph Latus, both   of Batley,   Howley,   ton, bd. at   fore 9 Dec., 1596 (? did she   BRIDGET, mar. to   Caterick, of
of Millum. Knight of the Shire for Cumberland   Yorks, bd. at   Yorks, knt.,   Muncaster,   re-marry at Muncaster, 28 May,   Philip Lovell, of   Stanwick,
1597. He was bd. at Muncaster 23 March, 1640/1,   Muncaster, 16   1st. hus-   19 Oct.,   1632, to Gabriel Skeldings).   Skelton, Yorks.   Yorks.
M.I., æt. 76.   Feb., 1625.   band.   1623).

WILLIAM PENNINGTON, eldest = KATHERINE, dau. of Richard   JOHN, bp. at Muncaster 21 Sep-   BRIDGET, bp. 26   BRIDGET, bp. at Mun- = Sir WM. HUDLESTON, of
son, born at Muncaster 14,   Sherburn, dau. of   tember, 1591, buried same day.   June, 1593, and   caster in 1596, and   Millum, co. Lanc., K.B.
and bp. there 23 July, 1590;   died 27 May, 1628, æt. 38,   JOHN, bp. 25, and bd. 26 Feb.,   bd. 1593/4.   mar. there 21 Feb.,   at the battle of Edge
bd. 14 August, 1652.   M.I., Mitton, Lanc.   1594/5.   1624.   Hill.

JOSEPH PEN- = MARGARET,   BRIDGET = 2. ALAN PEN- = ANNE (2nd   ANNE, dau. = 3. RICHARD, = LADY   MARY   4. WILLIAM, of Gray's   4. BRIDGET, M.I.,
NINGTON,   dau. of John   (1st wife),   NINGTON, M.D.,   wife), dau.   of Robert   M.I., an utter   BRADSHAIGH, pro-   Inn 1652, M.I., d.   mar. at Muncaster
compounded   Fleetwood,   dau. to ——   Queen's Coll.,   of John   Blundell,   barrister of   bably relict of Sir   1683.   30 Jan., 1644/5, to
for his estate,   of Penwor-   Aleworth   Oxon., 1651,   Legh, of   of Ince,   Gray's Inn,   Roger Bradshaigh,   1. ISABEL, M.I., d. in   Thos. Heber, of
£6. 3s. 4d.   tham, Lan-   of Somer-   living at Chester   Booths,   Blundell,   lg. at Salford   second Bart., who   London, bd. in Mun-   Stainton, co. York,
b. at Wiggles-   cashire, by   set.   1664, bp. at   and widow   co. Lanc.   1664. (1676,   d. 17 June, 1687,   caster chancel 21   and was bur. at
worth, Yorks.   Anne, dau.   Muncaster 19   of John   June 16,   and dau. and co-   March, 1689.   Marton, co. York,
bp. at Long   of Wm.   Sept., 1622, and   Dichfield,   Richard   heir of Hy. Mur-   2. CATHERINE, mar.,   4 Sept., 1662.
Preston,   ffarrington,   d. 12 Nov., 1696,   of Man-   Penington,   ray, Gent. of the   as 1st wife, to Sir   3. ELIZABETH, M.I.,
Yorks, 11   of Worden,   M.I., St. John's,   chester,   Esq., bd. at   Bedchamber to   Jeffery Shakerley, of   mar. 1647, to Sir
Aug., 1615,   m. at Pen-   Chester, bd. the   mercer   Manchester).   Charles I., living a   Hulme and Shaker-   Roger Bradshaigh,
died 1658, M.I.   wortham, 16   same day. Ad-   (lic. 9 Feb.,   A son and 3   widow, 1706.   ley, governor of Ches-   of The Haigh, co.
   Nov., 1652.   mon. granted to   1669/70),   daughters   ter, and died 3 April,   Lanc., cr. a bart.
     Anne, his widow,   d. 21 Dec.,   died young.   1673, buried at Ne-   17 Nov., 1679. He
     13 July, 1697.   1728, bd. at   ther Peover, co.   died 31 March,
      St. John's,   Cest., M.I.   1684.
      Chester, 23.

A   B   C

CONTINUED ON NEXT PAGE.

CONTINUED FROM PRECEDING PAGE:—

A   B   C

Sir WILLIAM PENNING- = ISABEL, elder dau. and heir of John Stapleton, of Warter, co. York, died Easter Monday, 28 March, and bd. at Waberthwaite, 12 Ap. 1687.
TON, æt. 9 at Dugdale's Visitation of Lancashire in 1664, bp. at Muncaster 16 March, 1655, created a baronet 21 June, 28 Chas. II., 1676, and died at Muncaster 1 July, 1730.

WILLIAM, son and heir, æt. 4 an. 9 Sept., 1663, of Brasenose Coll. 1680. Capt. in a Foot Reg., bd. St. John's, Chester, 21 Aug., 1713, will dated 13 June, 1713, and proved 6 Aug., 1714.

ALAN, of Piccadilly, druggist, 1714.

JOSEPH, of St. Margaret's, Westminster, 1714, bp. St. Bridget's, Chester, 4 June, 1678.

RUTH (1st wife), = only dau. and heir of Peter Legh, of Booths. (His w. d. 28 Dec., 1714, pd. 11 Sept., 1716.) She was buried St. John's, Chester, 8 March, 1715.

THOMAS (PENNINGTON) LEGH, of = HELENA (2nd wife), Chester, Capt., bap. at St. John's 15 April, 1680, took the name of Legh by Act of Parliament 1724, bd. at Knutsford 17 Feb., 1742/3. His widow, Helena Legh, renounced admon. of her husband, Thomas Legh, of Norbury Booths, in favour of her only son, Peter Legh, on 21 May, 1752.

HELENA (2nd wife), dau. of Sir Willoughby Aston, bt., mar. at St. John's, Chester, 26 Sept., 1720, bd. at Knutsford 12 Jan. 1764/5.

[pedigree chart — see original]

John de Ponyngton · *Robt d' Peres* · *Ric̄ Porore* · *Robt de Perpoune* · *Symon de Perpoune*

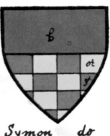

Walt Portobay · *Ric̄ Porcoval* · *Henry de Percye* · *mic̄s de Peres* · *Rico Potto*

Rauf Parot · *will'm de Port* · *nicole pefon* · *will Poffun* · *Richard de Pevenefe*

*Pennyngton, Sir William de—(E. II. Roll) bore, or, five fusils conjoined in fess azure; Parly. Roll; tricked also as a fess fusily and a fess indented. JOHN differenced with a label (3) gules (F.); Jenyns' Ordinary. Sir JOHN bore the field argent and a label (5) gules in the Ballard Roll.

[Penrice, Sir Robert de, 1326 (PENREES) —bore, per pale indented argent and gules; Neath Abbey Tiles, p. ix.]

Penzret, Sir John de, of Cumberland— (E. II. Roll) bore, gules, a bend battely argent; Parliamentary Roll.

Percehay, Sir Wauter—bore, at the battle of Boroughbridge 1322, argent, a cross patonce gules and in the dexter chief point, an inescocheon of ATON—or, a cross sable; the cross patonce is tricked patée in Ashmole MS. F.

Percehay, Sir Walter, knighted at the capitulation of Calais 1348—bore, argent, a cross patonce (flory in the trick) gules, in the cantel an inescocheon quarterly sable and or. F.

Percehay, Walter—(E. III. Roll) bore, argent, a cross patonce (flory in the trick) gules; HENRY COLVILE of Cambridgeshire bears the same arms, which are in dispute; Jenyns' Ordinary.

Percehay, Walter—(E. III. Roll) bore, argent a cross patonce (flory in the trick) gules, in the cantel a lozenge of the second all within a bordure engrailed of the last; Jenyns' Ordinary.

*[Perceval, Richard (Hen. IV.)—bore, argent, on a chief indented gules three crosses patée of the first; ascribed to Sir ROGER as per Seal E. I.—Shirley.] F.

Percy, Henry, of Topcliffe, banneret, baron 1298-9—bore, at the battle of Falkirk 1298, and at the siege of Carlaverock 1300, or, a lyon rampant azure.—F. (Nobility, Parly. and Arundel Rolls), being the arms of BRABANT, with which he sealed the Barons' letter to the Pope 1301, pp. xvii, xxiv. Ascribed also to THOMAS in the Surrey Roll, and to Sir PIERS at the first Dunstable tournament 1308. (1) HENRY differenced it with a label (3) gules; (2) RAFFE with a mullet or, on the lyon's shoulder, both in the Surrey Roll; and (3) WILLIAM differenced his brothers' arms with a bordure "recersele" gules; Cotgrave Roll. See MONTFORT.

Percy, Henry de, SR. DE LUCY, Earl ot Northumberland 1399-1408—(R. II. Roll) bore, or, a lyon rampant azure, *quarterly with* LUCY, gules, three lucies hauriant 2 and 1 argent; Surrey Roll.

Percy, Sire Nichol—bore, at the battle of Boroughbridge 1322, undée (6) argent and azure. F.

Percy, Henry, of Wiltshire—(E. I. Roll) bore, argent, five fusils conjoined in fess sable (or, in Camden); Jenyns' Ordinary; engrailed in Jenyns' Roll; JOHN bore the reverse, see below.

Percy, Walter de—(H. III. Roll) bore, azure, five fusils conjoined in fess argent; Arden and St. George Rolls. A WALTER took up the cross in the last Crusade 1270.

‡Percy, Sir Henry, of Spofford—(H. III. Roll) bore, azure, five fusils conjoined in fess or; Dering and Howard Rolls; indented in Grimaldi Roll; engrailed in Glover Roll, for HENRY.

Percy, Arnold, of Kildale—(E. III. Roll) bore, gules, five fusils conjoined in fess argent; Jenyns' Ordinary.

Percy, Robert, of Sutton-upon-Derwent— (E. III. Roll) bore, or, five fusils conjoined in fess azure; Jenyns' Ordinary; fess engrailed in Glover Roll.

Percy, Arnold and Robert—(H. III. Roll) bore, or, five fusils conjoined in fess sable (F.); Arden and St. George Rolls. Same arms as RICHARD DAUTREY; Jenyns' Ordinary.

‡Percy, John de—(H. III. Roll) bore, sable, five fusils conjoined in fess argent; Dering Roll; a fess of fusils in Howard Roll.

Percy, Sir Richard de—bore, at the first Dunstable tournament 1308, and at the battle of Boroughbridge 1322, quarterly argent and sable, in the cantel a mullet (vij. in Nativity Roll) gules (pierced or, at Dunstable) (F.); another Sir RICHARD (of co. Leic.) bore it when knighted at the capitulation of Calais 1348; Parly. and Harl. Rolls; EDWARD bore it undifferenced at the siege of Rouen in 1418.

Peres, Sir Thomas de (or PRYERS), of Essex—(E. II. Roll) bore, vert, a bend argent cotised or; Parliamentary Roll.

Periam (——) an Essex Knight—(H. VI. Roll) bore, gules, three crescents argent; Arundel Roll.

Perke, Henry de (or PARKE)—(H. III. Roll) bore, argent, a stag's head cabossed gules; Dering and Howard Rolls.

Perpont v. Pierpont.

Perpont (——), of Iklyng, and Symon— (H. III. Roll) bore, azure, a chief checquy or and gules; Howard and Ashmole Rolls. ‡ ROBERT bore the chief counter-compony (F.) in Dering Roll. SYMON ‡ bore the reverse, viz., checquy or and gules, a chief azure. (F.) Dering Roll; per fess in the tricks.

Perreres v. Perers.

Perrot, Rauf, baron 1297—bore, quarterly indented or and azure; Nobility Roll. To Sir RAUFE of Beds is ascribed quarterly per fess indented or and azure (F.), in Parly. and other Rolls; and to RAUF, dancettée in Dering Roll.

Pert, William de—(E. I. Roll) bore, argent, on a bend gules, three mascles or (F.); Jenyns' Roll.

Peshale, —— (R. II. Roll) bore, argent, a cross flory engrailed sable; Surrey Roll.

Peshale, Adam—(R. II. Roll) bore, argent, a cross flory sable, on a quarter gules a lyon's head erased of the first, crowned or; Surrey Roll.

†Peson, Nicole de — (H. III. Roll) bore, ermine, a fess azure. (F.) Dering Roll; thereon three lyonceux rampant argent (F.) in Howard Roll, and thus ascribed to WILLIAM in Arden Roll.

Petham, John de (POTHAM) —(H. III. Roll) bore, azure, six annulets or; Howard Roll. See PECHAM.

Petit, Thomas—(E. III. Roll) bore, gules, a fess between three annulets 2 and 1 or; Jenyns' Ordinary.

Pette, Thomas—bore, at the second Dunstable tournament 1334, ermine an engrêle gules (F.)—tricked as a fess indented, dancettée is probably intended.

‡Pevense, Richard de—(H. III. Roll) bore, azure, a chevron or square fretted gules, between three crosses moline argent; Howard Roll—crosses recercelée (F.) in Dering Roll— square fretted may be an error in the trick for fretty.

John Poveroll

Johan Pickard

Rog Pichard de stondone

Ffo Pikworth

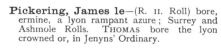

Henri Pirpund.

Hue Peverel.

Roger Poytwyn

Goffrey Pichford

Joan d' Pichford.

Robt Porpoynt

Henry de Pyers

Geffory Pigot

Robt Pygot

Pevere *v.* **Peyvre.**

Peverell, —— (E. III. Roll) bore, quarterly 1 and 4, vairé or and vert—2 and 3, gules ; Ashmole Roll.

Peverell, Sir John—bore, at the battle of Boroughbridge 1322, gyronny (8) argent and gules. F.

‡**Peverell, Thomas** — (H. III. Roll) bore, gyronny (12 or 16) argent and gules, a bordure sable bezantée ; Dering and Howard Rolls.

Peverell, Henry—(E. III. Roll) bore, argent, on a saltire sable five mullets or pierced gules ; Jenyns' Ordinary.

Peverell, Hugh—(H. III. Roll) bore, azure, three garbs argent banded gules, a chief or. (F.) St. George Roll.

Peverell, Sir Robert, of co. Leic.—(E. II. Roll) bore. gules, a fess argent between six crosses patonce or ; Parliamentary Roll.

‡**Peyferer, William**—(H. III. Roll) bore, argent, three fleurs-de-lys 2 and 1 sable ; Arden and Camden Rolls—six in Howard and Dering Rolls. Sir WILLIAM, of Kent (R. II. Roll) bore, argent, florettée sable ; Parliamentary Roll. Sir FOUKE differenced with a label (3) gules.

Peyton, Sir John de, of Suffolk—(E. II. Roll) bore, sable, a cross engrailed or, a mullet argent (Parliamentary, Arundel and Surrey Rolls) in the first and second quarter, in Jenyns' Ordinary—probably a mistake. One of these names took up the cross in the last Crusade 1270.

Peytwyn, Sir Roger, of Lincolnshire—(H. III. Roll) bore. ermine, three chevronels gules (four (F.) in Jenyns' Ordinary) ; Arden and Parliamentary Rolls.

Peyvere, Sir Philip, of Norfolk—(E. II. Roll) bore, or two bars sable between six martlets 3, 2, 1 argent ; Parliamentary Roll — an addition.

Peyvre, John, baron 1298-9—bore, argent, on a chevron gules three fleurs-de-lys or ; Nobility Roll. Ascribed also to Sir JOHN and Sir ROGER, both of Beds., in Parliamentary Roll ; THOMAS, in Jenyns' Ordinary, and WILLIAM in Glover Roll.

Phelip, Sir William, K.G. 1418—bore, quarterly gules and argent, in the first an eagle displayed or ; K. 401 fo. 16.

Pichford, Geffrey—(H. III. Roll) bore, checquy, or and azure, on a fess gules three lyonceux rampant argent. (F.) Arden and Camden Rolls.

Pichford, John de—(H. III. Roll) bore, sable, semée of quartrefoyles and a cinquefoyle pierced or ; St. George Roll—crusily (F.) in Arden Roll.

Pickard, Roger—(H. III. Roll) bore, argent, three lozenges sable ; St. George Roll. JOHN differenced with a label (5) gules. (F.) Segar Roll.

Pickarde, Sir Myles (or PICHARD), of Salop, **Richard** and **Roger**—(E. II. Roll) bore, gules, a fess or between three escallops argent. (F.) Parliamentary and Jenyns' Roll. [Sir JOHN differenced with a label of 3 azure—sometimes or.] ROGER, of Stondon, bore the fess argent ; Arden and St. George Rolls.

Pi(c)kenham, Raffe, of Thornton Watlass —(E. III. Roll) bore, or, on a chief indented azure three crescents of the field ; cinquefoyles pierced in trick ; Jenyns' Ordinary—see WAT-LOUS or WATLASS.

Pickenham, —— (PYKNAM), a Knight — (H. VI. Roll) bore, azure, a lyon rampant holding in its fore-paws a cross patée fitchée all or ; Arundel Roll.

Pickering, James le—(R. II. Roll) bore, ermine, a lyon rampant azure ; Surrey and Ashmole Rolls. THOMAS bore the lyon crowned or, in Jenyns' Ordinary.

Pickering, Sir Thomas de—(E. II. Roll) bore, or (sometimes argent) a lyon rampant sable, a bordure gules bezantée ; Harl. 6137. In Harl. 4033—argent, a lyon rampant sable, a bordure of the last bezantée.

Pi(c)kworth, Sir Thomas—(E. III. Roll) bore, argent, three picks gules ; Ashmole and Surrey Rolls. ROBERT, differenced with an annulet ; Surrey Roll.

Pickworth, John—(E. I. Roll) bore, gules, a bend between six picks (3 and 3) or. (F.) Jenyns' Roll—argent in Jenyns' Ordinary.

Pierpont, Henry (PERPUND)—(H. III. Roll) bore, burulée (16) argent and gules, a lyon rampant sable debruised of a baston or. (F.) Arden and St. George Rolls.

Pierpont, Sir Edmond, Henry and **Thomas**—(E. III. Roll) bore, argent, a lyon rampant sable, within an orle of six-foyles gules (the reverse ascribed to EDMOND in the Surrey Roll) ; Ashmole Roll and Jenyns' Ordinary—cinquefoyles in Cotgrave Roll, where to " the NEPHEW " is ascribed argent, a lyon rampant sable a baston gules.

Pierpont, Sir Robert—bore, at the first Dunstable tournament 1308, argent, a lyon rampant sable debruised by a baston or (F.) ; Cotgrave and Nativity Rolls.

Pierpont, Sir Robert (PEYPOUNDE)— (E. II. Roll) bore, argent, a lyon rampant sable (powdered with roses gules, Harl. 6137) ; a bordure of six roses gules, Harl. 4033 ; Parly. Roll.

Piers, Mons., LE CAPITOW DE BOUCH, K.G., *v.* **Greilly.**

Piers, Henry (PYERS)—(E. I. Roll) bore, azure, a bend argent, cotised or, between six martlets 3 and 3 of the second (F.) ; Segar Roll.

Pigot, Sir Robert (PYGOT), slain at the siege of Calais 1347—bore, gules, three picks 2 and 1 argent (F.), borne also by BALDWIN ; Surrey Roll

Pigot, Geffrey, of Melmerby—(E. I. Roll) bore, sable three picks (picois) argent (F.) ; Grimaldi and Jenyns' Rolls ; and by RANDOLF in Surrey Roll.

Pigott, Sir J. (PYGOTT)—(H. VI. Roll) bore, or, on a cross azure five crescents argent ; Atkinson Roll.

Pigott (——), Sr, of Norfolk—(E. II. Roll) bore, argent, two bends engrailed gules ; and in a marginal note, " 3 molles sable " ; Parly. Roll, an addition.

Pigott, Sir Baldwin, of Yorkshire, and **John** of Doddington—(E. II. Roll) bore, azure, two bars or in chief three besants ; Parly. Roll and Jenyns' Ordinary.

Peīs Pigod.

willt Pigott

Kauf Pipard

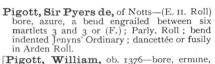

Joan d Piricon

Edmund de Ploico

Alox Pilkington

Tomes de Pin

Thomas d Pin

Ꝑ de Plukenoi

Hic du Playb

Huo de Plesis

John Plowdon

Kobert le Poer

Pigott, Sir Pyers de, of Notts—(E. II. Roll) bore, azure, a bend engrailed between six martlets 3 and 3 or (F.) ; Parly. Roll ; bend indented Jenyns' Ordinary ; dancettée or fusily in Arden Roll.

[**Pigott, William,** ob. 1376—bore, ermine, three fusils conjoined in fess sable.—Shirley.] F.

*[**Pilkington, Sir Alexander** 1301—bore, argent, a cross patonce voided gules. —Shirley.] F.

Pilkington —— (E. I. Roll) bore, argent, three bends gules and on a canton (or !) a cross voided sable ; Harleian Roll.

✝**Pin(e), Thomas de**—(H. III. Roll) bore, gules, a chevron argent, between three pine cones or (F.F.) ; Arden and St. George Rolls.

Pinkeney, Sir Henry de, of Northants, baron 1299—bore, at the battle of Falkirk 1298, or a fess " engréle " gules (F.) *i.e.* five fusils conjoined ; Nobility Roll and Jenyns' Ordinary, with which he sealed the Barons' letter to the Pope 1301, pp. xxii, xxiv ; a fess dancettée in Harl. MS. 6137 fo. 52ᵇ, and indented on fo. 22ᵇ.

Pinkenei, Robert—(E. I. Roll) bore, or, six fusils conjoined in fess gules, and THOMAS differenced with a baston sable (F.) ; Segar Roll.

Pipard, Sir Rauff, baron 1299—bore, at the battle of Falkirk 1298, argent, a fess and a demi fess, on a canton azure a cinquefoyle or (F.) In the Nobility and other Rolls—two bars ; " une fees et demi " in Jenyns' Ordinary, the cinquefoyles pierced in Arden and St. George Rolls. Signed but did not seal the Barons' letter to the Pope 1301, page xxiv.

Pipe, Sir Thomas de la, of Staffs—(E. II. Roll) bore, azure crusily 3, 3, and a fess or ; Parly. Roll ; crusily fitchée ; Jenyns' Roll.

Piritone, Joan de—(H. III. Roll) bore, or, a pear-tree vert fructed gules (F.) ; Arden and St. George Rolls.

Pitlysden (——) a Knight—(H. VI. Roll) bore, argent, a fess between three pelicans azure vulning themselves ; Arundel Roll. JOHN DE PYVELSDON took up the cross in the last Crusade 1270.

Placetis *v.* **Plessetis.**

Plaice, Sir Edmond de—bore, at the first Dunstable tournament 1308, argent, a bend between six annulets 3 and 3 gules (F.) ; bend azure in H. 5848.

Planche, Sir James de la, of Bucks, Kt.— (E. II. Roll) bore, argent, billetty and a lyon rampant sable ; Harleian and Segar Rolls ; crowned or, in Parly. Roll ; in Segar Roll the billets are more like guttée de poix, they even suggest ermine. F.

Plantagenet, *v.* enamelled tablet, GEOFFREY, Count of Anjou, page xxxviii.

Playz, Giles de, baron 1297—bore, per pale or and gules, a lyon passant argent ; Nobility Roll ; borne also by his son Sir RICHARD, a baron 1317, at the battle of Boroughbridge 1322 (F.)—lyon passant gardant in Parly. Roll, ascribed also to JOHN in Ashmole and Surrey Rolls.

Plays, William—(E. III. Roll) bore, azure, on a chief argent, three chaplets gules ; Ashmole Roll and Jenyns' Ordinary. F.

Plesington, Robert de—(E. III. Roll) bore, azure, a cross flory between four martlets argent ; Jenyns' Ordinary.

Plessetis, Hugh de, baron 1299—bore, argent, six annulets gules (F.) ; Nobility and other Rolls ; ascribed to Sir JOHN in Glover Roll—three annulets in Norfolk Roll, under PLACETIS, PLESCY, PLESCIS, and PLESSIS.

Plecy, Sir Henry or Hugh de, of Oxon— (E. II. Roll) bore, argent, six torteaux ; Sir JOHN differenced with a label (3) azure, and his son with a baston azure ; Parly. Roll.

*[**Plowden, John**—(E. III.) bore, azure, a fess dancettée florettée at the points or.— Shirley.] F.

Plugenett, Sir Alan de (or PLUKENET), banneret, baron, 1295—bore, ermine, a bend engrailed gules (F.), Nobility Roll ; a banneret, Arundel Roll ; blasoned as a bend fusily in Segar and St. George Rolls ; as a bend of fusils (F.) in the Howard Roll, and as a bend sinister fusily, probably erroneously, in Dering and Guillim Rolls. HUGO took up the cross in the last Crusade 1270.

Plumpton, Robert de and **Sir William** —(H. III. Roll) bore, azure, five fusils in fess or, on each an escallop gules ; Ashmole, Arundel and Surrey Rolls, and Jenyns' Ordinary.

Plumpton, Sir Robert—(E. II. Roll) bore, azure, six fusils conjoined in fess or, on each a mullet gules ; Parly. Roll—a fess indented in Harl. MS. 4033 fo. 51ᵇ.

‡**Poer, Robert le** — (H. III. Roll) bore, quarterly ermine and azure, two leopards' faces or. (F.) Dering Roll.

Pogeys, Sir Robert, of Bucks—(E. II. Roll) bore, lozengy argent and gules ; Parly. Roll. (F.) YMBERT PUGEIS bore the reverse in the Howard Roll.

Poinings and **Pointz** *v.* **Poynings** and **Poyntz.**

Pole *v.* **de la Pole,** and **Pull.**

Pole, Michael de la, baron 1366—bore, or, a lyon rampant gules ; Nobility Roll—borne also by Sir JOHN at the first Dunstable tournament 1308 ; ascribed to WILLIAM in Jenyns' Ordinary ; borne also by JOHN MUSCEGROS and GRIFFITH OWEN, le fitz. Sir LEWIS, of Cheshire, differenced with a baston sable ; Parliamentary Roll.

Henry de Pinkenoi

willt Playb

Jabe de la Planro

Alan Plokenet mᵉ Alayn de Plokenott

Kobert Pogeyb

John de la Pole

wal' d' la Pulle

John Polhill

w Porter

vis de Pozo

Lucas Pultimore

John Potonhold

Sir Polwhele

Ouuel Pouuel

John Popham

michael Poynings

Robt Pourtel.   *Porcer*   *Porchester*   *Joan d' Pordone*

*Poole, Sir Thomas of—(E. IV. Roll) bore, azure, florettée and a lyon rampant argent, *quarterly with,* argent, a chevron sable between three bucks' heads cabossed gules—*with crest ;* Ballard Roll.

*[Pole, Sir John de la—(E. III.) bore, argent, a chevron between three crescents gules.—Shirley.] F.

‡Pole, Walter de la—(H. III. Roll) bore, gules, a saltire argent, within a bordure sable bezantée. (F.) Dering Roll. POYLE in Howard Roll and PULLE in Arden and St. George Rolls.

Poley, Rauff—(R. II. Roll) bore, argent, on a bend gules, three crosses patée or ; Surrey Roll.

Poleyn (——) a Knight—(H. VI. Roll) bore, or, a fess gules and a bendlet sable ; Arundel Roll.

*[Polhill, John—(Hen. VI. Roll) bore, or, on a bend gules three crosses crosslet of the first.—Shirley.] F.

Poltimore, Richard de—(H. III. Roll) bore, or, a lyon rampant vert ; Arden Roll.

‡Poltimore, Lucas de and Richard—(H. III. Roll) bore, sable, a lyon rampant or. (F.) Dering and Howard Rolls.

Poltimore, Sir Richard de, of Devon—(E. II. Roll) bore, or, a cross engrailed gules, a baston gobony argent and azure ; Parliamentary Roll.

*[Polwhele, Richard de (E. III.)—bore, sable, a saltire engrailed ermine.—Shirley.] F.

Pomerey, Sir Henry and John Pomeray—(E. III. Roll) bore, or, a lyon rampant gules, a bordure engrailed sable ; Ashmole and Surrey Rolls.

(Pomfret ?) —— (R. II. Roll)—bore, argent, three cocks 2 and 1 sable ; Surrey Roll.

Ponchardon *v.* **Punchardon.**

Popham, John de—(E. I. Roll) bore, argent, a fess gules, in chief two bucks' heads cabossed or ; Jenyns' Roll.

Popham, Raffe de—(E. I. Roll) bore, argent, on a chief gules three bucks' heads cabossed or ; Jenyns' Roll. POPHAM, a Suffolk Knight, carried a besant between the two bucks' heads ; Arundel Roll.

Popham, John—bore, at the siege of Rouen 1418, gules, besantée (6, 4) and a chevron argent, *quarterly with,* argent, on a chief gules a besant between two stags' heads cabossed or. F.

Porcel, Robert—(H. III. Roll) bore, ermine three torteaux. (F.) Arden and St. George Roll.

Porcher —— (H. III. Roll) bore, argent, a cinquefoyle pierced gules. (F.) St. George Roll.

Porchester, Sr. —— knighted at the capitulation of Calais 1348—bore, or, eight barrulets sable. F.

Pordone, John de—(H. III. Roll) bore, gules, a fess or, between three mullets (6) argent. (F.) St. George Roll.

Porter, Sir W.—(H. VI. Roll) bore, sable, three bells 2 and 1 argent ; Atkinson Roll. F.

Potenhall, Sir John—bore, at the siege of Calais 1345-8, or, on a fess azure three decrescents of the field. F.

Potenale, Sir John—(E III. Roll) bore, argent, on a chevron azure three cinquefoyles pierced or ; Ashmole Roll.

Pountney, John de—(E. III. Roll) bore, azure, a fess dancettée gules, in chief three leopards' faces sable—on the fess in trick ; Jenyns' Ordinary.

Pouuel, Sir Ouuel—bore, at the battle of Boroughbridge 1322, paly (6) or and azure on a bend gules, three martlets argent. F.

Pouslyne, Sir William (PONSCYN, POUSCYN or PUSLINCH), of Herefordshire—(E. II. Roll) bore, quarterly argent and azure, a lyon rampant gules ; Parliamentary Roll.

Powell, Sire Walter de, of Oxon—(E. II. Roll) bore, undée (6) or and sable a bend argent ; Parly. Roll—tricked nebulée.

Power (——) a Suffolk Knight—(H. VI. Roll) bore, gules, on a chief argent three mullets pierced sable ; Arundel Roll.

Power (PORE), Richard de—(H. III. Roll) bore, gules, a fess and in chief two mullets argent. (F.) Arden and St. George Rolls.

Powis, Le Sr. de—(H. VI. Roll) bore, or, a lyon rampant gules ; Nobility Roll. See Monumental Brass, JOICE, Lady TIPTOFT.

Powtrell, Sir Robert, of Derbyshire, and **Roger** (E. II. Roll) bore, or, on a bend azure three fleurs-de-lys argent ; Parly. Roll and Jenyns' Ordinary.

Poyerd ——, (E. III. Roll) bore, azure a bend or between two indents (cotises indented) argent—and another with a label (3) gules ; Ashmole Roll.

Poynings, Sir Michael, of Surrey—bore, at the first Dunstable tournament 1308, barry (6) or and vert, a bend gules. On the same occasion his brother Sir THOMAS bore on the bend three mullets argent (Parly. Roll) ; at the second tournament 1334, another THOMAS bore the undifferenced coat, when his brother MICHAEL differenced with a bordure engréle (indented) ermine.

Poynings, Sir Michael, baron 1339—bore, at the siege of Calais 1345-8, the paternal coat barry (6) or and vert a bend gules (F.) Sir JOHN (or CHRISTOPHER) bore the same, he and his brother Sir THOMAS were knighted at the capitulation (of Calais), when the latter differenced with a baston gobony argent and gules.

Le Sire de Poynings

Robt. Pulsford

Sir F Anleston

Oliver Ponchardon

Rob Pundolardo

Howgs de Poyns

John Prideaux

witt de Quontin

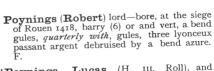

witt de Preston

Robt de Quincy

Poynings (Robert) lord—bore, at the siege of Rouen 1418, barry (6) or and vert, a bend gules, *quarterly with*, gules, three lyonceux passant argent debruised by a bend azure. F.

†**Poynings, Lucas** (H. III. Roll), and **Thomas** (E. III. Roll) bore, barry (6) or and vert, a bend gules ; Dering Roll and Jenyns' Roll, probably erroneous when tricked, or three bars vert, a baston (bend) gules in Howard Roll for LUCAS, and in Jenyns' Roll for JOHN.

Poyntz, Hugh, of Cory Malet, baron 1295—bore, barry (8) gules and or ; Nobility Roll ; the reverse is ascribed to him as having been borne at the battle of Falkirk 1298, and at the siege of Carlaverock in 1300 (F.) ; signed the Barons' letter to the Pope 1301 ; these being the arms of FITZALAN were disputed. Notwithstanding this Sir NICHOL (as banneret) appears to have borne them at the first Dunstable tournament 1308 ; (Arundel and Parly. Rolls), indeed, his seal with these arms and a label (5) is said to have been attached by his father to the Barons' letter to the Pope of 1301, see pp. xx, xxiv.

***Predias, John**—(R. II. Roll) bore, argent, a chevron sable, a label (3) gules (F.) ; Surrey Roll.

Prendergast, Robert—(E. II. Roll) bore, gules, a bend cotised argent ; Jenyns' Ordinary.

Presmarsh, Sir Reynold de—(E. I. Roll) bore, bendy (8) or and azure, on a chief of the second two palets between as many esquires based of the first, over all an inescocheon argent ; Holland Roll. (F.) See MORTIMER which is barry.

Preston, Piers de (ioust), JUXTA WENDESLAWE (E. III. Roll), and **Sir William de** (E. I. Roll) bore, gules, crusily and a bend or (F.) ; Grimaldi and Holland Rolls ; crusily fitchée in Howard Roll, and perhaps crusily potent in Dering Roll for a WILLIAM. ‡

Preston (——) a Suffolk Knight—(H. VI. Roll) bore, ermine, on a chief sable, three crescents or ; Arundel Roll.

Preston, Thomas de—(R. II. Roll) bore, gules five fusils in chief and three in base argent ; Surrey Roll.

Prestwolde, Hugh de—(E. III. Roll) bore, sable, a chevron or fretty gules, between three garbs argent ; Jenyns' Ordinary.

Preyers, Sir Henry, of Rutland—(E. II. Roll) bore, gules, three escallops argent ; Parly. Roll. F.

Preyers, Sir John, of Essex—(E. II. Roll) bore, gules, a fess double cotised argent ; Parly. Roll.

Preyers, Sir Thomas de, of Essex—(E. II. Roll) bore, vert, a bend argent cotised or ; Parly. Roll.

Preys, Sir Philip de—(E. III. Roll) bore, paly (6) or and azure, on a chief gules a lyon passant argent ; Ashmole Roll. F.

Prideaux, John v. **Predias.**

Prowze, Sir William le (PREUZ), of Cornwall—(E. II. Roll) bore, sable, crusily and three lyonceux rampant argent ; Parly. Roll.

Pudsay, John—(E. III. Roll) bore, vert, a chevron between three spur-rowells or ; Jenyns' Ordinary and Ballard Roll.

Pugeis v. **Pogeys.**

Puleston, Sir Richard, of Cheshire—(E. II. Roll) bore, sable three mullets argent ; Parly. Roll. (F.) JOHN DE PYVELSDON took up the cross in the last Crusade 1270 ; or PITLYSDEN.

Pulsford, Sir Robert, of co. Lancs.—bore, at the first Dunstable tournament 1308, sable, a cross flory or ; patonce in Parly. and Jenyns' Rolls (F.), said to be same as ROBERT SWINNERTON who bore the cross florettée, which see.

Pull, William de—(H. III. Roll) bore, or, three eagles displayed azure ; Howard Roll.

†**Punchardon, Oliver de**—(H. III. Roll) bore, sable platey 4, 3, 2, 1 ; Arden and St. George Rolls (F.) ; 3, 2, 1 in Jenyns' Ordinary.

Pundelarde, Robert—(H. III. Roll) bore, per pale argent and vert, a lyon rampant gules ; Howard Roll. F.

†**Queney, Robert** (or QUINCY)—(H. III. Roll) bore, gules, a cinquefoyle (ermine in Glover Roll) argent, in Howard and Camden Roll ; pierced argent in Dering Roll. F.

Queney, Walder de (or QUERYNE)—(H. III. Roll) bore, or, a cinquefoyle gules ; Glover Roll.

Quentin, Sir William—(E. III. Roll) bore, gules, on a chevron argent three martlets sable ; Ashmole Roll.

Quilly, Sir Roger—(E. III. Roll) bore, argent, a chevron between three mullets sable ; Ashmole Roll—pierced in Harl. Roll.

Quincy, Roger de, Earl of Winchester—(H. VI. Roll) bore, gules, seven mascles conjoined 3, 3, 1 or ; Nobility Roll—3, 2, 1 in Ashmole (E. III.) Roll.

Quisance, William de—bore, at the second Dunstable tournament 1334, sable a bend engrailed argent, a label gules. F.

Quitricke, John (or WHITRICK)—(E. I. Roll) bore, argent a fret and a quarter gules—fretty in trick ; Jenyns' Roll.

Qukin, Roland (or QUENKIN)—(E. I. Roll) bore, bendy (6) gules and ermine. (F.) Segar Roll.

Quixley, John de—(E. III. Roll) bore, gules, three greyhounds courant in pale argent, collared gobony or and sable. (F.) ADAM differenced this with an escallop sable on the shoulder of each hound—the collars, checquy or and sable.

witt de Quisance

Pet de Preys

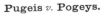

Roland Qunkin

John de Quixley

Bishop Odo, holding a club, rallies the young soldiers. After the Bayeux Tapestry.

— R —

John Radcliffe

Henri d. Roleie.

Sire de Ramorne

John Ratclyffe

†**Rabayn, Ellis de**—(H. III. Roll) bore, argent, a fess between three escallops gules; Glover Roll.

Racel *v.* **Rocel.**

*Radcliffe, Sir John**—(E. III. Roll) bore, argent, two bends engrailed sable, a label (3) gules. (F.) JOHN of Ordsall bore the same, his brother ROBERT of Smithills bore it undifferenced and his son NICHOLAS of Chadderton, differenced with a fess gules; Harl. MS. 1481 fo. 68.

Ragan, John—(E. I. Roll) bore, argent, a chevron between three bucks' heads couped sable; Jenyns' Roll.

‡**Ralee, Henry** (or RALEY) and **Sir John de** —(H. III. Roll) bore, gules, crusily or, a bend vair. (F.) Dering (Ashmole copy), Howard and St. George Rolls—tricked also probably in error, (1) gules, a fess vair, and (2) ermine a bend vair.

Ralee, Sir Simon, of Devon—(E. II. Roll) bore, gules, a bend lozengy (4) argent; Parly. Roll—engrailed in Harl. MS. 4033 fo. 33.

Raley, John—(E. III. Roll) bore, checquy or and gules, a bend undée (4) argent and azure; Jenyns' Ordinary—blasoned azure and argent in COTGRAVE.

Rayle, Sir Thomas de—(E. III. Roll) bore, checquy or and gules, a chief vair; Ashmole Roll.

Rame (——) an Essex Knight—(H. VI. Roll) bore, azure, three rams' heads cabossed argent; Arundel Roll.

Ramerne, Sire de ——, (E. I. Roll) bore, argent, a lyon rampant sable, oppressed by a baston sable. (F.) Camden Roll.

Rameston, Thomas de—(R. II. Roll) bore, argent, a chevron sable, in the cantel a cinquefoyle pierced of the last; Surrey Roll. Ascribed also to Sir THOMAS RAMPSTON, K.G. 1402; K. 400 fo. 25.

Rande, William—(E. III. Roll) bore, gules, three chevronels argent, a bordure engrailed sable; Jenyns' Ordinary.

Randolph, Sir John, of Wilts—(E. II. Roll) bore, azure, on a cross argent five mullets sable; Parly. Roll.

Ratclyffe, Sir John—bore, at the siege of Calais 1345–8, argent, a bend engrailed sable. (F.) Borne also by RADCLIF of the Tower; Ballard Roll; and by Sir JOHN, K.G. H. VI. See also RADCLIFFE.

Ratelysdown —— (E. III. Roll) bore, azure, six escallops 3, 2, 1 or; Ashmole Roll.

Ravenscroft (——), of Cheshire—(F. IV. Roll) bore, argent, a chevron sable between three ravens' heads erased proper—with crest; Ballard Roll.

Ravensholme, Sir John—bore, at the siege of Calais 1345–8 vert, on a fess or a lyon passant gardant gules. (F.) Harl. MS. 3968 fo. 123; a marginal note in the Ashmole MS. ascribes to him—argent, on a fess double battely gules, a lyon passant gardant or, as in Jenyns' Roll and Ordinary.

[**Rawdon, Michael de** (E. III.) —bore, argent a fess between three pheons sable.— Shirley.] F.

Ray, John de—(E. III. Roll) bore, quarterly argent and azure, on a bend gules three fleurs-de-lys or; Jenyns' Ordinary.

Raynes, John (REYNES) and **Sir Thomas** —(R. II. Roll) bore, checquy or and gules, a canton ermine; Ashmole and Surrey Rolls. Another coat with a canton argent in Ashmole Roll.

†**Raynes, Roger de**—(H. III. Roll) bore, azure, fretty sable and a bend vaire potent counter potent or and gules; Howard Roll.

Raynsford, Henry — (E. I. Roll) bore, argent, a cross p'my and a bordure sable; Jenyns' Roll—another coat argent, a cross sable—with crest; Ballard Roll. For parmy see also CONSTABLE, and DACRE.

Rede (——) a Suffolk Knight—(H. VI. Roll) bore, azure, three pheasants 2 and 1 or; Arundel Roll.

Redisham, Sir Edmond, of Norfolk— (E. II. Roll) bore, argent, florettée gules; Parliamentary Roll, additional.

Redesham, Walter de—(E. I. Roll) bore, checquy argent and gules. (F.) Camden Roll.

Redford, Henry de (RYDFORD)—(R. II. Roll) bore, argent, fretty and a chief sable; Surrey Roll.

Redham, William de—(H. III. Roll) bore, gules, an inescocheon within an orle of martlets argent. (F.) Arden and St. George Rolls.

John Ravon Ssolmo

miss Rawdon

Walter de Redesham

Will d. Redham

Richard Redman

Howel ap Res

Baldwin de Godders.

Joan de Boginghall.

Adam de Boroughby

Joan d Reveshale

Redman, Richard—bore, at the siege of Rouen 1418, gules, three lozenge-cushions ermine tasselled or. (F.) Surrey Roll and Jenyns' Ordinary. In the Parliamentary Roll (E. II.) they are ascribed to Sir MATHEW of Cumberland, and tricked as three square cushions or ; Parly. Roll, in Harl. MS. 4033 ; lozenge ermine, &c., in Harl. 6137. See also Glover Roll (H. III.).

Redman, Mathew—(R. II. Roll) bore, gules, a chevron argent between three lozenge-cushions ermine tasselled or ; Surrey Roll.

Rednesse, William de—(E. III. Roll) bore, sable, a chevron between three leopards' faces argent ; Cotgrave Roll.

Redvers, Earl of Devon and lord of the Isle of Wight. See DEVON and ISLE.

Redvers, Baldwin de—(E. II. Roll) bore, or, a lyon rampant azure ; Parly., Segar and St. George Rolls (F.) ; the LORD PERCY carries the same.

Rees, Howel ap—(H. III. Roll) bore, gules, a chevron between three spur-rowells argent (F.) ; St. George Roll.

Reigate v. **Rygate.**

Rekell or REKETT ——— a Kentish Knight— (H. VI. Roll) bore, gules two barrulets sable between three annulets argent ; Arundel Roll.

‡**Renci, Sire de** (RENTI)—(H. III. Roll) bore, gules, three broad axes erect 2, 1, edges to the dexter argent ; or in Ashmole MS. ; Dering Roll.

Repinghall, John de—(E. I. Roll) bore, sable two bars argent, in chief three plates (F.) ; Camden Roll.

Repps, Sir John, of Norfolk—(E. II. Roll) bore, ermine, three chevronels sable ; Parly. (*additional*) and Ashmole Rolls and Jenyns' Ordinary.

Reresby, Sire Adam de—bore, at the battle of Boroughbridge 1322, gules, on a bend argent three crosses (patée) sable (F.) ; Jenyns' Roll and Ordinary ; usually tricked as the modern patonce. THOMAS and WILLIAM both LE FITZ differenced with a label (3) or ; Jenyns' Roll and Ordinary.

Reresby, Thomas—(R. II. Roll) bore, gules, on a bend argent three mullets pierced sable ; Surrey Roll.

Resonne, Sir John de—(E. II. Roll) bore, gules, a lyon rampant or, in the cantel a cross patonce vair—in another trick, a cross patonce vert on the shoulder of the lyon ; Parly. Roll.

Restwold, Richard—(E. I. Roll) bore, per saltire ermine and gules ; Jenyns' Roll.

Retford, John de—(E. III. Roll) bore, quarterly argent and gules a bordure engrailed sable ; Jenyns' Ordinary.

Retford, Thomas de, of Ashby—(E. I. Roll) bore, ermine, on a chevron sable three escallops argent ; Jenyns' Roll.

Retour, Richard—(E. I. Roll) bore, argent, three tree stumps (racynes) eradicated sable ; Jenyns' Roll.

Revel, Sir John—(E. III. Roll) bore, ermine, a chevron gules, a bordure engrailed sable ; Sir WILLIAM differenced with a mullet or on the chevron ; Ashmole Roll.

Rever, John, v. **Rider.**

Reveshall, John de—(H. III. Roll) bore, or, a cross gules, a label (5) of France (F.) ; Arden and St. George Rolls.

Reydon, Sir Robert de, of Suffolk—(E. II. Roll) bore, checquy argent and gules, a cross azure ; Parly. Roll ; another REYDON coat, azure, a cross counter-compony argent and gules ; Ashmole Roll.

†**Reymes, Roger de,** v. **Raynes.**

Reynell, John—(E. III. Roll) bore, ermine, a chevronel gules, a chief indented sable ; Jenyns' Ordinary.

Reynham, Edmund de — (R. II. Roll) bore, sable, three mallets 2 and 1 argent ; Surrey Roll.

Reythinge v. **Roynger.**

Ribbesford, Sir Henry, of co. Leic.— (E. II. Roll) bore, ermine, a chief gules fretty or (F.) ; Parly. Roll ; RIBEFORD in Arden and St. George Rolls.

Riboo, Richard, of Newbegging—(E. III. Roll) bore, argent, a chevron gules between three torteaux ; Grimaldi Roll ; RYBO in Jenyns' Ordinary.

Richmond, Roald le, Constable of the Honour of—(H. III. Roll) bore, gules, two gemelles and a chief or ; St. George Roll. SIR THOMAS DE RICHMONDE bore the same at the siege of Carlaverock 1300 (F.) ; Nativity and Parly. Rolls.

Richmond, Earl of, v. **John de Bretagne.**

[**Richmond, Earl of, Peter** of Savoy, maternal uncle to ELEANOR, Consort of Hen. III.—bore, an eagle displayed within a bordure—died at Chillon, in the pays de Vaud 7 or 9 June 1268, buried in the Abbey of Hautecombe in Savoy, see Bookplate.]

Riddell, Sir William (RYDELL), of the North—bore, at the first Dunstable tournament 1308, and at the battle of Boroughbridge 1322, gules, a lyon rampant within a bordure indented argent (F.) ; Parly. Roll and Jenyns' Ordinary.

PETER OF SAVOY, EARL OF RICHMOND.

IN THE COLLEGIATE CHURCH OF AQUABELLA, IN SAVOY, 1268.

From the " Archæologia."

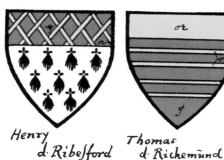

Henry d. Ribesford

Thomas d. Richemund

william Bidoll

Bidley

walt de Ridmore   Joan d·Riuers   Donnsub Riuers   Rochford   Thō de Rochford   Raffe de Rochford

Robsart

Rauf Racel.

Thomas Rocelin

Will Rosselyn

Theobald Rochcourt

Riddell, Sir John (RYDELL), of Beds.—(E. II. Roll) bore, paly (6) argent and gules; Parly. Roll.

Riddell, John (RYDELL)—(E. I. Roll) bore, argent, a fess azure between three garbs gules; Jenyns' Roll.

Rider, John (REVER)—(E. I. Roll) bore, argent, on a bend azure cotised gules three crescents or; Jenyns' Roll.

Ridemore, Sir Walter de (RYDEMOR)—bore, at the first Dunstable tournament 1308, gules, three stirrups argent (F.); also tricked as escallops.

Ridmer, Reynaud de—(E. III. Roll) bore, azure, a chief argent, a bend sable; Grimaldi Roll.

Ridmer, Reynald de—(E. III. Roll) bore, argent, a chief indented azure, a baston sable; Jenyns' Ordinary.

Ridware, Sir Thomas de, of co. Cambridge—(E. II. Roll) bore, azure, an eagle displayed argent; Parly. Roll.

Rigby (——) a Knight—(H. VI. Roll) bore, argent, on a cross patonce sable five mullets or; Arundel Roll.

Rigmayden, Thomas—(E. I. Roll) bore, argent three bucks' heads 2 and 1 cabossed sable; Jenyns' Roll; of Wedacre, in Ballard Roll.

Ripley, Sir (——) Knighted at the capitulation of Calais 1348—bore, or, three lyons rampant azure.

Ripley —— (REPPLEY), an Essex Knight—(H. VI. Roll) bore, ermine, a fess between three toads (tortoise in trick) sable; Arundel Roll.

Ripley, Sir John (RYPEL)—(E. III. Roll) bore, or, two chevrons and a canton gules; Ashmole Roll.

Rivers, Sir Joan de, of Aungre (Onger), banneret, baron 1299—bore, at the battle of Falkirk 1298 and at the siege of Carlaverock 1300, masculy or and gules—generally tricked six (or 7) mascles 3, 2, 1 (F.) but also as lozenges (F.) and as fusils; Arundel and Parliamentary Rolls.

Rivers, Sir Donnet—bore, at the siege of Calais 1345-8, gules, a pale masculy or. (F.) For surname PAYNE ROET in Ashmole MS.; RUETT and RUVETT or RYVETT also occur as suggestions.

Rivers, Sir William de (RYZERE), of Lincolnshire—(E. II. Roll) bore, gules, a bend ermine, a label (3) or; Parliamentary Roll.

Roald, Constable of the Honour of Richmond —(H. III. Roll) bore, gules, two gemelles and a chief or; St. George Roll.

Robsart (——), knighted at the capitulation of Calais 1348, bore, vert, a lyon rampant or ("alii the reverse"); borne also by Sir JOHN, K.G., and Sir GEORGE, K.G. temp. H. V. F.

Rocel, Raf—(H. III. Roll) bore, argent, two bars fusily gules azure—in St. George Roll—sometimes dancettée. (F.) Arden Roll.

Roceline, Sir Peers (ROSSELYN), of Norfolk, and Thomas—(E. II. Roll) bore, gules, three buckles' heads 2 and 1 argent, tongues to the dexter; St. George and Parly. Rolls. (F.) Another THOMAS, in Jenyns' Ordinary, the tongues to the sinister.

Roceline, Sir William (ROSSELYN), of Norfolk—(E. II. Roll) bore, azure, three buckles or, tongues to the dexter in Harl. MS. 6137 fo. 16ᵇ, and to the base in Harl. MS. 4033; Parly. Roll. F.

Roche, Sir J.—(H. VI. Roll) bore, gules, three roach argent; Atkinson Roll. See also DE LA ROCHE.

Rochecourt, Sir Theobald—bore, at the siege of Calais 1345-8, sable, five fleurs-de-lys 2, 1, 2 in saltire or. F.

‡Rocheford, Gyles de—(H. III. Roll) bore, argent, burulée (9, 12) azure, a chief dancettée (4 indents) gules. (F.) Dering and Howard Rolls.

Rocheford, Guy le, le Poytevin—(H. III. Roll) bore, quarterly argent and gules; Glover Roll.

Rochford, Guy de—(H. III. Roll) bore, quarterly or and gules; Norfolk Roll.

Rochford, Sir Robert de—bore, at the first Dunstable tournament 1308, quarterly or and gules, a bordure indented sable (F.) on which occasion Sir ROGER bore the bordure indented argent.

Rochford, Sir Thomas de, knighted at the capitulation of Calais 1348—bore, quarterly or and gules a label (5) azure (F.); ascribed also to GUY in Howard Roll—and a label (3) azure to RAFFE in Jenyns' Ordinary.

Rocheford, Sir John and Sir Raffe, of Essex—(E. II. Roll) bore, quarterly or and gules, a bordure sable besantée; Ashmole, Atkinson and Surrey Rolls—another RAFFE, differenced with an annulet argent, on the gules quarters; Surrey Roll. Sir JOHN, of Essex, differenced with a martlet sable; Parliamentary Roll.

Rocheford, Raffe—bore, at the siege of Rouen 1418, gules, an eagle displayed or, *quarterly with*, quarterly or and gules, a bordure sable bezantée. (F.)

Rockley, Richard de (ROKELEY)—bore, at the siege of Carlaverock 1300, lozengy ermine and gules. (F.) JAMES of Wokingdon and Sir RICHARD of Suffolk bore the same; Jenyns' Ordinary and Parliamentary Roll; sometimes blasoned masculy, Glover Roll and Jenyns' Ordinary, and the tinctures reversed, as in Parly. and Ashmole Rolls.

†Rockley, Richard de la—(H. III. Roll) bore, lozengy argent and gules, a bend azure. (F.) St. George Roll.

Rockley, Robert de—(R. II. Roll) bore, lozengy argent and gules, a fess sable; Surrey Roll.

Rockley —— (E. IV. Roll) bore, argent, a fess sable between seven lozenges 3, 3, 1 gules; with crest; Ballard Roll.

‡Rocksley, John and Sir Richard, of Kent (H. III. and E. II. Rolls) bore, azure, a fess gules between six lyonceux rampant argent. (F.) Dering, Howard, and Parly. Rolls.

Rocliffe, John de and Sir Robert—(E. III. Roll) bore, argent, a chevron between three lyons' heads erased 2 and 1 gules; Ashmole Roll and Jenyns' Ordinary. Sir RICHARD differenced with a chess-rook or; Ashmole Roll.

Rocliffe, Robert—(E. III. Roll) bore, argent, a chevron and in chief two lyons' heads erased gules, an annulet or for difference; Jenyns' Ordinary.

Rodes, Sir Gerard de, Chevr. de France—(E. I. Roll) bore, gules; Nativity Roll.

†Rodes, William de—(H. III. Roll) bore, azure, a lyon rampant or; Dering Roll—debruised by a baston gules. (F.) Camden Roll.

Rodney, John de—(R. II. Roll) bore, or, three eagles displayed 2 and 1 gules; Surrey Roll. Sir WALTER bore the eagles purpure; Ashmole Roll.

Robt de Rochford

Richard Rokell

Ric. d la rokele

Jon de Rokelle

Will de Rokel

Roger Bozant   Thomas de Bovnye   Will. Rookwood   will de Ros   Will d. Ros

Robt Rokeby

Roger de Rome

Roger de Romenal

Thomas Ross de bousobye

Jogn le Ros

Edwin Roper

Roet, Payne v. **Sir Donnet Rivers.**

Rohaut, Sir Roger—(E. II. Roll) bore, or, two chevronels gules on a canton of the last a mullet pierced argent; Ashmole Roll. F.

*****Rokeby, Sir Robert de,** knighted at the siege of Calais 1348—bore, argent, a chevron sable between three rooks proper (F.); ascribed also to ALEXANDER in Grimaldi Roll, and to THOMAS in Ashmole and Surrey Rolls.

Rolleston, John and **William de**—(E. III. Roll) bore, sable, a saltire argent; Surrey Roll and Jenyns' Ordinary. ELYAS took up the cross 1270.

‡**Rome, Roger de** — (H. III. Roll) bore, argent, a fess sable and in chief a lyon passant gules. (F.) Dering Roll.

‡**Romenal, Roger de**—(H. III. Roll) bore, or, two chevronels gules, on a quarter of the second three cats' (or leopards') faces 2 and 1 or (F.); Dering Roll. Another, on the canton gules, a lyon passant of the field; Howard Roll.

Romesbury, John de (or RONNEBURY)—(E. III. Roll) bore, argent, a saltire gules, between four pyes (birds) sable; Jenyns' Ordinary.

Romsey, Walter—(E. I. Roll) bore, argent, a fess gules, a label (5) azure; Jenyns' Roll.

Ronye, Sir Thomas le—bore, at the first Dunstable tournament 1308, ermine, on a chief indented gules two escallops argent. F.

Rookwood, Sir William, of Suffolk—(H. VI. Roll) bore, argent, six chess-rooks 3, 2, 1 sable; Arundel Roll. F.

Ros, Sire George de—bore, at the battle of Boroughbridge 1322, argent, three water-bougets sable—borne also by Sir JOHN, of Notts, in Parliamentary Roll.

Roos, Robert and **Sir William,** banneret (both), of Ingmanthorpe—(E. III. Roll) bore, azure, three water-bougets or; Norfolk Roll and Jenyns' Ordinary. Sir WILLIAM of Youlton, also Yorks., bore the water-bougets argent, and a label (3) or; Parliamentary Roll.

Roos, John le—(R. II. Roll) bore, ermine, three water-bougets gules; Surrey Roll.

Roos, William, of Hamlake, banneret, baron 1285—bore, at the battle of Falkirk 1298, and at the siege of Carlaverock 1300, gules, three water - bougets argent. (F.) Sealed the Barons' letter to the Pope 1301, see pp. xvii, xxiv. Ascribed also to (‡) ROBERT in Dering, Norfolk and other Rolls. JOHN, 8th Lord, also bore the same at the siege of Rouen 1418. ROBERT fil WILLIAM bore a label (3) azure; Glover Roll—another WILLIAM differenced, with a crescent sable on the first water-bouget; Surrey Roll. See Tiles, Neath Abbey, p. vii.

Roos and Badlesmere, Le Sr. de—(R. II. Roll) bore, gules, three water-bougets argent, *quarterly with,* BADLESMERE—argent, a fess double cotised gules; Surrey Roll. Borne also by WILLIAM, Lord Roos, K.G. 1414.

Roos, James, Sir Robert, of Gedney, Notts, and **William**—(E. III. Rolls) bore, gules, three water-bougets ermine. (F.) Surrey, Parly. and St. George Rolls. THOMAS KNOVILE bore the same. ROBERT differenced with a label azure; St. George Roll.

Roos, John, of Youlton, and **Sir Richard**—(E. III. Roll) bore, gules, three water-bougets or; Ashmole Roll and Jenyns' Ordinary.

Roos, Robert, of Werke, and **Thomas,** of Kendale—(H. III. Roll) bore, or, three water-bougets sable; Glover Roll and Jenyns' Ordinary. JOHN, differenced with a crescent sable; Jenyns' Ordinary.

Ros, Sire Thomas de (of Yorkshire) — bore, at the battle of Boroughbridge 1322, gules, a fess vair between four water-bougets or—three (F.) only in Ashmole MS.—the latter borne also by Sir THOMAS and THOMAS DE BEUSEBY or BOUSEBYE; Nativity Roll and Jenyns' Ordinary.

Roos, Sir John le (le filz)—bore, at the first Dunstable tournament 1308, gules, three lyonceux rampant argent, a label (3) azure *sic.* (F.)

*[**Roper, Edwin**—(E. I.) bore, per fess azure and or, a pale counterchanged, three bucks' heads erased of the second.—Shirley.] F.

Rosehall, John de — (E. III. Roll) bore, azure, a fess between six martlets or (argent in trick); Jenyns' Ordinary.

Rosells, Henry—(E. III. Roll) bore, gules six roses 3, 2, 1 argent; Jenyns' Ordinary. JOHN (H. III. Roll) bore, argent, ten roses gules, pierced or. (F.) St. George Roll.

Rotherfield, Adam de—(R. II. Roll) bore, gules, three fleurs-de-lys ermine; Surrey Roll.

Roucliffe v. **Rocliffe.**

Rouge-Mayne, Charles de la, founder of the Abbey of Lakee in Ireland. v. **MacMoylin.**

Rous, Geoffrey, and **Sir John,** of co. Gloucester—(E. II. Roll) bore, per pale azure and gules three lyonceux rampant 2 and 1 ermine; Parly. Roll and Jenyns' Ordinary.

Rous, Giles le—(H. III. Roll) bore, per pale gules and azure three lyonceux rampant 2 and 1 argent; St. George Roll.

Rous, Roger le—(H. III. Roll) bore, per pale gules and azure a lyon rampant tail fourchée argent (F.); Arden and St. George Rolls.

MONUMENTAL EFFIGY OF ROBERT ROOS, BROUGHT TO THE TEMPLE CHURCH FROM YORK, 1682.
From Richardson.

Joan d Roseles   Rog le Rous

Peter Rous   Henry Russell

Rous, Sir Roger, of co. Glouc.—(E. II. Roll) bore, per pale or and azure three lyonceux rampant gules; Parly. Roll.

Rous, John de (or ROOS)—(E. III. Roll) bore, checquy gules and argent—tricked argent and gules; Jenyns' Ordinary.

Rous, John (or ROOS), of Tyde—(E. III. Roll) bore, barry (8) gules and argent, a chief of the last over all a bend engrailed azure; Jenyns' Ordinary.

Rous, Sir John de (ROOS), of co. Linc.—(E. II. Roll) bore, argent, three bars gules, a bend engrailed sable; Parly. Roll.

Rous, Sir Richard le, of Beds.—(E. II. Roll) bore, quarterly argent and sable, a baston counterchanged—sable in trick; Parly. Roll and Jenyns' Ordinary.

Rous, Sir Thomas le—(E. II. Roll) bore, ermine, on a chief dancettée gules three (sometimes two) escallops argent; Parly. Roll.

[**Rouse, Peter**—(E. III.) bore, sable, a fess dancettée or between three crescents argent.—Shirley.] F.

Routh, John de—(R. II. Roll) bore, argent, on a bend cotised sable three mullets of the field; Surrey Roll.

Routhe, John de—(E. III. Roll) bore, barry (6) or and azure on a bend argent three rooks proper; Jenyns' Ordinary.

Routhe, John de—(E. III. Roll) bore, barry (6) azure and or a bend gobony argent and of the first; Jenyns' Ordinary, Harl. MS. 6589 fo. 24.

Routhe, Piers de—(E. III. Roll) bore, argent, a chevron sable between three wolves' heads erased gules; Grimaldi Roll—lyons' heads instead of wolves' heads are ascribed to THOMAS in Jenyns' Ordinary.

Rowthings, ———(E. III. Roll) bore, argent, four palets gules; Ashmole Roll.

Roynge(r), Sir Rafe de, of Norfolk—(E. II. Roll) bore, argent, three bars and eight martlets in orle gules; Parly. Roll.

Rue, Amande de—(E. III. Roll) bore, argent, on a bend cotised sable three mullets of the field; Jenyns' Ordinary.

[**Rushall, Richard de**—bore, argent, a lyon rampant within a bordure engrailed sable, adopted by HARPUR.—Shirley.]

**Russell —— ** an Essex? knight—(H. VI. Roll) bore, gules, three palets argent, a chief azure; Arundel Roll.

Russell, Sir Geffray (ROSSELL), of Northants or Rutland—(E. II. Roll) bore, argent, a chevron azure between three roses gules; Parly. Roll (crosses crosslet fitchée instead of roses for THOMAS). Another THOMAS, bore it with the field or; Jenyns' Roll and Ordinary.

Russell, Hugh and **Thomas**—(E. II. Roll) bore, or, a chevron azure between three roses gules a label (3) argent; Jenyns' Roll and Ordinary.

Russell, —— (E. III. Roll) bore, or, a fess between six martlets sable; Ashmole Roll.

Russell, Sir John—(E. II. Roll) bore, or, on a cross sable five martlets argent; nullets in Harl. MS. 6137 fo. 5ᵇ.

Russell, Maurice and **Raufe**—(H. III. Roll) bore, argent, on a chief gules three besants; Howard and Jenyns' Rolls.

*[**Russell, Henry,** 1455—bore, argent, a lyon rampant gules, on a chief sable three escallops of the first.—Shirley.] F.

Russell, Robert—(R. II. Roll) bore, gules, on a bend sable, fimbriated or, two mullets of the last pierced of the field alternated with two swans argent; Surrey Roll.

Russival, Sire Thomas—bore, at the battle of Boroughbridge 1322; sable, a fess between six martlets 3 and 3 or.

Rutland, Earl of— ED. PLANTAGENET, K.G. 1390-1402—bore, France and England quarterly, a label (5) per pale argent (charged with nine torteaux) and gules, charged with three castles or; Surrey Roll; a label (3) per pale argent and gules, on the gules, six castles or, and on the silver, as many lyonceux rampant gules; K. 399 fo. 11.

Ryba, Richard—(E. III. Roll) bore, argent, a chevron gules between three torteaux; Grimaldi Roll and Jenyns' Ordinary.

Rydergens, Sir John, FRANCOYS—bore, at the battle of Boroughbridge 1322, azure, a bend argent, an inescocheon or charged with a bend engrailed sable; Ashmole MS. See LYDEVUSERS, another suggestion for this rather doubtful name is LYDERGAM.

Rye, Sir William de—bore, at the first Dunstable tournament 1308, gules, a bend ermine, a label (3) or (F.); azure in Nativity Roll.

Rygate, John, of Howke—(H. III. Roll) bore, argent a bend lozengy azure (bend engrailed in Harl. MS. 6589); Jenyns' Ordinary.

Rythre, Sir William de, banneret, baron 1299—bore, at the battle of Falkirk 1298, and also at the siege of Carlaverock 1300, azure, three crescents or (F.); Parly. Roll, &c. See Monumental Effigy. WILLIAM differenced with a label (5) gules. (F.) Arden and St. George Rolls.

Ryther, John de—(E. I. Roll) bore, argent, on a bend azure three crescents or (F.); Jenyns' Roll and Ordinary. See also WITHER or WYTHER.

SIR WILLIAM DE RYTHER.
IN RYTHER CHURCH, YORKS, 1308.
After Hollis.

Thomas Russival   witt de Ryder   william de Ry   witt d Rie   John de Ritgor

Here is Duke William. After the Bayeux Tapestry.

— S —

Andrew do Sabouile.

Amory de Sointe Amand.

Oliver do Sointe Amand.

Gilebt d'Sant Aubin.

Sacheverell —— (E. III. Roll) bore, argent, on a saltire azure five water-bougets or ; Jenyns' Ordinary.

Sackville, (Sir) Andrew (of Suffolk)—bore, at the first Dunstable tournament 1308, quarterly or and gules, a bend vair (F.) ; borne also by another (‡) ANDREW or ADAM in Dering Roll, by GEOFFREY of Sussex, and by JOHN, and THOMAS in Surrey Roll and Jenyns' Roll and Ordinary. An Essex knight bore the bend argent ; Arundel Roll H. VI.

Sackville, Bartholomew and **Thomas** —(H. III. Roll) bore, ermine, three chevronels gules ; Glover and Surrey Rolls.

St. Amand, Almaric, of Wodehay, banneret, baron 1299, sealed the Barons' letter to the Pope 1301, pp. xviii, xxiv. He bore, at the siege of Carlaverock 1300, or, fretty sable, on a chief of the last three bezants. (F.) See Monumental Brass ; the field argent in Nobility Roll. Sir WILLIAM bore the same in Jenyns' Ordinary, and the Lord St. AMAND is said to have borne them at the siege of Rouen in 1418, but the barony appears to have been in abeyance 1402-49. Curiously blasoned as, or a saltire and chevron interlaced—for fretty—but in Jenyns' Ordinary as, or three chevronels interlaced sable, &c., both in all probability erroneously tricked.

St. Amand, Sir Oliver de, of co. Glouc.— bore, at the first Dunstable tournament 1308, or, fretty sable, on a chief of the second two mullets argent pierced vert (F.)—three silver mullets unpierced in Parly. Roll.

St. Andrew, Sir John—(E. I. Roll) bore, gules, six mascles 3, 2, 1 or, a label (3) argent ; Ashmole Roll. ROGER bore 7 mascles and a label azure, in Jenyns' Ordinary ; and Sir ROGER of co. Leicester bore three mascles (sometimes lozenges) and the azure label ; Parly. Roll.

St. Andrew, John—(R. II. Roll) bore, argent, a cross flory engrailed sable, a bordure gules besanty ; Surrey Roll.

‡**St. Aubin, Gilbert de**—(H. III. Roll) bore, or, on a cross sable five plates (F.) ; Dering, St. George, and Surrey Rolls. Another GILBERT with bezants in Arden Roll. See ORKABLIN and WOLTAUBIN.

St. B——, Nicholl de—(H. III. Roll) wrongly blasoned burulée (15) argent and azure ; Howard Roll.

St. Clere, John and **Sir W.**—(E. I. Roll) bore, azure, a sun or ; Jenyns' and Atkinson Rolls.

St. Clere, Sir John de, of Suffolk—(E. II. Roll) bore, or, a lyon rampant, tail fourchée, gules collared argent ; Parly. Roll.

St. Cler, William—(H. III. Roll) bore, argent, a lyon rampant gules, a bordure sable (sometimes bezantée) (F.) ; St. George Roll ; lyon crowned or and bordure crusily or ; Arden Roll.

St. Cler, Thomas—(R. II. Roll) bore, gules, a fess between three leopards' faces or ; Surrey Roll.

St. Clere, William de—(H. III. Roll) bore, gules, a fess between three boars' heads or ; Howard Roll.

St. George, Sir Bawdwyn de, of co. Cambridge—(E. II. Roll) bore, argent, a cross patonce sable ; Parly. Roll.

St. George, Bawdwyn—(E. III. Roll) bore, argent, a chief azure, over all a lyon rampant gules, crowned or ; Surrey Roll and Jenyns' Ordinary—Sir WILLIAM, of co. Cambridge, bore the lyon uncrowned in Parly. Roll.

St. Helen, John de—(H. III. Roll) bore, gules, six lyonceux 3, 2, 1 rampant argent (F.) ; Arden and St. George Rolls.

St. Ive, John de (CEINTEYNO)—(H. III. Roll) bore, or, three lyons passant gules ; Arden Roll.

St. John, Sir John de, of Lageham, banneret, baron 1299—bore, at the battle of Falkirk 1298, and at the siege of Carlaverock 1300, argent, on a chief gules two mullets or, accompanied on the latter occasion by his son JOHN, who differenced with a label (3, 5) azure (F.), spur-rowells in Nicolas and in the Nobility Roll.

‡**St. John, John de**—(E. I. Roll) bore, argent on a chief gules, two mullets pierced or ; Dering Roll ; spur-rowells in trick (F.), not pierced for ROBERT in Grimaldi Roll.

witt Soint Clair

Jon de Sointe Holeno

Johan de Soint John

Johan do Soint John

Edward do Soint John

Roger do Soint John

QUI PANSE

THE HERALDIC ATCHIEVEMENT

OF

SIR WILLIAM ULICK TRISTRAM ST. LAWRENCE, K.P.

4TH EARL OF HOWTH AND 29TH BARON.

‡**St. John, Sir John de**, of Lageham—bore, at the first Dunstable tournament 1308, or, on a chief gules, two mullets pierced vert, a bordure indented sable ; Parly. Roll—engrailed in Harl. 6137 fo. 36. He may be identical with JOHN junior, who differenced with a label at Carlaverock, and with Sir JOHN DE LAGE-HAM, who bore at the battle of Boroughbridge gules, on a chief argent two mullets sable.

St. John, John, brother of HUGH of Basing, *f* JOHN—bore, argent, on a chief gules two mullets or pierced vert, a bendlet gules ; Harl. MS. 1481 fo. 73.

St. John, John de, of Hanak (Halnaker), junior, baron 1300, sealed the Barons' letter to the Pope 1301, pp. xvi, xxiv. He bore, (argent), on a chief (gules) two spur-rowells (or) ; a label (3) azure in Nobility Roll ; borne undifferenced by another JOHN and Sir R., in Norfolk and Harleian Rolls ; by others the mullets are pierced azure, sometimes vert.

St. John, Sir John—(H. III. Roll) bore, argent, on a chief gules two martlets (? in error) or a bordure indented sable ; Ashmole Roll. One of these names took up the cross 1270.

St. John, Sir Edward de—bore, at the battle of Boroughbridge 1322, argent, on a chief indented (dancettée, in the Surrey Roll) gules, two mullets (6) or (F.) ; pierced vert in Surrey Roll.

St. John, Sir Roger de (of Wilts)—bore, at the first Dunstable tournament 1308, ermine, on a chief gules, two spur-rowells or pierced vert. (F.) Parly. Roll, borne by HUE and RICHARD, with mullets unpierced ; St. George and Segar Rolls.

St. John, St. Germyne (EYMIS), of Wilts —(E. II. Roll) bore, argent, crusily sable, on a chief gules two mullets or ; Parly. Roll.

St. John, Edmond, is said to have borne, at the second Dunstable tournament 1334, ermine, a chief gules—the blason is evidently imperfect.

St. John, Giles—(R. II. Roll) bore, gules, two bars argent, a quarter ermine ; Surrey Roll.

St. John, Hugh (SEINGEINE)—(H. III. Roll) bore, gules, three spur-rowells 2 and 1 and a chief dancettée or ; Norfolk Roll.

St. John, Walter de—(H. III. Roll) bore, azure, three buckles or ; Norfolk Roll.

ALMARIC, LORD ST. AMAND.
IN ELSING CHURCH, NORFOLK,
OB. 1382.
From a rubbing from the Hastings Brass.

‡**St. Leger, Sir Raffe**, of Kent, ‡**William** and **Robert**—(H. III. Roll) bore, azure, fretty argent and a chief or (F.) ; Dering Roll. ROBERT bore the same in Parly., Arundel, and Arden Rolls ; erroneously tricked with three chevronels interlaced in Jenyns' Ordinary.

St. Leger, Sir John, of Kent, and **William**—(H. III. Roll) bore, azure fretty argent and a chief gules ; Howard and Parly. Rolls. THOMAS bore the chief argent in Jenyns' Ordinary ; RENOLD and Sir THOMAS of Kent bore the chief or, in the cantel a spur-rowell gules ; Surrey Roll ; but a mullet in Parliamentary Roll.

St. Lo, Sire Rauf de (ST. LOUH)—bore, at the battle of Boroughbridge 1322, gules, a fess between three escallops argent (F.) ; borne also by ROGER and by Sir THOMAS of co. Lincs. ; Jenyns' Ordinary and Parly. Roll.

St. Lo, Hugh—(E. III. Roll) bore, azure, two bars argent, a chief gules ; Cotgrave Roll.

St. Loe, Sir John—(E. I. Roll), bore, gules vij fesses (barrulets) argent, three escallops of the second ; Nativity Roll.

St. Marcyl, William—(H. III. Roll) bore, gules, a fess argent, a label (5) or. (F.) Arden and St. George Rolls. ST. MARTILL in Harl. MS. 4965, the fess sometimes or. DE SAUTE MAREIS in St. George Roll.

St. Martin, John, Sir Renaud, of Wilts, and **William de** — (H. III. Roll) bore, sable, six lyonceux rampant 3, 2, 1 or (F.) ; St. George and Parly. Rolls, Jenyns' Ordinary (gules for WILLIAM in the Arden Roll) ; the reverse of LAYBOURNE of the North and of THOMAS MALLORY.

St. Martin, John de—(H. III. Roll) bore, argent, two bars gules, a label (5) azure. St. George Roll. See also MARTIN and WINTER-HULL.

St. Martin, Thomas de—(H. III. Roll) bore, gules, on a bend argent three escallops vert ; Arden Roll. F.

St. Maur *v.* Seymour.

St. Maure, Sir John de, knighted at the capitulation of Calais 1348, bore, ermine two chevronels gules. (F.) Also in Harl. Roll and 6th Nobility Roll (H. VI.). Sir RAUFFE, of Suffolk (E. II. Roll), differenced, with a label (3, 4 or 5) azure (F.), (the field argent in the Howard Roll), and by NICHOLAS, with a label of France, *i.e.* on each pendant three fleurs-de-lys or (F.) ; Harl. MS. 6137 *ff* 50, 81ᵇ ; Segar and Parly. Rolls—the field argent in Ashmole and St. George Rolls (F.)—the name is often spelt SEIMOR and SEYMOR in these entries.

Huo de Seymort

Herebert d'Sentqumt

Joan d'Semwaleri

mircol Salforde

Priors Saltmarsh

Roger Salosbury

Lorenz de St. mircol

Thomas Saintomer

Joan de St. Owen

Joan d' St. Owen

St. Maur, Sir Lawrence and **Sir Nicholas,** of co. Glouc. (E. II. Roll), and **Sir William**—bore, argent, two chevronels gules a label (3 or 5) vert ; Holland and Parly. Rolls—the label azure for (‡) LAURENCE in Ashmole and Howard Rolls, and for HUE in Segar Roll—a label (4) azure. The name is often spelled SEIMOR and SEYMOR in these entries. LAWRENCE DE ST. MAUR took up the cross 1270.

‡**St. Michell, Lawrence de**—(H. III. Roll) bore, gules, a cross or fretty azure. (F.) Dering Roll, Ashmole MS. and Howard Roll.

St. Nicolas —— a Kentish Knight—(H. VI. Roll) bore, ermine, a chief quarterly or and gules ; Arundel Roll.

St. Omer, Sir John de—(E. I. Roll) bore, azure, on a cross or five mullets gules ; Nativity Roll.

St. Omer, Thomas and **William**—(H. III. Roll) bore, azure, crusily and a fess or. (F.) St. George Roll and Jenyns' Ordinary—(JOHN CLINTON bears the same arms)—a different trick in Ashmole Roll for THOMAS—crosses flory 3, 3.

St. Omer, William—(H. III. Roll) bore, azure, billettée and a fess or ; Glover and Grimaldi Rolls.

St. Omer, William—(E. I. Roll) bore, azure, a fess gules billettée (4, 3) or ; Jenyns' Roll.

St. Owen, Sir Gilbert de, of co. Glouc., and **Thomas**—(E. III. Rolls) bore, gules three chevronels or ; Parly. Roll and Jenyns' Ordinary.

St. Owen, John de—(H. III. Roll) bore, barry (6) gules and or. (F.) St. George Roll. RAF bore, or three bars gules ; Arden Roll.

St. Owen, Sir John de (of Herefordshire) —bore, at the first Dunstable tournament 1308, gules, a cross argent, in the cantel, a shield of CLARE (or rather GRANVILLE) or, three chevronels gules. (F.) Parliamentary Roll.

St. Philibert, Hugh de, of Oxon, baron 1299 — bore, bendy (6) argent and azure ; Nobility and Parly. Rolls. Sir JOHN, of Oxon., bore it also at the battle of Boroughbridge 1322. F. See SYUSIWARDE.

St. Pierre, Sir Uryan de, banneret—bore, at the first Dunstable tournament 1308, argent, a bend sable, a label (3) gules—of five points in H. III. Roll (F.), Arden, Howard, and St. George Rolls ; ascribed to Sir THOMAS in Ashmole Roll.

St. Pole, Count de—(E. I. Roll) bore—the arms of COUNT DE BLOIS (*i.e.* gules, three palets vair, a chief or) with a label (5) azure ; Camden Roll.

St. Quintin, Sir Geffrey and **William** —(E. I. Roll) bore, or, a chevron gules, a chief vair ; Nativity and Surrey Rolls. JOHN and THOMAS differenced with a mullet or ; Jenyns' Ordinary and Surrey Roll.

St. Quintin, Edward—(E. III. Roll) bore, or, two chevrons gules, a chief vair ; Jenyns'. Ordinary.

‡**St. Quintin, Sir Herbert**—(E. II. Roll) bore, or, three chevronels gules, a chief vair (F.), Dering, Howard, and Parly. Rolls ; his brother (1) WILLIAM, of Fishide, bore two chevrons, and (2) ALEXANDER, of Harpham, bore one as aforesaid.

‡**St. Quintin, Herbert**—(E. III. Roll) bore, argent, a lyon rampant rere-regardant purpure, sable in trick ; Jenyns' Ordinary.

St. Valeri, Sir Richard de, of Oxon.— (E. II. Roll) bore, or two lyons passant gules ; Parly. Roll. JOHN bore the lyons gardant (F.) ; Arden and St. George Rolls.

Salesbury, Roger—(E. I. Roll) bore, gules patée (patonce in trick) argent between four leopards' faces or ; Jenyns' Roll. F.

Salford, Sire Neel de—bore, at the battle of Boroughbridge 1322, argent, on a chevron gules three escallops or. F.

Salisbury, Earls of, v. Longespée and Montagu or Montacute.

Salkeld, John—(E. I. Roll) bore, vert, a fret or ; fretty in trick ; Jenyns' Roll.

Salman, Thomas — (R. II. Roll) bore, argent, an eagle displayed sable, on its breast,. a tyger's or leopard's face or ; Surrey Roll.

*****Saltmarsh, Sir Piers de** (of Lincolnshire) —bore, at the battle of Boroughbridge 1322, argent, crusily and three six-foyles gules (F.) ; (roses in Parly. Roll)—ascribed also to THOMAS in Jenyns' Ordinary.

Saltmarsh, Sir Robert—(E. III. Roll) bore, argent, three six-foyles between four crosses crosslet fitchée within a bordure engrailed all gules ; Ashmole Roll.

Salveyn, Sire Anketyn— bore, at the battle of Boroughbridge 1322, argent, a chevron between three boars' heads couped gules (F.) ; Jenyns' Ordinary.

*****Salvayn, Sir Gerard,** of Yorkshire—(E. I. Roll) bore, argent, on a chief sable two spurrowells or, sometimes argent (unpierced mullets in Parly. Roll) ; Ashmole, Surrey, and Jenyns' Rolls and Ordinary.

Salveyn, Sire Gerard de (of co. Durham) —bore, at the battle of Boroughbridge 1322, argent, on a chief azure two mullets (6) or, a bordure indented gules (F.) tricked engrailed —the chief sable in the Arundel Roll.

*****[Salwey, William,** (E. I.)—bore, sable, a saltire engrailed or.—Shirley.] F.

Saly, William—(R. II. Roll) bore, quarterly argent and sable, a bendlet gules ; Surrey Roll.

Samby, Sir John, knighted at the capitulation of Calais 1348, bore, argent fretty azure. F.

Gerard de Salveyn

Willm de Salwey

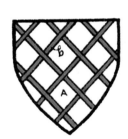

John Samby

John de St. ffulbert

Urian d' St peire

Aubotyn Salpayn

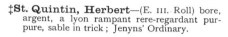

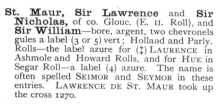

Samforde, Sir Thomas—(E. III. Roll) bore, argent, a chief gules; Ashmole Roll. See SANDFORD.

Samforth ——, a Kentish Kt.—(H. VI. Roll) bore, per chevron sable and ermine, in chief two boars' heads erased argent (perhaps or) (F.) Arundel Roll.

Samson —— (E. III. Roll) bore, paly (6) argent and azure a canton gules; Cotgrave Roll.

Samson, Sir John, of Yorkshire—(E. II. Roll) bore, or, a cross patonce sable; Parly. and Ashmole Rolls.

Samson, William, baron 1299—bore, argent, a cross moline sable (F.); Nobility Roll —probably father of

Sampson, Sir William, Da fʒ (? la fʒ) banneret—bore, at the battle of Falkirk 1298, sable, a fer-de-moulin or—(the reverse in Parly. Roll)—as a banneret, he carried, or a cross moline (recercelée) sable pierced of the field, in the Arundel Roll.

Samsson, William—(H. III. Roll) bore, argent, a fess and in chief two mullets (6) sable (F.); St. George and Arden Rolls.

Samur, Raufe de—(H. III. Roll) bore, azure, on a chief indented or, a crescent gules; Howard Roll.

Sancerlis, Piers de—(H. III. Roll) bore, gules, a fess or between six escallops 3, 3, argent; Arden Roll. Surname doubtful.

Sandacre, —— **de**—(E. III. Roll) bore, argent, a lyon rampant purpure and a baston vert; Cotgrave Roll.

‡**Sandars, Thomas de**—(H. III. Roll) bore, or, on a chief azure, three lyonceux rampant argent (F.), Dering Roll; the colours, or, gules, or, in Howard MS.

Sandeby, Sir Robert, of Lincolnshire, and **Sir Thomas**—(E. III. Roll) bore, argent fretty azure; Parly. and Ashmole Rolls, and Jenyns' Ordinary.

Sandes, Richard de—(E. III. Roll) bore, argent, a fess dancettée (4) between three crosses crosslet fitchée gules; Jenyns' Roll.

Sandford, William de—(E. I. Roll) bore, ermine, on a chief gules two boars' heads couped argent; Jenyns' Roll.

Saunford, Gilbert—(H. III. Roll) bore, undée (6) argent and azure; Arden Roll; argent and gules for NICHOLAS and WILLIAM in Glover and Norfolk Rolls; NICHOLAS fil. WILLIAM differenced with a label gules; Glover Roll.

***Saunford, Sire William de**—bore, at the battle of Boroughbridge 1322, quarterly indented azure and ermine. (F.) Probably per fess indented is intended.

‡**Sandwith, John de**—(H. III. Roll) bore, argent, a chief dancettée azure in Dering Roll; the field or (F.) in Howard and Camden Rolls.

‡**Sandwith, Rauf de**—(H. III. Roll) bore, azure, a chief dancettée (4) or—another trick as if per fess dancettée; Dering Roll; THOMAS bore three lyons on the chief (no tinctures); Howard Roll; he probably took up the cross 1270.

‡**Sansaver, Hugh** and **Sir Raffe,** of Surrey or Sussex—(H. III. Roll) bore, azure crusily and three crescents or (F.); Dering, Howard, and Parly. Rolls; crusily fitchée for HUGH in Jenyns' Ordinary. RALPH LE SAUSER took up the cross 1270.

Sansaver, Robert—(H. III. Roll) bore, gules, a bend between six escallops argent; Howard Roll.

Santon, Sir John de (SAUNTON or SAUMSON), of Lincolnshire—(E. II. Roll) bore, or, a chief azure; Parly. Roll.

Saperton, John de—(E. III. Roll) bore, or, an eagle displayed vert, membered gules, a baston gobony (6) argent and gules; Jenyns' Ordinary.

Sapi, John—(E. I. Roll) bore, gules, three buckles, tongues to the dexter or; Jenyns' Roll and Ordinary.

Sapi, John de—(H. III. Roll) bore, argent, billettée and a lyon rampant gules (F.); Arden Roll.

Sapie, Robert—(E. III. Roll) bore, argent, on a bend vert, cotised gules, three eaglets displayed or; Jenyns Ordinary.

Sarcilun, William—(H. III. Roll) bore, argent, a fess and in chief two mullets (6) sable; Arden Roll. See SAMSSON.

Sarnesfeld, Nicoll and **Walter**—(H. III. Roll) bore, azure, an eagle displayed or (F.); Surrey and St. George Rolls. Sir NICHOLAS, K.G., 1387, bore the eagle crowned argent. K. 399 fo. 18.

Sarren, William de—(H. III. Roll) bore, azure, three crosses or; Glover Roll.

Sassenau, Sir Otes de (CASANOVA)—bore, at the battle of Falkirk 1298, " d'or ou lez pies de sable."

Saunzaver, Ralph, baron 1294. See SANSAVER.

Savage, (Sir) Ernaud—bore, at the second Dunstable tournament 1334, argent, six lyonceux sable (F.); Ashmole and Surrey Rolls; ascribed also to Sir ROGER of Kent in the Parly. Roll, and the reverse to LAWRENCE in Jenyns' Ordinary.

Savage, Sir John—(E. IV. Roll) bore, argent, a pale lozengy sable; with crest; Ballard Roll.

Savage, Sir John, of Kent—bore, at the first Dunstable tournament 1308, ermine, on a chief azure, three lyonceux rampant argent (F.); ascribed also to (‡)RAUF in the Dering Roll, and with the lyons or in the Howard Roll.

Savage, Sir Piers de—(E. I. Roll) bore, gules, a cross moline argent; a cross argent in Glover Roll.

Savage, Robert de—(H. III. Roll) bore, barry or and gules; Glover Roll.

***Saville, John**—(R. II. Roll) bore, argent, on a bend sable, three owls of the field (F.); another JOHN differenced with a label (3) gules; Surrey Roll.

Sawney, Amys de and **Henry de**—(E. I. Roll) bore, argent, an eagle displayed sable (F.); Camden Roll.

SIMON SCROOPE, OF DANBY SUPER YORE, IN COM. EBOR. ESQ.ᴿ 1698.
quarters as his Complete Atchievment, by right of Descent from Heirs
General, these several Coats of Arms, viz.

1. Scroope, of Bolton; Baron. 2. Tibetot, of Langar; Baron. 3. Badlesmere, of Leeds-Castle; Baron. 4. Fitz-Bernard, of Kingsdown; Baron. 5. Clare, Steward of the Forest of Essex; Baron. 6. Gifford, Earl of Buckingham. 7. S. Hillary; a Noble Family. 8. Clausit, Earl of Gloucester. 9. Fitz-Hamon, Earl of Carboil. 10. Marshall, Earl of Pembroke. 11. Strongbow; Earl of Pembroke. 12. Mac-Morogh, King of Leinster. 13. Lacy, Earl of Lincoln. 14. Fitz-John, Constable of Chester. 15. Nigel; Baron of Halton. 16. Lizures; a Noble Family. 17. Quincy, Earl of Lincoln. 18. Bellamont; Earl of Leicester. 19. Waleran; Earl of Mellent. 20. Waher or Guader, Earl of Norfolk. 21. Fitz-Osborn, Earl of Hereford. 22. Grantmesnel, of Hinkley; Baron. 23. Chester, Earl. 24. Lupus, Earl of Chester. 25. Leofric, Earl of Mercia. 26. Fitz-Maurice-Fitz-Gerald, Justice of Ireland. 27. Conyers, of Danby. 28. Scroope, as before.

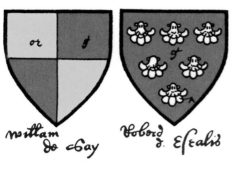

william
de Say

Robert
d. Escalis

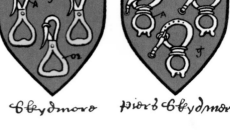

Scydmore

Piers Scydmor

Saxton, —— (E. IV. Roll) bore, argent, three wreaths gules between two bastons sable ; with crest ; Ballard Roll.

‡**Say, Sir William de**—(H. III. Roll) bore— MANDEVILLE'S coat—quarterly or and gules (F.) ; Dering, Glover, and Howard Rolls ; borne also by Sir GEOFFREY, banneret (baron 1313) at the first Dunstable tournament 1308, and at the second (1334) by his son GEOFFREY who was possibly knight (? banneret) at the capitulation of Calais 1348, bearing the same coat. One of this surname, a Suffolk Knight, bore, in the first tournament, a lyon passant azure (gardant in Harl. 4033 fo. 39ᵇ) ; Parly. Roll.

[**Say, Sir John,** of Herts., 1473—bore, per pale (argent and gules) three chevrons voided all counterchanged. See Monumental Brass.]

Saye, Sir William de, NORREYS, (sic)— (E. III. Roll) bore, gules, a cross patonce argent ; Ashmole Roll. There seems probable confusion here with SYWARD.

Scales, Robert de, of Musells, banneret, baron 1299, bore, at the battle of Falkirk 1298, and at the siege of Carlaverock 1300, gules, six escallops argent (F.) — Nicolas names 3 only—9 in Harleian Roll, 10 in St. George Roll. See knights banneret in Arundel Roll ; sealed (with 6 escallops) in Barons' letter to the Pope 1301, pp. xx, xxiv ; and so ascribed to THOMAS, last Lord SCALES, K.G., in K. 402 fo. 4.

Scargill, Waryne and **William de**— (E. III. Roll) bore, ermine, a saltire gules ; Grimaldi and Surrey Rolls ; Sir WALTER differenced, with a mullet or, in Ashmole Roll.

Scargill, Sir William—(E. III. Roll) bore, ermine, a saltire engrailed gules ; Ashmole Roll.

Scarsbricke, James of—(E. IV. Roll) bore, gules, three mullets between two bendlets engrailed argent ; with crest ; Ballard Roll.

‡**Scorenci, John de**—(H. III. Roll) bore, argent (sometimes or), a chevron gules ; Dering Roll.

Scott, John le, Earl of HUNTINGDON — (H. III. Roll) bore, paly (6) or and gules a bend sable ; Glover and Jenyns' Rolls ; in Jenyns' Ordinary the arms are tricked, or three piles meeting in base gules ; and as Earl of CHESTER, 1232-7, azure, three garbs or, are ascribed to him in Jenyns' Ordinary.

‡**Scotto, Robert de**—(H. III. Roll) bore, ermine, on a cross gules five martlets, or (F.) Dering Roll — SCOTHE in Howard Roll, ESTOTOT and STOTTOT in Arden and St. George Rolls.

Scremby —— **de** (E. I. Roll) bore, azure, three barrulets and a bend or ; Jenyns' Roll.

*****Scrope, Richard le**—(R. II. Roll) bore, azure, a bend or ; Parliamentary and Surrey Rolls ; and so ascribed to WILLIAM, K.G., Earl of WILTSHIRE, in K. 399 fo. 13 ; and to JOHN, 5th Lord Scrope, of Bolton, K.G. 1461, see title page.
 (1) HENRY, differenced with a label (3) argent.
 (2) JOHN, with a label ermine ; Surrey Roll.
 (3) HENRY LE, differenced with a label (3) argent, each charged with as many barrulets gules ; Surrey Roll.
 (4) HUGH, of Ruthen, slain at the siege of Calais 1347 —bore, a martlet for difference, and a label (5) or. F.
 (5) STEPHEN, differenced with a mullet ermine ; Surrey Roll.
 (6) THOMAS, differenced with a label (3) argent, charged with an annulet sable ; probably on the bend ; Surrey Roll.
 (7) —— differenced with a lozenge ermine, on the bend ; Surrey Roll.

Scrope, Sir Henry le, of Bolton—(E. I. Roll) bore, azure, on a bend or, a lyonceux passant purpure ; Nativity and Parliamentary Rolls and Jenyns' Ordinary. Sir RICHARD LE SCROPE, 1st baron, was thrice challenged as to his arms—first (as to crest) at the siege of Calais 1347 ; second, by CARMINOW in Paris 1360 ; and third, by GROSVENOR in 1385, but was never worsted.

Scrope, William le—(R. II. Roll) bore, gules, three armed legs conjoined argent, garnished or a label (3) argent ; *quarterly with*, SCROPE and a label (3) gules ; Surrey Roll.

Scudamore, Walter—(E. I. Roll) bore, gules, three stirrups, or, with the "cuires" argent ; Jenyns' Roll. (F.) Sir PIERS bore the stirrups argent ; Ashmole Roll. F.

Scures, Sir John de (of Wilts.)—bore, at the first Dunstable tournament 1308, azure, fretty, or. (F.) Parliamentary Roll and Jenyns' Ordinary. Borne also by another Sir JOHN, knighted at the capitulation of Calais 1348.

*[**Sebright, Peter,** 1294—bore, argent, three cinquefoyles pierced sable.—Shirley.] F.

Seckford, Sir George, of Suffolk—(H. VI. Roll) bore, ermine, on a fess gules three escallops argent ; Arundel Roll. F.

Sees, Sir Diggory—(R. II. Roll) bore, azure, platey 4, 3, **2,** 1 a chief or, issuant therefrom a demi-lyon rampant gules ; Jenyns' Ordinary —six plates and the demi-lyon sable in Arundel Roll.

Sefoule, Sir Ralph, of Norfolk—(E. II. Roll) bore, argent, a cross patonce vert, in the cantel a sea-fowl gules ; Parly. Roll. F.

Segni, Le Sire de—(H. III. Roll) bore, argent, a cross sable—"a merlos sable bordeaus" probably martlets — in orle sable ; Norfolk Roll.

SIR JOHN SAY.
IN BROXBOURNE CHURCH, HERTS, 1473.
After Waller.

Robt. de Scotto

Howge Scrope

Peter Sebright

John de Scures

George Seckford

Raffe Sefoule

niclolas Seigrave

nicola de Segrane

Esteven de Segrane

Henry de Segrane

SIR ROBERT DE SEPTVANS.

IN CHARTHAM CHURCH, KENT, 1306.

†Segrave, Nicholas—(H. III. Roll) bore, sable three garbs argent (F.); borne also by GEOFFREY and GILBERT; Dering, Norfolk, Glover, and Howard Rolls.

Segrave, Sir John de, banneret, baron 1296-1325, sealed the Barons' letter to the Pope 1301, pp. xviii, xxiv. He bore, at the battle of Falkirk 1298 and at the siege of Carlaverock 1300, sable, a lyon argent crowned or; as did his brother NICHOLAS, baron 1295-1322, with a label (3) gules, he signed but did not seal the famous Barons' letter 1301, p. xxiv; he bore the arms also at the first Dunstable tournament 1308 and at the battle of Boroughbridge 1322—a label (5) gules. F.

Segrave, Sir Stephen— bore, at the first Dunstable tournament 1308, sable, a lyon rampant argent, crowned or, charged on the shoulder with a fleur-de-lys gules (F.); ascribed also to Sir JOHN, of co. Leic., in Segar and Parliamentary Rolls.

Segrave, Sir Henry de, of co. Leic.—bore, at the first Dunstable tournament 1308, sable, a lyon rampant argent, crowned or, debruised by a bendlet engrailed gules (F.) in Harleian and Parly. Rolls; and also for HUGH, whose brother JOHN (ƒJohn) differenced with a baston or, as did Sir SIMON, also of co. Leic. (Harl. MS. 1481 fo. 77).

Segrave, Nicole de—(E. I. Roll) bore, sable, a lyon rampant argent; Dering and Howard Rolls.

Segrey, John and Simon de—(H. III. Roll) bore, ermine, a lyon passant gardant gules; Arden and St. George Rolls. (F.) SYMON bore a lyon rampant in Jenyns' Ordy.

Seilly, John de—(H. III. Roll) bore, azure, semée of mullets (6) and a lyon rampant or; Howard Roll. See SULLY.

*Selby, Sir Walter—(E. III. Roll) bore, burrulée (14) or and sable. (F.) Ashmole Roll.

Senefylde, Sir Guy de, of Essex—(E. II. Roll) bore, vert, an eagle displayed or; Parly. Roll. NENESFELD, NEVESFELD or STENEFELDE.

Seneschal, William le, v. Steward.

Sennyle, Sir Symon de (SENCILLE), knighted at the capitulation of Calais 1348, bore, azure, crusily fitchée (3, 3) and a bend or.

‡Septvans, Sir Robert, of Kent—(H. III. Roll) bore, azure, three corn-fans or. (F.) Dering and Arundel Rolls—tricked crusily or, in Howard Roll—see Monumental Brass, after *Waller*.

Servington, Sir Oliver—(E. III. Roll) bore, ermine, on a chief azure three bucks' heads cabossed or; Ashmole Roll.

Seton, Sir John—(E. III. Roll) bore, gules, a bend argent between six martlets or; Ashmole and Surrey Rolls.

x[Seimor, Sir Roger, 23 H. III.—(Seal), gules, two wings conjoined in lure of the first.—Shirley.] F.

Seymour v. St. Maur.

Seymour, Thomas—bore, at the second Dunstable tournament 1334, argent, three chevrons gules, a label vert. F.

Seymour, Sir Thomas (SEMOR)—(E. III. Roll) bore, argent, a chevron gules, a label (3) azure; Ashmole Roll.

Seynanse, Sir William de—(E. III. Roll) bore, gules, on a chevron or three martlets sable; Ashmole Roll. F.

Seys, Hemar (SCEYS)—(H. III. Roll) bore, gules, two palets vair and a chief or; Howard Roll.

Shakerley, William—(E. IV. Roll) bore, argent, three shakebolts 2 and 1 sable—with crest; Ballard Roll.

Shardelow, Sir John—(E. III. Roll) bore, argent, a chevron gules between three crosses crosslet fitchée azure; Ashmole Roll. JOHN CARBONELL bears the same arms.

Shardelow, Sir J.—(H. VI. Roll) bore, gules, a cross argent, a bordure engrailed or; Atkinson Roll. See also CARBONELL.

Shardeston, Fouke de—(H. III. Roll) bore, gules, a saltire engrailed argent; Glover Roll.

Sharingbourne, Andrew de—(E. III. Roll) bore, gules, a lyon rampant or, a quarter ermine; Ashmole Roll and Jenyns' Ordinary.

Sharnfield, John de—(E. III. Roll) bore, azure, an eagle displayed or membered gules; Jenyns' Ordinary. JOHN DE WOLVERTON bears the same.

Sharshall, Sir William—(E. III. Roll) bore, undée (6)—now barry nebulée—argent and gules, a bordure sable besantée. Sir ADAM differenced with a mullet (6) or; Ashmole Roll. See SARASSWELLE.

Shastowe, Robert de—(H. III. Roll) bore, gules, on a bend argent three mullets azure; Glover Roll.

Sheffield, Sir Thomas de (SHEFELDE)— bore, at the first Dunstable tournament 1308, gules, a fess between three garbs or. (F.) (Sir ROBERT bore the reverse; Parly. Roll.) JOHN and Sir THOMAS bore six garbs 3, 3, with the colours reversed; Parly. Roll and Jenyns' Ordinary.

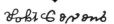

Simon d Segre

Robt Corvons

Roger de Soimor

Tho de Seymour

Will de Seynanse

Tho Sheffeild

Sheffield, Thomas—(E. III. Roll) bore, argent, a chevron gules between three garbs 2 and 1 or—another with the field ermine ; Jenyns' Ordinary.

*[Shelley, Sir William, (R. II.)—bore, sable, a fess engrailed between three whelk-shells or.—Shirley.] F.

Sheme, Sir (——) of Sheppey, in Kent—(H. VI. Roll) bore, azure, four lyonceux rampant argent a canton ermine ; Arundel Roll. Surname doubtful, see SHIRLAND.

[Shelton, Sir Ralph, of Norfolk, 1423—bore (azure) a cross (or). See Monumental Brass.]

Shepey, Sire John de—(E. II. Roll) bore, azure, a cross or fretty gules ; Parly. Roll. See STEPEY.

Shepey, Sir John—(E. III. Roll) bore, gules, a fess between three garbs argent ; Ashmole Roll.

*[Sherard, Sir Robert, 1343—bore, argent, a chevron gules between three torteaux.—Shirley.] F.

Sherborne, Sir John—bore, at the siege of Calais 1345-8, vert, a lyon rampant gardant argent. F.

Sherburne, Sir Richard, of Stonyhurst—(E. IV. Roll) bore, argent, a lyon rampant or *quarterly with,* vert, an eagle displayed argent ; with crest ; Ballard Roll.

Shillighelde, Yvon de, *v.* Silligheld.

Shillithorne, William—(E. III. Roll) bore, argent a cross checquy argent and sable,—counter-compony in trick ; Jenyns' Ordinary.

Shirbrook, Robert de—(H. III. Roll) bore, vair, a chief or, over all a bend gules (St. George Roll) charged with three mullets (6) ; Harl. MS. 6589.

Shirland, Sir Robert (of Kent)—bore, at the first Dunstable tournament 1308, azure, six lyonceux rampant argent, a canton ermine. Said, by G. E. C. to have been at the siege of Carlaverock 1300. (F.) & Monumental Effigy, after *Stothard,* next page ; borne also by (‡) ROGER ; Dering and Howard Rolls.

Shirley, Sir Raffe, of Warwickshire—(E. II. Roll) bore, paly (6) or and sable ; Parly. Roll. *HUGH and Sir RALPH—with a canton ermine, (F.) in Surrey and Ashmole Rolls.

Sherley, William de—(H. III. Roll) bore, paly (6) or and azure, a bend gules ; Arden Roll.

Shottesbrooke, Sir Gilbert—(E. III. Roll) bore, ermine, a chief per pale indented or and gules ; Ashmole Roll (F.) ; Sir R. ermine (incomplete) ; Atkinson Roll. F. See also Harl. MS. 6163 ff 16ᵇ-44.

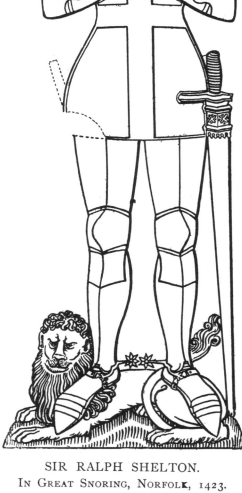

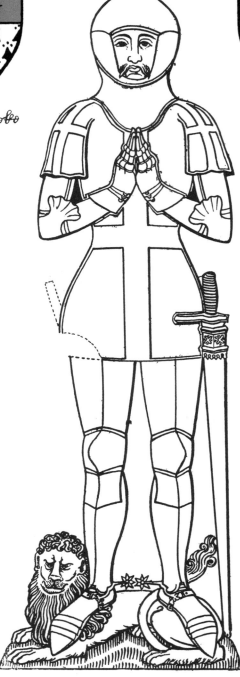

SIR RALPH SHELTON.
IN GREAT SNORING, NORFOLK, 1423.
After Cotman.

*[Shuckburgh, John de, (Ed. III.)—bore, sable, a chevron between three mullets pierced argent.—Shirley.] F.

Shyryak, Sir John—(E. III. Roll) azure, an inescocheon within an orle of martlets argent ; Ashmole Roll.

Sibbeton, Sir John de, of Herefordshire—(E. II. Roll) bore, or, an eagle displayed, a baston gobony argent and gules ; Parly. Roll.

Sidney ——, an Essex ? Knight (H. VI. Roll) bore, or, a pheon azure ; Arundel Roll.

Sifrewast, Richard de—(H. III. Roll) bore, azure, two gemelles and a chief or. (F.) St. George and Arden Rolls—NICHOLAS took up the cross 1270. See CIFREWAST.

Siggeston, Sir John—(E. III. Roll) bore, argent, a double-headed eagle displayed gules (sable, in Jenyns' Ordinary) ; Ashmole Roll.

‡Silligheld, Ivon de—(H. III. Roll) bore, azure, six cats' or leopards' faces 3, 2, 1 or (F.) ; Dering Roll ; men's heads couped in Howard Roll.

Silton, Sir John de—bore, at the first Dunstable tournament 1308, or, an eagle displayed vert, a bendlet gobony argent and gules. F.

Simeon, Robert—(R. II. Roll) bore, gules, a fess or between three lyons rampant argent ; Surrey Roll.

Sindlesham, Sir Robert de, of Berks—(E. II. Roll) bore, argent, on a fess between three escallops gules, as many martlets or ; Parly. Roll.

Skelton, Sir Rauf, of Suffolk—(E. II. Roll) bore, azure, a cross or ; Ashmole and Parly. Rolls. Another RAUFF with a label (3) argent ; Surrey Roll.

Skelton, Clement de—(E. I. Roll) bore, azure, a fess gules between three fleurs-de-lys or ; Jenyns' Roll.

Skette, John—(E. II. Roll) bore, argent, a cross crosslet sable ; Surrey Roll.

Skidburgh, Robert, of Saltfletby in Lincolnshire—(E. I. Roll) bore, azure, three closed helmets crested or ; Jenyns' Roll.

Skillithorne *v.* **Shillithorne.**

Skipton, John de—(E. I. Roll) bore, argent, an anchor erect sable ; Jenyns' Roll.

Skipton, John de—(E. III. Roll) bore, per base indented argent and purpure a lyon rampant of the last ; Jenyns' Ordinary. F.

[Skipwith, Sir William—(E. III.) bore, argent, three bars gules in chief a greyhound courant sable.—Shirley.] F.

Skirpenbeck, le Baron de—(E. I. Roll) bore, gules a cross patée (patonce in trick) argent, on a chief azure a lyon passant gardant or ; Jenyns' Roll.

Sleght, Robert—(R. II. Roll) bore, or, crusily (6, 4) and a chevron sable ; Surrey Roll.

Sleghtes, Henry—(E. III. Roll) bore, gules, six crosses moline 3, 2, 1 or, in chief a lyon passant argent ; Jenyns' Ordinary.

Sleghtes, Robert, of Legbourne in Lincs.— (E. I. Roll) bore, gules, a chevron between three crosses moline or ; Jenyns' Roll.

Smalborough, William—(R. II. Roll) bore, sable a chevron between three bears' heads couped or ; Surrey Roll.

Smareys, Sir Herbert de—bore, at the first Dunstable tournament 1308, argent, a lyon rampant sable (F.) ; as DES MAREYS.

Smyth, Sir John, of Essex—(H. VI. Roll) bore, ermines, three bezants ; Arundel Roll.

Snaves, John de—(H. III. Roll) bore, sable, a chevron between six lyons rampant argent ; Howard Roll.

*[Sneyd, Richard de—bore, gules, a scythe argent, the coat of his mother ROSIA DE PRAERS, his descendant RICHARD DE TUNSTALL DE SNEYD, had the fleur-de-lys sable for Poictiers 1356.—Shirley.] F.

Snotterley, Sir Roger de, of Norfolk— (E. II. Roll) bore, gules, a fess between three buckles, tongues to the dexter argent ; Parly. Roll.

Snylly, Robert — (E. III. Roll) bore, or, two bars gules ; Jenyns' Ordinary. See SULLY.

Soardeby, John, v. Sywardby.

‡Sodon, Stephen, (SOWDON)—(H. III. Roll) bore, azure, three bendlets argent (F.) ; Dering and Howard Rolls ; bendy (6) argent and azure in Ashmole MS.

Sofhongell, Raffe — (E. III. Roll) bore, argent, a cross flory sable —now patée flory— "boutes florettes" ; Jenyns' Ordinary.

Soleni, Averay de—(H. III. Roll) bore, quarterly argent and gules ; Arden Roll and Jenyns' Ordinary.

Solers, Henry de—(H. III. Roll) bore, paly (10) or and azure a bend gules (F.) ; St. George Roll.

Soleys, Richard—(H. III. Roll) bore, or, a fess gules (azure in Harl. MS. 6137) ; St. George Roll. F.

Soltone, Sir John de—(E. II. Roll) bore, or, a lyon rampant azure, a chief gules ; Harl. MS. 4033. In Harl. 6137—or, a chief gules, over all a lyon rampant azure ; Parly. Roll.

Somervile, Roger de—(E. I. Roll) bore, burulée (12) argent and gules, on a bordure, azure eight martlets or ; Jenyns' Roll and Ordinary.

Someri, Henry de—(H. III. Roll) bore, sable, a bend between six martlets 3, 3 argent (F.) ; Arden and St. George Rolls.

Someri, Sir John, of Kent—bore, at the first Dunstable tournament 1308, quarterly or and azure, a bend gules (F.) ; ascribed to JOHN of Herts. in Parly Roll.

Somery, Sir John, knight banneret—(H. VI. Roll) bore, argent two lyons passant azure— Arundel Roll. Sir Percival, of Warwickshire—(E. II. Roll)—bore, azure, two lyons passant or ; St. George and Parly. Rolls. (Sir HENRY DE ERDINGTON bears the same ; Arden Roll) ; Sir JOHN of Herts., a baron 1308, and ROGER (‡) bore the reverse ; Parly., Dering, and Norfolk Rolls.

Somery, Sir John—bore, at the first Dunstable tournament 1308, or, three lyons passant azure (F.) ; Segar Roll.

‡Somery, Symon de—(H. III. Roll) bore, azure, fretty argent, on a canton or a fleur-de-lys gules. (F.) Dering and Howard Rolls.

Sor, John le—(H. III. Roll) bore, chequuy or and gules, a fess azure ; St. George Roll.

Sothill, Sire Henry de—bore, at the battle of Boroughbridge 1322, gules, an eagle displayed argent (F.) ; ascribed also to Sir JOHN, Ashmole Roll, and to WILLIAM—oppressed by a barrulet azure, in Segar Roll. F.

SIR ROBERT DE SHURLAND.
IN MINSTER CHURCH, KENT.

Stapleton, afterwards Stapilton, now Stapylton, formerly of Carlton, Wighill and Myton.

CONDENSED FROM "COUNTY FAMILIES OF YORKSHIRE."—EDITED BY J. FOSTER.

MILES DE STAPLETON = SARA, dau. of Anketien Mallory.

SIR NICHOLAS DE STAPLETON, Judge of the King's Bench, 1272–89, had free warren in all = ISABEL, dau. of Miles Bassett, of North Morton his domain lands of Stapelton, Wath, Kirkby Fleetham, &c., 1272, lived at West | and Hathelsay, Yorks. Hathelsay, sat on the trial of David, King of Wales, brother of Llewellyn, 30 Sept. 1283; died 1290. Palgrave: Parl. Writs.

SIBILL (1st wife), eldest dau. and co-heir of Sir John = SIR MILES DE STAPLETON, had summons to Parliament, 6 and 7, Ed. II., = CECILIA; masses performed at Dur- de Bella Aqua or Bellew, Knt., baron 22 Ed. I., | 1312–13, lord of Stapleton, &c., and of Carlton, in right of his wife; | ham, Dec. 1314, for Sir Miles and lord of Carlton juxta Snaith, by Larderine, | served in Gascony 1295, and in Scotland, at the siege of Stirling, and at | Cecilia, formerly his wife (*Reg.* sister and co-heir of Peter Bruce, of Skelton and | the battle of Falkirk 1298, one of those who received reward for the | *Kellawe*). Carlton. | capture of Sir William Wallace—slain at Bannockburn 14 July, 1314.

SIR NICHOLAS, aged 25, 1314, | SIR GILBERT DE STAPLETON, KT. of Bedale, = AGNES or MAUD, eldest dau. and co-heir of Sir Brian | SIR JOHN, of Melsonby, received summoned to a Council 1342, | and lord of Askham Bryan (9 E. II.), in | FitzAlan, lord of Bedale, &c., by his wife Anne, | presents of plate from E. II. but not to Parliament. = | right of his wife; dead 19 E. II., King's | dau. of John Baliol, King of Scotland. She re- | when he kept Christmas at West- | Escheator. | married to Sir Thomas de Sheffield. | minster 1318, *Archæologia.*

SIR MILES, never summoned to | SIR MILES DE STAPILTON, of Ingham, Norfolk, and | SIR BRIAN DE STAPILTON, K.G. 1382, a deponent in = ALICE, widow of Sir Stephen Parliament; died 1372. = | of Bedale, Yorks, Knight and one of the founders | the Scrope and Grosvenor Controversy; served at | Waleys, lord of Helagh, | of the Order of the Garter; served at Cressy and | the siege of Tournay 1340, at Calais 1345–8, at | 2nd dau. and co-heir of | at the siege of Calais 1345–8, and also in the | Cressy; Gov. of Calais temp. Ed. II.; purchased | Sir John St. Philibert. THOMAS, of Kentmere, never | French Wars 1356; died 4 Dec. 1364; buried at | Wighill 50 Ed. III.; died 25 July, 1394; made his summoned to Parliament; died | Ingham, Norfolk. = | will 16 May, 6 R. II. 1394; to be buried in Helagh *s.p.* 10 Aug. 1373. | | Priory.

SIR BRIAN STAPLETON, of Carlton, | SIR MILES STAPILTON, of Wighill, &c., letters of protection to = JOHANNA, eldest dau. and co-heir of Sir Gerard eldest son = | Portugal 1380, to assist the Duke of Lancaster in his pretensions to | Uffleet, of Wighill, and widow of William Beck- | the Crown of Castile; died 6 Feb. 1400. | with (? Brechnells). A QUO STAPYLTON, of Carlton.

SIR JOHN STAPILTON, of Wighill, KT., made his will 21 Feb. 1454–5; = MARGARET, dau. of Sir Richard Norton, of Norton Conyers, | MABEL. | MARGARET. proved 3 June following. · Inq. p.m. 33 Hen. VI. | Chief Justice of the Common Pleas; died Jan. 1465–6. | HELEN. | JOAN.

MARGARET (1st wife), dau. of = SIR WILLIAM STAPILTON, of = JANE (2nd wife), dau. of Sir Thomas | 2. MILES OF YORK, d. 1498. | 1. ELIZABETH. Sir James Pickering, of Oswald- | Wighill, KT.; died 16 Dec. | Tunstall, and widow of Sir Roger | 3. THOMAS, 1466. | 2. ISABELLA. kirk, Yorks, and Killington, | 1503, buried there; made his | Warde, of Givendale, Yorks; made | 4. JOHN, will proved 1508. | 3. CATHERINE, 1st wife of Westmorland; ob. 1474. | will 4 Dec. 1503; proved 19 | her will 24 Feb. 1507–8; proved 23 | 5. CHRISTOPHER, and | Thomas Roos, of Ing- | Dec. 1504. | March following. | 6. BRYAN. | manthorpe; his will | | | proved 14 Aug. 1505.

1. HENRY, d. 1481. | 2. SIR BRIAN STAPILTON, of Wighill, = JOAN, dau. and heir of Sir Lancelot Thir- | ELIZABETH: dispensation to | AGNES, wife of Ralph Reresby, 3. JOHN, of Wighill. | KT.; fought at Flodden; died 18 | keld, KT. (by Margaret Lady Vesey, | marry 16 Nov. 1509, Edward | of Thribergh, Yorkshire. | Sept. 1518, Monumental Slab in | dau. and heiress of Sir Henry de Brom- | Saltmarshe of Saltmarshe. | Wighill Ch.; made his will 4 July, | flete, Lord Vesey; she died 5 Jan. | 1518. | 1542–3.

ALICE (1st wife), dau. = CHRISTOPHER STAPILTON, of = ELIZABETH (2nd | BRIAN, ? a clerk. | WILLIAM, a | JANE, wife of Robert Con- | MARGARET, wife of John of William Aske of | Wighill, aged 33 in 1518; | wife), dau. of Sir | LAUNCELOT, of Wath. | lawyer. | yers, of Hooton Paynell. | Copley, of Hotham. Aske, Yorkshire; | made his will 30 July, 1537; | John Nevile, of | MILES, 1518. | RICHARD. | ELEANOR, wife of Thomas, | ISABEL, a nun. died 16 Nov. 1521. | proved 29 Jan. following. | Leversedge. | JOHN, clerk. | ROBERT. | 1st Lord Wharton.

A
CONTINUED ON NEXT PAGE.

CONTINUED FROM PRECEDING PAGE :—
A

SIR BRIAN, of Wighill, mar. (disp. 9 Dec. 1520), Margery, dau. of Sir John Constable, of Halsham, Yorks; died *s.p.*

SIR ROBERT, of Wighill, on the trial of Q. Catherine Howard, at Doncaster, 24 Nov. 1541; died 6 June, 1557; 1st husband. = ELIZABETH, dau. of Sir Wm. Mallory, of Studley; she re-mar. to Marmaduke Slingsby.

WILLIAM, was active in Aske's rebellion.

JOAN, d. 3 Jany. 1537–8, wife of (covenant 6 May, 1535) Henry Hamerton, of Hellifield; d. Aug. 1537.

ISABEL, wife of John Lamplugh of Lamplugh. ANNE, wife of John Irton, of Irton.

MARGARET wife of Henry Eser. ALICE.

CATHERINE (1st wife), dau. of Sir Marmaduke Constable, of Everingham. = SIR ROBERT, re-built Wighill and High Sheriff, 1580–1; a Capt. of the City of York, at the time of the Earls' rebellion, 1569; came under the ban of the Star Chamber in his quarrel with (Edwin Sandys) Archbishop of York, " next to Sir Philip Sidney, he had no superior in England "; buried at Wighill, 3 Oct. 1606. = OLIVE (2nd wife), widow of John Talbot, of Salwarpe, co. Worc., dau. and eventual sole heiress of Sir Henry Sherrington, KT., of Lacock, Wilts.

ELIZABETH, 1st wife of Bryan Hamond, of Scarthingwell; she died *s.p.* 11 Apl. 1601.

BRIDGET, wife (1st) of John Norton of Norton Conyers, and (2ndly) of Anthony Maude.

BRYAN STAPYLTON, of Myton, by purchase, matric. from Balliol Coll., 1604, receiver-general of the North for K. Charles I.; made his will 1 Feb. 1655–6; proved in London 26 Nov. 1658. = FRANCES, dau. of Sir Hy. Slingsby, of Scriven, BT.

ROBERT, matric. from Balliol Coll., ob. 1607. WILLIAM. EDWARD, reader of the Inner Temple.

OLIVE, wife of Sir Robert Dyneley, of Bramhope; he buried at Otley 28 Feb. 1616.

URSULA, wife of Sir Robert Baynard, of Lackham, Wilts; she re-mar. to Sir Garret Rainsford, of London, KT.

MARY. GRACE, died unmar.

SIR HENRY STAPYLTON, of Myton, created a baronet 22 June, 1660.
=
A QUO STAPYLTON, of Myton.

ROBERT, of Stapleford, co. Leic., royalist, matric. at Oxford, 20 June, 1634, M.P. Boroughbridge, 1659, *o.s.p.* 1691.

MILES STAPYLTON, J.P., Co. Pal. Durham, auditor and librarian to Dr. Cosin, Bishop of Durham. = ELIZABETH, dau. of Mr. Hynde, citizen of London; mar. at St. Olave's, Jewry, 8 Aug. 1655.

OLIVE, mar. (1st) to Sir William Vavasour, of Copmanthorpe, Yorks, KT. and BT., Major-General to the King of Sweden, killed before Copenhagen, 1658. She re-mar. to Richard Topham, of Westminster, and was buried at Chelsea, 26 Nov. 1714.

FRANCES, mar. (articles 13 Sept. 1651) to John Hutton, of Marske. URSULA, mar. 29 March, 1660, to Thomas Pepys, of Hatcham Barnes, Surrey.

---

1. MYLES STAPYLTON, D.D., Fellow All Souls', M.A. 1663, B. and D.D. 1700, Rector of Harpsden, Oxon, 1690, Canon of Worcester 1700–31; bapt. at St. Giles', Cripplegate, London, 6 Apl. 1658; died May, 1731.

2. BRYAN died unmar.
3. ROBERT, R.N., Capt. of the *Ursula*, father of Martin, said to be an Admiral.

4. HENRY STAPYLTON, born 1672, M.A. All Souls', 1694, Rector of Marske, 1694, and of Thornton Watlass, Yorkshire, 1703, until his death there 9 Feb. 1747–8. = MARY, dau. and heir of Rev. John Orchard, of Newbury, Berks; buried at Thornton Watlass 22 Dec. 1755.

JOHN STAPYLTON, M.A., University Coll., Oxon., 1732, Rector of Thornton on the death of his father 1748; bapt. there 19 Sept. 1707; died 3 Oct. 1767. = ELLEN, or ELIZABETH (1st wife), dau. of Roger Lee, of Pinchinthorpe. = LUCY (2nd wife), dau. of Thomas Wycliffe, of Gailes, Yorks; bapt. 23 Sept. 1725; mar. at Kirkby Hill, 4 Feb. 1754.

MARY, died unmar. 1723. ELIZABETH, wife of Rich. Tennant. FRANCES, died unmar.

SARAH, mar. at Watlass, 8 Aug. 1733, to Thomas Raisbeck, of Stockton. HENRIETTA, died young.

OLIVIA, mar. 13 Apl. 1738, to Rev. Thomas Robinson, Rector of Wycliffe. HENRIETTA, mar. 14 Feb. 1739–40, to John Soux, of London.

HENRY STAPYLTON, of Norton, co. Durham, J.P., matriculated from University College, Oxon. 1773, then aged 19; a student of Lincoln's Inn, 1775; died in Aug. 1835. = MARY ANN, dau. and heir of Robert Gregory, Capt. R.N., by his wife; dau. and eventual heir of Polycarpus Taylor, of Norton, Rear-Admiral R.N.; mar. 3 Jan. 1786.

THOMAS, died at Newcastle-upon-Tyne, 1780; aged 21.

---

1. JOHN, bar.-at-law, Inner Temple, 1822; M.A., Fellow University Coll. Oxon, 1811, until his death, Feb. 1836.
2. HENRY, Lieut. 68th Regiment. Killed in the French Wars, 23 Feb. 1814.

ROBERT MARTIN STAPYLTON, of the Army Pay Office; born 21 Sept. 1793; died 17 Jan. 1864. = MARTHA ELIZA, 2nd dau. of John Bockett, of Southcote Lodge, Berks, esq.; mar. at St. Mary, Reading, 16 Apl. 1814; died 21 Aug. 1879.

1. MARY FRANCES, wife of Marshall Fowler, of Preston Hall, co. Durham, who died 18 May, 1878, aged 89.
3. LUCY, died unmar. 1838.

2. OLIVIA, mar. 21 Apl. 1824, to Geo. William Sutton, of Elton Hall, co. Durham.
4. HENRIETTA SARAH, died unmar. 23 Feb. 1845.

HENRY MILES.
THOMAS WYCLIFFE.
JOHN SUTTON.
MILES.
All died young.

ROBERT GEORGE STAPYLTON, of Manchester, bar.-at-law; born 13 Aug. 1820; died 6 Jan. 1873. = MADALINA CLEMENTINA, dau. of Very Rev. George Hull Bowers, D.D., Dean of Manchester; mar. 24 May, 1855.

HENRY, of Sydney, N.S.W., 1834; has 3 married sons with issue.

MILES STAPYLTON, of H.M. Probate Court; born 9 Feb. 1836; mar. 1 Feb. 1868, Sarah Dorcas, 3rd dau. of Rev. Benjamin Bradney Bockett, M.A., Vicar of Epsom, Surrey. =

MARY ANNE, died young. HENRIETTA, died in 1893. ELIZA A. LUCY, died in 1899. MARY JANE. OLIVIA, died 1851.

ROBERT MILES STAPYLTON, 19th in direct lined descent from the first Miles Stapylton, and 15th from Sir Brian Stapilton, K.G., 1382, brother of Sir Miles, one of the founders of the Order, M.A. St. John's Coll., Oxon, 1890, Rector of Lolworth, co. Cambridge, 1895; born 15 Apl. 1864. = MARGARET, dau. of Rev. Hy. Isaac Sharp, Rector of Downham, and Hon. Canon of Ely; mar. 29 Sept. 1892.

1. OLIVE HARRIET.
2. HENRIETTA ELIZA, d. 1872.
3. MARY URSULA, mar. 25 June, 1884, to Walter Handel Thorley, of Blackburn.

BRYAN, b. 23 Nov. 1870, volunteered into Paget's Horse (19th batt. Imp. Yeo.) in the South African Guerilla War; wounded at Lichtenburg 12 March, 1901, died next day.

ALAN, born 16 May, 1872.

ELLA MARY.
MABEL DORCAS.
KATHLEEN-ELIZA

JOHN MILES, born 13 Nov. 1896.

MADALINA MARY, born 27 March, 1898.

Percyval Sowdan   John Spoke

Souch v. Zouch.

Southbury, Sir John de, of Beds.—(E. II. Roll) bore, ermine, on a chief gules, three roses or ; Parliamentary Roll.

Southleye, John de (SUTHLEYE)—(E. I. Roll) bore, or, two bends gules ; Segar Roll.

Southworth, Thomas—(R. II. Roll) bore, sable, a chevron between three crosses patonce argent ; Surrey Roll. Sir CHRISTOPHER, of Samlesbury, bore the same, with crest ; Ballard Roll (E. IV.), in which crosses flory are intended.

Sowdan, Percyvall—bore, at the siege of Rouen 1418, gules, a man's head wreathed argent, *quarterly with*, sable three cinquefoyles argent. F. See also SODON.

Spalding, Michael de—(E. III. Roll) bore, gules, two bars and in chief three annulets argent ; Jenyns' Ordinary.

Spayne, Sir Peter, a captain—bore, at the siege of Calais 1345-8, gyronny (8) or and azure, an inescocheon argent. F. See Espagne.

Spaygne, William de—(R. II. Roll) bore, argent, a fess dancettée between three spaniels' heads erased sable ; Surrey Roll. See ESPAGNE.

*[**Speke, Sir John,** (H. VI.)—bore, barry (8) argent and azure over all a double-headed eagle gules.—Shirley.] F.

Spencer v. Despencer and **Le Despencer.**

*[**Spencer, John** and **Thomas,** 1504—bore, azure a fess ermine between six sea-mews' heads erased argent.—Shirley.]

Spencer, Philip—(E. III. Roll) bore, barry (6) or and azure, a canton ermine ; Surrey Roll and Jenyns' Ordinary.

Spencer, Sir William—(E. III. Roll) bore, gules, on a cross engrailed argent five torteaux ; Ashmole Roll.

Spenythorne, Thomas de—(E. I. Roll) bore, argent, on a bend sable three mullets or ; Jenyns' Roll—on a bend argent three mullets gules, in trick.

Spigurnell, Sir Henry, baron 1297—bore, gules, two gemelles and in chief a lyon passant or ; Nobility Roll.

Spigurnell, Sir John, of Bucks—(E. II. Roll) bore, gules, fretty argent, on a chief or a lyon passant gardant gules. Sir HENRY, of Bucks, bore this with a baston azure ; Parly. Roll ; not gardant in Cotgrave Roll.

Sprigurnel (Sir) Rauf—bore, at the second Dunstable tournament 1334, azure, three bars or, a mullet argent. (F.) Ashmole Roll.

RALPH, LORD STAFFORD, K.G.
IN ELSING CHURCH, NORFOLK,
1347, 21 E. III.

After a rubbing from the Hastings Brass.

Rog Speegehose   Rauf de Stafford

Sporle (——) a Suffolk Knight—(H. VI. Roll) bore, azure, three estoyles of 16 rays, and a bordure engrailed or ; Arundel Roll. Spurrowells may have been originally intended.

Spring, Henry—(E. III. Roll) bore, azure an orle argent ; Jenyns' Ordinary.

Springe, Sir John, of Yorkshire—(E. II. Roll) bore, argent, a lyon rampant vert ; Parliamentary Roll.

Springhose, Roger—(H. III. Roll) bore, gules, two lyons passant argent, a label (5) azure. (F.) Arden and St. George Rolls.

Spysse, Sir Roger, of Essex, Kt.—(H. VI. Roll) bore, per fess argent and gules a pile counterchanged ; Arundel Roll.

Sqyrye (——) a Suffolk Knight (H. VI. Roll) bore, argent a squirrel sejant gules, cracking a nut or ; Arundel Roll.

Stackpoole, Sir Richard de, of co. Glouc. —(E. II. Roll) bore, argent, a lyon rampant gules, collared or ; Parly. and Harl. Rolls.

Stafford, Edmund, banneret, baron 1299 (sealed the Barons' letter to the Pope 1301, pp. xx, xxiv). He bore, or a chevron gules (F.) ; Nobility Roll ; (bore, or a chevron gules ermynée in Grimaldi Roll). RALPH, K.G., founder 1344, 2nd baron (1st Earl) bore it at the siege of Calais 1345-8. See Monumental Brass. Borne by (another ?) Sir RALPH, knighted at the capitulation in 1348, and by HUMPHREY, 6th Earl (Duke of BUCKINGHAM, K.G.), and then a youth of 16, at the siege of Rouen 1418, and on the same occasion by HUGH, within a bordure gules. F.

Stafford, Hugh, K.G. 1418-19, Baron BOURCHIER—bore, or, on a chevron gules, a mullet of the first for difference, *quarterly with*, argent, a cross engrailed gules between four water-bougets sable ; K. 401 fo. 27.

Stafford, Robert de—(H. III. Roll) bore, or, on a chevron gules three plates, Jenyns' Roll ; a label azure (F.) Arden and St. George Roll—ascribed in the latter Roll without the label to Baron de STAFFORD.

Stafford, Sir Robert de, of co. Cambridge —(E. II. Roll) bore, or on a chevron gules, three besants ; Parly. and Glover Rolls.

Stafford, Edmond de, clerk, and **Sir Richard,** of Pipe—(E. III. Roll) bore, or, a chevron gules between three martlets sable ; Ashmole and Surrey Rolls and Harl. MS. 1481 fo. 56.

Stafford (——) of Pipe, co. Staffs.—(E. III. Roll) bore, or, on a chevron between three martlets gules, as many besants ; Ashmole Roll.

Stafford, Humphrey de, of Hoke, *f* JOHN of Bromshall—(R. II. Roll) bore, or, a chevron gules within a bordure engrailed sable ; Surrey Roll. JOHN, of Frome, *f* RALPH, bore the bordure gules ; Harl. MS. 1481 fo. 56.

Stafford, Nicol de—(R. II. Roll) bore, or, a chevron gules, a chief azure ; Surrey Roll. RALPH, of Grafton (brother of HUMPHREY), bore a quarter ermine in lieu of the chief ; Harl. MS. 1481 fo. 56.

Stafford, Robert de—(R. II. Roll) bore, or, a chevron gules surmounted of a bendlet azure ; Surrey Roll.

Stafford, John de—bore, at the second Dunstable tournament 1334, argent, a chevron gules.

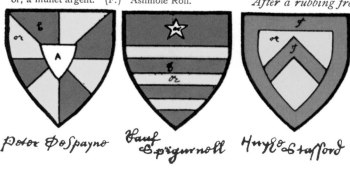

Peter Despayne   Rauf Spigurnell   Hugh de Stafford   Rob d' Stafford

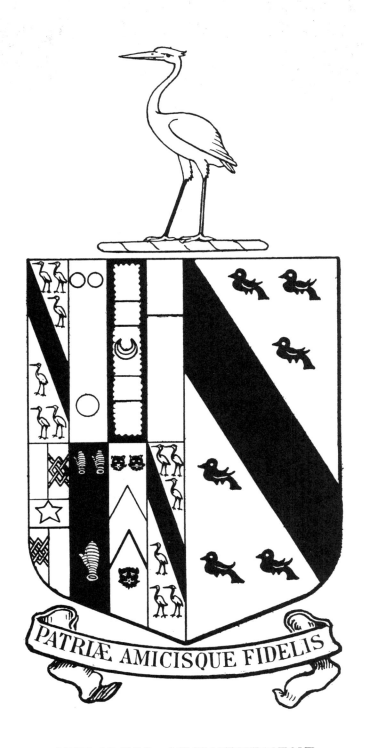

HERALDIC ATCHIEVEMENT

OF THE LATE

COL. LE GENDRE NICHOLAS STARKIE, OF HUNTROYDE, Co. LANC.

184

witt Stallingburgg

Stamford

Robt. de Stonegrave

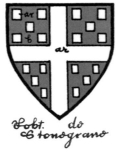

Robt Stanmorsse

Le Staple

How gr Standysse

John Stanhope

Rog Stanhope

Hereus d. Stanhowe

witt Stapleton

Robert de Stapleton

Coof Starbie

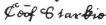

Robt de Stantoun

Robt de Stanhowe

Stallingborn, Sir Walter—(E. III. Roll) bore, sable, a chevron engrailed between three crosses botonnée all argent; Ashmole Roll—the trick may be intended for ordinary crosslets. Surname very indistinct in the MS.

Stallingburgh, William—(E. I. Roll) bore, sable, a chevron between three crosses crosslet fitchée argent; Jenyns' Roll—"iij bottones fyches" in Harl. MS. 6589 fo. 48ᵇ. F.

Stamford—— an Essex Knight—(H. VI. Roll) bore, gules, a saltire vair between four leopards' faces or; Arundel Roll. F.

Standish, Sir Alexander, of Standish—(E. IV. Roll) bore, sable, three standing dishes 2 and 1 argent, *quarterly with*, argent, a saltire engrailed sable, with crest; Ballard Roll.

Standish, Sir Christopher, of Duxbury—(E. IV. Roll) bore, azure, three standing dishes 2 and 1 argent (with crest); Ballard Roll. HUGH bore this at the siege of Rouen 1418 differenced with a label (3) or. (F.) In the Ashmole MS. squirrels sejant are the charges.

Standon v. **Stanton** and **Staunton**.

Standon, Robert—(H. III. Roll) bore, ermine, *quarterly with*, gules a fret or. STANHOWE in St. George Roll; STAUNDONE in Jenyns' Roll. See also STAUNDON.

Stangrave, Sir Robert (STONGRAVE)—bore, at the first Dunstable tournament 1308, and at the battle of Boroughbridge 1322, azure, billettée and a cross argent. (F.) Ashmole Roll, and of Kent in Parliamentary Roll.

*[**Stanhope, Sir Richard**, (E. III.)—bore, quarterly ermine and gules.—Shirley.] F.

Stanhope, John (E. I. Roll)—bore, quarterly gules and ermine, in the first and fourth a goat's head erased argent; Jenyns' Roll. F.

Stanhowe, Hervey—(H. III. Roll) bore, barry (6) or and azure, a bend ermine. (F.) St. George Roll.

Stanhowe, Robert—(H. III. Roll) bore, ermine, *quarterly with*, gules a fret or. (F.) St. George Roll. See STANDON.

Stanlade, Sir Rauf de (or STANLOWE, of co. Staff.)—bore, at the first Dunstable tournament 1308, argent, a lyon rampant tail fourchée sable (F.)—and renowée, in Parliamentary Roll. (F.) See STANLOWE.

*[**Stanley, Sir Humphrey**, of Aston—(E. IV. Roll), bore, argent, on a bend azure three bucks' heads cabossed or (BAMVILLE), with 3 quarterings; Ballard Roll. Sir JOHN, K.G. 1405, see title-page, bore STANLEY (i.e. BAMVILLE) *quarterly with*, LATHOM; as did his son JOHN at the siege of Rouen 1418—ascribed also to THOMAS and to Sir THOMAS; Jenyns' and Atkinson Rolls.

Stanley, Sir William, of Horton—(E. IV. Roll) bore, STANLEY (i.e. BAMVILLE) *quarterly with*, argent, on a bend vert three mullets or—with crest; Ballard Roll.

Stanlowe, Gerard—(E. III. Roll) bore, or, a lyon rampant tail fourchée sable; Jenyns' Ordinary. See STANLADE.

Stanmarshe, Robert—(E. III. Roll) bore, gules, on a fess dancettée argent three crescents sable; Jenyns' Ordinary. F. See NEWMARCH.

Stanmarche, Thomas—(E. III. Roll) bore, argent, a fess dancettée gules; Jenyns' Ordinary. See NEWMARCH.

Stanton, Helis de, and **Sir William**, of co. Leic.—(E. II. Roll) bore, vaire argent and sable, a canton gules; St. George and Parly. Rolls. See STAUNTON.

Staple, le (——) bore, at the siege of Rouen 1418, argent, two bars undée sable, on a chief gules a lyon passant gardant or. (F.) See also RICHARD STAPLETON.

*Stapleton, Sir Richard**—bore, at the siege of Calais 1345-8, argent, a lyon rampant sable—ascribed also to Sir MILES, of Yorkshire, and to NICHOLAS; Parliamentary Roll and Jenyns' Ordinary. In Ashmole Roll are two unidentified STAPLETON coats, the one differenced, with a label (3); and the lyon in the other, with a fleur-de-lys or. MYLES, K.G. (founder 1344), and BRYAN, K.G. 1382, differenced with a mullet, (M) or (B) gules on the lyon, in the Surrey Roll: undifferenced in K. 398, 399. see title-page. Another BRYAN and MYLES differenced with an annulet (B) argent (M) azure; Jenyns' Ordinary and Ashmole Roll.

Stapeltone, Robert de—(E. I. Roll) bore, azure, a lyon rampant or; Harleian Roll.

Stapleton, Sir Robert de (of co. Staff.)—bore, at the first Dunstable tournament 1308, azure, a lyon rampant tail fourchée or. (F.) Parly. and St. George Rolls. Borne also by JOHN, Jenyns' Ordinary.

Stapleton, Miles—(E. I. Roll) bore, sable, a lyon rampant tail fourchée argent. Harleian Roll.

Stapleton, Sir Richard de—(E. III. Roll) bore, argent, two bends undée (nebulée) sable; Ashmole Roll. WILLIAM DE HELLIFIELD bears the same arms, Jenyns' Ordinary; another coat for RICHARD in Jenyns' Ordinary is tricked, barry nebulée (6) sable and argent.

Stapleton, William, of Cumberland—(E. I. Roll) bore, argent, three swords conjoined at the pommel gules; Jenyns' Roll. F.

*[**Starky, Geoffrey**, E. I.—bore, argent, a bend between six storks sable.—Shirley.] F.

Staunton, Henry de, (STANDON)—(E. I. Roll) bore, argent, a bend double battaile sable; Jenyns' Roll and Ordinary.

Staunton, Robert de—(E. III. Roll) bore, sable, a cinquefoyle within an orle of martlets argent; Jenyns' Ordinary. F.

Raffe de Stanlade

Raffe de Stantord

Helis d. Stauntone

Tēp̃ do Stavile

Stoddaw

Jon do Tavorton

Staundone, Robert de—(H. III. Roll) bore, quarterly argent and gules fretty or, over all a baston sable ; Arden Roll. Ascribed to HUGH LE DESPENCER in Glover Roll.

Staunton, Sir Robert—(E. III. Roll) bore, gules, three crosses patée 2 and 1 argent, in chief a lyon passant or ; Ashmole Roll. See STAYNTON.

***Staunton, Sir Geoffrey de and Thomas de**—(E. III. Roll) bore, argent, two chevronels sable, a bordure engrailed of the last (F.) ; Ashmole and Surrey Rolls ; a plain border for Sir WILLIAM of Notts, 1326. See Monumental Effigy.

Staunton, Helis de and Sir William, of co. Leic.—(H. III. Roll) bore, vaire argent and sable, a canton gules (F.) ; St. George and Parly. Rolls.

Staveley, Adam de—(E. III. Roll) bore, barry (8) argent and gules, over all a fleur-de-lys sable ; Jenyns' Ordinary ; gules and argent in Grimaldi Roll.

Staveley, Sampson—(R. II. Roll) bore, paly (6) argent and azure ; Surrey Roll.

Stavile, Sir Thomas de—bore, at the first Dunstable tournament 1308, gules, a fess between three escallops argent (F.) ; also tricked or.

‡**Staverton, John de**—(H. III. Roll) bore, argent, fretty gules (F.) ; Dering Roll.

Stawel, Sir T.—(H. VI. Roll) bore, gules, a cross masculy argent, *quarterly with*, argent three bends azure ; Atkinson Roll.

Stenefeld, Sir Guy de (NENESFELDE or SENEFYLDE), of Essex—(R. II. Roll) bore, vert, an eagle displayed or ; Parly. Roll.

Stengrave, Sir John—(H. III. Roll) bore, ermine a lyon rampant gules (F.) ; St. George and Guillim Rolls.

Stepey, Sir John, of Notts.—(H. III. Roll) bore, azure, a cross or fretty gules (F.) ; Parly. Roll. WILLIAM DE STEPHEN bore the same ; Arden and St. George Rolls. F. See SHEPEY.

Sterlyng (——) a Suffolk knight—(H. VI. Roll) bore, azure, a cross patée between four estoyles or ; Arundel Roll.

Steward, Robert de—bore, at the siege of Carlaverock 1300, sable, a cross patée florettée argent (see also SYWARD), a cross flory in Nicolas.

Steward, William (LE SENESCHAL) —(H. III. Roll) bore, gules, on a cross argent five torteaux (F.) ; St. George Roll.

SIR WILLIAM STAUNTON.

IN STAUNTON CHURCH, NOTTS, 1326.

After Stothard.

Steyngrave *v.* **Stengrave.**

Steynton, Sir Robert—(E. III. Roll) bore, gules, three crosses patée 2 and 1 argent, in chief a lyon passant or ; Ashmole Roll.

Stockport, Waren, *v.* **Warren.**

Stodebuit, Raffe — (E. III. Roll) bore, burulée (12) argent and azure over all three lyonceux rampant gules—another purpure ; Jenyns' Ordinary.

Stoddaw (——) an Essex Knight—(H. VI. Roll) bore, gules, a chevron between three Cornish choughs proper, a bordure engrailed of the last ; Arundel Roll. F.

Stodham, Simon de—(H. III. Roll) bore, per pale or and azure, barry of six counterchanged, a chevron gules (F.) ; St. George Roll.

Stokes, Henry de—(H. III. Roll) bore, bendy (10) or and azure, a canton gules (F.) ; Arden Roll.

Stokes, William—(H. III. Roll) bore, vair, a chief gules (F.) ; Arden and St. George Rolls.

Stokes, William, of Kent, Knight—(H. VI. Roll) bore, gules, a demi-lyon rampant, tail fourchée, argent, a bordure sable bezantée ; Arundel Roll.

Stone, John de—(H. III. Roll) bore, gules, crusily argent, a lyon rampant or (F.) ; St. George Roll ; no crusily in Arden Roll.

Stone, Sir Nicholas de (ETONE), of Warwickshire — (E. II. Roll) bore, gules a chevron between three eagles displayed argent ; Parly. Roll.

Stone, Richard de—(H. III. Roll) bore, azure, crusily a bend or surmounted of another gules (F.) ; Arden and St. George Rolls. ESTONE, STONE, or STOWE, crusily a bend argent, &c. in Glover Roll.

Simon d. Stodham

Henri de Stoke

witt Shephep

Joan do Estongue

witt le Seneschal

witt d. Estoke

Joan d. Estone

Richard de Stone

186

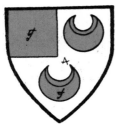

Rauf de Stopgam

Sr le Stratton

John Stryvohn

Adam de Strode

John de Strutgeley

Jo de Stopham

John Sturmy

Robt d. Stotevile.

John Sturton

Robt de Stotoville

John Sudburye

Counte de Estorne vel Strathorn

Joan d' Suteye

Stone, William de—(H. III. Roll) bore, argent, a lyon passant gardant sable ; Arden Roll.

Stongrave v. **Stangrave.**

***Stonore, John**—(E. III. Roll) bore, azure, two bars dancettée and a chief or (F.) ; Jenyns' Ordinary.

Stopham, John, Thomas, and **Sir William,** of Yorkshire—(E. III. Roll) bore, argent, a baston sable ; another JOHN and Sir JOHN of Yorkshire differenced with a label (3, 5) gules (F.) ; Segar and Parly. Rolls and Jenyns' Ordinary.

‡**Stopham, Rauf de**—(H. III. Roll) bore, argent, three crescents and a quarter gules (F.) ; Dering and Howard Rolls ; ascribed to Sir WILLIAM in Nativity Roll.

Stormyn v. **Sturmyn.**

Story, William—(E. III. Roll) bore, argent, a lyon rampant tail fourchée purpure ; Ashmole Roll—charged on the shoulder with a cross crosslet or ; Jenyns' Roll. RICHARD bore the cross patée or ; Surrey Roll.

Stoteville, Robert—(E. III. Roll) bore, burulée (10, 12, 14) argent and gules. (F.) Grimaldi and Jenyns' Rolls and Ordinary—six barrulets in St. George Roll.

Stotevile, Robert de—(H. III. Roll) bore, argent (5, 8, 9 or) 10 barrulets gules, over all a lyon rampant sable (F.) ; Dering and Howard Rolls.

‡**Stottot, Robert le**—(H. III. Roll) bore, ermine, on a cross gules five martlets or ; Arden and St. George Rolls. ESTOTOT and SCOTTO in Dering Roll.

Strabolgi v. **Atholl.**

Stradling, Sir Edward—(E. III. Roll) bore, paly (6) argent and azure, on a bend gules three cinquefoyles pierced or ; Ashmole Roll.

Strange v. **Le Strange.**

Strangray, John and **Raffe de**—(E. III. Roll) bore, azure, billettée and a cross argent ; Jenyns' Ordinary.

Stratherne, the Earl of, in Scotland— (E. III. Roll) bore, gules, two chevronels or. (F.) Camden Roll and Jenyns' Ordinary.

Stratton, Sr. le, (——) knighted at the capitulation of Calais 1348, bore, or, two bars and in the cantel an inescocheon gules. F.

Stretton, (——), a Suffolk Knight—(H. VI. Roll) bore, argent, on a cross sable five torteaux ; Arundel Roll.

Stratton, (——), a Suffolk Knight—(H. VI. Roll) bore, or, on a chief dancettée azure, three escallops argent ; Arundel Roll.

Strecche, Stephen — (E. I. Roll) bore, argent, a "chevron et demi" (2 chevronels in trick) azure, on a quarter of the last a fleur-de-lys or ; Jenyns' Roll.

Strechley, Sir John de (of Notts)—bore, at the battle of Boroughbridge 1322, argent, an eagle displayed sable. (F.) Parliamentary Roll—ascribed also to THOMAS in Jenyns' Ordinary.

Strelley, —— (E. III. Roll) bore, paly (6) argent and azure ; Jenyns' Ordinary.

***Strickland, Sir Thomas** and **Sir Walter** —(E. I. Roll) bore, sable, three escallops argent (F.) Jenyns', Ashmole, Nativity and Surrey Rolls ; see also Ballard Roll for quarterly coat.

Strickland, Sir Walter—(E. II. Roll) bore, argent, two bars and a quarter gules—in another trick three bars ; Parliamentary Roll.

[**Strode, Adam de,** E. I.—bore, argent, a chevron between three conies sable.—Shirley.] F.

Strother, Thomas de—(E. III. Roll) bore, gules, on a bend argent three eaglets displayed vert membered gules ; Jenyns' and Surrey Rolls.

Stryvelyn, Sir John de, baron 1342— bore, at the siege of Calais 1345-8, argent, on a chief gules three buckles, tongues to the dexter or. F.

Stryvelyn, Sir John—(E. III. Roll) bore, sable, crusily (fitchée in Cotgrave Roll) and three covered cups argent ; Jenyns' Ordinary—in Ashmole Roll three cups between three crosses fitchée.

Stukele, Nicoll—(R. II. Roll) bore, argent, on a fess sable three mullets of the field. Surrey Roll.

Sturmy, Sir Robert de—(E. I. Roll) bore, sable, a cross engrailed or, a label (3) argent ; Holland Roll.

Sturmyn, Sir Robert de, of Cheshire— (E. II. Roll) bore, gules, a chevron argent between three plates, Parliamentary Roll.

Sturmyn, —— (E. III. Roll) bore, gules, three inescocheons ermine ; Ashmole Roll.

Sturmin, Henry le — (H. III. Roll) bore, argent, three demi-lyons (rampant) gules ; St. George Roll—MERVILLE in Harl. 6137 fo. 89b.

Sturmyn, Sir John, knighted at the capitulation of Calais 1348, bore, sable, a lyon passant gardant argent — blasoned saliant argent in Jenyns' Ordinary. F.

Sturmyne, Sir Roger, of Suffolk—(E. II. Roll) bore, quarterly or and gules, on a bendlet azure three besants ; Parliamentary Roll.

***Sturton, Sir John**—bore, at the siege of Rouen 1418, sable, a bend or between six fountains. F.

Sudbury, Sir John—bore, at the first Dunstable tournament 1308,—ermine, on a chief gules three cinquefoyles or. Another, argent, on a fess dancettée gules three cinquefoyles or (F.) ; Harl. 6137 fo. 37b.

Sudeston, —— (E. I. Roll) bore, gules, fretty argent ; Harl. Roll.

Sudley, John de (SULLEE), banneret, baron 1299, sealed the Barons' letter to the Pope 1301, pp. xx, xxiv. He bore, or two bends gules. (F.) Nobility and Surrey Rolls. Borne also by his father, (‡) Sir BARTHOLOMEW SULEY and JOHN SULLEY, in many Rolls. (To BARTHOLOMEW and ROBERT bars are erroneously ascribed in Jenyns' Ordinary and Camden Roll.) Another Sir BARTHOLOMEW SULEY, of co. Worc., and Sir WILLIAM SULE differenced with a label (3) azure ; Parliamentary and Harl. Rolls.

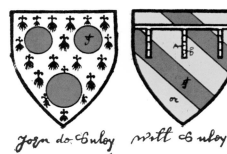

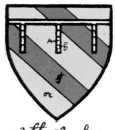

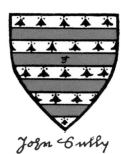

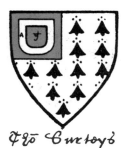

John do Suley · witt Suley · John Sully · F̃o Curtoys · John Sutton · John do Sutton

witt d. Smeli

Roland Sutton

John do Sutton

Sully, John—bore, at the second Dunstable tournament 1334, ermine, three torteaux. F.

Sully, Sir John (or SULBY), K.G., 1362—bore, ermine, four bars gules, K. 400 fo. 27. F.

Suley, Sir William de—bore, at the first Dunstable tournament 1308, gules, two bends or, a label (3) argent each pendant charged with 4 barrulets azure (F.); (another trick, or and gules)—the pendants gobony (4) argent and azure in the Parliamentary Roll.

Suneli, William de—(H. III. Roll) bore, azure, fretty or, a label (5) gules. (F.) St. George Roll.

Surrien, Sir Francis, K.G. (H. VI.)—bore, or three palets gules, on a chief argent three escallops sable; K. 402 fo. 28.

Surteys, Thomas—(E. I. Roll) bore, ermine, on a quarter gules, an orle argent; Jenyns' Roll. F.

‡**Susat, Sire de** (SUSANE) — (H. III. Roll) bore, sable, on a chief argent, a (demi) fleur-de-lys issuant gules. (F.) Dering Roll.

Sutton, Sir Avery de—(E. III. Roll) bore, quarterly argent and gules; Ashmole Roll.

Sutton, Sir John de—bore, at the first Dunstable tournament 1308, azure, on a chief or, a lyon passant gules. F.

Sutton, Sir Hamond de (of Essex)—bore, at the first Dunstable tournament 1308, vert, crusily and three covered cups argent. (F.) Parliamentary Roll.

Sutton (James) de—(H. III. Roll) bore, ermine, a canton sable. (F.) Arden Roll; as JAMES le fiz, in St. George Roll. *[ROLAND, (H. III.) bore, the field argent.—Shirley.] F.

Sutton, Sir John de, of Holderness, baron 1324, bore at the battle of Boroughbridge 1322, or, a lyon rampant azure, oppressed by a baston gobony argent and gules. (F.) Ashmole Roll and Jenyns' Ordinary.

Sutton, John de—bore, at the second Dunstable tournament 1334, or, a lyon rampant azure, oppressed by a baston gobony or and gules.

Sutton, Sir Richard, banneret — (E. II. Roll) bore, or, a lyon rampant tail fourchée vert; Parliamentary Roll.

Sutton, Sir John de, of Lincolnshire—(E. II. Roll) bore, or, a lyon rampant vert, a label (3) gules; Parly. Roll—probably also undifferenced by Sir RICHARD, knight banneret; Surrey Roll.

Sutton, Sir John—(E. I. Roll) bore, or, a lyon gules and a chief vair; Nativity Roll.

Sutton, John, BARON DUDLEY, K.G. (H. VI.)—bore, or, two lyons passant azure, *quarterly with*, argent, a cross patonce azure; K. 402 fo. 43.

Sutton, John de—(E. III. Roll) bore, azure, five fusils conjoined in fess or, a baston gobony argent and gules; Jenyns' Ordinary.

Sutton, Sir John de—bore, at the battle of Boroughbridge 1322, argent, a cross patonce azure (F.); ascribed also as a cross flory in trick and a cross patée in blason to RICHARD in Jenyns' Ordinary.

Sutton, John de—bore, at the second Dunstable tournament 1334, or three chevronels sable. (F.) Sir JOHN, knighted at the capitulation of Calais 1348, bore the same—as also JOHN, in Surrey Roll, and RICHARD, of Norfolk, in Jenyns' Ordinary. TERRY DE MANNY bore the same arms—Sir JOHN le fys differenced with a label (3) gules; Ashmole Roll.

Sutton (——) a Knight—(H. VI. Roll) bore, azure, two chevronels between three mullets argent; Arundel Roll.

Swalow, William—(R. II. Roll) bore, or, a fess between three swallows rising sable; Surrey Roll. F.

Swillington —— (E. I. Roll) bore, gules, a gryphon (segreant) argent; Cotgrave Roll. F.

Swillington, Adam, baron 1326, bore, argent, a chevron gules; Jenyns' Ordinary. Sir ADAM, of Yorks., differenced with a label (3) gules; Nativity and Parly. Rolls. ROBERT differenced with a label (3) ermine; Surrey Roll.

Swillington, Sir Hugh, of Yorkshire—(E. II. Roll) bore, argent, on a chevron azure, a fleur-de-lys or; Parly. Roll and a label (3) of the last; Harl. MS. 6137 fo. 21ᵇ.

Swinburne, Adam de—bore at the second Dunstable tournament 1334, gules, crusily and a swine's head argent. F.

Swinburne, Sir Adam de, of Northumberland—(E. II. Roll) bore, gules, three swines' heads couped argent; Parliamentary, Glover and Jenyns' Rolls.

Swinburne, Sir Robert, of Northumberland—(E. II. Roll) bore, gules crusily and three swines' heads couped argent; Parly. and Surrey Rolls. THOMAS bore it with a label (3) or; Surrey Roll. and Lansd. MS. 872 fo. 66ᵇ.

Swinbourne (——) bore, at the siege of Rouen 1418, or, a saltire engrailed sable, charged with an annulet, *quarterly with*, gules, crusily and three swines' heads couped argent.

***Swinbourne, William**—(E. III. Roll) bore, argent, a chief gules and three cinquefoyles counterchanged 2 and 1 (F.); Jenyns' Ordinary. In the Surrey Roll it is blasoned per fess gules and argent, three roses counterchanged.

John do Sutton

witt Swalow

Hamond do Sutton

James do Sutton

de Swillington

Adam de Swynobourn

witt de Swynobourne

Joan de Swynford

Robt. Swyneford

Robt. Gwynd of Hilton

Tho Swynythwaite

Gydney

Richard Gynard

Roger de Swinnerton

Roger de Swinnerton

Swynford, Sir John de, of Hunts.—(E. II. Roll) bore, argent, three swines' heads couped gules; Parly. Roll. F.

Swynford, Norman and **Sir Thomas de,** of Hunts.—(E. II. Roll) bore, argent on a chevron sable three swines' heads couped or; Jenyns' and Parly. Rolls. THOMAS differenced with a cinquefoyle, and WILLIAM differenced with a quarter sable charged with a cinquefoyle or; Jenyns' Roll and Ordinary. In the coat for Sir THOMAS, Harl. MS. 6137 fo. 22, the swines' heads are gules and between the chevron.

Swynhowe, Robert—(E. I. Roll) bore, sable three swine passant argent; Jenyns' Roll. F.

Swyne, Robert, of Hilton (in Holdernesse), founder of the abbey—(E. I. Roll) bore, or, three chaplets gules; Jenyns' Roll; HILTON bears the same. F.

Swynythwaite, Thomas — (E. I. Roll) bore, argent, a chevron between three swine passant sable; Jenyns' Roll and Ordinary. F.

Sydney (——) an Essex? knight—(H. VI. Roll) bore, or, a pheon azure; Arundel Roll. F.

Syfrewast, Robert — (E. I. Roll) bore, azure, three gemelles and a chief argent; Jenyns' Roll. See CYFREWAST and SIFREWAST.

Synsiwarde, Roger (SUISTYWARD)—(E. I. Roll) bore, bendy (6) argent and azure; Jenyns' Roll, (blasoned the reverse); same arms as St. PHILIBERT.

Swinnerton, Sir Roger de, baron 1337, bore, at the first Dunstable tournament 1308, argent, a cross (patée) florettée sable (F.); another ROGER bore it at the second Dunstable tournament 1334. Sir THOMAS bore it at the siege of Calais 1345-8, and Sir ROGER, knighted at the capitulation of Calais 1348, differenced it with a label (5) gules.

Swinnerton, Sir Roger, of Cambridgeshire —(E. II. Roll) argent, a cross patonce couped at the foot sable; Harl. 4033. In Harl. 6137, argent, a cross patée florettée at the ends sable; Parly. Roll. F.F.

Swinnerton, Adam de—(E. III. Roll) bore, argent, a cross flory sable (now patée flory) bouttes florettes; Jenyns' Ordinary. Sir ROGER bore argent, a cross patée sable; Nativity Roll. ROBERT bore the reverse (in Jenyns' Ordinary), being the same as PULFORD; the probability is that the crosses in these instances should be the same and are inaccurately tricked.

JOAN, the Fair Maid of Kent, wife, 1st, of Sir THOMAS HOLLAND, ob. 1360, and 2nd, of EDWARD the Black Prince.

Syward, Sir Richard, banneret (of Scotland)—bore, at the battle of Falkirk 1298, sable, a cross florettée argent (F.) He bore the same (tricked cross patée florettée) at the siege of Carlaverock 1300; the cross is variously tricked and blasoned cross flory, cross patonce, and fer-de-moulin; Holland Roll, &c. Called ROBERT in Harl. 6137 fo. 38b.

Syward, Sir Richard, a banneret—(E. II. Roll) bore, sable a cross florettée fitchée at the foot argent,—in trick a cross patonce couped at the foot; Parly. Roll; for a similar cross see Sir ROGER SWINNERTON.

Syward, Sir William—(E. III. Roll) bore gules, a cross patonce argent; Ashmole Roll with a note Sir WILLIAM DE SAYE, NORREYS.

Sywardby, John—(E. III. Roll) bore, argent, a bend cotised sable between six lyonceux (3, 3) of the last; Surrey Roll and Jenyns' Ordinary.

ANNE, daughter of THOMAS of Woodstock, wife, 1st, of EDMUND DE STAFFORD, K.G., fell at Shrewsbury 1403, and 2nd, of WILLIAM BOURCHIER, Earl of Eu.

ELIZABETH, daughter of JOHN of Gaunt, wife of JOHN HOLLAND, Duke of Exeter 1397.

MARY, Queen of France, youngest daughter of HENRY VII., ob. 1583, 3rd wife of CHARLES BRANDON, Duke of Suffolk.

Heraldic Atchievements of those Princesses through whom Royal Quarterings are transmitted; from unpublished drawings of the late Frater Anselm, of Mount St. Bernard Abbey, in Leicester.

"Here the French fight and those who were with Harold fell." After the Bayeux Tapestry.

— T —

Ric͠h Talebot

Lord Talbot

Talbot

Richard Talbott.

Tadington, Sir Peres de (TATYNGTON), of Suffolk—(E. II. Roll) bore, sable, a cross (moline) recercelée or ; Parliamentary Roll.

Talbot, Richard—(H. III. Roll) bore, or five bendlet gules. (F.) St. George Roll and Harl. MS. 6137 ff. 83, 89—bendy (10) argent and gules (F.) is the paternal coat of TALBOT, as attributed by the later Heralds. As Lord of ECKLESWELL, he sealed the Barons' letter to the Pope 1301, with the arms of RHESE AP GRIFFITH, Prince of South Wales, viz. : a lyon rampant within a bordure engrailed, pp. xix, xxiv.

*Talbot, Sir Gilbert (of co. Glouc.)—bore, at the first Dunstable tournament 1308, GIL-BERT, and his son RICHARD, with a label azure, bore at the second Dunstable tournament 1334, and RICHARD, lord steward of the King's Household, bore at the siege of Calais 1345-8, gules, a lyon rampant within a bordure en-grailed or (F.), being the bardic arms of RHYS, Prince of South Wales ; the border is often blasoned and tricked indented. GILBERT, K.G. (5th lord), bore at the siege of Rouen 1418, RHYS, *quarterly with* STRANGE, argent, two lyons passant in pale gules ; these are also as-cribed to RICHARD, in the Surrey Roll (R. II.). In the 6th Nobility Roll, LE SR. TALBOT bore the arms of STRANGE only and the Earl of SHREWSBURY those of BELISME only, azure, a lyon rampant within a bordure or ; JOHN, LORD TALBOT, K.G. 1424, bore this latter, quarterly with the first blasoned coat, see title-page.

Talbot, Sir John, knighted at the capitu-lation of Calais 1348, bore, gules, a lyon rampant or, a bordure engrailed of the last, and a bendlet azure. Jenyns' Ordinary as-cribes to another JOHN, the coat without the bendlet, the lyon charged with a mullet (argent).

Talbott, Richard—(H. III. Roll) bore, or, a lyon gules collared or, a bordure vert besantée ; Norfolk Roll.

Talbot, Sir Edmond—bore, at the first Dunstable tournament 1308, argent, three lyonceux rampant gules,—purpure, for another Sir EDMUND, of Lanc., in Parliamentary Roll and Jenyns' Ordinary.

Talbot, Sir (? EDMUND), of Bashall, in Lanc., knighted at the capitulation of Calais 1348, bore, argent, three lyonceux rampant 2 and 1 azure (F.) *vel* purpure. Sir JOHN, of Sale-bury, Sir EDMOND and Sir THOMAS, of Bashall, bore, the lyonceux purpure ; Ballard, Parliamentary and Surrey Rolls.

Talbot, Sir Richard—bore, at the battle of Boroughbridge 1322, gules, two bars vair. (F.) Ascribed also to Sir JOHN and WILLIAM ; and with a mullet pierced argent to GILBERT ; Ashmole and Surrey Rolls and Jenyns' Or-dinary.

Talbot, Gilbert—(H. III. Roll) bore, vaire, gules and or, a bordure azure ; Arden Roll.

Talbot, Sir John — (E. III. Roll) bore, argent, crusily fitchée (5, 7), and three fleurs-de-lys gules ; Ashmole and Surrey Rolls.

Talbot, Gilbert and (‡) **Robert**—(H. III. Roll) bore, barry (6) argent and gules ; Howard and Ashmole copy of Dering Roll—or and gules for ROBERT in Dering Roll. F.

Talboys, Walter—(R. II. Roll) bore, argent, a saltire gules, on a chief of the last, three escallops of the field ; Surrey Roll. HENRY bore the field or, in Jenyns' Ordinary.

Talboys, Sir William, SR. DE KYME—bore, at the siege of Rouen 1418, gules, crusily and a cinquefoyle or, *quarterly with*, KYME ; azure, crusily and a chevron or. F.

Talmache, Sir Hugh, of Suffolk—(H. III. Roll) bore, argent, fretty sable ; Arden and Parliamentary Rolls. Sir WILLIAM differenced with a label (3, 5) gules. (F.) Harleian and Segar Rolls.

Talworth, Sir William, of Essex, Kt.—(H. VI. Roll) bore, barry (6) or and azure, on a chevron gules three mullets (6) of the first ; Arundel Roll.

‡Tamworth, Giles de—(H. III. Roll) bore, argent, a fess dancettée between three cocks' heads erased sable ; Dering Roll. F.

*Tanckard, William, (H. III.)—bore, argent, a chevron between three escallops gules.—Shirley.] F.

‡Tancre, Bartram (TANQUERAY)—(H. III. Roll) bore, azure, two bends argent. (F.) Dering and Howard Rolls.

Robert Talbot

Lo E. de Rino

witt Talomarp

Giles de Tamworth

witt Tancard

Bertram Tancre

Robt d'Tateshale

John Tondring

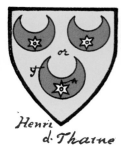

Gilbert d'Thaine

Henri d'Thaine

Robert Thornogam

Robt. Thornos

Robert Tatton

John de Tondring

Raffe de Thirtwall

Roger de Thorpe

Lucas Chani

Piers de Thornton

Sir Thorold

Roger de Thorpe

Tany, Sir John, of Essex, and **Lucas**—(H. III. Roll) bore, azure, three barrulets argent ; Parliamentary and Howard Rolls and Jenyns' Ordinary.

Tany, Sir Richard, of Essex—(H. III. Roll) bore, or, six eaglets displayed sable ; Guillim, Howard and Parliamentary Rolls — three eaglets in Jenyns' Ordinary.

Tarent, the Duke de—(E. IV. Roll) bore, quarterly gules and argent in the first an eagle displayed of the second ; Jenyns' Ordinary.

Tateshall, Sir Robert (TATTESHALL), of Buckenham, baron 1295—bore, at the battle of Falkirk 1298, as did his son Sir ROBERT at the siege of Carlaverock 1300, checquy or and gules, a chief ermine. (F.) Arden, St. George and other Rolls ;—this ROBERT the son differenced with a label (3) azure at Falkirk 1298, and so sealed the Barons' letter to the Pope 1301, pp. xvii, xxiv. ROBERT or ROGER LE FITZ differenced with a label (3) or, in Jenyns' Ordinary. Ascribed to RAFFE undifferenced, in Norfolk Roll.

Tateshal, Sir Hue de—(E. I. Roll) bore, checquy or and gules, a canton ermine ; Harl. Roll.

*[**Tatton, Robert**, E. III.—bore, quarterly argent and gules four crescents counterchanged.—Shirley.] F.

Tempest, —— (E. III. Roll) bore, argent, a chevron gules, between three martlets sable ; Cotgrave Roll.

*[**Tempest, Richard** and **William**—(E. III. Roll) bore, argent, a bend between six martlets 3, 3, sable ; Surrey Roll and Jenyns' Ordinary—bend engrailed for RICHARD also in Jenyns' Ordinary ; the birds are sometimes blasoned stormy petrels and storm finches.

Temple, the Auntient of the—(H. III. Roll) bore, argent, a cross passant gules and a chief sable.—The ANCIENT DEL HOSPITALL, bore, gules, a cross formée argent ; Norfolk Roll.

Tendring, Sire John—bore, at the battle of Boroughbridge 1322, sable, a fess between two chevronels or, a label (3) of France ; gules, on each pendant three fleurs-de lys argent. F.

Tendring, Sir John, a Suffolk Knight—(E. II. Roll) bore, azure, a fess between two chevronels or, a label (3) gules, on each pendant a fleur-de-lys argent. (F.) Parly. Roll.

Tendring, Sir William, a Suffolk Knight —(E. III. Roll) bore, azure, a fess between two chevronels argent ; Arundel, Ashmole and Surrey Rolls.

Tendring, Sir John, of Brenthall, Essex—(H. VI. Roll) bore, argent, on a fess between two chevronels azure three crescents or ; Arundel Roll, Harl. MS. 4205 fo. 20.

Terby, John, (TEREBY)—(E. III. Roll) bore, argent, an estoile or, on a chief azure three water-bougets of the second ; Jenyns' Roll.

Teringham v. **Tyringham**.

Teyes, Sir Walter de, of Stangreve, in Yorks., knight banneret, baron 1299—bore, at the battle of Falkirk 1298, or on a fess between two chevronels gules three mullets of the first ; argent in Arundel, Ashmole and Nobility Rolls ; (see also TYES), spur-rowells on his seal, attached to the Barons' letter to the Pope 1301, pp. xx, xxiv.

Teye (TAY) —— an Essex Knight—(H. VI. Roll) bore, argent, a fess between three martlets in chief and a chevron in base all azure ; Arundel Roll.

Thaine, Gilbert de—(H. III. Roll) bore gules, three mullets (6) argent (F.) ; ascribed also to GILBERT or GILES HAUNSARD or HASSELL ; St. George Roll.

Thaine, Henry de—(H. III. Roll) bore, or, three crescents gules, each charged with a spur-rowell argent. (F.) St. George Roll.

†**Thani, Lucas de**—(H. III. Roll) bore, azure, three bars argent ; St. George Roll. F.

Thani, Richard de—(H. III. Roll) bore, argent, six eagles displayed sable ; St. George Roll.

Thimbleby —— Knight—(H. VI. Roll) bore, gules, a chevron engrailed and a chief argent ; Arundel Roll.

Thirkeld —— (E. III. Roll) bore, argent, a maunch gules ; Ashmole Roll.

Thirkeld, William—(E. I. Roll) bore, argent, a maunch gules, a label (3) vert ; Jenyns' Roll—another, argent, a maunch burulée or and gules—or, three bars gules, in trick ; Jenyns' Ordinary.

Thirlewall, Raphe de—(E. I. Roll) bore gules, a chevron between three boars' heads couped bendways argent. (F.) Jenyns' Roll.

Thoresby, William, late Keeper of the Privie Seale—bore, at the siege of Calais 1345-8, argent, a chevron between three lyonceux rampant sable (F.) ; ascribed also to HUGH and PIERS ; Grimaldi Roll and Jenyns' Ordinary.

Thornburgh, William de—(E. I. Roll) bore, ermine fretty and a chief gules—tricked as three chevronels interlaced in base ; Jenyns' Roll.

Thornbury, John — (R. II. Roll) bore, argent, a chief or, surmounted by a lyon rampant azure, over all two bendlets gules ; Surrey Roll.

Thorne, Sir William de—(E. III. Roll) bore, azure, a bend argent between three lyonceux rampant or ; Ashmole Roll.

Thorneham, Robert, founder of Beigham Monastery, in Sussex—(E. I. Roll) bore, gules, a lyon passant between two lozenges in pale or. (F.) Jenyns' Roll.

[**Thornes, Robert**, 1357—bore, sable, a lyon rampant gardant argent.—Shirley.] F.

*[**Thornhill, Sir Bryan**—(E. III. Roll) bore, gules, two gemelles and a chief argent ; Ashmole Roll and Jenyns' Ordinary.

Thornton, Sir Piers de, knighted at the capitulation of Calais 1348, bore, argent on a bend gules three escarbuncles or. F.

Thornton —— a Knight—(H. VI. Roll) bore, sable, a chevron and a chief dancettée all argent ; Arundel Roll.

*[**Thorold, Sir Richard**, E. III.)—bore, sable, three goats salient argent.—Shirley.] F.

will de Thorpe

Edmonde Thorpe

Marmadue Thynge

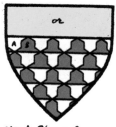

Jo de Tichebourne

Roger de Tilmanston

Thorpe (Sir) Edmond—bore, at the siege of Rouen 1418, azure, three crescents 2 and 1 argent. (F.) Ashmole, Surrey and Jenyns' Rolls. See Monumental Effigy, after Stothard, THORPE quarterly with BAYNARD.

Thorp, John, baron 1309—bore, gules, a fess between six fleurs-de-lys argent ; Nobility Roll ; checquy or and gules a fess ermine ; Parly. Roll.

Thorpe, Sir George de (of Norfolk)—bore, at the first Dunstable tournament 1308, checquy or and gules on a fess argent three martlets sable, as did Sir ROGER at the battle of Boroughbridge 1322. F.

Thorp, John de—(R. II. Roll) bore, azure, a fess dancettée ermine ; Surrey Roll.

Thorp, William de—bore, at the second Dunstable tournament 1334, burulée, or and sable. F.

[**Throckmorton, John,** (E. III.)—bore, gules, on a chevron argent three gemelles sable.—Shirley.] F.

Thurston (——) of Anderton—(E. IV. Roll) bore, sable, three shackbolts 2 and 1 argent *quarterly with*, vert, three bugles 2 and 1 argent stringed or—with crest ; Ballard Roll.

Thwaites, Thomas, of Coupland—(E. III. Roll) bore, argent, a cross fretty sable and argent ; Jenyns' Ordinary.

Thweng, Marmaduke, of Kilton, banneret, baron 1310—bore, gules, a fess argent between three popinjays vert ; Nobility Roll. All other Rolls give the reverse, viz., argent a fess gules, &c.

Thweng, Marmaduke de (called JOHN in the Roll), a baron 1307—bore, at the battle of Falkirk 1298, argent, a fess gules between three popinjays vert. See also FITZ MARMADUKE—ascribed also to Sir WILLIAM ; Ashmole Roll and Jenyns' Ordinary. F.

Thweng, Marmaduke, of Cornburgh—(E. I. Roll) bore, argent, on a fess gules between three popinjays vert as many escallops or ; Jenyns' Roll.

Tibetot, Sir Payn de (TIPETOFT), banneret, baron 1308—bore, at the first Dunstable tournament 1308, argent, a saltire engrailed gules (F.) ; Nobility and Arundel Rolls ; borne at the second Dunstable tournament 1334, by JOHN, the probable grandfather of John (baron 1426) who differenced with a label (3) azure at the siege of Rouen 1418. Ascribed also to ROBERT (‡) in the Dering and Howard Rolls. A JOHN and ROBERT took up the cross in the last Crusade 1270.

Tibtot, Paine—(E. III. Roll) bore, argent, a cross engrailed gules ; Jenyns' Ordinary —borne also by JOHN DE LA LINDE ; the cross probably a mistake for the saltire.

*[**Tichborne, Sir John de,** (E. II.)—bore, vair, a chief or.—Shirley.] F.

Tichesie v. **Tychesie.**

Tillioll, Piers and **Sir Robert**—(E. I. Roll) bore, gules, a lyon rampant argent, a baston azure ; Jenyns' and Ashmole Rolls.

Tilly, John—(E. III. Roll) bore, argent, a cross patonce (flory in trick) between four crescents gules ; Jenyns' Ordinary.

‡**Tilmanston, Roger de**—(H. III. Roll) bore, gules, six lyonceux rampant ermine (F.) ; Dering Roll ; argent in Howard Roll.

Tilney, Sir John — (E. III. Roll) bore, azure, three cinquefoyles pierced argent ; Ashmole Roll.

Timperley (——) knighted at the capitulation of Calais 1348—bore, gules, three inescocheons argent. F.

Tochelles v. **Touches.**

Todenham, Oliver—(H. III. Roll) bore, barry lozengy (6) argent and azure (F.) ; St. George Roll. JOHN bore it argent and gules. See TUDENHAM.

***Toke** (——) an Essex Knight—(H. VI. Roll) bore, per chevron sable and argent, three gryphons' heads erased counterchanged (F.) ; Arundel Roll. See also TOOKES and TOUKE.

Toni, Sir Robert de, of Castle Matill, banneret, a baron 1299, sealed the Barons' letter to the Pope 1301, pp. xvii, xxiv. He bore, at the battle of Falkirk 1298, at the siege of Carlaverock 1300, and at the first Dunstable tournament 1308, argent, a maunch gules (F.) ; Nobility Roll ; ascribed also to RAFE (‡) in Dering and Howard Rolls.

Tookes, Sir Robert (TOUK), of co. Cambridge—(E. II. Roll) bore, barry (6) argent and sable ; Parly. Roll, the reverse in Jenyns' Ordinary.

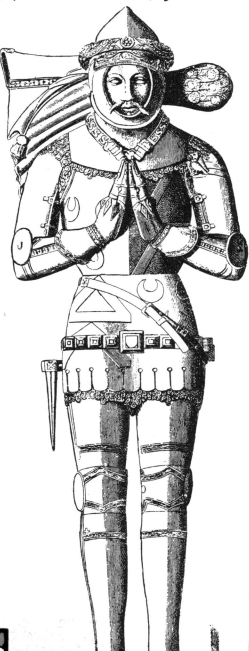

SIR EDMUND DE THORPE.
IN ASHWELLTHORPE CHURCH, NORFOLK,
1418.

John Throckmorton

Payn Tipotot

Timperley

Oliver Todeham

Toke

Robert Tonyo

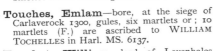

Torboc, Sir Richard, of Torboc—(E. IV. Roll) bore, or, an eagle's claw couped gules, on a chief dancettée azure three plates ; with crest ; Ballard Roll.

‡**Torpigni, Walter de,** (TURPIGNI)—(H. III. Roll) bore, azure, an inescocheon within an orle of escallops (9) argent (F.) ; Dering Roll, no escallops in Ashmole Roll.

Torrell —— an Essex Knight—(H. VI. Roll) bore, gules, a fess engrailed argent between three bulls' heads couped or, perhaps argent ; Arundel Roll.

Torry v. **Corry.**

Torts, Sir Raffe de, of Dorset—(E. II. Roll) bore, gules, a gryphon segreant or ; Parly. Roll.

Totesham —— (E. III. Roll) bore, sable; billettée and a cross argent ; Ashmole Roll.

Touches, Emlam—bore, at the siege of Carlaverock 1300, gules, six martlets or ; 10 martlets (F.) are ascribed to WILLIAM TOCHELLES in Harl. MS. 6137.

Touchet, William, lord of Levenhales 1299–1306, sealed the Barons' letter to the Pope 1301—crusily patée fitchée a lyon rampant, pp. xxii, xxiv, and Cott. Julius C vii. 277. The coat of martlets is ascribed to him in the Nobility Roll, and ermine a chevron gules in the Parliamentary Roll.

Touchet, Robert — (E. II. Roll) bore, ermine a chevron gules ; Jenyns' Roll and Ordinary, Surrey and Ashmole Rolls ; ascribed to Sir THOMAS of Northants, and to ROBERT (or ROGER) LE FITZ with a label (3) azure ; Parliamentary Roll.

Touchet, Sir William—(E. I. Roll) bore, gules, ten martlets 4, 3, 2, 1 or ; Parly. Roll ; six in the Arundel Roll—this latter is ascribed to EMLAM TOUCHES in the Carlaverock Roll 1300 and to WM. TOCHELLES in Harl. MS. 6137. F.

Toukes, Sir Walter, of Notts.—(E. II. Roll) bore, sable, billettée or, a canton ermine (F.) ; Parly., Holland, and St. George Rolls.

Tours, Eustace de—(H. III. Roll) bore, gules, an orle argent, in the cantel an inescocheon azure charged with a lyon rampant of the second crowned or, a label (5) of the last ; Glover Roll ; (this blason is rather obscure), identical with EUSTACE DE BALIOL DE TEAS.

*[**Townley, Richard de,** alias DE LA LEGH 1375—bore, argent, a fess and in chief three mullets sable.—Shirley.] F.

*[**Townshend, Sir Walter de,** c. 1400— bore, azure, a chevron ermine between three escallops argent.—Shirley.] F.

Tracheon v. **Treveynour.**

Tracy, Sir William, (co. Worcr.)—bore, at the first Dunstable tournament 1308, or, two bends and an escallop gules (F.) ; Ashmole and Parly. Rolls. Sir JOHN, knighted at the capitulation of Calais 1348, differenced with a label (5) azure.

Tracy, William—(H. III. Roll) bore, or, vo bends between nine or ten escallops gules (F.) ; Arden and St. George Rolls.

*[**Trafford, Edmund,** of Trafford—(E. IV. Roll) bore, argent, a gryphon segreant gules ; with crest. (F.) Ballard Roll.

‡**Traseme, Otes,** (TRAISINE)—(H. III. Roll) bore, or, three bends azure, within a bordure gules (F.) ; Dering Roll ; bendy (6) or and azure in Ashmole MS.

Travers, John de—(R. II. Roll) bore, argent, a chevron between four butterflies sable ; Surrey Roll.

Trayley, Sir (John) de, of Beds.—(H. III. Roll) bore, or, a cross between four martlets gules ; Arden, Parly. and Surrey Rolls.

*[**Trefusis, Peter de,** 10 E. III.—bore, argent, a chevron between three wharrow spindles sable.—Shirley.] F.

Tregoz, Sir John—bore, at the battle of Falkirk 1298, or, two gemelles and in chief a lyon passant gardant gules (GEOFFREY bore the same in the Norfolk Roll), and in all Rolls save the Nobility Roll, in which the colours are azure and or. The lyon is not gardant in the Dering nor Guillim Rolls. F.

Tregoz, Sir Henry, banneret, sealed the Barons' letter to the Pope 1301, pp. xiv, xxiv. He bore, azure, two gemelles and in chief a lyon passant gardant or ; Nobility, Dering and other Rolls ; gardant in Arden and Howard Rolls and Jenyns' Ordinary.

Tregoz, Robert de—(H. III. Roll) bore, gules, three gemelles or, in chief a lyon passant of the first (sic) probably or ; Glover Roll ; two gemelles in St. George Roll.

Trehampton, Ralph de—(H. III. Roll) bore, argent, a bend gules ; Glover and Grimaldi Rolls.

Trehampton, John de—(E. III. Roll) bore, argent, on a bend gules three cinquefoyles or ; Jenyns' Roll.

Trekingham, Sire Walter de—bore, at the battle of Boroughbridge 1322, argent, two bars gules, in chief three torteaux, over all a baston sable ; ascribed to JOHN (F.) in Jenyns' Ordinary.

*[**Trelawny, John,** E. I.—bore, argent, a chevron sable.—Shirley.] F.

Trellowe, Robert — (R. II. Roll) bore, azure, a chevron between three escallops argent ; Surrey Roll. See TRILLON.

*[**Tremayne, Perys,** E. I.—bore, gules, three dexter arms conjoined and flexed in triangle or, hands clenched proper.—Shirley.] F.

Trenton, Sir Raffe de (TREAUNTON), of co. Lincs.—(H. III. Roll) bore, argent, a bend gules ; Arden and Parly. Roll

Trevelyan

Thomas Trevett

mons Trumpington

Rog d. Trumpinton

SIR ROGER DE TRUMPINGTON.
IN TRUMPINGTON CHURCH, CAMBS,
1289, 17 E. I.
After Waller.

*[Trevelyan, Nicholas de,E. I.—bore, gules, a demi-horse maned and unguled or, issuing out of waves proper.—Shirley.] F.

Trevet, Thomas—bore, at the siege of Rouen 1418, argent a trevet sable (F.) ; ascribed to Sir JOHN TRYVETT in Ashmole Roll. JOHN bore it within a bordure engrailed sable ; Surrey Roll.

Treveynour, Sir John—(E. III. Roll) bore, argent, a fess azure between two chevronels gules ; Ashmole Roll. TRACHEON bears the same in PAPWORTH.

Trewent, Steven de—(E. III. Roll) bore, argent, a chevron between three double-headed eaglets gules ; Jenyns' Roll and Ordinary.

Trewlove, Robert—(E. I. Roll) bore, argent, on a chevron sable three quartrefoyles or ; Jenyns' Roll.

Trigot, Sir Henry—(E. I. Roll) bore, azure, two bars and in chief a lyon passant gardant or ; Harleian Roll.

Trillon, Sir John—(E. III. Roll) bore, argent, a chevron engrailed sable between three escallops of the last ; Ashmole Roll.

Triminell, Sir Nicholas, of co. Leicr.— (E. II. Roll) bore, or, a cross engrailed gules, a baston azure ; Parly. Roll.

Tromyn, Roger—(R. II. Roll) bore, sable, a saltire engrailed or ; Surrey Roll ; ascribed to JOHN TRUMWY in Jenyns' Ordinary.

Tromyn, Sir Humphrey—(E. III. Roll) bore, sable a saltire engrailed or, a bordure argent ; Ashmole Roll.

Troutbeck, Sir William, of Dunham— (E. IV. Roll) bore, azure three troutbeck intertwined argent, *quarterly with*, argent, a trefoyle sable between three moors' heads couped proper ; Ballard and Arundel Rolls.

Trumpington —— bore, at the siege of Rouen 1418, azure, crusily and two hautboys (or trumpets) addorsed or. F.

Trumpington, Sir Giles, of co. Cambridge (E. II. Roll) bore, azure, crusily and two hautboys chevronwise or ; Parly. Roll.

Trumpington, Sir Roger—bore, at the battle of Boroughbridge 1322, azure, crusily and two hautboys pileways or, a label (3) argent (F.) ; borne undifferenced by JAMES and Sir ROGER (see Mon. Brass) ; Camden and Howard Rolls. Sir JAMES bore it crusily fitchée in the Harleian Roll. A ROGER took up the cross in the last Crusade 1270.

Trumpington —— a Suffolk Kt.—(H. VI. Roll) bore, azure, crusily and two trumpets pileways or, *quarterly with*, argent, fretty sable, a canton gules, over all a label (3) azure ; Arundel Roll.

Trussebut, Robert—(H. III. Roll) bore, argent, three water-bougets gules (F.) ; Arden and St. Elms Rolls. One of these names Hereditary Standard-bearer temp. R. I. See Introduction.

Trussebut, Robert and Sir William— —(E. III. Roll) bore, argent, a fess dancettée between three water-bougets 2 and 1 sable. Sir ROBERT differenced with a label (3) gules ; Ashmole Roll and Jenyns' Ordinary.

Trussell, Sir William—bore, at the battle of Boroughbridge 1322, argent, a cross patée florettée gules (F.) ; Ashmole MS. ; ascribed also to Sir JOHN who was knighted at the capitulation of Calais 1348 ; Ashmole Roll, &c.

Trussell, Sir Waren and Sir William, of Cublesdon, (Northants)—bore, at the siege of Calais 1345-8, argent, fretty gules, bezanty at the joints (F.) ; (Sir WILLIAM differenced with a label (3) azure) and also Sir — TRUS- SELL knighted at the capitulation 1348 ; ascribed also to Sir JOHN, RICHARD, and Thomas ; Ashmole and St. George Rolls and Jenyns' Ordinary. AVERY bore the field or ; Surrey Roll.

*Trye, Mathew de—(H. III. Roll) bore, or, a bend azure. (F.) Dering Roll. REGINALD differenced with a label gules in Norfolk Roll.

Try, Seigneur de, DE BILEBATIA—(H. III.- Roll) bore, or,. a bend gobony argent and azure ; Norfolk Roll.

Tryvett, John—(R. II. Roll) bore, argent, a trivett within a bordure engrailed sable ; Surrey Roll. THOMAS bore it without the bordure at the siege of Rouen 1418, and it is so ascribed to Sir JOHN in Ashmole Roll. See TREVET.

Tudenham, John de—(H. III. Roll) bore, barry lozengy (6) argent and gules ; St. George Roll and Jenyns' Ordinary, in which latter it is blasoned barry (8) argent and gules indented counterchanged. OLIVER bore it argent and azure. See TODENHAM.

Tunstall, Richard, of East Bolton—(E. III. Roll) bore, argent, on a chief azure· three besants. In Jenyns' Ordinary, argent, on a chief indented azure four besants, three in trick.

Tunstall, Thomas—bore, at the siege of Rouen 1418, sable, three combs 2 and 1 argent. (F.) Surrey Roll and Jenyns' Ordinary.

Robt le Trussebut

Will Trussell

Waren d. Trussel

math de Trye

Thos Tunstall

194

Gilbt Taborvile

Aloyn de Twitham

Will Twyer

John Twifforde

Robert Tyas

Huo Turberville

Tho de Tregos

Henry Tyas

Hug de Torpinton

Turbervile, Sir Gilbert—bore, at the siege of Calais 1345–8, checquy or and gules a fess ermine (F.); ascribed to Sir PAINE, of co. Glouc., in Parly. Roll and in the Neath Abbey Tiles, p. ix—fess sable in Jenyns' Ordinary.

‡Turbervile, Hugh de—(H. III. Roll) bore, argent, a lyon rampant gules. (F.) Arden, Dering and Camden Rolls—crowned or in Howard Roll and Jenyns' Ordinary. ROBERT took up the cross in the last Crusade 1270.

Turberville, Thomas de—(H. III. Roll) bore, ermine, a lyon rampant gules; Howard Roll.

Turberville, Thomas—(E. III. Roll) bore, argent, billettée and a lyon rampant gules; Jenyns' Ordinary.

Turbervile, Geoffrey—(H. III. Roll) bore, sable, three lyons rampant or. (F.) St. George Roll.

Turberville, Henry v. Haberville.

Turk, Robert—(R. II. Roll) bore, argent, on a bend azure between two lyons rampant gules three besants; Surrey Roll.

Turpinton, Sire Hugh de—bore, at the battle of Boroughbridge 1322, argent, on a bend triple cotised sable six mullets or, on an inescocheon, the arms of MORTIMER azure and or. F.

Turvey, Sire John—bore, at the battle of Boroughbridge 1322, gules, a chevron between three bulls (passant) or. F.

Turvile, Sir Nicholas, of Warwickshire, and Robert—(E. II. Roll) bore, gules, two chevronels vair; Parliamentary Roll and Jenyns' Ordinary.

*Turvile, Sir Richard, of Warwickshire—(E. II. Roll) bore, gules, three chevronels vair; Parliamentary Roll.

Tutcham, Oliver de—(H. III. Roll) bore, checquy argent and gules a fess azure; ROBERT, on the fess three escallops or; Howard Roll.

Tuyley v. Cuilly.

Twyer, Robert and William—(E. III. Roll) bore, gules, a cross vair; Howard Roll and Jenyns' Ordinary. F.

Twyford, Sire John de (of co. Leicr.)—bore, at the first Dunstable tournament 1308 and at the battle of Boroughbridge 1322, argent, two bars sable, on a quarter of the second a cinquefoyle or. (F.) Another JOHN bore it at the second tournament 1334 on which occasion his son differenced with a label

gules (the cinquefoyle pierced in Ashmole Roll); ascribed also to RICHARD (" une barre et demi ") and to ROBERT—in Jenyns' Ordinary and Surrey Roll.

*[Twysden, Adam de, (E. I.)—bore, per saltire argent and gules, a saltire between four crosses crosslet all counterchanged.—Shirley.] F.

‡Twytham, Aleyn de—(H. III. Roll) bore, argent three cinquefoyles pierced sable. (F.) Dering Roll; six-foyles in Howard Roll.

Tyas, Francis, (TYEYS)—(H. III. Roll) bore, argent, a fess and in chief three mallets gules; Arden Roll.

Tyas, Robert—(E. I. Roll) bore, gules, a fess between three mallets bendways or—argent in trick. (F.) Jenyns' Roll.

‡Tychesy, Thomas de—(H. III. Roll) bore, gules, fretty vair. (F.) Dering & Howard Rolls.

Tyes, Sir Henry, of Chilton, banneret, baron 1299, sealed the Barons' letter to the Pope 1301, pp. xix, xxiv—bore at the battle of Falkirk 1298 and at the siege of Carlaverock 1300, argent, a chevron gules; (F.) as did his son HENRY (banneret) at the first Dunstable tournament 1308, at the battle of Boroughbridge 1322, and at the siege of Calais 1345–8; ascribed also to JOHN in Jenyns' Ordinary.

Tyndale, Sir William—(E. III. Roll) bore, argent, on a fess sable three garbs or; Ashmole Roll and Jenyns' Ordinary.

Tyndale (——) a Knight—(H. VI. Roll) bore, argent, three nails erect 2 and 1 sable; Arundel Roll. F.

Tyringham, Sir Roger de, of Bucks, and John—(E. II. Roll) bore, azure, a saltire engrailed argent; Parliamentary, Surrey and Arundel Rolls.

Tyrrell, Sir Roger (of co. Hereford), bore, at the first Dunstable tournament 1308, azure, a lyon rampant argent, a bordure indented or (engrailed Harl. MS. 6137 fo. 31ᵇ). (F.) Parliamentary and Ashmole Rolls.

Tyrrell, Roger (TIREL)—(H. III. Roll) bore, gules, a fess and in chief three annulets argent. (F.) Arden and St. George Rolls.

Tyrrell (——) an Essex Knight—(H. VI. Roll) bore, argent two chevronels azure and a bordure engrailed gules; Arundel Roll.

*Tyrwhit, Sir William, of Kettilby, co. Lincs.—(E. IV. Roll) bore, gules three tyrwhits 2 and 1 or (F.), with crest; Ballard and Arundel Rolls.

Tyndale

Johan Turney

Adam de Twysden

Roger Tyrell

Rog Tirel

Will Tyrwhitt

Here Harold was slain. After the Bayeux Tapestry.

— U—V —

Gerard uffloot

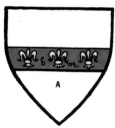

Robert de Offord

Thomas de Offord

Reinould de Ulggam.

Ufflete, Sir Gerard—(E. II. Roll) bore, argent on a fess azure three fleurs-de-lys or ; Parly. Roll and Jenyns' Ordinary—F.—fess sable in Nativity Roll. In the Surrey Roll—or, a bend between six martlets gules *quarterly with*, argent on a fess azure three fleurs-de-lys or, for another GERARD.

Ufford, Sir Robert de, baron 1309—bore, at the first Dunstable tournament 1308, sable, a cross engrailed or (F) ; as did his son ROBERT (after Earl of SUFFOLK, K.G.) at the battle of Boroughbridge 1322, at the second Dunstable tournament 1334, and at the siege of Calais 1345–8 (blasoned the reverse in Segar and Grimaldi Rolls). His brothers (1) Sir EDMUND differenced with a crown in the cantel argent and (2) Sir JOHN as in the next ; Harl. MS. 1481 fo. 34. A ROBERT DE UFFORD took up the cross in the last Crusade 1270 ; see also Dering Roll.

Ufford, Sir Thomas de—bore, at the first Dunstable tournament 1308, sable, a cross engrailed or, surmounted of a baston argent (F.) ; as did JOHN, at the second Dunstable tournament 1334 ; Ashmole Roll.

Ufford, Sir Edmund—(E. III. Roll) bore, sable, a cross engrailed or, a baston gobony argent and gules ; Ashmole Roll.

Ufford, Rauf de—bore, at the second Dunstable tournament 1334, sable, a cross engrailed or, an annulet argent. Sir THOMAS differenced with a label (3) argent and Sir WALTER with a ducal coronet or, in the cantel ; Ashmole Roll.

Ufford, John de—(H. III. Roll) bore, sable, a cross engrailed in the 1st and 2nd an escallop argent ; Arden Roll.

Ufford, John de—(H. III. Roll) bore, azure, on a cross engrailed or five escallops gules. (F.) St. George Roll.

Ughtred, Sir Thomas, K.G., baron 1343—bore, at the siege of Calais 1345–8, gules, on a cross patonce or five mullets of the field (F.) ; spur-rowells in Ashmole and Surrey Rolls and Jenyns' Ordinary. See OUGHTRED.

Ughtred, Sir John or **Robert,** (OUTREDE), of Yorkshire—(E. II. Roll) bore, or, on a cross patonce gules three mullets of the field ; four in tricks ; Parliamentary Roll.

Ulgham, Reinould de, of Northumberland —(E. I. Roll) bore, gules a cinquefoyle pierced or a bordure azure entoyre of horse-shoes argent.—Jenyns' Roll. (F.) See Gilbert de Umfreville.

Ulster, Earl of, Walter de Burgh—bore, or, a cross gules, the ancient arms of (BIGOD) Earl of NORFOLK ; Ashmole Roll and Jenyns' Ordinary.

Umfraville, Gilbert, Earl of ANGUS—bore at the battle of Falkirk 1298, gules crusily and a cinquefoyle or—in some Rolls the cinquefoyle is pierced (F.) ; (crusily patée in Guillim Roll), borne also by ROBERT, at the siege of Rouen 1418 (with a crescent for difference), and ascribed also to THOMAS,—crusily patée in Jenyns' Ordinary. Sir ROBERT, K.G., 1409–13, differenced with a baston azure, and Sir THOMAS, of Harbottle, Northumberland, differenced with a baston engrailed argent ; Harl. MS. 1481 fo. 75.

Umfreville, Gilbert de—(H. III. Roll) bore, or, a cinquefoyle gules, a bordure azure entoyre of horse-shoes of the second ; Glover Roll. See ULGHAM.

Umfrevile, Sir R.—(H. VI. Roll) bore, gules, a bend between six crosslets or ; Atkinson Roll.

Umfraville, de —(E. III. Roll) bore, party per fess or and gules 12 seysfoyles 3, 3, 3, 2, 1 counterchanged pierced ; Ashmole Roll.

Umfraville, Sir Ingram de—(H. III. Roll) bore, gules, an orle ermine, a label (3, 5) azure. (F.) St. George and Ashmole Roll and Jenyns' Ordinary—no label in Arden Roll. See INGRAM DE BALIOLL.

Upsale, Sir Geffrey and **John de**—(E. I. Roll) bore, argent, a cross sable. (F.) Segar, Nativity and Parly. Rolls ; Jenyns' Ordinary.

Upsale, Michel de, (OPSHALE)—(H. III. Roll) bore, argent, a cross sable fretty or ; Arden and St. George Rolls.

Upton *v.* **Hopton.**

*****Upton** —(E. III. Roll) bore, sable, a cross recercelée (now moline) argent. (F.) Ashmole Roll.

Urswicke, Robert de—(R. II. Roll) bore, argent, on a bend sable three lozenges of the field each charged with a saltire gules. WALTER, differenced with a crescent of the second ; Surrey and Ballard Rolls.

Uvedale *v.* **Dowdale.**

Robt. de Umfrevylle

Robt. de Umfreyville

Ingram d'Umfrauile

Joan d Offord

Johan do Opsalo

Cōte de Penbroc   *mōnsī de paloynb*

Henry Valoynb   *Johan de paloinb*

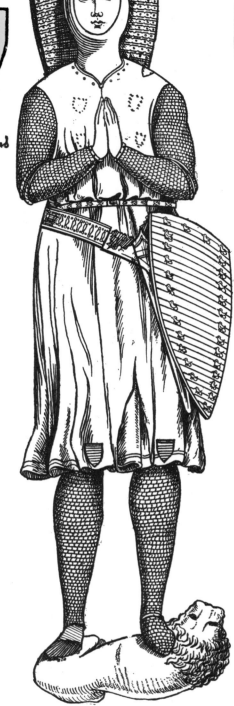

WILLIAM DE VALENCE, EARL OF PEMBROKE.

IN S. EDMUND CHAPEL, WESTMINSTER, 1296.

After Gough.

Vache, Hugh le—(E. III. Roll) bore, gules, three lyonceux rampant 2 and 1 argent; GRIMBALD PAUNCEFOTE bore the same; Jenyns' Ordinary—lyons crowned or in Arundel and Surrey Rolls. See DE LA VACHE.

Vale v. De la Val.

Vale, Nicol de—(E. I. Roll) bore, argent, on a cross gules five escallops or; Harleian Roll.

Valenan v. Velemane.

Valence v. Earl of Pembroke.

Valence, Aymer de, of Mountenake, banneret, baron 1299, Earl of PEMBROKE 1308, sealed the Barons' letter to the Pope 1301, pp. xv, xxiv. He bore, at the battle of Falkirk 1298 and at the siege of Carlaverock 1300, barry (10) argent and azure, ten martlets in orle 3, 2, 2, 3 gules, on his banner; Nobility and Parly. Rolls—burulée 12, 14, 16 or 20; ascribed also to WILLIAM (his father) Earl of PEMBROKE, who took up the cross in the last Crusade 1270; Grimaldi Roll (see Monumental Effigy)—(azure and argent) also to WILLIAM in Camden Roll and argent and gules in Glover Roll. (F.) For differences see Harl. MS. 1418 fo. 29.

Valence, Sir William de—(E. II. Roll) bore, argent, a chief dancettée (3) azure; Parliamentary Roll.

Valeys, William de—(H. III. Roll) bore, burulée (14) argent and azure, over all a saltire gules; Howard Roll.

‡**Valoines, Sire William de,** of Kent—(E. I. Roll) bore, paly wavy (ounde de longe of 6) argent and gules. (WILLIAM le fitz differenced with a label (3) or); RAFFE bore it within a bordure, ermine; all, Jenyns' Roll—three palets wavy in Dering and Camden Rolls.

Valoines, Sire Henry—bore, at the battle of Boroughbridge 1322, pale undée (6) or and gules, a label (6) argent. F.

Valoines, Stephen (VALONS)—(R. II. Roll) bore, or three palets wavy gules, a bordure ermine; Surrey Roll.

Valoines, Theobald—(E. I. Roll) bore, six peus undée or and gules—*vel*—or, three undées gulez—tricked, or three piles wavy meeting in base gules; Jenyns' Roll; and also for WILLIAM in Jenyns' Ordinary (F.); oundée (6) or and gules, in Grimaldi Roll.

Valoines, John de—(E. I. Roll) bore, sable, a maunch argent. (F.) Segar Roll.

Valoines, Richard de—(H. III. Roll) bore, burulée (14) argent and azure on a bend gules three mullets of six points (perhaps estoiles) or. (F.) St. George Roll.

Valoines, Richard de (DAVEREIGNES)—(E. III. Roll) bore, argent, a cross gules, a bordure engrailed sable; Jenyns' Ordinary.

Valoynes, Theobald—(E. III. Roll) bore, or, a cross gules a bordure azure entoyre of martlets of the first; Jenyns' Ordinary.

‡**Valoynes, Walrois de**—(H. III. Roll) bore, gules, fretty ermine. (F.) Dering Roll—WERREIS in Camden Roll and WILLIAM in Howard Roll—WARREN gules, fretty engrailed ermine; Ashmole Roll.

Van Halle, Sir Francis, K.G., 1360—bore, gules, a wyvern or, from its neck an escocheon pendent gules charged with a double-headed eagle argent, all within a bordure azure florettée alternated with lyons passant gardant all or. K. 398 fo. 53. F.

Varley, Sir Philip de (VERLEY), of Essex (E. II. Roll) bore, or, six eaglets displayed 3, 2, 1 sable, over all a bend gules; Parliamentary Roll.

Vascoil, Sir John (VASTOYLE), of Essex—(E. II. Roll) bore, argent, on a cross sable five nullets or; Parliamentary Roll.

Vauncy, Sire John (WANNCY)—bore, at the battle of Boroughbridge 1322, argent, an eagle displayed purpure.

Vauncy, William—(E. III. Roll) bore, argent, an eagle displayed azure, membered or; Jenyns' Ordinary.

‡**Vautour, John le**—(H. III. Roll) bore, or, a saltire gules. (F.) Dering and Surrey Rolls.

[**Vaux** (——) of Catterlen in Cumberland—bore, a fess checquy between six garbs. Incised slab at Newton Rigney—*from Boutell.*]

Ricard d'valoinb

Worron de paloynb

ffrā van Hallo

John de Vauls   John de Vaubt

witt manasor   Johan le poania soue

‡**Vaux, John** and **Robert**—(H. III. Roll) bore, checquy argent and gules. (F.) Dering and Norfolk Rolls. [Sir JOHN, of Notts, bore a label (3) azure; Parly. Roll.] FOULKE differenced with a quarter azure.

Vaux, Sir William de—bore, at the first Dunstable tournament 1322, or, an inescocheon within an orle of (8) martlets gules—the field argent for Sir WILLIAM, of Norfolk in Parliamentary Roll.

Vaux, Sir John de—bore, at the battle of Boroughbridge 1322, argent, an inescocheon within an orle of mullets gules. (F.) JAMES bore the same, blasoned argent an orle of martlets gules, a false escocheon; Jenyns' Ordinary.

Vaux, Sir John de, of co. Worc.—(E. II. Roll) bore, gules, on an inescocheon or two lyons passant azure, eight martlets in orle or; Parliamentary Roll.

Vaux, John and **Roland**—(H. III. Roll) bore, argent, a bend checquy argent and gules, counter-compony in trick; Glover and Jenyns' Rolls.

Vavasour, Sir William, banneret, baron 1299—bore, at the battle of Falkirk 1298 and at the siege of Carlaverock 1300, or, a fess dancettée (3) sable. (F.) Nobility and Parly. Rolls—ascribed to HENRY in Jenyns' Ordinary.

Vavasour, Sir William—(E. I. Roll) bore, argent, a fess dancettée azure; Holland Roll—a label (5) for another WILLIAM; St. George Roll.

Vavaseur, John le—(E. I. Roll) bore, or, fretty sable, a label (5) gules. (F.) Segar Roll.

‡**Vele, Robert le**—(H. III. Roll) bore, argent on a bend sable three calves passant of the field. (F.) Dering and Howard Rolls.

Velemane, Raffe, otherwise AUGUST or RUSTEN VALENAN — bore, at the siege of Rouen 1418 gules three birds in bend between two cotises argent. (F.) In the Ashmole MS. the trick is, gules, a bend cotised between two peahens argent.

Venables, Sir Hugh—(E. III. Roll) bore, azure, two bars argent; Ashmole Roll, and with crest in Ballard Roll. RICHARD of Bolyn (son of HUGH) differenced with two mullets pierced argent in the chief—and WILLIAM of Bradewall (brother of HUGH) bore two plates in chief; Harl. MS. 1481 fo. 35.

Venables, Richard—(R. II. Roll) bore, argent, two bars azure, on a bend gules three arrows of the field; Surrey Roll.

Vene, Sir Leysen de, of co. Glouc.—(E. II. Roll) bore, gules, three chevronels argent; Parliamentary Roll.

Venour, Sir Robert de, of co. Linc.—(E. II. Roll) bore, argent, crusily and a lyon rampant tail fourchée gules; Parly. Roll.

‡**Verdon, Sir Theobald de,** of Alton, banneret, baron 1295, sealed the Barons' letter to the Pope 1301, pp. xviii, xxiv—bore, at the first Dunstable tournament 1308, or, fretty gules (F.); ascribed also to JOHN in Surrey and Cotgrave Rolls, as or, a fret gules; who perhaps took up the cross in the last Crusade 1270.

Verdon, Sir Theobald de, of Webley, junior baron 1299—bore, at the battle of Falkirk 1298, or, fretty gules a label (3, 5) azure; Nobility and Guillim Rolls.

Verdon, Theobald de—(E. III. Roll) bore, or, fretty gules platey at the joints; Jenyns' Ordinary; and Tiles, Neath Abbey, p. ix.

Verdon, Sir Thomas de (of Northants) bore, at the first Dunstable tournament 1308, sable, a lyon rampant argent; Parly. Roll—borne also by JOHN (F.) at the second Dunstable tournament 1334 (and on the same occasion by his brother THOMAS—on the lyon's shoulder a chess-rook gules) and by Sir JOHN, knighted at the capitulation of Calais 1348; Jenyns' Ordinary.

Verdon, Christopher de, knighted at the capitulation of Calais 1348—bore, sable, a lyon rampant argent, on his shoulder a chess-rook gules. (F.) Borne also by THOMAS at the second Dunstable tournament 1334.

Verdon, Thomas de—(E. III. Roll) bore, sable, a lyon argent, holding in his paw a chess-rook gules; Cotgrave Roll.

Verdon, Sir Robert de (of Warwickshire) —(E. II. Roll) bore, argent, a cross azure fretty or Parly. Roll (Harl. 4033); and argent, on a cross azure five fleurs-de-lys or, Parly. Roll, Harl. MS. 6137.

Vere, Robert de, banneret, Earl of Oxford 1296—bore, at the battle of Falkirk 1298, quarterly gules and or, a mullet argent. (F.) Nobility and Parly. Rolls. See Monumental Effigy. Borne by an Earl of Oxford (? RICHARD 11th Earl, K.G. 1415) at the siege of Rouen 1418. This coat is often and erroneously blasoned the reverse.

ROBERT DE VERE, EARL OF OXFORD.

IN HATFIELD BROAD OAK CHURCH, ESSEX, OB. 1221.

Erected at a later date. After Stothard.

Jon le Vautour   Robert le Vele   Raffe Velemane   John Verdon   Johan de Verdon   Cristopher Verdon

Jorn do voro   Simon d. Ver   Robt le voro   Witt Videlon   Nich Villiers

Hue do voro

Thomas do voro

Ruchard do voro

Vere, Hugh de, of Swanscombe, banneret (brother of ROBERT), baron 1299, sealed the Barons' letter to the Pope 1301, pp. xvii, xxiv—bore, at the siege of Carlaverock 1300, quarterly gules and or, a mullet argent, all within a bordure engrailed sable. (F.) Harl. MS. 6137. (In NICOLAS, the field tinctures are reversed, the bordure indented.) Nobility, Arundel and Segar Rolls—indented, Parly. and Guillim Rolls.

Vere, Sir Thomas de—bore, at the first Dunstable tournament 1308, quarterly gules and or, a mullet argent, a label (3) azure; differenced with a label sable (F.), by Sir THOMAS le fiz le Count de Oxenford, at the battle of Boroughbridge 1322.

Vere, Aubrey le and **Sir Aufonso de,** of Essex—(E. II. Roll) bore, quarterly gules and or, a mullet ermine; Surrey and Parly. Rolls; argent, in H. 4033 fo. 38.

Vere, Sir Richard de, knighted at the capitulation of Calais 1348, bore, quarterly or and gules a bordure vair. F.

Vere, Robert de — (H. III. Roll) bore, argent, a cross gules; Glover Roll. NICHOL differenced with a label (3) azure; Jenyns' Ordinary.

Vere, Robert de—(E. I. Roll) bore, sable, three boars' heads couped or; Jenyns' Roll. F.

Vere, Simon de—(H. III. Roll) bore, gules three cinquefoyles (sixfoyles ermine in Glover Roll) argent (F.); Jenyns' Ordinary—pierced in Arden and St. George Rolls.

Verney, Sir Philip de—(E. III. Roll) bore, argent, a fess gules fretty or, in chief three mullets of the second; Ashmole Roll. F.

*****Vernon, John** and **Richard**—(E. III. Roll) bore, argent, a fret (fretty) sable, a quarter gules. (F.) Atkinson and Surrey Rolls and Jenyns' Ordinary. Lord VERNON bears it without the quarter.

Vernon —— (R. II. Roll) bore, or, on a fess azure three garbs of the field, *quarterly with,* argent a fret sable; Surrey Roll. VERNON quartering VERNON. F.

‡**Vesci, John, Eustace** and **Sir William,** banneret—(H. III. Roll) bore, or, a cross sable; Jenyns' Ordinary, Dering and Arundel Rolls. Another WILLIAM (‡) differenced with a label (5) gules. (F.) Dering and St. George Rolls.

Vescy, William de—(H. III. Roll) bore, gules, a cross patonce argent; Glover Roll. F.

Vescy, William—(E. III. Roll) bore, or, a lyon rampant azure, a baston gules; Jenyns' Ordinary.

Videlon, Sir William, of Berks—(E. II. Roll) bore, argent, three wolves' heads erased gules; Parliamentary Roll. F.

Vile, Ansel de—(H. III Roll) bore, argent, a fess between six spur-rowells gules; Dering Roll. See DEYVILE.

Villers, Sir Francis de, of Notts—(E. II. Roll) bore, gules, billettée and a cross or; Parliamentary Roll.

*****Villers, Sir Nicholas de,** of co. Glouc.—(E. II. Roll) bore, argent, on a cross gules five escallops or. (F.) Ashmole and Parly. Rolls and Jenyns' Ordinary.

Villers, Nichol de—(E. III. Roll) bore, azure, on a cross or five escallops gules; Jenyns' Ordinary—same as RANDOLF DACRE.

*****[Vincent, Miles,** (10 E. II.)—bore, azure, three quatrefoyles argent.—Shirley.] F.

Vipount, Sir John de—bore, at the first Dunstable tournament 1308, or, six annulets 3, 2, 1 gules a label (3) azure. (F.) Nativity and Parly. Rolls.

Vipount, Sir Nicholas, banneret (E. II. Roll), and **Sir Robert** and **John,** of Westmoreland (E. III. Roll) bore, or six annulets 3, 2, 1 gules; Ashmole, Arundel and Parly. Rolls, Jenyns' Ordinary.

Vyan, Sire le —— (E. I. Roll) bore, or, billettée and a lyon rampant gules. (F.) Camden Roll.

‡**Vyan, Lucas de,** (VYENNE)—(H. III. Roll) bore, azure, a fess dancettée argent; Howard Roll—in the Dering Roll azure, crusily and a fess dancettée or. F.

*****[Vyvyan, Sir Vyell,** 13th cent.—bore, argent, a lyon rampant gules.—Shirley.] F.

milos vincont

Jorn do Viponto

Vyel Vyvyan   Lucas do Vyonne   Sire do Vyan

Witt de Vesey   Witt d Vesse   Pet do Vernoy   R. Vernon   Vernon

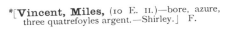
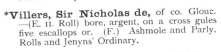

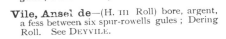

The English fled. After the Bayeux Tapestry.

— W—Y—Z —

Serard de
Wachessam

Simon
d' Waddone

Robert do
Wadeville

Wachesham, Sir Gerard—(E. II. Roll) bore, argent, a fess and in chief three crescents gules. (F.) Sir JOHN of Suffolk bore it with a baston azure; Parliamentary Roll.

Waddone, Simon de—(E. II. Roll) bore, sable, a cross engrailed or, in the first and second an escallop argent; St. George Roll. F.

Wadesley, Sir Robert de, of Yorkshire—(E. II. Roll) bore, argent, on a bend between six martlets 3 and 3 gules, three escallops or; Parliamentary Roll.

Wadeville, Sire Robert de—bore, at the battle of Boroughbridge 1322, argent, three chevrons gules within a bordure sable. F.

‡**Wadripun, Sire de**—(E. I. Roll) bore, or, two lyons rampant addorsed gules. Camden Roll (F.); called WATERIBONT in Dering Roll.

Wahull, Thomas de, of Beds., a baron 1297—bore, or, three crescents gules; Nobility and Parliamentary Rolls.

*****Wake, Sir John de**, banneret, a baron 1295—bore, at the battle of Falkirk 1298, or, two bars gules in chief three torteaux—borne also by BALDWIN(‡) and HUGH (F.); Dering and Glover Rolls. In the Arden Roll a Wake coat is tricked, azure two bars or and in chief three besants; this in Camden Roll with the field, gules for HUE WAKE.

Wake, Sire Thomas de Blisworth—bore, at the battle of Boroughbridge 1322, argent, two bars gules and in chief three torteaux, a bordure indented sable; as did THOMAS of Blisworth at the second Dunstable tournament 1334; the border is usually tricked engrailed; ascribed to THOMAS of Deeping, but with ogresses in lieu of torteaux, in Jenyns' Ordinary. F.

Wake, Sir Hugh, of Yorkshire—(E. II. Roll) bore, or, two bars gules, in chief three torteaux, a baston azure. Sir HUGH, the uncle, bore, gules two bars argent, in chief three plates; Parliamentary Roll.

Wake, Hue—(H. III. Roll) bore, argent fretty sable besanty at the joints; Arden Roll. F.

Wake, Jon—(H. III. Roll) bore, or, a fess gules in chief three torteaux; Arden Roll.

Walcote, John de—(R. II. Roll) bore, argent, on a cross patonce azure five fleurs-de-lys or; Surrey Roll.

*[**Walcot, John**, (H. V.)—bore, argent, a chevron between three chess-rooks ermine.—Shirley.] (F.) Checkmated the king with a rook, and so had these arms given him.

*****Waldegrave, Richard**—(R. II. Roll) bore, per pale argent and gules; Surrey Roll. Sir RICHARD DE bore this coat with a bend engrailed sable; Ashmole Roll, E. III.

Walden, Alexander—(R. II. Roll) bore, sable, two bars ermine, in chief three cinquefoyles pierced argent; Surrey Roll. F.

Waldeseuf, Alain de (or WALDESEFTH)—(H. III. Roll) bore, gules, two chevrons argent a label (5) of France; St. George Roll—borne also by EDMUND, in the Arden Roll.

Wale v. Waleus.

Wale, Sir Thomas, K.G., a founder—(E. III. Roll) bore, argent a cross sable; Surrey Roll. Sir THOMAS of Rutland bore, on the cross, five lyonceux or; Parliamentary Roll, E. II.

Wales, Edward, Prince of; v. England.

Wales, Prince of—(H. VI. Roll) bore, or, a lyon passant gules, *quarterly with*, gules, a lyon passant or; Nobility Roll. See also Neath Abbey Tiles, p. vii.

Waleis, Sir Steven—bore, at the siege of Calais 1345-8, gules, a fess ermine; borne also by Sir RICHARD of Sussex, a baron 1321; Parliamentary Roll (F.); ascribed to another RICHARD (‡) in the Dering Roll. HENRY bore gules a fess sable; Arden Roll.

Waleys, Sir Simon de, of Sussex—(E. II. Roll) bore, gules, a fess ermine, in chief a lyon passant gardant or; Parliamentary Roll.

Hue. Wake

Alex Waldon

John Walcot

Sire
do Wadripun

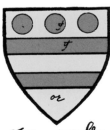

Johan Wake

Thomas Wake

Richard do Waleis

Alan
d' Waldesesp

THE HERALDIC ATCHIEVEMENT

OF

ROBERT HORACE, 5TH EARL OF ORFORD.

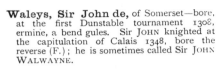

John do waleis   Jo͠an do waleis   Henry walpole   John walrond

JOHN WANTLEY.
IN AMBERLEY CHURCH, SUSSEX,
C. 1424, 2 H. VI.

After Stothard.

Waleys, Sir John de, of Somerset—bore, at the first Dunstable tournament 1308, ermine, a bend gules. Sir JOHN knighted at the capitulation of Calais 1348, bore the reverse (F.); he is sometimes called Sir JOHN WALWAYNE.

†**Waleis, Henry de**—(H. III. Roll) bore, burulée (14) argent and azure, a bend gules; St. George Roll. F.

Waleis, John de—(E. II. Roll) bore, gules, billettée or an orle ermine. (F.) Arden Roll. Called WALHOPE in St. George Roll.

Waleis, Stephen le, and **Sir Richard le**—(H. III. Roll) bore, quarterly gules and argent a bendlet or—F. (engrailed in Jenyns' Ordinary); Parliamentary and St. George Rolls and Jenyns' Ordinary. Sometimes tricked and blasoned argent and gules.

Waleis, William le—(H. III. Roll) bore, argent a fess between six martlets sable; St. George Roll. F.

Waleis, William de (GALEYS)—(E. I. Roll) bore, gules, a fess between two chevronels or; Segar Roll.

Walesborough, Sir John—(E. III. Roll) bore, gules, three bendlets a bordure engrailed sable; Ashmole Roll. See also WHALESBOROUGH.

Waleus, Sir John—(E. III. Roll) bore, vert, a lyon rampant or; Ashmole Roll.

Walkfare, Sir Robert de, of Norfolk—(E. II. Roll) bore, argent, a lyon rampant sable, on the shoulder a mullet or; Parliamentary Roll.

Walkingham, Sir John de—(E. II. Roll) bore, vair, two bars gules; Parliamentary Roll.

Walkington, William de—bore, at the second Dunstable tournament 1334, gules, a chevron argent. F.

Walkington, Sir William, knighted at the capitulation of Calais 1348—bore, gules on a chevron azure three mullets pierced argent. (F.) Another Sir WILLIAM bore, gules, a chevron between three mullets argent; Ashmole Roll.

Walhope v. Welhopp.

*Wallop, Richard de,** (2 Ed. III.) formerly BARTON, great-grandson of PETER (E. I.) who bore, argent, a bend wavy sable. See JOHN DE BARTON. Surrey Roll.

*[**Walpole, Sir Henry,** (E. I.)—bore, or on a fess between two chevrons sable three crosses crosslet of the first.—Shirley.] F.

*[**Walrond, John,**(E. I.)—bore, argent, three bulls' heads cabossed sable.—Shirley.] F.

Walrond, John and **Robert**—(H. III. Roll) bore, argent a bend fusily gules; Arden Roll; endented, tricked lozengy — Jenyns' Ordinary; engrailed in Glover Roll—all intended for one and the same—fusily.

Walsh, John—(R. II. Roll) bore, argent, a chevron between three fleurs-de-lys sable; Surrey Roll.

Walshe, Thomas—(R. II. Roll) bore, gules, two gemelles surmounted of a bendlet all argent; Surrey Roll.

Walsingham, Sir Richard de, of Norfolk—(E. II. Roll) bore gules, three chessrooks argent; Parliamentary Roll.

Walsingham, Roger de—(E. I. Roll) bore, sable a chevron argent between three cinquefoyles pierced or; Jenyns' and Surrey Rolls—not pierced in Jenyns' Ordinary.

Waltham, Ratcliff—(E. III. Roll) bore, gules, besantée and a lyon rampant argent; Jenyns' Ordinary.

Walton, William, of Essex, Knight — (H. VI. Roll) bore, argent, on a chief dancettée sable three besants; Arundel Roll.

Walton, Sir Adam de, of the North— (E. II. Roll) bore, argent, a cross patonce sable a bordure indented gules; Parly. Roll.

[**Wantley, John,** of Sussex, 1424, bore vert three leopards' faces argent. See Monumental Brass.]

Wanton v. **Wauton** and **Wawton.**

Wanton, Sir William de, of Essex— (E. II. Roll) bore, argent, a chevron sable; Norfolk and Parliamentary Rolls. Another WILLIAM (‡) in the Dering Roll.

Wanton, Sir William, knighted at the siege of Calais 1348, **Thomas** and **Sir John**—bore, argent, a chevron sable, in the cantel a martlet gules. (F.) Jenyns' Ordinary and Ashmole Roll. Another THOMAS differenced with an annulet sable; Surrey Roll.

Henri le waleif   Steuen le Waleife   will le waleif   will de wakington   will walkington   will de wantone

Witt do Wanton

Joan d' Wantone

William do Warren

Witt do Warren

Hugh do Wasonßam

Rog do Wapail

TBo do Warblington

Warberton

John Wassand

John do Wayz

Rog d' Wasseburne

Wanton, Sir William (of co. Glouc.)—bore, at the first Dunstable tournament 1308, argent, on a chevron sable three eaglets displayed or. (F.) Jenyns' and Parly. Rolls.

Wanton, William de—bore, at the second Dunstable tournament 1334, or, on a chevron sable three eaglets displayed of the field.

Wanton, John de—(H. III. Roll) bore, argent, on a bend sable three buckles, tongues to the dexter or. (F.) Arden and St. George Rolls.

Wapaile, Roger de—(H. III. Roll) bore, argent two chevrons ("a chevron et demy") gules over all a quarter of the last. (F.) Another differenced with a martlet sable; St. George and Jenyns' Rolls.

‡**Warbleton, Thomas de**—(H. III. Roll) bore, lozengy or and azure. (F.) Dering, Arden and Howard Rolls.

Warburton —— bore, at the siege of Rouen 1418, argent, three birds sable (F.); supposed to be cormorants.

Warburton, Geoffrey—(R. II. Roll) bore, argent, two chevronels gules, on a quarter of the last a mullet or; Surrey Roll.

Warcop, Thomas de—(E. III. Roll) bore, sable, a chevron between three covered cups argent; Jenyns' Ordinary. F.

Warde v. **de la Warde.**

Warde, Sir John—bore, at the siege of Calais 1345-8, azure, a cross flory or. (F.); (a cross patonce ascribed to JOHN in Surrey Roll)—a cross patée for Sir SYMON, banneret, patonce in trick in Parly. Roll, and flory in Jenyns' Ordinary.

Warde, Henry, of Swynythwaite—(E. III. Roll) bore, argent, crusily fitchée, 3, 3 and a fess sable; Jenyns' Ordinary.

Wardewick, John de—(E. III. Roll) bore, vert, three lyonceux rampant tails fourchée 2 and 1 argent; Jenyns' Ordinary.

Ware, William de—(E. I. Roll) bore, gules, a lyon rampant tail fourchée argent, debruised by a baston sable; Segar Roll.

Warre v. **de la Warr.**

Warren, John, Earl of, and a banneret; sealed the Barons' letter to the Pope 1301, pp. xv, xxiv—bore at the battle of Falkirk 1298 and at the siege of Carlaverock 1300, checquy or and azure (F.); (his only son WILLIAM was killed at a tournament at Croydon 15 Dec. 1285), as did his grandson JOHN Earl of Warren at the first Dunstable tournament 1308—colours reversed in the Arden and Guillim Rolls.

Warren, Reginald (brother of Earl WILLIAM) founder of the abbey of Castlecombe, bore checquy or and azure, a bordure engrailed gules; Harl. MS. 1481 fo. 32b.

Warren, Sir William—bore, at the siege of Calais 1345-8, checquy or and azure on a canton gules, a lyon rampant argent. F.

Warren, Sir William, le filz, knighted at the capitulation of Calais 1348—bore, checquy or and azure, a chief argent. F.

Warren, Sir John, of Poynton—(E. IV. Roll) bore, checquy or and azure, on a canton gules a lyon rampant argent (ermine in Ashmole Roll) with two quarterings and crest; Ballard Roll.

Warryne, Sir William — (E. III. Roll) bore, argent, a chief counter-compony or and azure; Ashmole Roll.

Waren (——) de Stockport—(H. III. Roll) bore, azure, crusily and three lozenges or; Arden Roll.

†**Warwick, (Thomas) de,** Earl of, "le veyl escu"—checquy or and azure, a chevron gules; Howard and other Rolls—a bend ermine in Reg. MS. 14 cvii. fo. 134. See also BEAUCHAMP.

Wasenham, Sir Hugh de—(E. III. Roll) —bore, sable, a fess dancettée (3) between three mullets argent; Ashmole Roll. F.

Washington v. **Wassington.**

Wassand, John—(E. I. Roll) bore, argent, a fess and in chief two crescents gules; Jenyns' and Ashmole Rolls. F.

Wasse, Sir John de (WAYZ)—bore, at the first Dunstable tournament 1308, gules, on an inescocheon or two lyons passant azure, all within 8 martlets in orle of the second. F.

Wasse, William de—(E. II. Roll) bore, "argent, an orle of martlets gules, a false escocheon of the same"; Jenyns' Ordinary.

Wasse, Sir William, of Bucks—(R. II. Roll) bore, barry (6) argent and gules on a canton of the last a mullet pierced of the first; Parliamentary Roll.

Wasseburne, Roger de—(H. III. Roll) bore, gules, besantée on a canton or a raven proper. (F.) St. George Roll.

Wassington, William de—(R. II. Roll) bore, argent, two bars in chief three mullets pierced gules (F.); Surrey Roll—colours reversed and the mullets unpierced in Jenyns' Roll. F.

Wassington, Walter (WESSINGTON) — (E. III. Roll) bore, gules, a lyon rampant argent, a bendlet gobony azure and argent; Jenyns' Ordinary. F.

John Warde

Mountoo do Warren

TBo de Warrcopp

Witt Wessyngton

Witt do Wassington

Watt do Wessington

THE HERALDIC ATCHIEVEMENT

OF

REGINALD LORD WELBY, G.C.B.

204

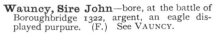

Estephn Wassingtone Robert Watevile Joran d'Waunei Goffray d'Waunei Wolbeworth

witt Le Wasteneis

Hardolf de wastenoys

witt de Watenald

witt Welby

witt Wold

Adam de Wells

Richard de Wells

Wassington, Stephen de—bore, at the second Dunstable tournament 1334, azure, " un rase " or.   F.

Wasteneys, Sir William (of co. Staff.)— bore, at the first Dunstable tournament 1308, sable, a lyon rampant argent collared gules. (F.) ; ascribed also to EDMUND and Sir THOMAS ; Segar and Ashmole Rolls.

Wasteneys, Hardolf de—bore, at the second Dunstable tournament 1334, sable a lyon rampant tail fourchée argent (F.) ; as- cribed also to Sir EDMUND and ROBERT in Parliamentary Roll and Jenyns' Ordinary.

Watenald, Sir William de, knighted at the capitulation of Calais 1348—bore, sable, a bend fusily or (F.) *alii* argent.

‡**Wateribont, Sire de**—(H. III. Roll) bore, or, two lyons rampant addorsed gules ; Dering Roll—called WADRIPUN in Camden Roll. (F.)

‡**Wateringbury, Bartholomew de** — (H. III. Roll) bore, argent, six lyonceux rampant sable. (F.) Dering and Howard Rolls.

****Waterton, Hugh** — bore, at the siege of Rouen 1418, barry (6) argent and gules, over all three crescents 2, 1 sable (F.) ; ascribed to ROBERT in Jenyns' Roll ; borne ermine and gules by (*Sir* ROBERT) a Yorkshire Knight Arundel Roll (H. VI.).

Watevile, Sir Geoffrey—bore, at the first Dunstable tournament 1308, sable, crusily and a lyon rampant argent.   F.

Watervile, Sir Robert, of Hunts, and **John de**—(E. II. Roll) bore, argent, crusily (5, 5) and a fess dancettée gules ; Parly. Roll and Jenyns' Ordinary.

Watevile, Sir John de, of Essex—(E. II. Roll) bore, argent, three chevronels gules ; Parly. Roll—inescocheons tricked in Harl. MS. 6137 fo. 13, and for Sir ROBERT and Sir ROGER named below.

Wateville, Sir Robert (of Essex) baron 1326—bore, at the first Dunstable tournament 1308, argent, three chevrons gules, a bordure indented sable—engrailed (F.) in trick ; Harl. MS. 6137 fo. 34, and so ascribed to ROGER in Jenyns' Ordinary.

Wateville, Sir Roger de (of Essex)—bore, at the first Dunstable tournament 1308, argent, three chevrons gules, in the cantel a martlet sable.

Watlass, Hervey de—(E. III. Roll) bore, or, on a chief indented azure three crescents of the field ; Grimaldi Roll and Jenyns' Ordi- nary.   See PICKENHAM.

Wauncy, Sire John—bore, at the battle of Boroughbridge 1322, argent, an eagle dis- played purpure.   (F.)   See VAUNCY.

Waunci, Gefrai de—(H. III. Roll) bore, gules, three dexter gauntlets aversant argent. (F.)   St. George Roll ; ascribed to JOHN in Arden Roll.

Wauncy, Nichole de—(H. III. Roll) bore, gules, three dexter gauntlets argent ; Howard Roll.

Wauncy, Sir Robert de, of Rutland— (E. II. Roll) bore, sable three sinister gauntlets aversant 2, 1 argent ; Parliamentary Roll.

Wauncye, Sir William de, of Suffolk— (E. II. Roll) bore, gules, six sinister gauntlets 3, 2, 1 argent ; Parliamentary Roll.

Wauton v. **Wanton.**

Wauton, John de—(H. III. Roll) bore, argent, on a bend sable three buckles tongues to the dexter or.   (F.)   Arden and St. George Rolls.

Wawton, John, and also **Gilbert de,** of Kerperby—(E. I. Roll) bore, gules. on a chief argent three torteaux ; Howard Roll and Jenyns' Ordinary ; no torteaux in the Ashmole and Grimaldi Rolls.

Wawton, Henri de (WAUTON)—(H. III. Roll) bore, argent, on a chief gules, a maunch of the field ; Howard Roll.

Wedone, Sir Raffe de, of Bucks—(E. II. Roll) bore, argent, two bars gules in chief three martlets sable ; Parliamentary Roll.

Welbewik —— (E. III. Roll) bore, azure, a fess engrailed argent between three escallops of the last ; Ashmole Roll.   F.

****[Welby, Sir William,** (E. I.)—bore, sable, a fess between three fleurs-de-lys argent.— Shirley.]   F.

****[Weld, William,** Sheriff of London 1352— bore, azure, a fess undée between three cres- cents ermine.—Shirley.]   F.

Welhopp, John de—(E. III. Roll) bore, gules, billettée or, an orle ermine ; Jenyns' Ordinary, same as JOHN DE WALEIS.

Welles, Sir Adam de, banneret, baron 1293, sealed the Barons' letter to the Pope 1301, pp. xix, xxiv.   He bore, at the battle of Falkirk 1298 and at the siege of Carlaverock 1300, a lyon rampant tail fourchée sable (F.) ; as did JOHN, 5th baron, at the siege of Rouen in 1418.

Wells, Sir Philip de, of Lincolnshire— (E. II. Roll) bore, argent, a lyon rampant tail fourchée sable, a baston gules ; Parly. Roll.

Welle, Sir John de, of Kent—(E. II. Roll) bore, gules, six crescents 3, 2, 1 argent, a baston gobony or and azure ; Parly. Roll.

Wells, Sir Richard—(E. II. Roll) bore, paly (6) or and gules on a canton argent a spur-rowell sable.   (F.) Ashmole Roll—argent and gules in Dering Roll—three pales for Sir RICHARD of Herts. in Parly. and Howard Rolls.

Welle, Robert de—(H. III. Roll) bore, argent, two bastons gules, besantée ; Glover Roll.

Well, Roger de—(E. I. Roll) bore, or, a male gryphon segreant vert ; Jenyns' Roll.

Bortolmew de walringbori Howgh Waltorton Goofferay Watervillo

Armine wollosburno

Thomas mosto

Thomas west

Johan de westune

will weston

Simon waltdone

william wone

walt wotwang

Johan wotowange

Wellesburne —— of the Montfort, slain at the siege of Calais 1347—bore, (purpure?) a lyon rampant tail fourchée argent.

Wellesbourne, Sir Armine, together with his namesake the Captain of Dover, were slain at the siege of Calais 1347—bore, gules, a gryphon segreant or, a chief checquy of the first and second, over all a bendlet ermine. (F.) The gryphon and the metal checque may be argent in the coat of the Captain of Dover, the colour has faded. This is a doubtful coat.

Wellesby, John — (E. I. Roll) bore, "amptie" = enté = per chevron sable and argent a lyon passant gardant or; Jenyns' Roll. See also WILSHIRE.

Wellington v. Willington.

Welnetham, Sir John (WELWETHAM), of Suffolk—(E. II. Roll) bore, or, on a fess azure three plates; Parliamentary Roll.

Welse, Sir John—(E. I. Roll) bore, ermine, a bend gules; Harleian Roll.

Weltdene, Simon—(E. I. Roll) bore, argent, a cinquefoyle pierced gules, on a chief of the last a demi-lyon rampant issuant of the first a bordure counterchanged of the first and second. (F.) Jenyns' Roll.

Welton v. Weston.

Welwike v. Welbewik.

Wene, Sire William—bore, at the battle of Boroughbridge 1322, ermine, on a bend gules three escallops or. F.

Wenlock, Sir Roger, slain at the siege of Calais 1348—bore, argent, on a chevron (sable) between three moors' heads erased proper those in chief regarding each other, an escocheon quarterly sable and argent. F.

Wennesley, Thomas de—(R. II. Roll) bore, ermine, on a bend gules three escallops or; Surrey Roll.

Wentworth, William, of Wentworth, Yorkshire—bore, sable, a chevron between three leopards' faces or; his brother, JOHN of Elmshall, bore it within a bordure argent; Harl. MS. 1481, fo. 69ᵇ.

Wentworth, Sir (——), of Suffolk—(H. VI. Roll) bore, gules, on a fess argent between three escallops azure, a spur-rowell of the second; Arundel Roll.

Werintone —— —(E. I. Roll) bore, azure, a bend between six escallops (3, 3) or; Harleian Roll.

Weste, Thomas—(E. I. Roll) bore, probably at the second Dunstable tournament 1334, azure, three leopards' faces jessant-de-lys or (F.); Jenyns' and Surrey Rolls. ROBERT bore it within a bordure gules; engrailed in the trick; Jenyns' Roll.

*[West, Sir Thomas, (E. II.)—bore, argent, a fess dancettée sable.—Shirley.] F.

Weston, Sir John de—bore, at the first Dunstable tournament 1308, argent, a fess sable within a bordure indented (engrailed Harl. 6137) gules, besantée (F.); (a plain bordure in the Parly. Roll). Sir JOHN, LE FIZ (of Hants. or Wilts.) bore it also at the battle of Boroughbridge 1322, as did THOMAS at the second Dunstable tournament in 1334, on which occasion his brother JOHN bore, a plain bordure and without the besants. WILLIAM (E. I. Roll) bore a plain bordure platey; Jenyns' Roll. A JOHN DE WESTON took up the cross in the last Crusade 1270.

Weston, Roger de—(E. III. Roll) bore, gules, crusily fitchée or, a lyon rampant argent, a baston engrailed sable; Cotgrave Roll.

*[Weston, Sir William, (E. II.)—bore, sable, a chevron or between three leopards' faces argent crowned or.—Shirley.] F.

Wetewang, John—(E. I. Roll) bore, sable, three lamps argent. (F.) Jenyns' Roll.

Wetwang, Sir Walter, "thresorer of the Wares," at the siege of Calais, 1345-8, bore, azure, a lyon rampant gardant tail fourchée argent, crowned or. F.

Weyer, Sir William de, of Staffs.—(E. II. Roll) bore, argent, a fess between three crescents gules; Parly. Roll.

Weyland, Sir John de—bore, at the first Dunstable tournament 1308, azure a lyon rampant or oppressed by a bendlet gules (perhaps the lyon argent in the Harl. Roll); ascribed also to ROGER (F.) in St. George Roll, and with a baston or, to Sir RICHARD of Suffolk, in Parly. Roll.

Weyland, Sir Nicholas de, of Suffolk— (E. II. Roll) bore, argent, on a cross gules five escallops or; Sir WILLIAM differenced with a label (3) azure; Parly. Roll.

Whalesborough (——) an Essex Knight— (H. VI. Roll) bore, argent, three bendlets gules, a bordure sable besantée; Arundel Roll. See also WALESBOROUGH.

Wharton, Thomas de, of Westmoreland— (E. III. Roll) bore, sable, a maunch argent; Jenyns' Ordinary.

[Whatton, Sir Richard de, of Notts., temp. H. III. bore, argent crusily gules on a bend sable three bezants. See Monumental Effigy.]

Rog' d' Welonde

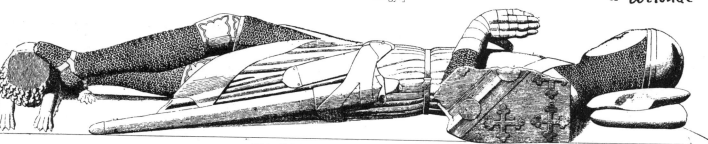

SIR RICHARD DE WHATTON.
IN WHATTON CHURCH, NOTTS, TEMP. H. III. *From Stothard.*

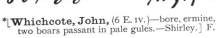

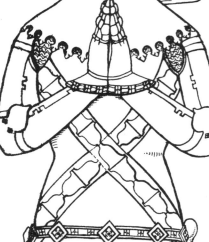
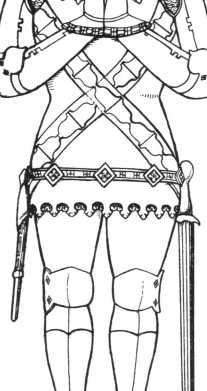

*[**Whichcote, John,** (6 E. IV.)—bore, ermine, two boars passant in pale gules.—Shirley.] F.

Whitacre v. **Witacre.**

White, Sir John (WHYGHT), of Norfolk—(E. II. Roll) bore, gules, a chevron between three boars' heads couped argent; Parly. Roll, additional.

Whitfeld, Sir William de—bore, at the battle of Boroughbridge 1322, sable, a bend engrailed or (F.) RICHARD bore five fusils in bend; Arden Roll.

‡**Whitfeld, Robert de**—(H. III. Roll) bore, sable, crusily and a bend fusily or (F.); Dering and St. George Rolls; a bend of lozenges conjoined in Howard Roll.

*[**Whitgrave, Robert,** 13 Aug. 1442 (20 H. VI.)—bore, azure, a cross quarterly pierced or between four chevronels gules, *per* grant from HUMPHREY Earl of Stafford.] F.

*[**Whitmore, John,** H. III.—bore, vert, fretty or.—Shirley.] F.

Whitney v. **Witney.**

Whitrick, (QUTRIKE) **John**—(E. I. Roll) bore, argent, a fret (fretty in trick) gules, a quarter of the last; Jenyns' Roll.

Wickston, John and **Robert de,** (E. III.—Roll) bore, argent, a chevron gules, in chief three torteaux; Jenyns' Ordinary. See WISTOWE.

Widdrington, Gerard and **John de**—(H. III. Roll) bore, quarterly argent and gules a baston sable; Jenyns' Ordinary; a bend in Ashmole—a bendlet in Surrey Roll.

Wigington, John de—(E. III. Roll) bore, argent, three mascles gules, sable in trick; Jenyns' Ordinary.

†**Wigton, Walter de**—bore, at the siege of Carlaverock 1300, sable, three mullets and a bordure indented or; (NICOLAS)—engrailed in H. 6137 fo. 4ᵇ (F.) three fleurs-de-lys and the bordure engrailed Harl. MS. 6137 fo. 40; the latter also in Arden, Jenyns' Nobility and St. George Rolls; ascribed also to Sir JOHN, banneret, in Nobility and Parly. Rolls.

*[**Wilburgham, Richard de,** 43 H. III.—bore, argent, three bends wavy azure.—Shirley.] F.

Williamscott, Sir Henry, of co. Glouc.—(E. II. Roll) bore, argent, three bars azure over all a lyon rampant gules, crowned or; Parly. Roll.

Willisthorpe, John—(E. I. Roll) bore, azure, a chevron between three lyons passant gardant argent; Jenyns' Roll.

Willington, Sir John de, banneret, baron 1329—bore, at the first Dunstable tournament 1308, (and by Sir HENRY at the battle of Boroughbridge 1322) gules, a saltire vair (F.) (see Monumental Effigy);—his son RAUF differenced at the second Dunstable tournament 1334, with a label or; ascribed to another RAUF (‡) in the Dering and Howard Rolls. Sir EDMOND, of co. Glouc. differenced with a mullet or; Parly. Roll. Sir JOHN, knight banneret, (H. VI.) bore, gules, a saltire sable (*sic*), in Arundel Roll.

Willington —— (E. III. Roll) bore, or, a saltire lozengy vair and gules; another differenced with a label (3) argent; Ashmole Roll.

Willington——(WELYNGTON)—(E. III. Roll) bore, sable, a bend engrailed argent cotised or; Ashmole Roll.

***Willoughby, Robert de** — bore, at the siege of Carlaverock 1300, or, fretty azure. F.

Willoughby, Sir Robert, knighted at the capitulation of Calais 1348—bore, gules, a cross recercelée argent, a bendlet sable (F.), and without the bendlet for Sir ROBERT, banneret (H. VI. Roll), as a cross moline; Arundel Roll; a fer-de-mouline in Parly. Roll.

Willoughby (Robert, 6th), Lord de—bore, at the siege of Rouen 1418, gules, a cross moline argent, *quarterly with*, or a cross engrailed sable (F.); the quarterings reversed in the Surrey Roll.

Willoughby, Richard de—(E. III. Roll) bore, argent, two bars azure, on each three cinquefoyles or; in another three cinquefoyles 2 and 1; Jenyns' Ordinary.

Willoughby, Edmund—(R. II. Roll) bore, or, two bars gules, charged with three waterbougets 2 and 1 argent; Arundel, Ashmole and Surrey Rolls.

Robd' Witefeld. Robt w Eitgrave.

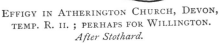
EFFIGY IN ATHERINGTON CHURCH, DEVON, TEMP. R. II.; PERHAPS FOR WILLINGTON.
After Stothard.

John w Estmore.   Wal d Wigetone.   Robt de Willoughby.   Robert de Wilobi.   Lodbirc de Willoughby.

Willoughby, William de—bore, at the second Dunstable tournament 1334, gules, a fer-de-mouline ermine. F.

Willoughby, Robert de—(H. III. Roll) bore, argent, a chevron sable. (F.) Arden and Segar Rolls. WILLIAM fil. ROBERT took up the cross in the last Crusade, 1270.

Wilshire, Sir John, slain at the siege of Calais 1347, bore, per chevron gules and argent the chief crusily patée (5, 2) of the second. RAFE bore it argent and azure (and another azure and argent—with crosses crosslet 4, 2) blasoned—argent and azure amptiz le chief crusily or; Jenyns' Roll. See WELLESBY.

Wilton, John de—(R. II. Roll) bore, gules, on a chevron argent three crosses crosslet fitchée of the field; Surrey Roll—colours reversed in Ashmole Roll.

Winceles, Edmond de (or WINSELES)—(H. III. Roll) bore, per pale argent and sable a fess counterchanged; St. George Roll—borne also by FITZ PAINE.

Winchester, Earl of, v. Quincy.

Windlesore, Hugh de—(H. III. Roll) bore, gules, a bend vair; Howard Roll.

Windsor ——— a Suffolk Knight—(H. VI. Roll) bore, sable, a saltire argent; Arundel Roll.

Windsor, Sir Richard de, of Berks—(E. II. Roll) bore, gules, crusily or, a saltire argent; Parliamentary Roll.

Wingfield, William—(R. II. Roll) bore gules, two wings conjoined in lure argent; Surrey Roll.

*[**Wingfield, Sir Henry,** (H. VI.)—bore, argent, on a bend gules cotised sable three pair of wings conjoined of the field.—Shirley.] F. See Monumental Brass for Sir JOHN.

*[**Winnington** ——— (E. IV. Roll) bore, argent, an inescocheon voided sable within an orle of martlets of the last (F.); crest; a retort azure; Ballard Roll. LYDULPH, E. I. Shirley.

Winsington, Sir John de, of co. Gloucr. —(E. II. Roll) bore, sable, three boars' heads couped argent; Parliamentary Roll.

Wintershulle, John de—(H. III. Roll) bore, or, two bars gules, a label (5) sable. (F.) St. George Roll. See MARTIN and JOHN ST. MARTYN.

Wisemale, Ernaud de—(E. I. Roll) bore, gules, three fleurs-de-lys argent. JOHN bore the lys, or; Camden Roll. F.

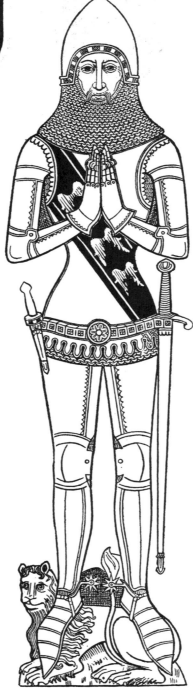

SIR JOHN WINGFIELD
IN LETHERINGHAM CHURCH, SUFFOLK,
c. 1400, 2 HEN. IV.

From Boutell.

Wisham, Sir John de, (of co. Glouc.)—bore, at the first Dunstable tournament 1308, sable, a fess between six martlets 3 and 3 or—argent (F.) in Jenyns' and Parly. Rolls—and so borne by WILLIAM at the siege of Rouen 1418.

Wistowe, John and **Robert de**—(E. I. Roll) bore, argent, a chevron gules, in chief three torteaux; Jenyns' Roll and Ordinary.

Witacre, Richard—(H. III. Roll) bore, argent, on a fess gules three besants, in chief two mullets (6) of the second. (F.) St. George Roll.

Withacre, Sir Richard, of Warwickshire—(E. II. Roll) bore, sable three mascles argent, —lozenges in trick; Parliamentary Roll.

Wither, Sire Thomas (WYTHER)—bore, at the battle of Boroughbridge 1322, argent, a fess between three crescent gules. (F.) Jenyns' Ordinary.

Wither, William—(H. III. Roll) bore, argent, three crescents gules. (F.) St. George Roll. See also RYTHER.

Witleburye, Aubrey de—(E. I. Roll) bore, azure; Camden Roll.

Witney, Sir Eustace de, of Cheshire—(E. II. Roll) bore paly (6) or and gules, a chief vair; Parliamentary Roll.

Witney, Eustace and **Robert de Whitneye**—(H. III. Roll) bore, azure, a cross counter-compony or and gules. (F.) St. George and Surrey Rolls; argent and gules in Arden Roll.

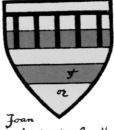

witt wither

witt wodeburh

Hugg wombwoll

witt wolrycgf

Robert morfmorte

John Wodehoufe

Roger Wrey

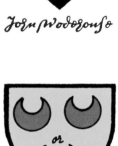

John do wodehulle

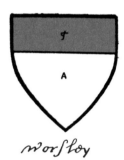

worfley

nichol do wobbowdono

Hugh Wrottefley

+**Wodeburgh, Rafe de**—(E. I. Roll) bore, burulée (10, 12, 14) argent and azure over all three lyons rampant gules. (F.) Jenyns' Ordinary – 6, 7 barrulets in Arden and St. George Rolls (crowned or in Dering and Howard Rolls); THOMAS burulée 12 (5 barrulets in trick), WILLIAM 14, Jenyns' Ordinary and St. George Roll; 9 barrulets and crowned or in Howard Roll. See also WOODEBURNE.

*[**Wodehouse, John**, 1415—bore, sable, a chevron or, guttée de sang between three cinquefoyles ermine.—Shirley.] (F.) Said to have been granted for valour at Agincourt.

Wodhull, John de and **Symon**—(H. III. Roll) bore, or, three crescents gules. (F.) Arden, Jenyns' and St. George Rolls.

Wodvyle. Sir Richard, of Kent—(H. VI. Roll) bore, argent a fess and a quarter gules; Atkinson Roll—(differenced in Arundel Roll—with a crescent of the first); and *quarterly with*, gules, an eagle displayed or; Jenyns' Ordinary; Lord RIVERS, K.G.; K. 402 fo. 32.

Wogges, Thomas de (?of Suffolk, Knight) —(E. III. Roll) bore, argent, a fess engrailed between three annulets sable; Jenyns' Ordinary and Arundel Roll.

Wokingdon, Sir Thomas, of Essex—(E. II. Roll) bore, gules, a lyon rampant argent crowned or; Cotgrave, Harleian and Parly. Rolls—ascribed to NICOLE in Segar Roll. F. See WYFRYNGDON.

Wokingdon, Sir Nicholas, of Essex—(E. II. Roll) bore, gules, a lyon rampant barry (8) or and azure; Parly. Roll—barry of six in Harl. Roll.

Wolterston —— an Essex ? Knight—(H. VI. Roll)—bore, sable, a fess nebulée between three wolves' heads couped or—a Suffolk Knight of the name bore lyons' heads; Arundel Roll.

Wolford, Sir William, a Gascoyne—bore, at the siege of Calais 1345-8, sable a fess, and in chief three fleurs-de-lys or. F.

Wol(l)aston, Sire John de—bore, at the battle of Boroughbridge 1322, sable, a chevron between three escallops argent (F.); estoyles of many points (F.) in the Ashmole MS. probably in error.

*[**W(o)lseley, Robert de**,1281—bore, argent, a talbot passant gules.—Shirley.] F.

Woltaubin, Gilbert de—(H. III. Roll) bore, or, on a cross sable five besants; Arden Roll. See ORKABLIN.

Wolverton, Sir John de, of Bucks—(E. II. Roll) bore, azure, an eagle displayed or, a baston gules; Parliamentary Roll.

Wolwardington, Sir Peers de, of Warwickshire—(E. II. Roll) bore, bendy (10) argent and sable; Parliamentary Roll.

Wombewell, Thomas—(E. I. Roll) bore, argent, on a bend between six martlets (3, 3) gules, three besants; Jenyns' Roll.

*[**Wombwell,** *alias* **Tawnell, Hugh** (6 H. IV. 1404-5)—bore, gules, a bend between six unicorns' heads couped argent.—Shirley.] F.

Woodeburne, John—(E. III. Roll) bore, burulée (12) argent and azure, over all three lyonceux rampant (2 and 1) gules; Jenyns' Ordinary. See WODEBURGH.

Woodstock, Thomas of, *v.* **Gloucester, Duke of.**

*[**Woolryche, William,** 1403—bore, azure, a chevron between three swans' wings elevated argent.—Shirley.] F.

*[**Worsley** —— a Lancashire Knight—(H. VI. Roll) bore, argent, a chief gules; Arundel and Ballard Rolls. F.

Worswick, Robert—(E. III. Roll) bore, argent, on a bend sable three lozenges of the first each charged with a saltire gules. (F.) Jenyns' Ordinary.

Wortley, Sir Nicholas de, of Yorkshire, and **Robert de**—(E. II. Roll) bore, argent, on a bend between six martlets (3, 3) gules, three besants; Parly. Roll and Jenyns' Ordinary —being the arms of FURNIVALL and three besants on the bend.

*[**Wrey, Roger,** (19 E. III.)—bore, sable, a fess between three poleaxes argent, helved gules.—Shirley.] F.

Wrialeye, Pers—(H. III. Roll) bore, azure, two bars or charged with five martlets, 3, 2, gules; Arden Roll—? being the arms of LEY with the martlets.

Wrokeshall, Geoffrey—(E. III. Roll) bore, ermine, two bars gules; Jenyns' Ordinary.

Wrokeshall, Geoffrey de—(H. III. Roll) bore, gules, two bars ermine over all a bend azure; Howard Roll.

Wroth —— a Kentish Knight—(H. VI. Roll) bore, argent, on a bend sable three tygers' (probably leopards') faces argent crowned or; Arundel Roll.

*[**Wrottesley, Sir Hugh,** K.G., founder 1344 —bore or, three piles, meeting in base sable and a quarter ermine—being the coat of his mother JOAN BASSET. K. 398 fo. 23; see title page. To another HUGH, or, a bend engrailed gules, is ascribed in Surrey Roll.

witt wolford

John do wolaston

Johan do wolaston

Henry wollaston

Robt do wolfoley

Wrottesley of Wrottesley.

CONTRIBUTED BY THE HON. G. WROTTESLEY.

SIMON, son of WILLIAM DE COCTON (Coughton, co. Warwick) occurs 1167 and 1172. =

WILLIAM, styled William de Verdon, William FitzSimon, and William de Wrottesley, occurs 1199 and 1242 = INGRITH, dau. of Robert FitzAdam, of Butterton and Waterfall.

SIR HUGH DE WROTTESLEY, KT.; died 1276 = IDONIA, dau. of Ralph de Perton.

SIR WILLIAM DE WROTTESLEY, KT.; died 1313 = 1. PETRONILLA, dau. of Sir John Audley, of Blore.
2. KATHERINE DE GLASELEY, neé Lestraunge, of Knockin.

SIR WILLIAM DE WROTTESLEY, KT.; died 1320 = JOAN, dau. of Sir Roger Basset; *or, three piles sable a canton ermine.*

1. ELIZABETH (1st wife), dau. of Sir John de = SIR HUGH DE WROTTESLEY, K.G.; died 1381; = 2. MABEL (2nd wife), dau. of Sir = 3. ISABELLA (3rd wife), dau. of Sir John
Hampton. *or, three piles sable a canton ermine.* Philip ap Rees. de Arderne.

HUGH, son of Mabel, died under age. HUGH, son of Isabella, died under age. JOHN DE WROTTESLEY, = ELIZABETH, dau. of Sir Robert de
died 1403. Standish.

HUGH WROTTESLEY, born 1400, died 1464 = THOMASINE, dau. of Sir John Gresley.

SIR WALTER WROTTESLEY, KT.; died 1473 = JANE, dau. of William Baron, of Reading.   HENRY WROTTESLEY, Sheriff of Worcestershire, 1460;
executed for treason at Southampton, 1470.

RICHARD WROTTESLEY, born 1457, died 1521 = DOROTHY, dau. of Sir Edmund Sutton, of Dudley.   WILLIAM, Esquire of the Body, Hen. VII.

WALTER WROTTESLEY; died in 1563 = ISABEL, dau. of John Harcourt, of Ranton.

JOHN WROTTESLEY; died in 1578 = ELIZABETH, dau. of Thomas Astley, of Patshull.

MARY, dau. and heir of Hugh Lee, of Woodford, co. Stafford, = WALTER WROTTESLEY, died 1630 = JOYCE, dau. of Sir Edward Leighton, co. Salop, widow of Francis
1st wife. Bromley, of Worfield, 2nd wife.

MARGARET, dau. of Sir Edward Devereux, of Castle = SIR HUGH WROTTESLEY, KT., d. 1633 = CLARA, dau. of Sir Anthony Colclough, and widow of William Sneyd, of
Bromwich, 1st wife. Keele, 2nd wife.

SIR WALTER WROTTESLEY, KT.; created a baronet 1642, died in 1659 = MARY, dau. of Ambrose Grey, of Enville, co. Stafford, 2nd son of Lord Grey, of Groby.

SIR WALTER WROTTESLEY, 2nd Bart., died 1686 = MARGARET, dau. of Sir Thomas Wolrich, Bart., of Dudmaston.

ELINOR, dau. and eventually co-heir of Sir John Archer, Kt., of = SIR WALTER WROTTESLEY, 3rd Bart., died = ANNE, dau. of Mr. Justice Burton, of Longnor, co. Salop
Coopersall, co. Essex, a Justice of Common Pleas (1st wife). 1712. (2nd wife).

SIR JOHN WROTTESLEY, 4th Bart., M.P. for co. Stafford, died 1726 = FRANCES, dau. of Hon. John Grey, and granddaughter of Henry, 1st Lord Stamford.

SIR HUGH WROTTESLEY, 5th Bart., died under age, 1729.   SIR WALTER WROTTESLEY, 6th Bart., died under age, 1731.   SIR RICHARD WROTTESLEY, 7th Bart., = LADY MARY GOWER, dau. of John, 1st
Dean of Worcester, died 1769. Earl Gower, died 1778.

SIR JOHN WROTTESLEY, 8th Bart., M.P. for co. Stafford, = HONBLE. FRANCES COURTENAY, dau. of William, 1st Viscount Courtenay,
died 1787. of Powderham, Devon, died 1828.

LADY CAROLINE BENNET, dau. of Charles, 4th = JOHN, 1st Baron Wrottesley, raised to the Peerage = JULIA, dau. of John Conyers, Esq., of Copt Hall, Essex, and
Earl of Tankerville, died 1818 (1st wife). 11 July, 1838, died 1841. widow of Honble. Astley Bennet, R.N., died 1860.

JOHN WROTTESLEY, 2nd = SOPHIA, dau. of Thomas Giffard, CHARLES, Lt.-Colonel ROBERT, in Holy Orders, WALTER, mar. Anne Lucy, EDWARD, mar. Ellen, dau.
Baron, President of the | of Chillington, died 1880. 29th Foot, died 1861, died 1838, *s.p.* dau. of Colonel Archer. of Charles Rush, of
Royal Society, a Founder | *s.p.* = Elsenham, co. Essex =
of the Royal Astrono-
mical Society, died 1867.

FRANCIS, in Holy Orders, LUCY.   ALFRED EDWARD, Major R.E.,
died 1873, *s.p.* EDITH.   died 1899

ARTHUR WROTTESLEY, 3rd Baron, = AUGUSTA ELIZABETH, CHARLES, Fellow GEORGE, Major- HENRY, Lieut. 43rd CAMERON, Lieut. Rl.   HUGH EDWARD,
in lineal (17th) descent from (Sir | dau. of 1st Lord of All Souls'. General. Regt., killed in the Engrs., killed at born 1882.
Hugh), one of the Founders of the | Londesborough. Kaffir War, 1852. Bomarsund, 1854.
Order of the Garter, a distinction
enjoyed by this family and no other;
born 17 June, 1824.

WILLIAM, Capt. 4th Dragoon Guards, BERTRAM, born 1864, VICTOR ALEXANDER, WALTER BENNET, EVELYN HENRIETTA,
born 1863, died 1898, *s.p.* died 1875, *s.p.* born 1873. born 1877. born 1866.

E E

THE HERALDIC ATCHIEVEMENT

OF

F. M. GARNET JOSEPH WOLSELEY, VISCOUNT WOLSELEY,

K.P., G.C.B., G.C.M.G., P.C., D.C.L., LL.D.,

COMMANDER-IN-CHIEF 1895-1900.

witt wyborgf   niet do wyfringdono   Simon la Souche   Alleyn la zouch   John Bourgf

Rich. d· Wikes

Wroughton —— a Somersetshire Knight—(H. VI. Roll) bore, argent, chevron between three boars' heads couped gules; Arundel Roll.

*[**Wybergh, William de,** (38 E. III.) –bore, sable, three bars or, in chief two estoyles of the last.—Shirley.] F.

Wycliffe, Robert — (E. III. Roll) bore, argent, a chevron between three crosses crosslet gules; Grimaldi Roll—the chevron sable and crosses botonnée in Jenyns' Ordinary.

Wyfryngdon, Sir Nichol de—bore, at the first Dunstable tournament 1308, gules, a lyon rampant argent crowned or. F. See WOKINGDON.

Wykes, Richard de—(H. III. Roll) bore, azure, a lyon rampant argent (Arden Roll); checquy argent and gules. (F.) St. George Roll—Sir JOHN, slain at the siege of Calais 1348—arms gone from Roll.

Wymale, Nicholas—(H. III. Roll) bore, argent, three cushions 2 and 1 gules. (F.) St. George and Jenyns' Rolls.

*[**Wyndham, John,** (38 H. VI.)—bore, azure, a chevron between three lyons' heads erased or.—Shirley.] F.

Wynseles v. **Winceles.**

Wythe, Sir Geffrey and **Oliver de**—(E. II. Roll) bore, azure, three gryphons passant in pale or membered gules; Arundel, Ashmole and Cotgrave Rolls. See FITZ WYTHE.

Wyther, Sire Thomas—bore, at the battle of Boroughbridge 1322, argent, a fess between three crescents gules. See RYTHER and WITHER.

Wivile, William de—(H. III. Roll) bore, argent, two bars sable, a bordure engrailed (gules). (F.) St. George Roll.

Wyvile, William—(E. I. Roll) bore, gules, fretty or, a quarter of the first (sic); Jenyns' Roll.

*[**Wyvill, John**—(E. III. Roll) bore, gules, three chevronels interlaced in base vair, a chief or (F.); Jenyns' Ordinary—erroneously blasoned, gules, fret vair, a chief or.

Wyville, Roger, slain at the siege of Calais 1347, bore, azure, three chevronels interlaced in base argent. F.

Yevelton, Robert le—(R. II. Roll, bore, argent, two bars undée sable, a label (3) gules; Surrey Roll and Harl. MS. 6163 fo. 34ᵇ.

York, Duke of, Richard Plantagenet, 1415–60—bore, France and England—a label (3) on each pendant three torteaux; Surrey Roll—these arms appear on the Rouen Roll 1418—this Duke born in 1412 succeeded in 1415!

Ypre, John de—(R. II. Roll) bore, argent, a chevron between three bulls' heads cabossed gules. RAUFF differenced with a mullet; Surrey Roll.

Zouche, Roger de la, at the second Dunstable tournament 1334, and **Sir Simon (la),** knighted at the capitulation of Calais 1348—bore, azure, besanté 4, 3, 2, 1 (F.); ascribed also to JOHN, of Sibthorpe (Jenyns' Ordinary), Sir ROGER (Ashmole Roll) and WILLIAM, of Haringworth, baron 1308 in Cotgrave Roll; 6 bezants in Howard Roll; ascribed to another WILLIAM (‡) in Dering Roll. See Tiles, Neath Abbey, p. vii. Sir WILLIAM, of Leic., differenced with a label (3) gules in Ashmole and Parly. Rolls.

Zouche, Roger la—(H. III. Roll) bore, ermine, on a fess gules three besants; Howard Roll.

Zouche, Sir Alan la, of Ashby, baron 1299, sealed the Barons' letter to the Pope 1301, pp. xviii and xxiv. He bore at the battle of Falkirk 1298, and at the siege of Carlaverock 1300, gules, besantée (4, 3, 2, 1) (F.); Parly. Roll; as did also his son Sire WILLIAM, banneret, of Haringworth, baron 1308, at the battle of Boroughbridge 1322 (six besants in Howard Roll)—ascribed also to HUGH and ROGER in Surrey and Arden Rolls, and to another ALAN (‡) in the Dering Roll. Sir WILLIAM bore it with a label (3) azure, at the first Dunstable tournament 1308; Parly. Roll.

Zouche, Sire Roger la—bore, at the battle of Boroughbridge 1322, and WILLIAM (5th baron) of Haringworth; bore, at the siege of Rouen 1418, gules, besantée and a quarter ermine (borne by one of the name with a mullet of 6 sable on the canton or quarter; Harl. Roll); ascribed also to Sir YVON (F.) in various Rolls, though he seems to have borne it with a label (3) azure at the battle of Boroughbridge 1322.

Zouche, John la—bore, at the siege of Rouen 1418, gules, besantée, a canton ermine, quarterly with, argent, a fess dancettée sable besantée. F.

Zouche, Sir William la, banneret, knighted at the capitulation of Calais 1348—bore, gules, besantée or, a canton "endente in base" ermine (F.)—a quarter ermine in Parly. Roll.

Zouche, Richard and **Thomas la**—(E. III. Roll) bore, gules, besantée and a chief ermine; Surrey and Ashmole Rolls and Jenyns' Ordinary.

Zouche, Sir Amory de la—bore, at the first Dunstable tournament 1308, gules besantée and a bend azure—though argent (F.) at the battle of Boroughbridge 1322; Parly. Roll. In Jenyns' Ordinary the coat is gules platey and a bend argent.

Zouche, Alan and **Roger la**—(H. III. Roll) bore, gules, besantée, and a fess ermine; Arden and St. George Rolls. F.

Zouche, Sir Oliver, of co. Leic.—(E. II. Roll) bore, gules, besantée and a chevron ermine; Parliamentary Roll.

Zouche, Sir Thomas, of co. Leic.—(E. II. Roll) bore, gules, besantée on a canton argent a mullet sable; Parly. Roll.

Sir Ywon la Zouche

witt la Zouche

Amory de la Zouch

Alan d la Souche

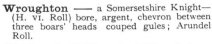
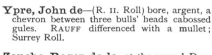

Nicol. d Wynhale

John wyndham   witt d· wivile   John wyvill   Roger d Wivile

212

RICHARD WELLYSBURNE DE
MONTFORT, c. 1265.
IN HITCHENDON CHURCH, BUCKS.
After Stothard.
A 19th Century imposture.

DE MONTFORT WELLESBURNE,
IN HITCHENDON CHURCH, BUCKS.
After Stothard.
A 19th Century imposture.

ERRONEOUSLY ASSIGNED TO GEOFFREY DE MAGNAVILLE OR MANDEVILLE, EARL OF ESSEX. c. 1144 In the Temple Church, London. *After Stothard.* See Effigy—Loveday, page 134 *ante.*

In Memoriam.

ROBERT FITZ HAMON.

In the Choir of the Abbey Church at Tewkesbury, ob. 1107.

After John Carter.

See also Clare, p. 47, and Gloucester, p. 95.

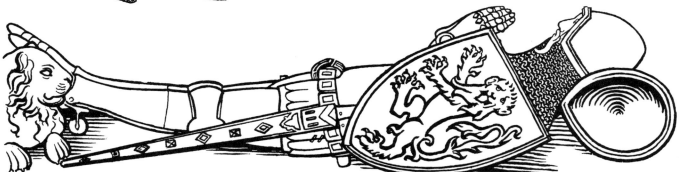

In Memoriam.—SIR BERNARD BROCAS, Beheaded 1400. *After Stothard.*

In the chapel of S. Edmund, Westminster Abbey; the effigy, which appears from its heraldry to be of modern date, may have been intended to supply the loss of a former work.

See also Robert de Vere, Earl of Oxford, page 197.

214

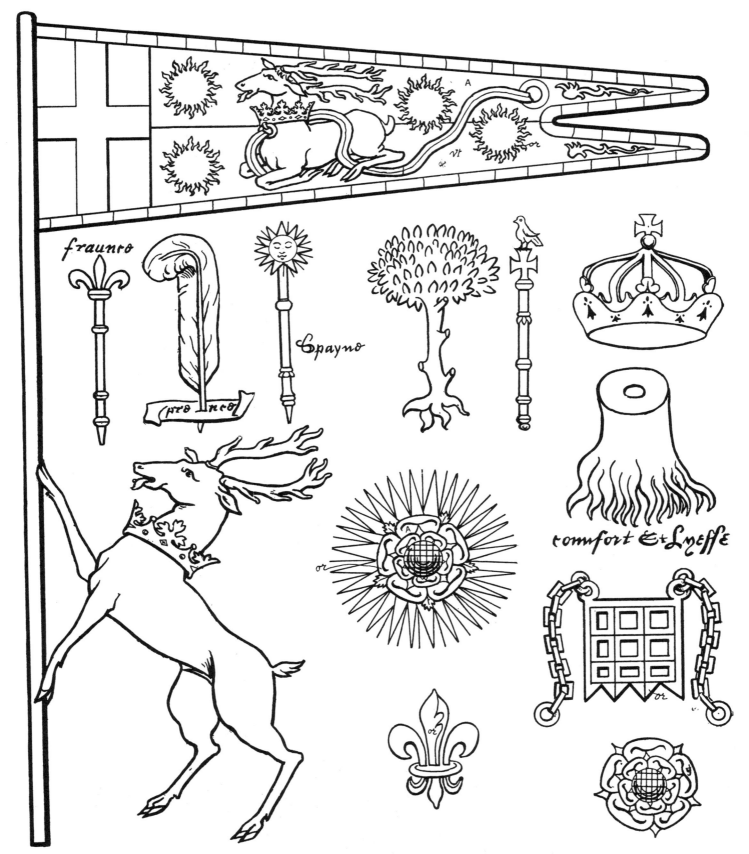

BANNERS, BADGES AND BEARINGS.

Men
of
Coat Armour:

THEIR BEARINGS AND BADGES

WITH MANY

CHART PEDIGREES AND ROYAL DESCENTS

AND

ADDITIONALLY ILLUSTRATED WITH

HERALDIC ATCHIEVEMENTS

MONUMENTAL BRASSES AND EFFIGIES

COMPILED BY

JOSEPH FOSTER Hon. M.A. Oxon

Author of
"Alumni Oxonienses" 8 Vols. ; "The British Peerage and
Baronetage" 2 Vols. ;
and many other Genealogical Works

FIRST LIST OF HERALDIC ATCHIEVEMENTS. &c.

MEN OF COAT ARMOUR AND ANCESTRAL FAMILIES.

PEDIGREES—FIRST LIST.

Examples from]   *[the Temple Church.*

MEN OF COAT ARMOUR—THEIR BEARINGS AND BADGES.

"Mr. Joseph Foster, after years of victorious fighting upon the side of the honest pedigree makers, enjoys a well-deserved reward of enormous labour in the shape of an honorary degree conferred upon him by the University of Oxford."—THE SPEAKER, 23 *March,* 1901.

NOW that I have completed "Some Feudal Coats of Arms," I shall issue as soon as practicable "Men of Coat Armour— their Bearings and Badges," similar to the specimen pages in this prospectus.

The notable or distinguishing feature of this volume will be illustrations of the Badges of Nobles, Knights and Gentle Men, as here indicated. This is an almost unexplored field in Heraldry, curiously so, as badges preceded coat armour, so called. Having then no rival in point of date, I often marvel that the Badge is not adopted in preference to a Crest by those families whose greater antiquity warrants them in so doing, for it affords precisely that simple distinction which is at once the emblem of the Age of Chivalry.

The drawings of the Arms and Crests of those distinguished persons, past and present, appearing in this work, will be based upon the choicest examples in the older Heraldic MSS. in the British Museum.

The fortuitous combination and numerical predominance of Arms of ancient families seems to be the appropriate setting for a selection of Pedigrees of representative families—I, on my part, will contribute the illustrations of arms, and Heads of families will contribute Pedigrees or Heraldic Atchievements, as their interest in the undertaking may incline them.

I shall be glad to hear from representatives of those families all over the Kingdom who in good faith have used arms for generations. To those whose arms do not appear on record in the College of Arms I can offer a crumb of comfort in the fact that not all arms granted by that institution are on record therein; not only does this apply to Visitation times, as witness the omission to record the arms granted in 1590 by Clar. Cooke to the five Regius Professorships of Cambridge, but it applies with equal force to modern times. In support of this statement, I quote from a volume of Docquets of Grants acquired by purchase, in which appears a pencil

trick of a grant in 1777 to Oliver Beckett of London; no trace of this is to be found in Grants Book XIII. (at the College), where it should naturally appear, nor does it occur in their Index to the Great Register itself, to a *copy* of which I have had unrestricted access for the purposes of this volume; the grant itself is, however, printed *in extenso* in the *Miscellanea Genealogica et Heraldica,* New Series Vol. II., 192, by Dr. Howard, Maltraver Herald.

Should the Heralds on this intimation succeed in unearthing the papers concerning the "business" of this grant, they may doubtless be able, thanks to me, to make good a gap in their records, but even so, this case does not stand alone. But I may go even further, and say that this *copy* of their Great Register contains an original reference slip to a grant, with the pencil memo, "insert when returned," but as it has not been returned, it of course has not been inserted, as I can testify; should an application be made to the College for this particular coat the answer would naturally be "not on record." I make the Heralds a present of these facts, as a side light on their absurd claim to infallibility.

I now frankly appeal to those representatives of "Men of Coat Armour" of the Victorian Era, whose names as grantees of arms I know, but the blazon of whose arms the College seemingly prefers to reserve for those whose procedure is that of "publicly insult- ing"* the Gentry and Man of Family, whereby its fees are increased. I am sure that a sense of fair- play will induce all to co-operate, as I have given abundant proof that in process of time almost every- thing leaks out of that institution by favouritism or other means.

This work will, I hope, as indicated, include the Arms and Badges of most County Families (ancient or modern), and just so many Pedigrees, Heraldic Atchievements, and Monumental Brasses and Effigies as will suffice to enhance the general interest in such a work.

JOSEPH FOSTER,
Hon. M.A. Oxon.

21 BOUNDARY ROAD, N.W.

* For strictures on this procedure see (1) "The Black Book of an Amateur Herald," *Saturday Review,* 25 February, 1899; (2) "Arms and the Gentleman," *Contemporary Review,* August, 1899; (3) "Order Arms," the *World,* 16 August, 1899; and (4) "A Reformed College of Arms," the *Contemporary Review,* July, 1900.

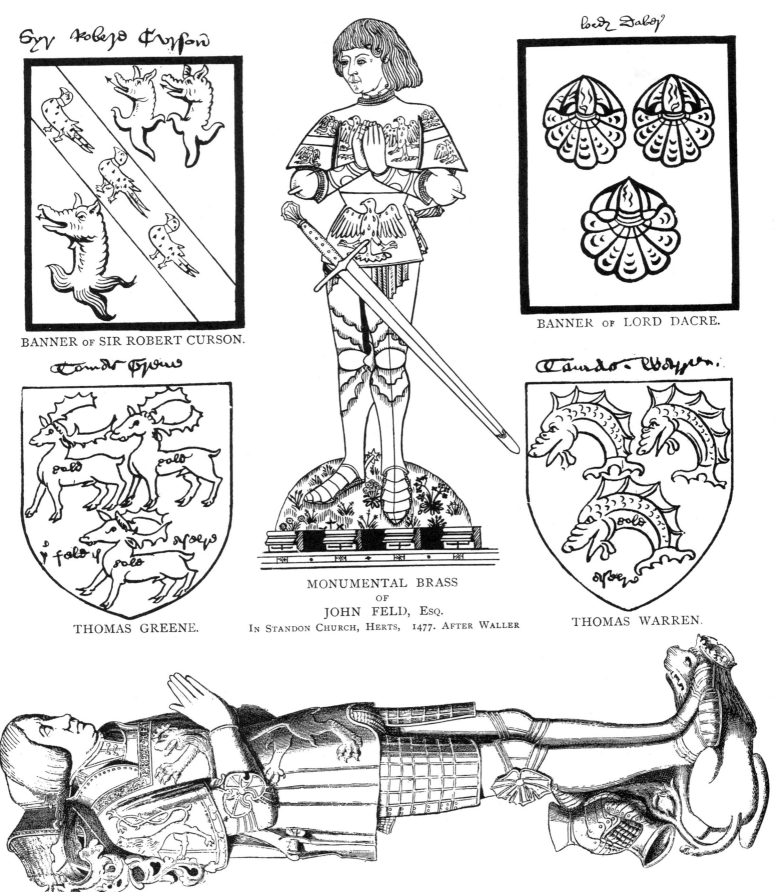

BANNER of SIR ROBERT CURSON.

BANNER of LORD DACRE.

THOMAS GREENE.

MONUMENTAL BRASS
OF
JOHN FELD, Esq.
In Standon Church, Herts, 1477. After Waller

THOMAS WARREN.

MONUMENTAL EFFIGY of SIR JOHN PECHE in Lullingstone Church, Kent, 1522, 14 H. 8. After Stothard.

BADGES.

COL. CHAS. J. BROMHEAD, C.B.

EDWARD NATHANIEL CONANT,
OF
LYNDON HALL, RUTLAND.

SIR J. W. PEASE, BART., M.P.

SIR J. E. BACKHOUSE, BART.

BANNERS, BRASSES, MONUMENTAL EFFIGIES, HERALDIC ATCHIEVEMENTS, AND PEDIGREES.

Talbot

Guch

or Guop o

Storton
or

wrloughby

darcio

fitb
ar

OUR

Ancestral Families

AND

THEIR PATERNAL COAT ARMOUR

PROFUSELY ILLUSTRATED WITH

ZINCO ETCHINGS

OF EFFIGIES BRASSES

BANNERS BADGES AND

HERALDIC ATCHIEVEMENTS

SOME CHART PEDIGREES

BY

JOSEPH FOSTER Hon. M.A. Oxon

Author of
"Alumni Oxonienses," 8 Vols.;
"The British Peerage and Baronetage, 1880-3," 2 Vols.;
and many other Genealogical Works

JAMES PARKER & CO.
OXFORD AND LONDON

Armour temp. Rich. II.   The arrival of the Saxons in Britain.   Cotton MS., Claudius B. VI.

ANCESTRAL FAMILIES.

ROBERT ABBOTT, 1654.

Abarough, Antony, 1623—bore, by right-heraldic; sable, two swords in saltire argent, hilted or, between four fleurs-de-lis of the second, within a bordure ermine. Seated at Castle Cary, *f* John, of Ditcheat, *f* John, of North Barrow, all in Somerset. Clar-Harvey made a grant of arms, 1 Jan., 1548-9, to John Aborrough, of Calleys.

Abarrow, Sir William, *c.* 1600—bore, by right-heraldic; sable, two swords in saltire argent, hilt and pommel gules, between four fleurs-de-lis or. Seated at North Charford, in Hants, Kt., *f* Anthony, *f* John, *f* Maurice, all of the same.

Abbot, Charles, see BARON COLCHESTER.

Abbott, Charles, see BARON TENTERDEN.

Abbott, Col. Henry Alexius, C.B. (1898), Indian Staff Corps, served in Afghan War 1878-80, Soudan Expedition 1885, &c., &c.—bears, by right-heraldic; ermine, on a pale gules, three pears or—notwithstanding the following grant by the intruded Bysshe, which is perhaps considered invalid!

Abbott, Robert, of London, gent—bore, by right-heraldic; ermine, on a pale gules, three pears pendant or, by grant 9 Aug., 1654, *p* Sir E. Bysshe, Clar and Garter. Guillim, 117.

Abbott, John, Braemar House, Lancaster Gate—bore, by right-heraldic; sable, on a pale or a crosier of the first, on a chief of the second three water-bougets of the field.

Abbott, Richard, 1623—bore, by right-heraldic; gules, a chevron between three pears pendant or. Seated at Guildford, in Surrey, *f* Richard, *f* Maurice, both of the same, the latter father also of Robert, Bishop of Salisbury, of George, Archbishop of Canterbury, and of Maurice, of London, who was the first knight made by King Charles. Matthew, of Hawkedon, Suffolk, bore these arms in 1664.

Abbott, Vernon and Christopher, of Highbury Cottage, Newland, co. Glouc., bore, by right-heraldic; per pale indented ermine and azure, on a chevron or between three pears ppr. as many crosses patée of the second.

SIR W. N. ABDY, BART.

Abbott, William, 1625—bore, by right-heraldic; sable, a cross voided or, between four eagles displayed of the last. Seated at Luffincote, in Devonshire, aged 19 in 1620, *f* Thomas, of the same, *f* William, of Hartland, *f* Waymond, brother of William, sergeant of the seller.

Abbys, Thomas, *c.* 1600—bore, by right-heraldic; gules, five fusils conjoined in fess, between three escallops all argent. Seated at Buxton, in Norfolk, *f* John, *f* Robert, *f* James, all of the same. The same arms were borne by William Abbys, " now maior of the Town of Bedford this 3 November, 1634, for the following year," seated at Stutfold, Beds, 1669, *f* Wm., *f* Thos., each mayor of Bedford.

Abdy, Sir William Neville, 2nd bart., of Albyns, Essex—bears, by right-heraldic; or, two chevronels between three trefoils slipped sable, which, with a crescent for difference, were used at the funeral of Roger Abdy, of London, merchant taylor, on Thursday, 26 June, 1595 or 1596, 4 days after Clar-Lee granted the crest to the sons of this Roger, viz. a griffin's head and neck ppr., beaked azure. Humphrey Abdy was seated at Stretham, Surrey, 1623; his brother Edmond was of Lincoln's Inn, *f* Roger, of London, afsd., *f* Roger, of Tickhill, Yorks; other branches were seated at Kingston-on-Thames, and at East Malling, Kent, those at Easterford and Albyns, Essex, being each represented by a baronet (both extinct), *f* Anthony, of London, Alderman.

A'Beckett, (Hon.) William Arthur Callander—bears, by right-heraldic; or, on a chevron gules between three lions' heads erased of the last, a fleur-de-lis, and on either side an annulet all of the first, within a bordure wavy of the second. Of Melbourne, &c., Justice of the peace and a J.P. Wilts, *f* Sir William, chief justice of Victoria. These arms are also borne by Arthur W. A'Beckett, of Eccleston Square.

Abeels, Nicholas, 1634—bore, by right-heraldic; argent, in a tree vert a bird gules, on either side of the trunk a cinquefoil of the last. Of London, merchant, *f* William, of Rouselaer in Flanders, *f* Nicholas, of the same, farrier to the Emperor of Germany,

HON. W. A. C. A'BECKETT, OF MELBOURNE.

ANT. ABAROUGH.

THOMAS ABBYS.

JOHN ABBOTT

[1]

Frances Thinne Herald of Armes

The Banner of Wales borne by y̆ viscount Bindon

The Lord Maior of London

THE BANNER OF WALES, CARRIED AT THE CORONATION OF
QUEEN ELIZABETH.

From a Contemporary Drawing in the British Museum.